Brown & Benchmark CourseKit Order Form For

Mass Communication: An Introduction
By Ronald T.

MW00723763

Brown and Benchmark is pleased to offer a black and white customized version of Mass Communication: An Introduction to the Field, Second Edition by Ronald T. Farrar. This book can be customized to include only the chapters you cover in your course. Other materials such as a course syllabus, your copyrighted materials, student studyguide, etc. can also be packaged to create a complete CourseKit tailored to meet the needs of you and your students. Ordering is easy. Just call 800-338-5371 and request a complimentary copy of the Annotated Instructor's Edition (ISBN 0-697-25987-0). Then, decide which chapters are most important for your course (a table of contents is provided on the back of this form) and use this form to place your order. If you need more information call your Sales Representative or our CourseWorks specialists at 800-446-8979.

Professor Name:_____

School:_____

Department:_____

Course Name:_____

Address:_____

City:_____ State:_____ Zip:_____

Phone/Fax:_____

Approximate Enrollment (please be as accurate as possible for ordering purposes): _____

Course Start Date:_____

Please indicate below which bookstores will be ordering the text, along with a phone number.

1._____ 2._____ 3._____

phone #_____ phone #_____ phone #_____

Please check the boxes below indicating extra material you wish to include in your CourseKit™.

☐ class syllabus   ☐ copyrighted material   ☐ other

Please describe in detail:_____

_____

━━ COVER INFORMATION ━━
(If needed to differentiate from other sections at your school.)

Professor or Course Name:

School:

━━ TO ORDER ━━

Please send order form to
Kate Finn • Brown & Benchmark Publishers • 2460 Kerper Blvd.• Dubuque, IA 52001
or, Call Toll-Free 1-800-446-8979
----over please-----

Mass Communication: An Introduction to the Field, Second Edition

by Ronald T. Farrar

Table of Contents

Please indicate numerically the order in which you would like your selected chapters.

<table>
<tr><td>_____</td><td>Chapter A</td><td>The Social Context</td></tr>
<tr><td>_____</td><td>Chapter B</td><td>Evolution of the Print Media</td></tr>
<tr><td>_____</td><td>Chapter C</td><td>The Wire Services</td></tr>
<tr><td>_____</td><td>Chapter D</td><td>Newspapers</td></tr>
<tr><td>_____</td><td>Chapter E</td><td>The Community Press</td></tr>
<tr><td>_____</td><td>Chapter F</td><td>Photographic Communication</td></tr>
<tr><td>_____</td><td>Chapter G</td><td>Magazines</td></tr>
<tr><td>_____</td><td>Chapter H</td><td>The Book Industry</td></tr>
<tr><td>_____</td><td>Chapter I</td><td>Growth of the Electronic Media</td></tr>
<tr><td>_____</td><td>Chapter J</td><td>Radio</td></tr>
<tr><td>_____</td><td>Chapter K</td><td>Recordings</td></tr>
<tr><td>_____</td><td>Chapter L</td><td>Television</td></tr>
<tr><td>_____</td><td>Chapter M</td><td>Films</td></tr>
<tr><td>_____</td><td>Chapter N</td><td>Public Relations</td></tr>
<tr><td>_____</td><td>Chapter O</td><td>Advertising</td></tr>
<tr><td>_____</td><td>Chapter P</td><td>Mass Communications and the Law</td></tr>
<tr><td>_____</td><td>Chapter Q</td><td>Ethics and Self-Regulation</td></tr>
<tr><td>_____</td><td>Chapter R</td><td>Communications Theory and Research</td></tr>
<tr><td>_____</td><td>Chapter S</td><td>Education and Professional Development</td></tr>
<tr><td>_____</td><td>Chapter T</td><td>Minorities, Women, and the Media</td></tr>
<tr><td>_____</td><td>Chapter U</td><td>International Communications</td></tr>
<tr><td>_____</td><td>Chapver V</td><td>Technology and the Future</td></tr>
</table>

Annotated Instructor's Edition

mass communication

Annotated Instructor's Edition

mass communication

an introduction to the field
second edition

Ronald T. Farrar
University of South Carolina

Brown & Benchmark
PUBLISHERS

Madison   Dubuque, IA   Guilford, CT   Chicago   Toronto   London
Caracas   Mexico City   Buenos Aires   Madrid   Bogota   Sydney

Book Team

Executive Publisher *Edgar J. Laube*
Acquisitions Editor *Eric Ziegler*
Developmental Editor *Mary Rossa*
Production Editor *Debra DeBord*
Proofreading Coordinator *Carrie Barker*
Designer *Jeff Storm*
Art Editor *Rachel Imsland*
Photo Editor *Laura Fuller*
Production Manager *Beth Kundert*
Production/Costing Manager *Sherry Padden*
Marketing Manager *Katie Rose*
Copywriter *M. J. Kelly*

Basal Text *10/12 Garamond*
Display Type *Template Gothic*
Typesetting System *Macintosh/QuarkXPress*
Paper Stock *50# Mirror Matte*

President and Chief Executive Officer *Thomas E. Doran*
Vice President of Production and Business Development *Vickie Putman*
Vice President of Sales and Marketing *Bob McLaughlin*
Director of Marketing *John Finn*

A Times Mirror Company

The credits section for this book begins on page C.1 and is considered an extension of the copyright page.

Cover photo © Lois & Bob Schlowsky/Tony Stone Images

Copyedited by Anne Cody; proofread by Janet Reuter

Printed in the United States of America by Times Mirror Higher Education Group, Inc., 2460 Kerper Boulevard, Dubuque, IA 52001

10 9 8 7 6 5 4 3 2 1

dedication

For Gayla Dennis Farrar

customized brief contents

contents

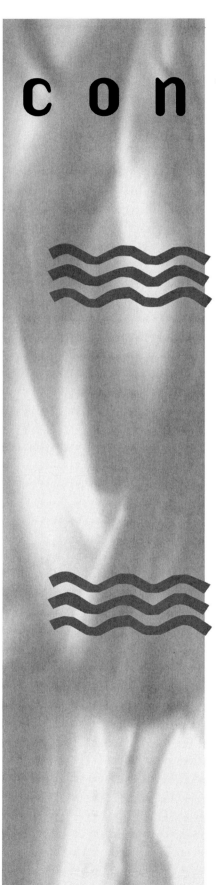

chapter C
The Wire Services

chapter D
Newspapers

chapter E
The Community Press

chapter F
Photographic Communication

chapter G
Magazines

chapter H
The Book Industry

chapter I

Growth of the Electronic Media

chapter J

Radio

chapter K

Recordings

chapter L
Television

chapter M
Films

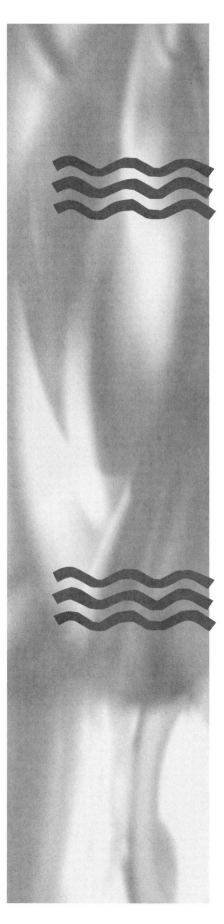

chapter N
Public Relations

chapter O
Advertising

chapter P

Mass Communications and the Law

chapter Q

Ethics and Self-Regulation

chapter R

Communications Theory and Research

chapter S
Education and Professional Development

chapter T
Minorities, Women, and the Media

chapter U
International Communications

chapter V
Technology and the Future

preface

This book is for students who want to know more about the mass communications media—how and why they operate as they do, and how they influence our society.

In a very real sense, we have become a media-driven nation. We cannot overestimate the influence the mass media exert over our politics, economy, and culture. To understand any of these areas, then, we must understand the mass media—and that is the central reason this book was written.

But just as the media drive our society, we define and drive the mass media. The choices we as consumers make determine whether a television series, a newspaper columnist, a magazine, or a radio station format succeeds or fails. The mass media compete for audience time and advertising dollars. Any description and interpretation of the media that did not take this into full account would be naive.

The student who hopes to enter the mass media field as a professional should find the chapters ahead a useful—and, I hope, uplifting—orientation. Many of the chapters specifically discuss career opportunities. But the book is written also for the communications *consumer,* the person who will spend a substantial portion of life watching television, listening to radio, reading magazines and newspapers and books, and absorbing (or tuning out) advertising messages. Tens of thousands of such hours lie ahead for each of you; this book is intended to help you make those hours more productive.

Jim Wright of the Dallas *Morning News,* in a flattering review of the first edition of this book, suggested in his syndicated column that this would be the ideal textbook for a course every American should be required to take called "Surviving Mass Communications," because, in Wright's words, "that's what we are all trying to do":

> This is the Information Age, and most of the information you get about events that occur outside your own neighborhood is brought to you by the various media of mass communications. You need this secondhand information, not only to be an informed citizen and voter, but to get through your daily routine. In our day, what you don't know can hurt you plenty.
>
> Yet the average U.S. citizen has a staggering lack of knowledge about how modern mass communications work. Few have even a nodding acquaintance with the processes, know anything about the hundreds of agencies competing for our attention and dollars, or understand the conflicting loyalties and pressures working on the people who make their living there.
>
> Even intellectuals who consider themselves thoroughly and completely educated have the most incredible delusions about the media sources of most of their current events information.
>
> Yes, I know you don't have to understand a carburetor or a differential to drive a modern car. But you do have to know to put gas in. And it is helpful to be able to distinguish between forward and reverse. A modern American who cannot tell the difference between a straight news report and an opinion column is operating at about the level of the motorist who has yet to figure out how the key fits in the keyhole.

Wright may or may not be accurately depicting today's mass media audiences, but we can make the case that the more we know about modern mass media, the better we will be able to cope with life in the twenty-first century. This book will not make you a mass media expert. It should, however, help you understand how the system works for—and upon—all of us.

The overall approach throughout the text is (1) to observe the industry's environment in its historical, technological, legal, economic, ethical, and social contexts and (2) to provide more specific portraits of various subgroups—television, newspapers, radio, magazines, advertising, public relations, films, books, and so on—that comprise the mass communications field. I hope the observations are reliable and the portraits interesting.

Beyond that, this edition also features:

- An increased emphasis on technology. This book will deal less with specific technical innovations—which will rapidly become dated—than on the cumulative effects that new technologies have on media content and ownership, along with the new ethical demands technology places on media professionals.
- An entire chapter devoted to minorities and women in the media. Women and minority group members remain woefully underrepresented in positions of mass media leadership.
- Separate chapters dealing with community journalism and photographic communication, fields far larger than generally acknowledged.
- Strong emphasis throughout on the mass media as business operations which must compete if they are to survive in a free society. It is important for all consumers to gain a realistic understanding of how the media are financed and how advertising dollars are allocated. Advertising creation and placement, market research, audience analysis, and other processes critical to a realistic understanding of the communications industries are discussed in these pages.
- In-depth discussions of media law and ethics, topics that affect all of society and not just journalists. From more than a quarter century of teaching, I know that students can handle this material and welcome exposure to it.
- A separate chapter dealing with mass communications as a global phenomenon, showing the vast gaps between the "have" and the "have not" nations of the world. This chapter examines economic, cultural, and political barriers to the free flow of information throughout the earth; it also discusses privatization and other global trends that were born or accelerated following the breakup of the former Soviet Union.
- A menu-driven format that gives instructors the opportunity to construct their own coursebook from a menu of 22 chapters. Selected chapters may be arranged in any order. Each custom-printed coursebook includes a full table of contents and an index.

A number of persons have helped with this book, far more than I can mention here. I am especially grateful to Donald McKinney, Donald Woolley, Bonnie Drewniani, A. Jerome Jewler, and Robert Jones, all friends and colleagues at the University of South Carolina; Roy L. Moore and the late Theodore Schulte of the University of Kentucky; John Carroll, now editor of the Baltimore *Sun;* Scott Cutlip, dean emeritus of the Grady School of Journalism at the University of Georgia; R. Dean Mills, dean of the School of Journalism at the University of Missouri; and a great many others. Their insights and expertise have been invaluable, and I am in the debt of these friends and associates who read and commented upon various portions of the book. Let me hasten to add that any errors that may have crept in are mine alone.

In addition, I would like to thank those professors who reviewed one or more drafts of the entire manuscript: Paul Anderson, University of Tennessee at Martin; Barbara Hartung, San Diego State University; James Hoyt, University of Wisconsin–Madison; Greg Lisby, Georgia State University; Jeffrey McCall, DePauw University; Maclyn McClary, Humboldt State University; Robert Ogles, Purdue University; Jerry Pinkham, College of Lake County; George Ridge, University of Arizona; and Paul Shaffer, Austin Peay State University.

For kindly granting permission to quote copyrighted material, the author is especially grateful to the Motion Picture Association of America, the Recording Industry of America, Inc., the Magazine Publishers of America, the Audit Bureau of Circulations, the Public Relations Society of America, WIS-TV in Columbia, S.C., the American Association of Advertising Agencies, and the National Newspaper Association.

A friend and former teaching colleague, Lloyd W. (Bill) Brown, has developed the special Annotated Teaching Edition of this book. Bill's expanded edition for teachers is a fine piece of work; teachers across the country will thank him for it, as I do. Special thanks also go to Jill Van Pelt, Larry Hoffman, and Anthony Henstock, each of whom served as research assistants. Their contributions to the theory, radio, recordings, and film chapters were particularly helpful. Still other people granted permission to use resource documents and to reprint copyrighted material. While these are acknowledged in the text, their cooperation and prompt responses are appreciated. Also, I want to thank the team at Brown & Benchmark that turned this manuscript into a book.

As ever, and most important, I want to thank my students. They have seen and heard the ideas in this book take form over the years, and their questions and comments, in the classroom and in countless informal conversations, have proved invaluable to me. One such former student, my daughter, Janet Farrar Worthington (now an author and editor in her own right) also provided a number of excellent suggestions for visual materials to accompany the text. My son, Bradley Farrar, contributed valuable—and free—advice on the finer points of communications law as I developed that portion of the manuscript. Finally, the entire project has benefited from the encouragement, insight, and perceptive editing of my wife and closest friend, Gayla Dennis Farrar, to whom this volume is dedicated.

Ronald T. Farrar

to the instructor

Numerous aids are available to instructors in mass communications courses. Some of the more common and valuable aids are listed here.

Media Magazines

Three weekly magazines are considered by many to be the primary sources of information about current media events. If your institution's library subscribes to one or more, read them regularly to provide additional information for class lectures or discussions. All three usually set special educational rates enabling students to subscribe at a considerable discount, either individually or in bulk. The three journals are

1 *Advertising Age.* Published by Crain Communications Inc., 740 Rush Street, Chicago, IL 60611–2590. Subscription information: Circulation Department, *Advertising Age,* 965 E. Jefferson, Detroit, MI 48207–3185; 800–678–9505.

2 *Broadcasting & Cable.* 1705 Desales St. N.W., Washington, DC 20036; 202–659–2340. Circulation: 800–554–5729.

3 *Editor & Publisher.* 11 West 19th St., New York, NY 10011; 212–675–4380.

If your library does not carry these magazines, you may wish to assign students to write a critique of one or more of the magazines. This will expose them to these sources at least once and will help them evaluate their usefulness.

Criticism of the media—constructive and otherwise—appears in two magazines: the *American Journalism Review* (formerly *Washington Journalism Review*), published by the University of Maryland; and *Columbia Journalism Review,* published by Columbia University Graduate School of Journalism. Both may be a bit too technical for beginning students, but they provide valuable insights into media actions.

Of course, many other media-related magazines are available. Most would probably be too technical for beginning students. National general-readership magazines such as *Newsweek, Time,* and *U.S. News & World Report* generally include media sections that are written in easily understood terms.

Reference Materials

The two major sources are

1 *Broadcasting & Cable Yearbook.* This volume lists all broadcast radio and television stations, cable systems, networks, and other program sources and includes synopses of Federal Communications Commission regulations and much more. It can be obtained from the *Broadcasting & Cable* magazine office listed previously.

2 *Editor & Publisher International Yearbook.* Lists all daily and weekly newspapers, magazines, and other print publications, multiple (chain) newspaper and magazine ownership, and much more. It is available from the *Editor & Publisher* magazine office listed previously.

These two volumes are excellent sources of information not only for the major national media, but also for local and regional media. A third reference book, particularly useful to the newcomer is *Webster's New World Dictionary of Media and Communications* by Richard Weiner, Simon & Schuster, 1990. The cover says it all: "The Most Comprehensive Source for Understanding the Language of Writers, Communications, and the Media Industries."

Audiovisual Materials

Many audio- and videotapes are useful in the classroom. The PBS video sales service will either rent or sell many media-related videotapes after broadcast. The nearest PBS broadcast station can give you further information on ordering tapes. (*Note:* Taping PBS programs off-air to show in class may be copyright infringement unless you have obtained specific permission. The same applies to most other off-air taping, except from C-SPAN.)

Cable-Satellite Public Affairs Network (C-SPAN) is a noncommercial cable network supported entirely by the cable industry. It carries gavel-to-gavel coverage of both the U.S. House of Representatives and the Senate. When Congress is not in session, C-SPAN covers key Senate and House committee meetings, many of which concern the media. C-SPAN has an education division, "C-SPAN in the Classroom." Any educational institution can tape and use all C-SPAN programs. Previous programs are archived at Purdue University. For full information, contact C-SPAN, 400 N. Capitol St. N.W., Suite 650, Washington, DC 20001; 202–737–3220.

Another source of audiovisual materials is any major broadcast network, along with cable channels such as the Discovery Channel, the Learning Channel, and Arts & Entertainment. Audiotapes of old radio programs are available from many suppliers, primarily through the mail. Excerpts from some of them can provide some lighter moments in a classroom discussion on the media.

Movies can also be useful from time to time. Unfortunately, most are too long to show in a single class session. Some instructors intersperse short sections with class discussion over several days. Some possibilities include:

- *The Front Page* (1931 version, starring Pat O'Brien). This film depicts the Chicago school of journalism—get the story first and the facts later.
- *Citizen Kane* (1941, Orson Welles). This story allegedly parallels the life of William Randolph Hearst. Supposedly, Hearst unsuccessfully tried to suppress it; it is now considered one of the greatest films of all time.
- *Teacher's Pet* (1958, Clark Gable, Doris Day). The stereotypical hard-nosed city editor disdains journalism education until a young protegée changes his mind. One scene includes an excellent explanation of who, what, when, where.
- *All the President's Men* (1976, Robert Redford, Dustin Hoffman). This film tells the story of the two *Washington Post* reporters who broke the Watergate story.

Many other movies have media-related plots. The older ones concentrate on newspaper and magazine reporters; later films feature radio journalism, and finally television.

Some teaching aids that were not available even a few years ago can also assist instructors. Consider the following possibilities:

- *Video camcorders.* Use these devices to videotape people and places—for example, printing plants, newspapers, radio and television stations, cable companies. Depending on the sophistication of the equipment, the location tapes can be played unedited (raw) in class, or edited and enhanced. In either case, the instructor could build up a library of tapes for use in later classes.
- *Audio cassettes.* Use them to record people on location if video equipment is unavailable. Numerous tapes about early and late radio programs are also available from several mail-order companies. One tape, *This Was Radio,* includes about an hour's worth of sounds from the early spark transmitters to the radios of World War II and later. Others feature old radio dramas, comedies, or commercials. Sometimes students themselves can provide audio- or videotapes to use in class.

Guest Speakers

The more media guests you can persuade to speak to your class, the better. However, be careful to choose speakers that relate well to students and that have something specific to communicate.

Other Sources

Use your imagination to find other supplementary materials. The national edition of the New York *Times* is an excellent source of current media news, particularly the Monday edition. Read the business section; a "business" story often has implications far beyond the stock market. In many areas, the national edition of the *Times* is available for daily delivery to classes at a special educational rate.

B&B CourseKits™

B&B CourseKits™ are course-specific collections of for-sale educational materials custom packaged for maximum convenience and value. CourseKits offer you the flexibility of customizing and combining Brown & Benchmark course materials (B&B CourseKits™, Annual Editions®, Taking Sides®, etc.) with your own or other material. Each CourseKit contains two or more instructor-selected items conveniently packaged and priced for your students. For more information on B&B Course-Kits™, please contact your local Brown & Benchmark Representative.

Annual Editions®

Magazines, newspapers, and journals of the public press play an important role in providing current, first-rate, relevant educational information. If in your mass media course you are interested in exposing your students to a wide range of current, well-balanced, carefully selected articles from some of the most important magazines, newspapers, and journals published today, you may want to consider *Annual Editions: Mass Media,* published by the Dushkin Publishing Group, a unit of Brown & Benchmark Publishers. *Annual Editions: Mass Media* is a collection of over forty articles on topics related to the latest research and thinking in mass media. *Annual Editions* is updated on an annual basis, and there are a number of features designed to make it particularly useful, including a topic guide, an annotated table of contents, and unit overviews. For the professor using *Annual Editions* in the classroom, an *Instructor's Resource Guide with Test Questions* is available.

Taking Sides®

Are you interested in generating classroom discussion, in finding a tool to more fully involve your students in their experience of your course? Would you like to encourage your students to become more active learners? to develop their critical thinking skills? Lastly, are you yourself intrigued by current controversies related to issues in mass media and society? If so, you should be aware of a new publication from The Dushkin Publishing Group, a unit of Brown & Benchmark Publishers: *Taking Sides: Clashing Views on Controversial Issues in Mass Media and Society* edited by Professors Alison Alexander of University of Georgia and Jarice Hanson of University of Massachusetts–Amherst. *Taking Sides,* a reader that takes a pro/con approach to issues, is designed to introduce students to controversies in media. For the instructor, there is an *Instructor's Manual with Test Questions* and a general guidebook, *Using Taking Sides in the Classroom,* which discusses methods and techniques for integrating the pro/con approach into any classroom setting.

Readings in Mass Communication

You create a mass media reader specifically for your course. Choose ten or more readings from a comprehensive menu of mass media articles compiled by Michael Emery, California State University–Northridge, and Ted Curtis Smythe, Sterling (Kansas) College. We will bind your selections into an 8.5″ × 11″ book with a sturdy wire coil binding. Copies of your customized book will be delivered within five weeks to the bookstore of your choice.

Lloyd W. (Bill) Brown

chapter

A

An Introduction to Mass Communication and the Social Context

During the early years of the nineteenth century, what we today call the "media of mass communications" consisted primarily of a relatively few newspapers and a smattering of magazines, and a frail book industry.

Objectives

When you have finished studying this chapter, you should be able to:

- Define communication and contrast it with mass communication

- Explain and compare four major concepts of mass communications operation and control used throughout the world today

- Understand the primary roles the mass communications system plays in our society

- Describe some of the current criticisms of mass media performance and ethical values

During the early years of the nineteenth century, what we today call the "media of mass communications" consisted primarily of a relatively few newspapers, a smattering of magazines, and a frail book industry. Yet even then, political leaders expressed concerns about the growing popularity of these emerging institutions and the power they wielded. As Thomas Babington Macaulay, the British poet, historian, and statesman, observed nervously in 1828, "The gallery in which the reporters sit has become a **fourth estate** of the realm"—right up there, in his judgment, with the leaders of the church, the nobility, and the House of Commons.[1] More than a century and a half later, our reliance upon the mass media has become almost total. Without them, governments would likely be paralyzed and laws unevenly and unfairly administered; education would be drastically curtailed; there would be no advertising and, as a result, less commerce; and we would enjoy much less varied entertainments. We live in a synthetic society, as Wilbur Schramm has reminded us, and the media of mass communications create that synthesis.[2]

The dimensions of the system are staggering. When Viacom sought to buy out Paramount in 1994 in one of the great corporate takeover battles in business history, the resulting conglomerate made one company:

- The biggest owner and operator of cable channels, including MTV, VH-1, Nickelodeon, and Showtime
- The world's largest producer of broadcast TV shows, accounting for forty hours of programming a week and including several hit programs
- The biggest book producer, publishing 26 of the top-selling 152 hardcover books sold in 1993
- The owner of the biggest video rental company (Blockbuster), taking in more annual revenue than the next 500 competitors combined
- The biggest retailer of interactive home video games
- One of the largest cable system owners, serving one in every fifty-two cable TV subscribers
- The owner of a television syndication library that includes "I Love Lucy," "The Twilight Zone," "The Cosby Show," and "Star Trek: The Next Generation"
- The owner of nearly 5 percent of the country's 25,200 movie screens[3]

While millions watched intently, television showed us the drama, as it began unfolding early in 1995, surrounding the trial of celebrity O. J. Simpson on murder charges. It was a media circus, but audiences seemingly could not get enough.

The Information Highway

Everybody knows what the telephone is for. It rings. You pick it up. A voice travels down a wire and gets routed and switched right to your ear.

Everybody knows what to do with the television. You turn it on, choose a channel and let advertising, news and entertainment flow into your home.

Now imagine a medium that combines the capabilities of phones with the video and information offerings of the most advanced cable systems and data banks. Instead of settling for what happens to be on at a particular time, you could select any item from an encyclopedia menu of offerings and have it routed directly to your television set or computer screen. A movie? Airline listings? Tomorrow's newspaper or yesterday's episode of *Northern Exposure*? How about a new magazine or a book? A stroll through the L. L. Bean catalog? A teleconference with your boss? A video phone call with your lover? Just punch up what you want, and it appears just when you want it.

Welcome to the information highway. It's not here yet, but it's arriving sooner than you might think.

Philip Elmer-DeWitt in *Time*, 12 April 1993.

Discussion

Ask your students whether they are aware of recent business deals involving the media. If so, what are they? What seems to be their effect on the public?

Discussion

Are these the *only* media of mass communication? If not, what are some of the others? Do billboards, direct mail, and telephone solicitation meet the criteria? Does timeliness have anything to do with it?

Teaching Idea

Survey the class to see what newspapers and magazines they read regularly, what radio stations they listen to, and what television channels they watch. Save the data for further use in chapters dealing with a specific medium.

The deal, involving around $10 billion in cash and stock, vividly underscores the many roles mass communications systems play in our lives—and the value colossal business interests now place upon such systems.

Communication and Mass Communication

Communication is the exchange of information—two minds seeking to share the same thought. This is not an easy task. Each of us experiences personal communication breakdowns: conversations in which directions and explanations are misconstrued, stories or jokes that somehow misfire. In **mass communication,** the task is even more difficult. The scale is bigger and less personal, the information flows mostly one way, and the possibilities for error are legion. We can define this ongoing, complex procedure in this way: *Mass communication is a process by which an individual or organization transmits messages to a large, diverse audience with limited opportunity to respond.* The media (means) of mass communications include (but obviously are not confined to) magazines, newspapers, radio and television, books, recordings, and films.

Our society enjoys all these media in abundance. For example:

- The 1994 combined circulation of all magazines in the United States exceeded 360 million—more than one magazine for every woman, man, and child. More than 90 percent of all adult Americans read magazines regularly, and the typical reader buys at least thirty-six issues per year.
- Daily newspaper circulation exceeds 60 million. More than 8,000 weeklies are published in the United States, adding millions more readers to this total. Only 14 percent of all adult Americans say they rarely or never read a newspaper.
- Television sets operate in 99 percent of all American households; 98 percent of households have at least one color set. The average household receives 30.5 channels, including cable channels. Television viewing averages nearly seven hours per household per day.
- One American in five, including teenagers as well as adults, bought a book in the past week.
- Ninety-six percent of all teenagers and adults report that they regularly listen to the radio.[4]

The mass communications field also encompasses advertising agencies; wire services; public relations and publicity firms; syndication houses that provide feature and photo material for print media or programs and movies for television; artists and graphic design consultants; research firms for product, audience, and message analysis; independent producers of movies and television programs; and program suppliers. The industry is large and pervasive.

Mass Media and the Interconnected World

Mass communication can divide us or bring us together. New technologies enable us to send and receive many more messages than before. If we do not like our leaders, we can let them know, talk back. Around the world, communication is becoming two-way, to the concern of autocratic leaders. In the United States, a single man from Texas, Ross Perot, in 1992 proved he could use communication technologies to bypass and challenge old political structures to reach large audiences. Audiences, through 800 or 900 telephone numbers, can talk back. Individuals and groups can communicate in many other ways as well. Mass communication is becoming more like person-to-person communication—exciting, involving, strange, unpredictable, challenging. International communication has entered a new era. Indeed, we all have.

Donald L. Shaw in *Journalism Quarterly*, Autumn 1992.

We will examine these and other specific media in some detail later. First, we must consider the mass communications system as a whole, learning what it does for us and why society exerts some degree of control over it.

The Social Roles of Mass Communications

In a pioneering study written in 1948, Harold Lasswell of Yale University identified three important social roles communications play: (1) surveillance of the environment, (2) correlation of the components of society in making a response to the environment, and (3) transmission of social inheritance.[5] In other words, the mass media act as:

- Sentinel. We rely on mass communications media to keep us alert to an impending snowstorm, a school board election, the movie schedule at the mall theaters, a department store sale.
- Arena. The communications media place events and controversies on the community agenda, focusing attention on issues so that consensus can be reached.
- Instructor. Through communications media, we learn what others are saying, wearing, doing. MTV has had an enculturating influence on many young people; Hollywood movies had a similar impact on their parents and grandparents. The media educate us, and, to a very great degree, help us function within our environments.
- Social and political regulator. This may be the most important role the mass communications media play. By providing their audiences with realistic information about society and politics, the media help keep leaders honest, social and governmental policies equitable. As eighteenth-century philosopher Jeremy Bentham put it:

Without publicity on the entire government process, no good is permanent; under the auspices of publicity, no evil can continue. Publicity, therefore, is the best means of securing public confidence.[6]

Communications control is also a hallmark of national power and leadership. As Walter Lippmann wrote in 1922:

Nothing affects more the balance of power between Congress and the President than whether the one or the other is the principal source of news and explanation and opinion.[7]

The successes and failures of every U.S. president since the television age began—Dwight Eisenhower, John Kennedy, Lyndon Johnson, Richard Nixon, Gerald Ford, Jimmy Carter, Ronald Reagan, George Bush, and Bill Clinton—have been at least partly connected to the skill with which they were able to articulate policies and "spin" them effectively to the voters via the mass media. In fact,

Discussion

Ask the class which medium they turn to in a local or regional emergency (storm, earthquake, or other event). Does one or more of the students have an interesting media-related emergency experience?

Example

Ask your students to find a current local or regional controversial subject, such as political misbehavior, and examine how the media have handled it. Ask the students how *they* would have handled the situation.

Discussion

Assign students to define *spin* and *spin doctor* in political terms. Ask them to locate recent examples of politicians (or others) allegedly using spin to control negative impressions.

Presents and other public figures utilize the mass media to help set the public agenda. Fewer White House occupants were more effective in communicating via television than John F. Kennedy.

Discussion

Ask the class how important photogeneity is to them. Would they vote only for a good-looking candidate? Why?

Ronald Reagan, president of the United States for most of the 1980s, bore the nickname The Great Communicator. Johnson, whose term ended in frustration with much he had hoped to accomplish undone, admitted that his greatest single failure as president was his inability to use television effectively. Many thoughtful observers worry that the American public now places so high a priority on media skills that we will no longer elect to governorships or the presidency individuals who, whatever other qualifications they might possess, are not reasonably photogenic and adroit at handling news conferences and television interviews. This reveals the impact communications media have had on our national values.

These concerns, though real, are not new; political leaders have confronted them, in different contexts and with varying degrees of success, for centuries. Early politicians didn't have to cope with television or radio, but every U.S. president since George Washington has found that newspaper journalists can be troublesome. Government leaders and mass communications professionals rarely coexist in perfect harmony. The media do not operate in a vacuum; they are part of the social, economic, and political structure, and they must define their role (or have it defined for them) within the countries where they do business. Every nation places limits of some sort on the freedom its mass media enjoy. In the paragraphs that follow, we will look briefly at the major philosophical theories that have evolved to describe what communications should be and do in the societies they serve.

Four Concepts of Mass Communication

In a thoughtful and widely quoted series of essays developed for the National Council of Churches, Fred S. Siebert, Wilbur Schramm, and Theodore Peterson examined the social systems the media of mass communications have functioned in, historically and philosophically. They found four distinct patterns of control: authoritarianism, libertarianism, the Soviet theory, and the social responsibility theory.[8]

Adolf Hitler on the Press

The organization of our [Nazi] press has truly been a success. Our law concerning the press is such that divergencies of opinion between members of the government are no longer an occasion for public exhibitions, which are not the newspapers' business. We've eliminated that conception of political freedom which holds that everybody has the right to say whatever comes into his head.

Adolf Hitler, *Reichstag* (parliament) speech, 1937.

Authoritarianism

In authoritarianism, the oldest and most common relationship between the communications media and society and government, the people are under the control of strong leaders. Individual men and women are regarded as ignorant and weak until they organize themselves into a state. Then, given a sense of direction and unity of purpose by their leader—king or queen, czar, emperor, or military dictator—the society can move forward. Benefits accrue to a united society, and eventually these benefits trickle down to individual members. The people obey their leaders, who in turn provide protection as well as guidance.

Authoritarianism is not necessarily evil. Many parents are somewhat authoritarian, at least to some extent; "Eat your vegetables," they might say, "Don't stay out too late," or "Don't drive too fast." If their offspring resist, such parents might respond, "Look, I know what's best for you. You'll need to do as I say, because you don't know what's best for yourself." Similarly, an old-time football coach's pregame pep talk might go something like this: "I don't want any hot dogs out there. No grandstanders looking for personal glory. We must block and tackle *as a team*. Team! Team! Pull together as a team today and we'll win!" Entire nations operate much like this.

The mass media in a society operating under **authoritarian theory** must contribute to the objectives of the state, or at least not hinder them. This means, for example, that the press may not print both sides of a story; *in an authoritarian society, there is but one side, and one side only.* Anything that suggests otherwise will undermine the progress of the state. Plato, among others, argued against free speech. He warned that unrestrained discussion encourages arguments, which in turn lead to factions; factions then threaten to divide the country, leaving it weak and vulnerable.

Authoritarian leaders expect to control the mass communications media, keeping them in line and silencing individuals who make waves. James Boswell, quoting Dr. Samuel Johnson on the subject, rationalized suppressing open discussion this way:

> Every society has a right to preserve public peace and order, and therefore has a good right to prohibit the propagation of opinions which have a dangerous tendency. To say the magistrate has this right is using an inadequate word; it is the society for which the magistrate is agent. He may be morally or theologically wrong in restraining the propagation of opinions which he thinks dangerous, but he is politically right.[9]

To our ears, this may seem a chilling notion, but dictators throughout history have endorsed the authoritarian position.

Libertarianism

Libertarianism represents another, diametrically opposed viewpoint about the nature of humanity. A product of the Age of Reason, **libertarian theory** places a much higher value on the individual. Men and women are inherently rational, say libertarians, and they can operate and develop without the state's heavy-handed direction.

Class Project

Assign students to find out which societies are strictly authoritarian today. England and other nations have monarchs—are they automatically authoritarian? Are there different degrees of authoritarianism?

Extra Information

Dr. Johnson, when reporting on the Parliamentary debates for a journal, is alleged to have said that the "Whig dogs" would never get the best of the debates he reported. Johnson himself was a staunch Tory. Question: What were "Whigs" and "Tories"?

If they are given the facts, individuals will usually respond properly and responsibly to them. In *Aeropagitica,* a rousing defense of free printing written more than three hundred years ago, English poet John Milton proclaimed:

> And though all of the windes of doctrine were let loose to play upon the earth, so Truth be in the field, we do injuriously be licensing and prohibiting to misdoubt her strength. Let her and Falsehood grapple; who ever knew Truth put to the wors, in a free and open encounter?[10]

During the Renaissance, philosophers turned their intellectual energies away from theological questions to study what happens on earth. Dramatic breakthroughs in publishing technology aided the search for truth through reason. Printing on a mass scale, enabled by Johann Gutenberg's development of movable type in the fifteenth century, speeded up the diffusion of ideas throughout the world. With respect for new ideas came respect for the individuals who created and reacted to them.

The media of mass communications play a role of the first magnitude in a libertarian society. By conveying a diversity of opinions to the community, the press creates a marketplace of ideas, the forum through which people debate opinions and in which truth will ultimately prevail.

Fortunately for mass communications in America, libertarian philosophy had reached a certain fruition by the time our national government was taking shape. Freedom of expression thus became an integral part of the new Constitution. In a famous and oft-quoted letter to Edward Carrington in 1787, Thomas Jefferson discussed the rationale behind free speech:

> The people are the only censors of their governors; and even their efforts will tend to keep these to the true principles of their institution. To punish these errors too severely would be to suppress the only safeguard of the public liberty. The way to prevent these irregular interpositions of the people is to give them full information of their affairs thro' the channel of the public papers, and to contrive that those papers should penetrate the whole mass of the people. The basis of our governments being the opinion of the people, the first object should be to keep that right; and were it left to me to decide whether we should have a government without newspapers or newspapers without a government, I should not hesitate to prefer the latter. But I should mean that every man should receive those papers and be capable of reading them.[11]

Libertarianism is the freedom to be wrong as well as right; views that are irresponsible, or even dangerous, can be offered for approval in the intellectual marketplace. The true libertarian is unworried by the clamor, serene in the belief that false

Discussion

In the real world, do the media actually provide a "marketplace of ideas"? What are some of the limitations of this marketplace?

Discussion

The last sentence in this Jeffersonian quotation is often eliminated. Is this sentence just as important as the preceding one? Explain.

Libertarianism: plenty to choose from in the marketplace of ideas.

ideas will be discredited and truth will sooner or later carry the day. It is a chancy philosophy, as we shall see, but our great system of mass communications was built on it and is permitted to exist because of it.

The Soviet Theory

As Siebert, Schramm, and Peterson pointed out, there are actually only two basic theories of mass communications, but each has both an older and a newer form. The newer form of authoritarianism is the **Soviet theory,** still operational in much of the world despite the disintegration of the former Soviet Union in the early 1990s. The Soviet theory differs from other authoritarian frameworks because it replaces mere regulation, which can be passive, with a vigorous activism. In authoritarianism, the government *controls* the media; under the Soviet theory, the government *is* the media.

As he attempted to establish Marxist philosophy in Russia in the years before and after the 1917 Communist Revolution, Lenin shrewdly employed the media of mass communications as a weapon, capable of imparting motivation—if not fear—and instruction to the people. Owned and operated by the government, the news media in a Soviet-style system are deeply involved in keeping the government functional. Under the Soviet theory, newspapers, magazines, radio, and television comprise a social force that defines goals, spurs workers to action, recognizes positive attainments, and criticizes sloppy performance. The media carry much more than merely the party line. As Schramm explains:

> The Soviet leaders believed, of course, that power is resident in people, latent in social institutions, and generated in social action. But it can only be realized when it is joined with the ownership of natural resources and the means of production, and when it is organized and directed. The media must therefore be owned and used by the state.[12]

Lenin's editorial philosophy, which ultimately failed in Russia, has nevertheless been picked up by political leaders elsewhere, especially in China and a number of developing countries. For example, some years ago, the editor of the only daily newspaper in a newly independent African country—a country so undeveloped it did not yet have its own currency but instead utilized the currency of its neighbors—explained to a group of U.S. editors and professors the role his newspaper had to play in attempting to modernize that society. "In our first issue," he said, "I published just one story on the first page. One brief story. The rest of the page was blank. That story read something like this: `We are no longer a European colony. We are a free nation now. And in a free nation we must have pride. People in free nations do *not* use the streets of the capital city as a public toilet.'" That particular mass communications medium did not concern itself with lofty editorials about international economics, the ozone layer, or nuclear disarmament—at least, not just then. More basic issues were at hand.

Under the Soviet theory, the media of mass communications may do much more than inform and entertain. They may serve as motivators, police, lecturers, and even nation builders.

Lenin on the Press

Why should freedom of speech and freedom of the press be allowed? Why should a government which is doing what it believes to be right allow itself to be criticized? It would not allow opposition by lethal weapons. Ideas are much more fatal things than guns. Why should any man be allowed to buy a printing press and disseminate pernicious opinion calculated to embarrass the government?

Nikolai Lenin, quoted in *Pravda,* 1921.

The Social Responsibility Theory

To work properly, libertarian theory requires that certain conditions be met. One is that all persons and all opinions must enjoy full and equal access to the intellectual marketplace. Another is that the audience—the public, the voters—must always seek out a wide range of viewpoints, then react intelligently to conflicting ideas. These assumptions, we learned in the mid-twentieth century, may be seriously flawed. First, as American society grew larger, more diverse, and more complex, it became harder to give voice to all viewpoints. The media of mass communications had grown into big businesses, expensive to own and operate. Media management was restricted, if not by law then by circumstance, to a privileged few. And Freudian research began to cast doubt on the idea that society is consistently rational. The public, in other words, might not react intelligently to what it hears.

Elmer Davis, a respected radio commentator who served as director of the Office of War Information during World War II, warned of the need for more care in communicating with the mass audience:

> Objectivity is all right if it is really objective, if it conveys as accurate an impression of the truth as can be obtained. But to let demonstrably false statements stand with no warning of their falsity is not what I would call objectivity.[13]

Social responsibility theory, then, represents an attempt to bring libertarianism up to date in modern society. It places an obligation on those who control the powerful communications media to make sure that (1) events are reported fairly and accurately and (2) all viewpoints, not merely media owners' opinions, are heard.

Earlier in this century, vigorously competitive newspapers were commonplace, even in smaller communities. If a Democratic candidate for governor made a campaign speech in the town, the Democratic newspaper would likely exaggerate the size and enthusiasm of the crowd. The Republican newspaper, in turn, could be expected to play down the occasion, underestimate the size of the audience, and characterize the crowd response as lukewarm. The intelligent reader could examine accounts in both papers, then decide that the truth probably fell somewhere in between.

Such comparisons are rare today, for only a tiny handful of U.S. communities can support competing newspapers. Far fewer newspapers are published in America than were a century ago; weaker papers have merged into stronger ones, other media have drained away advertising revenue and audience interest, and better highways have made it possible for larger papers to circulate over greater distances. Those newspapers that did survive, social responsibility theorists contend, have an obligation to the public to avoid abusing the privilege they enjoy. Events are too complex, and the stakes are too high, for media owners to distort the news so as to reflect their own biases. Classic libertarianism, the argument runs, is obsolete; changing events and conditions call for the media to play a different role. Mass communications leaders must take up the slack, discussing both sides of each issue and helping the reader to discern truth.

As may be expected, this theory is controversial. Some media owners regard freedom of the press as a personal right; they serve their audiences best, they feel, by presenting their own viewpoints for the public's acceptance or rejection. "Fairness," they argue, represents an artificial and perhaps even cynical exercise that can tie the media in knots. This position was staked out over two centuries ago by Benjamin Franklin, when a writer who disagreed with Franklin asked for space to present his differing view. "My newspaper," Franklin declared, "is not a stagecoach with seats on it for everyone."[14]

But the clear trend, acknowledged or not, has been toward more openness, fairness, and completeness. Newspapers and magazines often print guest editorials or **op ed** (opposite, or facing, the editorial page) columns and letters criticizing social

Discussion

Assign students to determine whether any competing news media exist in your area. Have students discuss what is meant by "competition."

How Powerful Is the Press?

America's social, political, and economic agenda today is largely established on the basis of what appears on the front page of the New York *Times* and (to a lesser degree) of other major newspapers, and on the covers of *Time* and *Newsweek,* and on the evening network news shows and "60 Minutes." Even radio talk shows can directly influence public opinion. . . . Most of the major media organizations are headquartered in New York, and once the journalistic titans there focus on an issue, the rest of the country is sure to follow. A story on an all-news radio station in New York becomes a headline in the New York *Post . . .* becomes a story on a local television news show in New York . . . becomes a page-one story in the New York *Times . . .* becomes a network news story . . . becomes a cover story in *Newsweek . . .* becomes a best-selling book. . . .

What influence the press retains owes far more to pervasiveness than to persuasion, far more to its role in setting agendas than in stating opinions. The press today may help determine what people *think about,* but only rarely does the press help determine what people *think.*

David Shaw in the *Gannett Center Journal,* Spring 1989.

and political events or even the publication's policies and performance. Publishers are not required to print such opinions, but a great many do. Broadcasters, who are obliged by federal law to operate in "the public interest, convenience, and necessity," do attempt to avoid being labeled as unfair, and often seek out opposing points of view on controversial issues. Some media owners must at times feel that their publication or broadcast station is less a private business than a quasi-public utility. In Theodore Peterson's words:

> Freedom carries concomitant obligations; and the press, which enjoys a privileged position under our government, is obliged to be responsible to society for carrying out certain essential functions of mass communications in contemporary society. To the extent that the press recognizes its responsibilities and makes them the basis of operational policies, the libertarian system will satisfy the needs of society. To the extent that the press does not assume its responsibilities, some other agency must see that the essential functions of mass communications are carried out.[15]

The "other agency" Peterson refers to, in a worst-case scenario, is likely to be government. And government's—any government's—definition of "responsibility" is almost certain to be very different from, and far more restrictive than, the definition most media people would proffer.

All four theories of mass communications are practiced in the world today. Some publications in the United States and western Europe, for example, energetically test the outer limits of libertarian theory in virtually every edition, while others possess a well-developed sense of what they regard as "social responsibility." The press of many nations, along with the broadcast operations of *most* nations, continues to function under some degree of authoritarian control. The activist Soviet theory, no longer in place in the former Soviet Union, nevertheless remains in effect throughout China and in a number of developing countries as well.

An Important and Dynamic Profession

The media of mass communications, then, do far more than merely report the news or provide an evening's entertainment. To a very great degree, they illuminate American society and help us shape individual and national priorities, develop our economy, and preserve our culture and our liberty. They create celebrities, define political and cultural agendas, and confer status on causes as well as individuals.

The mass media also make enemies. Powerful leaders of government, business, education, the clergy, organized labor, minorities, and environmental groups have complained, often bitterly, about what they perceive to be the media of mass communications' unfair attitudes and stereotypes, distorted coverage, and blatant invasions of privacy.

Class Project

Depending on class size, have either individual students or groups of students analyze one or more local or regional newspapers. What is the apparent political slant of the editorial page? What opinions appear on the op-ed pages? What kinds of editorial cartoons are featured? How many letters to the editor are printed, and do they criticize the newspaper? What percentage of the entire paper is given to advertisements? (Save this data for later use in chapter D.)

Publicity, Justice, and O. J. Simpson

The court of public opinion may be one of America's most maligned institutions. But in every high-profile case, it's still the place where everybody goes to plead. So with the nation largely—and for the most part, miserably—poised between affection for O. J. Simpson and revulsion at the bloody slicing of Nicole Simpson and Ron Goldman, a public game is in play between O. J.'s accusers and his defenders. The aim is to persuade people that they do not know what they *think* they know.

Richard Lacayo in *Time*, 4 July 1994.

A few of the specific charges focus on:

- Unfair attitudes: Political reporting, especially of presidential politics, is biased, critics charge.
- Distorted coverage: An investigative report on General Motors trucks that aired on "Dateline NBC" showed pictures of a truck bursting into flame due to a collision. Afterward, NBC executives admitted the demonstration had been rigged; the truck was outfitted with rocketlike "explosive devices" to ensure it would explode if the gas tank leaked.[16]
- Privacy invasion: Several years ago, members of the press threatened to disclose that tennis celebrity Arthur Ashe was afflicted with AIDS. Ashe, who had contracted the disease from a blood transfusion, hoped to protect his family from unwelcome attention. Ashe's notoriety, editors argued, made the newsworthiness of the story outweigh the tennis star's right to privacy. Many observers, both inside and outside the mass media field, disagreed.

Much media bashing is perpetuated by media people themselves. A Pulitzer-prize-winning journalist and senior editor of *Time,* William A. Henry III, launched a cover story, "Accusing the Press," by summarizing what critics were saying in this stinging paragraph:

> They [journalists] are rude and accusatory, cynical and almost unpatriotic. They twist facts to suit their not-so-hidden liberal agenda. They meddle in politics, harass business, invade people's privacy, and then walk off without regard to the pain and chaos they leave behind. They are arrogant and self-righteous, brushing aside most criticism as the uninformed carping of cranks and idealogues. To top it off, they claim that their behavior is sanctioned, indeed sanctified, by the U.S. Constitution.[17]

One of the most discussed books of the early 1990s was *Feeding Frenzy,* by Larry Sabato, in which he compared journalists to a swarm of bloodthirsty piranhas closing in for the kill when a politician is in trouble. A 1994 Gallup poll concluded that only about a third of the country would give TV reporters and commentators, journalists, and newspaper reporters high marks for professional ethics.

The saturation television coverage given to the legendary sports and broadcasting figure, O. J. Simpson, accused of two murders in 1994, was so excessive that legal scholars and judges wondered if the defendant could conceivably find jurors that had not heard of the case and formed an opinion about it.

Yet for all its critics and their concerns about sound bites, bias, and media symbolism, the American mass communications system is the envy of the world. In 1989, as social and political upheavals rocked China and Eastern Europe, the rest of the world knew about these events largely because American and other western journalists were there to report them, from Tiananmen Square to the Berlin Wall. Indeed, the youth-led uprisings in China, which resulted in the deaths of hundreds of university students, were a plea for democratic reforms and, especially, for more freedom of expression. By reporting on certain conditions in this country and

Discussion

Ask the class for their definition(s) of "good" and "bad" news reporting. Then have them analyze one or more issues of a daily newspaper to see what items fit their definition(s).

Discussion

Assign your students to explore any recent examples of a media "feeding frenzy" in national, regional, or local media. What effects does this have?

Town crier to the world. Cable News Network, among other global reporting agencies, reaches audiences in virtually every country.

Often perceived as pushy and relentless, U.S. journalists nevertheless are regarded as the most effective in the world.

abroad, the media of mass communications have helped improve them. Even the harsher critics, including some whom we have cited here, find far more good than bad in the media system. Asked once what had caused the stunning collapse of communism in Eastern Europe, Polish leader Lech Walesa pointed to a nearby TV set. "It all came from there," he said.[18]

Ethical and performance standards for the media will be discussed throughout these pages. We will focus on shortcomings as well as achievements; illustrations of each abound. It may be, to paraphrase Thomas Jefferson, that the country gets the kind of political leadership, and the kind of mass communications, that it deserves. There is ample room for improvement all around, provided society retains the freedom to choose, to grow and change.

One point is clear. The freedom we enjoy cannot long survive without freedom of communication. And freedom of communication, in the final analysis, is linked to the understanding the general public has of how and why the mass communications media operate as they do.

The chapters that follow are devoted to that end—to helping you understand the mass media. We will begin by placing the media—and especially the newspaper, which established so many of the patterns the others follow—into historical perspective.

Discussion

Survey the class to ascertain their feelings about the trustworthiness of various individuals and professions. Include lawyers, politicians, journalists, used car salespeople, and others. Which are most trustworthy and why? (Save the results, and ask again at the end of the term to see if students feel the same.)

summary

Communication is the exchange of information—allowing two minds to share the same thought. Mass communication is a process by which an individual or organization transmits messages to a large, diverse audience with limited opportunity to respond. The mass communications system in the United States reaches virtually every citizen and serves as a collective sentinel, public forum, teacher, and social and political influence.

Historically, mass communications systems around the world have reflected one of four important philosophies. Under authoritarianism, the government controls the press (or mass media) system. The press must support government policies to avoid factions, which could

prevent the attainment of social and political goals. Under libertarianism, free discussion is encouraged in the belief that individuals will choose from the marketplace of ideas those that will attain appropriate goals for the society. Under the Soviet theory, still in effect in China and other nations though not in the former Soviet Union, the mass media are active participants in the attainment of the government's objectives. And finally, under the social responsibility theory, the mass media operate freely but assume a responsibility to emphasize fairness and accuracy and bring to their audiences often conflicting points of view in an attempt to serve the total public.

? questions and cases

1. John Adams, president during the early years of the republic (1797–1801), deplored the time he spent dealing with the press. On 27 August 1800 he wrote to a friend: "If he [the president] must enter into a controversy in pamphlets and newspapers, in vindication of his measures, he would have employment enough for his whole life, and must neglect the duties and business of the nation." Comment on modern day presidents and the mass media. Do today's mass media have too great a claim on the time and energies of the chief executive? too little? Discuss this issue.

2. List several individual media professionals (editors, columnists, TV anchors) that you believe are

particularly effective in communicating via the mass media. What qualities, in your judgment, make them successful?

3. List several celebrities (political leaders, entertainers, other celebrities outside the mass communications field), who you believe are particularly effective in communicating via the mass media. What qualities, in your judgment, make them successful?

4. Do you agree that libertarianism as a theory of mass communications has become obsolete? Explain why or why not.

5. Does the concept of a socially responsible mass communications system worry you? Why or why not? How would *you* define "social responsibility"?

chapter glossary

authoritarian theory   For our purposes, one of four principal theories explaining the relationship between the mass media and the social and political structure. Under authoritarianism, the ruling class controls the information and ideas presented to the public.

fourth estate   Traditionally, an informal name for the press, referring especially to its role as watchdog.

libertarian theory   For our purposes, a belief that the public is best served when there is open access to all information and ideas.

mass communications   The process by which an individual or organization transmits messages to a large, diverse audience with limited opportunity to respond.

op-ed page   (opposite the editorial page) In many newspapers, a forum for columns, essays, and

commentaries—some of which may not agree with the paper's editorial policy.

social responsibility theory   A theory that contends that the media of mass communications have an obligation to present news and opinions fairly, fully, and accurately, taking pains to assure that all shades of opinion are heard and false information is exposed. This contrasts with libertarian theory, which holds that media owners should be free to report as they choose, that society will take the responsibility to seek out all points of view and separate the good ideas from the bad.

Soviet theory   An activist form of authoritarianism in which the mass media function as an integral part of the government.

notes

1 Quoted in Frank Luther Mott, *The News in America* (Cambridge: Harvard University Press, 1952), 6.

2 Wilbur F. Schramm, *Mass Media and National Development* (Stanford, Calif.: Stanford University Press, 1964), 5.

3 Paul Wiseman, "Redstone's Triumph of Tenacity," *USA Today,* 16 February 1994.

4 Figures reported by the American Newspaper Publishers Association, American Magazine Publishers Association, National Association of Broadcasters, and the Book Industry Study Group, respectively.

5 Harold D. Lasswell, "The Structure and Function of Communication in Society," reprinted in Wilbur Schramm and Donald F. Roberts, *The Process and Effects of Mass Communication,* rev. ed. (Urbana: University of Illinois Press, 1971), 84–99.

6 Quoted in John L. Hulteng and Roy Paul Nelson, *The Fourth Estate* (New York: Harper & Row, 1983), 2.

7 Walter Lippman, *Public Opinion* (New York: Macmillan, 1922), 289.

8 Fred S. Siebert, Theodore Peterson, and Wilbur Schramm, *Four Theories of the Press* (Urbana: University of Illinois Press, 1956), 36.

9 Quoted in James Boswell, *Life of Johnson* (New York: Alfred Knopf, 1992), vol. 1, p. 249. Originally published in 1791 in Edinburgh, Scotland.

10 John Milton, *Areopagitica: A Defence of the Liberty of Unlicensed Printing,* pamphlet issued in 1644. Quoted in Frank Luther Mott and Ralph D. Casey, *Interpretations of Journalism* (New York: Croft, 1937), 3.

11 Reprinted in Calder M. Pickett, *Voices of the Past: Key Documents in the History of American Journalism* (Columbus, Ohio: Grid, 1977), 63.

12 Siebert, Schramm, and Peterson, *Four Theories, op. cit.,* 122.

13 Elmer Davis, *But We Were Born Free* (Indianapolis: Bobbs-Merrill, 1954), 174.

14 Benjamin Franklin, *Autobiography,* reprinted in Mott and Casey, *Interpretations of Journalism, op. cit.,* 105.

15 Siebert, Schramm, and Peterson, *Four Theories, op. cit.,* 94.

16 Elizabeth Kolbert, "A Tabloid Touch in the Nightly News," New York *Times,* 14 February 1993.

17 Reprinted in William A. Henry III, "Why Journalists Can't Wear White," Freedom Forum *Media Studies Journal,* Fall 1992, 18.

18 John Lippman, "TV: The Third Superpower," Los Angeles *Times,* 27 December 1992.

The programming
format of a modern
radio station, the
prime-time
scheduling policies
of a television
network, the
editorial
philosophies of a
national
magazine—all
reflect to some
degree values

chapter

B

Evolution of the
Print Media

Objectives

When you have finished studying this chapter,
you should be able to:

Objectives

When you have finished studying this chapter,
you should be able to:

@ Explain prior restraint, why it existed,
and how it was first overcome in the
United States

@ Discuss the legal and symbolic implications
of the trial of John Peter Zenger

@ Describe the role the press played in the
American Revolution and in articulating
the debate over formation of the new
governmental structure

@ Explain how the penny press developed,
and discuss its importance to the mass
media then and now

@ Discuss Pulitzer and Hearst; the positive,
and sometimes the negative, effects a
media crusade can generate; and the
phenomenon known as "yellow journalism"

@ Analyze journalistic coverage of modern
war and how that coverage has changed
since World War II

@ Outline the reasons reporters turned
toward interpretive styles in coping with
twentieth-century news trends

The programming format of a modern radio station, the prime-time scheduling policies of a television network, the editorial philosophies of a national magazine—all reflect to some degree values established and battles won long ago by newspaper men and women. We begin our study of the mass media, then, with a look at the evolution of print journalism in the United States. It is a colorful story, and the entire mass communications industry owes much to it.

"The history of the American newspaper," declared journalism historian John Tebbel, "is a record of the Establishment's effort to control the news and of private individuals to disclose it without reservation."[1] While Tebbel's thesis may appear unduly combative, the fact is that the journalist's way has never been smooth. Consider, for example, the case of Englishman John Twyn, who in 1663 published a slender volume entitled *A Treatise on the Execution of Justice.* This treatise suggested that perhaps the king might find it within himself to become more accountable to his subjects. For this unsolicited advice, Twyn was charged with treason, despite the fact that he himself did not write the book but merely printed it. (He never did reveal the author's name.) The law's savage fury at uncontrolled printing came down full force in the judgment pronounced on Twyn:

> The court have found you guilty; therefore the judgment of the court is . . . that you be led back to the place from whence you came, to be drawn upon an hurdle [a sled] to the place of execution; and there you shall be hanged by the neck, and, being alive, shall be cut down, and your privy-members shall be cut off, your entrails shall be taken out of your body, and, you living, the same to be burnt before your eyes; your head to be cut off, your body to be divided into four quarters and your head and quarters to be disposed of at the pleasure of the King's majesty. And the Lord have mercy on your soul.[2]

This type of sentence led other publishers of the period to proceed with a certain caution. Yet newspapers of a sort, legal and illegal, called **corontos,** continued to appear and to sell briskly in Britain and throughout Europe. Less than thirty years later, on 25 September 1690, the first newspaper was printed in the American colonies. It lasted one issue.

The publisher was Benjamin Harris, a bookseller by trade and a fast-buck confidence man by inclination. He had served time in England for printing and selling anti-Catholic materials to Pope-hating Protestant extremists. Scholars remain unsure as to whether Harris was driven by true religious zeal or, as seems more likely, hopes of making money by pandering to ignorance and religious bigotry. Along with patent medicines, Harris sold, with equal enthusiasm, playing cards with anti-Papal messages printed on the back. For all his faults, Harris was smart, ambitious, cocky, and unimpressed with governmental authority. But in 1686 Harris found himself again behind bars following still another disagreement with the London police. This prompted him to emigrate to the colonies, where he prospered briefly as proprietor of a coffee house and bookshop in Boston.[3]

A few years of this placid existence, however, and Harris restlessly turned his attention to bigger things. Abruptly, and without bothering to consult the colonial

Extra Information
Courts doled out punishments to printers and journalists both in England and America. Most were not as painful as Twyn's.

John Kennedy on the Press

It is never pleasant to read things that are not agreeable news, but I would say that it is an invaluable arm of the Presidency—to check really on what is going on in the administration. And things come to my attention that give me concern or give me information. So I would think that . . . there is a terrific disadvantage not to have the abrasive quality of the press applied to you daily, to an administration, even though we never like it, and even though we wish they didn't write it, and even though we disapprove, there isn't any doubt that we could not do the job at all in a free society without a very, very active press.

John F. Kennedy, in response to a question at a presidential news conference, 1962.

Discussion

Should modern-day papers leave space for such "pass-along" news?

Background

English licensing laws remained in effect for many years. Even today, the British government can prevent journalists from printing news the government considers a matter of national security. There is no "First Amendment" right in England.

authorities, he brought out a newspaper, *Publick Occurrences, Both Foreign and Domestick*. Lively reports filled its three pages (the fourth page was left blank, so the reader could pencil in some more news before passing the copy on to a friend). These reports included an account of a British officer's mutilation of some Canadian Indians, an epidemic, a suicide, two fires, an essay speculating on England's difficulties with Irish rebels, and a steamy description of the king of France's recent extramarital affairs. Harris promised further disclosures in subsequent issues, adding that his newspaper's unflinching honesty would "cure that Spirit of Lying, which prevails amongst us."[4]

But there would be no subsequent issues. The merits of *Publick Occurrences*, such as they were, did not impress the royal governor. He summarily ordered the paper banned, announcing that Harris had taken it upon himself to publish "reflections of a very high nature." More to the point, Harris had failed to obtain a license, which colonial law then required. Harris was not thrown in jail for this effrontery, but he was made to feel unwelcome. Eventually he sailed back to England to engage in further publishing adventures while renewing his interest in pushing patent medicines. He had more brushes with the law. Harris died in poverty and disgrace, with little to show for the life he had led—little besides that brief, impulsive moment in 1690 when he launched the press in America. Or, at least, he tried to, and we remember him for the effort.

It was fourteen years before someone else dared publish another newspaper in the growing community of Boston.[5] This time the publisher was John Campbell. In temperament and operating style, Campbell and Harris were light years apart. Where Harris was bold and rebellious, Campbell was prudent in the extreme. Harris frequently did business on the wrong side of the law; Campbell was a model citizen. Harris's newspaper was suppressed after a single edition; Campbell's lasted nearly twenty years.

Campbell had been appointed Boston's postmaster, a position of some importance, and part of his responsibility was to keep his constituents informed. For a time he mailed out to various residents handwritten summaries of news and comment he gleaned from British newspapers and official dispatches that came through his office. Close with his money, Campbell soon hit upon the idea of printing and selling this material, in hopes that the twopence he charged per copy would cover his printing costs. But before printing the first issue of his Boston *News-Letter* in 1704, he judiciously checked with the royal government and secured proper permission. Campbell offered to clear the contents of each week's *News-Letter* with the governor's office, a gesture that assured him the law's full protection—and virtually guaranteed that his newspaper would be dull and noncontroversial. This arrangement was fine with Campbell, who was hardly a crusader. He was content to publish brief notices of ship arrivals and departures, weather reports, court actions, proclamations, and texts of sermons, all under the large boldface line, "PUBLISHED BY AUTHORITY."

News: Unrefined, Unruly, Irrepressible?

After all, the exchange of news, with all its limitations, remains an expression of our desire for awareness. . . . If the past is any guide, many future data banks will be stocked with gruesome murder stories, and more computer-organized news services will concentrate on Hollywood and baseball than on American politics. For no matter how sophisticated news organs become, unless human beings are also rewired, they are likely to continue to satisfy their desire to remain aware with a spicy, hastily prepared mix of the portentous and the anomalous similar to that with which they have satisfied that desire for the past few thousand years.

The more profound, more sober side of our nature may never succeed in transforming news into an ideal vehicle for its concerns. Still, is there not something wonderfully human in this image of a future in which layer upon layer of finely worked circuitry is placed at the service of subject matter as unrefined, unruly, and irrepressible as news?

Michael Stephens, *A History of News* (Penguin Books, 1988).

Campbell's *News-Letter* was dreary reading. Often he fell behind and had to warn his readers that there was no room in this week's paper for recent developments because he hadn't caught up with the old news yet. In some copies the news fell several months in arrears. Campbell printed it all anyway, and most of it was accurate and has become a valuable record. He possessed a strong sense of history and felt an obligation to his two hundred or so subscribers to present information fairly and responsibly. His journalism was that of a stodgy bureaucrat, but he was shrewd enough to sidestep potential clashes with authority which no mere journalist could hope to win.[6]

After fifteen years, Campbell was replaced as Boston's postmaster. His successor, William Brooker, also elected to produce a newspaper. Campbell stubbornly kept on with the *News-Letter,* and for several years Boston could boast of competing newspapers, both officially sanctioned. This condition, where there is prepublication control over content, or **prior restraint,** came under serious challenge in 1721 through the efforts of a bold, headstrong printer named James Franklin. Annoyed by the loss of some official printing business, Franklin retaliated by launching a newspaper of his own, the *New-England Courant.* It was a lively paper, filled with sparkling political and literary essays and irreverent humor pieces turned out by a clique of bright, rebellious young Bostonians. Among his contributors was sixteen-year-old Benjamin Franklin, who wrote for the paper anonymously while serving as an apprentice in his brother's print shop.

The new paper's free-wheeling comment and criticism at once evoked the wrath of Boston's religious leaders. Sunday after Sunday, they denounced the *Courant* from the pulpit, branding its writers members of a "Hell-Fire club" bound for eternal damnation. But because Franklin's *Courant* was such a refreshing departure from Boston's dreary semiofficial publications, it soon caught on with a large and appreciative audience. Sensing the paper's popularity and unwilling at that moment to risk a confrontation, the royal government backed away from issuing an order of suppression. The *Courant* was not published *by* authority, but in spite of it. Prior restraint had been dealt a serious blow.

The Trial of John Peter Zenger

The most significant media-related event of this period was a drama played out in a courtroom in New York, where John Peter Zenger, publisher of the *Weekly Journal,* faced charges of **seditious libel.** Zenger had been a printer at the government-supported *Gazette.* Infuriated by the dictatorial policies of the royal governor, William Cosby, several lawyers and landowners quietly arranged to begin a rival newspaper. They installed Zenger as publisher, with the understanding that he in return would provide space for the occasional, anonymously written item that might poke fun at the Cosby regime. These satirical barbs would seem mild today, but the thin-skinned Cosby was outraged. He tried unsuccessfully to persuade a grand jury that Zenger should be indicted for treason. When this brazen attempt failed, Cosby issued a warrant for Zenger's arrest and kept the publisher locked up for months before bringing him to trial. Such strong-arm tactics created widespread sympathy for Zenger. The trial, when it finally began in August 1735, had grown to encompass far more than one printer's liberty. Indeed, it would symbolize the plight of a people who were feeling increasingly oppressed by their British masters.

Governor Cosby's intolerance, though repugnant today, was fully supported by British law then on the books. The idea that Zenger had only printed the truth was not an acceptable defense against seditious libel charges. Beyond that, the jury was not permitted to determine whether the offending material was indeed treasonous; that decision was left to the judge, whom the governor had handpicked. The jury's role was limited merely to deciding who had printed the offensive statements, and there was no doubt Zenger had printed them. For his defense, however,

Although his genius extended into many areas of commerce, science, and diplomacy, Benjamin Franklin was first and foremost a printer— and one who understood the role of the press in a democracy."If all printers were determined not to print until they were sure it would offend nobody," he once wrote, "there would be very little printed."

Extra Information

A major prior restraint case involved the "Pentagon Papers," a set of documents detailing the government's handling of the Vietnam war that the Nixon White House tried to prevent newspapers from printing. The case went to the U.S. Supreme Court, which upheld the right of the press to print. Nine different reasons shaped the Court's decision. Check if a copy of the decision is available; it makes interesting reading.

Extra Information

Seditious libel continued to be a legal offense in the early days of the United States. Several publishers were jailed for "libeling" the government. Fortunately, the *Alien and Sedition* Acts were repealed and the publishers released.

Zenger's friends and silent partners retained Andrew Hamilton of Philadelphia, then eighty years old and perhaps the most distinguished lawyer in the colonies. Faced with a case that seemed unwinnable under existing law, Hamilton dramatically took the offensive. Rather than defend Zenger directly, he attacked the unfairness of the law and the haughtiness of the British authorities. In an emotion-packed closing argument, he appealed to the jury:

> It is not the cause of the poor printer, nor of New York alone, which you are now trying. No! It may in its consequence affect every freeman that lives under a British government on the main of America. It is the best cause. It is the cause of liberty, and I make no doubt but what your upright conduct this day will not only entitle you to the love and esteem of your fellow citizens, but every man who prefers freedom to a life of slavery will bless and honor you as men who have baffled the attempt of tyranny, and by an impartial and uncorrupt verdict have laid a noble foundation for securing to yourselves, our posterity and our neighbors that to which nature and the laws of our country have given us a right—the liberty—both of exposing and opposing arbitrary power . . . by speaking and writing truth.[7]

Inspired by Hamilton's oratory, the jury disregarded its instructions from the judge and found Zenger innocent. This was a heady victory for the jury system—and for those colonials, growing in number, who yearned for independence from British rule. Contrary to the widely held view, the Zenger trial did not result in an immediate change in the libel laws, nor did it generate more immediate freedom for the colonial press.[8] But the spiritual impact of the trial was tremendous. Revolt was in the wind, and newspapers, in their new role as public defender, became the defining force in the struggle for change.

The Press and the American Revolution

Anti-British sentiment intensified with the 1765 Stamp Act crisis, and Patriot editors and pamphleteers grew more strident in their demands for action. Royalist, or Tory, journalists replied in kind, while those in the middle—who resented British rule, but at the same time respected British investment and property rights—found it difficult to be heard. Benjamin Franklin, by now publisher of his own thriving paper, the *Pennsylvania Gazette,* carried this lament:

> Pamphlets have madden'd round the Town,
> And drove poor Moderation down.[9]

Boston's journalistic community, bristling with such gritty newspaper veterans and pamphleteers as Benjamin Edes, John Gill, Samuel Adams, and Isaiah Thomas, led the way in preparing the reading public to accept the notion of political independence. These leaders wrote with such passion as to leave little room for fairness, accuracy, balance, and other traits associated with a more detached form of journalism. Consider the following, a report in Isaiah Thomas's *Massachusetts Spy,* as the fighting broke out:

> AMERICANS! Forever bear in mind the BATTLE OF LEXINGTON!—where British troops, unmolested and unprovoked, wantonly, and in a most inhuman manner, fired upon and killed a number of our countrymen, then robbed them of their provisions, ransacked, plundered and burnt their houses! Nor could the tears of defenseless women, some of whom were in the pains of childbirth, the cries of helpless babies, nor the prayers of the old, confined to the beds of sickness, appease their thirst for blood! —or divert them from the DESIGN of MURDER and ROBBERY![10]

Fewer than three dozen newspapers existed in the colonies during the Revolutionary War; most of these, including perhaps the best written, James Rivington's *New York Gazeteer,* were devoted to the Tory cause. But what Patriot papers lacked in numbers they made up for in feverish intensity. Their pages rang out with dramatic appeals for recruits and supplies for the army, spirit-lifting essays such as Thomas Paine's *The Crisis,* texts of the Declaration of Independence and other vital

A Free Press: The Constitutional Guarantees

Amendment I (1791)
Congress shall make no law respecting an establishment of religion, or prohibiting the free exercise thereof; or abridging the freedom of speech, or of the press; or the right of the people peaceably to assemble, and to petition the Government for a redress of grievances.

Amendment XIV (1868)
SECTION I . . . No State shall make or enforce any law which shall abridge the privileges or immunities of citizens of the United States; nor shall any State deprive any person of life, liberty, or property, without due process of law; nor deny to any person within its jurisdiction the equal protection of the laws.

The First Amendment forbids Congress from enacting legislation repressive to freedom of expression. The Fourteenth Amendment now is interpreted to mean that federal guarantees of freedom of speech and press likewise cannot be impaired by the states.

documents, plus enthusiastic news reports that depicted their cause in the best possible light. The editors and pamphleteers were joined by the clergy, who made the pulpit a formidable political as well as religious forum. (Speakers and writers of this period foreshadow the later development of **propaganda** and even public relations. Newspaper journalism, in other words, is a strong but not exclusive forerunner of many of the communications activities that will be described later.) All told, the mass communicators helped mightily to hold the colonies together during the long, bitter struggle. A British journalist, visiting New York in 1776, wrote home to Lord Dartmouth: "One is astonished to see with what avidity they [the colonial newspapers] are sought after, and how implicitly they are believed, by the great Bulk of the People. . . . [The English] Government find it expedient, in the Sum of things, to employ this popular Engine."[11]

A Press for the Classes

When the battle for independence was finally won, the leaders of the infant nation faced a different kind of challenge: developing responses to crucial questions concerning the form the new government would take, the role of the individual states, relations with the British and the French, and who would wield political and economic power. Badly torn after six years of war, the American society found itself divided once more as arguments raged over the design and operation of the emerging governmental structure. The conflict pitted shopkeepers against farmers, English sympathizers against admirers of the new libertarianism that had emerged in France, and advocates of a strong central government against those who favored vesting the balance of power at the state and local levels.

Newspapers fueled the debate. Although the biggest political story, the drafting of the federal Constitution, developed behind closed doors because the convention delegates were fearful that premature disclosure in the press would ruin the delicate negotiations, political leaders of all persuasions afterward turned to newspapers to drum up enough popular support to get the new Constitution properly ratified. The *Federalist,* a series of essays that brilliantly explained and supported the Constitution, were written for such papers as the *New York Independent Advertiser* and reprinted widely. Throughout the nation, first-class minds used the press as a vehicle for articulating and resolving issues of national import. News was a secondary consideration; informed, if highly partisan, political commentary was paramount.

As the various factions jockeyed for positions of power, they created additional newspapers to rush their messages to the voters. Editors were flagrantly biased. "Professions of impartiality," confessed *Federalist* editor William Cobbett, "I shall make none." And in their **editorializing** excesses, they turned American journalism into a bare-knuckled political brawl. Not even war hero and first president George Washington was spared; when he retired after eight years as president, anti-*Federalist* editors such as Benjamin Franklin Bache were delighted to see him go:

> If ever there was a period for rejoicing this is the moment—every heart in unison with the freedom and happiness of the people ought to be high, with exultation that the name of Washington from this day ceases to give currency to political iniquity, to legalize corruption. . . . It is a subject of greatest astonishment that a single individual should have cancelled the principles of republicanism in an enlightened people, and should have carried his designs against the public liberty so far as to have put in jeopardy its very existence.[12]

Discussion

Are the media villifying, excoriating, or maligning the current president? Can the class separate politically motivated villification from warranted exposure?

Such rough-and-tumble rhetoric, in the republican view, was healthy in that it cut leaders down to size and restricted their power. As Thomas Jefferson said of his favorite editor, Philip Freneau: "His paper has saved our constitution, which was galloping fast into monarchy, and [monarchy] has been checked by no means as powerfully as by that paper." But not all editorialists were astute, and not all journalistic motives were lofty. In time, partisan journalism went into decline; too many newspapers became elitist, shrill, boring. As Professor Frank Luther Mott described it, "The whole period of 1801–1833 was in many respects disgraceful—a kind of Dark Ages of American journalism. Few papers were ably edited; they reflected the crassness of American society of the times. Scurrility, assaults, corruption, blatancy were commonplace. Journalism had grown too fast."[13]

Discussion

Do today's supermarket tabloids fit this description? Ask students to bring some to class for analysis.

A Press for the Masses

As journalism grew, the country was growing, too. Immigrants poured in, and cities began taking shape. Industrial development swept across the land. While these and other social changes were occurring, too many blindly partisan newspapers simply lost touch with their audiences.

Into this void moved Benjamin Day, a New York printer with ideas that changed forever the scope and mission of the American press. Day's modest little paper, the New York *Sun,* first appeared on 3 September 1833, and it did not look much like the revolutionary product it would prove to be. Day had started the paper primarily as an adjunct to his job-printing business, but he gave the *Sun* some important new wrinkles:

1   *It was sold by the copy—not through yearly subscriptions.* Other papers cost five to ten dollars a year, a price well out of reach for most New Yorkers. But the *Sun,* at a penny a copy, was eminently affordable. Day sent newsboys onto the streets to hawk the paper; an aggressive lad who sold a hundred papers could make thirty-three cents profit. Within four months, the

The newspaper that launched a revolution: the premier edition of the New York Sun.

Sun's highly motivated young sales force was moving papers at the rate of 15,000 a day, far more than any other newspaper at the time.

2 *It had no political affiliation; the selling point was news, not political commentary.* The paper attempted to give the ordinary reader an unvarnished portrait of life. Abuses in politics, government, churches, courts, and business were all reported. There were no sacred cows.

3 *Human interest items were emphasized.* The Sun's columns abounded with stories about ordinary people. Day hired George W. Wisner to cover the police courts and write about domestic squabbles, petty thefts, drunks, and fistfights as well as happier episodes in the human drama. Wisner's wry, low-key reports hit home. For the first time, ordinary readers found a newspaper that considered their lives, even the seamier aspects, newsworthy.

Background

A "sacred cow" is generally something the newspaper publisher has strong feelings for or against. For example, if the boss's daughter is a Girl Scout, the publisher might refuse to print negative stories about the Scouts. The term comes from India, where Hindus regard cows as sacred animals and refuse to harm them.

Figure 1 How newspapers and magazines were financially supported prior to the penny press era.

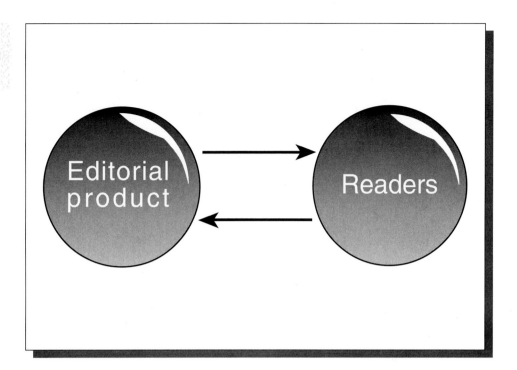

Within four years, Day's *Sun* had attracted a circulation of 30,000—and a number of imitative competitors. Significantly, none of the older, established New York papers lost circulation during this time, indicating that the **penny press** publishers, as they came to be called, were simply filling a vacuum of major proportions.

The penny press also wrought a fundamental shift in newspaper economics. Before 1833, papers were supported primarily by their readers, with occasional subsidies from a political party or government printing contracts awarded as patronage. Advertising income made up only a small portion of a newspaper's financial support. The financial equation looked like the depiction in figure 1.

The penny press barons, however, regarded their audiences in a different light. A marketing strategy evolved: *Do whatever it takes to attract large numbers of readers. Price the paper dirt cheap, be sure to include material appealing to the widest possible audience, and you will generate a consumer market advertisers will find irresistible.* Figure 2 illustrates how the new revenue cycle operated.

Not every aspect of the penny press was admirable. In their frantic maneuvering to sell papers to everybody, penny press editors regularly resorted to sensational and irresponsible reporting; even outright hoaxes masqueraded as important news developments. Editors catered to a lowest-common-denominator audience in ways that observers, then as now, would consider reprehensible. *Penny press publishers conditioned American readers, for better or for worse, to expect their mass media to be paid for chiefly by others—that is, advertisers.* But they also liberated the newspaper from its elitist role as mouthpiece for government or political parties or special interest groups. The press became a press for the masses.[14]

More Giants Emerge

The revolution Ben Day triggered soon passed him by. While his New York *Sun* remained popular, a series of remarkable newcomers would soon take over the personal leadership of New York journalism.

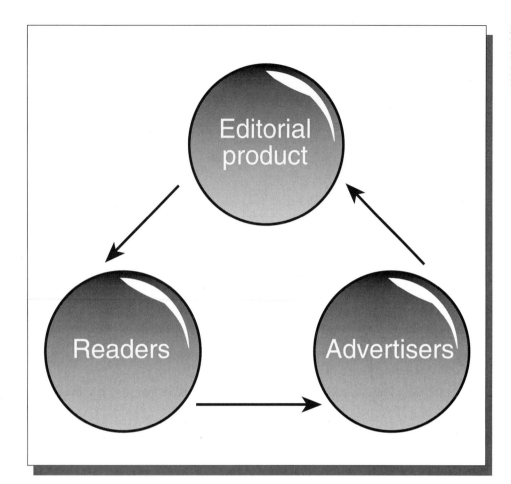

James Gordon Bennett

At age 40 and with $500 of borrowed money, James Gordon Bennett created the New York *Herald* and pushed it into becoming the dominant paper of its time. Like Day, Bennett blitzed the masses with sensational news at an affordable price. But where Day was by trade a printer, Bennett was a born editor. He organized a news staff and raised the *Herald*'s coverage to spectacular heights. His paper's courier service included swift sailing vessels that met incoming ships in Newfoundland and then raced to New York with the latest news from Europe. Pony express service to the far West also confounded rival publishers; they lost scoop after scoop to Bennett's enterprise. He expanded the *Herald*'s content to include reports of horse races and other sporting events, society news, and the latest financial reports, all presented in a style ordinary readers could understand and enjoy.

Life at Two Newspapers: *The Morning Glory and Johnson War Whoop*

"Ah," said he, "that is that scoundrel Smith, of the [newspaper] *Moral Volcano.* He was due yesterday." And he snatched a navy revolver from his belt and fired. Smith dropped, shot in the thigh. The shot spoiled Smith's aim, who was just taking a second chance, and he crippled a stranger. It was me. Merely shot a finger off.

Then the chief editor went on with his erasures and interlineations. Just as he finished them a hand-grenade came down the stove-pipe, and the explosion shivered the stove into a thousand fragments. However, it did not further damage, except that a vagrant piece knocked a couple of my teeth out.

"That stove is utterly ruined," said the chief editor.

Mark Twain, "Journalism in Tennessee," reprinted in John Nerone, *Violence Against the Press* (Oxford, England, 1994).

Extra Information

Some of Bennett's classified ads looked like invitations from prostitutes . . . and they probably were. This caused the moralists of the day to threaten Bennett with dire punishment, including horsewhipping. Bennett laughed all the way to the bank.

Bennett's high-voltage reports of crime and sex scandals offended a number of New York's clergy, who reacted by declaring what they described as a moral war against the *Herald*. Bennett counterattacked with a broadside of articles mocking the religious establishment, a tactic which gained him even wider circulation—and more enemies. Bennett emerged from the moral war with circulation and ego intact, his whirlwind energies undiminished. In 1837, as the *Herald* moved into handsome new quarters, he reflected on his performance thus far:

> This success [of the *Herald*] has undoubtedly arisen from the entire novelty which I have infused into the daily press. Until this epoch of the world, the daily newspaper press has been a mere organ of dry detail—uninteresting facts—political nonsense—personal squabbles—obsolete news—tedious ship news—or perhaps meagre quotations of the market. I have changed all this. I have infused life, glowing eloquence, philosophy, taste, sentiment, wit and humor into the daily newspaper. . . . Shakespeare is the great genius of the drama—Scott of the novel—Milton and Byron of the poem—and I mean to be the genius of the daily newspaper press.[15]

Which, of course, he was. Personal insufferability aside, Bennett became the founder of the modern American newspaper. His rivals in New York and elsewhere were forced to copy his concepts and strategies or find themselves hopelessly outclassed in the battle for circulation. Bennett made the *Herald* so vital and informative that friends and enemies alike were loath to be without it.

Horace Greeley

When he founded the New York *Tribune* in 1841, Horace Greeley provided the country with a superb, separate editorial page and, to a degree not achieved previously, a journalistic conscience. Unrelenting in his idealism, Greeley was, as one historian described him, "a fascinating, mercurial, neurotic prophet crying aloud in a wilderness of slaveholders, rum-sellers, autocrats, and ignoramuses."[16]

Born to impoverished parents in Vermont, Greeley learned printing in his youth and quickly grasped the potential of low-cost, mass audience newspapers as an educational weapon for the public good—or, at least, Greeley's vision of the public good, which might best be defined as inconsistent. His economic philosophy, an off-the-wall brand of socialism, led him to hire as his London correspondent Karl Marx, who held body and soul together by selling articles to the *Tribune* while trying to finish *Das Kapital*. Greeley's views, though elegantly expressed, were full of contradictions. He astonished his employees by insisting that they organize themselves into a union for protection—against management. His financial accounting practices were a disaster, and only through periodic miracles were the *Tribune*'s bills paid. Greeley's ill-fitting clothes, squeaky voice, vacant stare, and awkward manners made him appear a somewhat ridiculous figure outside the *Tribune* office.

Yet rarely has an editor been more beloved. Readers joked about Greeley's odd looks and erratic behavior, but they sensed that he identified with their concerns and respected their intelligence. They understood that the *Tribune*'s editorial page was less an advocate than a great national forum in which ideas could be presented. Many of those ideas were superb and some were atrocious, but all were worth looking into. The daily *Tribune* eventually served about 40,000 households in the New York area, far fewer than the *Sun* or Bennett's *Herald*. But a weekly version of the paper, featuring Greeley's editorials and the various political and economic essays Greeley and his stable of correspondents developed, reached some 200,000 subscribers throughout the land.

Greeley supported the candidacy of Abraham Lincoln and wrote powerful editorials demanding an end to slavery. He also personally signed the bail bond of Jefferson Davis, president of the Confederacy. In 1872, both the Liberal Republican and the Democratic parties nominated Greeley to run for president against Ulysses S. Grant, but the editor's health was failing badly and he lost by a decisive margin. He died that same year. His legacy was not his improbable presidential campaign, but the *Tribune*'s distinguished editorial page. It wielded, in the words of one historian of the period, "a power never before or since known in this country."[17]

Henry J. Raymond

At midcentury, Bennett's *Herald* was attracting handsome numbers of readers and advertisers, while Greeley's *Tribune* had attained a position of moral leadership. The New York *Evening Post,* under the thoughtful editorship of William Cullen Bryant, commanded respect. Benjamin Day had wearied of cutthroat competition and sold out to Moses Y. Beach, but the *Sun* held on to its circulation lead, largely by offering its readers sure-fire features such as Horatio Alger's serialized rags-to-riches stories. James Watson Webb's *Courier and Enquirer* continued to thrive, as did a number of special interest publications. Though the city had grown to half a million population, there hardly seemed room for still another newspaper. But a trio of businesspeople, led by Henry J. Raymond felt otherwise. With $100,000 in start-up capital, Raymond and his partners proposed to establish a journal that was less volatile than Greeley's, more authoritative and thorough than Bennett's, and more appealing than the financial and special interest press. Thus was born the New York *Times.* Referring to its editor, Greeley later wrote, "Abler and stronger men I may have met; a cleverer, readier, and more generally efficient journalist I never saw."

Where many journalists of the period were born poor and received little formal education, Raymond grew up in comfortable circumstances. At the age of three he could read; he achieved regional fame as a public speaker at five, became an honors graduate of the University of Vermont and a schoolteacher at sixteen, and traveled widely before settling in New York at twenty-one to commence his newspaper work with the *Tribune.* Greeley soon promoted him past others twice his age to the position of chief assistant editor. The two men formed an effective team, but they were too different in emotional intensity and operating style for the relationship to endure. Raymond longed to be on his own. Noting in 1850 that the *Tribune* had recorded an annual profit of $60,000 in spite of Greeley's cavalier management, Raymond took the plunge with his *Times.* His journalistic mission was not to entertain or persuade, but to inform. He was determined to make the *Times* synonymous with serious news. In his first issue, Raymond promised fairness, balance, and restraint:

> We do not mean to write as if we were in a passion, unless that shall really be the case; and we shall make it a point to get in a passion as rarely as possible. There are very few things in this world which it is worth while to get angry about; and they are just the things that anger will not improve. In controversies with other journals, with individuals or with parties, we shall engage only when, in our opinion, some important public interest can be promoted thereby; and even then, we shall endeavor to rely more upon fair arguments than upon misrepresentations or abusive language.[18]

Raymond had gauged his audience accurately. Within three months, the *Times* enjoyed a circulation of 20,000, enough of a base to assure survival. On the paper's first anniversary, Raymond could announce with satisfaction:

> Its [the *Times*'] readers are among the best portion of our citizens—those who read it because they like it, and not because it panders to any special taste, and least of all to any low or degrading appetite. It is made up for all classes, and it is designed to cover all departments. Whatever has interest or importance for a considerable portion of the community has found a place, according to its limits, within its columns.[19]

As Willard G. Bleyer has observed, "whatever has interest or importance for any considerable portion of the community" constitutes as useful a definition of news as has ever been framed.

Though deeply enmeshed in Whig and Republican politics for most of his career, Raymond kept his partisan opinions out of the *Times* and insisted upon reporting the facts fully and fairly. Eventually becoming disillusioned with the politics of

Extra Information

The motto of the current New York *Times* is "All the news that's fit to print." Cynical people say it really means "All the news that fits, we print." However, the *Times*, the Washington *Post*, the Los Angeles *Times*, and the *Wall Street Journal* are considered the most influential newspapers in the nation.

that stormy era, he severed his party responsibilities and devoted all of his considerable energies to the newspaper, a decision that elevated the *Times* to a new plateau of excellence. In 1869, the long years of overwork caught up with him, however, and he died before reaching his fiftieth birthday. But Raymond had lived long enough to develop the New York *Times* into a model of independence, moderation, and integrity.

Reporting the Civil War

The dynamism of the New York press transformed newspapers throughout the country. Many journals, established merely to help develop a town or promote a candidate, grew aggressive and powerful. The Chicago *Times,* edited by the heavy-drinking, hard-driving Wilbur F. Storey, picked one fight after another. "The function of a newspaper," said Storey, "is to print the news and raise hell." He added, perhaps unnecessarily, that in his opinion "a journalist should not be popular."[20] His main competitor was Joseph Medill, who created a journalistic dynasty with his Chicago *Tribune,* a flag-waving conservative paper that came to dominate vast portions of the Midwest and did much to build the Republican party and elect Abraham Lincoln.

As newspapers prospered, they enlarged their staffs, adapted to the telegraph, and refined techniques for presenting the news. The Civil War gave the reporter a new stature and a heightened sense of urgency. More than 150 correspondents served with Union army units, providing eyewitness reports from combat zones. Southern war reporters, fewer in number but no less brave, often pooled their information through a cooperative known as the Press Association to publishers who had to deal with dire shortages of paper, ink, and editing staff. Reporters on either side received little help from the military. Journalists had to compile their own casualty counts and piece together, usually without official briefings, their own conclusions as to a given battle's outcome and strategic significance. Often the reporting was inaccurate.

By-lines developed during this time, not to reward outstanding performance so much as to fix responsibility for factual error. The home office purposely slanted some of the material to make it conform to the paper's editorial policy on the war. Yet many of the pieces were vivid and informative, and more than a few were brilliant. Whitelaw Reid's dispatches from Shiloh and Gettysburg are regarded as classics. Henry Villard scored a clean *beat* (scoop) on the battle of Fredericksburg; he rushed on horseback for miles over virtually impassable roads, defied General Burnside's orders to keep news of the defeat from going north, outwitted his less resourceful fellow correspondents, talked his way onto a boat bound for Washington, and sent his story by train to the offices of the New York *Tribune.* Reporting had come of age.[21]

Joseph Pulitzer

Had it not been for a cruel prank, Joseph Pulitzer would never have gone to St. Louis at all. He was a young adventurer who emigrated from Hungary during the Civil War by collecting a $500 bounty for selling himself into the Union army to replace someone who could afford to hire a substitute. When the war ended, Pulitzer found himself destitute in New York, surrounded by other jobless immigrants with English as halting as his. In disgust he resolved to make his way to another city, preferably one less rife with foreigners. Someone suggested St. Louis as a joke, for St. Louis boasted one of the largest concentrations of German immigrants in the country, but Pulitzer took the advice seriously and hitched his way west by freight train. There was no turning back. He stuck it out for three years, sustaining a meager existence through part-time work before falling into a news reporting job on the *Westliche Post,* a German-language newspaper owned by noted political leader Carl Schurz.

Class Project

Have student(s) research journalistic use of the electric telegraph before and during the Civil War. Were carrier pigeons ever used to carry news?

Background

General W. T. Sherman hated reporters, claiming they had stigmatized him as "crazy" in the early days of the war.

For the first time in his young life, Joseph Pulitzer met success. News reporting came naturally to him, blessed as he was with insatiable curiosity and boundless energy. He pushed himself hard, in spare hours studying law and government. Before long, Pulitzer was the best-known reporter in the city. He made many friends, enough to get him elected to a seat in the state legislature, and for a while he seemed bound for a political career. But in 1878 he bought himself a newspaper, and from then on was to absorb himself in journalism to the exclusion of all else.

The paper was the St. Louis *Dispatch,* which cost him $2,500 at a sheriff's auction. There was little evident potential to the *Dispatch,* and it was encumbered with $30,000 in outstanding debt, but it did possess one important asset, an Associated Press membership. A few days later, Pulitzer formed a partnership to merge his paper with the St. Louis *Post,* a journal with some promise but no Associated Press connection and therefore no reliable source of world news. The merger paid off. Within a year Pulitzer gained complete control, and within three years the *Post-Dispatch*'s annual profit rose past $45,000, then to $100,000 and beyond. Spurred on by Pulitzer's driving energy and his impassioned local crusades, the *Post-Dispatch* became a formidable newspaper.

Not yet forty, the restless Pulitzer sought new challenges. It was at this point that he bought the New York *World,* a once-proud journal now skidding downhill, both in editorial quality and in profits, under the surprisingly apathetic management of business tycoon Jay Gould. Gould had bought the paper for political reasons, but it threatened to lose $40,000 a year and was not helping him politically either; he was relieved to unload it. The Pulitzer formula caught on quickly in Manhattan, where journalism had fallen into the doldrums following the deaths of Raymond, Greeley, and the elder James Gordon Bennett. In four months, Pulitzer doubled the *World*'s circulation of 20,000. By 1884, the figure hit 100,000; two years later it passed a quarter of a million and was still climbing.

While relying heavily on titillating headlines and purple prose, Pulitzer insisted that his motives were pure. He regarded sensationalism as a means to an end, a dancing temptress luring passersby into the temple. Once inside, he was convinced, his mass audience would receive instruction for the public good through well-researched investigative reports and a thoughtful editorial page. His results were indeed successful, but Pulitzer suffered great personal difficulty in rationalizing what he had to do to obtain them. Throughout his later years, he was troubled by physical disorders, thought at the time to be largely psychosomatic. But he and the *World* never let up.

A Pulitzer crusade was a major commitment. "Never drop a big thing," he insisted, "until you have got to the bottom of it." The goal was to mobilize the staff into presenting an irrefutable case, then let nature take its course. His editors were ordered to bear down relentlessly:

> Always tell the truth, always take the humane and moral side, always remember that right feeling is the vital spark of strong writing, and that publicity, *publicity,* PUBLICITY is the greatest moral factor and force in public life.[22]

Pulitzer crusaded against public officeholders, tax policies that favored the very rich, vote frauds, stock swindles, abuses committed by utilities and other corporate monopolies, slum landlords, police brutality, corruption wherever he found it. But he authorized crusades *for* causes, too; in one, the *World* raised more than $100,000 to finance a foundation and a suitable environment for Bartholdi's gigantic sculpture, "Liberty Enlightening the World." Some 120,000 contributors, most of them giving small amounts and many of them immigrants, as Pulitzer himself had been, responded to the *World*'s crusade to develop what became the country's symbol of opportunity and freedom, the Statue of Liberty.[23]

Background
An AP membership was exclusive—only one to a city, at that time. Thus, a paper with the AP service could provide more and better news than its competitors.

William Randolph Hearst

Pulitzer's achievements, so dazzling that they were described as the "new journalism," won him riches, fame, power—and the envy of publishers and would-be publishers everywhere. Few had the will or resources to challenge him. One who did was William Randolph Hearst. Born to immense wealth in California, young Hearst had seen much of the world by the time he enrolled at Harvard. His massive ego, fed by an imperious father and a doting mother, was not compatible with Harvard's then-harsh disciplinary code. At one point Hearst sent some chamber pots with pictures of his least favorite professors pasted to the bottoms over to the faculty club. The professors were not amused; soon afterward, they had him expelled. Before leaving the East, however, Hearst discovered journalism. He came to admire, then covet, the power Joseph Pulitzer wielded through his New York newspaper.

When Hearst returned to California, he asked for and received one of his family's lesser properties, the San Francisco *Examiner*. From that moment, the publisher's office became his natural habitat. Throwing wads of money into the operation, Hearst hired a top staff, then astounded his growing audience with one sensational scoop after another. He ignored the deep pools of red ink on the *Examiner*'s ledgers, at least for the moment. When a famous hotel in nearby Monterey caught fire, Hearst chartered an entire train to shuttle his journalists to the disaster. Taking full advantage of improvements in photographic and engraving technology, he filled the *Examiner*'s columns with pictures splashier and newsier than anything the competition could offer. Before long, the *Examiner* had recouped its financial losses and was turning a profit. Satisfied that he had learned his trade, Hearst was now ready to take on the master.

He established his eastern base of operations with the New York *Journal,* which he bought in 1895. To brighten the paper's dreary graphic design, he imported some of his star editors from San Francisco. Then, to let Pulitzer know he was serious, Hearst hired away, at top salaries, several of the *World*'s key executives. Pulitzer retaliated by cutting his paper's price, forcing Hearst to dig deeper into his family's finances in order to compete. The battle was joined. In his anger, each man misjudged the other. Hearst regarded Pulitzer's empire as superficial, built on sensationalism alone. Pulitzer, on the other hand, badly underestimated Hearst's financial staying power. He was convinced that Hearst's family would soon call a halt to the young publisher's extravagance. Both were wrong. Pulitzer was far more resourceful than Hearst had reckoned, and Hearst's cash supply proved more than ample to stay the course.

What followed was an expensive and ugly war for circulation leadership in New York, with each paper claiming to outdo the other in news and in special **features** offered to its readers. One such attraction was a cartoon, the "Yellow Kid," a forerunner to today's comic strip. Drawn by Richard F. Outcault, the nightshirted Yellow Kid proved highly popular, and Pulitzer and Hearst each vied for Outcault's services. The frenzied bidding war was soon nicknamed **yellow journalism,** a label that has survived to symbolize exploitative, demagogic, sensationalistic press performance.

Hearst, like Pulitzer, was a dynamic crusader, urging public ownership of utilities, more money for schools, stronger bargaining power for unions, and tax reform. Then he attempted to set foreign policy by mounting a loud crusade for United States intervention on behalf of the rebels in Cuba in their struggle against their Spanish rulers. Pulitzer joined in the fray with equal ardor. The slanted news stories, inflammatory editorials, and lurid photographs that filled their columns amounted to, as one historian put it, "the most incandescent display of unabashed jingoism in the history of American journalism, and the most effective." The thundering demands for action spread from New York across the land, and soon even President

Discussion

Ask students whether any current media fit this definition of yellow journalism.

McKinley became caught up in the unstoppable tide rushing toward war with Spain. When the fighting broke out, the *Journal* and the *World* exploited it to the hilt, dispatching reporters by the boatload to Cuban shores. The expense was staggering, but so was the ensuing circulation gain; Hearst and Pulitzer each sold more than a million and a half copies on eventful days. This was yellow journalism at its worst. Edwin L. Godkin, respected editor of the *Evening Post,* wrote in cold fury:

> Nothing so disgraceful as the behavior of two of these newspapers this week has been known in the history of American journalism. Gross misrepresentations of the facts, deliberate invention of tales calculated to excite the public, and wanton recklessness in the construction of headlines which even outdid these inventions, have combined to make the issues of the most widely circulated newspapers firebrands scattered broadcast throughout the country. . . . It is a crying shame that men should work such mischief in order to sell more papers.[24]

Eventually Pulitzer retreated to the higher ground from whence he had come. Leaving the garish sensationalism to Hearst—who was better at it anyway—Pulitzer devoted his remaining years to good works, solid reporting, and legitimate campaigns in the public interest. Except for an occasional lapse, he held fast to his stirring editorial philosophy:

Those Muckraking Magazine Writers

Now [in 1902], suddenly, there appeared in certain magazines a new, moral, radical type of writing by men and women who yesterday had been entirely unknown or had written less disturbingly. These writers savagely exposed grafting politicians, criminal police, tenement eyesores. They openly attacked the Church. They defended labor in disputes which in no way concerned them personally, decried child exploitation, wrote pro-suffragist articles, and described great business as soulless and anti-social.

These writers, using the most sordid details to make their points, shocked and bewildered the conservative reader. So far as he knew, they were supposed to be merely writers; it was no business of theirs if someone's factory was a firetrap. He preferred to read his magazines for relaxation, not for argumentative lectures. To the common people, however, the new writing was as gripping as it was educational; they had never known that business and politics could be so interesting.

Louis Filler in *Crusaders for American Liberalism* (Harcourt Brace, 1939).

[This newspaper] will always fight for progress and reform, never tolerate injustice or corruption, always fight demagogues of all parties, never belong to any party, always oppose privileged classes and public plunderers, never lack sympathy with the poor, always remain devoted to the public welfare, never be satisfied with merely printing news, always be drastically independent, never be afraid to attack wrong, whether by predatory plutocracy or predatory poverty.[25]

Hearst, on the other hand, was just getting up to speed. Exhilarated by his success in New York, he extended his empire from city to city. At one time, he owned twenty-six daily newspapers, thirteen magazines, eight radio stations, a Sunday supplement, a wire service, two motion picture studios, several estates, New York hotels, a world-class art collection, Egyptian mummies, a private railroad line, an entire abbey—purchased in Spain, taken apart, then gently reassembled on one of his places in California—and a zoo. In all, he had been in journalism for nearly seven decades when he died in 1951. Active to the end, he was shamelessly dictatorial with his editors, often commanding them to distort the news and to support ludicrous causes and unfit political candidates.

On the positive side, some of his editorial campaigns produced constructive results. He fostered many technical improvements, especially in photojournalism, and he sold copies of newspapers to many who would not otherwise have been interested. One of Hearst's biographers, William Swanberg, concluded a sensitive study of the publisher's enigmatic career with not one, but two obituary profiles— one fulsome in its praise, the other a severe condemnation—then asked the reader, "Which one is the real Hearst?" Both versions are persuasive.

Suggested Audiovisual Aid

If possible, show part or all of the movie *Citizen Kane*, allegedly based on the life of W. R. Hearst.

Magazine Journalism

Less noisy but arguably more effective crusades were being mounted on the pages of the opinion magazines, where a band of talented and idealistic writers impressively exposed commercial, social, and political evils. These journalists/social reformers became known as muckrakers, a pejorative label President Theodore Roosevelt, who darkly suspected such negative thinking of being unpatriotic, applied to them in 1906. The term **muckraker** derives from a character in John Bunyan's *Pilgrim's Progress,* a stable hand who was too intent upon raking up moist manure to look up at the stars to consider his heavenly crown. Their patriotism long since vindicated, the muckrakers did uncover serious flaws in the American system, and between 1890 and 1914, they presented their findings with skill and conviction. Their **investigative reporting** included "History of the Standard Oil Company," by Ida Tarbell, a devastating disclosure of corporate malpractice; "The Shame of the Cities," by Lincoln Steffens, a shocking series on machine politics; and "The Great American Fraud," Samuel Hopkins Adams's inside look at the patent medicine business. Such activist writing opened the eyes of thoughtful readers everywhere and led to enactment of much progressive legislation, including antitrust laws and the creation of federal agencies, to monitor food and drug standards and a variety of other business practices.

The muckraking movement eventually ran out of steam. Too many editors rushed into print with insufficiently researched articles, and the reading public wearied of magazines that seemed to be constantly carping. But for a bright moment, the muckrakers united the country and brought it a painful step closer to maturity.

Magazines have been around since colonial days. Their growth accelerated as the railroads moved west, creating advertising markets that became regional, then national, in scope. *Dial,* a Transcendentalist organ, provided a regular outlet for the essays of Margaret Fuller and Ralph Waldo Emerson. *Godey's Lady's Book,* forerunner to the modern women's magazines, quietly promoted feminist causes while assisting nineteenth-century housewives with home and family management. *Harper's,* made famous by Thomas Nast's political cartoons, gave the nation the most dramatic coverage of the Civil War. These magazines and dozens of others like them helped pave the way for the muckrakers, who, in turn, did much to create the intellectual climate in which newsmagazines and modern journals of ideas and opinion would thrive.[26]

The Jazz Age Comes and Goes

In June 1919, the tabloid era, a more or less natural extension of yellow journalism, arrived in New York. Its vanguard was the *Illustrated Daily News,* an Americanized version of London's profitable *Daily Mirror.* The **tabloid** was racy, to the point, easy to read on a crowded subway, and filled with spectacular photographs and short, hard-hitting articles described as "by turns sobby, dirty, bloody, and glamorous." Hearst promptly jumped in with a tab of his own, the New York *Mirror,* which copied the *News* format but boasted its own credo: "Short, quick, and make it snappy." A third tabloid hit the streets in 1924 when Bernarr Macfadden, who had made millions creating the confessions magazine field with *True Story,* brought out the *Daily Graphic.* Steadfast in his belief that contemporary audiences were interested in sex and money, in that order, Macfadden produced a newspaper that gave new meaning to the word *lurid.* Readers nicknamed it the *Porno-Graphic,* and they bought copies by the tens of thousands. Thus was born the period known as jazz journalism, in which much of the nation's press cheerfully reflected the country's rollicking, gamy, morbid postwar moods.[27] Here's how one 1928 Manhattan paper described the death of famed murderess Ruth Brown Snyder in the electric chair:

> "Jesus, have mercy!" came the pitiful cry. Ruth's blue eyes were red with weeping. Her face was strangely old. The blond, bobbed hair, hanging in stringy bunches over her furrowed brow, seemed almost white with years of toil and suffering as the six dazzling, high-powered lights illuminated every bit of Ruth's agonized lineaments. . . .
> Tightly corseted by the black leather bands, Ruth was flabby and futile as the blast struck her. Her body went forward as far as the restraining thongs would permit.
> The tired form was taut. The body that had once throbbed with the joy of her sordid bacchanals turned brick red as the current struck. Slowly, after half a minute of the death-dealing current, the exposed arms, right leg, throat and jaws bleached out again.[28]

After the stock market crash of 1929, the New York *Daily News,* which had leaped to the highest circulation in the country, shrewdly changed course. "We're off on the wrong foot," wrote Captain James Patterson, the paper's founder and publisher, in a memorandum to his staff. "The people's major interest is no longer in the playboy, Broadway, and divorces, but in how they're going to eat, and from this time forward we'll pay attention to the struggle for existence that's just beginning."[29]

While newly serious papers such as the *Daily News* were discovering the importance of reporting the Great Depression in the early 1930s, others in the press sensed the need to try and explain it. **Objective reporting,** the distinguishing characteristic of

Discussion

Can students identify any muckrakers around today? Do the supermarket tabloids contain real muckraking, or just muck?

Class Project

Ask your class to bring copies of various supermarket tabloids to class and compare their headlines. Do the stories bear out the headline?

Sudden Death of Viscount Morley : Special Memoir.

DAILY GRAPHIC

No. 10,535.   *   Registered as a Newspaper   MONDAY, SEPTEMBER 24, 1923.   ONE PENNY

FIRST PICTURES OF DISASTER TO U.S. DESTROYERS.

An unprecedented photograph of American destroyers which were flung on the rocks of Santa Barbara, California, while racing to the help of the Cuba, a Pacific liner. Seven of them being drowned in their bunks. | destroyers were caught in a tidal wave which followed the Japanese earthquake, and to add to their terrible ordeal a dense fog prevailed. Twenty-five men lost their lives, some of them being drowned in their bunks.

A group of the survivors. Some are asleep in their blankets. Inset: A. Peterson, of the destroyer Young, who swam to the Chauncey and brought a lifeline back to his ship.

Passengers in a lifeboat from the wrecked liner Cuba were picked up by the American destroyer Reno, which escaped the disaster, and took them into port.

A relatively tame edition of the New York *Graphic*, an often lurid competitor in the jazz journalism era. Photojournalism got a big boost during the Roaring Twenties. "Play pictures big," one managing editor advised his staff. "If the pictures are good they deserve big play. If they're bad, they need it."

Discussion

Ask your students to bring copies of *Newsweek*, *Time*, and *U.S. News* published in the same week. Have the class compare and analyze their content and any overt bias.

most American journalism for a century, simply was not adequate. A great need arose for analysis and interpretation, for significance and meaning. The facts could not always speak for themselves, and a straightforward presentation of raw information was apt to create more questions than it answered.

Because many newspapers could not, or would not, respond to the challenge posed by **interpretive reporting,** their readers turned elsewhere. It was no coincidence that *Time* magazine, short on objectivity but long on analysis and conclusion, prospered during the Depression and, in spite of the harsh economic difficulty of the period, became a huge national success. So did *Newsweek,* another magazine created primarily to interpret the news. The circulation of *Reader's Digest* and other monthly and weekly magazines increased, as did the number and readership of newsletters and topical, analytical books. Syndicated columns and depth reporting developed into distinctive trends. Until now, reporters could usually produce an acceptable news story by answering four simple questions: who, what, when, and where. Now other, more sophisticated responses were called for: how and why.

The Media and the Military

The public's appetite for interpretive reporting continued as the nation recovered from the Great Depression. Soon the press would face an even greater challenge: covering World War II.

World War II

The second world war was the deadliest, most destructive, most expensive war ever fought. Before it ended in 1945, it affected more people and brought about more far-reaching change than any other war in history. World War II was remarkable in another respect, too: The media coverage of it was, in the view of some historians, the most impressive achievement the American press ever recorded. While the reporting was uneven and flawed now and then, the coverage in the aggregate was authoritative, thorough, accurate, and, at times, brilliant. World War II was the best reported of all wars, before or since.

The journalistic heroes were many: combat photographers and newsreel camera operators who captured the drama on film, often at close range; daring wire service correspondents like Walter Cronkhite, who parachuted behind enemy lines with a battalion of rangers the night before the main force struck the beaches of Normandy to begin the liberation of Europe; thoughtful magazine writers who were able to synthesize the fast-breaking war news and give it depth and perspective.

Two of the greatest, and certainly among the most beloved, correspondents were Ernie Pyle and Edward R. Murrow. They won the adoration of their audiences not by creating probing strategic analyses of the war, but by simply getting close to the action and telling the American people what they saw and heard. Pyle's reporting technique was direct, unpretentious, and uncannily effective. He would attach himself to combat units and identify with them so completely that his columns, for Scripps-Howard and many other papers, seemed less like newspaper reports than personal letters from the front lines to families back home. As one analyst explained it:

Perhaps the most famous combat photograph of all time: Joseph Rosenthal's "Raising the Flag on Iwo Jima."

> A shy, gnomelike little fellow with an almost bald pate, Ernie Pyle was the idol of GI's on a dozen fronts. He deliberately avoided the command post in favor of the foxhole. He wrote only about what he personally witnessed and experienced. He lived with the men who fought and he accompanied them into battle. He reported what the GI's felt, what the war meant to them, and what they were dreaming about.
>
> Pyle's dispatches were filled with homely details—the GI's home town, his address, the names of members of his family. He noted little acts of kindness and unselfishness, the sadness, loneliness, and ennui of men bored to distraction behind the lines, the raw courage of boys who, in battle, became men. . . . He pictured tired, dirty soldiers who didn't want to die, and he wrote of heroism, anger, wine, cussing, flowers, and many, many graves. This was the human side of the war.
>
> For all this the GI's loved the bald little reporter from Indiana. He was one of them.[30]

Equally effective was Ed Murrow, whose radio reports from Europe made his voice among the best known in the country, before and during the war. Not only a brilliant reporter, Murrow was also a far-sighted editor who organized a radio network of correspondents in the capitals of prewar Europe. These journalists overcame obstacles posed by physical danger, confusion, and censorship. As a result, no audience was so well informed of events during World War II as the American people.[31]

Korea and Vietnam

The highly unpopular Korean war, 1950–53, was fought in a remote land, on difficult terrain, for a cause only dimly understood by much of the American public. It posed a monumental challenge to the journalists who attempted to cover it. The frustrations of the troops themselves—they described it as "a war we can't win, can't lose, and can't quit"[32]—were reflected in the media coverage. Indeed, technically, the Korean war was not a war at all, but a police action waged by the United Nations to halt aggressor forces from North Korea who had invaded the South. Sixteen nations sent forces on behalf of the United Nations, but 90 percent of the troops, equipment, and supplies came from the United States. Correspondents hated the war, largely because they could not get a handle on it, and the trade journal, *Editor & Publisher,* called it the most dangerous ever covered.[33] Seventeen correspondents, including ten American journalists, were killed attempting to describe the action, which often occurred in isolated skirmishes and ambushes. It was a tough, bloody conflict, which ended in 1953 with a cease-fire and a political settlement—and a great deal of frustration on the part of the U.S. military and the American public.

The Vietnam war, which the United States became embroiled in a few years later, proved far worse. After years of civil strife, the Vietnam war began in earnest in 1957, when forces supported by Communist North Vietnam attacked the government of South Vietnam. These northern units, the Viet Cong, waged a bloody, highly effective, guerilla campaign against the South Vietnamese Army, which asked for and received U.S. assistance. By 1965, U.S. combat units were deployed in a prolonged, but never officially declared, war. U.S. forces, in support of an unpopular South Vietnamese government, fought gallantly and well—but to an increasingly skeptical American public, the struggle appeared not only unnecessary but pointless.

The public's frustrations were intensified by the journalism of the era; Vietnam was the first war covered by television. Through vivid, on-the-scene reports on evening newscasts, American television audiences witnessed the carnage of what became known as "the living room war." Torn between "doves," who wanted the United States to pull out of Vietnam altogether, and "hawks," who demanded all-out warfare against North Vietnam, administrations in Washington held grimly to a middle course, attempting to confine the combat to South Vietnam while seeking an acceptable political solution. The struggle, all but futile under those circumstances, ended in 1975 with the fall of South Vietnam's capital city, Saigon.

The war and its aftermath was a wrenching experience for the United States. Many in the government and the military blamed the American mass media, and especially television news, for the outcome, contending that sensational and biased coverage nurtured the antiwar movement in the United States and undermined the war effort. Journalists and their news directors and editors hotly denied the allegations, contending that the message (government policy) was at fault, not the messenger.

Antipress feelings persisted within the military, however. When the United States again took up arms in 1983 to rescue Americans believed to be in danger on the island of Grenada, and in 1989 to capture the dictator Noriega in a massive raid on Panama, journalists were denied full access to combat zones. And in the Persian Gulf war of 1991, reporters, and especially camera crews, found their access to combat units sharply limited.

Reporting under fire in the Persian Gulf war.

While the Pentagon in 1992 agreed to provide prompter and fuller access to journalists in future engagements, the relationship between the military and the media was still characterized by a degree of mutual distrust. Media credibility, discussed elsewhere in these pages, had been severely tested by war.

Meanwhile, the center stage of news reporting shifted from New York to Washington, where the ranks of journalists swelled into the thousands. There was much to write about: the nuclear age; the decline of colonialism and the emergence of developing nations; cold war diplomacy and the astounding disintegration of the Soviet empire; poverty; Korea; holy wars in the Middle East and Northern Ireland; civil war in Latin America, Somalia, Yugoslavia, and Rwanda; drug wars on the streets of our cities; racism; inflation; Vietnam; Afghanistan; hostages; terrorism; AIDS; Watergate; recession; economic warfare with Japan; immigration; the women's movement; the environment; the trustworthiness of leadership and institutions. Reliable and complete information was hard to come by at times, even in the days of satellite communications and all-news television networks. Journalists often found themselves caught up in the struggle, as John Tebbel had described it a generation earlier, between "the Establishment's effort to control the news and private individuals to disclose it without restriction." How the media of mass communications have handled these questions, and how they have adapted to radio, television, satellites, and other techniques and technologies, will be dealt with later in these pages.

If the complexity of the news and the means of reporting it have changed, the fundamental mission of American journalism remains the same as it became with the birth of the penny press in 1833—that is, to attempt to make available all the news to all the people. Democratization of the press, like the democratization of other American institutions, had never been attempted on so vast a scale. The experiment has not been a total success. The miracle is that the attempt was ever made, and is being made, at all.

● ●

summary

The history of journalism in the United States is largely a struggle against prior restraint, or censorship. Notable successes in that struggle include James Franklin's *New England Courant,* the first newspaper in America to publish without an official license from the government, and John Peter Zenger, whose trial for criminal libel helped mobilize public support for the freedom to criticize authority. Fears of government control of the press were instrumental in the adoption of the First Amendment to the Constitution, the ultimate basis for U.S. press freedom.

Two significant periods followed the American Revolution: the party press, in which newspapers championed political views in defining national issues and institutions, and the penny press, when newspapers became available to the mass audience. The popular press was often a sensational press, as the yellow journalism and jazz journalism eras later proved. Throughout its history, powerful personalities have shaped the industry, including James Gordon Bennett, Horace Greeley, Joseph Pulitzer, William Randolph Hearst, and many others. Their publications reached millions of Americans and helped influence national policy.

News reporting styles have likewise evolved from the advocacy style of the party press era to the more straightforward presentations facilitated by the invention of the telegraph, to the more interpretative style of the modern era, wherein complex events often spawn extensive analysis and explanation.

? questions and cases

1. Are newspapers better today than they were a century ago? Justify your answer.

2. Discuss Joseph Pulitzer's strategy that the ends (good investigative reporting, an inspirational editorial page, crusades in the public interest) justify the means (sensationalism to lure readers into buying the newspaper). Is such a publishing philosophy defensible? Why or why not?

3. Compare and contrast media coverage of World War II, Vietnam, and the Persian Gulf war. Has the journalist's role changed? If so, how?

4. Wilbur F. Storey said that the purpose of a newspaper is "to print the news and raise hell." What do *you* think the purpose is? Explain.

5. Compare the point of view, content, objectives, and style of the New York *Sun* in 1833 with this season's prime-time television programming schedule. From the point of view of the mass media consumer, is one better than the other? Explain.

chapter glossary

Alien and Sedition Acts   Laws passed in 1798 designed to discourage criticism of the government. Directed primarily at Jeffersonian editors, they posed a potentially dangerous threat to freedom of the press during the formative years of the U.S. government. The last of the series of acts expired in 1802.

by-line   A line printed at the top of a newspaper or magazine article telling who wrote it.

corontos   Forerunners of the newspaper, corontos were single-sheet publications, usually devoted to a single story, popular in Holland and England during the early seventeenth century.

editorialize   To insert one's opinions into a news or feature article that normally would be presented without personal commentary.

feature   Newspaper or magazine article which provides background material or a light human-interest dimension. Less timely and often more literary than a straight news report.

Federalist Papers   (*The Federalist*) Series of 85 articles, written for newspapers in 1787 and 1788, explaining the proposed Constitution of the new United States and urging citizens to vote for its adoption.

interpretive reporting   A technique in which the journalist provides background on and analysis of complex news stories.

investigative reporting   News reports based on disclosure of material that was unusually hard to locate and piece together or which wrongdoers had concealed.

muckraking   Refers to investigative reporting which searches for corruption of public trusts. The term was applied by Theodore Roosevelt to a small band of magazine writers near the turn of the century who exposed massive wrongdoing in government and business.

objective reporting   Straightforward presentation of news in which the journalist's views, attitudes, biases, values, and other colorations are not reflected in the copy.

penny press   Important period in communications history when newspapers slipped away from their partisan orientations to seek broader audiences. The New York *Sun,* which appeared in 1833, was the first important penny paper.

prior restraint   Censorship. Attempts by government to prevent publication and/or circulation of information and ideas.

propaganda   Printed or broadcast material slanted to favor or disfavor a cause, a country, a political party, or an individual.

seditious libel   Published material deemed by government to stir up discontent, resistance to official policies, or rebellion. Considered treason—betrayal of one's country—in some societies.

tabloid   A newspaper about half the dimensions of the normal broadsheet, usually featuring highly condensed articles and proportionately more photos than standard-sized papers.

yellow journalism   Term applied to lurid circulation war waged between Hearst and Pulitzer near the end of the nineteenth century in New York; still used to describe sensational and demagogic treatment of the news.

notes

1 John Tebbel, *The Compact History of the American Newspaper* (New York: Hawthorn, 1969), 3.

2 Quoted in Harold L. Nelson and Dwight L. Teeter, *Law of Mass Communications,* 5th ed. (Mineola, N.Y.: Foundation Press, 1986), 34.

3 The most readable account of Harris's checkered career is in Tebbel, *American Newspaper,* 5 ff.

4 Quoted in Bernard A. Weisberger, *The American Newspaperman* (University of Chicago Press, 1961), 2.

5 The discussion that follows is drawn especially from Frank Luther Mott, *American Journalism* (New York: Macmillan, 1961); and Edwin Emery and Michael Emery, *The Press and America,* 5th ed. (Englewood Cliffs, N.J.: Prentice-Hall, 1984) along with Weisberger, *American Newspaperman;* and Tebbel, *American Newspaper.*

6 Weisberger, *American Newspaperman,* 4.

7 Tebbel, *American Newspaper,* 24.

8 John D. Stevens, "Freedom of Expression," in *Mass Media and the National Experience,* edited by Ronald T. Farrar and John D. Stevens (New York: Harper & Row, 1971), 18, pointed out that the "Zenger trial had about as much impact on American press law as the Boston Tea Party had on American etiquette."

9 Quoted in Mott, *American Journalism,* 108.

10 Reprinted in Louis L. Snyder and Richard R. Morris, *A Treasury of Great Reporting* (New York: Simon & Schuster, 1949), 29.

11 Quoted in Mott, *American Journalism,* 108.

12 Quoted in Willard G. Bleyer, *Main Currents in the History of American Journalism* (Boston: Houghton Mifflin, 1927), 116.

13 Mott, *American Journalism,* 169.

14 Ibid., 215–316. See Michael Schudson, *Discovering the News* (New York: Basic Books, 1978), for a superb analysis of the economic implications of mass journalism.

15 Quoted in Bleyer, *Main Currents.* Excellent and highly readable profile sketches of Bennett, Greeley, and other giants of the era may be found in Kenneth Stewart and John Tebbel, *Makers of Modern Journalism* (New York: Prentice-Hall, 1952).

16 Weisberger, *American Newspaperman,* 101.

17 Vernon L. Parrington, *Main Currents in American Thought,* 3 vols. (New York: Harcourt Brace, 1927–30), 2:247–57.

18 Quoted in Bleyer, *Main Currents,* 240–41.

19 Ibid., 242. See also: Francis Brown, *Raymond of the Times* (New York: W. W. Norton, 1951), 94 ff.

20 Justin E. Walsh, *To Print the News and Raise Hell: A Biography of Wilbur F. Storey* (Chapel Hill: University of North Carolina Press, 1968), 2.

21 Mott, *American Journalism,* 333.

22 Ronald Farrar, *Reluctant Servant: The Story of Charles G. Ross* (Columbia: University of Missouri Press, 1968), 106 ff. See also William A. Swanberg, *Pulitzer* (New York: Scribner's, 1967).

23 Ibid.

24 Bleyer, *Main Currents,* 377. Hearst's career is brilliantly captured in W. A. Swanberg, *Citizen Hearst* (New York: Scribner's, 1961). A brief but especially perceptive appraisal of Hearst's career may be found in Emery and Emery, *Press and America,* 427.

25 This paragraph appears in each edition of the St. Louis *Post-Dispatch.*

26 Two valuable studies of this era are Louis Filler, *Crusaders for American Liberalism* (Antioch, Ohio: Antioch College Press, 1939); and John Harrison and Harry H. Stein, *Muckraking: Past, Present, and Future* (University Park: Pennsylvania State University Press, 1973).

27 William H. Taft, *American Journalism History: An Outline* (Columbia: Lucas Brothers Publishers, 1968), 54.

28 Gene Fowler in the New York *American,* 13 January 1928. Reprinted in Snyder and Morris, *Treasury of Great Reporting,* 445.

29 Stewart and Tebbel, *Makers of Modern Journalism,* 326.

30 Snyder and Morris, *Treasury of Great Reporting,* 619.

31 Mott, *American Journalism,* 710.

32 Philip Knightley, *The First Casualty* (New York: Harcourt Brace Jovanovich, 1976), 336.

33 *Editor & Publisher,* 12 August 1950, 58.

chapter C

Few share a call to mind the glamor and excitement of the communications business more than the wire service teleprinters, those magical machines that tirelessly clatter out bulletins and

The Wire Services

Objectives

When you have finished studying this chapter, you should be able to:

@ Explain the importance of wire service reporting to modern society

@ Trace the development of the Associated Press and United Press International

@ Describe how wire services function today, and analyze characteristics of wire service writing style

@ Discuss supplementary wires and their impact

@ Outine career opportunities in the wire service field

Few images call to mind the glamor and excitement of the communications business more than the wire service teleprinters, those magical machines that tirelessly clatter out **bulletins** and terse news updates from the far capitals of the globe. Like many images, however, this one belongs to the past. Today's teleprinters are smaller and much faster, and the clicking noises they make are different. In fact, the term *wire service* itself is something of a misnomer, since most of the news is no longer transmitted over the wires but through space, captured by satellite dishes and transferred swiftly from one computer to another. But if the old symbolism has become technically inaccurate, the fundamental purpose of the wire service remains unchanged: to serve broadcasters and newspapers by extending their eyes and ears from one end of the planet to the other.

Almost every radio station, television station, and daily newspaper in America receives one or more wire service reports, and thus even the smallest communities are alerted immediately to news breaks from the state, region, nation, or world. No one publication or broadcaster could afford to fund these expensive operations. Pooled resources and shared costs, however, give local broadcasters and newspaper editors instant access to a wealth of news from wherever it occurs.

The wire services are staffed by a small army of men and women deployed throughout the world and determined to gather the facts, large and small, and to report them accurately, concisely, and swiftly. Wire service **correspondents** are acutely aware that their customers are at any given moment apt to be rushing an edition of a newspaper to press or putting a newscast on the air. Delays in transmitting a story can prove costly; too many missed **deadlines** and an angry editor might cancel one wire service outright and shift his or her business to another. Individual wire service reporters wage competitive struggles every day, with victories and defeats measured in terms of minutes, occasionally even seconds.

While the dramatic growth in television news and the emergence of around-the-clock global operations such as the Cable News Network have altered the mission of the wire services to contemporary audiences, wire services still provide us with the early alerts to what is news, no matter when and where the news breaks out. Much of what we know about what happens in the world is what the wire service people tell us. While they are trained to report the news without comment and to keep their personal opinions out of their copy, the wire service reporters and editors nevertheless exert considerable indirect influence simply by calling our attention to certain events and thus placing them on the political and economic and social agenda. For these and other reasons, the wire services are worth examining in some detail.

Teaching Idea
Bring a copy of your local paper to class and point out the origins of the news stories. Are the major ones from AP, UPI, or some other source?

A portion of the Associated Press New York bureau.

"Yes, young man," a famous statesman said to a reporter who sought to interview him some years ago. "I'll be glad to prepare a statement for you. Just tell me when is your—what do you newspapermen call it?—your deadline?"

The reporter sighed. "I'm from the United Press," he replied. "Our deadline is now. Someplace around the world at this instant a newspaper is going to press. We've got a deadline every minute."

Joe Alex Morris, *Deadline Every Minute: The Story of United Press* (Doubleday, 1957).

How Wire Services Developed

Several wire services sprang up in the United States during the late nineteenth and early twentieth centuries. Among them are the Associated Press, the world news cartel, United Press International, and International News Service.

The Associated Press

In 1848, New York City was a vigorous and competitive newspaper market, an arena where rival publishers had been known to do battle not only in the columns of their newspapers but also, on more than one occasion, with fists and canes in the street. In May of that year, however, these rivals agreed to a momentary truce. Six representatives of the city's leading newspapers gathered uneasily around a conference table in the office of the New York *Sun,* their journalistic differences temporarily overshadowed by a larger problem: how best to utilize a recent invention, the telegraph. While the telegraph opened up dramatic new vistas for newspapers, making possible the rapid transmission of news over long distances, the costs were proving too steep for any one newspaper to bear alone. As a result, the six publishers struck a deal to form an organization that would share both telegraph news and telegraph line charges. They named their organization the Associated Press.[1]

The cooperative quickly took on a life of its own. In 1849, the Associated Press opened its first foreign bureau at Halifax, Nova Scotia, where many ships first put into port after crossing the Atlantic. The AP correspondent, Daniel Craig, interviewed the captains, crews, and passengers for news from Europe, then telegraphed the reports to AP member papers long before the ships reached New York harbor. Within a year, Boston newspapers were asking to join the New York publishers' association, and a number of similar regional news cooperatives were forming in the South and West. By 1853, the AP had hired a Washington correspondent, Lawrence Gobright, who would later win fame for his reports on the Civil War and the assassination of President Abraham Lincoln. Associated Press circuits soon stretched from coast to coast.

With the AP's rapid growth, however, came certain problems. Beyond the Alleghenies, a group of publishers had created a regional news cooperative, the Western Associated Press. Western AP members, and especially publishers of the powerful Chicago dailies, resented what they regarded as the second-class treatment the New York headquarters accorded them. Though they paid heavy assessments, members received news reports they felt were inadequate, inferior, and frequently biased. Victor Lawson, publisher of the Chicago *Daily News,* was appointed to investigate the inequities, and his research turned up a scandal of major proportions: The national distribution of Associated Press news was controlled by a trust whose members had cut a covert deal among executives of a private news agency—the United Press—and of the Associated Press and the Western AP. They secretly awarded blocks of stock to insiders. Far more than a

Background

"Telegraphs" did exist before Morse's invention. The British and French navies had mechanical telegraphs covering hundreds of miles, beginning in the late 1700s and lasting until the mid-1800s.

Teaching Idea

If any of your students are amateur (ham) radio operators, or if any know one, ask them to bring a telegraph demonstration code set to class and explain the modern uses of Morse code transmission. If you wish, distribute copies of the Morse code to your class and let students send and receive messages. (You could send "Class dismissed" at the end of the period to see how many alert students leave.)

Death of a President

The Washington correspondent of the Associated Press, Lawrence A. Gobright, was seated in his office just after 10:15 the evening of 14 April 1865, when someone rushed in with a report that President Abraham Lincoln had been shot. Gobright rushed to Ford's Theater, nearby, entered the president's box and secured possession of the pistol the assassin had used. He then dashed to the president's bedside, interviewed witnesses, then began filing dispatches as more details became available. Here are three of the first seven reports:

> **First Dispatch**
> *To the Associated Press*
> WASHINGTON, FRIDAY, APRIL 14, 1865—The President was shot in a theater tonight, and perhaps mortally wounded.

> **Third Dispatch**
> *Special to the New York Tribune*
> The President was shot at Ford's Theater. The ball entered his neck. It is not known whether the wound is mortal . . .

> **Fifth Dispatch**
> *To the Associated Press*
> WASHINGTON, APRIL 15, 12:30 A.M.—The President was shot in a theater tonight, and is perhaps mortally wounded. The President is not expected to live through the night. Secretary Seward was also assassinated.
> No arteries were cut.
> Particulars soon.

> **Seventh Dispatch**
> WASHINGTON, FRIDAY, APRIL 14, 1865—The President attended Ford's Theater tonight, and about ten o'clock an assassin entered his private box and shot him in the back of the head. The ball lodged in his head, and he is now lying insensible in a house opposite the theater. No hopes are entertained of his recovery. Laura Keene claims to have recognized the assassin as the actor, J. Wilkes Booth. A feeling of gloom like a pall has settled on the city. . . .

Louis L. Snyder and Richard B. Morris, *A Treasury of Great Reporting* (Simon & Schuster, 1949).

conflict of interest, this was a crisis that threatened the fundamental integrity of newsgathering. Furious, Western publishers withdrew, and in 1892 obtained a charter for the Associated Press of Illinois. This organization would be a true, nonprofit cooperative, collecting and distributing news for its members. Each member would have a voice in the cooperative's management, and the daily news reports were required by charter to be unbiased and truthful. Melville E. Stone, destined to be a monumental figure in newsgathering history, became the general manager. Warring factions, including those from New York, soon rallied around the reconstituted Associated Press. A tradition for impartial reporting, carried on to this day, had begun.[2]

The matter of admission to the cooperative, however, would not be settled for many years. AP members had the power in their local communities to blackball prospective member publications. In some cities, they denied AP wire service to a rival newspaper and thus seriously crippled that paper's ability to keep its readers informed. This monopolistic practice was challenged in various courts for decades until, in 1945, the Supreme Court ruled that Associated Press membership must be open to all qualified U.S. newspapers. The Court affirmed an earlier ruling in which the distinguished federal judge, Learned Hand, struck down the notion that the press could not be muzzled, even if other newspapers did the muzzling:

> The [newspaper] industry serves one of the most vital of all general interests: the dissemination of news from many different sources, with as many different facets and colors as possible. That interest . . . presupposes that right conclusions are more likely to be gathered out of a multitude of tongues, than any kind of authoritarian selection. To many this is, and always will be folly; but we have staked upon it our all.[3]

The World News Cartel

Background

A *cartel* is an international monopoly.

Background

After Britain cut the undersea cable, the Germans used a powerful radio station in Germany to send news to the United States. This lasted until the United States entered the war in 1917.

Background

Each U.S. wire service keeps close tabs on the other. Example: A UPI local bureau message to headquarters might say, "ROX TOPS STRIKE, FOLDS NATO." This means that the local paper has printed the AP story on a strike at the top of the first page, and run an AP story on NATO on the bottom half (below the fold). "ROX" is a play on the name of early AP manager Melville E. Stone.

Extra Information

Edward W. Scripps, unlike W. R. Hearst, bought or founded mostly afternoon papers, encouraged local ownership, and gave local editors editorial control.

Another monopoly situation, this one with worldwide implications, plays an important role in Associated Press history. Beginning in 1871 and formally reaffirmed by contract in 1893, the AP agreed with a British agency, Reuters, to an exclusive exchange of world news. Reuters, meanwhile, had negotiated with other European wire services—the Havas Agency in France, Wolff News Bureau in Germany, and Stefani in Italy, among others—not only to share news but, in effect, to carve up the world among themselves. Each wire service, by mutual agreement, was given exclusive rights to certain countries with the understanding that it would share its news from those regions with the other members of the cartel. While this arrangement permitted the agencies to operate efficiently and to avoid costly duplication, it also produced a gigantic, interlocking network that was essentially designed to monopolize distribution of world news. Since most of the European news agencies operated under government control, the agencies were prone to transmit only those dispatches that reflected official views. In short, much of the reporting was distorted, biased, and heavily laced with political propaganda. Little could be done about it.

The AP's general manager, Melville Stone, made several trips to Europe to attempt to promote better and more independent reporting, but the pre–World War I biases and half-truths remained. Eventually the British, angered at the pro-German news slant the monopoly was dispensing to such pivotal nations as the United States, halted the German propaganda barrage in August 1914 simply by cutting the German-Atlantic cable. As a result, dispatches written on the European continent had to be routed through London, where the British could tone them down, before they were sent to the United States. But this solution was unsatisfactory to American editors, many of whom felt the British were merely substituting one type of slanted reporting for another.

After chafing under these self-imposed restrictions for years, and feeling the pressure from a rival U.S. wire service that was busily signing foreign newspaper clients, the AP decided to challenge the world news monopoly. In 1919, it "invaded" South America, which, under cartel arrangement, was largely the private preserve of the French agency Havas. By 1933, the AP's general manager, Kent Cooper, had obtained permission from his board of directors to move a bureau into Japan, and after that the world news cartel was broken.[4] The Associated Press has since competed freely throughout the world. Its most vigorous competition, however, has come from another American agency.

United Press International

Until the Supreme Court put an end to the Associated Press's practice of choosing its own members, newspapers outside the AP fold had to scramble for themselves to gain effective access to telegraph news. Early efforts to organize non-AP members were largely unsuccessful, but in 1882 a rival agency, the United Press, formed. Overcoming numerous obstacles, it managed to develop a viable economic base and a strong foreign service. For a time, it competed effectively with the AP. But internal problems, notably the uncovering of a scheme in which several top executives of both agencies secretly shared news and United Press stock, angered subscribers and led to the 1897 dissolution of the United Press, even as it had pushed the New York Associated Press over the brink.

In 1907 another United Press, unrelated to the original, was born. Edward Wyllis Scripps, who had built a publishing empire in the Middle West and West, developed two small, regional wire services to provide his own papers with national and world news. Irritated by what he perceived as the ultraconservatism of the Associated Press, and convinced that the AP wire released news bulletins to favor morning papers—while Scripps's papers were mostly afternoon dailies—he mounted a major assault on the AP. Combining his own wire services with the Publishers Press Association, made up of non-AP papers in the East, Scripps formed the United Press Associations.

A year later, Scripps turned management of the wire service over to Roy Howard, a dynamic individual then only twenty-five years old, and the ambitious Howard soon developed the United Press into a formidable and aggressive news agency. Unencumbered by any ties to Reuters or the world news cartel, and without a conservative board of directors to slow him down, Howard boldly established United Press bureaus in a number of world capitals. He met with considerable success, especially in South America, and before World War I signed up some 250 newspapers as United Press clients. Like Scripps, Howard considered the Associated Press wire dull and hidebound. He developed for the United Press a daily news report that contained not only serious news, but also bright features, background articles, and lively interpretive pieces. United Press pioneered other innovations as well: It began mailing out news photographs in 1925, two years before the AP, and moved quickly to sign up clients in the rapidly emerging field of radio, long before the Associated Press consented to offer service to broadcasters. UP technicians also introduced numerous improvements in the transmission of words and pictures.[5]

International News Service

In the meantime, another powerful press baron, William Randolph Hearst, initiated a wire service of his own. Using wire facilities already leased to communicate with his widespread publishing empire, Hearst formed his International News Service in 1909. INS wires hummed with spectacular reports from the highly paid stars on the Hearst national staff, gifted writers such as Damon Runyon, Paul Gallico, Bob Considine, and dozens of others who were among the glamorous figures in the journalism of their day.

But while INS could be counted upon for sparkling, hard-hitting coverage of the big story, it never possessed the depth, in numbers of bureaus and field reporters, to furnish editors with the hundreds of smaller, daily spot news items that make a wire service indispensable. For most publications, INS was at best a secondary service, something to add spice to the meat and potatoes that came from AP or the United Press. INS continued to lose money after World War II, though it had about two thousand print and broadcast customers throughout the world and some of the most talented writers in the business. Retrenching, the Hearst people sold INS to a competitor, United Press. The resulting agency, United Press International, picked up some of the INS staff and many former INS clients, and gained enough momentum to sustain its long and intense rivalry with the Associated Press for another generation.[6]

Rising costs and inflationary pressures exacted their toll, however, and by 1982 Scripps-Howard had grown weary of absorbing UPI deficits; they sold the service to a group of private investors. After some executive reshuffling, UPI announced plans to offer a variety of electronic services along with news, features, and photographs. But great numbers of new clients were not forthcoming, and the new owners were unable to attract sufficient working capital to reorganize UPI's troubled finances. In April 1985, after severe cost-cutting programs failed to stem the tide of red ink, UPI's board of directors filed for protection from the agency's creditors under the federal bankruptcy code. The move kept the wire service in operation, but its fiscal condition remained shaky and its future uncertain.

In 1986, a Mexican newspaper publisher, Mario Vazquez Rana, bought 95 percent of UPI's stock. Though he pledged not to interfere in the editorial affairs of the wire service, Vazquez Rana was soon accused of forcing resignations of key news and management executives who were not in sympathy with his plans to reorganize operations. He denied the allegations, asserting that he was attempting to streamline the wire service to make it more efficient. Morale at UPI was reported at low ebb in wake of management upheavals; between September 1984 and June 1987, UPI had six different presidents.[7] With bankruptcy at hand, UPI looked desperately for a well-heeled buyer with fresh capital. In the summer of 1992, after a number of prospective investors had considered UPI and then declined to buy into it, the service was sold to Middle East Broadcast Center, a London-based television news and entertainment company that specialized in broadcasting in Arabic throughout the Middle East and Europe. The new owners, Saudi businesspeople, indicated that the wire service operations, which financial hard times had curtailed in recent years, might again be expanded and the UPI's mission as a worldwide newsgathering operation would be sustained.[8]

The Wire Services Today

Teaching Idea
Invite the bureau chief of the nearest AP or UPI bureau to speak to the class.

Both major U.S. wire services serve their customers in similar ways. From a general desk—the AP's is in New York, UPI's in Washington—news moves through trunk distribution circuits to the major metropolitan daily newspapers, large broadcast operations, and state bureaus. In these state bureaus, editors select the most important national and foreign articles from the trunk circuit, insert additional items developed locally, and send out a report reflecting a balance of international, national, regional, and state interests. The most important state stories from bureaus around the country are forwarded to the general desks, where they may receive national distribution.

Each day's flow of news is divided into **cycles,** the A.M. cycle for morning papers and the P.M. cycle for papers published in the afternoon. At the beginning of each cycle, the general desk provides a tentative **budget,** or **schedule (sked),** of significant stories in the works. If, for instance, the Senate will take an important vote about noon, and the president will hold a news conference early in the evening, the general desk can alert editors to these stories in advance so they can arrange to hold space in their newspapers for them. **Spot news** stories—reports of unanticipated news incidents—are relayed as they develop. Wire service reporters and editors are keenly aware of newspaper deadlines, which mostly occur toward the end of each cycle, and they prepare their major articles accordingly. On breaking stories—developments in progress—the wire service tries to weave together details to the best possible extent with a **wrapup** piece before the cycle ends. Broadcast wires are geared toward early morning, noon, late afternoon, and late night newscasts, with brief updates and weather reports presented hourly.

Services and Structure

Wire service fees are based on the size of the newspaper or broadcaster and the range of services provided. A large metropolitan daily might require the main trunk service, one or more state services, special wires for sports and business news, plus a news photo service. A smaller paper may need only one all-purpose wire which carries a more generalized combination of services.

The Associated Press remains a nonprofit cooperative, owned and governed by its members. Members agree to provide the cooperative with their own local news as they develop it, and members can vote to decide AP policy. Associate members simply receive the service without having to contribute news to it, and they have no voting rights. The AP forecasts each year how much it will need for operating expenses, then assesses each member and associate an appropriate share of the total. United Press International is a private business which sells its various services and hopes to make a profit. UPI customers are referred to as clients. And while they have no voting rights, UPI clients can and do make their wishes known to the owners. Member or client advisory groups continuously monitor both associations' performances.

Since 1990, Agence France-Presse has been supplying photographs to clients throughout its European network, and later
around the world, via digital transmission—a technology that
has improved both speed and quality. Likewise, the Associated Press PhotoStream process has made it possible to

- Transmit black-and-white pictures in thirty-five seconds,
  color photographs in under two minutes, and compressed
  pictures in seven seconds.

- Transmit about 300 pictures, including 50 color
  photographs, to AP members daily.

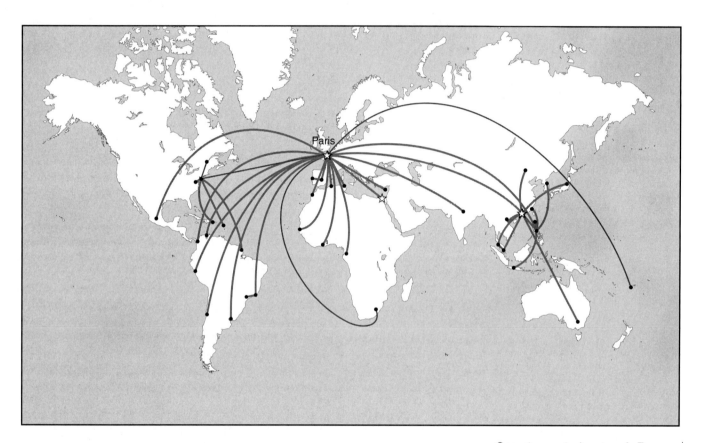

Paris

One wire service's outreach. From
its headquarters in Paris, Agence
France-Presse transmits a million
words of news a day in various
languages to its clients around the
globe.

Computers and Satellites

In their formative years, the wire services moved news by pony express, carrier pigeons, and Morse code messages across telegraph lines. In the 1990s, however,
news agency technology continues to develop at an astonishing pace. Reporters
write their stories on **video display terminals (VDTs)** and move each piece, as it is
finished, into a computer. There, the reporter or others can call up the piece immediately for editing, updating, or rapid distribution to customers everywhere. Editors
transmit the news stories and photographs by bouncing them off a **synchronous
satellite,** in fixed orbit 22,300 miles overhead, into receiving dishes at newspaper
and broadcast plants throughout the globe. Using portable terminals, reporters and
photographers can also transmit on-the-scene copy, voice reports, or pictures from
remote locations directly into wire service computers or, for that matter, through
portable transmitters straight to the satellite.

A Wire Service in Every Home?

By the year 2000, interactive television will be commonplace. You'll be able to push a button to order up a CD while watching a hot music video, or to vote in an instant nationwide poll during the evening newscast. You'll shop via on-screen merchandise catalogues that offer sound, text, and moving video. Running up bills will even be easier: The TV will already know your credit card number and address.

And you'll be able to access the news of the day—perhaps the full Associated Press report, for example—or call up specific portions of it (sports, business news, the latest science and medical reports, consumer bulletins).

Within a few years, wherever the TV is within your home will become a room with a very different view.

Adapted from Michael Rogers, "A Simple Guide to the Television Technology of the Future," *TV Guide,* 23 January 1993.

New high-speed transmission devices have dramatically expanded the types of services the news agencies can offer. To cite just one example, in the fall of 1984, the AP began offering its members a digital stock service that operates at a rate equivalent to 12,000 words a minute. Thus the entire New York Stock Exchange tables, which once took one or more skilled operators most of a cycle to put onto the wire, could be transmitted in four minutes.[9]

Characteristics of Wire Service Writing

As with other forms of journalism, wire service work involves accurately reporting newsworthy events. But the wire services make additional demands, and the men and women on wire service staffs soon learn that their writing must be fast, concise, impartial, readily edited, and frequently updated.

Competitive pressures, and the deadlines of editors and broadcasters who depend on the wire services, dictate that most copy be developed swiftly. Sometimes a reporter may have an hour to prepare an article; more often only a few minutes are available. Perhaps a reporter would prefer to hold off on a story, waiting for one or two additional details, but not infrequently a desk editor will point to the clock, then give the order, "Go with what you have."

Wordiness is a luxury wire service people can seldom afford. Effective writing for the wires is crisp and lean, making its point without wasting a word. Note how much verbiage can be removed from the paragraphs in figure 1.

The editing, shown in figure 1 with a pencil, would in fact be performed electronically. When editing saves space, the savings mount up: If five words are trimmed from each of five stories, then another twenty-five word item can fit into the paper.

Wire service journalists learned long ago that it simply is not possible to write articles that always agree with each customer's personal and political biases. The AP's first Washington correspondent, Lawrence Gobright, put it this way more than a century ago:

> My business is to communicate facts. My instructions do not allow me to make any comment upon the facts. My dispatches are sent to papers of all manners of politics. I therefore confine myself to what I consider legitimate news and try to be truthful and impartial.[10]

A 750-word wire service dispatch may appear in full in one customer's newspaper, be trimmed to 500 words in another, and be slashed to 150 words in a third. Realizing that each local editor's news requirements differ each day, the wire service writer usually includes the most important elements of the story at the top,

Discussion

Does wire service competition hurt accuracy or keep both services honest?

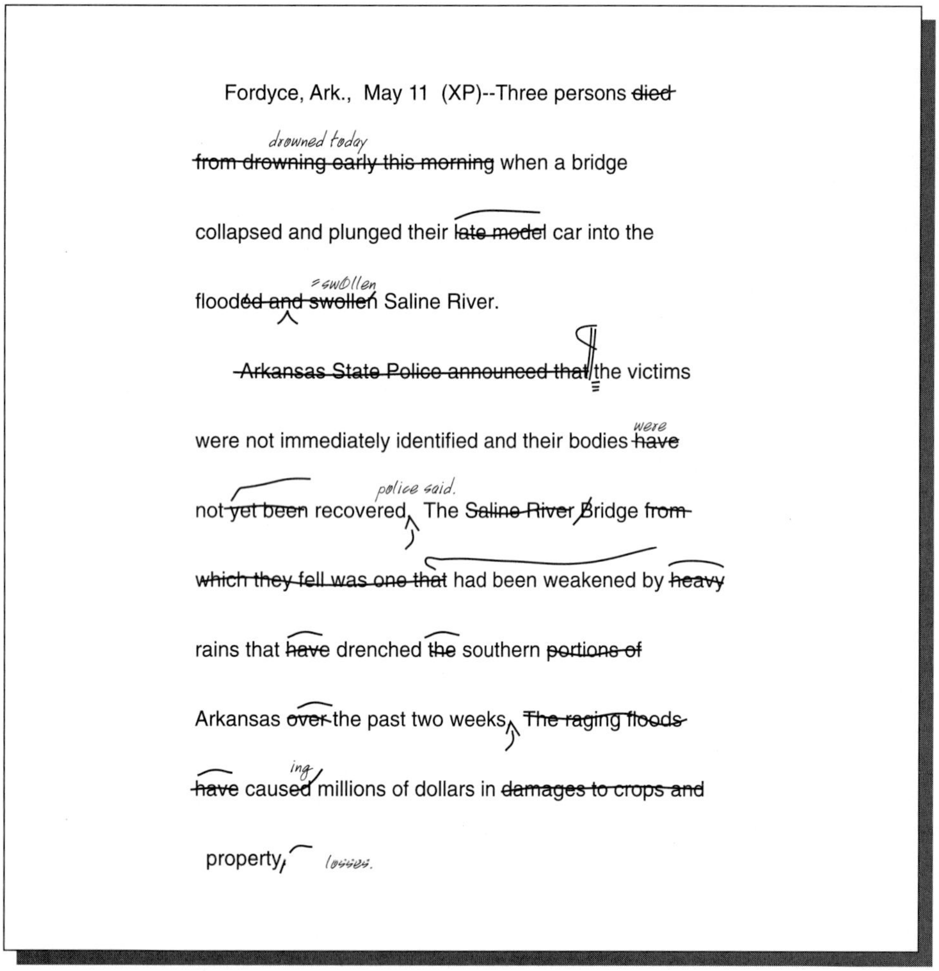

Figure 1 An example of newspaper editing: saving space is paramount.

Fordyce, Ark., May 11 (XP)--Three persons ~~died~~

drowned today
~~from drowning early this morning~~ when a bridge

collapsed and plunged their ~~late model~~ car into the

≠swollen
flood~~ed and swollen~~ Saline River.

~~Arkansas State Police announced that~~ the victims

were
were not immediately identified and their bodies ~~have~~

police said.
not yet been recovered. The ~~Saline River~~ Bridge ~~from~~

~~which they fell was one that~~ had been weakened by ~~heavy~~

rains that ~~have~~ drenched ~~the~~ southern ~~portions of~~

Arkansas ~~over~~ the past two weeks. ~~The raging floods~~

ing
~~have~~ caused millions of dollars in ~~damages to crops and~~

property, *losses.*

permitting the editor to fit the piece to individual space requirements without losing the essentials of the story. Note the following hypothetical example of the **inverted pyramid** writing style the wire services often utilize:

> Lincoln City, Mar. 9 (XP)—Striking police men and women came to terms on a new labor contract here today.
>
> The new agreement, signed in the office of Mayor Gary Burnett, calls for wage increases averaging $45 a week for the city's 750 police officers, who had walked off their jobs at dawn yesterday.
>
> The contract was ratified by more than 70 percent of the officers, the mayor said. Minutes after the pact was approved, police began returning to work, ending the 31-hour walkout.
>
> National guard troops, mobilized when wage talks broke down Monday, patrolled city streets during the strike. There was no reported violence, and criminal activity remained at normal levels, according to Mayor Burnett.
>
> "But we are glad to have come to an agreement," he added. "The entire community is happy this is settled."
>
> The new contract also calls for modest wage increases for police office workers, most of whom remained on the job during the walkout. . . .[11]

Thus constructed, the story could be terminated at nearly any point, even at the close of the brief opening paragraph, and the vital elements would remain intact. What the wire service writer would *not* do is begin the article with background information explaining how the wage dispute developed, leaving the climax of the story—that the strike has ended—late in the piece, where it might not survive cuts made by a hurried editor trying to fit a long story into a tiny space.

Class Project

Clip the longest wire service story from your local or regional daily paper. Ask the class to shorten it by cutting paragraphs from the bottom. How short can the story be and still contain all the important information?

Wire service history is filled with the names of heroes, famous and not so famous, who were at risk while attempting to report the news. Associated Press correspondent Terry Anderson was captured and held hostage for 2,455 days by Middle Eastern terrorists. This photo shows his joyous return to AP headquarters in New York.

Wire services attempt to inform their customers of important news breaks as swiftly as possible. They fire off the main points immediately. Details are filled in as they become known, leaving to individual editors and broadcasters the task of putting the fast-breaking story together. The following example, from Associated Press dispatches, illustrates how this process works. The story broke in late August 1992, during a tense moment in the Middle East. United Nations forces, massively supported by the United States in the wake of the Persian Gulf war, had imposed "no fly" zones, banning Iraqi aircraft from patrolling certain areas of that country. Allied forces were convinced that the Iraqi ruler, Saddam Hussein, was ordering Iraqi aircraft attacks on dissident factions of Shiite Muslims in the area to destroy internal political opposition to his regime. Toward noon Eastern Daylight Time in the United States, the AP warned editors and broadcasters of a dramatic development in the story:[12]

> APNews Alert
> Saddam Hussein vows to resist no-fly zone, says Allies plotting to control Iraqi oil.

Moments later, this bulletin moved on the wire:

> URGENT
> Saddam Rejects No-Fly Zone, Says Allies Want to Control Oil
> NICOSIA, Cyprus (AP)—Iraqi President Saddam Hussein vowed Sunday to resist the no-fly zone imposed over southern Iraq by the U.S.-led Allies.
> He said they were trying to partition the Arab world and control the region's oil, Baghdad's official media said.
> MORE

Shortly thereafter, more facts became known and could be added to the report. (Note that this next **take** to the story will become the "1st **add**"; it provides a pickup point from the previous dispatch.)

> Iraq-Saddam, 1st add
> URGENT
> NICOSIA, Cyprus: media said.
> In an address delivered by an unidentified spokesman on his behalf, Saddam also warned Arab governments against supporting Operation Southern Watch, which was launched Thursday to protect Shiite Muslim dissidents from Iraqi attacks.
> It was not immediately clear why Saddam did not deliver the speech himself.
> It was the first reaction from Saddam himself to the flight ban, although government officials and the state media had earlier taken the same defiant stance.
> The official Iraqi News Agency, carrying highlights of the speech, quoted the president as saying: "The leadership is determined to reject the bold aggression and confront it with all means available and on all levels."
> The agency, monitored in Nicosia, quoted him as saying:
> "We will not be deceived by the slogans they have raised justifying their ban on flights in southern and northern Iraq. These slogans are a conspiracy to eliminate Iraq's historical role . . . and partition the region to seize control over its oil wealth."
> MORE

Additional takes will arrive, as the concluding "more" message indicates. In a few moments, the "2nd add" to the story is moved:

> Iraq-Saddam, 2nd add
> URGENT
> NICOSIA: oil wealth.
> Despite the fiery rhetoric, Baghdad has so far made no signs of breaching the "no-fly" zone clamped on southern Iraq Thursday to protect Shiite Muslims who have risen up against Saddam.
> A U.S.-led coalition has threatened to shoot down any Iraqi planes that enter the zone, south of the 32nd parallel.

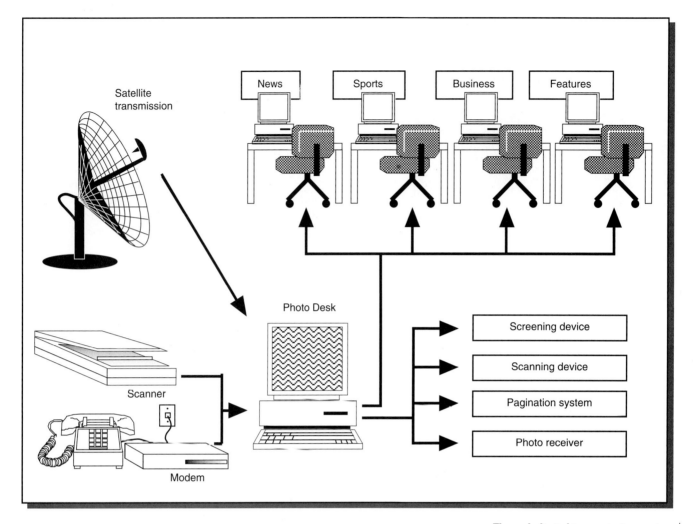

News   Sports   Business   Features

Satellite transmission

Photo Desk

Scanner

Modem

Screening device

Scanning device

Pagination system

Photo receiver

U.S. Navy and Air force pilots on Saturday detected the first Iraqi air activity near the zone but reported no encounters.

Senior U.S. military officers have said they do not expect Saddam to lash out at the U.S. air patrols because the situation could escalate quickly beyond his control. . . . MORE

Through digital transmissions, wire services can provide their clients with several hundreds of news and feature photos each day.

Still later, these developments and other information—reaction from the Pentagon, the White House, and other sources, plus additional background material—were gathered and combined in a lengthy, polished wrapup story. The earlier dispatches, which broke the story piecemeal and had to be fit together by editors in local newsrooms, could now be discarded in favor of the more polished update. All of these dispatches, from the opening news alert to the complete story, moved across the AP wire within a total elapsed time span of less than ten minutes.

Not every story requires this sense of urgency, but wire service men and women must react quickly, responsibly, and with considerable resourcefulness during times of crisis, assimilating information from a variety of sources and moving it onto the circuits without delay. This can be demanding work, and only a relative few are skilled enough to handle it.

Criticisms of the Wire Services

Even the harshest of journalistic fault finders have given both the Associated Press and United Press International generally meritorious ratings for their day-to-day performance. Still, over the years, some critical themes have been sounded.

A Preoccupation with Being First

The intense competitive pressure has spurred peak performance from most U.S. wire service reporters and editors, and they are widely regarded as among the hardest-working, most productive journalists in the world. Yet that same pressure has led to some costly mistakes. Roy Howard, determined to scoop the Associated Press, flashed word that World War I was over four days before it actually was. A generation later, an overly anxious AP correspondent prematurely flashed the end of the second world war in Europe. Both relied upon fragmentary information that had not been thoroughly checked. Similar, though less spectacular, lapses have occurred—not many, perhaps, considering the hundreds of stories transmitted each day, but enough to cause some concern that the competitive struggle might at times provoke reckless handling of important news.

In that same vein, the Cable News Network was criticized during the Persian Gulf war for showing raw footage—unedited material, shown live—of fast-breaking news stories. Critics charged that raw footage, presented without background information or context of any kind, can be dangerously misleading. But, again, the pressure a media organization feels to be first with breaking news is powerful stuff, even if the pressure is self-imposed.

Conformity

Because there is such heavy dependency on the two major wire services for state, national, and foreign news, the contents of many daily newspapers around the country, as well as the contents of radio and television newscasts, may be strikingly similar. In the deepest sense, wire service journalists are gatekeepers; what they send to their customers, and what they choose not to send, is important. Precious little evidence has been introduced through the years to suggest that wire service editors and reporters have used their positions for personal or political gain. But many editors and broadcasters place great faith in the news that comes in from the wire services. Through their internal reviews, advisory boards, and monitoring committees, the wire service executives seem determined to make certain the faith is not misplaced.

Oversimplification

Another worrisome problem, one that the wire service people frequently mention themselves, is that they may trivialize the events and people they cover. "I fear that I won't get through clearly to my editors and readers," one foreign correspondent explained. "I try to be clear, and as a result sometimes I know I get blunt instead. That's when all of us fall back onto using such words as 'hawk' and 'dove' and other stereotypes that oversimplify complex meanings in the news."[13] Much of the news *is* complicated, and many significant situations don't lend themselves to terse dispatches and the bang-bang inverted pyramid style of writing. Sensitive to charges that they sometimes oversimplify for a lowest-common-denominator audience, the wire services in recent years have begun developing more investigative pieces, interpretative articles, and background reports.

Crisis Journalism

Conflict is a key element in the news, and wire service writers, like journalists in other fields, have been accused of overemphasizing personality traits and creating more suspense and tension in a situation than might be warranted. Not every discussion is a "clash," and not every policy disagreement becomes a "bitter feud." In earlier years of this century, reporters embroiled in hotly competitive situations did not hesitate to inject a certain amount of hype (high promotion) into their copy. While the practice has by no means disappeared, it does seem less common today.

Despite these criticisms, the American wire services enjoy a favorable reputation for fairness, accuracy, and diligence.

Foreign Wire Services

So far we have discussed only the Associated Press and United Press International. Although the United States is the only nation to boast more than one world class wire service, other such agencies are presently in operation.

Reuters was established by Paul Julius Reuter, an enterprising German youth who sold bankers on the idea of using his carrier pigeons to wing stock quotations and other financial intelligence throughout Europe. By 1851, Reuter had moved to London, retired his pigeons in favor of telegraph cables, become a British citizen, and formed a full-fledged, international news service. His resourcefulness, accuracy, and thoroughness won him great popularity and spread his fame across the expanding British Empire. In 1941, several generations of Reuters later and following the agency's nefarious role in the world news cartel, Reuters became a cooperative owned by the British mass media, somewhat like the Associated Press. Reuters has moved aggressively to expand during the last few years; a number of U.S. clients subscribe to various Reuters services, notably its sports wire, which is heavy on horseracing news, and its worldwide financial reports.

Agence France-Presse (AFP) is the direct descendant of the Havas Agency founded by Charles Havas in 1835, which was the first news agency in the world. Headquartered in Paris and nominally controlled by the French government, Agence France-Presse beams out nearly a million words a day in six languages to audiences and clients in 120 countries. AFP has 50 bureaus in Africa and 39 in Asia, reflecting the wire service's relatively strong position in those areas.[14]

TASS, or Telegrafnoie Agentsvo Sovetskava Soiuza, the Russian news agency, formed in 1935 from a merger of five internal wire services in the Soviet Union. A highly political extension of the Soviet government as well as a busy news agency, TASS at one time claimed 5,000 subscribers, most of them newspapers in Eastern Europe. TASS reporters, many widely suspected of being intelligence agents as well as journalists, were deployed throughout the world. TASS's fortunes, intimately linked to those of its government, took a dramatic downturn on 25 December 1991, when the Union of Soviet Socialist Republics officially ceased to exist as a political entity. TASS, along with four television channels in Moscow, continued to be fully state-subsidized, but TASS's clientele, the news media of the former Soviet Union, began to change at a dizzying pace. The fall of the communist system brought about the

Extra Information

AFP has an overt connection with the French government, and Reuters is alleged to have a covert connection with the British government. A good research project might be to try to find out whether evidence exists that the latter is true.

demise of many newspapers and other media clients. Other media voices, responding to the spirit of *glasnost* and the historic propensity of the Russian people to read newspapers, rushed in to fill the void. By 1993, between 30 and 40 daily newspapers were being published in Moscow alone.[15] Most were marginal enterprises with shaky futures. TASS reporters continued to cover the news around the globe, but their numbers, like their influence and their political role, were greatly diminished. TASS clients, for the most part, had been government-funded. The battle to succeed in a market economy would not be an easy one.

Other Wire Services

On a more modest scale are a number of specialized press services, such as *AP-Dow Jones,* a New York-based agency that sends financial news over the globe, and *Interlink,* which focuses on news from and about Third World countries. Inter Press Service, based in Rome, serves a number of clients in Latin America and elsewhere with a wire service reflecting strong concern with news of political and social reform. Additional wires serve clients on the Pacific Rim and in the Middle East, among other regions. At least eighty-five nations have their own domestic wire services, but only a handful maintain networks or bureaus outside their immediate sectors of the world.

Supplementary Wire Services

As large newspaper groups continued to expand in recent years, a marked increase has occurred in the number of supplementary wires in use. Unlike the AP and UPI, these supplementary services make no attempt to establish bureaus everywhere or to provide comprehensive spot news coverage. Instead, they furnish their subscribers with features, analysis, and background material that add to, rather than compete with, traditional wire service offerings.

Suppose, for example, that the chief of a foreign nation is overthrown in a political coup. U.S. editors would expect, and receive, a prompt, straightforward account of the incident from United Press International and the Associated Press. But some editors might want an explanation as to why the coup occurred: an analysis of living conditions in the country, philosophies of the contending political factions, perhaps a cause-and-effect chronology of events that led to the overthrow. The Los Angeles *Times* and the Washington *Post* correspondents would likely develop just this kind of interpretative analysis for their newspapers—and the *Times-Post* supplementary wire service could make this in-depth reporting available to other newspaper subscribers as well.

Several newspapers and newspaper groups with unusually talented and expensive staffs have decided to compile the top news and feature pieces their writers produce each day and sell the package to editors everywhere. Besides the New York *Times* and the Los Angeles *Times*-Washington *Post* services, Knight-Ridder News Service, Gannett News Service, Scripps-Howard News Service, Copley Press, and others do so.

The supplementary wire reports can be impressive and appealing, and many editors have signed up for them even though doing so frequently means cancelling one of the two primary wires. Midsized and large dailies often subscribed to both AP and UPI; more recently, with the increase in supplementary wire popularity, the editors might elect instead to rely on one primary wire and one or more supplements. The Los Angeles *Times*-Washington *Post* service, as an example, in 1992 offered its hundreds of subscribers a package containing investigative reports and in-depth news features by top-of-the-line reporters, 162 regular columns, a graphics service including color photos, and other contributions from the *Post,* the Los Angeles *Times, Newsday,* the Baltimore *Sun,* and *The Sporting News.* This kind of competition has hit United Press International especially hard.

Teaching Idea

Ask your class to examine a local or regional daily newspaper to see if it uses any supplemental wire services, such as those run by Cox, Knight-Ridder, the New York *Times,* Washington *Post*–Los Angeles *Times.*

Journalism at Wholesale: The Feature Syndicates

Newspapers have three traditional functions: to inform, to persuade, and to entertain. Wire services provide much of the information; newspaper feature syndicates provide many of the persuasive and entertainment elements. Operating in an intensely competitive market, dozens of syndicate houses sell newspapers material ranging from comic strips to profound political commentary. Syndicate houses survive because they

- Make it possible for even the smallest newspapers to afford the services of expensive artists and writers.

- Supply newspapers with an extensive range of features, some of interest to everyone. Syndicated material, in other words, attracts more readers to the newspaper.

Development of Feature Syndicates

While editors have always "borrowed" items from other publications, the first systematic sharing of features and columns began in Wisconsin in 1865. Ansel Nash Kellogg established an independent agency that sold ready-to-print features, poetry, serial fiction, and household hints columns to community newspapers. Editors of these smaller papers, their staffs decimated by the Civil War, welcomed the wealth of material the A. N. Kellogg company could provide at low cost.

Metropolitan newspapers, too, learned to appreciate the economics of syndication. By splitting costs among papers in different markets, it became possible to amass the kind of money that would interest top literary talent in newspaper writing. Mark Twain, Rudyard Kipling, Robert Lewis Stevenson, Bret Harte—all wrote columns and feature pieces for newspaper syndicates. By the mid-1920s, syndicated material of all types was readily available, including:

- Political columns, representing all persuasions.

- Comics—for many, the most popular feature in the paper.

- Service features, from lonely-hearts columns, to advice on buying personal computers, to bodybuilding, to cooking tips.

How Syndicates Work

Syndicated features are born in one of two ways. A syndicate house might decide it needs a certain type of feature to round out its collection—adding, say, a columnist who specializes in single parenting. Or, more commonly, artists or writers themselves originate syndicate features. They develop good ideas for columns or comic strips, perhaps feature them in a few local papers, then persuade the syndicates to take them on for national audiences. Once under contract, the artist or writer prepares the material and forwards it to syndicate headquarters. The syndicate staff makes publication-quality copies, distributes them by mail or electronically to the clients the syndicate's sales force has lined up, and collects the proceeds, splitting them with the artist or writer. In the usual arrangement, the author receives 40 to 60 percent of the gross income, though some artists are able to negotiate more favorable terms. Publishers pay for the syndicated features they buy on the basis of their newspaper's circulation: a daily with five thousand subscribers would pay far less than a metropolitan paper with half a million. The relatively few syndicated columnists and comic strip artists with vast national circulations can earn hundreds of thousands of dollars annually.

The Enormous Stakes Involved

AP's annual budget runs well in excess of $200 million a year, and the U.S. media economy may be unable to sustain two major, comprehensive, competing wire service organizations. Yet for all its waste and duplication, the historic competition between AP and UPI has been healthy. Certainly it has prevented either of the giants from becoming complacent. Given the heavy reliance that editors, broadcasters, and the public have upon the major wire services, that is no small accomplishment.

Career Opportunities in the Wire Services

Wire service writers, editors, and photographers are chosen and retained largely on their ability to respond to events quickly, to handle a range of responsibilities, and to understand news values—that is, what kinds of material are likely to be of interest to a wide variety of readers and listeners. Wire service work often resembles newspaper work, but there are differences—for example, a wire service never has a final edition. Wire service bureaus are frequently open twenty-four hours a day, and even relatively new employees may find themselves working alone, responding to tests of skill and judgment.

Occasionally the AP or UPI hires brand new college graduates; the norm, however, is to require one or more years of newspaper experience first. Wire services do employ college students as interns during the summer months and may hire part-time **stringers** as well. Eventual assignment to an overseas bureau is possible, though beginners seldom are picked to be foreign correspondents. Fluency in at least one foreign language is expected for overseas employees.

Wire services tend to promote from within, and they conduct individual employee training with that in mind. New reporters do a certain amount of editing as well as writing, and they cover stories in person as well as over the telephone. Promising new people soon receive additional responsibility—as night desk editors, for example—and might later earn a promotion to chief of a small bureau or perhaps a major reporting assignment in a large bureau. Capital bureau chiefs, Washington bureau chiefs, foreign correspondents, senior management—all come up through the ranks.

Wire service starting salaries are higher than starting wages for all but the largest newspapers. Beyond that, wire service training and experience are highly prized throughout the mass communications industry. Many of the top newspaper political reporters, television anchor people, and senior newsmagazine editors have spent a significant part of their careers with a wire service. And while they may resent the demands and harsh discipline of wire service reporting at the time, they tend to be grateful in later years for the opportunity to develop their journalistic talents in a fast-paced and often exciting environment.

summary

Almost every radio station, television station, and daily newspaper subscribes to one or more wire services, and thus even the smallest communities are alerted immediately to news breaks from the state, nation, and world. Pooled resources and shared costs have given local broadcasters and editors instant access to a wealth of news from wherever it occurs. What we know about world events is, to a large degree, what wire service people tell us.

The Associated Press, America's first wire service, came into being soon after the development of the telegraph. Soon United Press, a private company, vigorously competed with the AP cooperative. Foreign wire services also offer news and other features to clients around the globe.

Wire service reporters must be swift and concise writers, able to develop impartial accounts of fast-breaking news stories and update them continuously.

Though sometimes criticized for oversimplifying events and making occasional mistakes—often prompted by a competitive rush to be first—U.S. wire services have earned generally high marks for the speed and overall accuracy of their reports. Wire service journalists have won many awards for their enterprise and courage.

In recent years, supplementary wire services, such as those the New York *Times,* Knight-Ridder, Washington *Post*-Los Angeles *Times,* and other organizations have offered, have added a different dimension to the field, providing more interpretation and analysis to complex news events.

? questions and cases

1. Governor Roberta Winton, trailing badly in the polls in her campaign for reelection, today accused her popular opponent, V. Stephen Johnson, of planning a massive state tax increase if he takes office. "My opponent may deny it, but he is lying if he says he doesn't have his tax increase legislation package already prepared." Governor Winton, who looked desperate, talked to a small crowd at the Lincoln City square. Despite her current standing in the public opinion surveys, Governor Winton declared she would win "this dirtiest of all political campaigns" and that she intends to file a lawsuit for slander against Johnson before election day next week. The threatened lawsuit arises from a televised debate earlier in the week in which Johnson accused Governor Winton of mishandling state funds.

Extra Information

Stringers are paid by the word or the story rather than at a weekly or monthly rate. The print media often employ stringers.

Assuming you are a wire service reporter assigned to cover Governor Winton's campaign:

a. How would you begin your story on the governor's speech? How would you organize and develop the body of your story?

b. How would you handle your impressions that Governor Winton (1) probably is going to lose the election and (2) appeared desperate as she made her speech? Explain and defend your treatment of these impressions.

c. Suppose, as you traveled with the governor on her campaign bus, she told you and other reporters a joke with racist overtones. You are convinced she is a bigot as well as an inept governor and, in short, you simply don't like the woman. What are your professional responsibilities in this situation? How do you reconcile them with your personal feelings?

d. Would you write your story differently if you were a reporter for the New York *Times* or Washington *Post?* Explain.

2. Do you agree with the critics who contend that the wire services are too competitive? too crisis oriented? Does knowing the wire services are under pressure to be first with the news trouble you? Discuss.

3. How, in your opinion, could editors and broadcast news directors interest their audiences more in international news?

chapter glossary

add   Material to be added to a story already written. Adds are numbered as they are developed: "first add," "second add," or sometimes "add 1," "add 2," and so on.

budget, or **news budget**   In our context, a listing of anticipated stories to be covered and reported that day. The AP and UPI transmit their news budgets early in each cycle. UPI's budget is referred to as a *schedule,* or *sked.*

bulletin   The first news report transmitted about a new and important development. Bulletins, which may interrupt normal news traffic, are high-priority items. An even higher-priority item is the *flash,* usually ten words or less about a story of momentous import. The flash is seldom utilized.

correspondent   A news reporter stationed at some distance from the publication's headquarters. The term also can be applied to a part-time journalist who may not be on salary but is paid per article submitted.

cycle   Used by wire services to describe a regularly recurring series of reports. The A.M. cycle, designed for morning newspaper customers, begins in the early afternoon and runs until early the following day. Then the P.M. cycle begins.

deadline   The last moment that copy may be accepted in order to meet a particular edition (see newspaper chapter glossary).

inverted pyramid   News writing style in which the reporter provides the most important elements of the story at the beginning, then presents the remainder of the facts in descending order of importance. Opposite of the suspended-interest format, which begins with small details and builds to a climax at the end.

schedule, or **sked**   UPI's term for a budget.

spot news   News that breaks without warning, such as an airplane crash.

stringer   A part-time correspondent often paid on a piece-work scale; in this case, by the total length of the articles accepted for publication or wire service transmission each month.

synchronous satellite   A satellite moving above the earth at the same speed, relatively, as the earth's rotation, thus appearing to hover in space over one fixed point. Signals can be bounced off the satellite directly into receiving dishes.

take   A short section of copy that is not a complete story in itself. A breaking story may be moved by a wire service in takes—that is, reported in separate developments as they become known.

video display terminal (VDT)   For our purposes, the newsroom keyboard and monitor connected to a central computer. As reporters write articles, they enter them into the computer, where they can be called up later for editing and production purposes.

wrapup   A piece that weaves together the details of a breaking story as a wire service cycle ends.

notes

1   The May 1848 founding date comes from the Associated Press's own officially prepared history. Other scholarship, notably that of Richard A. Schwarzlose ("Early Telegraphic Dispatches: Forerunners of the AP," *Journalism Quarterly* 51:4, Winter 1974) contends that newspaper publishers in upstate New York had been exchanging news before this time, and that the New York City newspapers were sharing telegraph messages as early as 1846.

2   Oliver Grambling, *AP: The Story of News* (New York: Farrar and Rinehart, 1949), 73. An excellent biography of Melville Stone, by Michael Kirkhorn, appears in *American Newspaper Journalists, 1901–25* (Detroit: Gale Research, 1984), 268–80.

3   U.S. *v.* Associated Press, 52 F. Supp. 362, affirmed in 326 U.S. 1 (1944).

4   The fullest report on the cartel appears in Kent Cooper, *Barriers Down: The Story of the News Agency Epoch* (New York: Farrar and Rinehart, 1942).

5   Joe Alex Morris, *Deadline Every Minute: The Story of United Press* (Garden City, N.Y.: Doubleday, 1957), 2 ff.

6   Frank Luther Mott, *American Journalism,* 3d ed. (New York: Macmillan, 1961), 818. See also Edwin Emery and Michael Emery, *The Press and America,* 5th ed. (Englewood Cliffs, N.J.: Prentice-Hall, 1989), 516.

7   Alex S. Jones, "Mideast Broadcaster Gains Control of UPI," New York *Times,* 24 June 1992.

8   Ibid.

9   Associated Press news release, *ca.* 15 June 1984.

10   Grambling, *AP: The Story of News,* 39.

11   From Norman J. Radder and John E. Stempel, *Newspaper Editing, Make-up and Headlines* (New York: McGraw-Hill, 1942), 131.

12   All of the following are Associated Press dispatches, 30 August 1993.

13   Dr. Hans Tusch, Paris correspondent for the *Neue Zurcher Zeitung,* interview with the author.

14   Background materials supplied to the author by AFP, Reuters, AP-Dow Jones, United Press International, and the Los Angeles *Times*-Washington *Post* News Service.

15   M. L. Stein, "The New Moscow Media," *Editor & Publisher,* 11 July 1992. For a history of the Soviet wire service, written during a tense period of the Cold War, see Theodore Kruglak, *The Two Faces of TASS* (Minneapolis: University of Minnesota Press, 1962).

chapter D

'Evidently the newspaper is an institution that is not yet fully understood," decided sociologist,

Newspapers

R. E. Park. "What it is, or seems to be, for any one of us at any time, is determined by our differing points of view . . . One

Objectives

When you have finished studying this chapter, you should be able to:

- Describe economic and social changes that have affected the newspaper industry, and how newspapers have responded to them

- Discuss the factors contributing to the rise in chain ownership of daily newspapers

- Explain the workings of the five major departments found on most U.S. daily newspapers

- Analyze industry trends, specifically in such areas as technological innovation, competition for advertising dollars, and the emerging national press

"Evidently the newspaper is an institution that is not yet fully understood," decided sociologist, R. E. Park. "What it is, or seems to be, for any one of us at any time, is determined by our differing points of view. . . . One reason we know so little about the newspaper is that it is a very recent manifestation. Besides, in the course of its relatively brief history it has gone through a remarkable series of transfigurations."[1] Park wrote these words in 1925—before network radio, talking motion pictures, television, stereo, computers, satellites, VCRs, digital imaging, fiber optics, and fax machines. The "remarkable series of transfigurations" he referred to goes on and on. The newspaper adjusts, then adjusts some more, changing and yet somehow staying much the same. Newspapers serve the country as watchdog and people's champion, providing more information and commentary than all other mass communications media combined.

The newsroom at the New York *Daily News.*

Newspapers also remain the leader, though the gap is narrowing, in terms of total advertising volume. At its 1992 level of more than $30 billion, the newspaper industry ran ahead of television, its nearest rival, by $3 billion. Newspapers also represent one of the nation's largest employers, with a combined work force estimated by the Labor Department at 462,500. In most U.S. cities and towns, the local newspaper is a major manufacturing plant with one of the bigger payrolls in the community.

More than 113 million Americans, according to figures compiled by the American Newspaper Publishers Association, read newspapers every weekday. Some 1,586 daily newspapers are currently published in the United States. Their combined circulation is 60.6 million.[2] An average of 2.14 persons read every copy, and the typical consumer spends forty-five minutes a day reading one or more newspapers. Advertisers are aware that their newspaper audiences are demographically attractive: The higher one's education and income levels, the more time one is likely to spend reading the daily newspaper. Too, advertisers, especially in the local and regional markets, appreciate newspapers' ability to reach highly specific segments. In most metropolitan areas, they can even target individual neighborhoods or suburbs with **zoned editions.** Newspapers also are improving their appearance and their capacity to produce quality color work. They know their audiences and,

Teaching Idea

Invite people from the local or regional daily newspaper to speak to the class. A good selection would be a young reporter who is enthusiastic about his or her job. Others would be the managing editor, sports editor, and circulation manager.

Background

Ownership and circulation figures for all U.S. daily and weekly newspapers are in the *Editor & Publisher Yearbook.* This reference work should be consulted for the latest and most complete information on newspaper chains, supplemental wire services, and many other things which could supplement the text information.

The Glory of Transmitting the Fact

Though I've returned to other media, I don't doubt that I'd jump at the chance of a newspaper job again today. For sane, sober, and secure though this [newspaper] business has become, it has lost none of the glory that is its essence, the glory of transmitting the fact, of telling the truth so that the people will know it, and—one must confess-of being on the inside when news is made. I have to say this deprecatingly within earshot of colleagues who profess to be cynics, lest we be seen as men and women with a mission or dedication.

But none of the fun has gone out of newspapering, either. If anything, the company is better, the wit is more sophisticated, the joking less juvenile, the iconoclasm more judicious, and the occasional bender all the better for its occasion. And something has been added, a sense of service beyond one's self and a consciousness of craft: In short, professional pride.

Judith Crist, author, editor, critic, and former New York City newspaper reporter, from an article for a Columbia University forum on the twenty-fifth anniversary of The Newspaper Guild.

for the most part, command local prestige. Readers like the newspapers' cheapness and portability and the readers' control of when, where, and how rapidly they read their newspapers. An individual can scan columns, pages, even entire sections—or leaf through the paper at a leisurely pace, reading selected articles with great care and repeatedly referring back to an individual piece or advertisement or coupon. According to one recent poll, 84 percent of the U.S. public profess to have some or even great respect for newspapers.

But newspapers face problems, too. High production and distribution costs and lifestyle changes have forced some dailies out of business. Readership time is declining; Americans continue to buy papers but read them less. The credibility of newspaper articles has come under sharp attack. The press is widely perceived as arrogant, an allegation not exactly new. "In America the President reigns for four years," observed Oscar Wilde in 1891, "and Journalism governs for ever and ever."[3] Technological innovations, notably improvements in electronic transmission of news reports, pose a continuing challenge to the industry's capacity to endure. Thus the newspaper field's "remarkable series of transfigurations," as Park put it nearly three quarters of a century ago, seems to be just beginning.

Economic Revolution

"The American newspaper business," a publisher recently asserted, "was built on three conditions that no longer exist: cheap paper, cheap gas, and cheap people." That assessment is glib and facetious, but it contains some truth. Newsprint sold at $179 a metric ton in 1970; by 1992, the price had more than tripled to $685. The low-cost paper, 60 percent of it imported from Canadian mills, permitted U.S. newspapers, unlike their counterparts elsewhere in the world, to develop the tradition of fat daily newspapers filled with lots of features and financed by big-volume advertising sold at relatively low unit prices.

Between 1947 and 1960, U.S. newspaper press runs jumped from 1.5 to 2.5 billion pages a day, and the average number of pages grew from 29 to 43 per issue. (In Europe and Asia, papers are much thinner, commonly ranging from 8 to 24 pages per issue.) American newsprint consumption continues to increase at a rate slightly higher than the national economic growth index, but rising paper costs have been passed on to consumers. The great majority of dailies sold for 10 cents a copy in 1970; by 1992, all but a handful of publishers had raised single copy price to at least 25 cents, and the national average was about 35 cents. These increases, accompanied by comparable rises in home delivery prices, have met with a certain amount of consumer resistance. During the 1970s and 1980s, newspaper circulation increased, but at a pace far below the growth rate of the adult population. Then, in 1991, daily newspaper circulation actually dropped—to 60.6 million, down from 62.3 million in 1990. (Table 1 lists the top twenty circulation leaders for 1992.)

Cheap transportation costs for most of the century encouraged newspapers to create elaborate home delivery networks, even in distant communities. Some newspapers, such as the Des Moines *Register* and the Louisville *Courier-Journal*, prided themselves on making copies of their papers available each day in virtually every community in their respective states. Such service brought the papers justifiable prestige and enhanced their political leadership. When gasoline prices rose sharply in the 1970s, however, the far-flung delivery systems became too expensive to maintain. Metropolitan retail advertisers, the papers' prime source of revenue, paid ad rates based on total circulation, and they could not realistically regard subscribers in remote shopping areas as potential customers. For these and other reasons, newspaper publishers began to retrench, concentrating on audiences in the more immediate, and more commercially promising, metropolitan area.

Newspaper staffs in all departments have tended to be large, and salaries historically have been low. Relative efficiency has improved somewhat in recent years,

Extra Information
Ask your students to find out how much your local or regional daily pays for newsprint, and any recent fluctuations in the price. If possible, find a picture of a roll of newsprint that indicates its actual size.

Teaching Idea
If your local or regional daily prints zoned or suburban editions, ask your students to bring one to class and compare it with a regular edition.

table 1   The Top 20 U.S. Newspaper Circulation Leaders*

Daily Newspapers	Average Circulation	Sunday Newspapers	Average Circulation
1. *Wall Street Journal*	1,795,206	1. New York *Times*	1,741,989
2. *USA Today*	1,506,708	2. Los Angeles *Times*	1,515,220
3. Los Angeles *Times*	1,146,631	3. Detroit *News & Free Press*	1,189,937
4. New York *Times*	1,145,890	4. Washington *Post*	1,141,089
5. Washington *Post*	802,057	5. Chicago *Tribune*	1,109,622
6. New York *Daily News*	777,129	6. New York *News*	969,341
7. *Newsday*	758,358	7. Philadelphia *Inquirer*	964,475
8. Chicago *Tribune*	724,257	8. *Newsday*	844,618
9. Detroit *Free Press*	580,372	9. Boston *Globe*	812,021
10. San Francisco *Chronicle*	556,765	10. Dallas *Morning News*	809,188
11. Chicago *Sun-Times*	528,324	11. Newark *Star-Ledger*	720,174
12. Boston *Globe*	508,867	12. San Francisco *Examiner & Chronicle*	707,881
13. Philadelphia *Inquirer*	502,149	13. Atlanta *Journal & Constitution*	689,258
14. Newark *Star-Ledger*	481,027	14. Minneapolis/St. Paul *Star-Tribune*	687,027
15. Dallas *Morning News*	479,215	15. Houston *Chronicle*	607,502
16. New York *Post*	437,918	16. St. Louis *Post-Dispatch*	559,142
17. Houston *Chronicle*	419,725	17. Cleveland *Plain Dealer*	545,849
18. Minneapolis/St. Paul *Star-Tribune*	410,920	18. Phoenix *Arizona Republic*	533,890
19. Cleveland *Plain Dealer*	410,237	19. Chicago *Sun-Times*	531,226
20. Detroit *News*	398,630	20. Seattle *Times/Post-Intelligencer*	517,742

Source: Used with permission of Audit Bureau of Circulations.

*For period ending 30 September 1992.

especially in production departments. Typesetting is simpler and faster; fewer skilled people are required to ready the paper for the press. One authoritative study reports that papers have about half as many production employees now as they did before they adopted the new technologies. Further declines are expected as **pagination** systems and other technological innovations become more commonplace. No one has yet found a way to fully automate the news departments, however. The journalistic strength—and, to a certain extent, the economic vulnerability—of the newspaper lies in the depth of its reporting and editing staff, the men and women who regularly frequent state capitols, city halls, federal buildings, courthouses, police stations. No other medium commits so many people to covering the news. In 1992, base salaries for reporters with one to four years' experience on daily newspapers averaged $30,816, a figure that actually was lower than the previous year, presumably because more junior staff members were entering the field.[4] Entry-level salaries on daily newspapers tend to be higher than those on weekly newspapers, radio, and television stations, and slightly lower than those paid by advertising and public relations agencies.

Beyond the entry level, daily newspaper pay in recent years has increased markedly, especially on larger papers. Many of the gains can be attributed to the negotiating efforts of the **Newspaper Guild,** which represents some 33,000 journalists

Extra Information

Ask your local or regional daily what it pays a beginning reporter. Is prior experience required?

Flanked by word-processor terminals, a Detroit *Free Press* editor reads a hard-copy printout of a feature story.

Background

Most newspapers, particularly large metropolitan dailies, print several editions at different times for different audiences. For example, the first edition of a morning paper, printed before midnight, would be sent to outlying regions by truck. Later editions, with more late-breaking and local news, would be placed on local rack sales and sent out for home delivery.

Example

Assign students to obtain copies of morning and afternoon daily newspapers. Compare the way the front pages are laid out as well as the overall contents. Which is the most visually attractive? Why? Are there other differences between the two?

and other newspaper staff members, mostly employed in metropolitan areas. While many well-paying newspapers are not covered by Guild contracts, the Guild's leadership has been influential in raising compensation levels throughout the industry.

Salaries paid to the reporting and editing staff may account for only 20 percent or less of the total newspaper budget. Many publishers feel pressure to raise salaries, because attracting and retaining good people is essential to the newspaper's continued survival. But salary increases—like increases in newsprint, gasoline, and all other administrative, production, and distribution costs—have made newspapers more expensive, and thus for many an expendable luxury.

As newspapers have become more costly, many Americans have cancelled their newspaper subscriptions, choosing instead to buy one or more single copies a week, on grocery shopping days, for example. In any event, newspapers are massively affected by social and economic trends, and a given newspaper's rise or fall in daily circulation may depend on factors entirely unrelated to editorial excellence.

These considerations and others, including the emergence of television as a ferocious competitor for reading time and advertising dollars, have led to major changes in newspaper production cycles and ownership patterns.

Evening Circulation Declines

In 1965, U.S. newspaper weekday circulation totaled just over 60 million, 24 million morning papers and 36 million papers delivered in the afternoon. By 1992, the total circulation was still about 60 million, but the morning/evening ratios were almost precisely reversed. Several prominent afternoon papers had converted to morning or all-day publication, and a number of other P.M.s folded outright. The afternoon dailies in large cities were hardest hit. More than a few metro P.M.s ceased publication, while publishers in other cities merged their morning and evening papers, strategic moves that caused the afternoon papers, for the most part, to simply disappear.

Morning newspapers, with their longer production and distribution cycles, historically have enjoyed greater prestige. Afternoon papers, many of which rely to a great extent on street sales, are inclined to be splashier. This is true in other countries as well. In a remarkable story which broke late in 1986, Britain's royal physician in 1936 revealed, half a century later, that he had actually "timed" the death of King George V so that the news would break in the morning press. The moribund king was injected with fatal doses of cocaine and morphine to assure him a painless death which could be announced "in the morning papers rather than the less appropriate evening journals."[5] Numerically, however, afternoon papers dominate the field; there are about twice as many P.M.s as A.M.s published in the United States. But morning papers are gaining circulation, in the aggregate, while afternoon sales slide. A number of factors have contributed to the decline:

1 Delivery problems. For an afternoon paper to be read, it must arrive at home well before families turn on their television sets for the evening. Traffic congestion forces delivery truck drivers to leave earlier to reach their dropoff points by mid-afternoon. This forces earlier deadlines, which in turn usually means less spot news in the paper. The copy deadline for some editions may be 10 A.M. or even earlier, while the offices for government officials might not open until 9 A.M. This leaves the P.M. reporter precious little time to develop breaking stories.

2 Changes in living and working patterns. Much of the U.S. economy is transforming itself from a manufacturing to a service orientation. For newspaper publishers, the change is profoundly important. People holding down office jobs tend to start and end their working days later than employees engaged in manufacturing. An executive whose work day begins at 9 A.M. probably will prefer to read the paper at breakfast; there may not be time when he or she comes home from the office at 6:30 P.M. By contrast, in cities where the manufacturing economy remains robust, the afternoon paper has a better chance. Plant workers who begin their shifts before 7 A.M. and are off by 3 P.M., for example, will likely favor afternoon papers. This is the situation in Detroit and Seattle, among other heavily industrialized cities.

3 Changing patterns in the availability of news. In many cities, mayors and other leaders have begun to schedule their press conferences and policy announcements for late afternoon, a shrewd ploy to grab prime exposure on local television evening newscasts. The afternoon paper is already off the presses by this time, and thus is left in the unenviable position of having to present its readers with warmed-over reports nearly a full day later. In addition to its other problems, the P.M. paper can get caught in a news-flow squeeze as well.

Group Ownership

Of all the changes in American journalism, perhaps the most startling has been the ascendancy, and now the sheer dominance, of newspaper chains. In 1960, the total circulation of U.S. dailies represented by chain-owned newspapers was 46 percent; by the mid-1990s, it was more than 75 percent. Several factors have contributed toward making the family-owned newspaper largely a thing of the past.

Economics of Scale

Chains can provide top-of-the-line expertise, especially in production, purchasing, accounting, sales, and administrative areas. In the newspaper field, as with grocery markets and drug stores, chain ownership tends to be more efficient. A local publisher with the resources of an entire chain behind him or her is in a stronger competitive position. Publishers can utilize profits from prosperous member papers to nurture weaker papers along. Collective profits quickly become a substantial pool of capital, providing ready cash leverage as well as loan collateral for additional investments.

Tax Laws

Profits from a newspaper chain can be paid out to stockholders as dividends, which are taxable, or plowed into the purchase of still more newspaper properties. The latter spares the stockholders from some income tax payments and earns them even more money because they now own part of a still larger company and because their stock has increased in value. Inheritance taxes are another important factor. When the owner of a family newspaper dies, the survivors may be forced to sell the paper to pay the inheritance duties on the property. A number of families have sold their papers before the publisher's death, placing the proceeds of the sale in a trust or other vehicle to minimize inheritance taxes. This trend intensified late in 1986 following passage of a tax reform bill which reduced capital gains tax benefits.

Fortified by tremendous sums of investment capital, chain ownerships can offer purchase prices that independent publishers often find irresistible. With these vast capital resources, the larger newspaper chains can afford to take the long view, paying far more than a paper might be worth but taking comfort in the knowledge that the eventual return on the investment will be substantial. The Gannett Company has emerged as the acquisitions leader. By 1986, when the fiercely competitive Allen H. Neuharth stepped down as president, Gannett controlled 81 daily newspapers

....
Extra Information
Direct students to examine the masthead of your local or regional daily newspaper to see whether it is part of a chain.

with a combined circulation of well over 6 million. Knight-Ridder Newspapers owned fewer newspapers (28), but their total circulation exceeded 5 million. Newhouse Newspapers owned 26 newspapers with a combined daily circulation of 3.8 million, and the Times Mirror Company's 9 dailies had a combined circulation of 3.5 million. Dow Jones, the Chicago Tribune Company, Cox Enterprises, Hearst, McClatchy Newspapers, Freedom Newspapers, Copley, and others were among the nation's largest chains—growing, prospering, still buying—and paying enormous sums. The New York *Times* bought the Boston *Globe* in June 1993 for $1.1 billion—the highest ever paid for a U.S. newspaper.

Social critics have long since expressed fears about chain ownership. "The press in Europe is gone the way the newspapers are going in the United States," wrote Lincoln Steffens in 1931, "into the hands of men who buy and run newspapers, not to protest evils, but to get in on them."[6] Early twentieth-century press lords, such as William Randolph Hearst, who brazenly used his papers to promote his own political causes in news as well as editorial columns, provided genuine cause for concern.

Even worse, in the view of some, is the reduction of a proud and honorable craft to little more than a series of entries on a corporate balance sheet. According to Jim Ottaway, Jr., chairman of the highly regarded Ottaway Newspapers, aggressive expansionism and a relentless pursuit of larger profits threatens newspaper quality. "The invasion of investment bankers into the buying and selling of American newspapers has led to too much talk about 'realizing asset values' or 'building asset values.' We ought to be publishing newspapers—not running banks," he declared in an angry speech to a group of journalists and journalism educators. He particularly assailed Thomson Newspapers and the Donrey Media Group for publishing what he called "some of the highest profit-margin, lowest quality newspapers in America today."[7]

Other contemporary chain managements receive higher marks for corporate responsibility. Knight-Ridder, in particular, has a reputation for improving most of the properties it acquires. Knight-Ridder newspapers, notably the Philadelphia *Inquirer* and the Miami *Herald,* regularly win Pulitzer prizes and other distinguished awards. The Freedom Forum, a foundation funded chiefly by the Gannett chain, has donated tens of millions of dollars to journalism education, scholarships, building and equipment improvements, and important research projects and has moved decisively to promote minorities and women into key leadership positions. The better chains have bolstered news coverage by pooling their resources to establish bureaus in Washington and overseas. They have also installed the latest technical and production equipment, rendering their papers more handsome as well as more efficient. Employee training programs on chain-owned newspapers are much improved.

On the other hand, some chains seem interested exclusively in fat, short-term profits. To attain them, their executives specialize in cutting costs, assigning a low priority to news coverage and editorial leadership. But the worst fears about chain ownership, that a handful of powerful press barons would use their papers as means to political ends, seem to be unfounded. Most modern newspaper chain executives tend to maintain a low profile, at least politically, and to hold local autonomy in high regard where editorial policies are concerned.

Diminished Competition

In the early years of the century, nearly every city of any size had two or more competing newspapers. But by 1994, only a handful of cities could boast more than one newspaper, and several of those were communities where the newspapers were published under a court-approved Joint Operating Agreement. JOAs allow separately owned newspapers in economic distress to merge their production facilities; printing, advertising, and circulation forces; and accounting departments—everything but their editorial staffs—to reduce duplication and save on operating expenses.

Background

The federal law allowing JOAs has been called both the Newspaper Preservation Act and the Failing Newspaper Act.

The JOA is a legalized exemption from antitrust laws designed to preserve some semblance of editorial diversity in communities where that commodity is about to disappear. An outgrowth of the Great Depression, a joint operating agreement provides some protection for newspapers in financial difficulty on the theory that the public is better served when more than one editorial voice exists in the community. It is an arrangement many press critics find disturbing; after all, they argue, newspapers are businesses and should not receive preferential government treatment. Criticism of Joint Operating Agreements exist even within the industry, on the grounds that a combined operation will become so prosperous and powerful it will preclude the possibility of any future competition.

Other media voices are available, as publishers are quick to point out. Massive population shifts have resulted in a hefty increase in suburban newspapers, many of which are both editorial and commercial successes. And audiences have access to plenty of radio and television choices. The fact remains, however, that in all but a tiny few U.S. cities, little or no direct, head-to-head daily newspaper competition has survived.

Newspaper Organizational Structure

While no two newspapers, even under group ownership, are precisely alike, most dailies organize their staffs along the following lines.

General management, headed by the publisher, coordinates the other departments; determines business—and often editorial—policies; and, in the main, keeps the paper at least solvent if not prosperous. Other business executives—personnel, accounting, payroll, promotion—may also be part of the general management team.

News-editorial is responsible for all the nonadvertising matter that appears in the paper. The editor is in charge of all content except advertising. The managing editor normally directs the news operation. Working for the managing editor are the **beat** and assignment reporters, photographers, copy editors, and news clerks as well as various subdepartments such as wire news, sports, women's news, business news, entertainment, the features desk, and so on. On a newspaper of any size, an intervening layer of supervision lies between the managing editor and the reporters—city or metropolitan editor, news editor, sports editor, special sections editor, features editor, Sunday editor. The editorial writers may have their own supervisor, often called the associate editor or the executive editor, who reports directly to the publisher.

The advertising department handles the sale of space in the paper to individuals and other business organizations. The advertising manager presides over the retail and national sales force, the classified advertising staff, and possibly a number of support personnel such as market researchers, artists, and sales promotion people.

The production department converts the advertising and editorial matter into type and prints the newspapers. Subexecutives in this area include the chief of the **composing room,** where the type is set; the pressroom supervisor, and the supervisor of the mailroom, where the papers are bundled for delivery.

Circulation people distribute the paper. At one time, the circulation manager's job was purely logistical; he or she ensured that copies reached subscribers and newsboxes on time. In recent years, however, the circulation manager has become a marketing manager as well, relied upon for pricing and promotion strategies in addition to maintaining a reliable delivery network. Reporting to the circulation manager are various district managers, who supervise carriers as well as motor route contractors.[8]

In many newspaper offices, these functional distinctions blur. On a small daily, for example, the publisher may also serve as editor or advertising manager, while editorial employees may handle some of the composing room duties. Recent advances in computer technology have led some publishers to adopt total pagination

Background

On most daily newspapers, the amount of advertising sold on a given day determines the number of pages in that day's edition. (If you invite an advertising person from the local paper to visit the class, he or she can explain how this is done.)

Class Activity

Ask students to bring in Monday and Thursday editions of your local or regional daily (Wednesday instead of Thursday if grocery ads are run then). How many pages are in each addition? What percentage of each day's paper is given to advertising (excluding classified ads)?

Example

Ask your students whether any of them are now carrying or have ever carried a daily newspaper delivery route. How did they feel about the hours and the pay? Did the newspaper treat them as actual employees, or independent businesspeople?

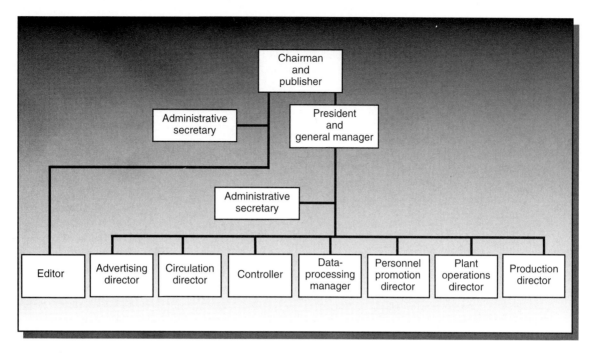

How one newspaper is organized.

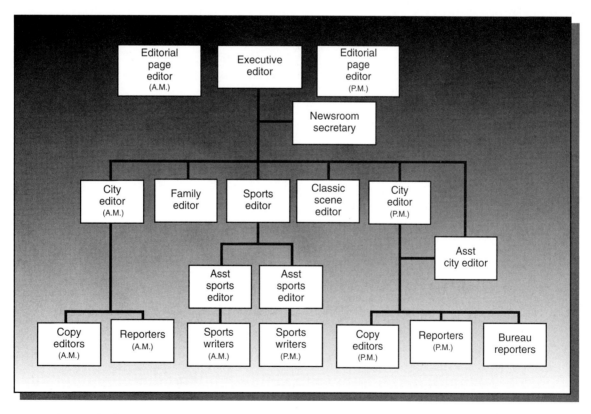

How one newsroom is organized.
This chart is for a company that
produces a morning (A.M.) as well as
an evening (P.M.) newspaper. A few
editors serve both papers.

systems, which allow composers to set text and graphics at newsroom terminals and then transfer the material directly to plates ready for the press. The composing room, under such systems, can be bypassed altogether. This trend will accelerate as competitive pricing makes pagination technology more widely affordable.

The Sunday Papers

Unremittingly determined to wring the last ounce of circulation out of a sensational murder trial, the New York *Transcript* jettisoned its regular publication schedule on 8 June 1836 to issue an extraordinary Sunday edition. The paper ran 24 columns, 15 recounting in steamy detail the trial testimony given earlier in the week, the other 9 prudently devoted to advertising. With this sellout edition, the *Transcript,* and soon its rivals in the penny press era, demonstrated that the market for news exists seven days a week. As the Sunday paper concept took hold, the content came to reflect less hard news and more features and family reading material—and much more advertising.

Joseph Pulitzer and his innovative editors on the New York *World* provided the first color photographs printed on high-speed presses, experiments which led also to the first color comic sections. Circulation for the Sunday *World* topped 600,000 in 1897. The New York *Times* recorded another advance in 1914 by introducing a rotogravure section in its Sunday paper. (The "roto" process, imported from Germany, involves printing from a depressed surface, such as a copper or steel plate, in which the impression is produced by chemically etched cylinders affixed to rollers of a rotary press. The technique produced high-quality photographic reproductions in great quantity.) By 1925, rotogravure sections were appearing in at least seventy-two Sunday newspapers.[9]

Modern Sunday papers are huge and profitable and in larger markets are dramatically increasing in circulation. In 1992, 875 Sunday papers were being published with a combined weekly circulation of 62 million. Sunday papers offer broad audience appeal through massive doses of news, sports, commentary, entertainment, travel, food, culture, and other service features. Often there is room in the Sunday paper for a detailed investigative report or thoughtful news feature—longer pieces that would not fit into the tighter weekday editions. Sunday papers exceeding three hundred pages are not uncommon.

Because they do consume great quantities of newsprint and often require a separate editor and additional staff, Sunday papers are expensive to produce. But in most cases advertisers support the effort by committing a substantial portion of their total ad budgets to the Sunday press.

The Press and the Public

"Newspapers are the schoolmasters of the common people," proclaimed the great nineteenth-century cleric, Henry Ward Beecher, "a greater treasure to them than uncounted millions of gold."[10] As the United States races toward the twenty-first century, however, the newspapers' social net worth, on the surface at least, seems to be depreciating. These ominous signs have arisen:

- A total of 2,580 daily newspapers were being published in 1914; by 1961 there were 1,761, and by 1992 just 1,586.
- Daily newspaper circulation in 1970 totaled 62.1 million with the total population estimated at 203.8 million. In 1992, U.S. population had increased by about 20 percent, while daily newspaper circulation was down by 4 percent.
- A national Nielsen organization survey taken in 1991 indicated that 69 percent of the U.S. public turn to television, not newspapers, as the source of most of their news, while other studies indicated that the public ranks television as the most believable of all news sources.

Teaching Idea

Assign students to bring in Sunday editions of several different newspapers. What are the similarities and differences in content? What kinds of feature articles and news analysis does each include?

Newspapers and the Human Condition

There are too damn many lonely people in the world who just can't handle it, who are afraid of other people, who don't understand what is going on, who fear change. It doesn't help them to get a newspaper plopped on their front stoops every day that reduces the whole rich, human, comic, tragic, absurd, exasperating, and exciting parade of one day's events into a dehydrated lifeless set of unrelated facts. We keep writing about events as though they were pictures on a wall, something we could stand off and look at, when in fact they are the stuff of our lives. The news gets sanitized, homogenized, pasteurized, dehumanized, and wrapped in cellophane. No wonder people forget they're human.

Molly Ivins, from *Molly Ivins Can't Say That, Can She?* (New York: Random House, 1992).

Discussion

Discuss each of the six criticisms noted in the text, using your local or regional daily as the basis for discussion. Ask the class for examples that demonstrate each criticism.

The economic statistics could be explained: Weaker papers were merging into stronger ones, resulting in a daily newspaper field that was leaner, more efficient, and in robust financial health. Newspaper profit margins were excellent. When newspaper properties changed hands, sales prices reflected enormous optimism. The believability/credibility rating, however, hit the newspaper industry hard. In an effort to develop a deeper understanding of public attitudes toward the press, the Times Mirror Company of Los Angeles commissioned the Gallup Organization during the early 1990s to perform a series of national surveys, arguably among the most comprehensive and thoughtful research ever done on the subject.

The survey respondents graded press performance harshly in six areas:

1 Political bias reflected in the news columns

2 Reporting that seemed to favor one side in a controversy over another

3 Attempts to cover up mistakes rather than admit and correct them

4 Influence from powerful outside pressure groups

5 Too much attention to bad news

6 Invasions of personal privacy

"The public expresses few doubts about [newspaper] accuracy," the report noted, "but it harbors serious reservations about other press practices such as fairness and objectivity."[11]

On the other hand, respondents expressed widespread support for the press in a number of areas, notably for care in handling facts and for patriotism. "On these fundamental qualities," the report said, "the public sees newspeople as decent citizens and news organizations as trying to do a responsible job."[12]

The general public, the report asserted, isn't very well informed about newspapers and what they do:

- Knowledge about the press is meager—even basic terminology is misunderstood. Fifty-nine percent of the respondents did not know that an editorial is an opinion piece which represents the viewpoint of the paper on a given issue. Only three Americans in ten are aware that the First Amendment is the part of the Constitution that mentions freedom of the press. Seventy-three percent do not know that the libel laws are different for public and private persons.

- The press does not attract as much public attention as it believes it does. Large elements of the population are indifferent to it and to issues that concern it.

- But the public values the ideas that governments should stay out of the newsroom and that the press should play an important watchdog role.[13]

Individuals who responded with supportive views of the press were twice as numerous as the critics. "To the degree that the press has a credibility problem," the report said, "it is because its critics are more vocal, intense, and involved with press issues than its supporters. Given who the critics are, there is no reason for complacency. We do not see a crisis. We do see an issue that needs continuing attention."[14]

In conclusion, the report stated, "Americans like the press and its practitioners. They like the product and its consequences. But most Americans do see a dark side to their free and commercial press. That may sound like the ultimate enigma in news media opinion. But in the last analysis, it's ultimately the American point of view."[15]

Industry Trends

"As a mental discipline, the reading of newspapers is hurtful," complained the Reverend T. T. Munger nearly a century ago. "What can be worse for the mind than to think of forty things in ten minutes?"[16] Publishing a newspaper has never been easy, but it has become increasingly difficult in the age of television. If there is, as the communications researchers contend, a Principle of the Least Effort, then Americans would seem to prefer someone to read the news to them rather than to read it for themselves. In spite of the difficulties, the newspaper industry remains vigorous and aggressive, confident in its leadership role, its commercial viability, and its capacity to adjust to whatever new challenges may lurk ahead.

Increased Competition

In the face of an aggressive and successful push by television and other media, newspaper advertising volume continues to increase. For example, newspaper classified ads (so-called because they are arranged by certain types of goods and services—help wanted, used cars for sale, positions wanted, and so on) were up 25 percent in 1984 alone. But shopping guides, **marriage mail** (which combines circulars and other notices from a variety of advertisers into one postal packet), direct response advertising, and a whole array of both old and new electronic media competitors assure newspapers that warfare for advertising income in the years ahead will be, if anything, intensified (see table 2).

Example

Bring the classified ad section of your local or regional daily to class and demonstrate how many and what kinds of ads it carries. Does it contain any unusual ads?

Stop the Presses? Not Just Yet

Alvin Toffler, futurologist and author of a best-selling book, *The Third Wave,* argues that the newspaper business is "the last of the smokestack industries"—decrepit, dated, destined to die. He is not alone. Analysts less excitable than Mr. Toffler have long predicted that newspapers would some day face an onslaught of newer media, from satellite and faxes to computers and cable TV. In this flashy future, the boring old broadsheet would look as anachronistic as a town crier on CNN.

. . . But gloom is not necessarily a twin of doom . . . Ad agency space buyers reckon that most TV channels likely to arrive in the years ahead will be financed by subscription fees.

If so, there is good reason to think that newspapers will soon dig in and hold their ground with advertisers. Because most papers are local, they are indispensible to many firms that have no need (and anyway cannot afford) to reach a national audience. As advertisers try to define their customers more precisely, they will turn increasingly to regional papers . . . to help them do so. That is good news for newspaper groups.

The Economist (London), 31 October 1992.

table 2 — Media Advertising Expenditures

Medium	Millions of Dollars
Newspapers	$32,281
National	4,122
Local	28,158
Television	28,405
Direct mail	23,370
Radio	8,726
Magazines	6,803
Yellow Pages	8,926
Outdoor	1,084
Miscellaneous*	<u>19,045</u>
Total	$128,640

Source: American Newspaper Publishers Association, 1990.

*Includes weeklies, shoppers, pennysavers, bus and cinema advertising, farm publications, and trade journals

Traditionally, newspapers have been strongest in attracting local advertising revenue and less successful in obtaining national ads. One reason for this was the bewildering variety of column widths, formats, and page depths in newspapers around the country. A national advertiser would have to produce one size ad to run in newspaper X, a slightly wider or deeper ad for newspaper Y, and so on. Rather than deal with so many production problems, some advertisers simply commit their national budgets to broadcast media, where a thirty-second spot in New York is obviously the same as a thirty-second spot anyplace else. In an effort to improve this situation, representatives of the newspaper industry in 1984 adopted a **Standard Advertising Unit (SAU)** system, a combination of uniform advertising sizes and dimensions, to make it easier for advertisers to plan and order newspaper advertising space. The SAU concept was not an immediate success—some publishers refused to go along with it, others found technical problems mitigated against changing page dimensions on their presses—but the size conformity has simplified print advertising placement and encouraged more national advertising in newspapers.

Another weak selling point for newspapers has been poor color reproduction. Convinced of the power of color sales messages, advertising executives are applying increased pressure on publishers to improve their color printing capabilities. Better qualities of newsprint are readily available now, and more publishers are upgrading their printing stock. In addition, highly skilled production chiefs and graphic design experts have joined many newspaper staffs. As advertisers are fond of saying, the buying public sees all of life in color save one thing—the daily newspaper. The newspaper of the future will print far more color, and print it better, than today's paper typically does.

More A.M. Papers

In recent years, literally hundreds of daily newspapers have converted from evening to morning publication, a truly remarkable development in an industry so characterized by tradition. A number of papers that publish on weekday afternoons are also providing their readers with Saturday morning coverage, either by starting new

Example

Ask students to bring copies of some daily papers that use color illustrations. Are they all attractive, or do you see significant quality differences? (Color pictures in most newspapers are made by separating the three primary colors of a photograph and making three printing plates. The plates are put on three separate presses, each with a different color ink. If the presses are synchronized—or registered—correctly, the result will be a true color reproduction. If not, one or more of the colors will seem smeared.)

newspapers or by converting Saturday afternoon editions to the A.M. cycle. Some previously P.M. papers have launched additional morning editions, in effect converting to an "all day" publication schedule. Of the country's twenty largest newspapers in terms of daily circulation in 1993, seventeen were morning dailies, two more were all-day papers, and only one, the Detroit *News,* had a P.M. publishing schedule. Given the dramatic growth in morning newspaper circulation around the country, the trend toward A.M. publication seems certain to increase.

A Softer News Package

"Soft news" is the term describing human-interest stories, interpretative pieces, and other articles, while "hard news" is the term for reporting solid facts of immediate import. Because so many persons receive their hard-news bulletins from the electronic media, newspapers are turning more and more to interpretation and features. In other words, much newspaper content is not, strictly speaking, news. Given the warm welcome readers gave to *USA Today* and the influence it has on other papers, the soft news trend is likely to continue.

An Emerging National Press

In most countries, a very few large papers circulate across, and provide powerful editorial leadership for, an entire nation. The U.S. press developed differently. We have many newspapers, most focusing tightly on their home towns and immediate surroundings. A few rose to exert considerable regional influence: the Chicago *Tribune* in the upper Midwest; the Denver *Post* in the Rocky Mountains, the Memphis *Commercial Appeal* in the mid-South. But no truly national newspaper dominates in the United States, at least not one operating at the influence level of a London *Times* in Great Britain, an *Asahi Shimbun* in Japan, or a Toronto *Globe and Mail* in Canada. In recent years, two major factors have combined in ways that could change that pattern:

- *Technology.* Satellite transmissions to subsidiary plants around the country make it possible for high-speed production and same-day distribution service.
- *Sophistication.* Owing in part to travel, films, and television, much of the reading audience has become cosmopolitan in outlook, interested in more worldly treatments of news and features.

The *Wall Street Journal,* appealing to vastly expanded business and financial interests, spearheaded the national newspaper concept. Now published in nearly two dozen plants, the *Journal* in 1992 boasted a circulation of 1,853,000, second largest of any daily newspaper in the country. The New York *Times* national edition, a scaled-down version of the city editions printed in several regional plants, is now available in most U.S. cities. Long regarded as one of the most thoughtful and reliable newspapers ever published, the *Christian Science Monitor* has for many years reached a smaller, but still countrywide, audience. The Washington *Post* in the 1980s developed a weekly edition for a national constituency.

By far the most ambitious entry in this select field, however, has been *USA Today,* which the Gannett Company launched in 1982. Spright editing and some of the most effective graphics and high-quality color ever to roll off newspaper presses quickly made *USA Today* a rousing popular success. Well over 100,000 bright blue *USA Today* newsboxes sprang up on street corners and in airport corridors all over the country. Within months, the publication had passed half a million in daily circulation, and by the end of 1992 it had eclipsed all daily newspapers in the United States in total circulation, averaging more than 1.9 million copies per issue.

USA Today articles are trendy and brief, to the dismay of some critics who dismiss the publication as superficial. The paper has been compared to junk food—fast

A heightened interest in visual communications—photographs, illustrations, graphics, design—has made newspapers more attractive. Infographics specialists now are regarded as essential on many newspaper staffs.

and convenient and even tasty, but of doubtful nutritional value; indeed, some editors of other publications refer to *USA Today* as a *McPaper*. But if *USA Today* is like television in print, it has also shown that newspapers can be interesting as well as informative. With its tightly written news summaries from around the country, beautifully produced weather maps and charts, and slam-bang sports coverage, *USA Today* has already exerted a powerful influence on other U.S. dailies. "They call us McPaper," noted *USA Today* Senior Editor Taylor Buckley, "but they're stealing our McNuggets."[17]

USA Today's features reflect a service philosophy; like articles in some popular magazines, they provide useful information readers feel they need to cope with a given situation. In tone and content, the paper is consistently upbeat. Allen H. Neuharth, Gannett's driving force during its most dynamic years, professed little use for what he called "the journalism of despair."[18]

USA Today is edited for mobile, cosmopolitan readers, an audience Neuharth was convinced existed in sufficient numbers to make a national newspaper viable. Despite *USA Today's* glittering debut and its undoubted popularity with readers across the country, the publication was not an early commercial success. Unlike the *Wall Street Journal,* which could offer advertisers regional as well as national coverage, *USA Today* was designed initially to carry only national advertising, and national advertisers were reluctant to allocate massive expenditures to this spectacular but experimental new daily. Industry estimates place *USA Today's* initial losses as substantial, perhaps $250 million or more during its first year of operation alone. But Gannett has deep pockets and was determined to give *USA Today* the time and resources it needed to establish itself. In 1992, as the paper happily observed its tenth anniversary, it had become a leader, along with other important national dailies—the *Wall Street Journal,* the New York *Times,* the *Christian Science Monitor,* and other publications existing or on the drawing boards—in a field that seemed destined to give the United States a formidable, lively, and varied national daily press.

Further Technological Evolution

In its twenty-fifth anniversary issue, the *Columbia Journalism Review* noted that twenty-three video display terminals (VDTs) graced U.S. newsrooms in 1970—compared to an estimated 60,000 in 1986. In the early 1990s, virtually all U.S. daily newspapers adopted, at least to some extent, the concept of the electronic newsroom. Articles are now written, edited, and set in type via computer-assisted composition equipment. Pagination systems permit newspaper editors to arrange entire newspaper pages electronically on videoscreens, ready for transmission to the press, and thus streamline the production process still further.

Other changes will follow on their heels. More and more newspaper plants will be equipped with digital imaging camera systems, allowing photographers and picture editors to process pictures electronically, bypass chemicals and darkrooms altogether, and transmit edited, ready-to-print photos directly to the pressroom. Reporters armed with portable computers and cellular telephones will transmit more and more stories directly from the scene to the newsroom. Satellite receiving

Discussion

What will newspapers be like in five years? Will video news replace the printed page?

And Now, the Latest from Mercury Center

In May, 1993, the San Jose *Mercury News* opened up what it called "Mercury Center," an online electronic extension of the paper for readers who own personal computers with modems.

The service, which was offered initially for a base price of $9.95 per month, offered such features as:

- Additional stories, texts, and documents that relate to articles printed in the newspaper, for readers who want more background information on a given article.

- Collections of useful articles published in the past, ranging from business coverage to Dave Barry columns.

- Virtually the full text of each morning's newspaper, including classified ads, with news updates by the afternoon newspaper staff.

- Bulletin boards that offer readers an opportunity to tell editors, reporters, and managers at the *Mercury News* what they think

about coverage or what about the newspaper they'd like to see changed. There are also message boards for readers to exchange views with other readers on any topic.

- Electronic mail, which lets readers send notes, letters, and computer files instantly to any subscriber to Mercury Center.

- "Chat" rooms where members can sign on for live discussions of topical subjects—or subjects of their own choosing.

- A "personal researcher" which allows readers to find in the newspaper's library any article published in the *Mercury News* since June 1985. (There is an additional charge for this service.)

- Many other services, at no extra charge, from Mercury Center's partner, America Online, Inc.: stock quotations, wine database, airline reservation service, encyclopedia, and thousands of downloadable freeware and software PC programs.

Promotional material provided by the San Jose *Mercury News.*

"Welcome to Your Paper" menu suggests the possibilities available to interactive newspaper customers.

• Click on the **Your Paper** button under the **Your Paper** icon on the **Welcome** window. Explore the area of the service devoted to news, business and events in the area.

systems, now already in place to capture wire service reports and feature material, may be used to receive national advertising proofs and entire page layouts from afar.

Computers also may permit newspapers to offer their readers "tailored" issues containing news and advertising packages that reflect the wishes of individual subscribers. One reader might prefer heavier-than-usual sports coverage, for example, while a "news junkie" might want more reports from the state capitol and Washington. A third subscriber could want more women's news and service features; a fourth might request a hefty diet of business news. A number of major U.S. dailies have this capability already, though the evolution of the tailored newspaper has been slower than predicted.

Computers also make it possible for newspapers to store their daily input and develop a massive database for libraries, scholars, attorneys, research agencies, and individual consumers who wish to have instant access via computer to authoritative, current information.

Recycled newsprint, though relatively expensive, will become more and more prevalent. About half of all Americans in 1992 said they regularly saved newspapers for recycling, and an additional 14 percent said they do so occasionally.

Dramatic progress seems likely in printing technology as well, especially with a still-experimental process known as flexography. "Flexo" presses are already on line at the world's largest commercial newspaper, Japan's *Yomiuri Shimbun* (13.5 million readers); they operate on the direct impression system, much like letterpress. The Washington *Post,* Miami *Herald,* and New York *Daily News,* among other major U.S. dailies, have for some time been testing flexographic presses, which reportedly produce sharper and truer colors. And, because it operates with water-based as opposed to oil-based inks, "flexo" could neutralize readers' most common complaint about their newspapers—ink rubbing off onto their hands. That breakthrough alone should do much to assure the newspaper industry a bright and prosperous future.

summary

Newspapers serve the country as watchdog and people's champion, providing more information and commentary than any other mass communications medium. About 1,600 U.S. daily newspapers have a combined circulation of 60.6 million, and newspapers as a group lead all other media in attracting advertising revenue.

In recent years, however, the newspaper industry has undergone profound change. Readers are spending less time with their newspapers, and many afternoon papers have folded or become morning papers. Powerful groups of newspapers, such as Gannett, Knight-Ridder, Cox, Newhouse, and others, have gained control of the great majority of newspaper properties, making the family-owned daily newspaper largely a thing of the past. Direct competition between daily newspapers owned by different publishers exists in only a handful of U.S. cities. Still, buyers are willing to pay huge prices to acquire newspapers, underscoring the long-term strength of the industry.

While no two newspapers are organized exactly alike, most dailies have news and editorial departments, along with advertising, circulation, and production operations. The publisher is in charge of the newspaper, though the editor often makes news decisions.

Newspaper industry trends include:

- Still more technological change, including electronic pagination, digital photography, and, in some markets, an interactive newspaper where individual readers can choose content as well as respond to newspaper advertising messages from their home computers.
- Countrywide newspapers, such as *USA Today,* the *Wall Street Journal,* and the New York *Times* national editions, which give Americans from coast to coast regular access to a lively and varied national press.

? questions and cases

1. Based on your reading of this chapter and your understanding of the responsibilities newspaper people face, what qualities do you think are positively essential for success as a newspaper reporter? an editor? a publisher? Are the qualities the same for each? Explain.

2. Does the vast increase in chain ownership of newspapers worry you? Why or why not?

3. Allen H. Neuharth of the Gannett newspaper chain has written that "a company in the information business that Gannett so diligently pursues will not long be successful if it ignores or neglects any segment of its audiences." Discuss this statement. In your opinion, are audience segments now being neglected? If so, which ones? Given the geographical limits most newspapers must operate within, how would you begin to correct these imbalances?

4. Comment on the strengths and weaknesses of the newspapers you personally read. If you were named editor of your local paper, what changes would you make? What new priorities would you adopt? How would you implement them?

chapter glossary

beat   A reporter's regular run, such as police headquarters, city hall, or the courthouse. Besides beat reporters, a newspaper or TV news operation may utilize special assignment reporters in such areas as sports, business, or education, and general assignment reporters, who are available to cover news wherever it occurs.

composing room   Area where production workers prepare news and advertising for publication. Sometimes, especially on smaller papers, referred to as the "back shop."

marriage mail   Combines (marries) several advertising circulars into one packet for inexpensive third-class mail distribution. Many coupons and other saturation marketing messages are distributed in this fashion.

Newspaper Guild   Labor union representing editorial and some other employees on certain newspapers.

pagination   Arranging pages for printing. In recent years, computer-generated pagination systems permit page layout on a videoscreen; the layouts are then transferred directly to the pressroom for plate making and printing.

Standard Advertising Unit (SAU)   Adopted by the newspaper industry in the 1980s, the SAU attempts to solve the problem of variations in page sizes and column widths around the country by standardizing advertisement space units. More than fifty possible SAU sizes and shapes are available.

zoned edition   A newspaper edition targeted at an individual community or neighborhood.

notes

1 Robert E. Park, "The Natural History of the Newspaper," reprinted in *Interpretations of Journalism,* edited by Frank Luther Mott and Ralph Casey (New York: Crofts, 1937), 124.

2 The figures used throughout this chapter are drawn in large part from *Facts About Newspapers,* published by the Newspaper Association of America, 1992.

3 Quoted in *The Reader's Digest Dictionary of Quotations* (New York: Funk and Wagnalls, 1968), 467.

4 George Garneau, "Average Pay for Reporters Declines," *Editor & Publisher,* 5 September 1992, 12.

5 New York *Times,* 28 November 1986.

6 Lincoln Steffens, *The Autobiography of Lincoln Steffens* (New York: Harcourt Brace, 1931), 703.

7 Mark Fitzgerald, "Chain Chairman Critical of Other Chains," *Editor & Publisher,* 14 February 1987, 11.

8 Herbert Lee Williams, *Newspaper Organization and Management,* 5th ed. (Ames: Iowa State University Press, 1978), 8–26; also, Ardyth Sohn, Cristine Ogan, and John Polich, *Newspaper Leadership* (Englewood Cliffs, N.J.: Prentice-Hall, 1986), 6–54.

9 Willard G. Bleyer, *Main Currents in the History of American Journalism* (Boston: Houghton Mifflin, 1927), 182, 339–57, 422.

10 Quoted in Tyron Edwards, *The New Dictionary of Thoughts* (New York: Standard Books, 1954), 422.

11 *The People and the Press: A Times Mirror Investigation of Public Attitudes Toward the News Media, Conducted by the Gallup Organization* (Los Angeles: Times Mirror Co., 1986).

12 Ibid.

13 Ibid.

14 Ibid.

15 Ibid.

16 Edwards, *New Dictionary of Thoughts,* 423.

17 Quoted by Allen H. Neuharth in his *USA Today* column, 11 September 1992.

18 Address to the Association for Education in Journalism and Mass Communication national convention, East Lansing, Michigan, August 1983.

chapter E

The Community Press

Despite the lowering importance of the New York *Times* and other great metropolitan dailies to our life and thought, the United States remains a nation of community newspapers, those weeklies and small

Objectives

When you have finished studying this chapter, you should be able to:

- List and discuss the seven primary roles of the community newspaper

- Explain the news philosophies the typical community editor holds

- Explain technological developments, including desktop publishing, and how they have influenced the community press field

- Debate the strengths and weaknesses of Total Market Coverage and free newspapers

- Analyze the career opportunities in the hometown press field

Despite the towering importance of the New York *Times* and other great metropolitan dailies to our life and thought, the United States remains a nation of community newspapers, those weeklies and small dailies which faithfully report events in towns, suburbs, and neighborhoods. And while foreigners often accuse U.S. newspapers of being the most parochial in the world, our readers continue to expect detailed and extended local coverage. Proximity is fundamental to American journalism. Readers are likely to read a news story of a car wreck in which a neighbor suffered a mild concussion far more intently than a piece about an earthquake that killed hundreds of persons half a world away.

The national newspaper concept, prevalent in Europe and Japan, where a handful of newspapers published in capital cities can dominate an entire country, has never fully caught on in the United States. More than 8,500 American newspapers, weeklies and dailies, have circulations of 10,000 or less. Of the 1,586 daily newspapers in the United States, only about 120 of them, well under 9 percent, exceed 100,000 in circulation.[1] Ours is, emphatically, a hometown press.

The Many Roles of the Community Newspaper

Community newspapers serve their readers and communities by:

1 Reporting local news items that would appear in no other newspaper

2 Developing details of local news items not included in articles other newspapers print

3 Serving local shoppers as an advertising medium for a community's merchants and other businesspeople

4 Promoting local welfare and improvement projects

5 Giving recognition to those who work on community programs, thus encouraging others to join in

6 Stimulating thinking, particularly on local problems and projects

7 Serving as a unifying force in the community

This list, adapted from the writings of Kenneth R. Byerly, describes a type of journalism that is far more intimate, and far less detached, than is normally found in the metropolitan media of mass communications.[2] Joseph Pulitzer, publisher of the St. Louis *Post-Dispatch* and the New York *World* at the turn of the century, insisted that his staff members remain "drastically independent" of the events they wrote about.[3] The community journalist, on the other hand, may well prefer (or feel pressure) to become deeply involved in local activities, to be a participant as well as a chronicler.

Background

How many weekly newspapers are published in your area and state? Do any print two or three times a week? Your best sources of information for this chapter are your state press association and the *Editor & Publisher Yearbook*.

Teaching Idea

Invite the publisher or editor of a weekly newspaper to speak to your class about how it operates.

Discussion

Ask your students to bring copies of several small-town weekly newspapers to class. Compare their contents with the seven roles cited in the text.

The Country Paper

To the modern historian the informal accounts of everyday events presented in the rural weeklies are much more significant source material than many pretentious essays composed consciously as histories. Scarcely a town or county in the South can produce public records that can serve alone as the basis of a satisfactory history. They are entirely too impersonal to give more than a skeletonized picture of the region. They seldom go beyond restricted subjects. There is, in fact, only one door through which the local historian can pass with satisfaction to much of the everyday world of the past, and that is the country paper.

Thomas D. Clark, *The Southern Country Editor* (Bobbs-Merrill, 1948).

What Do Community Newspaper Readers Want?

Research on suburban newspapers, by Ruth Clark of Clark, Martire and Bartolomeo, produced these suggestions for community newspapers, both daily and weekly. She said her study indicated that readers prefer the following:

- Local news handled importantly
- Serious material, but neighborliness and a social quality
- No junk fillers
- Listings on where to go, what to do, and how to get things done—such as church news, road repairs, quality and price of restaurants

- People news, such as weddings and engagements
- Family coverage
- Police and fire blotters and how the figures compare to other towns
- Housing news and real estate transactions
- Detailed day trip and family outing suggestions
- Local columnists
- Detailed local government coverage
- No editorials

Reported in *Suburban Publisher,* December 1988.

Background

Handling such duties is known as "paying your dues" and may be helpful later in moving up.

Teaching Idea

Assign students to find out if there is a weekly paper in the region which still uses hot type and letterpress. If so, have them obtain a copy of the paper. Compare the quality with a weekly that uses offset.

The community newspaper is a business, and perhaps one of the larger manufacturing plants in the town, but it is a cultural and educational force as well. Community journalists not only report the news, they give their readers a sense of direction and even a feeling of hope for the future.

Inside the hometown newspaper office are relatively few specialists. Staffs are small, the tasks to be performed are many, and the typical community journalist soon becomes adept at handling a variety of jobs. A sports reporter might also cover the courthouse and the police beat and, on the smaller papers, handle some advertising sales as well. **Pasteup** and **layout** duties, normally restricted on larger papers to production experts, are frequently shared by the entire staff at the community press level. The community journalist, in other words, is a generalist, someone who has, or quickly gains, a working knowledge of the entire newspaper's operations.

Technological Developments

Until a generation ago, most community newspapers were printed on ancient flatbed presses. News, editorials, and advertisements were laboriously "set" in heavy metal type, and pictures, when they were used at all, required a costly and time-consuming engraving process. Under this **letterpress** system, metal ingots were heated to the melting point, then "cast" into type that could be assembled as articles, headlines, and advertisements. Later these were arranged into columns, secured inside steel page forms, and locked onto the press. The type was then inked, paper placed on it, and pressure applied so that the ink transferred onto the paper. The process was slow, expensive, and cumbersome, and only very skilled printers could obtain consistently good reproduction quality. Not until the late 1950s did dramatic new developments in production revolutionize the printing industry, and community newspapers quickly took the lead in adopting the new technology. Prominent among the innovations were

1 **Cold type** composition. Compact new typesetting systems produced images on photographic paper or film, thereby eliminating the need for metal type. These "cold type" composition machines—named to contrast them with the letterpress typesetters, which require "hot type"—were much cheaper to purchase and operate. Also, they were markedly faster. Where a good **Linotype** operator may have been able to set six lines of

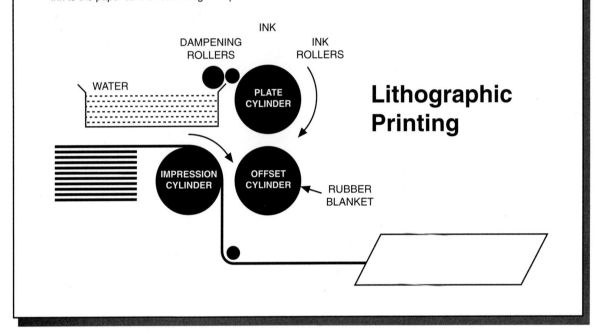

Offset lithography is a printing process based on the principle that oil and water do not mix. The images to be printed—words and pictures—are exposed onto light-sensitive plates, much like developing a photograph in a darkroom. The offset plate is coated with an oil-like chemical which *attracts* ink (printer's ink has an oil base). The non-image portion of the plate is uncoated metal; this attracts water, which *repels* ink.

The thin metal plates, one for each page, are mounted on the press. As the press begins to turn, an ink roller and a water roller apply a mixture of both substances onto each plate. The ink sticks to the image portions, then the ink transfers onto a rubber blanket, or cylinder. The blanket *offsets* or transfers the ink to the paper as it is fed through the press.

INK

DAMPENING ROLLERS

INK ROLLERS

WATER

PLATE CYLINDER

Lithographic Printing

IMPRESSION CYLINDER

OFFSET CYLINDER

RUBBER BLANKET

How offset printing works.

hot type a minute, state-of-the-art computers ran cold type machines that could produce hundreds of lines per minute.

2 **Offset lithography.** Sophisticated presses using the offset lithography process gave community newspapers greater flexibility and sharply improved production quality. By eliminating the need for photoengraving, offset printing allowed community editors, many of whom were without engraving facilities, to use pictures extensively. Once the exclusive province of metropolitan dailies and magazines, photojournalism became an integral part of the hometown newspaper.

3 The central printing plant. As high-speed offset presses became readily available, more and more community publishers abandoned their creaking, outmoded presses—and their attendant operating and maintenance problems—in favor of centralized printing facilities. One multiunit offset press could serve the needs of a dozen or more community publishers, offering them access to good-quality printing, including color capability, at relatively low cost.

The new technology is still evolving, as we shall see later. Already it has brought massive improvements in quality, effectiveness, and profits for the community newspaper industry.

I. F. Stone on Weekly Journalism

One of the most outspoken, and most widely quoted, weekly newspaper editors in American history was I. F. Stone. On the occasion of his retirement, he outlined his journalistic philosophy:

To give a little comfort to the oppressed, to write the truth exactly as I saw it, to make no compromises other than those of quality imposed by my own inadequacies, to be free to follow no master other than my own compulsions, to live up to my idealized image of what a true newspaperman should be, and still be able to make a living for my family—what more could a man ask?

Philosophically I believe that a man's life reduces itself ultimately to a faith—the fundamental is beyond proof—and that faith is a matter of aesthetics, a sense of beauty and harmony. I think every man is his own Pygmalion, and spends his life fashioning himself. And in fashioning himself, for good or ill, he fashions the human race and its future.

Quoted by Andrew Patner in *I. F. Stone: A Portrait*
(Pantheon Books, 1986)

Approach to the News

Example

If a newsworthy event has taken place in your area, assign students to obtain a copy of a daily and a weekly that covered it. How does the coverage differ?

While the technical means of producing hometown newspapers have undergone radical change, hometown editors' news philosophies have not. Currently and historically, most community journalism reflects strong beliefs that:

- Lots of names should get into the paper. At one time, cynics contended that all one needed to do to operate a successful hometown paper was to make sure that every subscriber's name was mentioned in print at least once a year. Community editors and their readers know better today; names alone do not make news. Even so, most community editors put forth a concerted effort to publish as many local names as possible in the context of reporting each day's or week's news. A localized, personalized outlook is a community editor's stock in trade. Local readers want to read about themselves and those around them. A metropolitan editor may ignore homely articles about anniversaries, scholastic honors, and the like. The community editor probably won't.

- Details are important. Big-city dailies, which carry a large volume of news each day in relatively little space, continually urge writers to summarize, condense, "boil it down." At the community level, newspapers often take the opposite approach. They develop articles in more leisurely fashion, with as much specific detail as possible. Writing about the winter's first snowstorm, for example, the metropolitan reporter might summarize the essentials into a few crisp paragraphs—school closings and power outages, traffic tie-ups, numbers of accidents reported, and other salient facts. The community writer, by contrast, might develop the story in much greater depth, perhaps sharing with readers pertinent anecdotes—one motorist's difficulties with a snowbound car, or how neighbors helped a physician get to the hospital in an emergency. The readers are never far away. Writing for and to them tends to be more relaxed, less brusque, warmer.

- The feelings of those involved in the news, and of their friends and families, should be considered. Because they are writing about friends and neighbors, community journalists tend to play down the sordid aspects of some news stories, repressing the temptation to write vividly about accidents and crime if doing so would cause undue hurt inside the community. Suicides, gruesome car wrecks, even unhappy but nonviolent stories such as business failures and personal bankruptcies—all likely will be handled with delicacy at the hometown newspaper. Some journalistic critics accuse community editors of glossing over unpleasantness, and frequently such criticism is warranted. Community editors, on the other hand, argue that they must deal tactfully with their readers' emotions—and that the big-city media, in turn, should become more sensitive. In any case, hometown newspapers are characterized by a sympathetic relationship between journalist and audience not often found elsewhere.

Editorials and Columns

Although many community newspapers are justifiably proud of their hard-hitting local editorials, perhaps half of all community papers carry no editorials at all. Publishers who refuse to editorialize often claim that small communities resent editorial badgering. Others fear alienating readers and advertisers. Still others say they haven't time to develop polished, well-researched editorials on a regular basis. Many publishers are leaders in the commercial and political lives of their towns and are so much a part of the local power structure that their editorials would not be persuasive anyway.

Those who do editorialize assert that editorials and opinion columns give personality to their newspapers and leadership to their communities. Indeed, some of the most inspired writing this country has produced—the "Crisis" essays of Tom Paine, the Federalist Papers explaining and defending the Constitution, the stirring commentary of William Allen White of Kansas—first saw the light of day as editorial or column material in a community newspaper. Courageous hometown editors regularly win Pulitzer prizes and other professional honors for crusading editorials on local issues. The editor's column, an alternative to the formal editorial on many hometown papers, can generate another type of journalistic leadership simply by praising good works and gently, or not so gently, calling attention to situations that seem unfair.

The vigorous local editorial page and the outspoken local columnist, however, are the exceptions rather than the rule in community journalism. Too many community newspapers blandly ignore local problems and issues and neglect to provide their communities with a public conscience and a sense of editorial responsibility. It should be added, though, that speaking out at the community-press level requires more than a little courage. It's one thing to attack the mayor in print from the safety of a metropolitan daily's skyscraper office, and quite another if the editor is almost certain to encounter the mayor personally in a small town's Main Street coffee shop the next morning. In community journalism, as local editors are fully aware, there are not many places to hide.

Example Discussion

Assign students to bring several different weeklies and to examine them for editorials and comment. Do they cover controversial topics?

Teaching Idea

Ask students to read and report on two humorous stories about country journalism—Edgar A. Poe's "X-ing a Paragrab," and "Journalism in Tennessee" by Mark Twain.

The Field Today

There is no such thing as a typical community newspaper, but an extensive survey of the field, conducted in 1991 for the trade magazine *News, Inc.,* suggested this composite profile: an 18-page weekly paper with a circulation of 2,800, which can be projected into a total readership of more than 8,000 persons, with an editorial staff of five or six persons, a publisher who also does some commercial printing on the side, and a primary purpose of reporting local news and opinion.[4]

Suburban papers typically are larger, averaging 16,000 circulation, with median staff size at about 100, including 26 editorial employees.[5] The average base salary for the publisher of a single weekly in 1991 was $39,630; publishers of groups of weeklies averaged $73,900, while entry-level reporters ranged between $15,000 and $16,000.[6]

The staff titles may resemble those on metropolitan dailies, but on community papers the duties likely will be expanded. The managing editor of a community weekly may also write news reports and take photographs, for example, as well as oversee page layouts. The publisher may also develop editorials as well as keep an eye on the account ledgers, and the sports editor may have some circulation/distribution responsibilities as well.

Weekly newspaper readership, unlike that of U.S. dailies, is increasing substantially—up 30.3 percent since 1980 to a 1991 total of 63.5 million—and advertising revenues continue to improve (see table 1 for circulation figures). "Weekly publishers feel strongly that they're onto a good thing," declared *News, Inc.,* summarizing its massive 1991 study, "and their responses reflect a lack of the handwringing and self-criticism that characterizes the mainstream press right now . . . there is little question that they offer the best source for entrepreneurial energy in newspapering today."[7]

Community radio. The strengths of the community newspaper—closeness to the audience and deep concern with local matters—make community radio a vital part of small towns and suburbs.

table 1   U.S. Weekly Newspapers and Circulation, 1960–92

Year	Total Weeklies*	Average Circulation	Total Weekly Circulation
1960	8,174	2,556	20,974,338
1965	8,061	3,106	25,036,031
1970	7,612	3,660	27,857,332
1975	7,612	4,715	35,892,409
1980	7,964	5,324	42,347,512
1985	7,954	6,359	48,988,801
1986	7,711	6,497	50,098,000
1987	7,600	6,262	47,593,000
1988	7,498	6,894	51,691,451
1989	7,606	6,958	52,919,846
1990	7,550	7,309	55,181,047
1991	7,476	7,323	54,746,332
1992	7,417	7,358	54,577,034

Used with permission of National Newspaper Association.

*Includes paid and free circulation newspapers

Press Associations

Nearly every community weekly and daily newspaper is a member of its state press association, an organization which confers the political and commercial benefits of size on a large group of relatively small operations. While each state's press association is different, most of them provide:

1 *Legislative representation.* By pooling resources through a single statewide organization, community publishers can create a powerful lobbying force with lawmakers. Press association lobbyists have been instrumental in obtaining passage of open-meetings and open-records acts as well as shield laws and other legislation of concern to press and public.

2 *Advertising representation.* Because there are so many community newspapers, and because they go to press on different days and charge different space rates, placing advertising in hometown papers can become a nightmarish bookkeeping chore. State press association representatives solicit advertising on behalf of all their members, and their central offices are geared to handle the details smoothly.

3 *Weekly or monthly newsletters.* These carry job placement information, listings of equipment needed or for sale, and news reports about association activities, among other regular features.

4 *State conventions.* In addition to one or two statewide meetings a year, the press association also may be counted upon to schedule a number of special interest and regional meetings to foster continuing education, an exchange of ideas, and the discussion of problems.

5 *Contests and awards.* These recognize member newspapers' outstanding professional performance in a wide range of categories.

6 *Legal advice.* The state press association may provide counsel on questions community publishers face regarding potentially libelous articles, questionable advertising claims, and so on, since few community publishers have their own legal departments.

In some states, the press association also administers statewide readership and marketing studies, clipping services, group insurance programs for member newspaper staffs, and a variety of other support programs.

Teaching Idea
Contact your state's press association and invite the manager to visit the class. If you can't arrange a visit, ask for information on the six major activities discussed in the text.

Suburban Newspapers

In the decades since World War II, a different type of community newspaper, the suburban, has come prominently on the scene. Blending the homeyness and localized appeal of the country weeklies with the editorial and advertising aggressiveness of the metropolitan dailies, the suburban press has become the fastest-growing segment of the newspaper industry. Many of the suburban papers are also among the most profitable, reaching affluent readers whose buying capabilities make them prime targets for retail advertisers. In 1992, the Suburban Newspapers of America counted about 200 member companies. They publish about 1,100 suburban daily and weekly newspapers and reach a combined total of 18 million households.[8] Suburban readership has doubled since 1970. A number of suburban papers have generated enough economic base to increase their publication frequency from weekly to daily; some suburban newspaper groups have emerged as the dominant retail advertising media in their markets.

Example
Do you know of any suburban daily or weekly papers in your area? If so, ask students to bring them to class and point out similarities and differences between them and a small town weekly.

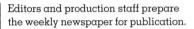

Editors and production staff prepare the weekly newspaper for publication.

Alternative newspapers are another form of community journalism.

Many suburban papers have expanded their news staffs, hired trained reporters, editors, and photographers and sharply improved a frumpy image once described this way by a magazine editor:

It was not too many years ago that, with rare exception, the suburban newspaper was thought of as a "nice, little" community sheet one could depend on for birth and death announcements, high school sports scores, school lunch menus, and a few items about zoning hearings and the like. What little reporting it did was usually dull, colloquial, or both. In short, that condescending impression was, with rare exception, well-founded.[9]

The situation is far different today. Many suburban papers now encourage investigative reporting, bright features, and in-depth editorial analysis. Suburban writers and photographers regularly win state, regional, and national awards for professional excellence.

Less bound by tradition than most community papers, the suburbans have adopted the chic graphic design of the more progressive metropolitan dailies. They've also followed the "metros" in such trends as TV viewing guides, lifestyle, arts, entertainment, sports, business, and recreation sections. One promotion-minded group in suburban Kansas City in a single year published more than 160 special advertising/editorial sections on fashions, jobs, careers, women's achievements, sports, and the like. Market research studies show that suburban newspapers have "as much or more sales message impact in their respective markets as the premier metro newspaper" in such characteristics as sales message recall, and brand linkage.[10]

Many of the suburban newspapers' gains with advertisers and readers have come at the expense of the metropolitan dailies. To compete, many medium-sized and big-city newspapers launched zoned editions, specially designed sections that carry local news for separate suburbs and offer neighborhood advertising to merchants in a particular retail area at sharply reduced rates. In the early 1990s, 70 percent of the metropolitan dailies with circulations of 100,000 or more were publishing zoned editions as a defensive marketing strategy against the suburban press.[11] Another successful response has been *regionalization*—inserting a tabloid section for a particular suburb inside the larger metropolitan edition. Beyond that, a number of metropolitan dailies decided to buy out the competition; Gannett, Knight-Ridder, Harte-Hanks, the Chicago Tribune group, and other large newspaper chains own much of the suburban press.

Suburban Newspapers of America, with offices in Chicago, is the trade association for the suburban press. Founded in 1971, SNA serves as an information clearinghouse; conducts training sessions and market research studies; and assists in editorial, advertising, and circulation promotion for its members in the United States and Canada.

Total Market Coverage

Many community newspapers, especially suburban weeklies, have in recent years decided simply to give away their papers to every household in the circulation area. Other publishers have gone to a system of voluntary pay, which means distributing the paper to all households, then collecting from as many as are willing to pay. In a number of cases, publishers provide an improved paper, with news and features, for those who do pay; all other households receive a product that is mostly advertising.

The switch to saturation delivery usually comes when powerful advertisers such as large discount houses, supermarkets, and major department stores strongly urge newspaper publishers to guarantee them *total market coverage (TMC)*.

In this area, the community newspaper faces competition from a variety of sources. Some companies produce **shoppers**—free newspapers containing primarily advertising—while others utilize marriage mail—several advertising messages and circulars combined (married) into a package for shipment by third class postage to every home in the region. For advertisers interested in saturation coverage (to promote a coupon offer, as an example) and without concern about any sort of editorial or service material, marriage mail can be an efficient medium.

Giving away newspapers goes against the grain of many publishers, who feel that one of the newspaper's great strengths as an advertising medium is the fact that subscribers seek out the paper and are willing to pay money to receive it. But the overwhelming success of couponing and other advertising promotions that depend on broad, saturation penetration of the market has prompted many publishers to rethink their views on free newspapers. In 1994, fewer than half the member publications of the Suburban Newspapers of America were fully paid for by their readers. About a third were given away entirely, while the rest were circulated through voluntary pay and **controlled circulation** plans—meaning, in effect, that readers might be asked to pay for their subscriptions, but even if they did not do so the papers came in the mail anyway.[12] Within the industry considerable feeling now exists that free community newspapers, already an established trend in England, will become the dominant pattern in the United States in the years to come.

> ## Extra Information
> A shopper usually contains mostly advertising with little or no editorial matter and is distributed free. The advertisers pay the entire cost of publication and distribution. Ask your students to bring a shopper to class and compare it with a standard weekly.

Technology: The Desktop Revolution

Historically, two of the most persistent problems facing the community newspaper editor have been (1) getting news and advertising set in type swiftly and cheaply and (2) providing readers with more imaginative typefaces and design features—in the absence of staff artists and other graphic arts support found on larger papers and magazines. In the mid-1980s, remarkable advances in personal computers and laser printers combined to alleviate both problems. The result was a change in the way many organizations, not just community newspapers, prepared materials for publication. The innovations became known as **desktop publishing.** Typically, the desktop system comprises:

- A personal computer with at least 512 kilobytes of memory
- A laser printer
- Computer software including word processing, graphics, and page-layout programs

> ## Teaching Idea
> If any unit in your institution uses desktop publishing, invite a representative to bring some portable items (computer, laser printer) to class for a demonstration.

Desktop publishing. Newsletters, small newspapers, brochures, and a host of other publications are ideal vehicles for desktop publishing technology.

This type of package, which in 1994 could be purchased for $5,000 or less, can outperform professional typesetting systems that previously cost $30,000 or more and can reduce typesetting page costs drastically. Desktop publishing permits individuals, even those with limited technical skills, to produce professional-quality typesetting, charts, headlines, borders, shadowboxes, and graphs—slick, attractive, complete publications, ready for the camera and the press. Economic experts forecast that desktop publishing sales, which exceeded $5 billion a year in the early 1990s, will grow even faster in the years ahead as newer breakthroughs find their way swiftly into use throughout the industry.[13]

Many headline faces can be packed onto desktop discs; these and computer-generated charts, borders, and other devices give even the most modestly budgeted desktop publisher access to a vast, unprecedented range of design effects. Striking improvements in low-cost laser printers, which triggered the desktop publishing boom, can reproduce these graphic effects with a clarity and precision hitherto found only in large magazine and book publishing houses.

While the community journalist is among the chief benefactors of the desktop publishing revolution, others gain from it also. Editors of church, organizational, and educational newsletters are finding the desktop publishing systems attractive, as are advertising and public relations agency people and others engaged in business communications. Scholastic publications, most of them operating on tight budgets, especially lend themselves to desktop publishing.

Larger media, too, have discovered that desktop publishing could streamline their graphics departments and offer them more effects, faster and cheaper. A spokesperson for the Knight-Ridder newspaper group estimated that 80 percent of all newspapers with 100,000 or more circulation are utilizing desktop systems for graphics production. The Associated Press, which strongly influences daily newspapers throughout the country, announced plans to beam charts, graphs, and other illustrative devices via satellites to subscriber papers. The astonishing success of Gannett's *USA Today* has demonstrated that U.S. audiences respond to well-done graphic effects, and the new technology is making them liberally available to publications everywhere.

Career Opportunities in Community Journalism

For most of this century, aspiring young journalists accepted jobs on hometown papers only as a last resort. Even then, they were apt to look upon the community newspaper as a temporary stopover, a place to sharpen skills for a time until something exciting opened up on the glamorous dailies in the major cities. In recent years, however, more and more men and women have come to regard the community press as a worthy career field in and of itself. And community publishers who previously ran small, family operations have expanded their staffs and begun actively recruiting college-trained people for news and advertising positions. Starting salaries, though improving, remain below those usually offered by metropolitan dailies, magazines, wire services, public relations firms, and broadcasters. But those individuals who do join the community-press ranks report a number of other advantages:

1   *Freedom and flexibility.* These are relative terms, because the deadlines on small newspapers can be as relentless as those anywhere. There is, however, a difference in the kind of work community journalists perform. While the metropolitan daily newspaper staff is a massive, finely tuned machine

requiring each person to complete highly specific tasks, community papers generally offer far more latitude. A reporter who doesn't like writing about crime may yet have some crime news to cover, but he or she also has opportunities to write features and perhaps sports news as well. Community journalists rarely become pigeonholed; most are expected to be versatile enough to handle all types of stories, and, as a rule, community journalists welcome the opportunity to tackle a diversity of assignments.

2 *A closeness to the audience.* Fire destroys a family home, leaving a couple and its children in desperate straits. A community newspaper reporter writes about them; when the story is published, a dramatic outpouring of support from the community helps the stricken family back on its feet. Situations such as this occur throughout journalism, but they happen with greater frequency, and perhaps with more intensity, at the community-press level. Hometown journalists write about people and situations they truly know. Their local newspaper work requires them to appreciate the importance of human life and experience. In the process, the journalists promote the social integration of the community.

3 *Opportunities for growth.* The informal atmosphere of most community newspaper offices makes them ideal learning laboratories for individuals willing to expand their capabilities. A reporter can readily acquire some knowledge of the advertising department—and news photography, production, circulation, and accounting in the process. In short, he or she can develop into a generalist as well as a specialist, and this is the stuff top managers are made of.

4 *The community environment.* Quality of life means profoundly different things to different people. While some young men and women find small towns stuffy, conservative, conformist, and dull, others regard them as wholesome and convenient, good places for working and raising a family.

5 *A chance for ownership.* Community newspaper prices have risen dramatically in recent years. Million-dollar pricetags on community weeklies are not uncommon, and powerful, acquisition-minded newspaper chains have moved aggressively into the community press market, making it more difficult than ever for an individual to buy his or her own

newspaper. Still, many opportunities remain. The classified ads in every issue of *Publisher's Auxiliary* and *Editor & Publisher* list literally dozens of smaller newspaper properties for sale. An ambitious, able young man or woman who has learned community journalism and who can convince local bankers to lend financial backing may still become the owner of a community newspaper.

Also, the relatively low cost of modern typesetting equipment—desktop publishing systems—and the ready availability of leased press time at a central printing plant combine to make starting a new community publication an attractive option under some circumstances. Launching a new publication from scratch, with all that requires in terms of building a circulation and advertising base, is risky business, and a number of such ventures fail. But the dozens of new publications that successfully begin each year prove that it can be done.

By whatever means one arrives there, the community journalism field for some will prove a remarkably satisfying endeavor. Community newspapers, like the small towns and suburbs they serve, are easy to misunderstand and underestimate. One of the wisest of all the community editors, the late Henry Beetle Hough of the *Vineyard Gazette* in New England, once put it this way:

> All generations before this one have found it difficult to understand size, bigness. The human conception has been able only with difficulty to cope with the tremendous figures, cities, steamers, wars, rates of production, and so on. But I wonder if the time has not come when it is more difficult for most people to formulate an idea of smallness. Things have been big for so long now. For instance, a great many people are not only unable to imagine what a small weekly newspaper and a small town are like, but they do not even try, because they assume that anything small is simply an early and imperfect version of something big. I doubt if there are many who know that these particular small things, and of course others, are more different in kind than in size. They are not underdeveloped. They are mature, complete specimens of what they have always been and will always be.[14]

William Allen White, famed editor of the Emporia, Kansas, *Gazette,* was even more emphatic. He spoke for many of his fellow community editors, then and now, when he wrote in 1911: "What we want, and what we shall have, is the royal American privilege of living and dying in a country town, running a country newspaper, saying what we please when we please, how we please and to whom we please."[15]

summary

While great metropolitan daily newspapers continue to influence our country's life and thought, the fact remains that the United States is also a nation of community newspapers, the weeklies and small dailies which serve small towns, suburbs, and neighborhoods. There are more than 8,500 U.S. newspapers, both dailies and weeklies, with circulations of 10,000 or less.

Community newspapers succeed by reporting local news, in detail, that likely would appear in print nowhere else, by giving local readers a forum for dealing with local problems and issues and by providing them with an effective advertising medium.

In recent years, the community press has prospered because of technology, chiefly the revolution in offset printing, and further technological change, such as desktop publishing, has made producing a community newspaper easier and more efficient.

Hometown newspapers are close to their audiences and often communicate with them in a writing style that is warmer and more relaxed than that of the metropolitan dailies. Suburban newspapers, blending community pride with metropolitan daily newspaper slickness and sophistication, are booming: Suburban readership has doubled since 1970.

As a career field, community journalism has much to offer, including an opportunity to learn all phases of the business quickly, and, for some, a chance at owning their own newspaper.

? questions and cases

1. Your small town's high school this year has an undefeated football team—one so newsworthy, in fact, that sports writers from the capital city and two out-of-town television news crews have begun to carry reports on the team's games. These reports are widely noted in your community. Given the fact that your newspaper is a weekly—thus your football scores and reports are stale news by the time your paper appears—how can you provide your readers with fresh, effective sports coverage in the face of such stiff competition from the city?

2. As a new advertising salesperson in a prosperous suburb with intense competition for advertising dollars (two metropolitan dailies serve this area, as do more than a dozen radio stations and three television network affiliates), you are preparing to call upon your first account, a sporting goods store in a busy shopping mall. What selling points will you try to make in behalf of your newspaper? What negative questions and comments might you receive? How would you counter them?

3. Does your community newspaper always work for the best interests of its readers? What specific projects in your hometown do you wish the newspaper would support? Discuss.

4. Are you influenced by the editorial recommendations (proposals for change, political endorsements, and so on) printed in your community newspaper? Why or why not?

5. Should community newspapers adopt different policies from those of metropolitan dailies in reporting crime news?

6. You are a teacher in the public schools of your community. Like many of your colleagues, you are upset with the local school board for not authorizing salary raises and, indeed, for not providing adequate support for the school system generally. How would you work with the local community newspaper to get your point of view across to the citizens of your town? Discuss some strategies you might adopt.

chapter glossary

cold type   Composition system in which letters are produced photographically, as opposed to molten lead linecasting (hot type) for printing.

controlled circulation   Publication limited to a certain audience, usually sent free to members of that audience.

desktop publishing   Procedure by which personal computers and laser printers, utilizing advanced typesetting and graphics capabilities, can produce polished, complete, camera-ready publications.

layout   Drawing which shows how a given page should look when filled with text and headlines. To "lay out" a page or an advertisement is to place all the elements (copy, headlines, art work) into a pleasing and workable arrangement. A diagram of the plan for an entire publication is often referred to as the *dummy*.

letterpress   Printing from a relief, or raised, surface. Raised letters are coated with ink and paper is applied, as with a rubber stamp. One of the oldest printing processes.

Linotype   Mechanical typesetting machine, developed by Ottmar Mergenthaler about 1886.

offset lithography   Printing process in which the image is transferred from a printing plate to a rubber blanket, then to the page.

pasteup   Process by which text, headlines, and other elements produced via cold type composition are affixed on a grid sheet. The pasteup is then photographed for platemaking, and the plate is attached to the press for printing.

shopper, or **shopping guide**   A local publication consisting primarily of advertising.

notes

1 American Newspaper Publishers Association, *Facts About Newspapers, '92* (Reston, Va.: American Newspaper Publishers Association, 1992), 1–7.

2 Kenneth R. Byerly, *Community Journalism* (Philadelphia: Chilton, 1961), 5.

3 Ronald T. Farrar, *Reluctant Servant: The Story of Charles G. Ross* (Columbia: University of Missouri Press, 1968), 106–9.

4 "Weeklies: A Special Report," *News, Inc.,* November 1991, 2–13.

5 "SNA: An Industry Profile," (Chicago: Suburban Newspapers of America, 1989), 20.

6 "Weeklies," *News, Inc.,* 8.

7 Ibid., 4.

8 "SNA: An Industry Profile," 2.

9 Craig Shutt, "Dateline: Suburbia," 7 April 1978. Background material provided by the Suburban Newspapers of America.

10 "SNA: An Industry Profile," 10.

11 Suzanne Donovan, "Holding Their Own," *Editor & Publisher,* 7 July 1990, 16.

12 "SNA: An Industry Profile," 11.

13 Van Kornegay, "Desktop Revolution," *The Carolina Reporter,* 28 January 1987; since updated by the author.

14 Henry Bettle Hough, *Country Editor* (New York: Doubleday, 1940), 2.

15 Quoted in Bruce M. Kennedy, *Community Journalism: A Way of Life* (Ames: Iowa State University Press, 1974), 3.

chapter F

"Does a photographer take a picture or make a picture?" A well-known photojournalism professor often poses this question to his students on the first day of the new term. A hand goes up. "Sure, photographers

Photographic Communication

Objectives

When you have finished studying this chapter, you should be able to:

◉ Trace the historical development of photography in general and photojournalism in particular

◉ Discuss the types of photographic communications work professionals in the various media do today

◉ Define the basic terminology of the field and be able to describe the impact changes in lighting, shutter speed, and cropping make on a given picture

◉ Discuss the changes in photo processing digital imaging makes possible and the impact computer retouching can have on photojournalistic ethics and news values

"**Does** a photographer *take* a picture or *make* a picture?" A well-known photojournalism professor often poses this question to his students on the first day of the new term. A hand goes up. "Sure, photographers create some pictures," a student ventures. "But other pictures are just snapshots. A photographer points the camera and takes the picture."

"Just fires away, does she?" smiles the professor. Then he pounces. "At *what*? The very decision to shoot the picture in the first place represents a creative action. Of all the photographic possibilities out there, *why this one?* How much of the subject will be included? What will be left out—and why? Which angle will the photographer choose? What lighting effects will she utilize? range? shutter speed? At what precise moment will the photographer decide to press the trigger?" The questions go on and on, and the point is nailed down: Photography is an intensively originative undertaking.

Teaching Idea
Invite a photographer from your local or regional daily paper to discuss newspaper photojournalism with your class.

The harsh brutality of the Vietnam war was brought home by photos—none more emotionally charged than this one, capturing the execution of a Viet Cong officer.

Photography (meaning "drawing or writing from light") touches and enriches our lives in numerous ways—in science and medicine, industry, commerce, teaching. Millions regard photography, justifiably, as an art form. The great majority of U.S. households contain one or more cameras, and amateur photography has become one of the most popular hobbies in the world. Photographs capture moments, preserve memories, express ideas. In this chapter, we shall look at just one aspect of photographic communication, *photojournalism;* a term that has come to mean *the combination of pictures and words to communicate information.*

Example
Examine any issue of a daily newspaper to see what types of photojournalism it contains. Are *all* pictures in a newspaper (other than ads) considered photojournalism?

Photojournalism today is taken for granted. When a new president is sworn in, fire destroys a city landmark, or the winning touchdown is scored, we *assume* there will be pictures available in the next edition and on the next newscast. "A major drug bust downtown," the local TV anchor announces during prime time. "We'll have live-action footage at eleven." News photographers climb mountains with guerrillas in Bosnia, duck from sniper fire in Somalia, doggedly cross the deserts of Kuwait and Iraq, and canvass equally harsh urban American crime zones to bring the glamorous and unglamorous, exciting and

Eyewitness to Humanity

Photojournalists sum up a news event in a manner the mind can hold, capturing that portrayal [as described by Harold Evans] "rich in meaning because it is a trigger image of all the emotions aroused by the subject." . . . From the photographer's framework, to capture the newsworthy moment is an important self-discipline. Photographers are trained not to panic but to bring forth the truth as events dictate. They are schooled to be visual historians, and not freelance medics or family counselors.

Clifford Christians, Kim B. Rotzoll, and Mark Fackler, *Media Ethics: Cases and Moral Reasoning* (Longman, 1991).

routine, hard news and soft news pictures we have come to expect as a matter of course. Ours is a visual culture. Today's audiences *expect* lavish use of pictures to illustrate the news and give added dimension to it. We want to be shown as well as told.

Technical Evolution

News consumers have not always expected or appreciated visual reporting. At one time, a substantial body of thought regarded illustrations as crude, tasteless, even counterproductive devices that led audiences to ignore reading and writing.

The stubbornest barriers to photojournalism's evolution were not intellectual, however, so much as technical. Reproducing an illustration upon a printed page, an artistic attainment in itself, was not achieved easily or swiftly. For most of its history, printing was done primarily by the letterpress system, wherein characters were cut in relief from blocks made of wood, or later, of metal. Printers then inked the raised surfaces and pushed paper against them. The process has speeded up a great deal in the thousand years or so since the Chinese first devised letterpress printing, but the basic principle remains the same and is still in operation today.

To reproduce illustrations for letterpress printing, artists must create relief etchings, or **engravings.** These engravings were originally called woodcuts. Many contemporary editors, even on publications now using different printing systems, still refer to an illustration as a **cut.** The Boston *News-Letter* carried the first cut in an American paper in January 1707; it depicted a naval flag. The first political cartoon published in an American newspaper was a highly emotional appeal to colonial unity; it came to symbolize an entire revolutionary movement. Based on the popular superstition that a snake slashed in two would come to life if the pieces were joined before sundown, the crude woodcut depicted a snake in eight sections representing the various, often bickering colonial governments, and carried the caption "Join or Die." Other papers widely copied the illustration as sentiment shifted toward the fateful break with England.[1]

Cameras, in primitive fashion, at least, have been around for five hundred years or more. The earliest version, called the *camera obscura* (meaning "dark chamber"), was a blackened, boxlike device with a small hole in one wall to let in light. When the light rays hit the opposite wall of the chamber, they formed an image of the scene outside. Artists could trace the outlines of the image, apply colors, and thus produce a remarkably lifelike portrait. The camera obscura proved a boon to artists. Leonardo da Vinci was using the technique early in the sixteenth century; many credit him with inventing it. Scientists, meanwhile, searched for ways to make the images permanent yet portable. A French physicist, Joseph Nicephore Niepce, is believed to have been the first to produce a light-sensitive metal plate to fit inside the back wall of a camera obscura; he sensitized the plate by coating it with silver chloride, then added a mixture of nitric acid in an attempt to "fix" the image. This earliest of all photographs, produced in 1826, remains legible today.

Another Frenchman, Louis J. M. Daguerre, is credited with giving the world the first popular, readily usable form of photography. His pictures, called *daguerreotypes,* were achieved by exposing the image to a light-sensitive plate and applying mercury vapor to "develop" the picture and then salt to fix the image permanently. Daguerreotypes first appeared in 1839. That same year, William H. F. Talbot, a British scientist, successfully used light-sensitive paper; coated with silver nitrate and salt, this *film* would eventually give photographers the freedom and flexibility they needed to make pictures under all types of conditions.[2]

News photos began appearing in newspapers and magazines as early as 1842. They reproduced poorly. To print a picture, an editor had to turn the photograph over to a skilled craftsperson to carve a likeness of the picture onto a block of wood, which could then be mounted onto a press and, with luck, print up as something

How Many Words Is a Picture Worth?

Probably Confucius never said a picture was worth a thousand words; and if he did, it was one of the slips a wise man sometimes makes. A very good picture—like Joseph Rosenthal's "Flag Raising on Iwo Jima"—is worth a good many thousand words in the average newspaper, though not as much as the 265 words of the Gettysburg Address. On the other hand, a group picture captioned

"Prominent Members of the State Dental Convention Now Meeting at the Grand Hotel. Left to right: James Whoosis, Charles Doke, and Frank Zilch," in which Whoosis looks as though his dentures were paining him, Doke looks like a pallbearer suffering from a hangover, and Zilch has his eyes shut, is not worth more than one noxious word—"lousy."

Frank Luther Mott, *The News in America* (Harvard, 1952).

more or less resembling the photograph. Only solid blacks and solid whites would reproduce; the other, subtler shades, called **halftones,** could not be rendered. Some of the early newspaper and magazine woodcuts were remarkably good, however. Civil War photographs and war maps carried by *Harper's Magazine,* the Philadelphia *Inquirer, Scribner's Monthly,* and other publications gave audiences a glimpse of what journalistic illustration might achieve.[3] Soon readers would demand better.

Joseph Pulitzer and William Randolph Hearst accelerated the tempo of photojournalism's evolution by making aggressive use of the new halftone engraving process. With this revolutionary system developed primarily by the British, photographic images could be swiftly transferred to light-sensitive metal plates and mounted on high-speed presses to reproduce not only blacks and whites but intermediate shades of gray with considerable fidelity. Ignoring the objections of such lofty publications as *The Nation,* which declared that pictures were infantile, Pulitzer and Hearst dispatched legions of photographers to provide saturation picture coverage that astonished newspaper audiences. Pages of New York's yellow press were gaudy with photographs and diagrams of crime and gore, often enhanced by arrows pointing helpfully to the spots where the bodies were found. "It is just this sort of journalism that fosters the idea in the minds of the general public that a newspaper man has no conscience," fumed *The Journalist,* a trade paper of the day, "and that when he enters the house it is a good idea to lock up the spoons."[4] But pictures sold newspapers. As *Harper's Weekly* observed before the turn of the century, "The question of 'cuts' in the columns of the daily newspapers, if not exactly a burning one, excites more animated comment than many of more importance. It has been settled in favor of their use now."[5]

Faster film and smaller, more convenient cameras such as the Speed Graphic, introduced in 1912 and destined to become the mainstay of newspaper photography for more than fifty years, spurred rapid growth of the field prior to World War I. So did spectacular news stories such as the *Titanic's* sinking in 1912; photojournalists obtained pictures showing rescue efforts in the icy waters of the North Atlantic and printed dramatic portraits of some survivors. News photographers in 1914 followed U.S. troops into Mexico on a "punitive expedition" against Pancho Villa. Three years later, they went to France when the United States entered the war against the Central Powers. When President Woodrow Wilson signed the Treaty of Versailles, formally ending the Great War, two U.S. newspapers scooped their competition by arranging to have news pictures of the ceremony flown to New York on the R-34, the first dirigible ever to cross the Atlantic Ocean.[6]

The 35-mm camera, much smaller and less obtrusive than the Speed Graphic, though somewhat less reliable and far more difficult to use effectively, first appeared in the 1920s. Equipped with faster lenses and highly sensitive film, the miniature camera could use available light and thus produce pictures showing people in informal, realistic, off-guard situations. These "candid camera" shots were perfect for the

Teaching Idea

A halftone picture in a newspaper is made up of patterns of individual ink dots. (A dot-matrix computer printer uses the same principle.) To demonstrate this to your class, either enlarge a newspaper picture in a copy machine or use a magnifying glass.

Teaching Idea

Ask a local photographer whether he or she has any older cameras to demonstrate to your class. If the demonstration could include the older flash powder and flashbulbs, so much the better.

The drama of student protest in China was symbolized by this brave young man, who faced down a column of tanks in Tiananmen Square in 1989. The victory was short-lived; the tanks returned and the students, who were crusading for more freedom of expression, were silenced.

jazz journalism of the Roaring Twenties. New York's *Illustrated Daily News,* which ushered in the tabloid era just after World War I, attracted an enormous circulation. So did its imitators, chiefly Hearst's *Daily Mirror* and the New York *Daily Graphic,* fellow champions of overblown, often steamy, news and feature photographs. At least some of these photos were doctored, and others were faked altogether.[7] The older yellow journalism pales in comparison.

Times were worse during the Great Depression of the 1930s, but the photojournalism was better. Two unrelated decisions led the country to a deeper and more sympathetic understanding of photographic communications. One came from an unlikely quarter when the Farm Security Administration arranged for a small, gifted band of photographers to travel across the country recording on film the dust storms and resultant soil erosion and their tragic impact upon crops and farm families. A controversial federal agency, the FSA operated in the face of heavy criticism, mostly from staunch conservatives in Congress who feared that some of the Roosevelt administration's programs to help tenant farmers were impractical, communist-inspired efforts to undermine the country's traditional economic system. The FSA photographers' mission was to provide the White House and Congress with hard-hitting documentary evidence that a true emergency existed. Under the direction of Roy L. Stryker, and including such talents as Dorothea Lange and Walker Evans, the FSA photographers produced more than a quarter of a million negatives and 150,000 prints; they brought home to the American people the true devastation of rural poverty. As social statements, and as grim, sensitive works of art, the FSA photographs are profoundly important.[8]

Equally significant, although in a different way, was Henry R. Luce's decision in 1936 to establish *Life* magazine, which emerged as photojournalism's greatest vehicle for more than a generation. *Life's* original managing editor, John Shaw Billings, is believed to be the person who coined the term *photojournalism.* (Others argue that Professor Cliff Edom of the University of Missouri originated the term.) Blessed with lively creative talents and lavish expense accounts, *Life's* editors hired some of the finest photographers who ever lived, then dispatched them to picture-story assignments around the globe. The magazine's dramatic success—its circulation at one time hit 8.5 million—spawned many imitators. Chief among these was *Look,* which generated a distinguished history of its own. Most important, *Life* showed a vast audience of Americans what was happening here and abroad. Week after week, its picture stories set new standards of photographic and journalistic excellence; today many of them are properly regarded as classics.[9]

Life's popularity, however, could not withstand the challenge television presented in the years following World War II. A TV newscast may not have reflected the creative flair of a *Life* picture essay, but TV news was quicker, the images moved and talked, and TV offered news to the consumer free of charge. As readers and advertisers began drifting away, *Life* soon faced a cash flow problem it could not overcome. The magazine suspended weekly publication in 1972, though it reappeared later, in a different package. *Look* was already gone by then. Few magazines ever enjoyed more successful runs than these two. Their traditions live on and are reflected today in such superlative picture-conscious magazines as *National Geographic* and *Sports Illustrated.*

Heroes and Heroines of Photojournalism

The history of photojournalism, only touched upon here, is graced by any number of heroes and heroines. Following are a few of the most outstanding.

Mathew Brady preserved much of the Civil War on film for future generations. Working under wretched combat conditions—and using primitive equipment often housed inside horse-drawn wagons used as darkrooms—Brady and his assistants took more than 3,500 photos of camp and battle scenes. The negatives, now stored in the Library of Congress, comprise an invaluable historical record.

Alfred Stieglitz pioneered the photograph as creative art; his pictures are regarded as among the most meaningful ever produced. In 1902, he and his associates, among them Edward Steichen, formed the Photo-Secession, a group active in promoting the artistic aspects of photography. Their "Family of Man" exhibit, shown in New York's Museum of Modern Art in 1955, is one of the most influential collections ever assembled.

Henri Cartier-Bresson, a French photographer, brilliantly employed the miniature camera to capture what he called "the decisive moments" in people's lives. Through his rare ability to record feelings and events, he exerted powerful influence on modern photojournalism in Europe as well as the United States.

Robert Capa packed a legendary career into a tragically short lifetime. Hungarian-born Capa established his reputation through daring, close-up combat photographs of the Spanish revolution. Later, his World War II pictures set new standards for courage under fire. The grim, vivid photographs Capa sent back from the combat zones of the world reflect his personal bravery, quick eye, sensitivity, determination, and leadership in the grim world of wartime photojournalism.

Margaret Bourke-White, the first accredited woman correspondent to see combat overseas in World War II, was one of the original staff of *Life* magazine. She survived aerial combat missions and a ship torpedoing, and gave U.S. audiences some of the most dramatic action photographs ever made.[10]

Many others have also molded the field. Jacob Riis was one of the first ever to use flash powder, and his dramatic photographs of the squalid New York slums during the 1890s led to housing reforms and more humane treatment of immigrants. Lewis W. Hine is believed to be the first to utilize the picture story as a journalistic form; his 1908 photo essays on coal miners and immigrants influenced enactment of several powerful social justice reform programs.[11] The tradition continues. In the 1980s and early 1990s, events in Latin America produced outstanding work from a number of resourceful and courageous U.S. photojournalists, men and women who won awards for their coverage of such important and dangerous stories as civil war in Nicaragua, a volcanic eruption in Colombia, famine victims in El Salvador and Somalia, and the poverty much of the world was living in.

Background

Show the class a few books on Civil War photography. (Perhaps the best is William C. Davis's six-volume series, *The Image of War,* which includes examples of photographs taken by photographers on both sides of the conflict.)

Photojournalism and the Community Newspaper

Subscribers like to *see* evidence of their community in action as well as read it. Here, from the young editors of the *Harvard Post*, are some tips for using photos to good advantage.

- Make it a goal to find and use at least one good photograph on your front page every issue. It doesn't have to depict a particular news event; a candid shot of a person in town or a seasonal landscape can add a nice touch to the front page.

- Try to avoid using too many photographs of people or groups of people simply standing and looking straight at

the camera. Encourage your photographers to catch people actually doing things.

- Use photographs that have a good range of tonal values, from white to black. Photographs that have a uniform tone of grey throughout, without much contrast, will be difficult for your printer to reproduce well. . . .

- You'll often find that scenes photographed from a low angle seem to produce better, more lively shots.

Editors of the *Harvard Post* (Harvard Common Press, 1978).

The Field Today

Contemporary photographic and publishing techniques—and audience expectations—combine to present attractive opportunities for today's photojournalists.

Teaching Idea

Assign students to bring weekly newspapers to class and examine their photos. Can they identify any differences between "feature" and "news" photos?

Community Newspapers

Today, virtually all country and suburban weeklies and small dailies are published by offset lithography, a procedure by which photographs can be reproduced inexpensively and with excellent fidelity. Thus a community journalist is usually expected to make good photography a part of the job in addition to writing the story. Many community newspapers now routinely publish thirty or more news and feature photographs per issue. The old country weekly proverb, "names make news," might be updated to "names *and faces* make news." Some young journalists hired onto community newspapers primarily as writers are dismayed to learn that they will be required to become proficient with the camera as well; later, they discover the photographic part of their work to be fully as creative and satisfying as the literary aspects. In any case, the news picture has become an integral part of the community newspaper, and both the publications and the audiences are better served as a result.

Metropolitan Dailies

On larger newspapers, photojournalism is more of a specialty. Photographers may work individually, moving in radio-equipped staff cars to report spot-news assignments such as fires, auto accidents, or crime stories. Or reporter-photographer teams may be assigned to cover important news events. Even when working alone, however, the photojournalist must double as both reporter and photographer, gathering full and accurate details needed to caption the news photos. Back at the office, the photojournalist must process the film, personally or with the aid of a photolab technician, and submit the best prints to various editors.

Most newspaper photographers can also expect a number of sports assignments. On some papers, sports is a top-of-the-line priority, and a good action shot of the local football team may well displace a routine news picture on page one. Remembering that at one time too many sports pictures consisted of posed groups or posed action, many editors embarked on determined efforts to increase the percentage of sports shots showing athletes in motion. Fast-film and sequence cameras have helped. The ideal sports photographer is not only a dedicated technician with lots of energy, but he or she also has a shrewd understanding of the flow of the contest and some keen insights about the players, coaches, officials, and fans. In sports photography, every moment is potentially "the decisive moment."

Newspapers also encourage photographers to take "enterprise" photos, that is, pictures of scenes they observe on their own, without an editor specifically assigning them. Many brilliant news and feature pictures owe their origins to hard-working, self-starting photojournalists who spotted a promising subject or situation and instinctively began taking pictures. Whether on duty or off, experienced photojournalists usually have their cameras with them.

Magazines

Less concerned with spot-news pictures, the magazine photographer may well spend weeks or even months on a single assignment, enough time for the magazine to show a dimension to the subject not available anyplace else. The photographer may shoot thousands of negatives, and top editors may review hundreds of prints, choosing perhaps only a handful to be published. Not all magazine photography is so elaborately conceived, however. Many of the photos are simply shots of one person passing an award to another, or two leaders shaking hands—"grips and grins," they are called. Most magazines employ only a handful of staff photographers; the largest picture magazine of them all, *Life,* at its peak had a photography staff numbering fewer than three dozen. The remainder of the pictures are supplied in large part by freelance photographers, men and women who work for no single company or publication but are free to sell pictures to any and all clients. Shrewd magazine editors cultivate a stable of trusted freelancers, competent professional photographers who can be relied upon to handle specific shooting assignments on a contract basis. Often freelancers themselves suggest the assignments, perhaps in queries much like those freelance writers make.

Wire Services and Picture Agencies

Picture agencies supply useful supplements to the efforts of newspaper and magazine photographers. They amass thousands of prints from staff photographers and freelancers, then sell the publication rights to newspapers, magazines, book publishers, and others. One of the largest of these agencies is Wide World Photos, established by the New York *Times* in 1919. Agencies such as this have in stock, or can quickly lay claim to, a selection of photographs needed to illustrate a given article or book chapter.

The Associated Press and other major wire services maintain photojournalism staffs to cover state, national, and world events and transmit their pictures to members or clients around the world. Electronic transmission of news pictures began in the 1920s, and the Associated Press launched its famous Wirephoto network in 1935. The first spot-news pictures transmitted in color—they showed President Roosevelt welcoming King George VI of England on a state visit to Washington—were sent in June 1939. Wire transmission made it possible for newspapers across the country to publish news pictures within minutes, gave news developments additional impact, and provided wire service photographers with national audiences.[12]

Associated Press and the Electronic Darkroom

At the heart of the [photojournalism] revolution is the **AP Leaf Picture Desk**, an electronic darkroom system—a color edit station and a file server—that combines state-of-the-art technology with unmatched economy. This remarkable machine performs all the conventional photo-handling tasks: size, crop, tone, touch up, and burn and dodge. It receives AP photos as well as those from other photo services. And, with an input scanner, it can handle your local photos too.

Best of all, the **AP Leaf Picture Desk** outputs images directly to pre-press and pagination systems.

In the United States, the **AP Leaf Picture Desk** is receiving **PhotoStream**, which delivers a black-and-white photo in 35 seconds and color in 1 minute and 45 seconds. Satellite transmissions are digital, preserving all the quality of the original photo.

What does this add up to? Fast delivery, high quality, ease of handling, direct output and cost savings for many newspapers.

AP Phototechnology, an Associated Press promotional brochure.

Advertising and Public Relations Photography

Creative directors, public relations managers, and account executives also rely heavily on freelancers to handle their photographic needs, which may be highly specialized. An expert in tabletop photography, as one of a bewildering number of possible examples, is of critical import in food advertising. Other photographers have developed particular talents for photographing heavy machinery, motel interiors, fashion models, mountain ranges, scientific experiments, engineering procedures, tropical beaches, tall buildings, or supersonic aircraft. Much public relations photography, on the other hand, consists of routine shots to illustrate press releases, corporate annual reports, employee newspapers and magazines, and the like. Again, freelancers, who may also operate portrait and general commercial photography studios, often produce pictures for public relations organizations.

Tools of the Trade

Most people can learn the basic skills of photography rather quickly. Focusing the camera, choosing exposure settings, developing the film, making enlargements and performing related procedures are not complicated, and most individuals can achieve minimal competence in short order. But early successes with photography, like success in building a simple birdhouse, can be misleading. Professionals set a

"See Only Through the Camera"

Early during the fighting in Tunisia, during World War II, photographer Eliot Elisofon of *Life* magazine wrote to his picture editor at *Life,* Wilson Hicks:

I have just finished my second attempt to photo a battle. The most important thing I have found is to see only through the camera. . . . Two days ago we were bombed too damn close at Sened. We had no foxholes and no time to run so Will [Lang, a writer for *Life*] and I flopped. I was on my back ready to photo hits near us, but when I saw the bombs come out and start right for us, I must admit I turned over, put my entire body under my helmet and said "Maybe this is it. . . ." Of course I missed a great picture of bombs coming to the camera. . . . My picture quality is going to stink. One of my cameras is jammed. I was changing lenses in a foxhole as some planes approached and a soldier slid into the hole, throwing sand into the open camera. . . . Some of my pix of American casualties . . . are enough to make any American fighting mad. . . . Plenty of blood, believe me. Too damn much. . . . I have not been able to photo from a tank. They will not allow one into battle with the window open, for which I cannot blame them.

Robert T. Elson, *The World of Time, Inc.* (Atheneum, 1973).

When the flash won't reach (or is not permitted), the photographer must use fast film and existing light.

A fast shutter speed (1/1000 sec.) "freezes" the action. A slower speed would blur the action.

high standard of excellence, not only in technical ability but in sustained superlative production. A snapshot is not usually a fine picture, just as a birdhouse is not usually superb carpentry. A photojournalist has much to learn.

Entire books have been written on the subject of *photographic lighting.* An underexposed negative can produce prints that are too dark, while an overexposed negative is so dense as to lose its medium tones and produces a flat or gray-looking print. Natural light can give the picture realism and candor. Artificial lighting, on the other hand, may be needed to produce good detail in difficult-to-capture situations where the existing light is low. Studio lighting—front, top, back, side, or fill—creates diverse effects, especially in portrait and product photography. A photojournalist must understand lighting.

A photojournalist must also understand the relationship between shutter speeds and *apertures (f/stops).* Faster shutter speeds, up to 1/4000th of a second on some modern cameras, "stop" action more precisely than a slower shutter speed. A shutter speed of 1/60th of a second will not stop most action; if the subject moves, the picture may blur. A speed of 1/125 may capture a slow-moving vehicle, while 1/1000 will usually capture an Indianapolis race car exceeding 200 mph on the straightaway.

Apertures help determine the overall clarity of the picture. As the lens opening becomes smaller, the zone of sharpness behind and in front of the subject becomes larger. This is called *depth of field.*

The combination of selected shutter speed and f/stop determines the *exposure* of the film. The photojournalist must understand the options available when setting the camera. Sometimes, to free action by using a fast shutter speed, the photojournalist must sacrifice depth of field. These decisions can be made only with a thorough understanding of the photographic process.

Still another variable lies in how the picture is edited, or **cropped.** The photographer can crop a photo, composing the picture in the viewfinder, or choosing one area of the negative to print from in the darkroom. The photo editor can also crop, simply trimming away unwanted portions of the picture. These methods all strive toward concentrating attention on one aspect of the picture. Most cropping is for esthetic reasons, to get rid of wasted space at the top, bottom, right, or left of the subject. But cropping can completely alter the meaning of a photograph. The old cliché "photographs don't lie" is not necessarily true if the proper context has been cropped out of the picture.

Cropping can completely alter the meaning of a photograph. Most cropping, however, is done for aesthetic reasons to eliminate wasted space and to focus on the strongest aspect of the picture.

All photographers are affected by these and a hundred other considerations, matters such as optics, color theory, and photographic processes, which in turn presuppose a certain familiarity with applicable physics and chemistry. Photojournalists must bring to their work certain other talents as well:

- *An understanding of news values.* There is a story, told in newsrooms for generations, about a cub photographer assigned to shoot a picture for the entertainment section to illustrate the opening of a local dramatic production. Upon his return to the newspaper office, someone asked the photographer when his prints will be ready. "Oh, I didn't shoot any," he explained. "Nothing happened. The building collapsed, so the performance was called off." That story is probably a bit too pat to be true, but it does make a point: The photojournalist cannot be merely an unthinking technician; he or she must know news and must react to newsworthy situations, with or without instructions to do so. Traditional criteria for news articles—immediacy, consequence, proximity, and conflict—apply with equal rigor to news photographs. The effective photojournalist is more than a photographer; he or she is a reporter with a camera, someone fully briefed on current events, on newsworthy personalities and situations, and is someone who knows what is of interest and important to the audience.

- *A feeling for the decisive moment.* No one can train a photojournalist precisely when to snap a picture. Recognition of the perfect opportunity, the split second referred to as "the decisive moment," comes only after trials and errors, a few lucky successes and many near misses, and the shooting of hundreds or thousands of pictures that *almost* caught an expression: a fleeting glance, an emotion, or the climax of an event. At this precise moment, the story is told best, and the shutter must be tripped. Yosuf Karsh, one of the world's great portrait photographers, explained his renowned sense of the decisive moment in a *Reader's Digest* article some years ago: "Within every man and woman a secret is hidden, and as a photographer it is my task to reveal it if I can. The revelation of it, if it comes at all, will come in a small fraction of a second with an unconscious gesture, a gleam of the eye, a brief lifting of the mask that all humans wear to conceal their innermost selves from the world. In that fleeting interval of opportunity the photographer must act or lose his prize."[13]

Rapid Technological Change

The mechanics of photographic communication have been simplified by a dramatic series of technological improvements. During the 1980s, camera companies introduced new models that offered still more automated features, such as automatic focusing and built-in electronic flash lighting. Improved lens attachments enhanced the photographer's ability to produce wide-angle, zoom, and other effects more quickly. Better sensitization processes made possible color film that was not only faster but provided richer tones and finer grain. Most far-reaching of all, however, are the opportunities—and the dilemmas—created by the introduction of computer technology to photographic communication.

Teaching Idea/Example

Ask a local camera store owner or manager to bring various types of modern cameras to class and explain their features. If a computerized camera and playback unit is available, so much the better.

Technological change—such as an improved lens attachment—can alter the outcome of a photograph. Here, a star filter provides an added effect.

Morphing: When Seeing Cannot Be Believing

Just as genes are being spliced into the fruits and vegetables we eat, so dazzling and strange new images are being seamlessly woven into the movies, video, and commercials we consume. Such modern cinematic processes, including "morphing," in which one image can be digitally changed into another by a computer, may turn out to be more than pleasing special effects.

The techniques are already changing the way products are sold and candidates are packaged. (Shall we make the President's eyes an honest, direct blue or go for a sexier blue-green?) But these same techniques are also subtly changing the nature of reality as experienced through moving images. . . .

It is now possible for the gorgeous models in a cosmetics ad to be made even more beautiful, or to take the bouncing blondes in a beer commercial and have their breasts enhanced, their waists and thighs narrowed. Ideal beauty, already considered an impossible standard by some, may be becoming literally impossible: the person in the ad doesn't exist.

Woody Hochswender, New York *Times,* 23 June 1992.

Discussion

Should the government set legal limits on the media's use of computer imaging?

Digital Imaging and the Ethical Problems It Poses

Still-video systems (SVS) came on the market in 1986 and are now widely available throughout the industry. These systems record images on magnetic disks, somewhat like those used in personal computers. As many as fifty images may be captured on a single disk, which is then inserted in a playback unit for immediate viewing on any television set, or run through a high-speed, electronic, full-color printer or transmitted over telephone lines to a distant newsroom computer. Once inside the publication's data system, the image can be transmitted, through pagination, directly to a plate to go on the press. In other words, this system can permit the photojournalist to bypass darkrooms and chemicals altogether.

Well beyond this, the photojournalist can alter the picture with great precision: A good technician can add or take away elements, change colors, or subtly or materially alter the entire scene. The storage discs used by still-video cameras can be used again and again, erased, and recorded over and over. *With this system, there is no equivalent of the original photographic negative.* As a result, the image changes can be done quickly, easily, and without detection: It is virtually impossible to discover whether an electronic image was recorded by a camera or enhanced by a computer.[14]

For the most part, photojournalists use such enhancements to make the photograph stronger and more attractive—adding a moon to a silhouette of a Western landscape, or, as *National Geographic* did on a famous cover shot from Egypt, moving two pyramids closer together,[15] orchestrating a photograph to suit esthetic or editorial needs. But other, far more sinister, possibilities exist as well: doctoring a photograph to place a political leader in a compromising position, for example, or fabricating what appears to be a conspiratorial meeting between two rival business leaders who have never met. The possibilities are endless. The belief that "cameras don't lie" now can be called into sharp question. Computer imaging of photographs can change our view of the reality we once found in photographic communication.

News at the Movies

Motion picture photography has been around since the late 1880s. Various inventors in Europe and America, notably Thomas Alva Edison, experimented with devices that made pictures appear to move. A breakthrough of major proportions occurred when another American, George Eastman, perfected a technique for producing flexible film. The new product replaced the glass plates previously used for fixing images and made it possible to record still pictures in quick succession. By the turn of the century, motion pictures, employing Edison's **kinetoscope** (a forerunner of the movie camera) and Eastman's film, were being exhibited around the country.

If Edison and Eastman were the technological midwives to the movie industry, a director, D. W. Griffith, was its founding artistic genius. Up to this point, films had been produced with camera and lights in fixed position, recording the scenes from a single point of view. Griffith changed this procedure completely. By moving cameras in and out, adding more cameras for different angles and new insights, and then editing to create drama and tempo and flashbacks in time, Griffith devised essential movie-making techniques that remain in use today.

Newsreels

As early as 1907, movie cameras in Europe were photographing current events; the film was then tightly edited into a brief **newsreel** to be shown in movie houses. A French entrepreneur, Charles Pathé, is believed to have shown the first newsreel in this country in 1911. In 1927, the year *The Jazz Singer* would usher in the era of "talkies," the movie industry ceased being merely an amusing diversion and, instead, became a prominent part of American life. Firmly affixed to the coattails of the feature films, these ten-minute newsreels also grew rapidly in popularity. Paramount ("The Eyes and Ears of the World"), Fox Movietone, Universal News, and other companies packaged slick, fast-moving film clips that fascinated movie audiences with action footage of natural disasters, sporting events, world leaders, celebrities, high fashion trends, and assorted news and feature pieces on a wide range of topics. Television news eventually blew away newsreels, but from the 1930s to the mid-1950s newsreels delighted and informed millions of Americans, showing them people and situations they would never have known much about otherwise. Newsreel photographers were especially effective during World War II; a number were honored for their bravery under fire.[16]

Documentaries

Not all movies were fiction. As early as the 1920s, some filmmakers devoted their talents to producing **documentaries,** movies that present factual information in a dramatic manner. Some early, powerful documentaries were produced under government auspices. *The Plow That Broke the Plains,* first shown in 1936, movingly depicted the Dust Bowl tragedies in the South and Midwest during the Depression years. *The River,* made the following year, showed the flood-swollen Tennessee River in a way that won public support for proposals to build hydroelectric dams for flood control and to bring electricity to a largely impoverished area. Government filmmakers also used movies during World War II for training purposes and to help civilians and military alike understand why the nation was at war. Shorter documentaries became a traditional part of the bill at many U.S. movie theaters during this period. One of the most successful efforts in this regard was *The March of Time,* a movie dimension of *Time* magazine. Using real events, but usually professional actors, this remarkable series provided U.S. moviegoers sharp, if sometimes biased and often controversial, interpretations of world figures and major events. Each episode closed with a line that became a part of the culture: "Time . . . marches on!" The hard-hitting, crisply edited series established a tradition that later characterized television documentaries.[17]

Suggested Audiovisual Aid

PBS Video has a very interesting documentary on newsreels, hosted by Bill Moyers.

Background

When television news began, TV networks and stations hired many of the newsreel camera operators, as videotape was not invented until much later. Many of the aggressive tactics of the newsreel people carry over into today's TV news.

Electronic Journalism

From a purely technical point of view, the electronic photojournalist shares many of the concerns of his or her counterpart in the print media: Both must know news values; both must have a feel for the decisive moment.

Like print photojournalists, television news photographers and the editors who supervise their work face the constant ethical problem posed by context. What best illustrates a news story? Is it the three hours of peaceful discussion, or the twenty seconds when the two city council members erupt into an angry shouting match? The obvious and understandable expectation is that both photographers and editors will opt for the confrontation; the routine is seldom newsworthy ("News from the airport: All the planes landed safely again today"). Television is by definition a visual medium, and the temptation to overplay action footage is at times irresistible. The situation is compounded by the severe shortage of available air time most stations face. A brisk, fast-moving news program, the kind that outside consultants often prescribe and audiences seem to prefer, may pack twenty to forty items into a few minutes of air time. Individual news stories must be cut, often to the bone. The action pictures remain, but their perspective and context may be slashed. All journalists face this problem, but television journalists find it particularly acute.

Television news photography remains an emerging discipline—the first coast-to-coast telecast, showing President Truman opening the Japanese Peace Treaty Conference in San Francisco, did not air until 1951—but spectacular achievements have been recorded. Nowhere was this more evident than during the Persian Gulf war, when gritty TV news photographers brought the horrors of combat into millions of American homes, at times keeping their cameras rolling when one or more SCUD missiles were known to be threatening the area, or, as was the case with a brave CNN crew, reporting the Allied air attack on Baghdad from a hotel room as missiles bombarded the city.[18] U.S. television audiences now routinely anticipate realistic, close-up reporting of virtually all news events, dangerous or not. Electronic photojournalists tend to be fiercely competitive individuals; they battle not only rival print media and other TV news operations but, perhaps most of all, their own rising expectations and performance standards.

Dramatic technical innovations have helped. **Electronic newsgathering equipment (ENG),** especially the minicam (a lightweight, portable camera), permits TV journalists to send live pictures to the station directly from the scene. In addition to having a built-in microwave transmitter, the minicam utilizes videotape, which, unlike film, needs no processing. Some television stations in 1994 successfully implemented digital technology that permitted them to bypass videotape altogether. These features give TV field reporters greater flexibility—though there is the risk (as happened on occasion during the Persian Gulf war), when live, unedited footage goes directly on the air, that audiences could easily be misled by the lack of explanation and context. What a newscast might gain in immediacy it could lose in an overemphasis on the dramatic without an accompanying sense of perspective.[19]

Career Opportunities

News photographers for both print and electronic media tend to be creative, self-starting individuals with the capacity for sustained hard work. Hours are wildly unpredictable; spot news does not always break within the normal nine-to-five workday. The professional photojournalist must be prepared to react quickly in crisis situations and must be assertive enough to obtain top-quality pictures under often less-than-ideal conditions. This does not mean that news photographers are required to be pushy and rude, though some are, and this stereotype is often the one the public sees. But the photojournalist is not often passive. The photojournalism field is highly popular, and competition for positions, especially on larger newspapers and television operations, is keen.

News photographers with leadership ability can move into editorships, supervising not just other photographers but, in some cases, entire news operations. A heightened interest in graphic design also has conferred improved status upon photographers. Often picked from the ranks of photographers, graphics editors possess considerable stature on many large newspapers and on virtually all magazines.

On community papers, acquired photographic skills make news reporters more effective. Photography can develop the senses; by merely focusing a lens on a scene—even without snapping the shutter—the photographer stretches his or her awareness of the scene, looking and feeling and living that moment in a special way.

....

summary

Photojournalism—combining pictures and words to convey information—has added a vital dimension to the news, and audiences now want to be shown as well as told what is happening around them. Skilled, courageous, and highly professional photojournalists roam the world in search of the news and feature pictures we have come to expect as a matter of course.

Photojournalism is a creative activity requiring careful use of such variables as lighting, shutter speeds, and cropping. The most successful photojournalists have a keen sense of timing and a feel for the decisive moment in shooting a picture.

Electronic photojournalists, working for television stations and networks, have likewise evolved into skilled, competitive individuals, battling not only rival print media and other TV news operations, but their own rising expectations and performance standards as well.

Technological change has given photojournalists another tool, electronic processing. Through digital imaging—including computer retouching—photographers can dramatically alter pictures. Indeed, they can change photographs easily (and virtually without detection) to reflect something other than what the camera actually saw. With this system, there is no equivalent of the original photographic negative, and the old phrase "cameras don't lie" can now be called into sharp question. While the industry has welcomed digital imaging, its possible impact on news values and photojournalism ethics is not yet clear.

....

? questions and cases

1. Discuss events and situations that are contrived (or staged) for the cameras—photo opportunities, ceremonies, presentations ("grips and grins"), and the like. Are such pseudoevents necessarily bad? What guidelines should editors use in deciding whether to cover them?

2. Assume that you and a fellow photojournalist are contacted by an obviously distraught individual who threatens, as a protest against unemployment, to set himself on fire. He douses his clothes with lighter fluid, then touches off the blaze with a match—while your camera is running. What would you do? (This actually happened, in March 1983. The photographers kept filming for more than half a minute before one of them tried to put out the fire. The victim, an unemployed laborer, suffered severe burns over more than half his body. The photographers contended they thought the event was a stunt staged for their benefit and that they were unaware the man's life was in jeopardy.)

3. To what extent do you believe that photojournalism distorts reality? Discuss the ethical implications of electronic imaging, enhancing a photograph to make it more appealing. Are such enhancements ever justified?

4. Cite examples of situations when you believe photojournalists have invaded the personal privacy of news sources, persons you read about in print and watch on television. Suggest how these photojournalists might have covered such stories differently.

chapter glossary

crop   To trim an illustration in order to emphasize certain aspects of it and/or to eliminate nonessential background.

cut   A piece of art, usually a photograph, ready for printing.

documentary   A nonfiction TV program or film that reconstructs events that actually happened, though often with artistic embellishments.

ENG   Electronic newsgathering equipment, such as minicams and microwave relays, that greatly enhances the capability of TV journalists to present live pictures from the scene.

engraving   Cutting a design in metal for purposes of printing an illustration or type. After engraving, the printing plate has a raised surface, which can be inked and printed.

halftone   A photoengraving, photographed through a screen that breaks up the image into tiny dots, thus creating the effect of halftone values between black and white.

kinetoscope   First workable motion picture camera, invented about 1887. Some historians credit Thomas Edison with creating the device, others say the honor should go to his assistant, William K. L. Dickson.

newsreel   A brief motion picture, usually shown in movie houses along with feature films, depicting current events.

notes

1 Frank Luther Mott, *American Journalism* (New York: Macmillan, 1962), 54.

2 Ibid., 44.

3 Edwin Emery and Michael Emery, *The Press and America,* 5th ed. (Englewood Cliffs, N. J.: Prentice-Hall, 1984), 204.

4 Time-Life Books, *Photojournalism* (New York: Time-Life Books, 1971), 13.

5 Mott, *American Journalism,* 54.

6 Time-Life, *Photojournalism,* 16. See also Craig T. Norback and Melvin Gray, eds., *The World's Great News Photos, 1840–1980* (New York: Crown Publishers, 1980), 1–34.

7 William H. Taft, *American Journalism History: An Outline* (Columbia, Mo.: Lucas Brothers Publishers, 1962), 54; and Time-Life, *Photojournalism,* 15.

8 Emery and Emery, *The Press and America,* 462. See also Arthur Rothstein, *Photojournalism* (New York: American Photographic Book Publishing, 1956), 2–6.

9 The most copious history of *Life* magazine is Robert T. Elson's *The World of Time, Inc.,* vols. 1–2 (New York: Atheneum, 1968, 1973). Volume 1, which covers the period from 1923 to 1941, details the magazine's founding.

10 Alfred Eisenstaedt, *Witness to Our Time* (New York: Viking, 1966), 3; see also Rothstein, *Photojournalism,* 62–116.

11 Norback and Gray, *World's Great News Photos,* 45.

12 Oliver Grambling, *AP: The Story of News* (New York: Farrar and Rinehart, 1940), 381–97; 419–22.

13 Reprinted in *The Reader's Digest Dictionary of Quotations* (New York: Funk and Wagnalls, 1968), 231.

14 Fred Ritchin, *In Our Own Image: The Coming Revolution in Photography* (New York: Aperture Foundation, 1990), 5–17. See also Andy Grundberg, "Ask It No Questions: The Camera Can Lie," New York *Times,* 12 August 1990.

15 *National Geographic,* February 1982, front cover.

16 Emery and Emery, *The Press and America,* 456–58.

17 Elson, *World of Time, Inc.,* 253–68.

18 "History as It Happens," *Time,* 6 January 1992, 24.

19 Ibid.

chapter

G

Magazines

An interviewer in 1962 asked Henry Luce, who had founded Time nearly half a century earlier, about allegations that the magazine he produced was politically biased. Perhaps the interviewer was seeking a righteous

Objectives

When you have finished studying this chapter, you should be able to:

- Discuss the sense of personal involvement audiences feel with the magazines they read

- Explain how the magazine industry developed and how magazine staffs function today

- Outline recent changes in the nature of the industry, especially niche marketing to increasingly fragmented audiences

- Explain how the industry is organized and the various categories by which magazines are classified

- Analyze current industry trends, especially the use of computers in graphic design and in targeting audiences

- Discuss some of the possibilities—and difficulties—freelance writers face

An interviewer in 1962 asked Henry Luce, who had founded *Time* nearly half a century earlier, about allegations that the magazine he produced was politically biased. Perhaps the interviewer was seeking a righteous denial, but one was not forthcoming. "I am a Protestant and a free enterpriser," Luce replied coldly, "which means that I am biased in favor of God, Eisenhower, and the stockholders of Time, Inc., and if anyone who objects doesn't know this by now, why the hell are they still spending thirty-five cents for the magazine?"[1]

Time's editorial position has shifted somewhat to the left since then, and each copy now costs considerably more than thirty-five cents, but Luce's point remains valid: A magazine, more than any other medium of mass communications, can be a highly personal work. An individual or a very small group of people usually launch a magazine to give form to an idea that burns deep inside. The radical visionary John Reed unleashed *The Masses* in a determined attempt to remake our social and political structure. Henry Luce and another then-recent graduate of Yale, Britton Hadden, began what would become the vast publishing empire of Time, Inc., confident that they had discovered a new way to report current events. When DeWitt Wallace, the son of a Presbyterian minister, was wounded during World War I, he whiled away his convalescent hours reading, then rewriting and trimming articles from magazines he found in the hospital day room. He and his bride-to-be, Lila Bell Acheson, borrowed $5,000 in 1921 to start a magazine that would present "condensed articles of permanent and popular interest" culled from the country's other magazines. They spent their wedding day mailing out circulars for charter subscribers to their experimental publication, which they named the *Reader's Digest*.[2]

These magazines and thousands of others that have come and gone shape our culture as well as our individual personalities. They tell us how other Americans live, think, behave, and dress. Magazines reflect our tastes and often anticipate them, helping us grow and change. We, in return, have involved ourselves more intimately with magazines than with any other form of mass communications. A newspaper or television network must gather its audience through broad appeal. A magazine, in contrast, might attract only those who have a special interest in skiing, fishing, women's fashions, needlepoint, conservative politics, or foreign travel. The magazine may not command a wide following, but its audience is likely to be knowledgeable about the subject and enthusiastic about the publication. The **Magazine Publishers Association** can cite authoritative studies suggesting that more than nine out of every ten readers *react* to their magazines in some tangible manner—clipping out an ad, a coupon, or an article; sending for a product or information advertised in the magazine pages; cutting out and/or using a recipe. Magazines, in short, reach out to their audiences in a special way.

Teaching Idea

Assign students to visit a newsstand and count (1) how many magazines relate to their hobby or avocation and (2) how many total magazines the newsstand carries. Discuss the results in class.

One Magazine's Philosophy

The personality and character of each magazine is different. Here is an editorial profile of one:

The *Reader's Digest* is not things which it does not pretend to be. It does not go into exhaustive detail on any subject. It is not often analytical. It is not bitter or cynical or superior, or up-to-the-minute with its news and interpretations of the news, or even splendidly pictorial. . . . Millions of readers, consciously or unconsciously, recognize these as characteristics they know and share. They are sometimes afraid and want to be brave. They are depressed and want to be cheered. They worry about sex, fear it, exult in it. They hope. They relish the humor in life when they can find it. They hate unfairness and resent the abuse of the weak by the strong. They like miracles and thrill to high adventure. They have a high regard for facts. . . .

The *Reader's Digest* does not reach its world audience . . . by being profound, esoteric, and difficult to understand, or by espousing unpopular causes or adopting viewpoints either outmoded or too far advanced. . . . It reaches it partly through the compression that means that only the high points of a discussion can be presented, and these set forth in black and white clarity.

James Playsted Wood, *Of Lasting Interest: The Story of The Reader's Digest* (Doubleday, 1967).

Magazines of all kinds continue to enter the market, catering to virtually every conceivable reader need or interest. More than 500 new titles are launched each year, more than one new magazine a day. Many do not survive. Others grow old and die, their vitality often connected to the life cycle of the founder and the founder's idea. Despite the attrition, however, the magazine field keeps on growing. In the early 1990s, some 12,000 different magazines were published in the United States, an increase of more than a thousand over the previous decade. Eighty-eight percent of adult Americans read magazines, each buying an average of thirty-six copies a year. Despite economic hard times and a few well-publicized magazine failures, the industry grows, with new magazine starts exceeding magazine closings. Total magazine circulation has nearly doubled in the last ten years, and publishers head for the new century armed with statistics showing that magazines can deliver highly targeted, quality audiences with more product-purchasing power than any other mass media.[3]

How the Field Developed

Benjamin Franklin, responsible for so much in the national experience, planned to publish the first magazine in the colonies. In Philadelphia, a rival printer named Andrew Bradford got wind of Franklin's idea and was able to beat him, in February 1741, with the *American Magazine*. Franklin's *General Magazine* appeared three days later, although neither magazine lasted a year. Like the newspapers, these and other pioneer magazines were heavily influenced by British publications in that they carried literary pieces, poetry, and political commentary. Isaiah Thomas, the extraordinary newspaper publisher and revolutionary leader in New England, carried the first magazine engravings in the pages of his *Massachusetts*.

Publishers had founded more than three hundred magazines in the United States by 1830. Most of them represented literary, abolitionist, temperance, or other movements. Rarely were enough readers sufficiently interested, or sufficiently prosperous, to give a publisher a dependable economic base, and as a consequence the magazine mortality rate was high. A few pre–Civil War publications, however, had genuine impact. One was New York's *Knickerbocker Magazine,* which printed the

Teaching Idea

Assign students to look through several different dictionaries (OED if possible), abridged and unabridged, for definitions of the word *magazine*. Your class may be surprised at the results.

Want to Start a Magazine? Beware the Pitfalls

Success in launching a new publication or entering a new market depends on many factors, including effective market analysis, hard work, good luck, smart timing, and sufficient capital. But it also depends on avoiding common mistakes that have hampered—and sometimes torpedoed—other magazine launches:

- Choosing the wrong editor.

- Assuming effort is equal to size. In truth, it takes almost as much effort and oversight to plan and start a small magazine (though usually less investment) as it does to launch a large one.

- Too high a frequency, which puts pressure on the staff to produce the next issues, without time to consider feedback, read results, or correct mistakes.

- Believing there's not competition. It's important to recognize that there's always competition—if not with another magazine, then for people's time and money.

Barrie J. Atkin, "New Market Smarts for Publishers," *Folio,* 1 June 1993.

Women and the Golden Age of Magazines

Another development in this [nineteenth century] golden age of magazines was the rapid rise of periodicals for women. Earlier attempts to reach this audience were dwarfed by the giants which now arose, challenging the general magazines and arousing not only their competitive antagonism but also the ire of those who thought it preposterous to serve women with magazines at all. Charles A. Dana, soon to be one of the most famous of newspaper publishers, deplored in the *Harbinger* for August 8, 1846, the assumption these magazines "constantly put forth of being designed for *ladies*, and of representing in some way the women of the country. . . . Heaven protect us from such literature!"

While feminists today would agree with Dana, the women for whom the new magazines were intended disagreed. Some of the material offered them was appallingly bad, but there was plenty of good reading, too, and they were delighted with the idea of large, well-printed magazines directed especially at them.

John Tebbel, *The Media in America* (Crowell, 1974).

works of such writers as William Cullen Bryant, Washington Irving, Henry Wadsworth Longfellow, and John Greenleaf Whittier. Its counterpart in Richmond was the *Southern Literary Messenger,* which Edgar Allan Poe edited for a time. *The Dial* in Boston articulated the Transcendentalist philosophy of such brilliant writers as Ralph Waldo Emerson and Margaret Fuller. *Godey's Lady's Book,* with its fashion and household hint departments and its quiet but persuasive crusades for women's rights, became the forerunner of the modern women's magazine.[4]

The years after the Civil War turned out to be a golden era for the magazine industry. Railroads linked the country together, giving magazine publishers, for the first time, a sporting chance to cultivate national audiences and national advertisers. Improved literacy and an expanded middle class meant more Americans were intellectually curious, and more could afford the price of a magazine subscription. Perhaps most important of all, as Theodore Peterson points out in his definitive *Magazines in the Twentieth Century,* Congress in 1879 stimulated the growth of periodicals by enacting a provision for mailing them at low cost.[5] *The Nation* was founded during this period, as were *Scribner's Monthly, Smart Set, Harper's Bazaar, Collier's,* and the *Ladies' Home Journal.* Great editors emerged: Edwin L. Godkin of *The Nation,* Edward Bok of the *Journal* and the *Saturday Evening Post,* Bret Harte of *Overland Monthly,* young H. L. Mencken of *Smart Set.*

Just after the turn of the century, a handful of influential magazines published lengthy investigative pieces which exposed wrongdoings in both business and government. Abuses of corporate monopoly, insurance frauds, collusions between employers and union leaders, big-city bossism—writers ventilated these and other social ills on the pages of *McClure's, Munsey's, Cosmopolitan,* and similar hard-hitting magazines. Many of these pieces were brilliantly researched, and they achieved impressive results. For example, Lincoln Steffens, one of the most famous magazine writers of this period, wrote a series entitled "The Shame of the Cities," in which he attacked municipal corruption in Chicago, Minneapolis, New York, Philadelphia, Pittsburgh, and other cities. Following these exposés, good-government groups formed, new officials were elected, and many of the old political machines were destroyed—though, obviously, some resurfaced later. These aggressive, idealistic journalists became known as "muckrakers," and their reporting efforts were widely thought to have helped create a political climate in which progressive legislation was enacted and reform-minded political leaders were able to win local and national elections.[6] Some scholars believe that environmentalism and comparable public interest movements of the 1990s have their spiritual and intellectual roots in the crusading magazine journalism of the muckraking period.

Extra Information

Ask students to visit the local post office and find out how much it costs to mail magazines, newspapers, and other printed matter. Do nonprofit magazines receive different rates?

Teaching Idea

Assign students to read some of the articles early magazine muckrakers wrote, and report to the class. Do any of the problems these early writers dug up still exist today?

PITTSBURG: A CITY ASHAMED

McCLURE'S MAGAZINE

MAY

LINCOLN STEFFENS'S exposure of another type of municipal grafting; how Pittsburg differs from St. Louis and Minneapolis.

THE END OF THE WORLD, by Professor Newcomb. A powerful story, yet a scientific prediction; pictures by the famous French artist, Henri Lanos.

IDA M. TARBELL on the Standard tactics which brought on the famous oil crisis of 1878.

SIX SHORT STORIES

PUBLISHED MONTHLY BY THE S.S. McCLURE CO., 141-155 E. 25th ST., NEW YORK CITY

Most famous of the muckraking magazines was *McClure's*. In this famous 1903 issue ran famous investigatory pieces by Lincoln Steffens and Ida M. Tarbell.

Teaching Idea

Ask students to bring sample copies of their favorite slicks and pulps to class. Compare differences in paper quality and content.

Muckraking hit its peak about 1906. In the years that followed, the country seemed to tire of internal reform. World War I's aftermath brought a flock of new magazines representing a more cosmopolitan spirit. The *New Yorker,* founded in 1925, offered a satirical, urbane look at the happenings of the day. *Time,* a rousing success almost from its first issue in 1923, paved the way for others in the newsmagazine field. *Reader's Digest,* with 1,500 charter subscribers responding to the Wallaces' circular, became the largest-selling magazine in the world; its worldwide circulation reached 28 million and each edition was printed in sixteen languages. The *Saturday Evening Post,* an effective blending of light fiction, humor, and highly readable reporting, at one point reached millions of homes each week. So did *Life,* a fabulously successful picture-oriented magazine Luce started in 1936. Women's magazines, notably *McCall's, Good Housekeeping,* and the *Ladies' Home Journal,* also saw their circulation figures and advertising incomes soar.[7]

The years after World War I were good for well-produced mass-audience magazines. Within the trade, these were known as *slicks*—a reference to the high-quality paper they were printed on—as contrasted with some western, detective, adventure, and/or confessions magazines called *pulps.*

The Boom Ends—for Some

After World War II the slicks' premier position in national advertising came under massive challenge from the new medium of television.

A commercial on a hit network program might reach more potential customers than a full-page ad in a slick magazine, and the TV commercial could demonstrate the product as well as merely describe it. Television grew at a spectacular pace, and much of the growth came at the expense of ad revenues drained away from the lavish national magazines. The slicks were particularly vulnerable because almost every copy sold for less money than it cost to produce and distribute it. Publishers depended on advertising dollars to make up the difference.

Attempting to match television's huge audience increases, many national magazines embarked on expensive promotional campaigns to attract new subscribers. By the early 1960s, magazines had lowered their prices so much that readers were contributing only a small fraction of the publication cost. *Life,* at one point during this period, was selling for nineteen cents a copy. These promotional efforts siphoned off profits. Worse still, the new subscribers had to receive their copies of the magazine right away, often before advertising space could be sold at the higher rates.

Magazine advertising charges are based, to a very great extent, on a publication's *circulation guarantee*—that is, the number of copies that will be sold. The larger the guarantee, the higher the charge per ad. Publishers invariably deliver more copies than they guarantee, allowing a fair-sized cushion in case business should drop suddenly. When the magazine consistently exceeds its guarantee, the publisher will raise ad rates for the future. But there are times when a magazine's increased circulation—again, following a costly promotional effort—runs too far ahead, that is, before the magazine obtains new advertisers and before it renegotiates old advertising contracts. Eventually the situation should correct itself, but the magazine publisher may face a cash flow crisis until it does.

This, among other factors, contributed to dramatic changes in the magazine industry during the 1960s. Several of the biggest slicks—the *Saturday Evening Post, Collier's, Life,* and *Look* among them—closed outright or became shadows of their former selves. Ironically, most of the magazines that folded did so at a time when they had attained their largest circulations. Other magazines that had appealed to broad general audiences shrewdly repositioned toward a narrower, but potentially more loyal, segment of the market. *Redbook,* for instance, successfully took aim at what it called "young marrieds," and *Cosmopolitan,* whose motto was once "The world is my country and all mankind are my countrymen," now sought an audience consisting largely of single women.

By the early 1970s, publishers had assessed the economic damage and embarked on two new strategies: (1) trim away waste or marginal circulation and (2) begin raising the price to the consumer. The single copy price of *McCall's,* 50 cents in 1969, had climbed to $1.50 in 1994; *Time,* meanwhile, rose from 25 cents a copy to $2.95 during that same period. Like other industry giants, *McCall's* and *Time* were readjusting the income formula: While readers were paying 10 to 15 percent of the total costs a generation ago and advertisers paid the remaining 85 to 90 percent, today's readers and advertisers provide the revenue in roughly equal amounts.

Television not only grabbed the bigger audiences, it busily replaced the main function general-interest magazines traditionally served—entertainment. In 1948, for example, the *Saturday Evening Post* usually ran four or five short stories and two serials per issue, plus a number of light, relatively superficial articles. Television could provide more—if not necessarily better—entertainment, faster and cheaper. General-interest magazines were forced to dig deeper than television—with probing investigative articles, for example—and to rethink their entire philosophy about reaching the mass audience.

But while the giants were realigning themselves, smaller and more specialized magazines prospered. They went after personalized shares of the total market, a market that network television could often reach only at the most superficial level. No longer a handful of general-interest publications attempting to be of universal appeal, dominate the magazine field. Instead, the industry now reflects a rich diversity of magazines that may serve relatively fewer readers each but will almost certainly know those readers better.

The Industry Today

Magazines are classified by frequency of publication, and, more important, function. Some of the functional categories include consumer magazines, businesspapers, company publications, and newsletters.[8]

Consumer Magazines

These are the publications one sees on the newsstands, magazines aimed at audiences that buy products for personal use. This is the best-known category, though not the largest, and it comprises numerous subgroups:

- *General-interest magazines,* such as *Reader's Digest, People, TV Guide,* and the *National Enquirer,* which appeal to across-the-board circulation groups.
- *Newsmagazines,* including *Time, Newsweek,* and *U.S. News & World Report.*
- *Shelter magazines,* such as *Better Homes & Gardens,* which are involved with family living.
- *Men's magazines,* including the outdoor and sports magazines *(Field and Stream, Sports Illustrated)* and the "urbane and sophisticated" magazines *(Esquire, Playboy, Penthouse).*
- *Women's magazines,* including the fashion magazines *(Vogue, Glamour),* traditional leaders *(McCall's* and *Good Housekeeping),* magazines for women who work outside the home *(Ms., Savvy, Working Woman, Working Mother).*

Class Project

What back copies of major magazines are kept in your institution's library? Have students chart price increases for some of them during the past twenty (or, if possible, fifty) years.

Teaching Idea

Ask students to compile examples of magazines in each category that your institution's library carries. What audience does each intend to reach?

Teaching Idea

If the library carries back issues of the *Reader's Digest,* ask one or more students to chart changes over time in this popular magazine. When did it begin accepting advertising? What percentage of articles were abridged (condensed) from other publications, and how many were staff-written both now and in past years? Editorial writers for the *RD* may have articles published in other magazines, then reprinted in the *RD.* Can your students find any examples?

One of journalism's premier
showcases: the cover of *Time*.

- "Class" magazines for select or special interest audiences (*Atlantic, National Geographic, Harper's*).
- Farm publications, such as *Successful Farming* and *Farm Journal*.
- Topical magazines, such as *Scientific American, Catholic Digest, Ebony,* and a raft of others.

Industry leaders and advertisers would add far more categories than we can discuss here, among them travel magazines, in-flight publications, city magazines, magazines for teenagers and magazines for retired people, a classification that includes the massively successful *Modern Maturity* and the *American Association of Retired Persons' Bulletin*. Even within each category, considerable distinctions exist; *Esquire*'s audience differs from *Playboy*'s, and both are hugely unlike the readers of *Penthouse* and *Hustler*.

table 1   The Top 25 Magazines' Circulation*

Rank	Magazine	Circulation
1	Modern Maturity	22,450,000
2	NRTA/AARP Bulletin	22,174,021
3	Reader's Digest	16,306,007
4	TV Guide	15,353,982
5	National Geographic	9,921,479
6	Better Homes and Gardens	8,003,263
7	Family Circle	5,151,534
8	Good Housekeeping	5,028,151
9	McCall's	5,009,358
10	Ladies' Home Journal	5,002,900
11	Woman's Day	4,751,977
12	Time	4,248,565
13	Redbook	3,841,866
14	National Enquirer	3,706,030
15	Playboy	3,498,802
16	Sports Illustrated	3,444,188
17	Newsweek	3,420,167
18	People	3,235,120
19	Star	3,207,951
20	Prevention	3,109,562
21	The American Legion Magazine	2,984,389
22	Cosmopolitan	2,679,356
23	First for Women	2,393,722
24	Southern Living	2,385,058
25	U.S. News & World Report	2,351,922

Source: Used with permission of Magazine Publishers of America.

*As of 1 July 1991; subscription and single copy sales combined

Circulations of consumer magazines can be enormous (table 1). *Modern Maturity,* for persons fifty years of age and older, in the early 1990s enjoyed a circulation of well over 20 million; so did *Parade,* a supplement to Sunday newspapers regarded as a magazine. The U.S. edition of *Reader's Digest* and *TV Guide* averaged over 15 million, while *National Geographic* neared the 10 million mark.

Important as it is, raw circulation may not be as decisive to a prospective advertiser as total audience. In the vigorously competitive women's magazine field, for example, *Good Housekeeping* traditionally has enjoyed the highest number of readers per copy, and thus the lowest advertising cost per thousand. The situation can be much like a horse race, where one is twelve lengths ahead and the others are scrambling for place and show. *McCall's* recently had 4.5 million circulation and *Good Housekeeping* only 3.7 million, but *Good Housekeeping* could still claim the larger

Teaching Idea

Obtain current circulation figures for the top 100 magazines from the Magazine Publishers Association. Before showing them to your class, ask the class what magazines *they* think would be among the top 10, 20, or 30. The results may surprise them.

The business press. Trade journals comprise a most important segment of the magazine industry. Though the general public might be unaware of the business press, executives in all lines of work rely on trade journals to keep abreast of developments in their field.

overall audience. Total audience figures, as measured by Simmons and other research firms, probably account for advertising rates and sales as much as or more than guaranteed circulation.

Businesspapers

This is larger, in terms of numbers of magazines, than the consumer field, and in recent years has been the fastest-growing segment of the industry. While business publications such as *Forbes, Fortune,* and *Business Week* enjoy national popularity, most—and there are more than three thousand different titles—are designed to serve highly specialized audiences within a particular trade or profession. As Stanley H. Slom, editor of *Chain Store Age Executive,* points out:

> For years we in business and trade journalism were sort of third cousins to the consumer press, but more and more the differences are blurring. We expect the same ethics and objectivity of our reporters and editors as do consumer publications. We do interpretative reporting, as does the consumer press. Probably the biggest difference is that the audience for the business and trade press is more expert at what they do than the general public so our reporters and editors have to be more exact at what they see and write.[9]

The Business Press Educational Foundation can point to numerous award-winning investigative reports, information-packed trend and roundup pieces, and human interest stories that any editor would be proud to publish. Following are three examples:

- "Inside Japan," in *Automotive Industries,* toured Japanese automobile factories, comparing them with their U.S. counterparts. The conclusion: Japan's secret weapon is not better technology or more robots, but more efficient use of resources.
- "The Right to Die," in *Nursing Life* magazine, probed the feelings of nurses and patients' relatives on this highly emotional issue.

Class Project
Assign students to visit your institution's library and see how many nonconsumer magazines it carries. How many are mass-media related?

- "The Counterfeiting of America and Elsewhere" is an exposé in the *Commercial Carrier Journal* of the flood of copycat, fake merchandise pouring into the United States from the Far East. Posing as New York businesspeople, two *CCJ* editors traveled thousands of miles, to Hong Kong, Singapore, and Taiwan, as well as to the Chinatowns in large U.S. cities, on the trail of the purveyors and financiers of counterfeit products.[10]

Virtually every trade or professional association or industrial group has at least one magazine to provide news and other useful information about new products and services, management innovations, labor relations, corporate strategies, legal problems, personnel profiles, and so on. The bigger business publications provide international coverage and maintain bureaus in Washington to report on pending legislation, pertinent decisions of courts and regulatory agencies, Congressional trends, and other matters of importance to a given business audience.

Company Publications

In terms of numbers of titles, this is by far the largest segment of the industry. Members of the International Association of Business Communicators alone—and they comprise only a fraction of the total—in one recent year produced on a regular basis an estimated 28,660 external and internal publications. These had a combined circulation conservatively estimated at more than 300 million, about four-and-a-half times the circulation of all the daily newspapers in the United States and Canada.[11]

External publications are company magazines commercial organizations produce for their customers, prospective customers, friends, suppliers, and users of their products. Circulations vary from a few thousand to half a million or more. These magazines feature successful case histories and how-to articles; often, especially in the fast-breaking electronics field, the magazines help customers keep abreast of new developments. At General Electric, for example, each division produces a customer magazine; the Industrial Power Systems Division publication is aimed at engineers and other key executives, and its content focuses on state-of-the-art developments. Mobil Oil sends its dealers a handsomely produced magazine on coated paper, with illustrations in full color, filled with management tips and money-making ideas. Other company externals adopt an institutional approach, using their company magazines as a soft-sell public relations exercise to build good will among customers and prospects.[12]

Internal publications, as the name suggests, are primarily for employees. They attempt to build morale, to present the company and its policies and products in an appealing way, to recognize employee achievement, and to promote a sense of corporate teamwork. Often called *house organs,* these magazines range from homely to lavish. They continue to improve, reflecting top management's appreciation of their public relations value and a heightened professionalism among their editors.

Newsletters

Somewhat outside our scope here, but worthy of mention, are newsletters—the oldest of the print media and, in recent years, the most resurgent. Two factors have combined to account for the astonishing growth in the newsletter industry:

- *A need for quick information.* Because of the complexity of business and government, where so much happens so rapidly, swift, expert media can explain the latest developments for selected audiences. Publishers can produce these newsletters, typically four to twelve pages, quickly and cheaply, although some humble-looking newsletters may carry a price tag of several hundred dollars a year; these highly specialized insider publications serve such industries as petroleum, aerospace, financial analysis, and electronics. The subscriber pays for the information, not necessarily the literary style or production values.

- *Technological improvements in production and targeting specific audiences.* The computer not only permits rapid typesetting, including graphic effects; it also can store vast databases, which in turn provide automated mailing lists and precise identification of selected readers.

Many newsletters are like small, folded magazines on special topics. The *Oxbridge Dictionary of Newsletters* lists about 14,000 titles, and these represent only the commercial ventures, a relatively small share of the total field. Add to that the many thousands of newsletters churches, schools, clubs, and other non-profit organizations publish, and the newsletter becomes the most pervasive mass communications print medium of them all.

Current Trends

After some rocky going during the recession of the early 1990s, consumer magazines were recovering nicely and industry leaders were predicting steady long-term growth for the foreseeable future. Substantial increases in production and distribution costs, and especially in postal rates, caused higher subscription and single copy charges. These increases, for many publications, affected circulation; single copy sales in the early 1990s slipped somewhat, presumably in response to the steep price increases. On the other hand, numbers of subscriptions—and subscriptions account for about 80 percent of all magazine sales—continued to increase. The long-term industry outlook, based on hopes for new gains in personal disposable income and predictions that nationwide educational levels will continue to improve, remains upbeat.

In the meantime, buzzwords such as *micromarketing, target marketing,* and *niche marketing* characterize the pitches of magazine industry sales reps. These terms describe an industry attempting to make more out of less, to be more precise and more effective in communicating with a viable segment within an increasingly fragmented total market. In 1993, as an example, the number of new automobile models was 50 percent higher than five years previously. In the food industry, total sales increase by less than 1 percent a year, yet nearly 7,500 new food products appear annually. As reader interests and product availabilities change, new magazines—or old magazines with new ideas—arise to address them. Magazine publishers pride themselves on offering attractive options in targeting and reaching tightly defined market segments.

Magazines on Demand

"Contract Publishing" is another element in communications programs to be accelerated by database identifications of highly involved target audiences.

Certainly special editions are not new to magazines. But publishers today can also create market-driven magazines on contracts for marketers with "captive" or special-interest target audiences. These can range from the employees of a large corporation to the owners of a type of automobile—or simply to readers interested in an event. . . . And customized binding will allow editors and advertisers alike to address specific groups within a magazine's circulation, matching a marketer's database with that of the magazine.

The 90s: The Smarter Decade, promotional material from the Magazine Publishers of America.

Growth, Change, and Technology

In what ways has the [magazine] business gotten better?

The explosion of international travel and communications, and the world's exposure to different cultures—all those developments spawned new magazines. And, as it turned out, the very technology that was to replace print (technology, computers, etc.) ended up increasing the importance of print. All the new technology has given tremendous flexibility and greater quality to the graphic capabilities and to manufacturing [of magazines] as a whole. Magazines that don't change and don't adapt die out.

Lawrence W. Lane, former publisher of *Sunset* and a leader in the magazine industry, from an interview reported in *Folio*, 1 June 1993.

These trends, among others, are expected to intensify in the years ahead:

1 *Paper/reproduction/graphic design improvements.* Desktop computer graphics are now augmenting better grades of paper and inks and continued improvements in printing quality. Computer-aided design allows magazine editors to develop, modify, and tailor graphic presentations, even to the point of customizing editions for specific geographic or specialized interest groups. Inkjet imaging developments permit publishers to localize both advertisements and personalized messages to readers.

2 *Increased involvement with readers.* Additional interactive devices—coupons, scents, product samples, pop-up response cards, three-dimensional viewing devices, even voice messages—are now routine options magazine publishers use to improve their marketing effectiveness with readers. Soon, the Magazine Publishers Association predicts, it will be relatively commonplace for magazines to carry ads that address the individual reader by name, not just by inkjet printing, but by voice.[13]

3 *More service journalism,* giving more information, ideas, and assistance to the reader. *Better Homes & Gardens,* an early and vigorous advocate of this philosophy, strived to make its articles relevant to the daily activities and lifestyle of its audience. Readers received articles and features that were not only informative, but helpful as well. Service journalism is by no means limited to the magazine field. All media to some extent attempt to help their audiences cope, but certain magazines seem to be particularly suited to adopt this philosophy and make it work. As *Better Homes'* managing editor, David Jordan, stated in a memo to his staff, "An important but subtle task . . . is to make the reader feel that what he is reading about is important, worthwhile, worth doing, and that the experience of reading about it and doing something about it will add to his self-esteem. . . . It is the sort of thing that makes a publication 'user friendly' and builds the long term loyalty without which no publication can survive."[14]

Magazine Staff Organization

While no two magazines are staffed precisely alike, a number of similarities in roles and functions are common throughout the industry. Here are a few key positions, as described by the Magazine Publishers Association:

- *Publisher.* Responsible for profitability of a magazine or group of magazines. The advertising, circulation, manufacturing, distribution, and editorial departments report to the publisher. He or she retains responsibility for policy setting and for ensuring the success of the magazine.

Teaching Idea
Assign students to find magazines with regional inserts obviously aimed at your geographical area. Does the class think these inserts make sense and achieve results?

Teaching Idea
If a local or regional firm regularly publishes a magazine, invite the publisher, editor, or other staff member to explain operations to your class.

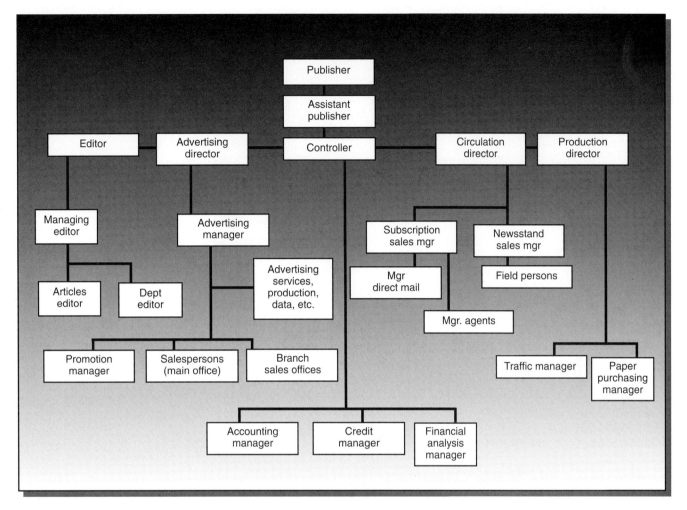

An organizational structure of a large magazine. Note that the editorial staff is typically small. Freelancers do much of the actual writing.

- *Editor-in-chief.* Responsible for editorial direction, content, and cover of the magazine; may also be responsible for special publications, books, and other reader products.
- *Managing editor.* Responsible for coordinating editorial, art, and production departments in turning out each issue of the magazine in acceptable form and on time. Supervises copyediting and proofreading staff to ensure that the magazine is factual and grammatically and typographically correct.
- *Senior editor.* Head of major editorial feature department. Plans and produces features in specialty areas; responsible for all editorial content in a subject area. Supervises associate editors, freelance writers/designers, and chief photographer. Many magazines have more than one senior editor; rather than reflecting specific functions, the title may recognize seniority and ability.
- *Associate editor.* Second-level editor in a major editorial department. Consults with senior editor on story plans. Researches and coordinates editorials; may organize photography shootings, find locations, select props, test projects. Stays on top of trends in specialty area; attends trade shows, press conferences. May write a column and/or handle reader mail.
- *Staff writer/reporter.* Researches, writes, and edits material in assigned subject areas. Attends functions, shows; keeps current on magazines and newspapers in assigned area. Checks layouts and pasteups.

Other key figures include the advertising director, circulation director, production chief, and head of promotion, as well as editorial copyeditors and art directors.

Most magazine staffs are not large. A relatively small cadre of editors and managers perform the work. The magazine often contracts for printing and production; few magazines own and operate their own presses. Most of the advertising is handled by **reps,** who may sell on commission for many different publications, and **freelancers** may do a great deal of the writing.

Freelancing for Magazines

Because large reporting/writing staffs are expensive to maintain, and because experts in every subject and geographical territory are hard to identify, many magazines have come to rely heavily on freelance writers. The term stems from the days of chivalry, when knights voluntarily chose to take up their lances in behalf of a cause, without personal attachment or allegiance. Today's freelancer writes for any number of magazines but might not be regularly employed by any of them. Instead, he or she negotiates each article or assignment individually. The arrangement is efficient for the magazine, which does not have to worry about paying a full salary with vacation time, medical coverage, fringe benefits, and the like.

It can work well for the writer, too, in that he or she is not tied down to a nine-to-five office routine and can instead follow whatever writing trails appear most interesting at the moment. In and of itself, however, freelancing is a tough way to earn a living. Most freelancing is done part-time by journalists and others who want the extra income and additional exposure and prestige that magazine writing can provide.

How does one become a freelancer? Simply by writing an article or short story and selling it to an editor—a process much easier said than done. The freelancer, who may not know a given editor's needs, could spend days or weeks on a piece only to learn that the editor has already arranged for another writer to deliver a manuscript on the same subject. Or the freelancer may not be familiar with the magazine's style or approach; editors reject many article ideas simply because the editor knows that his or her magazine's audience would find them inappropriate. A great many more manuscripts simply do not measure up to the publication's standard of quality. Despite these frustrations, editors keep reading freelance material. Most of

Teaching Idea

If you or your colleagues know of any full- or part-time freelance writers in your area who have sold articles to magazines, invite them to speak to your class on the joys and pains of freelancing.

For Freelancers: It Takes Discipline

Most writers, in the beginning, have trouble getting themselves to work on a regular schedule. . . . Discipline is absolutely necessary if a writer is going to produce with some consistency. Allen Churchill quotes the novelist David Graham Phillips:

"I write every night from eleven to five or six in the morning," he once told an aspiring writer. "Sometimes it is seven or eight. I write every night seven nights a week. Let me urge you to work the same number of hours every day and never, never, never to let anything interfere between you and those working hours. I don't wait for mood or inspiration and I don't give up because I don't begin right or am writing rubbish. I think it is fatal to give way to moods."

In ten years, this appalling schedule enabled Phillips to produce twenty-three books and several hundred short stories and articles. . . . I would hesitate to recommend such a schedule—but I do believe that the young writer should set aside certain periods of time when he will do nothing but write, and should stay on this schedule in spite of everything.

Richard Gehman, *How to Write and Sell Magazine Articles* (Harper, 1959).

the manuscripts are returned with a polite-but-firm rejection slip, but there is always the outside chance of finding a fresh idea, a creative new insight, a flawlessly written piece of copy. That's enough to keep writers writing and editors reading.

Often an editor prefers to see not the entire manuscript, but a **query** instead. A query letter explains briefly what the writer has in mind and how he or she would develop the story. It may also inform the editor of the writer's previous publication credits. In the query, the writer attempts to sell the editor on the idea. Here's a query that persuaded the editor of a magazine for veterans to buy an article on shortwave radio listening:

> Dear Sir:
> Tired of TV?
> Then you may be ready for short wave radio listening—a hobby that lets you tune in on the world.
>   Once, only those prepared to lay out a sizeable chunk of cash could afford short wave receivers. Not, however, transistorized radios, with powerful short wave bands, which begin as low as $40 and open up the excitement of international broadcasting to millions.
>   I propose to develop a brief, but information-packed, piece explaining what kinds of programming are available on short wave, what's needed to set up an effective rig, and why your readers will find it fun.
>   I am a newspaperman who has published in a dozen or more magazines, and would enjoy doing this piece, "Short Wave Means—Excitement!" for you. About 2,500 words, available within three weeks . . .
>
>   Sincerely,

The query affords the editor the opportunity to make at least a preliminary decision on an idea without investing a lot of precious time in the process. Also, it gives the editor a feel for the writer's style. If the writer can engage the editor's interest in one or two short paragraphs, there's a good chance he or she can interest the magazine's readers also. Finally, the query lets the editor have a say, early on, in how the writer develops the article. Perhaps the writer has missed an aspect of the story an editor thinks is essential. The query also helps the writer; if the story idea is not salable, then he or she can move on to something else without expending a lot of time on a project that doesn't seem to be leading anywhere.

There are psychological advantages to the query as well. When some editors receive a finished, unsolicited manuscript, they sense that the piece has already been rejected elsewhere; to them, an aura of defeat already surrounds it.

Freelancers who have made several sales and have begun building a reputation may be offered an assignment by an editor who needs a particular piece done by a reliable professional (although humor pieces are rarely assigned, and the same goes for personal essays and fiction). Established professionals sometimes retain *literary agents* to assist in marketing manuscripts. Agents, who receive a commission on all proceeds from the work, rarely take on unpublished newcomers as clients, however; those who do normally charge a fee for evaluating and/or attempting to sell a manuscript. For the most part, agents are reluctant to attempt magazine sales at all because the commissions don't justify the effort. Agents who cultivate magazine sales usually do so as a service to proven writers who are also generating substantial revenues through book royalties, movie rights, and so on.

Writer's Market, Ayer's Directory, and similar compilations available in most larger libraries can provide prospective freelancers with a great deal of information about various magazines and their editorial requirements.

Career Opportunities

At one time, young people hoping to enter the magazine field faced slim chances. Now, with more and more new magazines, the chances are better. Competition remains keen, but a number of jobs, especially with business magazines and company publications, open up each year. The International Association of Business Communicators, for example, is adding new members at the rate of about a thousand a year. More and more company managements are being held accountable for problems that range from sexual harassment to air pollution; many have responded by attempting to communicate better. Business publications are likely to continue their remarkable growth in the years ahead. Substantial numbers of journalism graduates, in particular, are landing jobs in this field.

Only about 20 percent of the consumer magazines recruit staff members directly from the ranks of new college graduates. Most editors prefer to allow a prospect to first gain some seasoning on a newspaper or a company or business magazine. A national survey of magazine editors, conducted by Edwin O. Haroldsen and Kenneth E. Harvey and reported in the *Journalism Educator,* found widespread dissatisfaction with the language skills recent college graduates, and journalism graduates in particular, generally possessed.[15] "The biggest single problem in magazine hiring today is finding young people who can spell, punctuate, clarify, proofread, and rewrite," said John Fay, editorial director of *Golf, Outdoor Life,* and *Ski.* "We are heading into a period when employers will have to start supplying courses in remedial English to make up for inadequacies in our schools and colleges." Another editor said of recent college graduates, "Their grammar is not sufficient to begin to instruct them in copy editing. Some cannot write a simple letter. It is pointless to teach editorial skills to such a candidate."

That survey was completed in 1979. Presumably things have improved since then, but in any case the message should be clear: Persons expecting to obtain and hold jobs on magazines must be able to present, along with a degree, an uncommonly good ability to handle the language. Beyond that, the successful applicant ideally should be a self-starter, capable of performing the independent research and analysis needed to develop a polished story. The editor-in-chief of *Popular Science,* Hubert P. Luckett, offered this advice: "Write, write, write, and write some more—preferably for publication. At least the articles should be submitted to a hard-nosed editor who will critique mercilessly."[16]

The editorial side of magazine publishing gets the most exposure, but hundreds of jobs each year open up on the business side of the industry.[17] In advertising sales, for instance, vast opportunities exist for men and women who are able to understand how a magazine relates to the reader, and who are able to communicate this effectively to the advertising client. Among the entry-level openings in magazine ad sales are junior account executives, ad sales coordinators, advertising production assistants, and sales records assistants. Sales support, on some publications an entirely different operation, provides job openings in market research, promotion, merchandising, and public relations/publicity. The circulation department offers jobs carrying such titles as circulation promotion assistant, fulfillment (customer service) rep, and subscription or single copy analyst. Production department positions include traffic assistants—who arrange shipping from plants to post offices and wholesalers, make-up assistants, and production cost analysts.

Those who do break into the field can usually expect to find it glamorous and exciting. It almost has to be, if today's magazines are to continue to be a step, or possibly two, ahead of their readers.

summary

Magazines reflect our tastes and often anticipate them. Readers involve themselves with magazines—through clipping articles or coupons, sending for more information about a product or service, and so on—more intimately than with any other mass communications medium. Eighty-six percent of adult Americans read magazines, buying an average of thirty-six copies a year.

During much of their history, magazines served large, general audiences. Since the advent of television, however, magazines have tended to target narrower markets and to engage the readers in these market segments at greater depth. Many new magazines appear each year, mostly niche publications aimed at increasingly fragmented audiences.

While consumer magazines—women's magazines, newsmagazines, general-interest publications, and so on—are the most visible part of the industry, they comprise only a fraction of it. Other groupings include business publications (trade and professional journals) and company magazines (house organs). Most magazines employ relatively small permanent staffs; much of the writing is done on a work-for-hire basis by contributing writers (freelancers).

Technological changes have enhanced magazine effectiveness in many areas, permitting sharper graphics and more precise targeting of audience segments. Computer-aided design lets magazine editors customize editions for specific regions or interest groups. Inkjet imaging developments permit publishers to localize advertisements as well as personalized messages to readers, and interactive devices—including voice messages and three-dimensional viewing devices—-allow magazine publishers to develop new marketing strategies and to communicate with their readers more effectively.

? questions and cases

1. If magazines must stay a step, possibly two, ahead of their readers, what does this require of the magazine editor? the freelance magazine writer?

2. Are there any specific audiences in society that magazines are not adequately serving? If so, what sort of magazine would, in your opinion, succeed with such an audience? How would you develop your concept and market it?

3. Analyze your favorite magazine. Why do you like it? What types of articles or stories would you like to write for it? How would you approach the editors with a story idea?

4. When did you first begin reading magazines? What magazines did you read? Why? How, if at all, have your magazine reading patterns changed recently?

chapter glossary

businesspapers   Sometimes referred to as business magazines, these papers are published for trade, professional, and industrial audiences.

external   A company publication aimed primarily at customers, potential customers, suppliers, and others outside the company.

freelancer   A writer or editor not under regular contract to a publication, but who sells specific writings and services to any buyer.

internal   A company publication written and edited primarily for staff and employees and often referred to as a house organ.

Magazine Publishers Association (MPA)   Trade association for the field. Headquartered in New York, as is the American Society of Magazine Editors (ASME).

query   A letter a freelance writer sends to an editor, outlining a possible article idea and attempting to interest the editor in the complete manuscript.

rep   A sales representative, or salesperson.

notes

1 Reprinted in *The Reader's Digest Dictionary of Quotations* (New York: Funk and Wagnalls, 1968), 125.

2 James Playsted Wood, *Of Lasting Interest: The Story of the Reader's Digest* (Garden City, N.Y.: Doubleday, 1967), 23.

3 Magazine Publishers Association, *The Magazine Handbook 1991,* 48.

4 See especially Frank Luther Mott, *American Journalism* (New York: Macmillan, 1962), 106, 138, 575. The most comprehensive study of the field is Mott's Pulitzer-prize winning *History of American Magazines,* 5 vols. (vol. 1, New York: Appleton, 1930; vols. 2–5, Cambridge: Harvard University Press, 1938–68).

5 Theodore Peterson, *Magazines in the Twentieth Century,* 2d ed. (Urbana: University of Illinois Press, 1964), 5–80.

6 John M. Harrison and Harry H. Stein, *Muckraking: Past, Present, and Future* (University Park: Pennsylvania State University Press, 1973), 11–23.

7 Peterson, *Magazines in the Twentieth Century,* 67.

8 These are highly subjective classifications for purposes of illustration. The student who wishes a detailed breakdown should consult the trade press, notably *Folio* magazine and the *Standard Rate and Data Service* yearbooks.

9 Letter to the author, 29 January 1985.

10 Background materials furnished to the author by the Business Press Educational Foundation.

11 *The Journal of Communications Management,* 12:1 (1982), 1–11; also *Profile,* a special report published by the International Association of Business Communicators.

12 M. Daniel Rosen, "Customer Magazines," *Communications World,* 1 March 1983, 2–18.

13 *Magazine Handbook '91,* and other background materials provided by the Magazine Publishers Association, 1993.

14 David Jordan, memo to the staff of *Better Homes & Gardens,* 1985.

15 Edwin O. Haroldsen and Kenneth E. Harvey, "Frowns Greet New J-Grads in Magazine Job Markets," *Journalism Educator,* 34:2 (1979), 3–8. These findings were challenged within the industry, notably by Robert E. Kenyon, executive director of the American Society of Magazine Editors, in "New, Qualified J-Grads DO Land Magazine Jobs," *Journalism Educator,* 34:4 (1980), 20.

16 Haroldsen and Harvey, "Frowns Greet New J-Grads."

17 "Guide to Business Careers in Magazine Publishing," pamphlet published by the Magazine Publishers Association, 1993.

chapter H

The Book Industry

Objectives

When you have finished studying this chapter, you should be able to:

◉ Trace the early history of books, especially noting such breakthroughs as the codex, movable type, and the Linotype

◉ Explain how the industry is organized and list the major divisions of it

◉ Understand the four major steps in book publication

◉ Discuss some concerns facing the industry, and cite at least five trends that appear favorable for the book industry's future

During the darkest days of World War II, President Franklin Delano Roosevelt urged the American people to produce more aircraft, ships, guns, ammunition—and books. In a spirited charge to the chairperson of the Council on Books in Wartime, the president urged that ". . . all who write and publish and sell and administer books . . . will rededicate themselves to the single task of arming the mind and spirit of the American people with the strongest and more enduring weapons." In that same message, Roosevelt added, "Books, like ships, have the toughest armor, the largest cruising range, and mount the most powerful guns."[1]

A copy of the first book ever printed using movable type—the Gutenberg *Bible*.

Of all the media of mass communications, books are clearly the oldest, arguably the most prestigious, and certainly the most lasting. Books transmit our culture from one generation to the next; help us to understand and function in modern society; teach us how to develop as individuals; and permit us to organize our lives, now and for the future. Books instruct us and entertain us, but beyond that, they challenge us. As President Roosevelt might have put it, in the battle of ideas and for the minds of men and women, books are the heavy artillery.

American book publishers bring out between 40,000 and 54,000 new titles each year. That may be too many, in terms of industry efficiency, but what choices this gives us! More than half of all American adults—nearly 100 million people—read an average of two books a year, and about one third of this large group reads an average of one book per week.

Extra Information

Ask students to find out how many new titles your institution's library purchased last year. How many were related to mass communications? How many were classified as popular fiction? Also, assign students to find out how many books the public library purchased last year. How many of them were popular fiction? A comparison might prove interesting.

The Role of Book Publishing

Publishers, although treated in government compilations as manufacturers, are really service companies. They assess the information needs of society, locate sources of that information (authors), process it into forms suitable for the market (editing), arrange for its production (printing and binding) and market it (selling and distribution). In this sense, they function much like contractors. . . . In particular, book publishers are involved with information of more than transient value, which may be unique in its content, and which is intended for the use of individuals in small or large groups who wish easily accessible, relatively inexpensive, highly portable and readily understood information in a durable, relatively permanent format. Other characteristics are precision, the use of symbols for speed of communication and accuracy, and other factors that make the book preferable to alternative media for purposes of information and dissemination.

Benjamin M. Compaine, *Who Owns the Media?* (Crown, 1979).

Not all of these reading hours are committed to the relentless pursuit of matters intellectual. To the contrary, many are pure pleasure time. In the spring of 1994, for example, the most popular books on the bestseller lists included:

- *The Bridges of Madison County,* by Robert James Waller, a novel about a photographer and a lonely farmer's wife in a remote region of Iowa.
- *Disclosure,* by Michael Crichton, about a computer industry executive whose boss charges him with sexual harassment.
- *Embraced by the Light,* by Betty J. Eadie, a nonfiction account of her near-death experience.
- *Zlata's Diary,* by Zlata Filipovic, the poignant journal of an eleven-year-old girl living in war-ravaged Sarajevo.
- *Schindler's List,* by Thomas Keneally, the story of a heroic man who saved Jews during World War II.

Politically oriented books filled the lists, too, such as *See, I Told You So,* by Rush H. Limbaugh, the conservative radio talk show star, and *Earth in the Balance,* by Vice-President Al Gore, a critical examination of current environmental conditions. Bestseller how-to books included *Stop the Insanity!* by Susan Powter, providing advice on women's fitness and health, and *First Things First,* by Stephen R. Covey, a primer on ways to organize your life for success. *Seinlanguage,* by Jerry Seinfeld, contained the television comic's observations on life's trials and pleasures, and one unlikely success story, *The Book of Virtues,* was a compilation by William J. Bennett of moral stories adapted from the *Bible,* the ancient Greeks, folklore, and literature.[2]

Interest in books, in other words, remains vibrant—a condition that must confound some scholars who, a generation ago, freely predicted that the electronic age would soon put an end to buying and reading books. Further dramatic, widespread changes will affect how information is processed, stored, retrieved, and utilized. But shifts in human appetites and behavior patterns are less easy to predict, especially where books are concerned. Or to put it another way, as Benjamin M. Compaine did in *Understanding New Media,* could we imagine curling up in front of a fire with a Tolstoi novel on the video screen?[3]

Technological competition is a serious problem for the book industry, but it is not the only one. Other concerns include conglomerate takeovers of publishing houses, rising costs, marketing and distribution changes, and illiteracy—not just those who cannot read, but the equally depressing problem group called **aliterates,** people who can read but don't. We will look at each of these concerns. But first, a brief sketch of the industry's long and honorable history is in order.

Early Forms of Books

The urge to bind information and ideas into permanent form is as old as humankind.[4] Writing began on the walls of caves and was later preserved in hard-baked clay tablets, perhaps first at Nineveh and Babylon nearly sixty centuries ago. In that same part of the world some years later, ancient Egyptians discovered that the pith of **papyrus,** a tall water plant of the sedge family that was abundant in the Nile Valley, could be soaked, pressed into thin slices, and woven into pages to make a far more portable writing surface. Longer weaves of papyrus could be pasted together into rolls; normally they were 1 foot wide and as much as 140 feet long, anchored by wooden rollers at each end. The *papyrus scroll,* which could house a great deal of information, served writers and recorders of history for many years. The Romans modified this idea by developing a writing surface from the cured skins of goats, calves, and sheep. This high-grade parchment, called *vellum,* was easier to write on and lasted longer. The Chinese, meanwhile, created books from rolls of silk.

Extra Information

The *New York Times Book Review,* included in the Sunday edition, includes both hardcover and paperback bestseller lists. Show these lists to your class. Have them track books over a two- or three-month period. How many remain on the list? Do they rise or fall in rank?

Teaching Idea

Fletcher Pratt and L. S. DeCamp wrote *Lest Darkness Fall,* which—among other things—gives modern students a good idea of the difficulties early printers faced without modern knowledge or technology. Assign a student to read it and report on the problems Harold Shea encountered in trying to put out printed matter.

Making a scrolled book required considerable labor; entire teams of copyists had to be trained, housed, and fed. Even reading a scroll was no easy task. The signs and symbols of written language were still evolving, slowly and inconsistently, and the reader had to roll backward and forward, very gingerly, to study a few passages at a time. Incredibly, a few great libraries were built, one of them during the reign of Ptolemy I. The pharaoh's great array of copyists duplicated virtually every book then known, and his library collection at Alexandria numbered several hundred thousand rolls.

The more immediate forerunner of the modern book was the **codex,** which emerged between the first and fourth centuries after the birth of Christ. A codex consisted of several sheets of vellum folded into a section called a *gathering;* gatherings were sewn together and bound on one side into a volume. This made books far easier to use, and the codex format, in outward appearance, at least, resembles today's book.

For most of its history, the book was handwritten, the scribe utilizing a quill or a reed; it often took months of painstaking work to prepare a single volume. The Chinese, who invented both printing and paper more than a thousand years ago, learned to produce books by *letterpress.* While this process was also slow—the carving required great patience and skill—the finished page form could be used again and again; each new book, in other words, no longer represented an entirely new exercise.

Mass Printing Arrives

In the fifteenth century in Mainz, Germany, Johann Gutenberg invented—or, at least, is widely credited with inventing—*movable type,* a system that uses individual letters produced and kept on hand as needed; the letters are assembled into words, locked onto a page form, printed, then swiftly sorted out for immediate reuse. The movable characters concept, like much else in printing, originated in Asia but developed in Europe, presumably because European languages were comparatively simpler. It took Gutenberg's contribution, combined with improvements in ink and paper, to launch printing on a mass scale.

Printers trained in Gutenberg's shop spread throughout Europe and published hundreds of titles, many of which dealt with the profound religious questions under discussion at the time. The great thinkers of the day argued the Protestant Reformation and Counter-Reformation positions in deadly earnest; these philosophical statements, increasingly written in the languages people were using rather than the more esoteric Latin and Greek, encouraged great numbers of concerned citizens to learn to read. And, largely because of the ferocity of the religious debate, this period also introduced the world to another new concept—censorship. More than a few books were banned, while others were seized and destroyed. All the books published before 1500 are known collectively as the *incunabula,* from the Latin word for cradle. They represent printing in its infancy.

For more than three centuries after that, printing technology remained essentially unchanged even though skilled typographers designed many new type faces, new presses were faster and more consistent, more books became available, and a bigger cross section of the general public was eager to read them. Those trends intensified in 1884, especially in the United States, with Ottmar Mergenthaler's invention of the Linotype—a machine that could set an entire line of type at once.[5] While this procedure reduced printing from an art form to more of a mechanical process—and the esthetic quality of books did momentarily deteriorate somewhat—automatic typesetting made cheap and plentiful books possible.

Extra Information
A palimpsest was vellum or animal skin used for writing. When there was a shortage of material to write on, scribes scraped off the first ink and wrote over it. Fortunately, scholars know how to bring out the original text as well as the overwrite.

Background
Both the Chinese and Japanese languages use a form of picture writing employing thousands of ideographs (or "characters") instead of our twenty-six letters. It is necessary to memorize thousands of characters to be fully literate; this made it difficult to design typewriters and computers using these languages.

Discussion
Is there a close correlation between the growth of printing and the rise of literacy?

Early Printing in America

Colonial publishing began in 1640 with Stephen Daye and the primitive but busy press he assembled on the campus of Harvard College near Boston. Some of the more famous pioneering newspaper proprietors also published books. Benjamin Harris, who started the abortive *Publick Occurrences* in 1690, printed almanacs and the acclaimed *New England Primer*. Benjamin Franklin for twenty-five years brought out his highly profitable *Poor Richard's Almanack*. Isaiah Thomas, fiery editor of the *Massachusetts Spy,* also published dozens of books, including a valuable two-volume *History of Printing in America,* at his plants in Boston and Worcester.

The nineteenth century saw the beginnings of true mass education in the United States. A sharp rise in the literacy rate, combined with rapid population growth and an increase in numbers of printers, triggered the emergence of the book as a popular medium. Libraries grew and changed during this period. Prior to the mid-1800s, libraries existed primarily to serve scholars, the relatively few college and university students, and the rich. But librarians, philanthropists, and key political figures combined efforts to build hundreds of new libraries and extend library services to anyone interested in using them. Public library growth and support, though uneven around the country, was nevertheless dramatic.

Other factors were involved. Newspapers, freed from partisan ties and now openly courting the widest possible audience, often ran novels in serial format. These popular entries were reprinted in book form following their newspaper publication. The rags-to-riches Horatio Alger stories, as an example, became popular newspaper serial fare, then even more popular books. Beyond this, U.S. book publishers enjoyed another, clearly dubious, advantage: Because the United States did not then participate in international **copyright** agreements, American book publishers were not legally precluded from pirating foreign books. Entrepreneurs in this country freely reprinted hundreds of popular European works and did not bother to pay royalties to authors. This practice ended in 1891, but before then a number of publishers lined their pockets with proceeds from the sale of books they had stolen, chiefly from British authors.

In the years just before the Civil War, books began to do on a national scale what other media of mass communications attempted to do—inform, persuade, and entertain. Support for public education, which always translated into good news for the book industry, came from several quarters: Pragmatic businesspeople appreciated the need to develop a skilled labor force whose members could read, write, and cipher; politicians knew that education for all carried powerful voter appeal; thoughtful government leaders, such as Horace Mann of Massachusetts, urged their states to pour money into schools. Education, Mann argued, "is the great equalizer of the conditions of men—the balance wheel of the social machinery. . . . It does better than to disarm the poor of their hostility toward the rich; it prevents being poor."[6]

Millions of American school children learned their ABCs, with heavy moralizing thrown in, via the McGuffey readers. As adults, many of them created a market for popular fiction. Long before the Civil War, a New York publisher, E. F. Beadle, launched a series of cheap, fast-paced adventure books called dime novels that a vast national audience read. Beadle's success has prompted some scholars to credit him with making the book a true medium for the masses in the United States. Other American novelists were meanwhile creating books that also became important, if in different ways. Herman Melville's *Moby Dick,* published in 1851, is widely regarded as the most commanding novel of the century. Nathaniel Hawthorne's psychological novels, notably *The Scarlet Letter* and *The House of the Seven Gables,* were also pub-

Extra Information
Assign students to research the current copyright law. What does such a law protect? If you have ever copyrighted any work, explain the procedure to students.

Example
Reprints of the McGuffey readers are available and might prove interesting to your class.

lished about that time. They achieved world distinction, as did Mark Twain's humorous stories of American boyhood, *The Adventures of Tom Sawyer* (1876) and *Huckleberry Finn* (1884). Stephen Crane's *The Red Badge of Courage,* published in 1895, was a powerful and realistic examination of war.

In terms of social and political influence, perhaps the most significant novel of the century was Harriet Beecher Stowe's *Uncle Tom's Cabin,* a melodramatic but powerful indictment of slavery that touched consciences in both South and North. Characters such as Simon Legree, Uncle Tom, and Little Eva became a part of the national experience. This novel, and the play George L. Aiken based on it, was accused of escalating the slavery issue into civil war—solemn testament to the strength of one book's impact.

By the turn of the century, a truly popular novel might sell as many as 600,000 copies in the English-speaking world.[7] Book publishing houses were well established. New York became, and still is, America's publishing capital, though Boston and Philadelphia are home to several large book companies. And with its heavy concentration of religious publishers, Nashville has emerged as an important publishing center as well.

The Twenty Most Influential Women's Books of the Last Twenty Years

When asked about the most important women's books they have sold over the last twenty years, booksellers mentioned the following titles:

The Courage to Heal: A Guide for Survivors of Child Sexual Abuse, by Ellen Bass and Laura Davis (Harper & Row, 1988)

The New Our Bodies, Ourselves, by the Boston Women's Health Book Collective (first edition New England Free Press, 1969; subsequent editions Simon & Schuster, 1973)

Rubyfruit Jungle, by Rita Mae Brown (first edition Daughters, 1973; subsequent editions Bantam, 1977)

Daughters of Copper Woman, by Anne Cameron (Press Gang, 1981)

Gyn/Ecology: The Metaethics of Radical Feminism, by Mary Daly (Beacon Press, 1978)

The First Sex, by Elizabeth Gould Davis (out of print)

Dialectic of Sex, by Shulamith Firestone (Morrow, 1970; out of print)

In a Different Voice: Psychological Theory and Women's Development, by Carol Gilligan (Harvard, 1982)

The Work of a Common Woman, by Judy Grahn (first edition Diana Press, 1978; subsequent edition Crossing Press)

Ain't I a Woman: Black Women and Feminism, by bell hooks (South End, 1981)

Their Eyes Were Watching God, by Zora Neale Hurston (first edition Lippincott, 1937; a revival of interest occurred in 1981 with the publication of Alice Walker's essay in *Ms.* magazine; currently available from HarperCollins)

Sister Outsider, by Audre Lorde (Crossing Press, 1984)

Brown Girl, Brownstones, by Paule Marshall (first edition 1959; reissued by the Feminist Press, 1981)

Lesbian/Woman, by Del Martin and Phyllis Lyon (first edition Glide, 1972; also available in a revised twentieth-anniversary edition Volcano Press)

Patience and Sarah, by Isabel Miller (self-published; reissued by Fawcett Crest, 1972)

This Bridge Called My Back: Writings by Radical Women of Color, edited by Cherrie Moraga and Gloria Anzaldua (first edition Persphone, 1981; subsequent edition Women of Color Press, 1983)

Sisterhood Is Powerful: An Anthology of Writings from the Women's Liberation Movement, edited by Robin Morgan (Random House, 1970)

Of Women Born: Motherhood as Experience and Institution, by Adrienne Rich (Norton, 1976)

Spiral Dance: A Rebirth of the Ancient Religion of the Goddess, by Starhawk (Harper & Row, 1979)

The Color Purple, by Alice Walker (Harcourt Brace Jovanovich, 1982)

Publishers Weekly, 11 May 1992.

table 1 — Book Publishing Industry Sales, 1982–91 (in millions of dollars)

Category	1982	1990	1991	Compound Growth Rate 1982–91
Trade books	1,513.0	3,892.8	4,248.5	12.2%
Religious	425.5	788.0	838.5	7.8
Professional	1,536.4	2,765.9	2,826.7	4.4
Book clubs	522.9	725.1	753.4	3.4
Mail order books	568.6	731.4	733.6	2.9
Mass market paperbacks	703.4	1,148.6	1,258.9	6.7
University presses	125.4	245.8	265.5	8.7
Elementary and secondary texts	1,108.2	2,025.8	2,060.2	7.1
College texts	1,206.1	1,991.3	1,997.3	5.8
Standardized tests	70.4	127.6	133.5	7.4
Subscription/reference books	306.9	540.5	552.4	6.7

Source: Association of American Publishers, Inc.

The Industry Today

While not a mammoth industry on the scale of aerospace or agribusiness, American book publishing nevertheless is a sizable enterprise. There are perhaps 2,000 active book publishing companies in operation today, and this doesn't count the growing number of desktop publishing authors who produce and sell their own books. Together they bring out about 50,000 new titles each year. Total 1991 industry revenues topped $16.1 billion, a hefty 9.6 percent gain over the previous year's sales (table 1).

Within the industry are a number of classifications.[8] The major ones include:

- **Trade books.** Usually hardcover, these are books of general interest, fiction and nonfiction, sold at bookstores.
- Mass market paperbacks. These popular books are available at drugstores, newsstands, department stores, and discount stores as well as at bookstores.
- Religious books. Bibles, hymnals, prayer books, theological interpretations, and denominational materials come under this category. Sold primarily by several hundred Christian bookstores, they are often available at general bookstores as well.
- Elementary and secondary textbooks. Known as **el-hi** division books, these books are purchased by school districts.
- College textbooks. This classification includes books and many audiovisual materials, maps, manuals, workbooks, and so on. Though it is estimated that the average college student spends only about 5 percent of his or her total educational costs on books, the totals mount up: In 1994, the combined revenues of college and university bookstores exceeded $2 billion.

Teaching Idea

If your institution has an academic press, ask the director or manager to visit your class and explain its operation.

Teaching Idea

If there is an independent (or locally owned) bookstore in your area, ask the owner or manager to visit your class and explain how he or she selects books to order. The manager of a chain operation would also be interesting, although his or her authority to choose books may be limited.

- Professional books. Legal, medical, scientific, technical, and business books are in this grouping. Many of these titles are automatically updated each year as new information becomes available.

- University press books. These scholarly works, while worthy, usually have little appeal to wide audiences. Most university presses operate on a nonprofit basis. They market aggressively, however, in hopes that a brisk sale of their more popular books will bring in enough revenue to underwrite other books which, though of narrow interest, are important for their scholarship.

Other classifications exist, including standardized tests and encyclopedias and **vanity press** books, which authors pay to publish. In addition, the industry also consists of various marketing or distribution divisions, such as:

- Book clubs, which sell books published by others, usually to specific audiences—the History Book Club, the Military Book Club, Mystery Book Club, and so on. Larger clubs, such as Book-of-the-Month and the Literary Guild, often sell several hundred thousand copies of individual selections.
- Mail order publications, which frequently sell books by the series directly to their customers. Tax law revisions and court decision updates that law and accounting firms buy are marketed this way.

In a typical year, trade books comprise the largest share of the industry's revenues. Professional books, college textbooks, el-hi texts, and mass market paperbacks follow, usually in that order.

How Books Are Produced

Book publication essentially involves four steps: finding a promising manuscript, editing it, manufacturing a book from it, and selling the finished product.

Getting the Manuscript

The process often begins with an *acquisitions editor.* This person examines the manuscripts and query letters that come in from freelance authors, directly or through a literary agent, who have an idea for a book and want to secure a publishing contract. Hundreds of such communications arrive **over the transom** in a large publishing house each year. Acquisitions editors dutifully read them. But the enterprising acquisitions editor does far more than this; he or she actively seeks out promising manuscripts as well. This requires an awareness of what is on the public's mind or, at a minimum, a sufficiently large share of the public to create a potential market for a book. Acquisitions editors read a great deal, particularly in their areas of specialization, and cultivate a network of reliable sources that they can count upon for advice on current trends, issues, and personalities. After the acquisitions editor has zeroed in on a topic that might be worth pursuing, he or she might then invite an author to develop a manuscript or a prospectus for a book on the subject.

Once the acquisitions editor is persuaded that the subject, the author, and the concept are right, he or she submits the proposal to the publishing firm's *editorial board,* which consists of the editor-in-chief, managing editor, and several senior editors. The board may approve the proposal, reject it, or, as is frequently the case, recommend changes in the tone, approach, or scope of the manuscript. A senior editor, who may or may not be the acquisitions editor who originally developed the proposal, might then be assigned to work with the author in preparing the final manuscript. The board authorizes a contract to spell out the terms of the agreement, including what **royalties** the author will receive, the anticipated dates the manuscript will be completed, and so on.

Editing

When the completed manuscript is in hand, the publisher must then arrange to have it copyedited. Because books are designed to last—unlike newspapers, which may put out several editions each day, permitting prompt correction of errors—editing a book manuscript is serious business indeed. The copyeditor checks facts, quotations, and references for accuracy. He or she rigorously examines the author's writing style and organizational development and, where necessary, improves them. In addition, the copyeditor corrects errors in grammar, spelling, and syntax—in short, polishes the manuscript to make it as appealing and effective as possible. The editor must do all this without destroying the author's style or point of view in the process. In Dessauer's lyrical explanation, "Nowhere is the essential midwifery of publishing more apparent than at that point where the editor must literally inhabit an author's soul and whisper as though from within, seeing the world and the subject with the author's eyes and hearing the cadences of language with the author's ears."[9] Copyediting, in short, requires heroic amounts of knowledge, judgment, skill, and tact.

Producing the Book

The edited manuscript is now ready to go into production. At this stage, the book is designed: Art work, pictures, maps, charts, and boxes are arranged for; complete publishing specifications are prepared. These are crucial decisions. Selection of the book's type face, for example, affects not only the readability of the work, but says something about the book's personality as well. An ultramodern typeface for a book about contemporary rock music stars reveals the publisher's feelings about the book—and the in-house image of those who might be expected to buy it. Choices of printing stock (paper) and cover design are likewise made with care. Not every type face or grade of paper makes a philosophical statement, but a sensitive book designer is aware of impressions the finished book, or any of its parts, can create.

Most publishers do not own their own presses. Instead, for each job they provide specifications to various printing companies and invite competitive bids. Once

Teaching Idea

Ask students to find out from a publisher or printer why a hardback costs more than a paperback. How do the paper and bindings differ in quality?

A book designer prepares a cover.

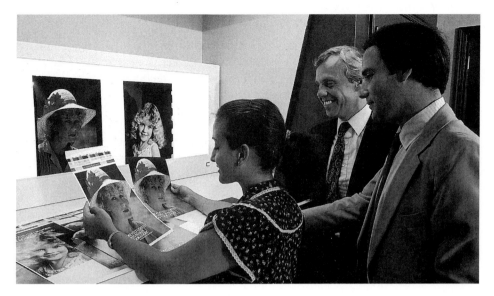

Type selection, typographic arrangement, printing stock—all are key decisions on book production.

the printing and binding contracts are awarded, a production department staff person within the publishing house serves as liaison with the printer and monitors the project to completion. Effective liaison requires the production editor to coordinate not only the printer but the artists and suppliers, and to keep track of costs and a multitude of administrative and logistical details so that the project is finished on schedule and within budget.

Selling the Book

Marketing people, meanwhile, have been drafting plans to promote the book, not only through the company's sales force but through the media of mass communications and the general public. They must also develop an advertising budget and agree upon marketing strategies. The marketing department sends publicity material out to the trade press as well as to the general media, some of it perhaps based on early reviews of the **galley proofs.** They may dispatch direct-mail pieces to librarians and other interested parties. Computerized mailing lists make it possible to target highly specific market segments. Copies of the book are sent to reviewers. Perhaps exhibits are prepared for conventions, book fairs, and other gatherings. Sales representatives, fully briefed, are then dispatched to call upon bookstores and other likely prospects.

Textbooks are marketed somewhat differently. El-hi sales representatives contact state and city school organizations, presenting books as candidates for adoption. Individual professors or a departmental committee chooses college texts, placing the order with the college bookstores. Textbook salespeople focus their efforts on the adopters rather than the bookstores.

Marketing people in the book industry are faced with a difficult task. In few other industries does a single company introduce several hundred new "products" a year, yet this is routine in book publishing. Although some books have already been presold when they appear, such as subscription publications for accountants and lawyers, most books require an individual marketing plan. Because publishers cannot project sales with great accuracy, advertising budgets, usually allocated as a percentage of anticipated sales, tend to be relatively small. Rarely will a company mount a blockbuster television ad campaign in behalf of a new book. Print advertising may be limited to trade publications and a carefully

Television talk shows are important vehicles for promoting books.

selected number of newspapers and magazines. As a result, those who market books rely on other strategies: author tours and appearances, especially on television talk shows and at autographing sessions; generating publicity about the book or the author in various media; promoting the book by whatever means possible. Book marketing and promotion people know that theirs is an unscientific and uncertain business. But it can be highly satisfying, especially when a bestseller, or even a good seller, comes along.

Paperbacks

Paperbacks have been around for centuries. During the 1490s in Venice, one of the most prominent of the incunabula printers, Aldus Manutius, was publishing pocket-sized, undecorated, paperbound books for his impoverished scholar-clients.[10] Several later European publishers, especially in France, similarly ignored fancy bindings to produce low-cost paper-covered books. Customers who wanted to preserve these books could bind them in any manner they chose. Many editions of the classics found their way to thrifty readers by this means. In 1837, Christian Bernhard Tauchnitz, a printer in Germany, founded what would become an enduring publishing house, its reputation and profits built on the sale of thousands of low-cost editions, many of them translations of British and American works. In the United States, the phenomenally successful dime novels showed the extensive market for modestly priced books.

Essentially, however, the paperback revolution is associated with twentieth-century publishers in this country. Many scholars fix the beginning of the modern era at 1939, when Robert de Graff founded Pocket Books. His firm brought out 34 titles that year and sold about 1.5 million copies, most at 25 cents each. By 1955, 13 major publishers produced paperback books; they issued 1,000 titles and sold some 250 million copies.[11] **Mass market paperbacks** had changed an entire nation's reading pattern.

Several factors account for the astonishing growth of the paperback trade:[12]

- The hardcover book business was stagnant. Many titles were long since out of print, and expenses of reissuing them for a limited or uncertain market were prohibitive. The cheaper paperback production costs gave publishers far more flexibility, and author royalties tended to be proportionately less. With a paperback, a publisher could get in and out of the market relatively efficiently.
- Increasing numbers of college students provided new audiences for textbooks. Publishers, faculty, and students alike saw the value of lower-cost texts that could be revised, updated, and reissued more readily in paperback form.

- World War II created a demand. Millions of paperbacks were published for military morale and entertainment purposes, giving the new paperback industry a solid economic base and introducing hundreds of thousands of military personnel to a new reading medium.
- New channels of distribution developed. In several respects, including price, paperbacks resembled magazines more than books. As a result, paperback publishers found they could plug into the magazine distribution system. Tens of thousands of additional, high-traffic outlets—drug stores, newsstands, discount houses, supermarkets—opened up as if by magic.

Early paperbacks sold for a quarter and were, for the most part, reprints of hardcover books that had already run their course. By the 1990s, however, paperback prices had risen significantly, and paperbacks were no longer regarded as second-class citizens. Younger men and women had grown up reading paperbacks in high school and college. A paperback, to them, was a *book*—not merely a cheap substitute for the real thing.[13]

Problems and Concerns

The book industry in the contemporary United States remains in vigorous health despite the difficult economic conditions of the early nineties. Predictions that books were doomed, ventured a generation earlier, in retrospect seem outlandish and misbegotten. To the contrary, industry leaders have strong reason to be pleased with the present and cheerfully optimistic about the future.

At the same time, there are problems and concerns that must be taken into account.

Consolidations and Takeovers

Big investment capital, much of it flowing from overseas interests, has gone a long way toward realigning the book publishing industry. The Bertelsmann firm of Germany purchased such giants as Doubleday, Bantam, and Dell. Another German company, von Holtzbrinck, bought Henry Holt. Rupert Murdoch, the Australian tycoon, added Harper & Row to his vast media holdings in the United States. Other respected book publishing houses have been absorbed by large U.S. and foreign corporate giants. General Electric bought into Silver-Burdett; ABC bought Chilton, and CBS bought Holt, Rinehart & Winston, while NBC acquired Random House.[14] In addition, several more major book publishers are believed to be takeover targets.

Stock market experts on the book industry point out that international acquisitions can offer authors attractive worldwide circulation options. Mergers also promise greater efficiency; nearly every large paperback house is now aligned with a trade book publisher. Financial analysts also say that many U.S. book publishers are not sufficiently profit conscious. By merging departments and functions and by eliminating jobs—steps some publishers have been reluctant to take—the book business could become far more lucrative. However, some industry leaders express concern that conglomerate management and bottom-line expediency might threaten the editorial integrity that has characterized most major U.S. publishing houses over the years.

Too Many Titles

In 1983, American book publishing hit an all-time high, with 53,380 titles issued. That number has dropped, but the feeling persists that more books are published than the industry needs or the public wants. Reviewers for the country's newspapers and magazines, men and women whose business is to identify promising books and call them to the attention of the mass audience, can write about only a tiny fraction of the annual total. Only about one new book in twenty-five, for example, can possibly be discussed in the *New York Times Book Review,* the most influential of the critical publications. So many mediocre and/or superfluous books are published, the argument runs, that the reading public may pass over the truly good ones. Too, the book industry's distribution system, already overloaded and inefficient, might be better served with fewer entries to handle.

There is no simple and direct solution to the problem (if, indeed, it is a problem; if so, it is the kind of problem other nations would like to have). Total book sales continue to increase. Moreover, an industry-wide agreement to cut back on new titles—and, inevitably, to charge more for those that are published—would amount to collusion and therefore be illegal. Besides, as Benjamin M. Compaine noted, a proposal to limit production would starve the patient in order to save it.[15] By 1992, signs indicated that individual publishers were choosing to bring out slightly fewer books each year. Perhaps the overproduction matter will eventually take care of itself.

Illiteracy—and Aliteracy

According to the U.S. Bureau of the Census, of the 170 million Americans aged 14 and older, 99 percent are literate. That means 1.7 million adult Americans are functionally illiterate, unable to read and write well enough to function in society. Many observers, especially teachers, believe that estimate is low, that illiteracy is far more widespread than the census figures suggest. In the 1980s, the American Library Association united eleven interested organizations into a Coalition for Literacy and launched a prolonged campaign to increase awareness of the problem and recruit volunteer tutors to combat it. This effort produced a number of individual success stories, as well as evidence that public awareness of illiteracy as a social problem increased dramatically. But whether this heightened sensitivity would translate into massive remedial programs remained an open question.

Aliterates, people who are capable of reading but don't, far outnumber illiterates. One study, sponsored by the National Commission on Reading, revealed that fifth graders spent only 1 percent of their spare time reading but averaged two hours and ten minutes each day watching television. This and other research has tended to confirm what teachers, librarians, editors, and members of the book industry have long suspected—that reading is a declining trend in American life, and that love of reading must somehow be cultivated in children, both in school and at home.[16]

How to Identify Adult Nonreaders

Following are some tips from the Metropolitan Atlanta Chapter of Literacy Volunteers of America:

- Never assume adults will come to you boldly stating they cannot read. The inability to read brings with it a great stigma. . . . Adults will go to great lengths to conceal their problem, and many have become extremely adept in hiding the fact.

- Catch phrases often used by nonreaders include:

  "I forgot my glasses."

  "I can't read that print."

  "I'll read it when I get home."

"You read it for me."

"I can't understand those big words."

"I don't have time to read that now."

- In questioning persons you suspect have literacy problems, try to ask them what area(s) of their lives they would like to improve.

- Any probing questions should always be asked in a confidential, one-on-one setting so that the information obtained can remain confidential and the person will not be embarrassed. So far as it is possible, keep any information obtained confidential, and assure the nonreader that you will do so.

Censorship

The 1980s saw a marked increase in attempts to purge school library shelves of books that some concerned pressure groups found offensive. These censorship activities—resulting in a thousand or more complaints a year, according to the American Library Association—were directed at books thought to be unsuitable for young people. Most of the complaints originated with the Moral Majority and other conservative groups. Their targets included such well-known works as J. D. Salinger's *Catcher in the Rye;* John Steinbeck's *Of Mice and Men;* Ken Kesey's *One Flew over the Cuckoo's Nest;* Mario Puzo's *The Godfather;* and *Our Bodies, Ourselves* by the Boston Women's Health Book Collective. In a different context, black parent groups have objected to Mark Twain's *The Adventures of Huckleberry Finn,* which, in their view, perpetuates racial stereotypes.

By 1982, one such challenge to a local administrative authority had reached the U.S. Supreme Court. The Island Trees, New York, school board had removed nine books from the high school library. These included *Best Short Stories by Negro Writers; The Naked Ape,* a book about anthropological evolution by Desmond Morris; and *Slaughterhouse-Five,* by Kurt Vonnegut. The president of the student council and several other students brought suit to get the books back on the shelves. The Supreme Court's ruling provided some guidance but left several questions unanswered. A majority of the Court held that a school board may not ban books from the school library merely because the board does not agree with the political ideas expressed but can remove books they deem "educationally unsuitable" or "persuasively vulgar." At the same time, the Court held that students have a First Amendment right to receive ideas and to prevent a school board from banning books purely on moral or political grounds. Unfortunately, the Court did not define "educationally unsuitable" or "persuasively vulgar," thus leaving school librarians and administrators still uncertain as to how they might resolve further controversies.[17]

Some pressure groups attacked certain el-hi textbooks, too, in an attempt to influence political and historical interpretations presented to school children. These highly publicized challenges were focused on state departments of education, school boards, and other groups responsible for school textbook adoptions. No one can measure the precise effect of such pressuring, but it is entirely possible that more than one publisher has modified controversial views contained in a text, lest they offend certain key decision makers and lose a large, profitable adoption.

Censorship and intimidation cannot be said to represent a widespread or massively threatening problem to today's book industry. However, in a field where new and potentially controversial ideas play so central a role, any outside pressure, or attempts to bring outside pressure, can be cause for concern.

Alternative Ways of Getting Information

Technology, which has profoundly affected newspapers, television, and the other media of mass communications, has the potential to drastically reshape the book industry most of all. Computers with access to enormous databases and linked to laser printers have given us a new term as well as an astonishing concept: *on-demand publishing.* This means that, for the first time since Gutenberg, books may be printed on a one-at-a-time basis; each reader can pick and choose, compiling a book from the mass of data available on a given subject. As Ithiel de Sola Pool pointed out in *Technologies of Freedom,* the most economical way of moving, storing, and displaying words is electronically.[18] The use of paper is becoming a luxury. Today's publishers print, warehouse, distribute, and market books; tomorrow's publishers may call up individual copies and transmit them electronically as requested. Publishing strategies, in other words, could change radically in the years ahead, and some of the adjustments will be difficult to make.

Discussion

When is it permissible for an elementary school, a middle school, or a high school to limit or censor the types of books the school library carries? Has anyone attempted to limit school books in your area? (School librarians can help answer this question.)

Example/Teaching Idea

It seems as if a book on a major news event takes only a few days to reach the newsstands. Assign students to check bookstores and newsstands and find books that have appeared following recent news stories. Students can discuss whether a "quickie" is of the same quality as other books.

Electronic books: the CD-ROM revolution.

Class Project

Assign a student to read Ray Bradbury's classic *Farenheit 451* and discuss the central idea in class. (An alternative would be George Orwell's *1984*.)

Throughout history, the paths traveled by authors and book publishers have rarely been smooth. Books have been banned and burned, publishing offices have been shut down or forced into bankruptcy. From Martin Luther in the sixteenth century to Alexander Solzhenitsyn in the twentieth, writers have been exiled, excommunicated, jailed, or even hanged because of the views they have expressed in books. Yet the industry has survived, perhaps because books actually deal less with manufacturing than with ideas. For this reason alone, as British poet John Milton insisted more than three centuries ago, books are as precious as life itself:

> As good almost kill a man as kill a good book: who kills a man kills a reasonable creature, God's image; but he who destroys a good book, kills reason itself, kills the image of God, as it were in the eye.[19]

What Is an Electronic Book, Anyway?

Some terminology may help:

CD-ROM: Think of a music CD; the music is digitally encoded onto the disc. A CD-ROM looks exactly like a music CD, but it can contain text, graphics and sometimes sound, even motion. It is played on a CD-ROM drive, a device very much like a musical CD player. The information, however, is "received" by a computer, rather than a stereo receiver. CD-ROMs can store huge amounts of information (all of Shakespeare's works can easily fit onto one). ROM stands for "Read Only Memory," which means that you can read from the disc, but not write on it.

Optical Media: This doesn't mean media that require use of your eyes. It refers to how the *computer* reads the information. On the typical floppy disc, the information is encoded magnetically. CD-ROM, however, is a technology that is read by a laser. Thus, a music CD is, paradoxically, an *optical* medium, since the CD player "reads" the discs via laser.

CD-I: An interactive compact disc. With CD-ROM, the user can read information and move around easily in the text. With CD-I, the user can interact with the disc. Broderbund's *Grandma and Me* allows a child to make things happen on the screen; clicking on to the mailbox, for example, allows a torrent of mail to descend, or, another time, releases an ocean of fish. An important note: you can't play a CD-I on a CD-ROM player.

Platform, Environment: When you buy a [music] CD, you do not have to worry about whether it will play on your particular brand of CD player. The same is not true for CD-ROM, CD-I or floppy discs. Technology types do not talk in terms of brands, but whether something runs on a particular platform (meaning type of machine) or environment (meaning the type of software that runs the machine).

Electronic Book: Any book that can be read on a computer or a handheld personal information product.

Publishers Weekly, 18 June 1992.

John Steinbeck: The Author as Reporter

As Mark Twain once remarked, "Truth is stranger than Fiction . . . because Fiction is obligated to stick to possibilities. Truth isn't." Yet the *Grapes of Wrath* is often truthful because it strives to emulate documentary genres: case study, informant narrative, travel report, and phototext. [John] Steinbeck wanted his migrant book to be honest and moral, an act of social expiation. As we wrote his agent, "I'm trying to write history while it is happening and I don't want to be wrong."

William Howarth in *Literary Journalism in the Twentieth Century* (Oxford, 1990).

Careers in the Book Industry

Today's book industry is a vital part of the country's mass communications system, and many of the same talents and skills needed in the other media—writing, editing, an understanding of the intellectual and entertainment values of the general public—can also qualify one for success in the book publishing field. Many persons engaged in other aspects of mass communications work are prominent authors as well: Bill Cosby, Dan Rather, Robert MacNeil, Jim Lehrer, Carol Burnett, James Reston, Tom Wicker, William F. Buckley, Jr., Jane Fonda, Andy Rooney, Jimmy Breslin, Bob Greene, Mike Royko, Tom Wolfe—the list could go on and on.

Others combine a love and understanding of books with reporting/editing jobs on newspapers, magazines, and broadcast operations. Reviewers and critics are an important adjunct to the book industry. Few books become successful, in terms of sales and readership, without at least some media exposure.

Still others work in the retailing end of the business. While bookshops at one time tended to be intimate family enterprises, today's book dealer may well be a high-powered national chain employing sophisticated market research and the latest retailing techniques. The mass marketing successes of major chains such as Waldenbooks and B. Dalton Bookseller have transformed the book publishing business. Not only have they revitalized book sales and distribution patterns, but their national presence has encouraged millions of Americans to shop in bookstores they might never have seen otherwise. On the other hand, the chains' combined buying power and influence have given them leverage, reflected in the deep discounts they can command, that reduces profit margins throughout the industry. Book retailers must be versatile—many stores now carry audio and video cassettes, computer software, games, cards, stationery—and must possess marketing knowledge as well as an appreciation for books and local audience interests.

Working for a Publisher

Though the book publishing field is relatively small—perhaps 100,000 combined full-time employees, roughly half of them production workers—several hundred positions open up each year. Many of these are for book *travelers,* salespeople who roam assigned territories contacting individuals and organizations who buy books. They also serve as their publisher's eyes and ears throughout the country, picking up trends, perhaps spotting a talented writer who might one day develop a manuscript. Thoroughly briefed at numerous sales conferences, and armed with catalogs and other promotional materials, travelers cultivate their contacts and land the orders the publisher must have to stay in business. Often a seasoned traveler will join the home office as an executive in the editorial, marketing, or some other department.

Editors have two primary functions which sometimes overlap: finding or selecting manuscripts, then polishing them for publication. Acquisitions editors perform the first chore. The approach they adopt depends on several factors. The idea for an el-hi or college text, for example, usually originates inside the publishing house; the acquisitions editor's job is then to locate a suitable author to deliver the manuscript. In a trade book division, on the other hand, the acquisitions editor may be more passive, carefully reading manuscripts and queries that authors mail in, then recommending the best for development. In the former case, the acquisitions editor may be knowledgeable in a given area, such as economics or one of the sciences, while the second type of editor might be more of a generalist. Copyeditors who whip the manuscript into shape for the press must possess a superb background in English and work within high standards of accuracy and thoroughness, along with a remarkable attention to detail.

Talented people are also needed in marketing and advertising departments of publishing houses. These individuals write publicity releases and jacket and other promotional copy; they also develop the company's catalogue and other sales materials. Marketing and advertising people also handle a variety of additional public relations jobs, such as media relations; they may handle an author's radio and television appearances, newspaper and magazine interviews, personal-appearance tours, autograph sessions, and related activities that directly or indirectly promote sales.

There is no one way to break into the publishing field. A number of colleges and universities conduct intensive, summer-long workshops in book publishing, and some graduates use these as a springboard into the book business. Others, with degrees in journalism or English, land jobs on the basis of their writing and editing promise. Graphics and design specialists often enter the field directly from highly specialized programs at such institutions as Cooper Union and the Rhode Island School of Design. *Publishers Weekly,* the newsy and authoritative trade journal, carries "help wanted" notices in every issue. Metropolitan dailies, notably the New York *Times,* Los Angeles *Times,* Washington *Post,* Chicago *Tribune,* and Boston *Globe,* can be helpful sources of job openings in specific areas of the country.

An Encouraging Outlook

Several factors make the industry's immediate, midrange, and long-term prospects appealing:

- *An expanding audience.* The 25-to-49 age group, especially important in book sales, will reflect an enlarged percentage of college-educated, affluent men and women in the years ahead. Production of CD-ROM books has enormous potential for customers who prefer to access their books via their home or office computers.
- *More international sales.* To an impressive degree, English has become the world's language of commerce and the arts. Now allied with multinational conglomerates, many U.S. book publishers have unprecedented access to global audiences.
- *Accommodation with the competition.* At one point, some experts feared that the newer media of mass communications would supplant the book. Now considerable evidence suggests that technology can complement rather than destroy the book industry. People who use audio and video cassettes are not necessarily foregoing books; they are simply spending more total time with all media. The market for serious fiction, as an example, has been far healthier in recent years than it had been in a generation.

- *Growth of submarkets*. The book market in the United States, unlike most countries, is largely a collection of submarkets, or micromarkets, and these continue to grow and expand.[20] As an example, sales of children's books, bolstered by a modest baby boom which began in the early 1980s, remained brisk in the years that followed; the religious book field has likewise enjoyed tremendous growth, which should continue; and the professional book market, already profitable, can look forward to further growth.[21]

Indeed, one respected forecast, issued in 1992 by Vernois, Suhler & Associates, predicted book sales would continue to increase by 7.6 percent a year well past 1996—thus continuing the strong upward trend in sales that began in the 1980s. The growth in the early 1990s, according to the forecast, showed "there is no evidence to suggest that the incidence of book reading or purchasing is declining or that the new technologies are replacing book reading." Similarly encouraging to industry observers was the report that 45 percent of book purchases were made by persons with incomes lower than $30,000 annually—proof that book buying seems to cut across the income distribution of the population.[22]

For these and other reasons, the book industry's bright future seems assured. Those who become a part of it can look forward to a career that combines prestige and service in a way few other jobs can match.

Discussion

Will other media eventually replace print entirely? How and when?

summary

Of all the media of mass communications, books are the oldest, arguably the most prestigious, and certainly the most lasting. Books transmit culture from one generation to the next, help societies function and individuals develop, entertain and challenge us. More than half of all adult Americans read two or more books a year. U.S. book publishers bring out about 50,000 new titles each year.

The major classifications within the industry include trade books (books of general interest), mass market paperbacks, religious books, elementary and secondary (el-hi) textbooks, college texts, and professional books to serve the legal, medical, scientific, and technical communities.

Major steps in book publishing include acquiring the manuscript, editing it, producing (designing and printing) it, and marketing the finished product.

While some recent trends have affected the industry adversely—such as still-widespread illiteracy rates and a decline in reading interests among many Americans—the long-term outlook appears positive. Encouraging signs include a rising education level, increased international sales, and healthy growth in submarkets such as childrens' books.

? questions and cases

1. Assume you have been named an acquisitions editor for a major book publishing company. Your first day at work, the editor-in-chief tells you, "We were particularly interested in hiring you because of your youth and because we think you are familiar with young people's tastes. Now, I want you to generate some ideas for books you think young people would find interesting. Please give me five or six topics you think we should develop manuscripts for." How would you respond?

2. Within the mass communications field, and especially among journalists, this question is often raised: For a prospective novelist, is a media career an advantage or a disadvantage? One "advantage" argument is that a media career provides opportunities for many varied and unusual and intense experiences—in other words, a media career can help give a novelist something to say. What possible disadvantages can you think of?

3. The U.S. Supreme Court, in *Island Trees v. Pico,* held that certain books could be removed from school library shelves if they were "persuasively vulgar" or "educationally unsuitable." However, the Court did not explain what these terms mean. How would *you* define them?

4. The chapter concluded with a highly positive prognosis for the book industry. Do you agree? Given certain negative factors—among them the decline in reading and the threat posed by newer technologies—would you forecast a different future for books? Why or why not?

chapter glossary

aliterate   Person who is technically capable of reading but doesn't.

CD-ROM (Compact Disc, Read-Only-Memory)   A disc with room for about 600 times as much data as a standard computer floppy disc. An important new format for presenting book-length materials.

codex   A forerunner of the book wherein pages were, for the first time, cut and bound on one side.

copyright   Legal protection procured to protect original creative effort, such as a work of fiction, a piece of music, or other original creative works.

el-hi   Textbooks published for elementary and high school students.

galley proofs   Sheets of type used to check a manuscript prior to publication.

mass market paperback   Paperbound book sold at places in addition to bookshops—chain retail outlets, newsstands, airports, etc.

over the transom   Unsolicited manuscripts received by book and magazine editors from freelance writers.

papyrus   Forerunner of paper, this writing material was developed by early Egyptians from a sedgelike plant growing in the Nile valley.

royalty   A share, usually expressed in percentages, of the proceeds from sales paid to the owner of a copyright or patent.

trade book   A book of general interest, fiction or nonfiction, sold primarily at bookstores or through book clubs. (Text and reference books are marketed through other channels.)

vanity press   Publisher who brings out books that the authors themselves pay for.

notes

1 Quoted by Frank L. Schick, *The Paperbound Book in America* (New York: Bowker, 1958), frontispiece.

2 *New York Times Book Review,* 3 April 1994, *inter alia.*

3 Benjamin M. Compaine, *Understanding New Media: Trends and Issues in Electronic Distribution of Information* (Cambridge, Mass.: Ballinger, 1984), 340.

4 Much of this passage dealing with book history was drawn from John P. Dessauer, *Book Publishing: What It Is, What It Does,* 2d ed. (New York: Bowker, 1981), 1–6; and Van Allen Bradley, "Books," *World Book Encyclopedia* (1974), 2:370.

5 A good interpretation of the significance of the Linotype is found in Frank Luther Mott, *American Journalism* (New York: Macmillan, 1962), 500 ff.

6 Quoted in John Blum, et al., *The National Experience,* 2d ed. (New York: Harcourt Brace, 1968), 260.

7 Dessauer, *Book Publishing,* 3.

8 The classifications that follow are drawn largely from Benjamin M. Compaine, *The Book Industry in Transition* (White Plains: Knowledge Industry Publications, 1978), 8–22.

9 Dessauer, *Book Publishing,* 39.

10 Schick, *Paperbound Book in America,* 4.

11 Ibid., 125 ff.

12 Ibid.

13 Trish Todd, "Fiction's New Look," *Publishers Weekly,* 6 February 1987, 26.

14 Dan Lacy, "From Family Enterprise to Global Conglomerate," in *Publishing Books* (New York: Freedom Forum Media Studies Center, 1992), 6.

15 Compaine, *Book Industry in America,* 4.

16 Associated Press report published as "Year of Reader Aimed at 'Aliterates.'" Columbia, South Carolina, *State,* 19 May 1987.

17 *Island Trees v. Pico,* 102 S. Ct. 2799 (1981). The interpretation here is drawn largely from Don R. Pember, *Mass Media Law,* 6th ed. (Dubuque, Iowa: Wm. C. Brown, 1991), 97.

18 Ithiel de Sola Pool, *Technologies of Freedom: On Free Speech in an Electronic Age* (Cambridge: Harvard University Press, 1983), 188–96.

19 John Milton, *Areopagitica: A Defence of the Liberty of Unlicensed Printing* (1644), quoted in Frank Luther Mott and Ralph D. Casey, eds., *Interpretations of Journalism* (New York: Crofts, 1937), 4.

20 *Publishers Weekly,* 3 July 1992, 21.

21 Ibid., 30 March 1992, 11.

22 Ibid., 29 June 1992, 14.

chapter

I

Radio works by
converting sounds
into
electromagnetic
waves, also called
radio waves, which
can be heard
(broadcast)
through space.
These waves travel
at the speed of
light, even
penetrating some

Growth of the
Electronic Media

Objectives

When you have finished studying this chapter,
you should be able to:

@ Trace the development of radio, especially
the problems leading up to the request for
government intervention

@ Explain the rationale for governmental
controls, and how those controls are
defined and implemented

@ Discuss how broadcasting networks
operate, why they arose, and how they
influence the economics of the industry

@ Evaluate the impact television has had on
the radio industry, as well as the changes
radio underwent in coping with TV as a
competitor

Radio

Radio works by converting sounds into electromagnetic waves, also called radio waves, which can be beamed (broadcast) through space. These waves travel at the speed of light, even penetrating some solid objects such as building walls.[1] When they reach a radio receiver, they change back into the original sounds. The waves can be transmitted at various *frequencies*—numbers of cycles per second—and a radio receiver can then *tune* the waves—that is, bring in one frequency at a time without interference from another.

No one person invented radio. Instead, the process evolved over a number of years, with many scientists contributing. A Scottish physicist, James Clerk-Maxwell, proposed as early as the 1870s that radio waves existed. Between 1886 and 1889, Heinrich Hertz of Germany demonstrated how to set radio waves in motion and pick them up again. In his honor, the scientific community later named the radio wavelength, or cycles-per-second frequency measurement, after him; today's broadcast frequencies are expressed in calibrations of **hertz** called megahertz and kilohertz.

But it was the vision of a brilliant, intense young Italian engineer named Guglielmo Marconi that led to the practical use of radio as a means of point-to-point (including ship-to-shore) communication. Convinced that the wireless process had vast commercial potential, Marconi journeyed about the globe, securing patents where possible and lining up customers to try out the new system. By 1899 the company called American Marconi, through its astute exercise of patent rights, controlled much of the wireless communication within the United States.

Other scientists were by then tinkering with the radio process, and the technology developed rapidly. Nathan B. Stubblefield of Murray, Kentucky, claimed to have transmitted the first words (as opposed to the Morse code radiotelegraphy then in use) as early as 1892. His message, "Hello, Rainey," was beamed to a neighbor, Rainey T. Wells. Stubblefield was unable to repeat his successful transmission, however, and as a result his claim was not widely accepted. By 1904, John Ambrose Fleming had invented the vacuum tube, which generated, modified, amplified, and picked up radio energy, freeing radio technology from the necessity of employing unwieldy moving parts.

Fleming's remarkable invention was modified by Reginald Fessenden, who in 1907 was credited with being the first person to transmit speech on a regular basis by radio wave. That same feat was achieved independently, and somewhat by accident, by Lee DeForest, five days later. Elated, he wrote in his diary, "My present task (happy one) is to distribute sweet melody broadcast over the city and sea so that in time even the mariner far out across the silent waves may hear the music of his homeland."[2] The energy, enthusiasm, and promotional skills displayed by DeForest at this critical moment have prompted some historians to credit him with being the father of AM radio.

Edwin H. Armstrong, then a student at Columbia University, developed a different system that permitted reception of radio waves without an elaborate outside antenna. This process eventually became known as FM radio.

The rights to the inventions of DeForest, Fessenden, and Armstrong were purchased by Westinghouse, General Electric, and American Telephone and Telegraph. American Marconi, meanwhile, had locked up the legal rights to a number of critical radio processes. These territorial disputes escalated into a nasty patent war, with the result that radio's development was bogged down in the courts during the years prior to World War I.

One early, dramatic incident demonstrated radio's potential to transmit important messages across land or sea: the *Titanic* disaster of 1912. The wireless distress signals reached the *Carpathia,* which was then able to rescue 711 of the *Titanic's* 2,201 passengers. The *Titanic's* signals also reached American Marconi in New York, and they passed the story on to U.S. newspapers and wire services. The *Titanic*

Extra Information

A kilohertz (KHz) = one thousand Hertz; a megahertz (MHz) = one million Hertz. The AM radio dial begins at about 550 KHz and goes up to 1700 KHz. The FM radio dial begins at 88 MHz and goes to 108 MHz.

Background

All early wireless (radio) communication used the International Morse Code, derived from the Morse telegraph code. Many amateur radio operators still use wireless code transmissions today.

Background

AM stands for amplitude modulation; *FM* stands for frequency modulation. Modulation refers to the method of adding intelligence to the basic radio wave.

Background

Other sources say Sarnoff's part in the *Titanic* disaster has been overrated. However, regardless of his role in that event, he was the originator of the "radio music box."

tragedy was the first big news story involving radio, and it showed what the medium could do. It also massively affected the life of David Sarnoff, the young radio operator in New York who for three days remained in nonstop contact with the rescue ship *Carpathia*. In a memorandum to his superiors at Marconi, he outlined a plan whereby radio could be developed as "a household utility in the same sense as the piano or the phonograph."[3] Later, as head of the vast company he would create—the Radio Corporation of America (RCA)—Sarnoff would fulfill his own prophecy.

World War I delayed the evolution of radio in one way but speeded it along in another. Commercial experimentation with the new medium was sidetracked while the nation's big companies allocated their resources to war mobilization. For purposes of national security, radio was awarded to the Department of the Navy. Taking its mandate seriously, the Navy cut a swath through the patent jungle, snapping up whatever systems and processes it needed, and when U.S. fighting ships put to sea, they were equipped with the finest wireless systems possible. The Navy's rousing success prompted widespread pressure to award the military permanent control over all radio. A formal proposal to that effect was introduced in Congress after the armistice. Following a long and often angry debate, the bill was tabled. Radio was returned, if somewhat grudgingly, to the private sector. This decision became a defining moment in radio's history.

At this stage, however, radio was for the most part merely a hobby. Amateur radio operators, called "hams," chattered over their crystal sets to colleagues and new-found friends in faraway places, tinkering with primitive radio equipment much as computer hackers do in the present day. One such amateur operator was Frank Conrad, a research engineer for Westinghouse in Pittsburgh, who enjoyed his radio set so much that each evening he began to transmit news, sports, and even his favorite recorded music. Before long, Conrad had attracted a considerable audience, and marketing executives at Westinghouse picked up on the profit potential; if radio listening could become a pleasure, something of interest to all members of the family, then manufacturers such as Westinghouse could sell radio sets by the thousands.

Thus inspired, Conrad and H. P. Davis, a Westinghouse vice-president, applied for a commercial radio license. It was the first awarded in the United States. Westinghouse heavily promoted their station, KDKA in Pittsburgh; the company even built them a much larger transmitter. KDKA signed on with a sure-fire news story: the

1920 presidential election returns. Not many Americans first learned via KDKA that Warren G. Harding had defeated James M. Cox, but the station's publicity coup captured the fancy of consumers everywhere. The market for radio receivers surged dramatically, and all types of institutions—newspapers, churches, colleges and universities, and business concerns—charged into the broadcasting field.

It was only a matter of time before someone realized that the growing numbers of radio listeners were, in fact, a potential advertising market. A New York station, WEAF, is credited with the idea of first trying to reach this concentration of consumers with a sales pitch; it began *toll broadcasting*—that is, selling air time to anyone who wanted to use it for commercial purposes. The first taker appears to have been the Queensboro Corporation, which in 1922 purchased ten minutes to promote the sale of some new condominiums in Jackson Heights. The copy for this flowery, soft-sell commercial opened this way:

> It is 58 years since Nathaniel Hawthorne, the greatest of the American fictionists, passed away. To honor his memory the Queensboro Corporation, creator and operator of the tenant-owned system of apartment homes at Jackson Heights, New York City, has named its latest group of high-grade dwellings "Hawthorne Court." I wish to thank those within sound of my voice for the broadcasting opportunity afforded me to urge this vast radio audience to seek the recreation and daily comfort of the home removed from the congested part of the city, right at the boundaries of God's great outdoors and within a few minutes by subway from the business section of Manhattan. This sort of residential environment strongly influenced Hawthorne, the greatest . . .[4]

The Queensboro commercial and others that followed did not touch off an immediate explosion—the industry was still too young and too experimental—but the advertising community nevertheless caught a glimpse of radio's grand potential. Some government officials, meanwhile, were furious. "It is inconceivable," fumed the Secretary of Commerce and president-to-be Herbert Hoover, "that we should allow so great a possibility for service, for news, for entertainment, for education, and for vital commercial purposes to be drowned in advertising chatter."[5]

Hoping to placate the hostile public mood, the National Radio Conference adopted a resolution to curtail radio advertising. As late as 1929, the new National Association of Broadcasters opposed the airing of commercial messages between 7 and 11 P.M. But advertising meant money, and radio commercials had come to stay.[6]

In the mid-1920s, the growth of radio was as rapid as it was uncontrolled. Starting a radio station was easy. Once on the air, an individual could broadcast at whatever frequency, and at whatever power, he or she wished. Often two or more stations broadcast on the same frequency, at the same time, in the same town. If a station owner sensed he was losing to a competitor, and if he had a mean streak, he might shift his broadcast frequency to precisely match his competition; in *kamikaze* style he could neutralize the enemy, at least for the moment. The air jam was ugly.

More to the point, it was unprofitable, and broadcasters decided to do something about it. At this critical juncture, radio broadcasters turned to the federal government and *asked* that their industry be regulated. This request is significant, because when radio station managers later complained about the heavy hand of federal regulation, Congress reminded them of their *request* for government controls. Congress did not respond to the request immediately; powerful arguments arose to leave radio alone and allow the principles of supply and demand to solve the industry's problems. But the pressure to bring radio under government regulation finally prevailed. In 1927, Congress established the Federal Radio Commission and enacted the legal basis for broadcast regulation in the United States. The **Radio Act of 1927** rested on several premises:

- *The airwaves belong to the people.* No one individual can own a channel or frequency.
- *Broadcasting is limited by the number of frequencies available.* In theory, everyone could publish a newspaper, for an infinite number of presses could operate at once. In radio, however, relatively few frequencies are available on the spectrum. (Technological developments that brought us cable television and other systems later undercut this argument.) Because broadcast frequencies are scarce, their use must be regulated. As one Supreme Court justice stated, "Regulation of radio was therefore as vital to its development as traffic control was to the development of the automobile."[7]
- *All people are entitled to expect benefits from the industry.* The government could have permitted a handful of superpowerful stations to blanket the nation. Instead, it decided to authorize a great many smaller stations, each intended to serve a given community or region. For national security and other reasons, about twenty-five strong **clear channel stations** were authorized, but the main intent was to decentralize radio, making it as locally oriented as possible.
- *Not everyone is eligible for a license.* Whenever a new license is to be awarded, the government attempts to find the best applicant for it. No federal model or prescription for operating a radio station is available. To a great extent, license decisions are made on the basis of each applicant's promises of stewardship. Each must explain how the station would be run if the license were awarded to him or her, and the applicant with the strongest answer wins.
- *Despite federal regulation, broadcasting has constitutional protection.* As with other forms of expression, the First Amendment guarantee of freedom of speech applies. Like newspaper and magazine people, broadcasters may be sued for defamation or invasion of privacy. But broadcasters, again like their counterparts in the print media, cannot easily be censored by the government. In other words, freedom from prior restraint extends to the broadcast media.
- *The government's regulatory powers are discretionary, not absolute.* The mandate from Congress is that broadcasting should be regulated "in the public interest, convenience, and necessity." That is an important phrase, perhaps intentionally vague, and we will return to it later.

The federal government's powers were clarified and broadened seven years later when the Communications Act of 1934 was adopted. This law eliminated the five-member Federal Radio Commission and replaced it with a seven-member **Federal Communications Commission (FCC).** The new agency had authority over not only the radio industry, but all telecommunications. The patterns and mechanisms for broadcast regulation were now firmly in place.

Networks Evolve

The Radio Acts of 1927 and 1934 did not solve all of radio's problems, but they did give the new industry a sense of structure and organization, which reduced the chaos of future growth. Now it needed to shore up programming. Heretofore, radio listeners had been content to bring in distant stations, largely for the sake of novelty, but most of the stations weren't broadcasting much other than high school bands, community choirs, trombone solos, poetry recitations, and banquet speakers. As audiences grew restive, station managers began to think in terms of pooling their resources. One of the earliest attempts came in the autumn of 1922, when stations at Newark, New Jersey, and Schenectady, New York, linked up via telegraph wire for a simultaneous broadcast of the World Series. A few months later, stations in Boston and New York arranged a telephone hookup to broadcast a concert. Neither effort was successful from a technical point of view, but the concept was clearly worth pursuing.

By July 1923, a special cable had been developed and installed along the coast from New York to Massachusetts. Several stations tied into the "network," and they quickly began sharing programs and advertising revenues. American Telephone and Telegraph, which had long lines already in place, moved to create a national network of its own—six stations sharing three hours of programming each day. This became known as the Red Network because, in one version of the story, the special telephone wires carrying the radio programs had red labels. Not to be outdone, the Radio Corporation of America established a Blue Network.

As others attempted to form radio syndicates, AT&T, which controlled telephone land lines, found itself in the uneasy situation of having to provide flawless service to competitors or face possible restraint of trade charges from the Justice Department. For this and other reasons, AT&T entered into a complex set of negotiations with RCA. When the smoke cleared, RCA had bought the Red Network from American Telephone and Telegraph; AT&T, in return for pulling out of the commercial radio broadcasting business, remained uncontested in the telephone land lines field.

RCA's Red Network became the National Broadcasting Company. The Blue Network, later sold, eventually became the American Broadcasting Company. Another group of stations banded together to form the United Independent Broadcasters; they soon worked out an agreement with the Columbia Phonograph Record Company where, under the astute leadership of William S. Paley, they emerged as the Columbia Broadcasting System. A fourth major radio network, the Mutual Broadcasting System, comprised primarily of smaller stations, developed in the 1930s. In addition to the four national networks, numerous state and regional networks were founded as well.[8]

A Change in American Life

Networks catapulted radio into an information, entertainment, and advertising force of heroic proportions. A radio network served its member stations, called **affiliates,** by developing high-caliber—or, at least, expensive—programs. The network transmitted these programs to the affiliates for local broadcasting. The networks also sold advertising time for their affiliates with major national clients.

A change in American life. Radio brings events and celebrities to audiences throughout the country. Here, Babe Ruth is interviewed by Graham McNamee, one of the greatest of the early sportscasters.

In exchange, the affiliates agreed to carry the network programs free of charge. It was a good bargain. The affiliates got slick, top-quality programming, a share of the advertising take, and the chance to sell their time locally during agreed-upon commercial breaks throughout the broadcast days and nights. The dozens of local affiliates combined to provide the networks with a ready-made audience, a vast, rich market that spanned from one coast to the other.

It is difficult to overestimate the impact that network radio had on American society from the 1920s through the 1940s. Millions of listeners were transported as if by magic to the faraway concert hall, baseball stadium, vaudeville house, night club, studio theater—to virtually anywhere one could haul a microphone and a portable transmitter. Radio wrought a transformation in national life, perhaps even more remarkable than the one television produced later.[9] Between 1930 and 1945, a period often referred to as "the golden age of radio," American families huddled before their living room receivers, riveted to broadcasts of action-adventure tales, comedies, mystery dramas, music, and variety shows. Homemakers could listen to romance serial dramas, called soap operas because detergent manufacturers sponsored so many of them. Youngsters raced home from school to tune in afternoon adventure programs. Families planned entire evenings around the network

Extra Information

Actually, families could participate in other activities as they listened since radio—unlike TV—doesn't require you to stare at it. Homemakers commonly ironed and cleaned while listening to soap operas.

Red Barber on Language

Regarded by many as the best baseball announcer in radio history, Red Barber was a fixture at Ebbets Field, where he called the Brooklyn Dodger games, and at CBS network radio for a generation. Audiences admired him not only for his wit and insight, but especially for his ability to choose just the right words, no more, to describe the action. In his autobiography, he explained how he learned his craft:

As soon as I got to CBS, Murrow [Edward R. Murrow, credited with building the News Division] sent for me. He didn't say much. All he said was, "Be careful of the adjectives . . . when you say something was a great riot, be damned sure it was a great riot . . . not a minor scuffle or a mere commotion or a handful of people milling around. It's the adjectives you have to watch to report the news properly. Be careful with the adjectives.

Red Barber, *The Broadcasters* (De Capo Books, 1970).

Allen's Alley

One of the most popular radio personalities of the thirties and early forties was Fred Allen, whose satiric sketches provided radio listeners with some of the nation's best radio comedy. Midway during his weekly radio program, he escorted his huge network audience through "Allen's Alley," a fictional neighborhood populated by such characters as Senator Claghorn, a windy Southern politician; Mrs. Nussbaum, an archetypical Jewish mother; Titus Moody, a taciturn New Englander, and Ajax Cassidy, an Irish American. Cassidy, portrayed by Peter Donald, always greeted Allen with a cheery "We-e-ell, how do ye do?" One of their more or less typical conversations went this way:

ALLEN:	Ajax, I heard you were sick.
CASSIDY:	I was at death's door . . .
ALLEN:	You were bad, eh?
CASSIDY:	The doctor gave me a big bottle of . . . pills.
ALLEN:	Uh-huh.
CASSIDY:	After every meal the doctor said to swallow one pill and drink a small glass of whiskey.
ALLEN:	How is the treatment coming along?
CASSIDY:	I'm a little behind with the pills.

Neil A. Grauer, *American Heritage*, February 1988.

prime time radio schedule. Entertainers such as Amos 'n Andy, Jack Benny, Jimmy Durante, Bob Hope, Bing Crosby, Red Skelton, and Fred Allen were beloved by huge network radio audiences. In a way that later generations may find difficult to fathom, radio commanded the attention and the affection of the American public.

Radio News

Radio was also bound for moments of greatness in the news field. Regular news analysis and commentary began in 1921. One of the earliest pioneers was Hans von Kaltenborn, a columnist for the Brooklyn *Eagle,* who developed a half-hour review of world events. Kaltenborn's terse, perceptive insights gave broader meaning to the news; powerful government leaders as well as thousands of ordinary citizens faithfully tuned in his broadcasts on WEAF in New York. Kaltenborn's commentary was at times controversial: Should a broadcaster, using the public airwaves, be permitted

Suggested Audiovisual Aid

Obtain cassettes of early radio programs and play some in class.

Background

After Germany became the villain in the late thirties, Kaltenborn dropped the aristocratic "von" and became plain H.V. Kaltenborn.

Jimmy Durante, one of the most popular radio stars of the 1940s, rehearses with that week's guest, a youthful Frank Sinatra.

to criticize specific government actions? Some highly placed observers thought not. Indeed, WEAF once pulled him off the air following protests from Secretary of State Charles Evans Hughes.[10] Eventually radio developed station managers strong enough to weather the attacks of those who would impose prior restraint, or censorship, on broadcast messages.

Regularly scheduled newscasts began a few years later. Lowell Thomas, a dashing adventurer and author blessed with an uncommonly authoritative voice, inaugurated his daily fifteen-minute newscast in 1930 on NBC Blue. The program remained on the air for more than forty years. Other networks launched evening newscasts shortly thereafter, and local stations were soon providing news reports during the day as well. News bulletins and flashes often interrupted regular programming.

Radio's speed, convenience, and dramatic quality soon began to affect newspaper readership, a development that gave publishers pause. One early victim of radio news was the newspaper "extra," a special edition brought out at any hour of the day or night that big news broke. But those "flashes" that once sold newspaper extras now reached the public first on the radio. Radio bulletins, in other words, drove the extras into extinction as audiences and advertising dollars drained away.

Some publishers shrewdly hedged against radio's threat by opening or buying stations themselves. Others, however, came to regard broadcasting as the enemy. Exerting their considerable leverage, publishers badgered the major wire services—Associated Press, United Press, and International News Service—to withhold service to broadcast networks. This heavy-handed tactic ultimately failed, but for more than a decade publishers bitterly and effectively contested radio news broadcasting.

The publishers, in fairness, did have a point. Most of the news broadcast on radio was lifted from the newspapers to begin with. The wire services were legally entitled to get carbons of the articles the moment the newspaper reporters were finished, and often stories were put on the wire, snatched off the ticker by a radio newscaster, and broadcast before the paper hit the streets. Too, many publishers felt that spoken news on the radio was little more than gossip, hastily and carelessly handled by newscasters more interested in entertainment values than news judgment.

For a while in the 1930s, the wire services permitted radio stations to broadcast only ten minutes of wire service news per day, and only after the stories had been published in a newspaper. These and other punitive measures were eventually overturned, and by the early 1940s radio news was unrestricted.[11] The newspaper industry's fears did not completely disappear; in many small towns even today, the local newspaper and local radio station vigorously compete for news. But the open warfare ended. Many publishers discovered that radio news could actually help sell newspapers; the person who caught a fleeting, but important, news bulletin on the radio was highly likely to buy a newspaper to obtain further details.

While waging their uphill battle for access to the wire services, radio networks gradually began building reporting teams of their own. By 1936, U.S. radio correspondents were broadcasting on-the-scene reports from the Spanish Civil War, and CBS was beginning to deploy a tiny but gifted cadre of reporters throughout Europe. Led by Edward R. Murrow, the CBS team quickly got on top of the political crisis that rocked Europe during the months leading up to World War II. Building a tradition that later formed the basis of *broadcast journalism,* Murrow's correspondents produced superior-quality evening roundups of news from the capitals of Europe. When the fighting broke out, they reported from the battlefields. The horrors of the Nazi blitz were brought home to millions of Americans through Murrow's brilliant accounts, sometimes broadcast under fire while an air raid was in progress.[12]

Background

United Press was the first to sell news to radio stations.

Teaching Idea

Does an all-news-and-talk radio station broadcast in your area? If so, have students find out what sources it uses to obtain the news it broadcasts.

Suggested Audiovisual Aid

Edward R. Murrow's "This is London" broadcasts during the 1940 air raids are available on cassette and still worth listening to.

Radio's public service capacity and its value as a unifying element within society were impressively demonstrated in the hours following the Japanese attack on Pearl Harbor. Network anchors pieced together fragmentary reports from throughout the Pacific to inform an anxious people about the events leading directly to the United States entry into the war. Using newly developed portable wire recorders, combat correspondents traveled with U.S. invasion forces in North Africa, the Pacific, and on the continent of Europe. Through transoceanic hookups, radio carried live broadcasts of the unconditional surrender of the Germans and Japanese in 1945.[13]

Television Takes Hold

At the end of World War II, radio was riding the crest of a wave of popularity, prestige, and profits. The industry's total income doubled between 1937 and 1944. Network advertising revenue was now handsomely augmented by the increasing millions of dollars that poured in from local retailers. Hundreds of license applications, bottled up by wartime restrictions, awaited FCC approval. Within sixteen months, reported the Federal Communications Commission in 1947, the total number of communities with local radio stations almost doubled. Radio appeared to be in an invincible position. It was not.

Television technology had been around for years—seventeen experimental TV stations were in operation as early as 1937—but only after World War II did TV begin to take hold with U.S. audiences. TV's gains were to become radio's losses. As reflected in national advertising revenue, radio's decline began in earnest during 1949; the industry recorded some $5 million less in ad revenue that year, and far more severe decreases lay ahead. "Hooperatings" and other audience measurements documented the exodus from radio to television. Between 1948 and 1951, the Jack Benny program, a top-drawer network radio attraction, lost the equivalent of three out of every four of its listeners.[14] Less popular radio personalities fared even worse.

The national networks covered their losses by moving into television programming themselves. This was a shrewd business move, but one hardly designed to inspire advertiser or audience confidence in radio's present or future. Ironically, network radio's profits were diverted to finance the growth of television. The industry seemed to be paying for its own funeral.

Radio's Remarkable Rebirth

With television rapidly gaining control over the mass audiences, radio got the leftover fragments—an unenviable position, but not necessarily a fatal one. Radio's renaissance began with the realization that these audience segments could, with careful and selective programming, be developed into potentially profitable submarkets. Deprived of its cherished role as family entertainer, radio was nevertheless able to hustle up different types of audiences by becoming more personal—good company for the solitary listener, no matter what his or her interests, indoors or out, daytime or night. National radio celebrity entertainers may not have been so readily available, but listeners soon created heroes anew—disc jockeys and local news and weather personalities. TV had the masses, but radio soon grabbed the "classes," the personalized audience segments comprised of teenagers, homemakers, country-and-western music fans, the news-hungry, and the devoutly religious. According to critic Richard L. Tobin, "Radio . . . seems to have grown up since TV took over its hackneyed situation comedy routines, its stand-up comics, its weekly musicals. What was worst in radio has deserted for the glamour of the picture tube. What is left is often the very best in music at many levels, news coverage, unparalleled in any other medium including TV and print, some of the most rewarding talk available anywhere, and a format so simple and comparatively inexpensive as to be indestructible."[15]

The Rise of FM Radio

Radio programs can be broadcast in different ways, depending on how the program signal and carrier wave are combined. **Amplitude modulation (AM)** radio operates by varying the strength (amplitude) of the radio waves to match the shape of the audio waves. In **frequency modulation (FM)** radio, the size and shape of the waves remain constant, but the frequency of the waves—the number of times they vibrate per second—changes to match the electronic waves transmitted from the studio.

A radio station antenna beams out *ground waves* and *sky waves,* but AM and FM waves behave differently. AM's sky waves bounce off a ceiling of electrical particles in the ionosphere (known as the *Kennelly-Heaviside layer,* it forms mostly at night) and return to earth in a broad pattern that may extend for many miles. Thus, AM waves have great range, particularly in the evenings. FM sky waves, in contrast, cut through the Kennelly-Heaviside layer and continue into space. An FM station's effective listening range is therefore limited to ground waves along the *line of sight*—that is, the signal cannot normally be transmitted beyond the horizon seen from the antenna. Despite this limitation, FM had certain strategic advantages:

1 It generally provided clearer, truer sound quality than AM and was less affected by static.

2 Its spectrum was broader, allowing for many channels.

3 The stations were less expensive to operate, generally, than their AM counterparts at the time.[16]

AM was the earlier process, and it enjoyed universal use during the industry's formative years. As research resolved FM's complex technical problems, AM owners, who feared that FM could render their operations obsolete, for years exerted their formidable political clout to delay FM's logical expansion. FM stereo broadcasts, for example, were not authorized until 1961. By the mid-1960s, however, FM radio had begun to realize its potential. Central to this was the adaptation of stereo sound, an advance encouraged by a new generation of appreciative music listeners, accustomed to high-fidelity sound recordings, who began tuning in to local FM stations. As the audience numbers increased, so did the advertising dollars. By the mid-1960s, new radio home receivers came off the assembly lines routinely equipped with FM as well as AM bands. The Federal Communications Commission welcomed FM's surge by shutting off further expansion in the crowded AM spectrum and granting new licenses only to FM station applicants. Once merely a novelty, FM had come of age.

FM greatly outperforms its older brother in many pivotal areas. During 1994, the Federal Communications Commission reported more FM than AM stations in operation. That year, 11,253 licensed radio stations operated in the United States; 4,969 of them were commercial AMs, 4,723 commercial FMs, and the remaining 1,561 noncommercial FMs.[17] FM stations, according to market research, boasted a dominant share of the market; one recent survey showed that AM stations commanded only 29 percent of the listening audience, while FM accounted for the other 71 percent. The total number of radio listeners was about the same as it had been ten years earlier, when FM had only about a third of the total. FM's growth came at AM's expense.

AM radio continues to be strong, however, in one all-important part of the day. During *drive time,* radio's most popular listening period, AM programming—especially news-talk—seems to work best. Many possible explanations come to mind. Perhaps, as James D. Harless has noted, "beautiful music does not always suit the bustle and hassle of life in the fast lane."[18] But by any standard, much of the credit for the radio industry's rejuvenation must go to the dramatic increase in the popularity of FM listening.

Example
Have your students ascertain the number of AM and FM radio stations in your area. Can they determine whether any recent additions or deletions have occurred?

Television: The Technology Evolves

Transmitting television sights and sounds requires three basic processes. (1) The TV camera gathers sound and sight waves as it scans the scene and converts them into electronic signals. (2) The camera transmits the signal to a receiver. The entire image is not reproduced at once; the TV camera can capture and send only one minuscule portion of it at a time. (3) The receiver then deciphers the signals and changes them back into the original sequence. On a photo-sensitized picture tube—coated with material that emits light when struck by electronic beams—the scene is reassembled, microscopic dot by microscopic dot. The scanning of the TV cameras is so swift—thirty complete pictures, or *frames,* are sent each second—that the effect is that of a single, continuous image. The flickers are minimized and the illusion is complete.[19]

Background
Motion pictures use the same process as still pictures, but they are projected at a 24-frame-per-second rate. In the early days of television, this caused some problems in televising movies.

Background

For several years, mechanical and electronic television battled in England. By 1935, electronic had won.

Background

Inventor Philo Farnsworth is generally credited with developing the first all-electronic TV system. RCA later bought many of the Farnsworth patents.

Color television takes the black-and-white (*monochrome*) process a step further, using the three primary colors of light—green, blue, and red—to develop full-color pictures. Various combinations of these three primary colors can produce any color of light. Color cameras and TV receivers possess the necessary electronic circuitry to activate the color components in addition to the normal monochrome transmissions. Stations today send out *compatible color* signals, which means monochrome sets can also receive the signals in black and white.

While television's overwhelming presence is a fairly recent phenomenon—the first nationally televised presidential address to Congress, for example, did not occur until 1950, and the first colorcasting began on a highly limited scale in 1953—the technology of television began to take shape more than a century ago. In the 1880s, various scientists, mostly in Europe, were experimenting with transmitting communications signals through the air as electromagnetic waves. In 1884, Paul G. Nipkow, a German, invented a scanning wheel for transmitting pictures by wireless. As Nipkow's wheel turned, spirally positioned holes each scanned one line. The unwieldy mechanical contraption prompted other scientists to experiment in this area. By 1915, Guglielmo Marconi, the brilliant entrepreneur who would do so much to establish radio, predicted that "wireless telephone" would one day transmit pictures as well as words. But television's true development was tied to general advancements in the electronics industry, and leadership in this effort would soon move from Europe to the United States.

In 1923, Vladimir Zworykin, who was born in Russia but became a U.S. citizen, patented the first **iconoscope;** a vacuum tube housed a photosensitive plate on which an image could be projected, and an electron "gun" scanned the image with a narrow-focused beam. A number of successful experiments followed the invention of this first workable television tube. The Bell Telephone Laboratories televised several news and special events programs during the 1920s; and WGY in Schenectady, New York showed the first television drama in 1928. These were costly and cumbersome ventures, but they suggested the new medium's vast potential.

The Radio Corporation of America was particularly impressed. Armed with profits from its thriving radio business, RCA in 1930 assembled a formidable engineering force, with Zworykin as its chief, to deal directly with all the technical and economic barriers to effective, publicly acceptable national television. The British Broadcasting Corporation, meanwhile, in 1936 became the first to offer its audiences regular, if limited, television service. After nearly a decade of expensive and intense research, the RCA task force triumphantly demonstrated at the 1939 New York World's Fair a high-resolution, all-electronic television system. The picture quality was far better than that available anywhere else, and the technical problems seemed largely a thing of the past. RCA and other electronics giants confidently began tooling up to manufacture television receivers on a considerable scale. The screens were small—with five- to nine-inch picture tubes—and initially the prices were high, but the public was captivated, and the new medium's immediate success appeared near at hand.

As measured by enthusiastic, nationwide acceptance, success did come, but not immediately. World War II harnessed the country's total engineering and manufacturing efforts, and television operations were suspended until after the fighting ended. When telecasting resumed in 1945, only eight stations provided regular programs to an estimated 10,000 operational TV sets. A few months later, broadcasters had dozens of stations, and TV receiver sales shot into the millions. Lifestyles were visibly changed; movie attendance took a drastic downturn, while crowds fell off at minor league baseball games and at evening civic club meetings. TV was reordering the cultural scene, and neither the government nor industry itself was prepared to deal with it. Fearful of repeating the mistakes made with radio a generation earlier, when broadcasting licenses were awarded without a clear technical plan and without adequate controls, the Federal Communications Commission on 30 September 1948 clamped a freeze on TV station expansion: no new licenses until the industry became better organized.

Over the next four years, the FCC developed engineering standards, reserved a number of stations for educational use, adopted uniform criteria for color systems, and approved a plan for allocating licenses more equitably. When the freeze was lifted in April 1952, the industry was positioned to expand, in more or less orderly fashion, to communities throughout the country. Telecasters had not been idle during the freeze years. In 1948, effective TV relay systems had been put in place, linking one part of the country with another and making network telecasting possible.

The first entertainer to attract a vast national audience was Milton Berle, an actor-comedian whose zany routines made his "Texaco Star Theater" enormously popular from 1948 to 1956. Millions of Americans bought television sets largely to view this one program, which often commanded an 80 percent share of the entire TV audience. Perhaps the most successful situation comedy of all time, "I Love Lucy," starring Lucille Ball and Desi Arnaz, premiered in 1951. "Lucy" reruns, shown in syndication, remain popular more than a generation later. Quiz programs, professional wrestling matches, and variety hours such as "Your Show of Shows," starring Sid Caesar and Imogene Coca; Ed Sullivan's "Toast of the Town"; and "Arthur Godfrey's Talent Scouts" attracted large followings and created new stars. Television dramas, notably "Playhouse 90," "The Kraft Television Theatre," "The General Electric Theater," and "Fireside Theater," aired scripts written by Paddy Chayefsky and other top literary talents, often shown in "live" performances. These programs enthralled millions of viewers and launched many successful acting careers.[20]

By the early 1950s, network TV reached 60 percent of all U.S. homes, and only a few years after that, the penetration of television, as defined by numbers of consumers reached, had become all but total.

Spectacular technological changes would soon have to be dealt with—adjustments to the possibilities offered by cable, satellites, fiber optics, interactive systems—but the regulatory and economic patterns defining the broadcasting industry were in place. Television was positioned, and radio repositioned, to face the challenges and opportunities ahead.

Television's first great star, Milton Berle. Millions of Americans bought their first television sets largely to see "Uncle Miltie" and his weekly variety show.

Teaching Idea

Several cable channels regularly replay some of these early programs from the golden age of TV. Consult your cable guide for particular programs your students could watch.

summary

No one person invented radio. Wireless broadcasting evolved over a number of years, with many scientists contributing to it. Prominent among them were James Clerk-Maxwell, Heinrich Hertz, John Ambrose Fleming, Guglielmo Marconi, Lee DeForest, and Edwin Armstrong, each of whom developed an important device or procedure that helped make radio a viable communications medium. Initially, patents secured these separate inventions, precluding any one company from totally integrating an effective system. During World War I, the Navy was awarded control over radio, empowered to cut through the patent jungle and develop an effective system. Impressed by the Navy's success, many government leaders favored keeping radio under government control, but Congress decided, by a narrow margin, to allow radio to remain in private hands.

The radio industry grew rapidly in the 1920s, but the growth was neither planned nor regulated, and soon broadcasters asked Congress to set broad guidelines for the new industry. The Radio Act of 1927, which provided for stations to be licensed "in the public interest, convenience, or necessity," affirmed that the airwaves belong to all the people, and license holders were to act as custodians for the public good.

Further growth, including the development of radio networks, permitted radio to become an entertainment, news, and advertising medium important enough to change American life. Millions of listeners were transported as if by magic to the faraway concert hall, baseball stadium, vaudeville house, studio theater, or night club. Few developments have influenced social and behavioral patterns as much as network radio began to do in the thirties and forties.

The networks and the scientific community, meanwhile, were busy conducting experiments that would make television feasible. In 1923, Vladimir Zworykin, a Russian-born U.S. citizen, patented the first iconoscope, which could project images onto video screens. A Radio Corporation of America task force was able to develop a high-resolution, all-electronic television system to demonstrate at the 1939 World's Fair. Further research was halted soon after, however, as the nation mobilized its resources for World War II.

After the war, television was introduced to U.S. audiences in a big way. The Federal Communications Commission awarded station licenses, following much the same philosophy and pattern established for the radio industry. By the early 1950s, network TV reached 60 percent of all U.S. homes, and only a few years after that, the penetration of television, as defined by numbers of consumers reached, had become all but total.

? questions and cases

1. Assume a new television channel is about to be made available in your community. You are interested in applying for the license to operate that channel. Given the historical context of earning a broadcast license, outline the main points you would make in your application to the FCC.

2. Comment on radio news as it is broadcast in your market. How thorough is it? how accurate? how professional in its presentation? If you were news director of the leading radio station in your market, would you change your newscasts? Explain.

3. Most broadcasting systems around the world are government owned or controlled. By a close vote in the Congress, U.S. radio remained in private hands. How might U.S. broadcasting history have been different if the federal government owned and operated the system? Evaluate the differences in terms of programming, advertising, and newscasts. Would we be better or worse off as a result of government ownership of broadcasting?

4. Do you agree with the basic premise of the Radio Act of 1927, that "the airwaves belong to all the people"? How effectively, in your view, have the broadcast companies served as "stewards" of the country's radio and television stations? Is the FCC's control too harsh? too lenient? What changes would you like to see in broadcast regulation? Discuss.

chapter glossary

affiliates   Stations that agree to carry a radio or television network's programming.

AM radio   Amplitude modulation radio; this oldest form of commercial radio transmits sound by changing the size of the radio wave, rather than changing its frequency (as FM, or frequency modulation radio does).

clear channel station   A maximum-power radio station with a point on the spectrum all to itself. Most stations are assigned local or regional coverage; for national defense and other reasons, however, a few clear channel stations are permitted.

Federal Communications Commission (FCC)   Government agency charged with the regulation of broadcasting; awards licenses to broadcasters, reviews their performance, and sets national broadcasting policy, subject to review by Congress and the courts.

FM radio   Frequency modulation radio; this form changes its frequency rather than its amplitude (see *AM radio*).

hertz   Frequency of radio waves per second. Named in memory of H. R. Hertz, German physicist who was a pioneer in radio development, these frequencies are measured in thousands (*kilohertz*), formerly called *kilocycles*. They describe a station's transmitting frequency and its location on the broadcast spectrum.

iconoscope   The camera tube in the initial television system developed by Vladimir Zworykin.

kinescope   Cathode-ray tube which served as an early television receiving unit. Its luminescent screen picked up transmitted light signals and reproduced them as televised images. (This term also refers to film recording of TV programs or advertising messages.)

Radio Act of 1927   Congressional determination that the airwaves belong to the people, not to individual station owners, and that the radio industry must be regulated at the federal level. This law, expanded in the Radio Act of 1934, provides the basis for broadcast regulation in the United States.

notes

1 This discussion of radio history was drawn from "The Fifth Estate," *Broadcasting/Cablecasting Yearbook,* 1993, A–1 ff; Sydney W. Head, *Broadcasting in America,* 3d ed. (Boston: Houghton Mifflin, 1976), 21–34 and 90–124; Erik Barnouw, *A Tower in Babel: A History of Broadcasting in the United States* (New York: Oxford University Press, 1966), 1–188; and an excellent essay by Robert L. Hilliard, "Radio," *World Book Encyclopedia* (1974), 16:78.

2 Barnouw, *Tower in Babel,* 23.

3 Quoted in John Tebbel, *The Media in America* (New York: Crowell, 1974), 359. Other historians suggest that Sarnoff's role in the *Titanic* disaster has been greatly exaggerated, however.

4 Barnouw, *Tower in Babel,* 111.

5 Ibid., 114.

6 Irving Settel, *A Pictorial History of Radio* (New York: Bonanza Books, 1969), 51.

7 Justice Felix Frankfurter, in delivering the majority opinion in *National Broadcasting Company v. United States,* 319 U.S. 190 (1943).

8 Barnouw, *Tower in Babel,* 143–53; Settel, *Pictorial History of Radio,* 55–69; Head, *Broadcasting in America,* 117–21.

9 Tebbel, *Media in America,* 362.

10 Barnouw, *Tower in Babel,* 141.

11 *Associated Press v. United States,* 326 U.S. 1 (1945).

12 An excellent biography of Murrow is Alexander Kendrick's *Prime Time: The Life of Edward R. Murrow* (Boston: Little, Brown, 1969). *A Treasury of Great Reporting,* edited by Louis L. Snyder and Richard B. Morris (New York: Simon and Schuster, 1949), carries the complete text of one of Murrow's superlative World War II broadcasts, 633.

13 Frank Luther Mott, *American Journalism* (New York: Macmillan, 1962), 708.

14 Head, *Broadcasting in America,* 153.

15 Reprinted in *The Reader's Digest Dictionary of Quotations* (New York: Funk and Wagnalls, 1968), 267.

16 For a full discussion of these differences, see Head, *Broadcasting in America,* 42 ff. In today's climate, where programming and management strategies are different, FM stations are not inherently less expensive to operate than AM stations. Nor does FM inherently provide truer sound. FM's fidelity is due to receiver design; wideband AM receiver sound is fully comparable to wideband FM reception.

17 Figures furnished by the National Association of Broadcasters, 1993.

18 James D. Harless, *Mass Communication* (Dubuque, Iowa: Wm. C. Brown, 1985), 269.

19 This passage dealing with the technology of television is drawn largely from Sydney Head, *Broadcasting in America;* "Brief History of Broadcasting and Cable," *Broadcasting & Cable Market Place,* 1992, xv, and Erik Barnouw, *Tube of Plenty: The Evolution of American Television* (New York: Oxford University Press, 1977).

20 Tim Brooks and Earle Marsh, *The Complete Directory to Prime Time Network TV Shows, 1946–Present* (New York: Ballantine, 1981).

chapter J

"The report of my death," cabled Mark Twain from Europe to an embarrassed Associated Press, "was an exaggeration."[1] So too, in the years after World War II, was the oft-heard prediction that a revolutionary new medium called

Radio

Radio

Objectives

When you have finished studying this chapter, you should be able to:

- Describe various contemporary radio formats and explain why they are employed

- Explain how radio news is written and presented

- Discuss public radio—its background, organization, contemporary situation, and primary purpose

- Comment on such current issues within the industry as deregulation and moral concern over content

- Explain some of the principal technological changes affecting radio

"The report of my death," cabled Mark Twain from Europe to an embarrassed Associated Press, "was an exaggeration."[1] So too, in the years after World War II, was the oft-heard prediction that a revolutionary new medium called television would soon smash radio into oblivion.

Radio was staggered by television, bent by TV, but not broken. Major adjustments were called for, and they were forthcoming. Radio reorganized itself, redefined its mission, and found new audiences by approaching them at different times in different ways, and soon the industry was off and running once more. In recent years, the renaissance of radio has been astonishing. Consider: In 1950, early in television's history and when radio was presumably at its peak, 2,867 radio stations were on the air. Despite the phenomenal growth of television after that, by mid-1994 the number of radio stations had *quadrupled,* to nearly 12,000, with construction permits for 1,419 more stations already authorized. Additionally:

- Radio advertising revenues continue to climb, and currently average about $9 billion a year.
- More than 96 percent of all Americans aged twelve and older are regular radio listeners—that is, they listen at least once a week, accounting for an estimated 39 percent of *all* time spent with mass media.
- Americans have more than 500 million radio receivers—twice as many radios, in other words, as population. Each household averages 6.6 radio sets, including car radios. Only one car in twenty is *not* equipped with a radio.[2]

Radio is a constant, portable companion that listeners count on for news, entertainment, service messages, consumer information, and commentary. Radio is more convenient than television and more immediate than newspapers—"When you hear it, it's news," boasts one radio promotion, "but when you read it, it's history." The medium touches virtually every aspect of our lives, making us aware of the world around us and keeping us in contact with it.

Radio's essential strength: portability.

Extra Information

Broadcasting and Cable publishes current figures on the number of operating and proposed radio and television stations each week.

Class Project

Survey the class on (1) exactly how many radios they own or have access to each day, and (2) how much time they spend listening to radio.

Radio and American Culture

Radio's cultural function is probably best illustrated by the popularity of Garrison Keillor, whose "Prairie Home Companion"—originally a local program on Minnesota Public Radio before going national—makes creative demands on the senses and encourages listeners to see, smell, and feel Keillor's imaginary hometown of Lake Wobegon, "where all the children are above average." In anyone's radio hall of fame, Keillor has first-rank inclusion, so strong is his influence on the character of the medium and its content. More or less alone on the radio stage of the 1990s, he does what radio did in the 1930s and 1940s, during the medium's so-called golden age.

"Radio: The Forgotten Medium," *Medium Studies Journal,* Summer 1993.

Talk Radio: Looking for Shared Values

The appeal of talk radio, beyond its value as entertainment, appears to be its old-time town-meeting quality. It is reminiscent of a time when people had shared sets of values, when people gathered regularly to exchange information, especially on local politics and social issues, and reaffirmed their sense of belonging—even when belonging meant bitterly disagreeing over what was best for the community. "The subliminal depths of radio," Marshall McLuhan wrote, "are charged with the resonating echoes of tribal horns and antique drums. This is the very nature of the medium, with its power to turn the psyche and society into a single echo chamber."

U.S. News & World Report, 15 January 1990.

Town Meetings of the Air

Nowhere is contemporary radio's vibrancy more evident than in call-in talk shows, both local and national. Radio talk shows are credited, or blamed, with influencing political events and social trends whenever and wherever they occur. Indeed, this programming genre has made it possible for audiences throughout the land to engage in a massive, practically continuous town meeting in which listeners of every political persuasion tirelessly debate the political and social issues of the moment.

Foremost among the radio talk show hosts of the early 1990s was Rush Limbaugh, whose conservative message was eventually heard over more than 600 stations, reaching virtually every radio market in the United States. His audience, estimated at 6 million or more each weekday, was fiercely loyal and effusive. One scholar in the field of radio described it this way:

> The political reasons, of course, are best known and most cited. Almost all who listen maintain fervently that he speaks the truth as he fulminates daily about militant homosexuals, the excesses of the feminist movement, "wacko" environmentalists, gun controllers, vegetarians or any of the other "liberal" cause-mongerers who exasperate him. Limbaugh's partisans listen with the rapt adoration usually reserved for a lover or a divinity. Almost all the calls he takes from listeners—about a dozen each program—are prefaced with "dittos," the Limbaugh idolizer's shorthand for "How do I love thee?"[3]

Teaching Idea

If there is a news-talk radio station in your area, ask your students to report on whether it is AM or FM and what national and local talk shows it carries. Do any students listen regularly?

Others were less impressed, vilifying Limbaugh as a bigot and a demagogue. But even his detractors, and there were many, conceded that he had the most powerful voice on talk radio. Some industry analysts even credit him with saving AM radio, where his weekday program could most often be heard, from extinction.

Satellites and 800-numbers have made it possible for radio talk shows to go national. Callers can share their views with listeners everywhere. Eager for the chance to reach the large, activist audiences that find talk radio irresistible, politicians and other celebrities have called to air their views on talk radio also. Larry King and G. Gordon Liddy, among many talk radio hosts representing various shades of political views, have drawn listeners by the millions. Perhaps the most controversial radio talk show host of the early 1990s was Howard Stern, whose shock-talk approach offended some listeners, made him wildly popular with others, and earned him an estimated $12 million a year. As a *Time* cover story explained, "For now, both Limbaugh and Stern make the . . . marketplace of ideas quirkier, livelier, more bracing, more free, more American."

A superstar of modern radio: controversial talk show host Rush Limbaugh, whose weekday audiences number in the millions.

But by no means are all talk radio programs national. Nearly every medium and large radio market now boasts its own local talk programs. And politicians are listening. Radio talk shows are just one dimension of public opinion feedback, but they are a lively and important dimension. "We elect officials to make hard decisions," writes one radio talk show star, Diane Rehm of WAMU-FM in Washington, D.C. "For them, sometimes insulated inside the beltway in Washington, D.C., or in state capitol offices in North Dakota, talk shows can provide an early gauge of whether an issue will be controversial and an accurate reading of what the folks back home are saying over the backyard fence."[4]

Other contributors to radio's survival in the 1950s and 1960s include "top 40" stations, which provided music and news and attracted loyal audiences. Radio's individual heroes included Bernice Judis of WNEW, Todd Storz at WHB, Gordon McLendon at XETRA and elsewhere, and Bill Drake at KHJ. These are just a few of the stars and executives whose innovations kept the industry alive.

Formats

A radio station's format is its personality, the programming formula it develops to appeal to a specific audience in a specific market. Formats are constantly adjusted in response to audience flow and advertiser demand, factors monitored more or less continuously: a dismal "book" (a report of audience listening patterns, compiled by a survey agency such as Arbitron) may well foreshadow a shakeup of programming, staff, or both, or perhaps the adoption of an entirely new format. *Broadcasting/Cable Yearbook* in the early 1990s listed more than sixty formats in use throughout the country—including "Eskimo," "Elvis," and "New Wave."[5] Among the most common major groups of formats, which might include many variations, are

- *AOR* (album-oriented rock). Adult-oriented selections from the top 100 albums.
- *MOR* (middle-of-the-road). No extreme hard rock music.
- *Contemporary*. More rock with emphasis on current recordings.
- *Country*. Formerly referred to as Country and Western (C and W), but purely "western" music is seldom aired today.
- *Gold*. Music of an earlier era, heavily laced with nostalgia.
- *African American*. Other targeted ethnic formats are Spanish-language and, less frequently, programming for Asian Americans.
- *Progressive*. Music reflecting new, usually improvisational, interpretations.
- *Religious*.
- *Beautiful music*. Lavish, melodic arrangements, mostly instrumentals; pleasant background sounds.
- *Classical*. Most often heard on public radio, though commercial classical music format stations are highly successful in some metropolitan markets.
- *News-talk*. Round-the-clock information, service, discussion, and audience call-in programming.

A station's format decision is crucial. The "sound" positions the station in the mind of the listener and advertiser and represents the station's potential access to a viable share of the market. If the format doesn't work—and audience ratings services provide prompt and ample testimony on that score—the station will soon modify or replace the format altogether. The format reflects a disciplined consistency throughout each phase of the station's operation. The music that is broadcast, **the playlist,** is carefully monitored, as is the style and patter of the *disc jockeys*—a term *Variety,* the authoritative and irreverent trade journal serving the entertainment industry, gave the world. Promotional announcements and campaigns, news presentations, and commercial announcements all remain consistent

Teaching Idea

If there is a news-talk station in your area, bring a radio to class and let students listen for a while. What are their reactions?

Teaching Idea

Assign students to listen to local stations to identify some of the formats listed in the text. Which formats are most popular with your students? Does more than one station use the same format?

Teaching Idea

Invite the program director from a local station, preferably the one with the most popular format, to explain how the station operates. If the person is willing, ask him or her to bring the latest rating book and advertising rate cards and explain their importance.

Edward R. Murrow, one of the legends of broadcast journalism. His courage and integrity set the standards for the field.

with the format. Radio today is an intimate medium, highly personal to most listeners; the format is a station's way of attracting and holding listeners whose particular interests it shares.

Radio News Writing

Reflecting a philosophy developed during radio's infancy when powerful newspaper publishers threatened to cut broadcast journalism off at the knees, most radio stations today prefer to present the news rather than gather it. The typical radio news department is small—from one to a dozen persons—and reporters prepare most of their newscasts from wire service reports, interspersing fast-breaking developments. Radio reporters do much of their work over the telephone. Where possible, **actualities**—brief reports from the scene, live or on tape—are inserted into the stories. Radio news reporters learn to write swiftly and concisely.

Women in Broadcasting

The greatest increases in participation for women in journalism were at radio and television stations. Broadcast organizations not only expanded their work forces more than print organizations, but also were under the most pressure to comply with affirmative action programs. In 1971, the FCC added women to its equal opportunity rule that originally applied only to racial and ethnic minorities. This order prohibited discrimination against women. . . . The FCC regulations requiring broadcast stations to apply the equal opportunity rule to women made the broadcast industry more accountable for its hiring practices than some other areas of communications, and the figures gathered for this study offer some support for the argument that affirmative action has been somewhat successful in achieving its goals.

David H. Weaver and G. Cleveland Wilhoit, *The American Journalist: A Portrait of U.S. News People and Their Work* (Indiana University Press, 1986).

The Radio Correspondent in Wartime

From the earliest moments of the war [World War II], CBS issued warnings to its correspondents and analysts to broadcast fairly and objectively. . . . Those warnings led Eric Sevareid [one of CBS radio's leading foreign correspondents] to note, "We must not display a tenth of the emotions that a broadcaster does when describing a prize fight . . . that [philosophy] was right," wrote Sevareid. "It was the only legitimate way to perform our function—but it was very hard."

Robert Slater, *This . . . Is CBS* (Prentice-Hall, 1988).

Radio writing is also simplified as much as possible. Too many facts and over-long sentences cannot easily be assimilated by a listening audience. At times the broadcast journalist must envy the print reporter, who can use more words and who knows the magazine or newspaper reader can reread the story if necessary. Compare the following stories:

Newspaper	Radio
CYNTHIANA—Industrial development in central Kentucky will soon necessitate the construction of a regional airport for Bourbon and Harrison counties, city and county officials and business executives learned today.	A regional airport for Bourbon and Harrison counties? . . . That's what officials in Paris and Cynthiana are talking about today . . . to provide more convenient access to the region for business leaders checking out prime industrial sites.
ROME—Italian authorities reported the arrest today of another Palestinian—perhaps the ringleader—in the "Achille Lauro" highjacking last week in which one U.S. citizen was killed.	From Rome today, another break in the Achille Lauro (AH-KEE-LAY LOW-ROW) highjacking. . . . Police nabbed another Palestinian . . . perhaps the mastermind of the cruise ship takeover . . . in which an American tourist died.

While a number of radio newscasts are prepared by golden-throated announcers who do little more than tear out wire service reports and intone them theatrically over the airwaves, many radio news people have long surpassed the "rip and read" stage and dived into genuine professionalism. The Radio-Television News Directors Association (RTNDA), concerned with the ethical and professional advancement of the broadcast news field, has done much to raise standards. Good local newscasts demonstrably bring their stations prestige and profits. And radio news journalists can take pride in the knowledge that their medium remains the fastest, the one through which most of the public will first be informed when the big news breaks.

Public Radio

Educational stations were prominent among the pioneers of the radio industry; the government had issued some 175 educational broadcasting licenses by 1925, and many institutions hoped to use radio to teach the masses. But public radio has not had an easy time in the United States. First, signal interference presented a problem in those chaotic days before federal control. Then, when advertising began bringing substantial dollars and more sophisticated programming to commercial radio, the public stations and their shoestring budgets were barely able to compete. Congress has seldom appropriated massive sums of money to support public broadcasting. The explanation for this may lie in the negative example of Adolf Hitler and other foreign dictators who used state-controlled radio as a destructive propaganda instrument. Or perhaps the commercial broadcasters were persuasive in their arguments that the federal government should not compete in an area that private enterprise could serve instead. For whatever reason, public radio, throughout most of its history, has had to scramble.

Teaching Idea

Assign students to invite the news director from any local radio station to explain radio news—present and future—to your class.

Teaching Idea

If there is a public or noncommercial radio station in your area, invite the program director to class to explain the station's programming.

After World War II, the Federal Communications Commission reserved twenty FM channels, between 88 and 92 megahertz on the spectrum, for public radio. The channels adjoined the commercial portions of the FM band, thus making it easy for listeners to dial in either sector or both. An additional incentive came in 1948, when the FCC began permitting educational radio stations to go on the air with 10-watt transmitters; commercial stations were required to broadcast using at least 250 watts.

While Congress has never sustained an active role in encouraging noncommercial broadcasting, in 1967 it did adopt the Public Broadcasting Act, following strong recommendations from the Carnegie Commission on Educational Television. The measure allowed government funds, for the first time, to go into program production. Perhaps more important, the act established the **Corporation for Public Broadcasting,** a vehicle that channels money from government and private sources into noncommercial programming. By creating an independent and distinguished board of directors and giving it power to supervise CPB, Congress attempted to remove the agency from politics.

In 1970, the Corporation for Public Broadcasting launched **National Public Radio** as a network and programming service for selected public radio stations. NPR offers about fifty hours of programming each week—mostly news and cultural material—to its nearly four hundred affiliates. NPR's **drive-time** news programs, "All Things Considered" and "Morning Edition," have been favorably compared to similar programs broadcast by the British Broadcasting Corporation and other worldwide radio services.

One of the stars of public radio, Garrison Keillor of "The Prairie Home Companion," surrounded by a youthful chorus.

National Public Radio's financial situation, always precarious, eroded further in the early 1980s through inflation and a series of budget cuts that bordered on the calamitous.[6] Too, public radio programming is frequently provocative; powerful critics, both inside and outside Congress, accuse NPR of reporting news and public affairs in a biased (in this case, a leftist) manner. The charge, which may or may not be warranted, has been a difficult one to dispel, and it has created still more problems for those who advocate an expanded, better-funded public radio system.

Meanwhile, brisk competition has emerged within the realm of cultural affairs programming. American Public Radio in 1981 began buying programs from local public radio stations and outside producers, then offering them by satellite to customers within the public broadcasting field. Until this point, National Public Radio, which produced programs for its affiliates, had taken what many thought was a too-narrow view of public radio programming. A classic case in point: Garrison Keillor's popular "Prairie Home Companion," produced by Minnesota Public Radio, was offered to National Public Radio for national distribution, but NPR declined the offer, arguing that the program had only limited appeal and that the production values were too low for national audiences. American Public Radio (APR), begun in 1981 as a subsidiary of Minnesota Public Radio, boldly approached other public radio stations, sold them "Prairie Home Companion" and, eventually sold them other programming, such as "Market Place," as well. By 1994, APR programs were aired in more than 450 public radio stations, and APR programming—high-quality classical music, comedy, and variety programs—constituted an average 13 percent of all public radio air time each week. Competition within the public radio field was proving to be healthy, not only for the stations, but for their audiences as well.[7]

Satellite Digital Radio?

The Federal Communications Commission . . . will propose assigning a block of frequencies for satellites to broadcast compact-disc-quality digital sound to homes and cars.

Digital satellite radio is still little more than a gleam in the eyes of entrepreneurs, but the technology is available and proponents say it offers numerous benefits to listeners. For one thing, they say, digital transmission produces sound that is free of static and clearer than that of AM or FM stations. Beyond that, satellite broadcasting reaches every part of the country, allowing people to tune in even if they are nowhere near a city.

But listeners will first have to buy entirely new radios, which do not yet exist. And the market for the new services remains unclear. So it is not certain when, or if, satellite radio stations will go on the air.

Edmund L. Andrews, New York *Times*, 8 October 1992.

Current Trends

Radio in the early 1990s was once again commanding large audiences, with advertising revenues still impressively high, despite a dip in national spot revenue. "We're becoming marketing companies with two strong tools," said Radio Advertising Bureau President Gary Fries in 1992, "our inventory and our listeners."[8]

Actually, radio can offer advertisers other advantages as well, among them lifestyle formats and a high degree of target marketing efficiency. While other media seem to be growing more remote from their audiences—newspapers, for example, are often perceived in market studies as cool and aloof—radio stations maintain strong ties with their listeners. The predictability and warmth of a comfortable radio format make a powerful selling tool. And the large number of radio stations in a given city no longer seems to be a serious drawback. As one observer put it, "Suddenly, a choice of 40 radio stations in a market seems a lot easier and more concentrated than a choice of 60 to 100 (or more) cable channels."[9]

New engineering advances should continue to enhance radio's portability, convenience, and sound fidelity, while multimedia packaging, special events and promotions, and partnerships with retailers are proving to be effective marketing

A modern-day radio news editor reports to her unseen audience.

strategies. The popularity of radio with young people bodes well for the years ahead. All in all, the industry seems in better shape now than it was more than a generation ago, when it was still picking up the pieces after being struck by the tornado that is television. Several factors, however, will influence radio's future to at least some degree.

Deregulation

Recent years have seen a marked easing of governmental requirements and controls, a trend likely to accelerate in the future.[10] Radio licenses, which until 1981 had to be renewed every three years—a costly and time-consuming business—now last for seven. The *7-7-7 rule,* which prohibited any single company from owning more than 7 AM, 7 FM, and 7 television stations, was replaced in 1992 by a policy allowing a single company to own as many as 30 AM and 30 FM radio stations.[11] Beyond that, the FCC has relaxed regulatory guidelines in such areas as:

- ***Ascertainment.*** An FCC rule required each broadcast license holder to undergo an elaborate survey procedure to determine the problems in the community that the station should address or explore in its programming. Detailed, formal survey regulations have been modified to permit ascertainment of community needs by far less rigid means.
- *Nonentertainment programming guidelines.* Formerly, 8 percent or more of radio programming had to be news and public affairs (6 percent for FM stations). These percentages have been abandoned.
- *Commercial guidelines.* Stations were once limited by the FCC to a maximum of eighteen minutes of advertising per hour. These rules no longer apply.
- *Program logs.* Detailed programming records are no longer required. Instead, the FCC now expects only an annual listing of five to ten public issues that the licensee covered, along with examples of programming dealing with those issues.

Other FCC deregulatory decisions may follow these. Strong, high-level sentiment exists in Washington to further streamline license-renewal procedures and to end the FCC's control over all program content. Behind these sweeping proposals lies the belief that the government is less effective in controlling broadcasting than the marketplace itself would be. In other words, poorly managed stations, or stations not operating for the public good, would sooner or later be driven out of business by more effective and socially responsible operators. The marketplace theory may or may not prevail over the long pull; in the meantime, deregulation has proved a boon to radio station operators in their crucial battle to hold down business costs.

Even so, radio remains a brutally competitive arena wherein a great many stations battle an uncertain economy, and each other, to stay afloat. A 1992 staff report, compiled by the FCC, concluded that more than half of all radio stations in the country were at that moment losing money.[12]

While FCC radio deregulation opened opportunities for people to buy new stations, it also triggered a buying frenzy in which speculators, equipped with bank credit but no radio management experience, flocked into the market, driving station prices to unrealistic levels.

As new stations crowded the airwaves, advertising revenues were sliced thinner. The Charleston, South Carolina, area, for example, in 1994 had no fewer than forty-six radio stations on the air, perhaps three or four times as many as that market could comfortably support.

Across the country, banks became increasingly skittish about making additional loans to radio station managements, a fear which, unless resolved, could deprive the industry of the venture capital it needs for the years ahead.[13]

Discussion

Does the new 30-30 ownership policy tend to create monopolies? What about the lack of a news-and-public-affairs requirement? What balance do students think radio stations should strike between commercials and entertainment?

Background

When a radio station goes off the air permanently, it is said to "go dark."

The situation grew more complicated in 1994 when the Federal Communication Commission announced plans for opening the broadcast license opportunities even more. Some two thousand additional local and regional licenses would become available, auctioned off by the FCC for "personal communication services," such as portable telephones, computer transmissions, and handheld messaging services. The auction could bring the federal treasury as much as $10 billion—or it could flood the market, dropping radio license values to an alarming degree.

Rapid technological breakthroughs have dramatically increased the numbers of radio frequencies that might be available. Only a tiny slice of the full radio band has thus far been useful for broadcasting purposes, because delicate higher-frequency signals are adversely affected by clouds and rain. As a result, most broadcasting signals operate at frequencies under 2 megahertz, or millions of cycles per second. New satellite systems, already in the works, would utilize a vast band of ultra-high frequencies—at 28 megahertz—that heretofore has been virtually unused. This super abundance of new channels is likely to have a profound impact on the economics of the radio industry. Experts are divided as to whether the increase in numbers of frequencies will be met by a comparable demand to use them.[14]

Shoring Up AM Radio

Halting the decline in AM listening audiences has become a top priority. The AM stations, which the industry was built upon and which today remain the backbone of the national emergency broadcast system, have lost 71 percent of their audiences to FM. Apart from drive time, AM is rapidly becoming a medium for older listeners who are, as one industry leader put it, fed a diet of "news, talk, and nostalgia."[15]

Some focus the blame for this state of affairs on the FCC, which did not adopt, early on, an industrywide stereophonic sound standard for AM as it did for FM broadcasting.

In the meantime, FCC and industry leaders are studying a number of other options to help AM, including possible reduction of interference from computers, telephones, and other appliances that use some of the same frequencies; expanding the AM spectrum; and permitting duplicate programming in all markets where the same owner holds AM and FM licenses. The **duopoly rule,** barring owners of stations in neighboring markets from overlapping signals, has been eliminated; this move should encourage AM to again become more of a regional, or even national, service. These and other reforms, plus innovative format changes, might reverse the audience declines that have weakened AM radio in recent years.

Satellites

By transmitting program material far less expensively than landlines can, satellites have prompted a resurgence in radio networks and syndicated services—even in entire formats. A communications satellite can cut transmission costs by 50 percent or more and can often deliver better sound quality. Thus, a small-town station might be able to purchase the entire format of a big-city operation—the well-produced music shows, highly professional disc jockeys, network quality news—for a tiny fraction of the original cost. The syndicated format presents an appealing package to advertisers, who can take advantage of numerous cut-in periods during the day for local commercials. Satellites give major radio networks increased flexibility, too, for delivering special-interest programming to targeted audiences.

Still More Technology

The future of radio, according to B. Eric Rhoads, publisher of *Radio Ink* magazine, is a brave new world, with technology offering great promise—and posing a threat as well. The threat lies in the *pace* of change: Radio technology could change so quickly that new systems would already be obsolete by the time they are on line. Some of the developments include:

- Radio Broadcast Data Service (RBDS), a technology making possible the transmission of data via radio signals. Already utilized in Europe, RBDS allows radio sets to be programmed to receive special interruptions: weather bulletins, news flashes, traffic updates. The radio receivers are equipped with tiny screens; listeners can insert a memory card into their radio, punch in a button or two, and, among other things, record and print out an advertising coupon to redeem with a participating merchant.
- Digital Audio Broadcasting (DAB), which would offer superlative sound quality. In time, some experts predict, DAB signals will dominate the industry, while FM and AM transmissions will ultimately be phased out.
- Direct Broadcast Satellite (DBS) transmissions, which would permit the reception of signals from satellites directly into home or car radios, making it possible to receive radio stations from across the country—or around the world.
- Regional radio companies, which could join forces to develop their own regional satellite networks. Listeners to interactive radio receivers could then gain ready access to programs and advertisements from many markets. Such a system would allow radio to enter the classified advertising field, for example; a listener could respond to a classified ad by punching in some buttons on an interactive radio. The charges would appear on the next month's telephone bill.[16]

Moral Concerns About Content

Still on the law books are most of the provisions of the Radio Act of 1927, including this one:

> No person within the jurisdiction of the United States shall utter any obscene, indecent, or profane language by means of radio communication.

The provision remained largely superfluous for nearly fifty years. During the 1970s, however, more outspoken programs and comedy routines prompted the FCC to define indecency standards more precisely. In 1976, the FCC began to judge a program indecent if it contained one or more of seven words dealing with bodily or sexual functions. (The "seven dirty words" case arose out of a twelve-minute monologue comedian George Carlin delivered on a New York radio station in 1973.) Howard Stern's shock radio antics, while bringing him large audiences, also incurred the wrath of the FCC, which fined his employer $1.1 million in 1992 for using language the federal agency found indecent.

The standard is highly controversial. Those opposed point out that it prevents the broadcast of a number of classic works as well as sexually explicit dramatic productions that may reflect worthy social goals ("The Jerker," for example, a radio drama about homosexuals living in an atmosphere of fright because of the threat of AIDS). Those favoring the standard accuse radio of becoming increasingly decadent—"raunch radio," some call it—and proclaim that too many announcers routinely insert heavy sexual or excretory innuendos into their comments.[17] Some have also raised strong objections to the lyrics of some of the recordings aired on radio, a problem discussed elsewhere in these pages.

"What Have You Done with My Child?"

Advancing technology and governmental deregulation can combine to make radio an attractive medium for investors. Hundreds of stations are bought and sold each year and, despite the shaky economy in the early nineties and the murderous competition inside the broadcasting industry, many radio stations remained highly profitable, with returns as high as 50 percent. Radio's advantage as an advertising medium is impressive; it has the ability to deliver prospects at a very low cost-per-thousand.

But radio has its down side. For all its space-age effectiveness, satellite syndicated programming could reduce radio to a sterile, remote medium. Of far more import is the recent industrywide decline in air time and resources allocated to news and public affairs programming.[18] FM commercial radio, now the dominant force in the industry, has shown relatively little concern for news. Many AM stations, faced with shrinking audiences, are reducing news staffs for economic reasons. Deregulation, especially in abandoning the standards for minimum time stations must devote to news, has made cutbacks easier for station owners to justify. So while the industry is by and large healthy, its historic mandate to serve "the public interest, convenience, or necessity" could be watered down considerably in the years ahead—a high social cost for radio's efficiency and prosperity.

It may be that American society expected more of radio than it can reasonably deliver. "What have you done with my child?" demanded Lee DeForest, one of radio's pioneering geniuses, of the National Association of Broadcasters. "You have made him the laughing stock to intelligence, surely a stench in the nostril of the gods of the ionosphere. . . . This child of mine is moronic, as though you and your sponsors believe the majority of listeners have only moronic minds."[19] That outburst came in 1941. Many might agree with it today.

But radio has its defenders, too. They point out that in countries undergoing revolution, the first target the rebels head for is the radio station——not the banks, the newspapers, the stores, or the schools, but the radio station. No other medium can reach as many people throughout the world, and reach them as quickly, as radio. In the far less dramatic circumstances that govern our everyday lives, radio is a trusted guide, cheerful companion, and vital and pervasive force in modern society. Americans continually search for contact with people whose values they share, and no medium of mass communications connects them nearly so quickly, nor, it can be argued, any better, than radio.

Background

In times of great natural or other disasters, amateur (ham) radio often becomes the only means of communication with the disaster area. The Russians used radio after their 1917 revolution as a cheap and effective way to spread the party line in outlying regions and anywhere people couldn't read.

Radio and the New Generation

The new generation, born between 1965 and 1985, is marked by diversity, divisions, and disenfranchisement, he [Gordon Link of the McCann-Erickson Worldwide advertising agency] said. "How do we reach a generation who cries out at us, 'I am not a target market!'" Link said, warning of "a generation we don't understand and can't talk to."

But Link said radio, along with niche magazines, is well positioned to adapt itself to the new generation. Because of its low cost structure, its capacity for appealing to distinct slices of the population and its ability to change and adapt quickly, radio may well outperform television as the new consumers come of age.

"I particularly think that radio can get ahead of the wave on this," he said.

Broadcasting magazine, 23 March 1992

summary

Widely predicted to become an endangered species after television arrived, radio reorganized itself, redefined its mission, and enjoyed a remarkable rebirth. By 1994, four times as many radio stations operated as in 1950, before TV's impact had been fully realized; advertising revenues had risen to an average of $9 billion a year, and more than 96 percent of all adult Americans had become regular radio listeners. Currently, twice as many radios as people exist in the United States, and 39 percent of *all* time spent with the mass media is spent listening to radio.

Radio stations have succeeded by niche marketing, targeting a specific audience through careful attention to format, to programming personality or "sound." Dozens of formats are in use today, including various kinds of rock music, country and western, and news-talk. News-talk formats have given rise to the popularity of such controversial radio personalities as Rush Limbaugh and Howard Stern, whose daily audiences number in the millions.

Recent trends in the radio industry include deregulation, a governmental philosophy which has reduced or eliminated many requirements broadcasters faced, including ascertainment of community needs, maintenance of comprehensive program logs, and ownership limits. Technological breakthroughs promise to open the broadcast spectrum wider, permitting more licenses; satellites, which can bring in big-city formats to local stations; and increased improvements in sound quality. Industry problems include an oversupply of stations in many markets—more than the advertising base can profitably support—and continuing moral concern, expressed by citizens groups and some government officials, over the possibly indecent content of certain recordings played over the airwaves.

? questions and cases

1. Analyze radio news as it is broadcast in your market. How thorough is it? how accurate? how professional in its presentation? If you were news director of the leading radio station in your market, what changes would you make in your station's newscasts? Explain.

2. Assume you are an advertising representative for the dominant radio station in your market. You are attempting to persuade a leading retailer to place a substantial portion of her advertising budget with your station. Heretofore, the merchant has advertised only in newspapers. Explain how you would prepare a sales presentation that might win her over.

3. How would your sales presentation be different if you were working for a local television station instead? Make a case for advertising on local television instead of local radio. Now argue the advertising advantages of local television over local newspapers.

4. Do you agree with Lee DeForest's bitter assessment that radio "is moronic, as though you [broadcasters] and your sponsors believe the majority of listeners have only moronic minds"? Discuss.

5. Is the so-called marketplace theory of radio regulation preferable, in your view, to other forms of control? Why or why not? How can the marketplace theory be reconciled with monopoly ownership in smaller communities? Or, conversely, given cable television's vast potential, is *any* form of control over radio necessary in today's society?

6. What strengths and weaknesses do you find in public radio? What changes, if any, would you implement in it? Should government be involved in broadcasting at all? If so, to what extent? Should public radio be required to pay its own way? If so, what changes might we see in public radio programming?

7. Describe the format of the radio station you like best. In as much detail as you can, explain the personality of the station, the audience segment it is attempting to reach, and how the station implements the format throughout the broadcast day.

chaper glossary

actuality   A live or taped report from the scene, incorporated into a radio newscast.

ascertainment   The Federal Communications Commission requirement that local broadcast operations determine systematically the needs and problems of the communities they serve.

Corporation for Public Broadcasting (CPB)   A government-created corporation that allocates funds to Public Broadcasting Service (PBS) to produce and distribute programs.

deregulation   For our purposes, a governmental broadcasting administration philosophy that favors fewer rules and controls in an attempt to let market forces regulate the industry.

drive time   The periods from about 6 A.M. until 10 A.M., and 3 P.M. until 7 P.M. Popular, and most expensive, radio daypart because of heavy car radio use.

duopoly rule   An FCC provision barring any party (individual or corporation) from owning more than one radio or one television station in the same broadcast market.

National Public Radio (NPR)   A network that provides news, educational, and cultural materials to member stations.

playlist   Periodic announcement of the recordings an individual radio station currently airs.

notes

1 Reprinted in the *Oxford Dictionary of Quotations,* 2d ed. (London: Oxford University Press, 1955), 550.

2 *Broadcasting/Cablecasting Yearbook,* 1991, A–3. The total number of radio stations in operation was provided by the National Association of Broadcasters, October 1992.

3 Tom Lewis, "Triumph of the Idol: Rush Limbaugh and a Hot Medium," *Media Studies Journal,* 7:3 (Summer 1993), 54. See also "Big Mouths," *Time,* 1 November 1993.

4 Diane Rehm, "Talking Over America's Backyard Fence," *Media Studies Journal,* 7:3 (Summer 1993), 63.

5 Marilyn J. Matelski, "Resilient Radio," *Media Studies Journal,* 7:3 (Summer 1993), 5.

6 This situation affected public television also. See John Weisman, "Public TV in Crisis," *TV Guide,* 1 August 1987, 2.

7 Stephen L. Salyer, "Monopoly to Marketplace: Competition Comes to Public Radio," *Media Studies Journal,* 7:3 (Summer 1993), 176.

8 Peter Viles, "Radio Looks to Marketing, Promotion for Revenue," *Broadcasting,* 24 October 1992, 11.

9 B. Eric Rhoads, "Looking Back at Radio's Future," *Media Studies Journal,* 7:3 (Summer 1993), 15.

10 Broadcast deregulation is discussed in depth in Don R. Pember, *Mass Media Law,* 6th ed. (Dubuque, Iowa: Wm. C. Brown, 1992), 540–615.

11 Edmund L. Andrews, "FCC is Permitting Broadcasters to Own More Radio Stations," New York *Times,* 12 March 1992.

12 Ibid.

13 Jim Davenport, "Radio Daze," Columbia, S.C. *State,* 1 June 1992.

14 Edmund L. Andrews, "For Sale. Cheap. Your Own Piece of the Airwaves," New York *Times,* 27 March 1994.

15 Brad Woodward of *Radio and Records* magazine, quoted in Reginald Stuart, "New Policies to AM Radio Are Studied," New York *Times,* 24 October 1985.

16 B. Eric Rhoads, *Media Studies Journal,* (Summer 1993), 15–21.

17 Alex Jones, "FCC Studies 'Indecency' on Radio," New York *Times,* 22 November 1986.

18 See especially Reginald Stuart, "Radio Stations Reduce Air Time Given to News," New York *Times,* 17 November 1985.

19 Irving Settel, *A Pictorial History of Radio* (Bonanza Books, 1969), 69.

chapter

K

Recordings

Objectives

When you have finished studying this chapter, you should be able to:

- Describe the size and scope of the recording industry and discuss some of its history

- Analyze trends in consumer buying behavior and technology where recordings are concerned

- Outline some of the marketing and promotional problems record companies face

- Discuss matters of current concern within the industry, such as counterfeiting and political and social pressure to monitor lyrics dealing with violence, drugs, and sex

When the one-hundredth United States Congress convened in January 1987, Senator Alan Cranston of California and Representative John Conyers of Michigan introduced and led to passage identical resolutions in the Senate and the House of Representatives, official appreciations of the importance of jazz in American life:

> It is the sense of the Congress that jazz is hereby designated as a rare and valuable national American treasure to which we should devote our attention, support, and resources to make certain it is preserved, understood, and promulgated.[1]

Though gracious, such formal acknowledgment was hardly necessary for jazz, any more than it would be for rock, country, or gospel music. Americans had already shown their appreciation in more tangible ways: in the early 1990s, for example, by buying 360 million cassettes and 333 million compact discs a year—in addition to nearly 200 million other recordings in various forms, ranging from vinyl singles to music videos. The total expenditures for recordings exceeded $5 billion annually, each year setting a new high for the industry.

Music, in our culture, is available anywhere, any time: on car radios, on portable transistorized tape players, on expensive home stereo systems, and as background sound in elevators and restaurants. Recorded music is the first thing many of us hear when we wake in the morning, the last thing we hear as we doze off at night. Music enriches our lives and improves our moods. Warning darkly that one who does not like music is not to be trusted, Shakespeare assessed music's therapeutic power in this stern language:

> Preposterous ass! that never read so far
> To know the cause why music was ordained!
> Was it not to refresh the mind of man
> After his studies or his usual pain?[2]

In this chapter we will look at one aspect of music, recordings—and at the artistic and business operations that create and market recordings to the public. The recording industry is a volatile part of the mass communications field; it carries a high profile and touches millions of Americans—some only peripherally, others profoundly—each day and each night. It is also an industry which, thanks to the compact disc and the continued strong support of the nation's youth market, is now flying high.

From the Phonograph to the Compact Disc

During his astonishing sixty-year professional life, Thomas Edison invented the electric light bulb, motion pictures, the telephone transmitter, the stock ticker, the mimeograph machine, and more than 1,090 other devices and processes, among them the first workable phonograph machine and the first recording.[3]

Edison first captured sound waves in 1877 by enlarging them through a vibrating diaphragm. This was connected to a tiny needle which hovered over a rotating metal cylinder covered in tinfoil. The sound waves caused the needle to vibrate and create small dents in the foil. When another needle was placed against the foil, it relocated the original dents and set the diaphragm vibrating again. These vibrations reproduced the original sounds.

Edison's objective was to invent a means of recording telephone messages, but he soon became absorbed with different projects. Other inventors pursued the recorded sound phenomenon. Emile Berliner, who had emigrated to the United States from his native Germany, in 1887 invented the gramophone, which used a flat disc instead of a cylinder. Like Edison's phonograph, the early gramophone was cranked manually rather than electrically powered.

In 1888, Jesse H. Lippincott obtained the franchise rights to both the phonograph and the gramophone. Lippincott regarded the recording machine exclusively

Thomas Alva Edison and his favorite invention, the phonograph.

The juke box brought recorded music to eateries and other hangouts for young people, providing popular music for generations.

as a piece of office dictation equipment and altogether ignored its entertainment potential. It was left to an unsung genius, as Roland Gelatt later described him or her, to conceive the idea of placing phonographs in public places, equipping them with coin slots, and offering professionally recorded renditions of popular musical selections on wax cylinders. This primitive form of jukebox proved that a market existed for recorded music and sent the new industry on its way.

The next few years were like a wild ride on a roller coaster. The recording business was awash in profits one moment, a hair's breadth from ruin the next. Soon after the turn of the century, highly popular artists from the United States and Europe were signed to recording contracts, opening up new markets and giving the industry needed prestige. The ballroom dance craze swept the country just before World War I, triggering widespread demand among young people for readily available popular music. Recording technology improved, and better sound quality generated more sales. By 1925, the major studios had begun to market the first electrically recorded music. Electric phonographs also became available that year.

The rapid emergence of radio in the early 1920s threatened to eclipse recordings as an entertainment medium; cooling public interest affected the recording industry for a brief, but critical, period. Following the stock market crash in 1929, the recording industry teetered on the brink of a financial abyss. But the home record collection, like the jukebox in diners and soda fountains, had become a part of the culture. Recorded music helped sustain weary Americans through the Great Depression of the 1930s, just as it would boost the entire country's morale a few years later during World War II.

Technological changes in the postwar era were rapid and far-reaching:

- *Speed and format evolution.* In 1948, Columbia Records introduced the long play (LP), which offered high-quality sound and nearly a half hour of playing time on each side. Designed to operate at 33 1/3 rpm (revolutions per minute), the LP forced massive retooling within the industry and

Teaching Idea

Survey your class to see if their parents, grandparents, or friends have old discs or cylinders they could bring to class. If an old player is available, demonstrate the early phonograph.

touched off a bitter internal fight among record producers. Until the LP came along, the industry standard speed had been 78 rpm. Made from a shellac and clay mixture, 78s were easily broken and even more easily scratched. Their sound quality was limited, and they were bulky; four or five 78s were required to record as much music as a single LP. Meanwhile, a rival company, RCA Victor, had sunk millions of dollars into research and development to come up with the vinyl 45-rpm record, a smaller, less fragile version of the 78. Besides operating at a different speed, 45s required a different record changer as well. When RCA took the offensive with an all-out promotional campaign for its 45, other record producers and the general public were caught in the middle. This unhappy and largely unprofitable condition prevailed until 1950, when the industry giants agreed on the 45 format for singles, the LP for albums.

- *High fidelity.* As early as the 1930s, record companies and some radio stations were using elaborate systems designed to extract the maximum fidelity—faithfulness—of sound reproduction from recordings. High-fidelity players (hi-fi, or *ffrr*—full-frequency-range recording players) became commercially affordable in the late 1940s and early 1950s. These vastly improved sound systems attracted new fans by the millions. Stereophonic hi-fi, which reproduces sounds from their respective directions, added depth, drama, realism, and clarity to recording production. Stereophonic systems and records caught on quickly following their introduction in the late 1950s, and less than a decade later, stereo recordings and playback systems were commonplace.

- *Magnetic tape.* Originating in Europe, magnetic tape further enhanced recording quality. It was first employed on a sizeable scale in the United States after World War II and dramatically changed the way recordings were produced. Because it can be easily cut and spliced, magnetic tape gave record producers enormous editing flexibility. No longer did recordings have to be created from a single, live studio performance. Instead, the audio could be recorded at different levels, portions of it at different times, and the various tracks could be mixed together to form a rich, errorless, multilayered rendition.[4]

- *Digital recording.* Instituted on a serious scale in 1979, digital recording made the computer a partner in the recording business. In digital recording, the signals represented by musical sounds are broken into tiny bits of information, encoded numerically in strings of 1s and 0s, stored on a computer disc (**compact disc**, or **CD**), and "read" back by a laser beam instead of a needle. The system assures high quality and all but eliminates unwanted background noise.

Background

Before the LP and audiotapes, radio stations used "transcriptions," or sixteen-inch diameter discs turning at 33 1/3 rpm. Each side contained about fifteen minutes of material. Entire syndicated radio programs were recorded on them and sent to local stations. The LP record, also known as "microgroove," just narrowed the groove in which the needle moved and made the needle and disc smaller. The transcription's grooves and needles were three one-thousandths of an inch in diameter; the LPs were one one-thousandth of an inch. The typical twelve-inch LP album played for about thirty minutes.

Background

Radio station turntables (record players) were already set for speeds of 78 and 33 1/3 rpm in 1948–49. Playing an LP album was easy—it just meant placing a smaller needle in the pickup arm. By contrast, adding 45 rpm to existing turntables was a mechanical nightmare; stations could buy new, three-speed turntables or just buy the cheap, consumer-type 45 rpm players.

Background

By 1960, almost all records were pressed in vinyl plastic, which was much stronger and quieter. Early stereo attempts used two separate pickup arms and records—this was known as a binaural system.

A Short Journey into Obsolescence

Shoppers who enter a Tower Records in Manhattan in search of a 33 1/3 record album are stunned to discover that, despite its name, Tower Records sells no records. "People are really shocked," said Victor Morales, 22 years old, a supervisor at the chain's Broadway store. "They'd say, 'What do you mean Tower Records doesn't have records?' Most of the people working here are young kids who don't even own records."

The recording industry's shift to compact discs has led to the virtual obsolescence of LP technology. Nine years ago, when compact discs were introduced, record companies shipped 295.2 million LPs and 800,000 CDs, according to the Recording Industry Association of America. In 1991, 4.8 million LPs were produced, compared with 333.3 million CDs.

Griffin Miller, New York *Times,* 18 July 1992.

Background

The Germans developed a magnetic tape recorder before WW II and used it to—among other things—record symphony orchestras. Americans listening to these broadcasts during the war were astounded at the quality of the broadcasts. After the war, using German research, the Ampex Company produced the first professional audiotape recorder in 1947–48.

Extra Information

In computer terms, today's CD is merely a ROM (read-only-memory).

The Industry Today

Rock music, which emerged after World War II, accounts for nearly two of every five recordings now sold in the United States.[5] A lively and sometimes rebellious offshoot of such other forms as gospel, country, folk, and blues, rock is believed to have acquired its name from the 1950s blues song "There's Good Rockin' Tonight." Bill Haley and the Comets, riding to global stardom on "Rock Around the Clock," was perhaps the first world-famous rock group, while Elvis Presley is regarded as rock's first important solo performer. Chuck Berry, a composer and blues singer, and Buddy Holly, who pioneered new recording and production techniques, were also major influences as the new medium took shape.

In a remarkably short time, rock music captivated audiences, especially young audiences, around the world. It articulated an entire generation's frustrations with the traditions, sentiments, and values of modern-day society. It influenced hairstyles, dress, language, and political and social behavior. It created international heroes, like the Beatles, inspired numerous films, and mushroomed into a multibillion-dollar industry. Rock is by far the most dramatic success story in modern music history. The field became so large, in fact, that it split into a number of subspecialty forms—hard rock, soft rock, acid rock, punk rock. Its dominance in the recording industry is reflected in a breakdown of music purchasing trends (table 1).

table 1 — Percentages of Retail Dollars Spent on Recordings

Recording	Percentage of Sales
Rock	36.3%
Urban contemporary	18.2
Country	12.5
Pop/easy listening	11.7
Jazz	4.3
Classical	3.9
Gospel	3.5
Children	.3
Other (soundtrack, foreign language, etc.)	7.7

Source: The Recording Industry of America, 1992.

table 2 Record and Tape Consumer Profile (percentage of dollar spent)

Age	Percentage of Sales
10–14	6.8%
15–19	17.1
20–24	18.7
25–29	15.2
30–34	12.6
35–39	10.4
40–44	7.1
45–49	3.7
50–54	2.8
55+	5.0

Source: The Recording Industry of America, 1992.

About 20 percent of all records are bought by direct mail, through record clubs, direct-response advertising messages, and the like. Mail-order buying patterns are similar to those at retail outlets, though buyers purchase proportionately more country and classical recordings by direct mail. As table 2 shows, persons under age twenty-five buy about half of all recordings.

Some 34.4 percent of all records, according to the RIAA, are sold in the South. The North, West, and East each account for just over 20 percent of total purchases. Males typically buy more records than females.[6] Beyond these buying patterns, which have remained fairly consistent in recent years, two new product trends can be identified:

- *Continued technological evolution.* The compact disc, which sold fewer than a million units in 1983 and 5.8 million in 1984, by the early 1990s was selling at a rate of more than 333 million a year, leading all forms in dollar volume. Cassette sales were declining somewhat, by 18.5 percent in 1991 over the previous year, for example, while sales of long-playing albums plunged by nearly 60 percent. Another recording form, the eight-track tape, illustrates the meteoric paths that burn throughout the recording industry: Bursting into prominence in the early 1970s, eight-track cartridges accounted for $489 million in total sales in 1973; by 1979, they hit $948 million; then they began to drop precipitously, sinking to $10.5 million by 1986.
- *Continual increases in unit costs.* Though overall revenues for the industry are up, total units manufactured and sold actually declined again in 1991, reflecting the growing affluence of the market and consumers' willingness to pay for compact discs and other more expensive recordings. Top sellers Garth Brooks's *The Chase* and Michael Bolton's *Timeless,* each retailing at $16.98 when they were released in 1992, were the highest-priced standard-length compact discs by single artists at that time.

Creating a Recording

A record company's "artists and repertoire" (A and R) people negotiate for talent and material, then try to match them appropriately. This involves continual contact with performing artists and their agents, managers, and songwriters in an attempt to

Teaching Idea

Survey the class to see if any of the students are members of a mail-order record club. Ask them to explain how the club works and whether the prices are lower than at retail record stores.

A recording session: Robbie Dupree.

secure the strongest possible recording combinations. When these arrangements are agreed upon, a producer chosen by the A and R chief brings together the performing and engineering talent for the recording session.

The objective of the recording session is to assemble the makings of what will become, with editing, a perfect **master** tape. In the studio, carefully placed microphones can provide versions of the material from as many as thirty perspectives at the same time. Some portions of the music might be recorded again and again to achieve perfection, and many tapes are created. Eventually these tapes are edited, spliced into sequence, mixed to attain the purest balance, then dubbed (copied) onto a master recording disc. This disc becomes the mold to be used in stamping vinyl records.

In the digital recording process, a computer converts the amplified sounds into digital bits—enough to cover an impressive range of possible sound variations: 16 bits per sample and about 50,000 samples per second. Because more bits than necessary are encoded on the magnetic tape, sound bit signals may be rerecorded many times without any appreciable loss in tone quality. Once the signals are edited and mixed, the finished version is transferred from tape to a master recording disc, where the sound signals create tiny indentations on the disc surface. Then, as with vinyl recordings, the master is used to form stampers for pressing duplicates.

Cassette duplication is less efficient. The finished tape is placed on a master playback unit located in a room with twenty or more slave units. To save time, the master plays at sixty-four times the normal cassette speed while the slave units are fed blank tape from long rolls. Once dubbed, the tapes are transferred to an editing machine, where they are cut into proper lengths for winding onto reels.[7] Each tape is then inserted automatically into its cassette housing, labeled, and boxed.

Marketing and Promotion

While artists and engineers work on the recording, art directors develop the sleeve/box design, and writers write and edit the jacket notes. Once the recording is both well produced and handsomely packaged, the task is to create a demand for it.

Marketing and promotion positions are the recording industry jobs mass communications graduates can most easily attain, though few jobs are likely to be open outside Nashville, Los Angeles, and New York.

In many respects, including a cumbersome distribution system, the recording industry and the book publishing industry have much in common. Unlike magazines and newspapers, which readers may subscribe to for a year or more at a time, each new recording, like each new book, is unique; it has its own personality, and it requires its own individualized marketing plan. The system is fraught with uncertainty and risk; as with books, recordings are rarely assured of massive advertising support. Nevertheless, promotional efforts must be designed and carried out so that large segments of the buying public can hear about the work, if only indirectly.

Copies of the recording and press releases about the recording are sent to such authoritative publications as *Spin, Rolling Stone, Down Beat,* and *Billboard,* and to the music critics of selected newspapers and magazines. Publicity parties may be scheduled and advertising purchased according to a budget. Promoters may arrange for television appearances by the artists, if possible.

The surest path to promotional success, however, is through radio. If a station plays the recording on the air, and plays it often enough, the recording will more than likely enjoy brisk sales in that market. Without radio exposure, the recording's

The Rolling Stones kick off their highly successful 1994 tour.

chances for success are slight. Radio stations are, in short, prime targets for the promotional campaign. Stations receive copies of the record, accompanying publicity material, and plenty of encouragement to let their audiences know about it.

The record company carefully monitors the recording's progress. Local radio stations often publicize their playlists, especially at locations that sell records. At the national level, the **charts**—weekly popularity tabulations published by the authoritative industry trade paper, *Billboard,* and other interested media—report on a recording's reception. Its sales momentum, as chronicled in the charts, is a powerful factor in producing additional sales. In the recording business, perhaps even more than elsewhere, popularity begets greater popularity, which becomes evident in sales, airplay, and surges in concert attendance.

Gold and Platinum

Where the book industry has its bestseller, the recording industry measures success in terms of gold and platinum. To qualify as a **gold record,** a recording must sell 500,000 albums or CDs; to qualify as a *platinum,* 1 million; and as multiplatinum, 2 million. A video single must sell 25,000 to be awarded a gold, while a video long-form must sell 50,000 copies. Recording Industry of America figures show that 1991 was among the biggest years for gold albums, with 217, and multiplatinum, with 138. Madonna's "Justify My Love" that year became the first video single to sell more than 400,000 copies. "Hammer Time" hit 10 million units, making Hammer the all-time top seller in the rap field; the largest-selling single remained "We Are the World," the 1985 megahit.[8] Artists and producers made huge sums of money: In 1992, for example, Prince reportedly earned more than $100 million from his six albums, his production company profits, and his executive talent-scout fees from Warner Brothers Records. Madonna's deal with Time Warner was estimated to be worth more than $60 million, including startup support for her own records and publishing company, Maverick.

Payola

In their zeal to get their company's records on the air, record executives have historically cultivated disc jockeys, plying them with kindnesses and flattery. In this industry, as with many others, stroking practices were regarded as an aggressive sales technique and accepted as a matter of course. During the 1950s, however, a congressional investigation turned up evidence of outright bribery—**payola,** as it was called—to encourage disc jockeys to play and promote certain recordings.

In the wake of the scandal, which momentarily shook the public's faith in the radio and recording industries, numerous stations dismissed or reassigned disc jockeys and recording companies toned down promotional efforts. Congress and the FCC drafted new rules in an attempt to stamp out the practice. Radio stations in many markets also conferred more authority on program directors, rather than individual disc jockeys, to control playlists. Another wave of payola charges resurfaced in the 1970s and again in the 1980s, indicating that a problem—no one knew precisely how severe—remained. The 1980s incidents did not all involve the record companies directly; instead, some of the charges accused independent producers, retained by record companies, of bribing disc jockeys to get air time for the recordings their clients produced. Following an investigation by the U.S. Senate, several major record companies decided to abandon the practice of hiring independent promoting organizations.

The payola scandals, despite what they tell us about ethical business behavior, underscore in a dark and unsettling way the importance of radio play to recording success. Many recordings are produced, and only a relative few can be chosen for on-the-air exposure to the buying public.

The Concert Tour

A tried-and-true promotional strategy is the concert tour, which not only sells recordings but can be enormously profitable in and of itself. Successful performers often play to sold-out arenas and may gross millions of dollars per tour. The money comes from admission fees, which can be pricey, and from souvenir sales. The Grateful Dead, a durable and popular rock group, in the early 1990s was still selling one thousand shirts per concert (T-shirts at $10 or more apiece, golf shirts at $20), and the group had completed some sixteen hundred live performances over the past twenty-five years. By aggressively marketing other souvenirs and paraphernalia, the Grateful Dead could make far more money than they do. The groups's merchandising manager told *Forbes* magazine that permitting fans to tape their concerts and refusing to sell certain types of trinkets may cost the group as much as $200,000 per performance in lost revenue.[9] Such decisions have created lasting goodwill among fans, however, and should pay additional dividends in time. Other groups are less restrained in their promotional efforts.

Road tours present grave risks for promoters as well as performers. For promoters, the gamble is mainly financial; if the tour flops, huge losses result from prepaid arena rentals and promotional expenses. For the performers, the risks are largely personal and emotional. The brutal travel schedule and the constant pressure to sing or play at peak form in a live setting can be wrenching experiences that have undone more than one recording artist. The extraordinary possibilities that road tours present for enhanced prestige and vast profits, however, are tempting—especially in a field where public adulation may last but a fleeting moment.

The Video

Another promotional vehicle, the video, emerged in the 1980s. By tieing rock music directly into film, the video creates a short, often imaginative, minidramatization of a recording. The musicians join actors and dancers on designed sets, providing audiences with pictures as well as words and music. The primary video arena has been MTV (Music Television), a cable channel launched in 1981 which broadcasts twenty-four hours a day to a potential audience of nearly half the country.

Produced by record companies at budgets typically ranging from $50,000 to $250,000 or more each, TV videos altered marketing and promotional strategies within the recording industry. The videos, introduced on the air by "veejays," are commercials for recordings, advertising designed to reach an affluent audience composed mostly of teenagers. Numerous success stories, as measured by record sales and a dramatic increase in an artist's popularity, are directly attributable to video exposure on MTV.

After more than ten years of spectacular success, however, signs appeared that MTV had peaked. The channel's ratings dipped from a high of 1.2 percent of the

total possible cable audience in 1983 and 1984 to 1 percent or lower in the early 1990s, though the network, which receives the videos free from record companies, continued to attract advertising and remained profitable. Two reasons have been offered to explain the audience slippage: increased competition from a second cable video network, VH-1, as well as late-night video programming on NBC, WTBS, and many local stations and cable channels; and a creative slump in the videos themselves. Many videos, as a *Time* magazine critic noted, seemed trapped in a yawn-provoking rut.[10]

Still, videos can be valuable. With programming needs around the clock, MTV can offer exposure to songs and talent that might not be heard otherwise. Most new recordings, especially those produced by major companies, include a video version as an integral part of the promotional plan. Videos often accompany the music in night clubs. The MTV audience may be declining somewhat, but it cannot be ignored, and the addition of video to music can result in a powerful sales appeal anywhere it is shown.

Two Industry Concerns

In the early 1990s, while thousands of songwriters, recording artists, and production companies waged their individual competitive struggles to succeed in a fiercely competitive arena, two larger, subtler problems confronted the industry as a whole: pressure group response to explicit lyrics and piracy and counterfeiting.

Explicit Lyrics and Pressure Groups

From the beginning, rock lyrics have reflected an impatience with the sentimentality inherent in other forms of popular music. Many rock songs are angry social dissent, and others deal openly and frankly with such topics as drugs, alcohol, sex, violence, and the occult. In the early 1980s, certain citizens' groups charged that some rock lyrics went too far, that they condoned violence, demeaned women, and promoted other forms of antisocial behavior, especially among children. The rap album "As Nasty as They Wanna Be," recorded by 2 Live Crew, aroused particular controversy with its graphic descriptions of sex, genitals, and sodomy, leading Florida authorities to prosecute. The rap band members were found not guilty,[11] but the conflict persisted. At issue were artistic freedoms versus a community's right to restrict what some regard as offensive material.

Teaching Idea

Survey the class to see which music video channel is the most popular and why. Are students more likely to buy a recording if they first see a video on TV?

President Bill Clinton publicly criticized rap artist Sister Souljah for what he called her racist remarks following the Los Angeles riots in 1992. She had been quoted in the press as taking the rioters' point of view: "If black people kill black people every day, why not have a week and kill white people?" She denied that she was issuing a call to arms to African Americans. Some radio stations, however, quit playing rap music, at least temporarily, until tensions eased—a gesture which, in itself, underscored the clout rap music was believed to have with audiences.

Some fifteen hundred record stores across the country refused to carry certain controversial recordings, including "Cop Killer" by Ice-T. Time Warner refused to pull the album, but Ice-T later requested that they remove the song "Cop Killer" from it. Time Warner claimed the record producer's employees received bomb and death threats as a result of the song.

The First Amendment right to freedom of expression does apply to songwriters and performers, but this issue was clouded by the fact that songs are broadcast by radio and television facilities licensed "in the public interest, convenience, and necessity." Should lyrics that seem to condone rape, incest, substance abuse, and comparable behavior be regulated? If so, by whom? using what criteria? And at what point do protective laws become censorship?

Following lengthy discussions in the U.S. Senate and with the FCC, the Recording Industry Association of America was urged to adopt a rating system, classifying recording lyrics along the lines used for motion pictures.[12] The RIAA at first opposed the ratings but later encouraged its members to voluntarily print warning labels or song lyrics on record covers. The label warning "Explicit Lyrics—Parental Advisory" did not have a deep impact on overall sales. Industry revenues continued to climb, though individual albums and artists may well have been affected. For example, in the 1980s, Wal-Mart Stores and several other large retailers removed recordings containing suggestive lyrics from their shelves.

Piracy and Counterfeiting

Illegal copies of records and tapes represent an enormous drain on the recording industry's revenues, a loss estimated at $400 million or more each year. The audio cassette, so easily dubbed, is especially vulnerable.

Is It a Fake?

Here, according to the Record Industry Association of America, are the common characteristics of a counterfeit recording product:

- Jackets, labels, and insert cards with blurred, smudgy printing, poor artwork or photos, and labels affixed at improper angles or not completely attached

- Insert cards made from paper rather than card stock

- Shrink-wrap packaging of inferior quality, with uneven or loose seal folds

- Unfamiliar or fictitious company names of alleged manufacturers or distributors listed—or no names listed at all

- Unauthorized compilations of different artists

The problem continues even in the face of tougher penalties adopted in the Piracy and Counterfeiting Amendments of 1982, which increased possible punishment to fines of $250,000 and prison terms up to five years for unauthorized duplication of recordings and films. Stepped-up enforcement efforts, involving the Anti-Piracy Unit of the RIAA in conjunction with the police, resulted in the seizure of 1.3 million bootleg cassettes in raids during 1991 alone. Beyond those confiscated by law enforcement authorities, some 78,385 more illegal cassettes were seized following civil litigation in trademark and copyright violation. Seventy-two percent of the criminal actions were taken against illegal street vendors. The industry estimates an additional $1 billion is lost each year in missed sales due to international piracy of U.S. recordings.[13]

The RIAA in 1983 advocated a royalty tax on recorders and tapes in an attempt to extract some revenues from unauthorized copiers. Others contend that home taping, as opposed to commercial piracy, does no real damage and that, to the contrary, it helps create new fans for the industry. After years of debate, Congress decided to act: The Audio Home Recording Act of 1992 authorized a tax on blank digital tapes and recording equipment; the proceeds were earmarked for royalty payments to music publishers, recording companies, and recording artists.

Digital audio tape (DAT), a home recording technology that can copy recordings with almost perfect clarity, in the late 1980s posed what appeared to be a monumental challenge. Worried industry lobbyists urged Congress to forbid the marketing of digital audiotape recorders unless they contained a built-in anticopying device (a copy code scanner chip) or *spoiler* that would impair duplication of copyrighted material. The spoiler developed by CBS Records inserts a signal in the master recording that, when encountered by a DAT recorder, interrupts the recording process for twenty-five seconds. CBS began encoding all its compact discs with spoiler signals during the summer of 1987.[14]

Other bills introduced in Congress would prevent importation and sale of DAT recording equipment without such safeguards for up to three years—enough time, the industry hoped, to develop a solution that would equitably reflect the interests of artists, record companies, and the listening audience.

DAT, meanwhile, proved far less a threat than expected. New technologies promised to be cheaper, more convenient, and more flexible, and DAT—once viewed as the ultimate copying vehicle—found itself quickly supplanted, and threatened with extinction, before it had ever really enjoyed its moment in the spotlight.

Background

In *analog* audio- and videotape terms, the original recording is the "master," and copies made from this master are "generations." Usually, any second or further generation copies begin to noticeably lose quality. In *digital* recording, copies of copies don't lose quality. The recording industry has thus traditionally opposed any technical advance which would allow consumers to copy and recopy material with no loss of quality.

Reasons for Industry Optimism

Those who attempt to predict the recording industry's prospects for the remainder of the century are apt to find more good news than bad. Technological innovation and relative, if unpredictable, periods of prosperity, especially in the youth market, indicate continued growth ahead. The next wave—and the one after that—should bring several innovations:

- Digital Audio Broadcasting (DAB), the digital radio of the future, broadcasts in digital rather than analog format. This produces a fidelity comparable to a compact disc and with a signal immune to many kinds of broadcast interference.[15]
- Digital Compact Cassettes (DCC), high-quality digital tapes that offer playback and recording of digital sound for up to ninety minutes per cassette, will play on standard analog as well as new machines. As the battle lines are drawn for a showdown between digital tape recorders and CD recorders, the music companies would prefer the winner to be tape. If tape succeeds in the marketplace, music companies could sell recorded music in yet another format, while a victory for CD recorders would leave the record companies with a single digital format—compact discs, which they already sell.[16]
- Additional computer utilizations, such as CD-ROM (Compact Disc–Read Only Memory), expand the CD format to include not only music but any kind of program material. CD-ROMs currently include primarily computer applications, and CD-I (Compact Disc Interactive) applications, a multimedia extension which permits simultaneous use and storage of audio, video, data, text, and graphics.[17] Audiophiles and sound engineers, not to mention the consumer public, could expect interesting times ahead.

The Compact Disc

Meanwhile, the industry charges ahead, driven—for now—by the startling success of the compact disc. The CD has given customers superior sound quality and created a surge of new business and profits for record companies, performers, and retailers. Consumers are willing to pay higher prices, with greater markups for both producers and sellers, to obtain the distortion-free clarity offered by digitally recorded compact discs. Classical music lovers seem particularly excited about CD quality. An estimated nine of ten classical recordings sold are compact discs.

The popularity of the compact disc should continue to increase as CD playback units become more affordable. The players dropped in price from $1,000 in 1983 to an average of $200 or less in the early 1990s; industry analysts noted in 1992 that one of every three U.S. homes was equipped with a CD player, as was one of every ten vehicles. Each CD player sale, as record company executives are well aware, triggers the immediate sale of many compact disc recordings. There is plenty of room to grow; the Electronics Industries Association forecasts that CD player sales should continue to increase at the rate of 12.5 percent a year, a glittering prospect indeed.[18]

Teaching Idea

Assign students to visit music stores to see whether any still sell LP albums or 45 singles. What are the prices for CDs? Do the stores carry clearly labeled used CDs? How much lower are they priced than new CDs? Previously owned CDs can be a headache for recording companies, as CDs don't lose quality until they are completely destroyed.

In a traditional compact disc, the zeroes and ones of digitized sound are represented by a pattern of pits on the underside of the disc. Once these pits are embedded, they cannot be changed. In Sony's recordable mini-disc, the pits are replaced by magnetic patterns, like the north and south poles of a magnet. These patterns can be changed, allowing the disc to be rerecorded.

On the underside of the new mini-disc, a laser moves from inner to outer edge, heating each segment of the disc, "softening" the surface film so that its magnetic pattern can be rearranged.

After the disc is heated by the laser, a magnetic head reads the incoming signal and records the desired north or south polarity.

Sources: Sony; and Adam Bryant, "Coming Soon: New Tapes and CDs," New York *Times,* 17 June 1992.

The Continuing Enthusiasm of the Youth Market

To a very great degree, young people helped create the record business. About the year 1900, American youths began clearly expressing their own tastes in popular music. Bored with the waltz, quadrille, and other European imports, they demanded new dimensions in popular music, mostly for dancing. Drawing upon Creole and Latin American rhythms, they developed in rapid succession such dances as the one-step, the turkey trot, and the cakewalk. Later, the fox trot, the shimmy, the Charleston, the shag, and the black bottom came upon the scene. These dances, and the exuberance they represented, also generated a demand for variety and accessibility in popular music that only recordings could satisfy.

Though severely strained over the years by murderous competition, ranging from early radio to new video games, the alliance between young people and recorded music has endured. The reasons today's youth buy recordings are different, and more sophisticated, than those of the dance-happy teens at the turn of the century. According to Allan Dodds Frank, a writer for *Forbes,* buying records is a form of social protest. "You know: U.S. out of Nicaragua. Down with Apartheid. End Hunger. Ban the Bomb. It's a way for the affluent young to feel virtuous and be self-indulgent at the same time."[19]

Such social concerns can be mobilized into powerful and affirmative action. In recent years, hundreds of recording artists and millions of their fans, most of them young people, have joined forces in a number of campaigns. These include raising money for hurricane relief; USA for Africa, a project to send food to impoverished nations; Farm Aid, organized largely by country music artists to assist financially strapped rural families; AIDS research and support for AIDS victims (1992's "Freddie Mercury Tribute: Concert for AIDS Awareness," televised in seventy nations, alone raised $35 million); and Amnesty International's Conspiracy of Hope tour to promote international human rights work.

Perhaps these motives have been analyzed too much. In the view of Ahmet Ertegun, chairman of Atlantic Records, observers like Frank may be making things more complex than they really are. Ertegun says, "Sometimes, socially conscious songs sell a lot of records, but that's accidental. Kids buy sound and rhythm more than messages. They like the idea that these [rock] groups have a social conscience, but they groove to the music."[20]

Discussion

Survey the class to determine the most popular current hits and artists. Are their favorite songs expressions of protest or rebellion, emotional appeals, or just good music?

Adolescents and Music

A recent study of high school teenagers found that music serves as a powerful communications medium, speaking directly to emotions. Both male and female respondents most often associated these emotions with music: excitement, happiness, and love. Females were somewhat more likely to associate emotions with music and to use music for "mood management." The results showed little difference in responses based on social class, race, and ethnic background. The study identified five emotional types where music is concerned: "self-assured," "angry," "romantics," "highly emotional," and "unemotional." There was some relationship between emotional clusters and musical preferences.

"Overall," the study concluded, "it is clear that for many adolescents who like popular music, it is a powerful tool for expressing and managing emotions."

Alen Wells and Ernest A. Hakanen, "The Emotional Use of Popular Music by Adolescents," *Journalism Quarterly*, 68:445 (1991).

summary

The recording industry is a volatile part of the mass communications field. It carries a high profile and touches millions of Americans each day and night. It is also an industry which, thanks to dramatic technological improvements and the continued strong support of the nation's youth market, is flying high.

While thousands of songwriters, recording artists, and production companies waged their intense (and often lucrative) competitive struggles, however, some persistent problems troubled the industry. One involved illegal pirating and counterfeiting of recordings. Illegal copying in the early 1990s cost the industry an estimated $400 million or more a year in lost revenue. Another difficult issue concerned explicit lyrics and pressure groups. Many rock and rap songs convey angry social dissent, or deal openly and frankly with such topics as drugs, sex, and violence. Some pressure groups alleged that certain recordings condoned violence, demeaned women, and promoted antisocial behavior. Precautionary efforts, such as parental advisory labels on certain recordings, were attempted; some large retailers removed controversial recordings from their shelves. But the First Amendment right to freedom of expression does apply to songwriters and performers, and free speech groups objected to any abridgment of creative expression. Determined to avoid censorship, the industry and government sought to preserve artistic freedom while at the same time allowing communities to exert some controls over objectionable materials.

The popularity of recordings, meanwhile, continued to grow. Further technological advancements, including digital audio broadcasting and digital audiotape, digital compact cassettes, and CD-ROM utilizations, provide a basis for optimism in the years ahead.

? questions and cases

1. Assume you are program director of a leading radio station in your community. Your station's playlist includes a number of rap recordings some residents in your community find offensive. Your station manager asks you to rethink your playlist, perhaps with a view toward banning controversial rap recordings altogether. What is your reaction? What arguments would you use in support of your position?

2. Does the issue of suggestive lyrics seem overemphasized to you? Why or why not? Is it possible to connect rock and rap music lyrics directly to worsening social problems (increases in teen-aged pregnancy, substance abuse, rape, violence)? Which regulatory measures, if any, seem both fair and consistent?

3. Experts attribute the high degree of interest that young people have in popular music to everything from rebellion to rhythm. What do *you* think are the primary motives driving young people to buy popular recordings?

4. Gary Shapiro, an executive of the Electronics Industries Association, thinks the record industry is wrong to oppose home taping (as opposed to commercial pirating) of recordings. In an essay published by *Billboard,* he argued, "For every sale displaced by an exchange of tapes with a friend, there is at least one gained." Do you agree? Others would levy a tax on blank cassette tapes and allocate the proceeds to artists and record companies in an attempt to remedy the damages caused by illegal copying. How, if at all, would *you* control unauthorized duplication of records and tapes?

5. The author stressed the importance of radio play to the sales success of a new recording. Do you agree with this emphasis? Does saturation exposure on radio prompt you to purchase a particular recording? How powerful is radio, in your opinion, as a record promoter? How effective is the concert tour? What other factors would you list?

chapter glossary

charts   Tabulations published by *Billboard* and other journals to report on a recording's popularity.

compact discs   Electronically produced recordings played back with a laser beam rather than a phonograph needle.

gold record   Generally, a single recording which has sold 1 million copies or an album that has sold 500,000 copies. Platinum recordings have sold 2 million singles or 1 million albums. The "multiplatinum" distinction applies to an album that sells 2 million or a single that sells 3 million copies.

master   The exact, original version of a recording after final editing and mixing. All copies are made from the master.

payola   Bribery money promoters paid to radio disc jockeys to obtain air time for certain recordings. Variations include *plugola,* to obtain favorable mention of the work, and *drugola,* in which the reward is tendered by means other than cash.

notes

1 Reported in *Down Beat,* January 1987, 12.

2 *The Taming of the Shrew,* act III, scene 1, lines 9–12.

3 This discussion of phonograph and recording history is drawn largely from Roland Gelatt, *The Fabulous Phonograph, 1877–1977* (New York: Macmillan, 1977); Robert A. Berkowitz, "The Phonograph," *World Book Encyclopedia* (1974), 15:363; Sydney W. Head, *Broadcasting in America,* 3d. ed. (Boston: Houghton Mifflin, 1976), 66 ff; and James D. Harless, *Mass Communication* (Dubuque, Iowa: Wm. C. Brown, 1985), 662.

4 J. G. Woodward, "Magnetic Recording" and "Disk Recording," *McGraw-Hill Encyclopedia of Science and Technology,* 5th ed. (New York: McGraw-Hill, 1982), 5:52 and 2:325.

5 Figures supplied to the author from the Recording Industry of America. The passages on rock music are drawn from Gelatt, *The Fabulous Phonograph;* Ralph Gleason, "Rock Music," *World Book Encyclopedia* (1974), 16:74; and other sources.

6 These figures, along with those cited earlier in the chapter, came from the Recording Industry of America, November 1992.

7 Woodward, "Magnetic Recording."

8 *Inside the Record Industry: A Statistical Overview* (Washington, D.C.: Recording Industry Association of America, 1991), 12.

9 Allan Dodds Frank, "And the Beat Goes On," *Forbes,* 18 May 1987, 40.

10 Richard Zoglin, "MTV Faces a Mid-Life Crisis," *Time,* 29 June 1987, 67.

11 New York *Times,* 21 October 1990, and elsewhere.

12 The matter was widely discussed in the trade press throughout the late eighties and early nineties. A good review is Bill Holland, "FCC Clarifies New Indecency Guidelines," *Billboard,* 12 May 1987, 1.

13 *Inside the Record Industry,* 20–23.

14 *Billboard,* 12 May 1987, 1.

15 *Inside the Record Industry,* 25.

16 Andrew Kupfer, "The Next Wave in Cassette Tapes," *Fortune,* 3 June 1991, 153.

17 *Inside the Record Industry,* 25.

18 Ibid., 16.

19 *Forbes,* 18 May 1987, 40.

20 Ibid.

chapter

Television

The story of television is a profoundly important and exciting chapter in the American experience. According to some studies, 69 percent of all Americans receive most of their news from TV, and 54 percent

The story of television is a profoundly important and exciting chapter in the American experience. According to some studies, 69 percent of all Americans receive most of their news from TV, and 54 percent regard it as the most believable of the mass media. Well beyond this, television has also become a universal instructor, dinner companion, salesperson, entertainer, and babysitter, our connection with the world outside. Members of the typical U.S. household in 1994 watched TV for an average of nearly seven hours each day of the year.[1] Nothing since the advent of the car has affected modern life so much.

Television's influence is everywhere. Ninety-eight percent of all U.S. households are now equipped with television receivers, and 65 percent have more than one set. Advertisers spend nearly $30 billion a year hawking goods and services via television. National advertisers, as opposed to local and regional, commit more money to television than any other medium. For all its faults, the much-maligned TV commercial remains the most spectacular means of reaching the greatest number of people at one time. Thirty-second commercial messages on the 1995 Super Bowl telecast sold for $1,000,000 apiece—an amazing figure, but so was the size of the audience for that telecast; more than 120 million people in the United States alone. Nearly that many were also riveted to their TV sets in June 1994 to witness a macabre series of events unfolding along Southern California freeways. While a small army of police trailed a white Ford Bronco with O. J. Simpson inside, the TV cameras made it possible for an American icon to become the most watched double-murder suspect in history.

The social effects of television, though still to be fully assessed, are staggering. Consciously or subconsciously, millions of Americans dress and talk and behave as they do because of what they have seen and heard on television. Television teaches, and

TV cameras make it possible for us to witness events as they happen such as the trial of confessed serial killer Jeffrey Dahmer.

Background

Broadcast television stations occupy **Very High Frequency (VHF)** channels 2 through 13, and **Ultra High Frequency (UHF)** channels from 14 up. Before cable, the most desirable channels were VHF, as their coverage was better than UHF; moreover, many early TV sets did not even have UHF tuners, keeping UHF stations at an economic disadvantage. Congress finally required TV manufacturers to include UHF tuners in 1960 to encourage UHF stations.

A Matter of "Live" and Death?

During the spring of 1993, the nation was shocked to see on television a tragic confrontation between federal authorities and a religious commune near Waco, Texas. After a prolonged standoff, which was fully covered by the media, federal officers stormed the Branch Davidian compound; the Davidian leaders set their buildings on fire, and most of those inside—all but a handful of the nearly one hundred members of the cult—perished.

In the tragedy's aftermath, there was considerable soul-searching throughout the media. The following, excerpted from the *American Journalism Review,* is an example:

In its grim, closing hours, the Waco story was treated on television like a sports event with play-by-play reporting; perhaps that's all that could have been expected as the compound was quickly engulfed in flames. But the tragic outcome also raised questions about the way the press, especially television, had played a role in extending the siege and contributed to its horrific ending. Was Waco just another big story that should have been covered in the usual way? Or do events of this type demand new thinking and new policies from television news managers?

"I have not resolved in my own mind how we fulfill the public's desire, if not need, to know when something as dramatic as Waco is happening and not at the same time encourage someone who wants headlines to do something atrocious," says veteran **CNN** correspondent Mary Tillotson, expressing what many reporters and producers are feeling.

Jeff Kamen, *American Journalism Review,* June 1993.

Science and TV Violence

After more than 1,000 scientific studies, the notion that violence portrayed in popular culture has an impact on behavior is finally coming through—although the picture is still a bit fuzzy. Research shows that not all kinds of violent depictions are equally harmful, not everyone is affected in the same ways and, ironically, the most influential displays of violence may be those that reinforce the moral message of right over wrong. . . .

The real danger of violence in popular culture may result from the fact that it sometimes reinforces existing prejudices. . . . Apparently, seeing images of a bad person being violently punished motivated viewers to mete out harsher punishments of their own. That's when the primordial urge for vengeance can get pushed too far.

U.S. News & World Report, 12 July 1992.

some of its lessons have helped show society a better way. Many scholars believe that genuine progress against racial and sexual discrimination, to cite just two examples, came about not through the preachments of politicians, but because television comedies and dramas began to depict the cruelty and ridiculousness of inequality. Television did not put an end to discrimination, but TV audiences have gone a long way toward laughing much of it into oblivion.

Not all of television's effects have been positive. Critics contend that certain personality types cannot handle the violence so ingrained in many television programs, that more than one brutal crime is directly attributable to an idea presented in a TV thriller. Hoping to avert a federally imposed ratings system for violence on television, the country's four major networks consented in the summer of 1993 to begin providing a warning to families when a violence-laden program was about to air. The warning was immediately criticized as inadequate: Many favored drastic censorship of violence instead. One network's dramatic films recently averaged twenty-one acts of violence per hour.[2] Some thoughtful observers argue that television violence has narcotized us into placidly accepting violence when it does occur in real life. The cumulative psychological effects of television on the lives of children are far from fully understood. Other critics blame television for overemphasizing differences between politician and voter, parent and child, labor and management, incumbent and candidate.

When television was new, John Tebbel pointed out, "it was viewed as a medium that would unite people as never before, but in fact it has splintered them beyond any real hope of unification."[3] That assessment may be unduly pessimistic, but a number of government leaders, including several recent U.S. presidents who never gained the national consensus they sought for implementing their policies, might well agree with it. Indeed, recent campaign advertising has taken on a decidedly negative tone. Television, as one candid political adviser put it, has reduced the audience's attention span to thirty seconds or less; given that incredibly narrow limit, a negative message might register better. We have become an audience overwhelmed not by complete news reports, but by sound bites.

Other observers resent the control television exerts over the scheduling of the events it covers. A politician will arrange an important news announcement to coincide with the evening newscast. A university's athletic director will cheerfully move the starting time of a football game to accommodate TV programmers, just as the referees will frequently whistle the game to a halt so that commercial messages can be presented on cue. In the gloomy view of some critics, television even threatens to isolate us into social nothingness. "It is a medium of entertainment which permits millions of people to listen to the same joke at the same time," despaired the great poet, T. S. Eliot, "and yet remain lonesome."[4]

While these criticisms cannot be ignored, they do not yet represent a serious threat to the love affair Americans have with their television sets. Collective viewing time, though it has dropped slightly in recent years, continues at near-record levels.

Background

In 1993, Congress held hearings on violence on both network and cable TV, and at least one senator threatened punitive legislation unless television cleaned up its act.

Discussion

In televised amateur sports, such as college football and basketball, is it ethical to allow commercial time outs that the players do not really need?

Popular TV personality Roseanne, whose "Roseanne" situation comedy (co-starring John Goodman, above) was a rating success story in the 1990s.

To an astonishing degree, individuals and entire families organize their meals, their evenings, and their social engagements around the daily television program logs. Their hurried conversations occur mostly during station breaks. TV's hold on contemporary society is powerful and pervasive.

Money, Money, Money

Well over a thousand commercial TV stations are currently operating in the United States; the great majority are network *affiliates*—that is, local stations that agree to carry network programs, following a pattern well-established by the radio industry. In addition to the four major networks—the National Broadcasting Company, the American Broadcasting Companies, CBS, Inc., and Fox Broadcasting Corporation—a number of regional and *ad hoc* networks assemble to present special events, such as a sports package or holiday spectacular.

Networks create some programs of their own and buy others from independent producers, putting together a rich variety of entertainment and news offerings. Affiliates agree to telecast several hours of the network's programs each day and night. Advertising sponsors purchase time on network programs, and the networks, in turn, share much of this income with affiliates, in effect paying local stations to carry network programming. In addition, the networks leave open a number of spots during the broadcast day for the local affiliates to sell commercial time independently. A local television station takes in money from:

1 Its *pro rata* share, based on the size of its market, of *network income;*

2 *National spot* advertising, from the independent sale of commercial time to national advertisers who are more interested in reaching specific markets than in working through a network, which could force them to buy more stations than they may want or need; and

3 *Local spot,* or retail, advertising.

Network advertising can reach great numbers of people at one time. If the total cost is enormous, so is the size of the audience. Individual TV stations may charge $20,000 or more per thirty-second announcement, although the normal rate, especially in secondary markets during slow viewing hours, is often no more than $25. Even so, advertisers are investing their money by the billions in television; in 1993, they invested more than $10 billion in network television commercials, and about $8 billion or more each in non-network, or **spot, announcements,** and in local advertising sales. With that kind of money at stake, advertisers understandably want to know, as precisely as possible, just who is watching. Hence the concern with **ratings.**

In an interview with *Broadcasting* magazine, TV producer Richard Rosenstock, who has been associated with a number of hit shows, described his frustrations in trying to succeed with "Flying Blind," a short-lived series that aired briefly in the early 1990s:

Q: What is the most disturbing practice in network television?
A: Testing. Maybe it's because I had that experience myself. One of the reasons I think this show [*Flying Blind*] got on the air is that we delivered the show very close to the date the network was going to announce, so I don't know if the network tested it or not. I think they kind of screened it and I believe kind of took the reaction in the room and said we can do this show. I've heard more horror stories about testing and the network reliance on testing as an indication of whether a show is going to work or not than any other thing. When I was at ABC with this last show there was this prevailing vision fueled by the research department that in this current channel-switching era, if someone isn't a fan of yours by the first two or three episodes they will never watch you again. A lot of shows, including mine, I think got swept away in that ridiculous sensibility. . . . They all claim research is just a tool. But it's not a tool. It's a blunt instrument they bang you over the head with.

Broadcasting magazine, 26 October 1992.

Television Audience Analysis

A newspaper or magazine publisher knows exactly how many copies of the last issue were printed and to a great extent—since most copies are home delivered—who received them. The broadcaster is less fortunate; once a program is telecast, information about its audience is harder to come by. Yet such data must be collected to bridge the gap between the station and its audience, to improve programming decisions, and, especially, to let sponsors know what they are getting for their advertising dollars.

Television viewing research usually involves monitoring a carefully chosen sample of the population, then projecting the results to the population as a whole. Four specific kinds of techniques have been most commonly employed:

1 *The telephone coincidental.* Interviewers call a predetermined sample of people. "Is your TV set on?" respondents are asked. "What channel are you watching? what program? How many persons are watching the set right now?" The telephone coincidental can provide quick—usually overnight—results for a given program or viewing hour, though obviously it does not generate the comprehensive information many sponsors would prefer.

2 *The meter method.* Electronic **meters** are installed on TV sets in selected households. The owners give their permission and receive nominal payment for their trouble. The meters record precisely when a set is on and what channel is selected. A computer scanning from the research firm's headquarters tabulates the results. Subscribers can obtain overnight reports on television viewing, based on data from these meters. The procedure is expensive. Also, it can only report what the set is tuned to, not whether anyone happens to be in the room watching. But it provides a great deal of information.

In the fall of 1987, industry researchers introduced highly controversial measuring devices called "people meters," tiny, portable minicomputers equipped with buttons that individual viewers can use to record what they are actually watching. Each person in the viewing sample can activate the meter when he or she begins to view a TV program, then turn off the machine upon leaving the room. Demographic data on each member of the viewing household are collected beforehand. When a visitor initiates a viewing entry, flashing lights prompt him or her to provide gender and age data. The meters can monitor and record VCR viewing as well.

3 *The diary method.* Preselected, consenting families agree to keep a notebook by their TV sets; each family member records the stations and programs they

Teaching Idea

Ask your class whether any of them, their parents, or friends have ever taken part in a media survey project, such as Nielsen or Arbitron. What did the survey require them to do?

actually watch. In addition, the diarists, who receive a modest monthly payment, provide information about their buying behavior. The diaries are mailed each month to the research firm, which compiles the entries into patterns and relays the totals to clients. Diaries generate much information relatively inexpensively, though they do require extensive cooperation from viewers. Too, the diaries depend on recollections, which are sometimes faulty.

4 *Personal interviews.* Interviewers ask viewers what programs they watched the day before. One form of this technique, the *roster recall method,* requires the interviewer to provide a schedule of programs televised the previous day and night for the respondent to use in reporting which he or she remembers seeing. Interviewers using the *unaided recall* technique provide no cues whatever; they depend entirely on the respondent's memory.

While an increasing number of firms are engaged in television audience analysis, the current giant of the industry remains the **A. C. Nielsen** Company. (**Arbitron,** for years a major presence in this area, elected in 1993 to relinquish the TV audience analysis business.) Ratings reports reveal the size of a program or network audience on a given day or night. Scholars and other observers concede that the statistical projections are correct most of the time.

In their determined efforts to define audiences with precision, the broadcast companies and the market researchers utilize their own jargon. Here are a few of the more commonly mentioned expressions:

- *Market.* The group of people reached by a given television station. Arbitron referred to it as that station's **ADI (Area of Dominant Influence):** the geographic area consisting of all counties the station can draw a preponderance of viewers from. Nielsen's term is **DMA (Designated Market Area).**
- *Sets in use.* The percentage of all households in the population with sets in operation at any time. This is sometimes referred to as HUT—Households Using Television.
- *Rating.* The percentage of TV households in an area tuned to a specific program. The significance of the rating varies with the time of day, depending on the number of sets in use. A program shown at 7:30 A.M. may gain a rating of 5, while a program at 9 P.M. may have a rating of 21, and both ratings would be regarded as good, given their relative viewing hours.
- **Market share,** *or share of audience.* The percentage of households using television (HUT) tuned to a specific station, program, or network. Assume we are in a market where there are one thousand television sets, half of which are turned on. Half of those, or one-quarter of the total number, are tuned to a particular program. That program would enjoy a rating of 25—one-quarter of the market. Its share would be 50—or half of the sets in use.
- **Cume ratings,** *or* **cume.** Cumulative audience, the number of (unduplicated) persons who tune in to a particular program for at least five minutes during a given time period, often one week. This rating is reported as a percentage.[5]

Teaching Idea
Broadcasting & Cable magazine prints weekly rating charts for network and cable programs. If you or your library subscribes, ask your students to estimate the ratings certain programs will earn. Then compare the class's predictions to the actual ratings.

Television ratings translate quickly into dollars. Here again, TV differs from print: Full-page advertisements in a national magazine cost pretty much the same; volume, purchase discounts, extra charges for certain production services, and a few other variables may affect the price somewhat, but the essential rate structure remains consistent. Not so with television. During a recent fall season, for example, a thirty-second spot sold for as little as $30,000 during one prime-time network program, or as much as $380,000 for a much higher-rated program during the same time slot on another network. The prices fluctuated wildly an hour later. Rates can rise if a show proves to be a hit or fall after an unfavorable ratings report during the season. Each rating point at the network level may mean millions in revenue gained or lost over the course of a year.

Advertisers understand ratings points and are prepared to pay for them. If a program reaches an audience of 14 million, for example, the network may charge one price per commercial. If the audience drops off, the advertiser would want to pay less and might also begin looking for a more promising vehicle to carry the client's sales messages. To draw ratings, networks and local stations redesign programs, move them to different time periods, or cancel them outright. Ratings companies don't kill TV shows, though they are sometimes blamed for doing so; network executives do. But in arriving at these critical decisions, the network executives rely heavily on audience analyses companies such as Nielsen provide. Any TV viewer whose favorite show is dumped from the network schedule because of low Nielsens may resent the fact that ratings carry such weight within the volatile, and often nervous, television industry. But they do. In spite of their flaws, which can include imperfect methodologies, faulty respondent memories, and other human errors, ratings do provide timely audience information. As a result, stations, advertisers, networks, and syndicators can better evaluate programming and buying decisions, compete more effectively, and learn more about how Americans use their TV sets.

Programming Policies and Procedures

The typical television station, which might be on the air from twenty to twenty-four hours a day, churns through a great deal of content. Only a small percentage of telecasts are locally produced—perhaps one to three hours a day of news and public affairs programs, possibly half an hour of local talk shows or community forums. The overwhelming bulk of the programming must be imported from the network and from various companies selling **syndicated programs.** Many programs are available, but selecting the right ones, singly and in pleasing combinations, requires considerable judgment and skill.

To make programming decisions—and maximize their inevitable corollary, advertising sales—networks divide the television cycle into viewing segments, or **dayparts,** as table 1 shows.

table 1 — Dayparts of Weekday Network Programming

Time Designation	Hours	Main Audiences	Types of Programs Shown
Early morning	Until 9 A.M.	Women, pre-school children	Juvenile, news, cartoons, games
Daytime	9 A.M.–4 P.M.	Women, elderly	Soap operas, game shows
Early fringe	4–7:30 P.M.	School children, adults	News, variety, game shows
Access	7:30–8 P.M.	Family viewing	Serials, sitcoms
Prime time	8–11 P.M.	Adult, teen	Serials, sitcoms, drama, specials, movies
Late news	11–11:30 P.M.	Young adults	News
Late late	11:30 P.M.– dawn	Singles, young adults	Movies, drama, talk shows

Note: A detailed discussion of television dayparts and programming, from which some of this discussion is adapted, may be found in Otto Kleppner, *Advertising Procedure,* 7th ed. (Englewood Cliffs, N.J.: Prentice-Hall, 1979), 122–26; and S. Watson Dunn and Arnold M. Barban, *Advertising: Its Role in Modern Marketing,* 6th ed. (Dryden, 1986), 604–30. Also, see Daniel Paisner, "The Pilot System, or $300 Million Guesswork," New York *Times,* 6 December 1992.

The patterns change somewhat on Saturday and Sunday mornings, when more children's and religious programs appear. Sports programming occupies many weekend afternoon time slots. **Prime time,** as the name suggests, attracts the heaviest audiences.

Network Programs

If a local station is affiliated with a network, then the network's offerings will be the major factor in the local station's programming decisions. The network itself does not have total control over its affiliates, however, except at the very few **O and O** stations, those owned and operated by the network. Instead, network affiliates sign a contract agreeing to carry a minimum number, but by no means all, of the network's programs. In actual practice, the typical affiliate will use about two-thirds of the network's offerings.

An affiliate station's management might decline a network program for any of several reasons. The network program may seem too controversial for a particular local audience. Or the station could have a policy of telecasting the entire schedule of a popular regional basketball team; these games would then replace network programming from time to time throughout the season. Or perhaps the local station might elect to telecast a movie or a special—a religious program, for instance, or a syndicated rerun of a popular old series—in place of one or more network shows during a given evening. The station may be able to sell a great deal of local advertising that pays better than the station's share of the network programs, or the affiliate may think its own programming will attract more viewers. In any case, the individual station, not the network, makes the final programming decisions.

Fully aware of the high stakes involved, networks spend a great deal of time and money attempting to create enthusiasm for network schedules among their affiliates. If the affiliate in a particular city elects not to carry a network program, the network loses advertising revenue, the dollars the client would have paid for commercial messages to reach the audience in that market. Too, the network's national ratings will be affected, because some viewers had no chance to see the program. As ratings drop, so do advertising rates and profits. It is thus in the network's urgent best interest to see that its affiliates are at least reasonably satisfied with network offerings. A complaint from an affiliate station manager receives a network executive's full attention, and more than a few complaints from affiliates about a network program may well bring about that program's demise.

Networks produce some of their own programs—chiefly news, sports, and public affairs programs—and purchase rights for others from private companies and film studios. These independent producers develop story ideas, prepare **pilots** (sample tapes to show what a series is like), and offer programs to the networks. A network may pick up the more promising pilots and incorporate them into the new season's entertainment schedule. Huge sums of money are involved, as much as $200 million in some years for pilots alone, and most of these will never air. Of the twenty or fewer picked for a given season's schedule, only a handful will survive more than a few episodes.

Syndicated Programs

The local station management can also choose from a wide variety of programs offered outside the network structure. These programs are sold or distributed by syndicate houses, which may or may not have had a hand in producing the programs originally, but own the rights to them now. Syndicated offerings include reruns of former network series, movies, interview shows, game shows, and other programs marketed to local stations and delivered on videotape or transmitted via satellite. Network affiliates might use syndicated programs to fill one-third or more of their broadcast schedules. Unaffiliated stations rely on the syndicators almost entirely.

Teaching Idea

Ask students to compare network and cable program listings with the text's daypart schedule. Is there a close correlation? Do any maverick stations or channels wildly deviate?

Teaching Idea

Assign students to monitor local network programs for a week. Do any preemptions of network programs take place? If so, for what reason? (*TV Guide* is a good source for checking scheduled network programs.)

Extra Information

In mid-1994, twelve broadcast stations, some in major markets, changed their network affiliation to Fox. (It might be interesting to have students see whether any others have changed since then.)

Teaching Idea

Ask students to analyze one day's programming on a local network affiliate. What percentage was obviously network? What percentage was syndicated? And what percentage was filled with locally produced news or other programs?

Background

The earliest network TV news programs were only fifteen minutes long. Visuals were charts, graphs, and film clips. It was a number of years before the news lengthened to a half-hour. Local affiliates have generally opposed hour-long network news programs.

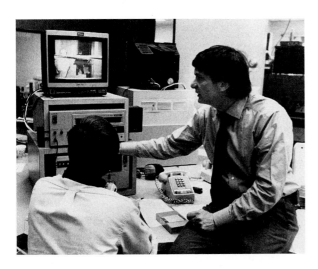

Directing a local newscast.

Often contracted at bargain prices, syndicated shows can prove highly profitable for the local station because all commercial breaks are open to sell local advertising messages. In other cases, the station **barters,** receiving the program without charge in exchange for letting the program provider sell half the commercial spots. The station gets no payment for carrying these messages, but it does get a program without cost and obtains the right to sell the remaining commercial time spots at lucrative local rates. Some network programs are offered in this manner.

Positioning

Besides selecting which program to show, television executives must also decide when to show it, a determination that can be crucial. More than one promising situation comedy or dramatic presentation has been victimized by landing in an unfortunate time slot, scheduled against an entrenched popular favorite.

Network program chiefs must consider a nightmarish combination of variables: type of program available (action-adventure, drama, western, police-detective, doctors-and-lawyers, situation comedy, variety, romantic serial); traditional viewing patterns; and what the competition might offer in each time period. Public tastes, moreover, constantly change. Western series and variety shows, hugely popular in the 1960s, became a rarity in the 1990s; a hard-hitting investigatory news program, "60 Minutes," succeeded brilliantly at CBS, but the same format flopped several times at NBC. For these and other reasons, the odds of making a smash on network are slim. In a typical year, a network may receive twenty-five hundred program ideas; the network may select a hundred to go into limited production, on speculation as possible series programs, and maybe choose twenty of the resulting pilots to add to the fall schedule. Most will not be renewed.

Network programmers are heavy players in a risky game. At times they must secretly yearn for a return to the early days of television, when a single variety show could entertain an entire nation, offering something for all. Today's TV viewers, with so many choices available, are harder to please.

Television News

Live coverage of an actuality, as Sydney W. Head describes it, remains television's unique dimension: "The most memorable high points of television's programming—the peaks of excellence that rise up out of the surrounding wasteland, as some would have it—are nearly all of this type, whether Olympic games or Congressional hearings, the first steps on the moon or the pageantry of great heads of state. Without exception, the most popular individual programs have all had this quality of immediacy and unpredictability."[6]

It is in the realm of news reporting that television comes closest to fully realizing its remarkable potential. Newspapers, which dominated for years, since the mid-1960s have been relegated to second place, and the gap is widening. Television news is faster, more dramatic, and usually far more convenient for the audience. Network news organizations have enormous resources at their command and can send correspondents throughout the world. Chartered jet aircraft, minicams, satellite uplinks, and a fierce competitive drive make it routinely possible for U.S. television journalists to show us news events wherever they happen. Many local television newscasters, once chosen more for their mellifluous voices than for news judgment, have become true professionals, respected by their fellow journalists and admired by their audiences. Despite, or perhaps because of, its undoubted

Writing for Television: A Look at One News Story

Following is the script for one brief, uncomplicated TV news story, a little "bright" or "kicker" aired near the end of a late-night newscast at WIS-TV, an NBC affiliate in a midsized market, Columbia, South Carolina.

Note that the script is formatted in two columns. All the instructions to the director, audio person, electronic graphics indicator, and so forth appear on the left side so the *anchor,* or person on camera, will not be distracted when reading off the **TelePrompter.** The right column carries the text to be read over the air. Material in the left column does not appear on the TelePrompter.

The *talent,* or on-the-air anchor, introduces the story, setting the stage for the tape to roll with a report from the scene of the story itself. *ENG* refers to the Electronic News-Gathering equipment, the camera used in the field for shooting the story. The *ENG UP FULL* cue calls for the audio technician to turn the volume all the way up on the videotape sound track. The anchor may talk above *sound under* but must quit talking for *up full.*

Frequently, in introducing a story, viewers will hear the anchor in a *VO,* or **voice-over** while seeing the action from the story itself.

Often a **character generator** (CG) is used to present key words and phrases to help the viewer follow the story more closely. In this example, the CG will be used to superimpose the location of the story, Cambridge, Massachusetts.

SOT refers to "sound on tape," the audio portion of the videotaped report *(VTR)* being shown. This particular tape came to the station from the NBC network feed.

After the taped portion has rolled, the director returns the anchor to the screen to wrap up the story.

KICKER TALENT=DAVID	JODIE FOSTER HAS WON HARVARD'S HASTY PUDDING AWARD AS WOMAN OF THE YEAR.
ENG=VOSOT CG=CAMBRIDGE, MASS.	THE AWARD IS GIVEN EACH YEAR BY THE HARVARD THEATRICAL GROUP. FOSTER IS AN ODDS-ON FAVORITE TO WIN AN ACADEMY AWARD THIS YEAR FOR HER ROLE IN THE SERIOUS THRILLER, THE SILENCE OF THE LAMBS . . . SHE SAID SHE TRULY APPRECIATES THE HUMOR IN THE GESTURE.
ENG=UP FULL SOT	"The truth is that I'm not that serious a person and people who know me know that I'm a goof. So, I think that that's what I like the most about this is that it is from peers and from people I respect; it's kind of a goof thing which is more of a celebration than almost anything else."
VTR OUT OUT Q=ALMOST ANYTHING ELSE. TALENT=DAVID	MICHAEL DOUGLAS, THE MAN OF THE YEAR, WILL PICK UP HIS BRASS POT NEXT WEEK.

Used with permission of WIS-TV.

impact and influence, television news receives a heavy measure of criticism from sociologists, political scientists, the clergy, and journalists themselves. Some of the principal themes include superficiality, a preoccupation with pictures, cosmetics, the quality of interviewing, and limited reporting staffs.

Superficiality

Even its staunchest defenders concede that television news is often little more than a headline service. A typical TV newscast that consists of less than twenty-three minutes of actual news time may present thirty or more items, some in twenty seconds or less and consisting of one or two sentences each. Complex stories may be hopelessly oversimplified or ignored altogether. A two- or three-minute piece, rare on TV newscasts, is regarded as reporting in depth. The text for an entire newscast, set in type, would take up far less space than a single newspaper page.

A Preoccupation with Pictures

Television's visual power, critics charge, can also distort news values. The question "Is it an important story?" may be less relevant at times than "Do we have good visuals for it?" Thus, a relatively ordinary auto accident with spectacular footage available may receive far more prominent play than a significant-but-dull analysis of next year's local school budget.

Local TV News Salaries

According to a survey conducted by Dr. Vernon A. Stone for the Radio-Television News Directors Association, the following were salary averages at local television station news departments around the country during the early 1990s:

Camerapersons	$21,400
Producers	24,620
Executive producers	37,750
Reporters	25,485
Anchors	48,600
High anchors (stars at their stations)	82,835
Assignment editors	27,815
News directors	51,745

The Communicator, Radio-Television News Directors Association, February 1992.

Teaching Idea

Assign students to watch and analyze a local station's news programs on a given day, comparing the programs to the criticisms noted in the text. How much actual news was reported within the scheduled length?

Teaching Idea

Ask your students for reactions to any interviews they have seen on TV recently. Did the interviewer ask any inappropriate questions?

Cosmetics

Television "news teams," as the on-camera readers are called, typically consist of one or two anchors who present news items or introduce reports from journalists in the field; someone to give the weather forecast; and a sports reporter. Station managers choose these on-the-air personalities with great care. Some studies conclude that among the factors that help viewers decide which newscast to watch, "liking the anchor team" is cited far more often than "newscast content." Often, the selection criteria seem more concerned with the team's attractiveness than with its journalistic competence. Cosmetic concerns also extend to the news set, the anchor desk, the pulsating weather map, and the lead-in music. Often outside consultants or "news doctors" prescribe them. Brought in to shore up a local newscast with sagging ratings, these individuals conduct polls to measure personal viewer reactions to such things as the personalities and voices of individual members of the news team. Fortified with reams of survey data, the consultants may recommend sweeping changes in the newscast: different on-the-air **talents,** fastidiously selected to present just the right image; new sets; a new basis for deciding what kind of news is most important; how long or how short certain types of stories should run. The result is a slick, attractive, fast-paced newscast, often augmented by preplanned, cheerful conversations among the anchors, so the news comes across in a friendly, comforting manner. Such contrived presentations are not necessarily evil—perhaps they have saved more than a few local newscasts from extinction—but thoughtful observers do worry when an institution as important as a television newscast is developed around entertainment, as opposed to journalistic, values.

The Quality of Interviewing

As television news reporters become more numerous, and rivalries with other media intensify, some experts express concerns about the propriety and intellectual content of some of the questions reporters ask while the cameras are turning. Thrusting a microphone into the face of a woman who has just seen her house destroyed by fire and demanding her reaction to the tragedy is tasteless in the extreme, but it happens. Badgering political leaders on live television likewise angers many in the audience. Too many reporters seem to want to put words in a subject's mouth ("Isn't it about time we began to see the light at the end of the tunnel, Governor?") or, worse, to ask an intimate personal question of an anguished private citizen ("What are your feelings now?"), leaving the cameras trained mercilessly while a confused, helpless person gropes for words to reply.[7]

Aggressive journalism requires tough questions, of course, and reporters from all media ask them. But TV news, especially when telecast live, provides few built-in safeguards to protect the subject or the audience from questions that invade personal privacy or offend common decency. For this reason, television reporters, editors, and directors must be especially alert to the possibly harmful effects of unfair interviewing.

Limited Reporting Staffs

Television news staffs tend to be smaller, in numbers of reporters, than newspaper staffs in comparably sized markets. As a result, TV reporters can cover fewer events in person, and they may be too rushed to spend more than a few minutes at the scene when they do. Efforts to stretch a reporting staff too thin can result in empty, oversimplified news stories.

In spite of these and other limitations caused by time pressures, economics, federal regulations, and the attention span of the mass audience, television news generally does a worthy job of summarizing and presenting the highlights of the news of the day. Network newscasts have earned high marks from their vast audiences, while great numbers of local newscasts have improved dramatically. The brilliant work of CNN's field reporters during the Persian Gulf war showed the world how competent television journalists can be. A number of local TV news reporters now consistently outperform their counterparts on local newspapers.

Public Television

Conceived as an alternative to private, commercially supported television, public TV has captivated a fair number of viewers but has never quite achieved the lofty goals periodically set for it. One mission statement, developed by the Carnegie Commission in 1967, proclaimed that public television

> should show us our community as it really is . . . [be] a forum for debate and controversy . . . bring into the home meetings, now generally untelevised, where major public decisions are hammered out, and occasions where people of the community express their hopes, their protests, their enthusiasms, their will . . . provide a voice for groups in the community that may be unheard. . . . [Public television] . . . can increase our understanding of the world, of other nations and cultures, of the whole commonwealth of man . . . should have the means to be daring, to break away from narrow conventions, to be human and earthy . . . should be an innovative laboratory for the analysis of the intellectual, artistic, and social institutions of our culture.[8]

This was a tall order which provoked some misgivings—especially in Congress and the White House, where strong opposition exists to governmental competition with private enterprise. Thus, public television has rarely received anything approaching adequate financial support; nor has there been any detectable groundswell of outrage from the voters as a result. Perhaps, as John Tebbel has noted, "the fact that the education stations have to struggle for their lives is proof

Teaching Idea

If your local cable system carries *CNN Headline News*, assign students to watch it and compare its content with national network evening news broadcast on the same day and at approximately the same time. What similarities and differences do students notice?

Background

In 1962–63, Congress appropriated funds to assist educational TV systems to construct over-the-air (broadcast) stations on channels the FCC reserved for them. Existing commercial stations supposedly helped the educational stations get on the air, so that the channel could not be assigned to another commercial station.

that most viewers do not want culture and education from the tube."[9] For whatever reason, public television remains a minority service in U.S. society, though much of its programming is high-quality and its audiences, if relatively small, still number in the millions.

KUHT in Houston, Texas, was the first educational television station to go on the air with regular broadcasting in May 1953. Alabama established the first statewide public television network in 1955. By 1994, more than 350 public TV stations were operating in the United States. Prohibited by law from carrying commercial advertising messages, they are supported by public contributions, government grants, and donations from large private corporations and foundations. The Corporation for Public Broadcasting (CPB) raises money from public and private sources and allocates funds for program production and distribution through the Public Broadcasting Service (PBS). In 1993, public broadcasting's total income was well under $2 billion; perhaps one-fifth of this came directly from federal funding.[10] This comprised only about 4 percent of the total income commercial broadcasting generated that year.

Despite the financial constraints, public television has managed to provide the country with innovative programming; much is of superb quality and probably would not have been available to American audiences otherwise. "Sesame Street" and other products of the Children's Television Workshop literally revolutionized children's programming, entertaining young audiences while teaching them. Handsomely produced dramatic programs, many of them imported from England, have met with enthusiastic receptions. Public television's cultural productions—concerts, ballets, operas, classical dramas—have also been enthusiastically received, while PBS debates, forum discussions, and documentaries, though of uneven quality, stimulate debate on important public issues.

In the realm of news and public affairs, "The MacNeil-Lehrer News Hour" has won more than fifty national awards for journalistic excellence. This program, which provides a general news overview and then deals with one topic at length, has clearly influenced commercial network news as well. Its adroit treatment of longer subjects prompted the commercial networks to create "special segments" that provide a deeper examination of one complex story. The single-subject theme of MacNeil-Lehrer was also later reflected in ABC's highly successful "Night Line."

On the other hand, critics of public television charge that too much of its programming is dull and esoteric; that PBS stations devote too much air time to

Teaching Idea

If your local PBS station carries the MacNeil-Lehrer News Hour, ask students to watch it and discuss its content in relation to other TV news programs.

fundraising appeals; and that the documentaries exhibit a political bias that some viewers and members of Congress find disturbing. Indeed, Republicans in the Senate, declaring that public television was permeated with liberal ideology and that the programming was occasionally obscene, proposed a drastic reduction, on the order of $400 million a year, in planned federal funding for the Corporation for Public Broadcasting. That proposal was decisively defeated, 75 to 22, as public television supporters throughout the country lobbied against it. Senator Daniel Moynihan of New York, a leader in the fight, called public television "the pride of Congress. . . . It's one of the few real winners we've come up with in a quarter-century."[11]

Though increasing, public television viewing remains relatively small, ranging from less than 5 to as much as 16 percent of the weekly audience for commercial TV. Contrary to what might be expected, surveys show that the viewers who watch public TV also watch a lot of commercial TV as well; the public TV viewer, in other words, is not an elitist who tunes in precisely at 9 P.M. for an episode of "Masterpiece Theater," then turns off the set promptly at 10. Instead, the typical public television viewer is much like TV viewers generally; public television is simply another available option.

In the larger sense, PBS is not a true, cohesive network so much as a collection of syndicated programs, offered to woefully underfinanced affiliates that may or may not be able to pay for them. Those that do order the PBS programs might not air them at uniform, or even predictable, times; Robert MacNeil's highly acclaimed series, "The Story of English," was shown during early evenings in some markets, late night in some, and on Saturday mornings elsewhere. Until public broadcasting is better organized and better funded—two conditions that show no immediate signs of improvement—it will remain a secondary service, enjoyed in a great many homes but something less than a viable alternative to the commercial networks.

Cable Television

As television began sweeping the country in the late 1940s, certain households were unable to pick up TV signals through the air. These included homes in remote or mountainous areas as well as urban households surrounded by tall office buildings. Enterprising businesspeople developed the concept of the **Community Antenna Television (CATV)** system: A powerful master antenna was positioned in an area with good reception, and the broadcast signals were picked up and redistributed, via coaxial cable, to subscribers who paid a monthly service charge. At the outset, cable television systems served merely to enhance reception by bringing in regularly scheduled television programs to audiences which could not receive them otherwise. While that remains its primary purpose today, cable television has become capable of far more. Dozens of channels, some of them highly specialized, offer access to programming never thought possible previously.

After the Satcom satellite was successfully placed in orbit in 1975, cable systems were able to pick up signals from far-off locations, allowing a CATV company to offer its subscribers programs from a rich variety of sources. By 1994, 56 million U.S. households—60.3 percent—were hooked into one of the 11,314 authorized CATV systems. Besides regular commercial network and local station programming, the cable system can also provide its customers:

- *Cable networks.* These produce programming often devoted to a single topic or aimed at a particular audience interest and use satellites for transmitting to cable operators. Arts and Entertainment, ESPN (sports and business), the Weather Channel, the USA Cable Network, Cable Network News, Nickelodeon (children's programming), C-SPAN (Cable-Satellite Public Affairs Network), and Black Entertainment Television are examples of this type of service.

Background

Several terms describe nonbroadcast television: *CATV*, which means Community Antenna TV; *MATV*, which means Master Antenna TV (primarily used in apartment buildings); *CCTV*, which means Closed-Circuit TV; and *narrowcasting*. *Cable TV* now commonly refers to any wired system.

- *Local access channels.* These may include round-the-clock news and weather wires, live telecasts of local school board and city council meetings, library channels, and other opportunities for local residents and organizations to reach a television audience.
- *Superstations.* Large, independent stations—such as WTBS in Atlanta, WGN in Chicago, and WOR in New York—beam their signals via satellite to subscribing cable companies.
- *Premium pay channels.* These offer films, sports programming, and entertainment specials for an additional fee. Home Box Office, which helped launch the satellite cable boom in 1975, remains the largest of the premium channels. Others include Showtime, the Movie Channel, Disney, Cinemax, and the Playboy Channel.

Additional programming, under the broad heading of STV (Subscription Television) is also available, through both over-the-air broadcasting and cable channels. STV signals are "scrambled," so that only subscribers with decoding devices attached to their TV sets can receive them. Some farmers, for example, pay for an STV service that presents current commodity price information and late-breaking agricultural news.

No federally prescribed model exists for a CATV system. Local governments award cable franchises, usually after competitive bidding. As a result, some communities are served by cable systems providing as few as twenty channels, though most offer thirty or more. In 1972, the Federal Communications Commission did issue an order requiring cable operators to make available public access channels, at least one per system, for anyone who wants to broadcast his or her own TV program. Churches, minority groups, civic organizations, school clubs—anyone with something to say—should have, in theory at least, an opportunity to utilize a public access channel.[12] In addition to public access opportunities, many cable operators also reserve channels for local government, school systems, and the public library.

Income and Expense

Individual cable operators charge subscribers a flat monthly fee for basic cable service—in 1993, the national average was $18 per household—plus extra charges for certain additional channels and for the premium movie channels.

About one in five cable companies generates extra income from local advertising, commercial slots sold on the public access channels, while most systems also sell advertising messages to fit in local time breaks scheduled by ESPN and other cable networks. Cable TV ad income is not large; for many operators, it represents 10 percent or less of total income.

Cable expenses run high. *Broadcasting & Cable Market Place* in 1992 estimated the costs of laying cable at $10,000 per mile in rural areas, $100,000 in urban areas, and up to $300,000 in communities where underground cable is required. In addition to user fees paid to cable networks, local cable operators must absorb the costs of public access programming, plus any copyright fee assessments, such as those the Copyright Royalty Tribunal charges for carrying an additional superstation signal. Eager to present the most attractive bid for the franchise, many cable companies initially promised a more elaborate package than they could prudently deliver. Too, high costs are associated with subscriber cancellations or changes in service, especially regarding the otherwise profitable premium pay channels. Customers moving in and out of the system—the percentage referred to as the *churn rate*—may run as high as 40 percent a year on some premium channels.

For these and other reasons, not all cable operations are prosperous. A great many, in fact, expect deficits for several years before they can ultimately project profits. On the whole, however, the industry thrives. Cable revenues in the 1990s were nearing $20 billion a year, and some individual cable companies—especially MSOs, or *Multiple System Operators*, as they are known—have grown to substantial size. Tele-Communications in 1993 was the largest of the MSOs, with more than 8.4 million subscribers.[13] Overall, the cable television industry entered the 1990s in robust health, with even brighter prospects for the century ahead. But technological and political climates can change rapidly, and, as we shall see, not all indicators are necessarily favorable.

An Industry in Transition

If the years ahead look bright for the cable industry, over-the-air telecasters can see only gloom. A far-reaching position paper issued in 1991 by two senior economists within the Federal Communications Commission, warned that "the broadcast industry has suffered an irreversible long-term decline in audience and revenue shares, which will continue through the current decade."[14] The report added that for ABC, CBS, and NBC, "the decline in audience share will probably slow over the decade as cable matures and as marginal independents go dark. . . ."

While the sluggish U.S. economy was a contributor, the principal player in broadcasting's decline was cable, which was drawing off advertising dollars and viewers to an alarming degree. Though cable penetration, now just over 60 percent, is expected to peak at no higher than 70 percent, the added income to the cable industry will permit cable companies to acquire and develop better programming, which will attract even more viewers and advertisers. Indeed, some observers speculate that the networks might ultimately become program *packagers*, supplying programs to cable networks rather than to their own affiliates.

The declining fortunes of over-the-air broadcasters are likely to force networks and individual stations to take massive cost-cutting measures, the report warned, but added that "large cutbacks in program expenditures may reduce the perceived quality and distinctiveness of network programming and further reduce the ability of networks to attract audiences."

The networks' problems were compounded by a series of Justice Department orders prohibiting the big three from acquiring a financial interest in and later syndicating network programs licensed from outside producers. Before this restraint—referred to as the fin-syn rule—was loosened in the early 1990s, the networks lost additional market power to program producers, who were able to raise prices and reap additional profits.

The long-term problems over-the-air broadcasters face cannot all be solved by enacting new laws, but Congress attempted some interim relief, at least, when it passed the Cable Act of 1992.

The Cable Act of 1992

Known formally as the Cable Television Consumer Protection and Competition Act of 1992, this measure placed some limits on the market power cable television operators could wield in dealing with programmers and consumers. In theory, it could result in reductions of up to 30 percent in cable system rates charged to subscribers and provide over-the-air broadcasters with an estimated $1 billion a year from the cable companies in payments for carrying their programs. Both possibilities were, at best, uncertain.

The rate structure, which the Federal Communications Commission would oversee, now involved a new, highly complex formula placing limits on charges for the *basic tier*, defined as local broadcast signals and PEG—public, educational, and governmental—channels. The FCC assumed responsibility for regulating extended cable service charges as well, and the agency was directed to make sure cable subscription rates would be reasonable and competitive.

Background

Cable penetration refers to the percentage of TV homes subscribing to cable, as compared to the total number of TV homes.

Extra Information

The 1992 Cable Act resulted when consumers complained to their senators and representatives that cable systems provided poor service and charged excessive fees. Unfortunately for the cable systems, many members of Congress lived in areas with poor service and high rates.

The act also required local cable operators to include all local over-the-air television signals in their coverage areas as part of their basic cable package (the "must carry" rule) or to negotiate payments to local stations for retransmitting their programs. Cable companies, in other words, could end up paying local television stations for programming previously available without cost.

Designed to take effect in stages over a prolonged period, the act also established technical standards for cable signal quality and provided privacy safeguards for cable customers, restricting the release of "personally identifiable information" about cable subscribers. Also, it required warnings when "indecent programming" might appear on premium channels unscrambled during free previews, and so on.[15] The Cable Act of 1992 was no cure-all—indeed, some observers argued that the new law was already out of date before it was passed—but it did represent an effort to curb the awesome power the cable industry had attained.

For the over-the-air broadcast industry, the act was an acknowledgment that the cable forces were now in control. It gave further ammunition to forecasters who were already speculating about the long-term future for a national television system based on the premise that the huge, mass audience for a single telecast would always be there.

Industry Trends

As the twenty-first century neared, few industries were more volatile than television. Technical innovations, the changing economics of home information services, new viewing patterns—these and other developments were rapidly redefining the traditional patterns of American television.

More Cablecasting, More Pay-per-View

In 1975 several cable companies arranged to beam a major sporting event—the heavyweight boxing championship match between Muhammad Ali and Joe Frazier, held in Manila, the Philippines—directly to subscribers, who paid an additional fee to receive the telecast. This procedure, which bypasses networks entirely, has since been termed *cablecasting;* cable companies deal directly with promoters and producers for the rights to certain spectacular programs, which they then offer to subscribers on an event-by-event basis. Pay-TV—cablecasting and the premium channels, such as Home Box Office and Showtime—might never topple network television directly, but they do threaten to drain off a number of viewers, notably higher-income families who are prime targets for advertising messages.

The money to be made is staggering. In 1991, an estimated 1,450,000 cable subscribers paid $34.95 each to view the heavyweight boxing match between Evander Holyfield and George Foreman—more than $50 million for that one event alone. Other pay-per-view offerings have been less successful—"only" 165,000 customers signed up for the fifteen-day triplecast of the 1992 summer Olympic games, for example.[16] But the potential profits from pay-per-view sales are too enticing to ignore; industry observers are predicting that major sporting events—the Super Bowl, World Series, college and professional basketball championships, the Indianapolis 500 and the Kentucky Derby, and perhaps even the regular season games of professional football and major league baseball teams—will become pay-per-view attractions. Rising costs, and especially the dramatic increase in player salaries, require team owners to seek out additional sources of revenue, and

More pay-per-view events, such as the 1994 Woodstock event, are likely for the years ahead.

pay-per-view is a logical next step. Unless Congress intercedes—and the legal implications of that would be complex—it's increasingly probable that American audiences soon will be expected to pay to watch the major events on television they now can view for nothing.

More Viewer Control

In the early 1990s, more than two-thirds of all U.S. television sets were equipped with handheld remote control units, giving the viewer instant and convenient opportunities to change the channels at will. Two manifestations of this high-tech viewer power are "zipping" and "zapping." A "zipper" is someone who switches frantically from channel to channel during commercial station breaks, checking to see what might be on elsewhere. "Zapping" occurs when a viewer, watching a network program taped earlier on the videocassette recorder, leans on the fast forward button during commercial breaks, effectively "zapping" the advertising messages.

Zippers and zappers may not appear to pose a major industry problem, but worried advertising and network executives have convened several conferences to discuss techniques for dealing with them. However, zippers and zappers do reinforce the theory some observers hold that a considerable number of persons thought to be watching television really aren't watching it at all, but merely "grazing" or "surfing" among the available program offerings. The term fragmentation, in other words, can apply to attention spans as well as to numbers of viewers.

Videocassette recorders (VCRs) also threaten to make the network audience, if not smaller, at least less predictable. In 1993 more than 70 percent of all U.S. households contained at least one VCR unit. By "time shifting," or taping a program to watch later, VCR owners can emancipate themselves somewhat from the rigors of network scheduling.[17] In the process, they add to the woes of those who attempt to track network audiences and to predict viewing patterns accurately.

Viewer control, however, will soon gain far more opportunities. News and information will be transmitted via satellite through cables or phone lines into the home, where a viewer could open a menu on either a personal computer or television keypad, using an electronic pointer to choose a news or information category— say, President Clinton's speech on events in the Middle East. The menu would offer detailed choices, such as the actual text of the speech, informed analysis of it, a videotape of the speech being delivered. The viewer might then choose to halt the speech momentarily, while calling up on the screen a political map of the territory in question—among many other possibilities that could be accessed. "TV won't be TV much longer," warned a writer from *USA Today*. "The old boob tube is about to change into multimedia, interactive TV, on-demand video, a knowledge navigator or who knows what else. It's enough to make your head spin out of vertical hold."[18]

Theme Networks[19]

More and more cable networks are likely to emerge in the years ahead, for two compelling reasons: (1) the increasing technological availability of additional channels and (2) the incentives the Cable Act of 1992 provides to cable companies to establish additional channel offerings. While requiring the cable companies to provide subscribers with basic and public access channels at minimum cost, the act allowed cable companies to charge additional fees for more channels, so long as these fees were "reasonable." Thus, in 1993, The Game Show Channel started, featuring reruns of TV's once-popular game shows, such as "What's My Line?" and "The Price Is Right." The Romance Classics cable network, featuring older movies such as "Love Story," old episodes of soap operas, and made-for-cable movies based on steamy

Extra Information

In 1994, one company claimed its VCR could cut out commercials while recording programs.

Background

Ampex developed the first practical videotape recorder in 1956, and the networks immediately used it to delay programs three hours for replay to the West Coast. Previously, networks filmed live programs (on kinescope) and rapidly developed the film. The early recorders cost in excess of $100,000 but immediately saved money for the networks. Reasonably priced consumer models didn't appear until the mid-eighties.

paperback romance novels, would be another entry, as would the How-To Channel and the Golden American Network, targeting older viewers. Broadcasting has become narrowcasting.

Further Technological Change: New Capabilities, New Players

Dramatic technological advances toward digital, interactive TV can offer literally hundreds of channels, allowing viewers to obtain nearly any programming or information on their TV sets at any time—a wide range of movies each night, for example, starting at fifteen-minute intervals, giving customers virtual on-demand video.[20] In just one application of this delivery system, top-rated programs could be "saved" on special channels for a day or two, allowing viewers to catch up on episodes they missed.

The technological capabilities, and the vast amounts of money involved, attract new competitors to the battle. Far more than a battle for television supremacy, the real battle is over who will control the next generation of communications services into the home.[21]

Giant interests are involved. The telephone companies, already wired to nearly every household in the country, would like to transmit movies and other cable television programming into the home. Under what is called the "video dial-tone" proposal, the phone companies could offer on-demand movies and telecasts of sporting events on a pay-per-view basis at a rate likely to be well below current charges for premium cable TV channels. The phone companies are experimenting with compression techniques that would permit TV signals to flow over conventional copper telephone wires. The long-term solution for interactive or high-definition television will likely require the phone companies to install high-capacity, fiber-optic telephone lines.[22]

The cable companies, meanwhile, push ahead with efforts to enter the telephone business with tiny, handheld phones that transmit calls to cable subscribers without interfering with regular cable service. Thus cable companies, already serving more than 60 percent of the nation's homes, claim they could deliver personal calls at rates far below those consumers are currently charged, giving the cable companies a crack at the vast revenue potential—in 1993, $100 billion—of the telephone industry.

Many legal and political barriers must be cleared before the phone companies and the cable companies truly invade each other's respective territory. But the conflict, which seems inevitable, apparently has the full approval of the Federal Communications Commission, on the theory that massive competitive struggle would provide customers with better service and lower prices. Industry leaders predict that consumers will soon have the same kinds of television viewing choices, via cable or telephone wire, they have come to expect from various long-distance telephone services.

Need for Programming

The real winners in the years ahead, however, are likely not to be those who have access to the hardware and delivery systems so much as those who can supply the programs, the entertainment and information packages (content) the increasingly selective viewer will want to watch. Each new wave of innovation means that the industry must work still harder to compete. Even as things stand now, television's appetite for fresh material is insatiable. The major commercial networks, as one broadcast executive recently calculated, will require an annual supply of television programs for prime-time alone that equals ten years of Hollywood film output or twenty-five years of theatrical productions on Broadway.[23] Add to that the programming needs of the cable networks, superstations, and local telecasters, and the industry's demands are indeed gigantic. Continuous infusions of new creative talent will be required for the years ahead.

The future of television can be exciting and brilliant, provided the industry responds to technological challenge with skill and imagination—and provided the public seeks out and applauds programming excellence. In television, as in much else, more is not necessarily better. Edward R. Murrow, whom many regard as the greatest of the broadcast journalists—and one of television's toughest critics—sensed a generation ago the pivotal role audiences would play as the television saga unfolded: "This instrument can teach, it can illuminate; yes, and it can even inspire. But it can do so only to the extent that humans are determined to use it to those ends. Otherwise it is merely lights and wires in a box."[24]

• •

summary

The story of television is a profoundly important and exciting chapter in the American experience. According to some studies, 69 percent of all Americans receive most of their news from TV, and 54 percent regard TV as the most believable of the mass media. Members of the typical U.S. family watch TV for an average of nearly seven hours each day of the year. Ninety-eight percent of all U.S.

households are equipped with television receivers, and 65 percent have more than one set. Advertisers spend an estimated $30 billion a year with the television industry.

Because of the huge amounts of money involved, advertisers want precise information about who is watching their commercial messages; hence, the concern with television ratings. While television ratings, and the decisions based upon them, are often criticized, precise audience analysis can permit networks and stations to make better programming and buying decisions and to learn more about how Americans use their television sets.

News reporting has permitted television to come closest to fully realizing the medium's remarkable potential—though television news is frequently criticized for being superficial and preoccupied with cosmetics. But in spite of the difficulties time pressures and other factors cause, network newscasts earn the high marks their audiences give them, and great numbers of local TV newscasts have improved dramatically.

About 60 percent of U.S. households are now connected to cable television, which provides clearer reception as well as a rich variety of additional networks for the viewing audience. Cable TV's remarkable growth has outpaced the government's ability to regulate the industry effectively. A number of legislative measures, such as the Cable Act of 1992, have been passed in attempts to serve both consumer and industry interests.

Technological advances in the early nineties promised more dramatic changes ahead. Chief among these will be increased viewer control over television reception; interactive TV, a primary characteristic of the new Information Highway, would permit individual viewers to choose their own news reports and programming, calling up selections from a wealth of on-demand possibilities. Indeed, the real industry battles ahead are predicted to be over who will control access to the programming, or content, viewers will be able to bring so easily into their homes.

? questions and cases

1. Does cable television provide enough specialized channels? Which interest groups, if any, do you think should be better served? Explain how you might develop a cable network to fill this particular gap. Include in your plan suggestions for financing this service.

2. Discuss your views regarding television's treatment of racial minorities, young people, women, the elderly—and any other group you think might be unfairly stereotyped in TV programming.

3. Do you think television networks rely too heavily on program ratings? Explain.

4. Some social critics believe that television transports us to a harmful degree away from the realities of life. Do you agree? Are young viewers emotionally and intellectually equipped to deal with television programming? Explain.

5. Reread the criticisms of television news outlined in this chapter. Apply the criticisms to your favorite network television newscast and to the news program you watch locally. Support or reject the criticisms, fully or in part.

6. Some educators believe television is second only to parents in shaping the values of young people. Do you agree? What influences have been most important to you? Where, if at all, does TV rank among them?

7. In that same vein, assume you are a parent with two preschool children at home. What restrictions, if any, would you place on their TV viewing? Suppose the children are older, in elementary school. How, if at all, would your TV viewing policy change? Be specific in terms of the amount of time, as well as types of programs, you might allow. Would you impose limits of any kind? Explain.

chapter glossary

Arbitron A leading audience research firm, historically associated with both TV and radio, now focusing on radio.

Area of Dominant Influence (ADI) Primary geographic area (defined by counties, usually) that a medium of mass communications serves. Used chiefly by Arbitron. Comparable to Designated Market Area (DMA) market definition utilized by the Nielsen research firm.

barter Trading advertising time or space for programming, merchandise, or other nonmonetary consideration. No cash is involved.

character generator (CG) Machine used to type letters and numbers onto a television screen. Provides textual information, as in electronic newscasts, as well as superimposing identifications and other information on a television picture.

Community Antenna Television (CATV) A system where one master antenna, strategically placed, can receive television signals and relay them via cable to subscribers.

cumulative ratings, or **cume** The number of households (or people) reached by a given program, publication, or advertising campaign over a specific time period, usually one to four weeks.

dayparts Time periods in which the television or radio day is split. The dayparts have different names (prime time, early fringe, and so on), different audience sizes, and different costs to advertisers.

Designated Market Area (DMA) Primary geographic area a medium of mass communications serves. Used chiefly by A. C. Nielsen Company; Comparable to Arbitron's Area of Dominant Influence (ADI).

market share Percentage of a market dominated by a product or company. Often referred to simply as *share;* for example, "The XYZ company enjoys a 60 percent share." This means that three out of every five widgets are sold by XYZ. In television audience analysis, market share means the percentage of all viewers watching TV who are tuned to a particular program.

meters Attached to certain television sets (or, as in the case of "people meters," operated by individual viewers) and monitored by research companies to indicate relative sizes of program audiences.

Nielsen The A. C. Nielsen Company, a leading communications and market research firm.

O and Os Broadcast outlets stations owned and operated by networks. No network may own more than five VHF stations, or twelve stations altogether.

pilot The first (sample) episode of a possible TV series.

prime time In television, the period from 8 P.M. until 11 P.M., which attracts the largest audiences and the highest advertising rates.

rating Percentage of households in a market reached by a given radio or television program.

spot announcement Radio or television advertising time bought from an individual station, as opposed to time bought from an entire network. Also refers to commercial messages generally.

syndicated program A program or series distributed outside the normal network structure. Often syndicated programs are former network shows that local television stations or cable networks lease for reruns.

talent For our purposes, an on-the-air personality.

TelePrompTer Screen mounted on or near the camera to aid newscasters or other performers; text of script scrolls across the screen where the talent can read it, yet he or she appears to be talking directly to the camera.

ultra high frequency (UHF) Television channels 14 through 83, broadcasting in the upper band of the electromagnetic spectrum.

very high frequency (VHF) Television channels 2 through 13.

voice over Narration by an off-camera speaker to illustrate a television news report, commercial, or portion of a program.

notes

1 A. C. Nielsen estimate, 1994.

2 Ray Benson, "CBN Network Has Most Violent Acts," Columbia, S.C. *Record,* 8 November 1986.

3 John Tebbel, *The Media in America* (Crowell, 1974), 360.

4 Reprinted in *The Reader's Digest Dictionary of Quotations* (Funk and Wagnalls, 1968), 257.

5 Background material provided to the author by the A. C. Nielsen and Arbitron rating companies, 1992.

6 Sydney Head, *Broadcasting in America,* 3d ed. (Boston: Houghton-Mifflin, 1976), 180.

7 Tebbel, *Media in America,* 180, is particularly cogent on this point.

8 Carnegie Commission on Educational Television, *Public Television: A Program for Action* (Harper & Row, 1967), 33.

9 Tebbel, *Media in America,* 370.

10 *Broadcasting & Cable Market Place,* 1993, xv.

11 Charles Trueheart, "Senate Backs Big Bird," Washington *Post,* 4 June 1992.

12 The ground rules for local access channels are set forth in Federal Communications Commission, *Cable Television Report and Order* 36 FCC 2d 143 (1972).

13 *Broadcast & Cable Market Place,* 1992, xv.

14 "FCC Report Concedes TV's Future to Cable," *Broadcasting,* 1 July 1991, 19–20.

15 Randy Sukow, "The Act's Aftermath: On to the FCC," *Broadcasting,* 12 October 1992, 32–33.

16 Stuart Elliott, "Pay TV Hopes for Financial Knockout," New York *Times,* 12 November 1992.

17 For a full discussion of the impact of the VCR on television programming and viewing, see James Lardner, *Fast Forward: Hollywood, the Japanese, and the Onslaught of the VCR* (Norton, 1987).

18 Kevin Maney, "TVs and PCs to Become Media Centers," *USA Today,* 19 November 1992.

19 See especially Elizabeth Kolbert, "Cable TV's Future: Theme Programming," New York *Times,* 5 January 1993.

20 Maney, *USA Today,* 19 November 1992.

21 Edmund L. Andrews, "Cable TV Battling Phone Companies," New York *Times,* 29 March 1992.

22 John Schneidawind, "Phone, Cable Giants Ready for Combat," *USA Today,* 15 July 1992.

23 Gene F. Jankowski, speech to the International Radio and Television Society, 15 July 1992.

24 Quoted in Fred W. Friendly, *Due to Circumstances Beyond Our Control* (New York: Random House, 1967), frontispiece.

chapter

Films

M

Darryl F. Zanuck, a Hollywood kingpin rarely given to understatement, once described movies as "the greatest political fact in the world today."[1] That may present an inflated view, but in truth the film industry in all its manifestations

Objectives

When you have finished studying this chapter, you should be able to:

- Explain trends in movie viewing, and relate them to recent theme, approach, and content changes

- Retrace early film history, noting especially the rise and decline of the studio system

- List the major steps and key personnel involved in movie production

- Comment on efforts to censor films, both inside and outside the industry

Darryl F. Zanuck, a Hollywood kingpin rarely given to understatement, once described movies as "the greatest political fact in the world today."[1] That may present an inflated view, but in truth the film industry in all its manifestations—including the blockbuster entertainment feature, the cartoon, the art film, social documentaries, industrial and educational and training films, and, especially, the made-for-television movie—does reach a colossal audience around the globe. Most films are created to entertain, but their influence extends to other areas as well. Motion pictures have changed ideas, attitudes, even cultural patterns. Students of international politics regard film as the most powerful propaganda medium of them all.

In this country, more people are watching movies than ever before, but fewer and fewer Americans are watching movies in movie theaters. In 1946, the peak year of moviegoing, 90 million Americans went to movie theaters. By the 1990s, the figure had dropped to around 20 million, a total audience smaller than one night's viewing of a typical prime-time television program. The number of tickets U.S. moviegoers bought declined from 8.4 per year in 1985 to 5.7 in 1992.[2]

The number of movie theaters is increasing, thereby dividing the ticket audience still further. Box office receipts continue to rise a bit, just over 1 percent a year, because of higher ticket prices rather than more customers. Meanwhile, the price of making and promoting movies is escalating at a far more rapid rate. In 1992, the average studio film cost $28.8 million to produce and $11.2 million to market; this $40 million price tag represents an increase of 5 percent over 1991. And that is an average. Some productions were far more expensive: *Terminator 3,* for example, cost $150 million.[3]

Quality and cost are not always directly related. Consider two remarkable films of the early 1990s directed by Steven Spielberg: *Jurassic Park,* a high-tech film about dinosaurs, cost about $70 million to produce; *Schindler's List,* shot without high-priced stars on location in Poland, was produced for an estimated $23 million, and it won the Oscar for best picture of 1993.

While costs spiral upward and the ticket-buying audience shrinks, however, some bright spots still appeared:

- *More older Americans, at long last, buying more tickets.* While few industry experts were predicting a return to movie themes of the 1940s, when entire families went to theaters together, many film releases of the early 1990s did reflect a certain appeal for all age groups: *Aladdin, Jurassic Park, Beauty and the Beast, Forrest Gump, Maverick, The Flintstones,* and *Home Alone* among them. The most obvious reason for the plethora of warm-hearted movies, one critic observed, was the uncertain national economy, which led studios to seek out scripts designed to attract the widest possible audience. This meant families, who need an alternative to *Basic Instinct* or *Lethal Weapon.*[4] For whatever the reason, **Motion Picture Association of**

Background

"Movies" or "cinemas" are nothing more than still pictures projected on a screen at the rate of twenty-four frames per second (fps). The human eye is fooled into seeing motion. (Television uses the same idea, but at 30 fps.) Early movies used lower frame rates, speeding up the action when projected today. The 24-fps rate, an international standard, is actually a compromise between a better-quality, higher rate that uses more film, and a cheaper, lower rate that can cause annoying "flicker" for the viewer.

Teaching Idea

Ask students what movies they have seen recently and what they think of them. What are the usual admission charges? How much does a "movie date" cost?

More Screens, Fewer Patrons, Higher Prices

There were 24,570 movie theater screens in operation in the United States in 1992, an increase of 3.7 percent over 1991.

Thirty-two theater companies own 100 screens or more. Largest of these in 1992 was United Artists Theatre Circuit, with 2,398 screens, followed by Odeon Theatres with 1,715.

Total attendance at U.S. movie theaters in 1991 was 981,900,000—falling below the one billion mark for the first time since 1976.

Ticket prices, topping $7 in some cities, have risen 81.8 percent since 1980 and averaged $4.892 in the U.S. in 1992.

International Motion Picture Almanac, 1993.

Young People and the Movies

Ticket buyers under age thirty continue to be the dominant force in movie attendance, though their numbers are declining slightly.

Moviegoers by Age Group (percentage of total yearly admissions)

Age Group	1991	1990	1989	Actual Percent of Population
12–15	12%	11%	11%	7%
16–20	19	20	19	9
21–24	12	11	14	7
25–29	12	14	16	10
30–39	19	20	18	21
40–49	13	12	11	15
50–59	5	5	4	11
60 and over	8	7	7	20
	100%	100%	100%	100%
12–17	17	18	19	10
18 and over	83	82	81	90
	100%	100%	100%	100%

Used with permission of the Motion Picture Association of America.

Extra Information

Copyright violations and piracy are major problems in foreign sales. A dishonest movie projectionist in this country can make an illegal videocassette of a hit movie and sell it internationally.

Background

In the late 1970s, Sony—maker of the first consumer VCR—was sued by major movie makers for alleged violation of copyright laws. After years of litigation, the U.S. Supreme Court said home taping of movies and other materials did not violate copyright restrictions. Sony won the battle but lost the war; its equipment was Beta, and VHS equipment captured much of the consumer market. Both Beta and VHS, in upgraded versions, are used in commercial and professional applications.

America figures released in 1993 showed that 30.4 percent of all tickets were purchased by moviegoers aged forty or older, up from 14.2 percent in 1985.

- *Continuing export revenues.* The United States doesn't produce more movies than any other country in the world—that distinction goes to India—but U.S. films are the most popular with international audiences. U.S. films each year generate hundreds of millions of dollars in foreign trade, making the film industry one of the country's leading exporters.
- *The home market.* U.S. videotape movie sales and rentals in 1992 zoomed to a record $17.2 billion, more than triple the domestic theater box office total that year of $4.9 billion. Indeed, a survey of viewing trends in 1993 reported that American families preferred watching movies on television to watching sitcoms, dramas, and other types of programming.

After first denouncing television in the 1950s, Hollywood producers eventually learned to live with it—first by selling TV rights to their older films, then by leasing out their back lots and sound stages to TV producers. Eventually, the movie studios began producing their own television movies and series programs. The home television screen, which once threatened to kill the motion picture industry, saved it instead.[5]

The demand for video rentals—$11.4 billion in 1992—and video sales—$5.8 billion—continued to increase in dramatic fashion, outstripping even the most optimistic industry projections. "The country is consuming [video] movies like there is no tomorrow," boasted Warren Lieberfarb, president of Warner Home Video.

Paradoxically, the surge in video rentals and sales came as some experts were forecasting that new technologies would soon sweep away videotapes—technologies such as movies on demand, transmitted via cable TV or telephone lines.[6] Pay-per-view showings of first-run movies were already popular in the early 1990s with many cable television customers. Further technological developments are expected to provide a vast range of movies, each offered in a variety of starting times.

Whether or not huge film libraries can be delivered to home viewers affordably remains an open question. Meanwhile, one thing is clear: No matter how the motion picture is delivered, or where it is seen, audiences are interested. Some of us watch movies for their artistic values, others for entertainment or momentary escape. Still others watch the movies because they are . . . well, movies.

The Movie Industry Evolves

Capturing the image of movement is a notion which has intrigued humans for centuries. The walls of some primordial dwellings were lined with sketches of sequences depicting figures in action. Motion pictures, however, did not come until late in the nineteenth century, as the result of a number of scientific experiments conducted in Europe as well as the United States. No one person is credited with having first produced and projected motion pictures in an effective, efficient way. But prominent among the industry's pioneers are the following people.

Eadweard Muybridge, a San Francisco photographer, successfully photographed motion in the 1870s. Through an elaborate arrangement involving twenty-four still cameras, Muybridge caught on film a series of photos of a running horse. The cameras were lined up on a racetrack, with strings stretched across the track and attached to the shutters. As the horse ran by, it tripped each string in succession, producing a sequence of still photos, which, taken together, depicted the action. The procedure was inordinately cumbersome, but it did prove that motion photography was possible.

Thomas Edison, who invented the phonograph in 1877, began working on a mechanism to make pictures seem to move—thus, in his vision, connecting sight to sound. His success came only after George Eastman invented flexible *film* to replace glass plates for capturing photographic images. Flexible film carried an emulsion that could hold images in a form that moved easily and swiftly through a camera, in effect making motion picture photography possible. Edison's staff developed two prototypes of a motion picture device: One could project images on a wall, and the other held them inside a box with a peep-show window. This device, the *kinetoscope,* was a box with 50 feet of film revolving on spools inside. Edison elected to develop only the peep show version on the theory that it would be easier to sell. It proved to be a bad miscalculation, but not as bad as his failure to spend an extra $150 to secure patent rights for his projecting device in Europe.[7] While kinetoscope parlors became enormously popular in New York and elsewhere, their novelty soon wore off. Edison's film projector invention, however, had not been patented outside the United States, so European inventors were free to use it, and improve upon it, in their own ways. Two such opportunists were the Lumière brothers, Louis and Auguste, who in 1895 were able to photograph simple movements—a train pulling into a station—and project them onto a screen to appreciative audiences in a Paris cafe. Their success prompted imitators, and soon motion pictures were being shown throughout Europe.

We are able to assimilate movements intellectually, as scholars such as the Roman poet Lucretius and the astronomer Ptolemy professed nearly two thousand years ago, through a process known as *persistence of vision:* The brain does not "see" a light until a fraction of a second after the light is turned on; the image persists inside the brain a fraction of a second after the light is turned off. Thus, a series of

Teaching Idea

Survey your class to see how many students rent movie videos and how often. Do any use pay-per-view services on a cable system? Do any record movies off-air and save them rather than playing them just once?

Background

Muybridge's photos were taken to win a $10,000 bet for California Governor Leland Stanford. The question was whether a running horse ever had all four feet off the ground.

individual images—a movie projector shows twenty-four images a second—register inside our brains as uninterrupted movement, for we still "see" the previous image as the succeeding image appears.

David Wark Griffith developed many aspects of film technique. The early film-makers simply recorded scenes as they transpired—vaudeville skits, ocean waves crashing against a rocky coast. But soon it became clear to a handful of industry pioneers that the camera could also present a story, complete with characters and plot—in effect, mass producing a drama. The industry's first true producer-director was D. W. Griffith, who developed such techniques as **zooming** cameras in and out for closeup and faraway views, **panning** cameras from side to side for additional perspective on the action, editing the film into sequences to provide narrative quality, and, indeed, conferring upon the new industry a certain prestige that elevated it from the peep-show and saloon audiences to popularity on a grand scale with family audiences. He also created many stars of the infant industry. With Griffith came the realization that film is preeminently a director's medium.

Griffith's great masterpiece was *The Birth of a Nation,* a three-hour melodrama about the Civil War and its aftermath. *The Birth of a Nation* was not the first movie to tell a story; that honor goes to *The Great Train Robbery,* an eleven-minute feature made by Edwin S. Porter in 1903. Though embarrassing to us today—the film has strong racist overtones—*The Birth of a Nation* was a magnificent technical success at the time, showing the industry what the new medium could do and attracting millions of Americans to the new movie theaters. It was a milestone in movie history and remains supposedly the biggest film money maker of all time.[8]

Along with these industry pioneers, other forces shaped early filmmaking. By 1912, the year *The Birth of a Nation* was completed, a number of moviemakers were in business, and their common interests moved them to seek a home for the new industry. New York, where most of them were then situated, had become an unfriendly venue, largely because of legal difficulties involving patents. At the time a minor suburb of Los Angeles, Hollywood was selected for its proximity to Mexico, in case troubles developed with the federal government, as well as for its variety of locations and splendid climate. As the moviemakers resettled in the West, Hollywood soon emerged as the film capital of the world, a distinction it was to hold until well into the 1950s. Throughout that time, the great majority of American films were made there. Independent producers merged into large studios powerful enough to control not only producers and actors, but patents on film cameras, projectors, film stock, and, to a remarkable degree, the way in which motion pictures were distributed and exhibited. Indeed, many movie theaters, especially in the larger markets, were owned outright by the studios.

The first movies were silent. Later, as the stories grew more complex, musical accompaniment was added—provided by a local piano player in each community where the film was shown. Creating music on the spot to match the mood of each scene required heroic effort, but local pianists, hundreds of them, were up to the task and the effect was remarkable. As one industry pioneer, Irving Thalberg, explained: "We'd finish a picture, show it on one of our projection rooms and come out shattered. It would be awful. Then we'd show it in a theater with a girl pounding away at a piano and there would be all the difference in the world. Without that music there wouldn't have been a movie industry at all."[9]

Silent film star Rudolph Valentino with Agnes Ayres in a torrid (for 1921) scene from *The Sheik.*

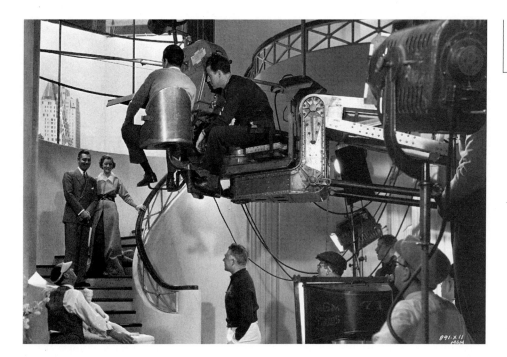

Efforts to add sound tracks to movies were underway as early as 1923. The major studios, however, were momentarily low on cash after purchasing hundreds of movie theaters and in no hurry to develop talking pictures; adding sound systems to their theaters and their studios would cost millions. But Warner Brothers, a smaller studio which did not own theaters, was less inhibited. In 1927, Warner brought out *The Jazz Singer,* starring Al Jolson, the first speaking and singing film. After that, silent pictures simply could not compete. Talkies created the biggest revolution the film industry has ever known, and if some film critics didn't care for talking movies—the sound quality at first was indeed raucous and unpleasant—the general public did. Talkies provided the industry with the fresh impetus it badly needed and ensured the popular success of the new medium.

Next followed Hollywood's Golden Age, the 1930s and 1940s, when the big studios produced efficient, unpretentious, and diverse entertainment. Most of the films were enjoyable and, for nearly everyone, affordable. Americans by the millions went to the movies, even throughout the Great Depression. During World War II, movie theaters served as collective morale builder as well as entertainer, and attendance hit new records.

Background

The earliest talkies used phonograph records allegedly synchronized with the film action. This system was clumsy and prone to error. Both RCA and Western Electric devised ways of optically recording the sound directly on the film. Much the same optical system is still in use today, even with stereo, Dolby, and surround sound.

Regarding Oscar

The golden symbol of fame conferred by the Academy of Motion Picture Arts and Sciences, Oscar was first presented in 1929. There are conflicting stories as to how the statuette got its name. Oscars weigh 8 1/2 pounds and cost about $350 each. The television audience for the Academy Awards is one of the largest of the year, estimated at hundreds of millions of viewers around the globe.

Here are some Oscar statistics:

- **Most Nominated Film:** *All About Eve* (1950), 14 (won 5).

- **Most Awarded Film:** *Ben Hur* (1959), 11.

- **Most Awarded Person:** *Walt Disney,* 30.

- **Most Awarded Performer:** Katharine Hepburn (4 best actress awards; also most nominated performer, with 12).

International Motion Picture Almanac, 1993.

Hollywood is still synonymous with moviemaking, but in fact, since the end of World War II, the city's position, like that of the movie business itself, has undergone drastic change. Television swept across postwar America like wildfire, massively affecting the film industry, reshaping and downsizing movie audiences to a drastic degree. **Block booking,** a heavy-handed marketing strategy by which studios forced theater owners to take weak movies along with stronger ones, was outlawed. Other factors reshaped the industry as well. Actors, who had long chafed under the strict studio system, broke away to become independent producers. The Supreme Court ruled that Hollywood studios could no longer own theaters, because such near-monopolistic power could restrain trade throughout the industry. Thus the major studios were forced to sell their movie theaters precisely when few buyers were willing to pay much for them. Then came the introduction of a superior new film process, CinemaScope. While CinemaScope gave movies a big new dimension,

Best Pictures

Following are the Oscar winners for best picture of the year, since the awards began:

1927–28	Wings	1962	Lawrence of Arabia
1928–29	The Broadway Melody	1963	Tom Jones
1929–30	All Quiet on the Western Front	1964	My Fair Lady
1930–31	Cimarron	1965	The Sound of Music
1931–32	Grand Hotel	1966	A Man for All Seasons
1932–33	Cavalcade	1967	In the Heat of the Night
1934	It Happened One Night	1968	Oliver!
1935	Mutiny on the Bounty	1969	Midnight Cowboy
1936	The Great Ziegfeld	1970	Patton
1937	The Life of Emile Zola	1971	The French Connection
1938	You Can't Take It with You	1972	The Godfather
1939	Gone with the Wind	1973	The Sting
1940	Rebecca	1974	The Godfather, Part II
1941	How Green Was My Valley	1975	One Flew over the Cuckoo's Nest
1942	Mrs. Miniver	1976	Rocky
1943	Casablanca	1977	Annie Hall
1944	Going My Way	1978	The Deer Hunter
1945	The Lost Weekend	1979	Kramer vs. Kramer
1946	The Best Years of Our Lives	1980	Ordinary People
1947	Gentleman's Agreement	1981	Chariots of Fire
1948	Hamlet	1982	Gandhi
1949	All the King's Men	1983	Terms of Endearment
1950	All About Eve	1984	Amadeus
1951	An American in Paris	1985	Out of Africa
1952	The Greatest Show on Earth	1986	Platoon
1953	From Here to Eternity	1987	The Last Emperor
1954	On the Waterfront	1988	Rain Man
1955	Marty	1989	Driving Miss Daisy
1956	Around the World in 80 Days	1990	Dances with Wolves
1957	The Bridge on the River Kwai	1991	The Silence of the Lambs
1958	Gigi	1992	Unforgiven
1959	Ben-Hur	1993	Schindler's List
1960	The Apartment	1994	Forrest Gump
1961	West Side Story		

In the Hollywood of the '30s and '40s stars were not born; they were mass produced. The machinery that swallowed up legions of girls with pretty midwestern faces and that ground out sultry vamps and sexy tomboys gave each young hopeful a buildup that can only be described as relentless. . . .

The full-dress Hollywood buildup usually amounted to a complete metamorphosis. The budding neophyte was subjected to make-up classes and voice classes; she took deportment lessons, posture lessons, and lessons in how to dress. But even more important than her transformation was her publicity. Studio press representatives had her squired to the right spots with the right dates and tried to wangle mentions of her in the columns of Hedda Hopper, Louella Parsons, and Sidney Skolsky. She was photographed in every imaginable pose, and a few unimaginable ones, and the results were sent to almost any publication with a circulation of over 10.

Life Goes to the Movies, by the editors of *Life* magazine

emphasizing the gap between films and the tiny TV set, it also had the ironic effect of making many studio-designed sets show up poorly on screen. As a result, producers felt the need to leave Hollywood's back lots for more authentic production locations elsewhere. Finally, the nation's political mood changed as the Cold War with Russia intensified. Strong anticommunist feelings, given direction by Congressional investigations, led to an ugly period in which many talents were **blacklisted.** Others simply left town, bound for other cities or other countries. Hollywood's Golden Age was over. The movie industry would survive, but it would not be the same.

How Movies Are Made

The process of making a movie[10] typically begins with the acquisition of a story or story line, which becomes known as a *property*. Developing the property into a movie involves many persons, among whom the following are especially important:

- *The producer,* who is in charge of the film's budget, among much else, and who is ultimately responsible for the total success or failure of the production. He or she hires and controls all personnel engaged in making the film and is instrumental in marketing it as well. The producer approves casting and design decisions, though usually delegating artistic responsibilities, principally to the following people.
- *The director* is normally the key creative person on the production. Directors supervise scripts, make casting and editing decisions, and control the photographing of each scene, guiding the performances of the cast. While many directors are comparatively unknown outside the industry, a few, such as Alfred Hitchcock, John Ford, and Walter Huston, became celebrities in their

Extra Information

CinemaScope and similar processes use special lenses to "condense" information onto regular 35-millimeter film and "expand" it when the film is projected. This caused problems for TV. Watch the opening of a CinemaScope picture—during the credits, the background figures look narrow, then widen immediately afterwards when the lenses are changed.

"3-D," or three-dimensional films, were a dramatic attempt to revive a floundering movie industry in the 1950s. While providing a sometimes vivid effect of depth, 3-D movies had a few disadvantages as well; one of them that the audience had to wear uncomfortable special glasses to get the full effect.

Twenty-Five Landmark Movies: A Producer's Selection

The Producer's Guild of America, an association of professional movie and television producers, selected what its members believe have been twenty-five landmark films produced between 1927 (the end of the silent film era) and 1980. Following are their choices:

All Quiet on the Western Front (1930)	*The Maltese Falcon* (1941)
Around the World in 80 Days (1956)	*Midnight Cowboy* (1969)
Ben-Hur (1959)	*Mr. Smith Goes to Washington* (1939)
The Best Years of Our Lives (1946)	*Mutiny on the Bounty* (1935)
Casablanca (1942)	*On the Waterfront* (1935)
Citizen Kane (1941)	*One Flew over the Cuckoo's Nest* (1975)
Fantasia (1940)	*Snow White and the Seven Dwarfs* (1937)
From Here to Eternity (1953)	*Stagecoach* (1939)
The Godfather (1971)	*Star Wars* (1977)
Gone with the Wind (1939)	*Sunset Boulevard* (1950)
The Grapes of Wrath (1940)	*The Treasure of Sierra Madre* (1948)
High Noon (1952)	*The Wizard of Oz* (1939)
The Informer (1935)	

Reported by Lawrence Van Gelder in the New York *Times*, 22 March 1991.

From one of Director Steven Spielberg's greatest successes: *E.T.: The Extra-Terrestrial*. E.T. tells Elliott (Henry Thomas) that he'll always be there.

own right. Film fans and, to an increasing degree, the general public appreciate that the director is normally the most influential creator of a movie.

- *The writer,* who develops the scenario, or screenplay.
- *The cinematographer,* who operates the cameras.
- *The cast,* actors and actresses.
- *The designers,* who create costumes and settings. Movie sets must not only provide the proper environment for the action but also must be constructed so that cameras can move about freely to capture the action.
- *The editor,* or *film cutter,* who works closely with the director in choosing the best shots of each scene. Then, when the shooting is finished, the editor and director weave these hundreds of shots into a coherent story.
- *The composer,* who prepares the score, or background music, for the film, fitting the music to the action and mood of the various scenes.

For much of the industry's history, all the talents were housed in big Hollywood studios, and financing, facilities, and filmmaking expertise could be quickly mobilized once the studio chief gave the go-ahead. Now, however, most films are produced by independents who must secure the financing and assemble the production team in a series of individual negotiations.

Metro-Goldwyn-Mayer, Universal, Paramount, United Artists, and other giants of Hollywood's Golden Age operated almost as if they were sovereign kingdoms with literally thousands of technicians, screenwriters, and actors and actresses under contract. Their prodigious payrolls had to be met whether the employees worked or not, so each major studio might crank out, as MGM did, one movie—sometimes more than one—a week. Some of these films were masterpieces, others ordinary, but there was intense demand for them from exhibitors, who might change their playbills several times each week. Often accused of cynically mass producing some pictures just to fill out a schedule, Hollywood's big studio moguls also felt free to experiment occasionally with a daring, avant-garde script, confident in the knowledge that, if one film bombed at the box office, other releases, through block booking arrangements, would soon come along to recoup any losses. Now far fewer films are released, and as a result independent producers have grown more cautious—or, rather, the moneylenders who hold the purse strings have become more cautious. As a result, financing expensive film ideas is difficult unless the backers can be assured of a bankable lead star or a proven director at the helm, and even then the money may not be forthcoming if the property appears too unconventional. While many major films are box office success stories, many more fail outright or achieve only limited commercial success. A great deal of money is involved, and financing a film can be a perilous undertaking.

Career Opportunities

To make it in the movie business, according to former actress and long-time Hollywood resident Billie Burke, "you need the ambition of a Latin-American revolutionary, the ego of a grand opera tenor, and the physical stamina of a cow pony,"[11] and, perhaps, a certain amount of good fortune, for the job market is relatively small; the total film industry work force in 1992 was listed at 388,600 persons, and a great many of those held only part-time positions. The field is highly competitive. Still, the industry does value young people and fresh ideas, and as a result will always demand, if only to a limited degree, new talent. Some who majored in mass communications in college have ultimately wound up as producers, directors, and cast members, though they likely began as publicity writers or promotion people.

Those interested in the production side need experience with cameras, editing machines, lighting equipment, and the like. The quickest route to technical proficiency for most is in studying film production in college. The American Film

Extra Information

Other film workers include *grips,* or stagehands; *gaffers,* or electricians; and *best boys,* who are apprentices. For a more detailed inventory of movie workers, watch the credits at the end of any recent major production.

Extra Information

TV and movies are similar in that a successful production is immediately followed by copies. TV shows result in "spinoffs," and movies in "The Return of," "Son (or Daughter) of," or "II, III, IV," and so on. The derivatives generally are not as profitable as the original.

Institute's *Guide to College Courses in Film and Television*[12] lists several hundred institutions of higher learning that offer this subject. The instruction usually involves esthetics of film as well as filmmaking, and often professors with contacts inside the industry teach these subjects.

The film industry encompasses far more than entertainment features associated with Hollywood. Hundreds of industrial and educational films are produced each year for academic organizations, the medical community, business, government, industry, and the military. These sponsored films represent an important, if less glamorous, segment of the industry and offer a number of career opportunities as well.

An increasing number of journalists, for both print and broadcast media, are finding it possible to combine their interest in the movies with their professional training to become film critics. Most larger newspapers, and many magazines and television news departments, presently have one or more staff persons who review current movies and write about the film industry. Readers and viewers welcome information and opinions about movies, especially as ticket prices continue to rise, and as a result, film criticism, once a narrow field, has expanded substantially in recent years.

The Movies and Censorship

The power and influence of films have troubled governments around the world, and every country has found it necessary to regulate the film industry to at least some degree. Censorship boards, designed to deal with films thought to be immoral, were established in some U.S. communities as early as 1907. In 1921, following a series of drug-related scandals in Hollywood, the movie industry organized the Motion Picture Producers and Distributors of America and named a powerful political figure, Will H. Hays, as president. The Hays Office, as it was called, was joined in 1934 by the National Legion of Decency, a Catholic-sponsored organization that protested films it deemed unsuitable. The industry responded with its own production code, which required a seal of approval before a film could be released. The code prohibited vulgar language and excessive violence and placed severe limits on scenes involving sex.[13]

Many producers regarded the code as unfairly repressive, however, and the Hays Office frequently revised its interpretations, especially as the film industry found itself struggling to present livelier fare than the competing television industry could offer for free. Aside from the economic pressures, particularly connected with Hollywood's courtship of the all-important youth market, code censorship posed serious First Amendment issues.

On 1 November 1968, member companies of the Motion Picture Association decided on a compromise: Creative expression would not be censored, but audiences would at least be warned of possibly objectionable aspects of a film's content. This ratings program required all pictures released after that date to carry one of four identifying symbols on all prints, trailers, and advertising, and at theater box offices. The four categories initially were *G* for general audiences; *M* for adults and mature young people, for which parental discretion was advised; *R* for attendance restricted to persons over 16, unless accompanied by parent or adult guardian; and *X*, to which no one under 16 would be admitted.

In 1970, the *M* rating was changed to *GP* (all ages admitted—parental guidance suggested) and later changed to *PG*. In 1984, a new rating was introduced, *PG-13*, which indicated parents needed to give special guidance to children under 13.

That pattern in one fairly typical year, 1989, resulted in these ratings: 9 of the films released were awarded a *G* rating; 84 were classified as *PG*; 93 were *PG-13*; 381 were rated *R*, and one was rated *X*.

In September 1990, the *X* rating was changed to *NC-17*, or "no children under 17," in hopes of removing the pornographic connotation of the *X*. But, like the *X*, the *NC-17* rating seemed to convey a stigma; in the first two years after the new rating became available, only one major studio film, *Henry and June,* was released with the *NC-17* rating. A few more films would later test the box office viability of *NC-17,* but most of the other bigger-budget films were toned down (edited) to receive the more commercially friendly *R* rating.[14]

Fair or Foul?

The ratings are subjective, of course, especially where sex and violence are concerned. Language is a bit easier to quantify: One use of the "F word," for example, automatically places a film in the *PG-13* category, while the use of two or more is almost always grounds for a rating of *R*. But the overwhelming majority of movie tickets are purchased by young people, and movie producers believe this youthful audience responds best to themes laced with sex, violence, and special effects. A character in the 1986 film *Sweet Liberty* proclaimed that a successful modern movie had to do three things: defy authority, destroy property, and take off clothes.

That assessment may be a bit cynical, but even so, the movies, which entire families once attended, have grown saltier. The 1992 release, *Laws of Gravity,* had more than 150 obscenities and at least 25 profanities (defaming the sacred), while the Oscar-nominated *GoodFellas* contained 294 uses of the "F word."[15] Some critics now regard the film industry as twisted and threatening. One of them, Michael Medved, put it this way:

> Our long-running romance with Hollywood is over. Few of us continue to view it as a magical source of uplifting entertainment, romantic inspiration or even harmless fun. Instead, tens of millions of Americans now see the entertainment industry, with its ugly obsessions, as an alien force that assaults our most cherished values and corrupts our children. The dream factory has become the poison factory.[16]

Medved's assessment evidently is shared by others. A 1989 Associated Press/Media General poll concluded that 82 percent of Americans felt movies contained too much violence, 80 percent found too much profanity, and 72 percent complained of too much nudity.[17]

Censorship is not the solution to the problem, if, indeed, it is a problem, but long-term economic forces may bring about change. The teenage audience, a base for the film industry, is diminishing, in relative terms, and a different demographic pattern may push the film industry toward a potentially wider audience. Indeed, between 1989 and 1991, the number of *R*-rated movies released slipped from 67 percent to 61 percent of the total.[18]

The Future

Despite occasional surges, the financial future[19] for the film industry in the 1990s has looked uncertain at best. Declining revenues in the wake of a prolonged recession at the beginning of the decade weakened advertising-driven media, especially broadcasters, and the movie industry proved anything but resistant to the trend. Escalating production costs and soft summers at the box office deflated the shares of the major studios, while debt problems torpedoed the share prices of a number of independent production companies. Despite record highs on Wall Street generally, many entertainment stocks languished, dispelling the notion that entertainment is a recession-proof industry.

Although it could boast two of 1991's biggest critical and box office successes, the multiple Oscar winners *Silence of the Lambs* and *Dances with Wolves,* Orion Pictures Corporation filed for bankruptcy that December, undercutting the old Hollywood saying "there's nothing wrong with the motion picture industry that a good movie can't cure." Carolco Pictures, which had the biggest movie of that year with

Background

It is no secret that a movie may be made and released in several different forms. For commercial TV stations, little violence and nudity is included. More is allowed in versions showing in movie houses, and even more in extreme versions for international release.

Teaching Idea

Have you class discuss the movie rating system. Can they devise a better one?

Partners

George Comstock, *What's News* (Institute for Contemporary Studies, 1981).

Terminator 2—which cost $150 million to make—saw its stock plunge 77.9 percent, due to mounting debt problems. *Batman Returns,* the biggest hit of 1992, was regarded as a financial disappointment. Despite its U.S. gross of $160 million, it fell nearly $100 million short of its 1989 predecessor, *Batman*.

There are more movie theaters in operation than a decade ago, but more, in this case, is not necessarily better. A national research study, conducted by the movie industry in 1993, disclosed that 16 percent of all U.S. filmgoers surveyed had endured a bad experience with the sound or picture quality at one of the last three movies they saw; in the face of ever-increasing ticket prices, such complaints must be taken seriously.

Bad news for the motion picture industry was good news for cable operators. In spite of the weak economy, cable operators in the early 1990s saw their cash flow increase by up to 15 percent as fewer people went to the movies.

Shrinking box office receipts and a decrease in the number of theaters, coupled with staggering corporate debt brought about through mergers and takeovers and spiraling production costs, combined to deal industry optimists a severe blow.

But with the movie industry, as throughout mass communications, technology was opening up dramatic new possibilities, among the more intriguing: interactive movies. Digital technology allows dozens—perhaps even hundreds—of plot alternatives to be stored on CD-ROM, a compact disc that a computer or an interactive

Jim Carrey is overcome with love in *The Mask,* a film featuring spectacular special effects.

home entertainment system can read. This technology, which combines the glamour of Hollywood stars with the participation of video games, would permit the viewer to shift the plot, leading to different conflicts and different outcomes, as the movie goes along. "We are redefining, in some ways, what Hollywood will be about in the twenty-first century," said Tom Zito of Digital Pictures. But this technology poses serious artistic and creative problems for the moviemakers. As David Landis of *USA Today* put it, "once a viewer takes control of a movie, it's not a movie anymore."[20]

Still, the movie industry has survived its conflict with television in the 1950s and 1960s, with cable in the 1970s, and the VCR in the 1980s—protracted struggles that left scars and wrought change, but nevertheless provided a degree of confidence for the 1990s. Too, international audiences still flocked to see American films, even those which had not done well with U.S. moviegoers.

It seems as though some form of cost-cutting measures will be essential for all but the most stable movie studios. Aside from the seasonal epic, and guaranteed blockbusters such as *Jurassic Park, Lethal Weapon 3,* or almost any Arnold Schwarzenegger vehicle, future movies seem destined to be comparatively small-scale affairs. This form of niche marketing, which radio and the magazine industry utilize so effectively, should lead to more demographically oriented movies, such as those designed to appeal to the African American audience. Movies such as *Do the Right Thing* and *Boyz N the Hood* can be made for a relatively modest outlay. And different audiences are taking shape: In 1992, the largest growth segment at the movie box office was Latinos. These niche-marketed movies address hitherto underserved audiences and often turn a healthy profit for producers and distributors as well. Perhaps the story of the film industry will have a Hollywood ending after all.

Teaching Idea
What do students think the future of the movie industry holds?

summary

More Americans are watching movies than ever before, but fewer and fewer are watching them in movie theaters. While theater attendance dropped—from 90 million in 1946 to about 20 million in the early 1990s—the industry continued to grow, largely because of the home video market and international exports. Hollywood remained the symbol of the movie business, but since the end of World War II, the city's position, like the industry itself, had undergone drastic change. With the passing of the old studio system and rise of independent filmmakers and on-location productions, Hollywood's Golden Age was over. The industry has survived, but it has not been the same.

Many persons are involved in making a movie, including the producer, director, writers, cinematographer, cast, designers, composer, film editors, and marketing people. With rising costs, moneylenders have become cautious about backing properties that may be too unconventional. While many major films are box office success stories, many more fail outright or achieve only limited commercial success.

The power and influence of films have troubled governments around the world, and every country has found it necessary to regulate the film industry to at least some degree. In the late sixties, in the face of protests from pressure groups and the threat of possible governmental action to suppress controversial film content, the U.S. film industry adopted a ratings code. The code did not authorize censorship or other abridgements of creative expression, but instead labeled films to alert audiences to possibly objectionable aspects of a film's content. The ratings, highly subjective, continue to be modified. Some critics insist that certain films undermine family values and corrupt children, but social scientists are split on the validity of the charge. Meanwhile, the film industry, hard-pressed to compete with television, continued to turn out vivid and, to some, controversial movies. The number of *R*-rated films, though declining, in the early 1990s was still about 60 percent of the total.

With the movie industry, as with mass communications, technology has opened up astonishing new possibilities. Among these are interactive movies; digital technology allows dozens of plot alternatives to be stored on CD-ROM discs, enabling individual viewers to move the film through different conflicts and various possible outcomes.

International audiences continue to flock to see American films, even those which do not do well with U.S. audiences. The film is regarded by communications scholars as the most powerful propaganda medium in the world.

? questions and cases

1. Compare what you believe would be the differences between writing a movie screenplay and writing a script for a television drama. Discuss, beyond the technical differences, degrees of relative freedom for the writer.

2. How effective is the present rating system in providing parents with an indication of a film's content? Did you or your parents pay any attention to film ratings when you were a teenager? What changes, if any, would you make in the movie rating system?

3. Will such technical improvements as high-definition TV and on-demand delivery of movies into the home kill movie theaters entirely? Why or why not?

4. Film critic Michael Medved, quoted in this chapter, once wrote that "the entertainment industry promotes every form of sexual adventurism and regularly ridicules religious believers as crooks or crazies." Do you agree or disagree with him? Explain.

5. What are some aspects of the human experience that have not yet been, but should be, satisfactorily portrayed in the movies? In other words, what kinds of persons, attitudes, or situations would you like to see more movies portray?

chapter glossary

blacklisting During the politically charged "Red Scare" era following World War II, a number of filmmakers and performers were accused of being in sympathy with the communists and were denied work in the film industry.

block booking A marketing practice, now illegal, whereby film studios forced film exhibitors to contract for some of the studios' weaker films in order to obtain the better ones.

Motion Picture Association of America (MPAA) Industry organization which, along with much else, developed the system for rating movies to indicate their suitability for children.

pan To move a camera to follow the action, or to obtain a panoramic view.

zoom Camera effect created by a swift move toward, or move away from, the subject.

notes

1 Quoted in *Halliwell's Filmgoer's and Video Viewer's Companion,* 9th ed. (New York: Harper & Row, 1988), 797.

2 Susan Spillman, "Moviegoing Slips; Audiences Growing Older," *USA Today,* 10 March 1993.

3 Ibid.

4 Bernard Weinraub, "Hollywood Testing the Financial Value of Family Values," New York *Times,* 12 November 1992.

5 This conclusion, along with many others mentioned in this chapter, was reached by Dr. John Stevens, professor of journalism at the University of Michigan, who wrote the chapter on film for the first edition of this book.

6 James Bates, "Video Sales, Rentals Top $17 Billion in '92," Los Angeles *Times,* 9 January 1993.

7 Stevens, *op. cit.*

8 *Halliwell's Filmgoer's Companion,* 501.

9 Ibid., 559–61; 1059.

10 For this passage, the author drew heavily upon the works of Professor Arthur Knight, especially *The Liveliest Art* (New York: Macmillan, 1957), a history of motion pictures.

11 Quoted in *Halliwell's Filmgoer's Companion,* 560.

12 Published in 1990 by Peterson's Guides, Princeton, N.J.

13 Jean Folkerts and Dwight Teeter, *Voices of a Nation: A History of Media in the United States* (New York: Macmillan), 420.

14 See especially William Grimes, "NC-17 Rating Declares a Film Is . . . What?" New York *Times,* 30 November 1992.

15 Larry Hackett, "Movies: Fair or Foul?" New York *Daily News,* 15 November 1992.

16 Michael Medved, "Hollywood's Fascination with Filth," *Reader's Digest,* October 1992, 177.

17 Ibid., 178

18 Hackett, New York *Daily News,* 15 November 1992.

19 The author is especially indebted to research assistants Anthony Henstock and Larry Hoffman for their work on this passage.

20 David Landis, "New Hybrids Lack a Single Direction," *USA Today,* 7 April 1994.

chapter

N

Public Relations

One of the ironies besetting the public relations field, where clear communication is of such obvious and vital importance is that the work itself is widely misunderstood. Even the name public relations is

Objectives

When you have finished studying this chapter, you should be able to:

- Define public relations and explain what public relations practitioners do

- List the various publics a typically large and complex organization must serve, and suggest ways of dealing with each

- Trace the development of modern, systematic public relations procedures

- Outline the kinds of services public relations departments and counseling firms offer

- List some of the personal and professional traits organizational recruiters look for in hiring employees for public relations positions

- Debate current criticisms of the public relations field

One of the ironies besetting the public relations field, where clear communication is of such obvious and vital importance, is that the work itself is widely misunderstood. Even the name *public relations* is somewhat confusing in that it suggests but one large, amorphous public to deal with. Actually, each organization affects, and is affected by, many publics. Consider your own college or university: At a minimum, it must adroitly juggle relationships among such diverse publics as:

- *Students,* who desire interesting and useful classes taught at convenient hours by competent professors, as well as comfortable housing, decent dining facilities, ample entertainment and recreational opportunities, counseling and medical care, and a multitude of other services.
- *Faculty,* whose concerns include teaching loads, salaries, research support, and opportunities for career advancement.
- *Prospective students,* who must be recruited into the fold if the institution is to maintain its reputation and its operating budget.
- *Parents of students,* who must remain convinced that their sons and daughters are receiving educational experiences that justify huge investments of time and money.
- *Other colleges and universities,* whose continuing respect is essential to the recruitment of new faculty and transfer students, and acceptance of the school's seniors into graduate and professional schools elsewhere.
- *The trustees* or governing board, who is responsible for the financial and academic integrity of the institution.
- *The surrounding community,* which can make life on campus pleasant or miserable by its handling of such matters as police and fire protection, parking, street and sidewalk repair, utilities, zoning laws, and the other services your college needs.
- Various other publics, including your school's *alumni, secretarial and maintenance and administrative support staff, agencies of state and federal governments,* and philanthropic *foundations.*

At times the interests of various publics may conflict. Many members of the student public might be delighted if your college or university abolished all disciplinary rules and sold cocktails in the student union—policies the parent public could find alarming. Lavish salary increases would make the faculty public happy, but not necessarily the trustee public, which would be required to come up with the money without alienating the parent, student, and prospective student publics.

Teaching Idea

Survey your students to see if they can identify any additional publics at your institution—possibly fraternities, sororities, athletes, sports boosters, student groups, and others.

The institution must frequently communicate with the various publics in different ways. A press conference and news release might be the most effective means of reaching the community public; a folksy newsletter may work best with faculty and staff, while a quiet, one-on-one conversation in the dining room of the state capitol might be the surest way to swing a key vote for a bill favorable to your school. Yet all of these techniques—the elaborate press conference and the intimate newsletter, the brassy press release and the soft-sell luncheon talk—are part of the complex career field known as public relations.

Success or failure of a press conference often depends to a great extent on the advance planning of staff public relations people.

A Publicity Primer

Been elected publicity director? Your job, to present your organization to the public, will be a challenge. Here are some tips that can help you get your story told in the mass media serving your campus and community:

1. Be the only person from your group to contact news media. Two members calling the same newspaper editor or program director are bound to bring conflict or confusion.
2. Be quick to establish personal contact with the right persons at each newspaper, radio, and television station in your area.
3. Be sure to write everything down. Train your memory, but don't trust it.
4. Be prompt in meeting every deadline.
5. Be legible. Type news releases. Erase and correct errors. Don't use carbons, except for your own file copy.
6. Be accurate. Double check dates, names, places before you submit your copy.
7. Be honest and impartial. Give credit where due.
8. Be brief. Newspaper space and air time are costly.
9. Be brave. Don't be afraid to suggest something new if you honestly believe you have a workable idea. Media people welcome original ideas when they're practical and organized logically.
10. Be business-like. Never try to obtain publicity by pressure of friendship or business connections. Never ask when a story will appear. Never ask for clippings.
11. Be appreciative of all space and time given your club's publicity. The media giving it also have space and time for sale.
12. Be professional. Members of the press are always invited guests. Never ask them to buy tickets or pay admission. Arrange a special Press Table for large banquets.

Publicity Handbook: A Guide for Publicity Chairmen, the Sperry and Hutchison Company, 1972.

Definitions and Duties

The terms *publicity, propaganda, promotion,* and *public relations* often are thought to be interchangeable, but technically they are not.

Publicity refers to news items or stories in the mass media about people or organizations. Although public relations people often prepare publicity releases, the public relations field goes far beyond publicity.

Propaganda is an expression of opinion deliberately designed to influence individuals or groups toward preconceived objectives. While propaganda materials such as broadcast messages, pamphlets, and news releases often come from reputable persons or organizations, the term *propaganda* has earned a sinister connotation through its incessant application in world wars and cold wars to dictatorships employing half-truths and distortion-filled tirades to prey upon bigotry, intolerance, hate, and fear. The field of public relations is broader and more positive than the mere issuance of propaganda.

Promotion includes all forms of communication, other than paid advertising, that call attention to sales or marketing ideas or in some way reinforce what is said in advertising messages. Arranging a luncheon for dealers to announce a new product would be considered promotion; so would a contest inviting salespeople to compete for the first-place prize—a junket to Hawaii. Unlike advertising campaigns, promotions are usually short-term, specific efforts connected to a special offer, such as a premium or coupon. Public relations people may become involved with promotion, but typically they do other things as well.

In the 1990s, many companies were blending their advertising and public relations operations into something called *integrated marketing communications.* But while advertising and public relations people may work closely toward a common goal, their procedures and tactics remain different, and each contributes to the collective effort in a different way.

The term *public relations* is used to explain both an organization's program of activities and a way of looking at that organization's performance. The trade journal *Public Relations News* defines it as "the management function which evaluates public

Teaching Idea

Discuss the text's definition of propaganda. Then ask students to bring examples of propaganda from the media to class. Students should explain why they considered their examples "propaganda." Are they "good" or "bad" propaganda?

attitudes, identifies the policies and procedures of an individual or an organization with the public interest, and plans and executes a program of action to earn public understanding and acceptance." Other, simpler definitions of public relations include "the engineering of public consent" and "doing good and getting credit for it." The Public Relations Society of America in 1988 formally adopted its own definition: *"Public relations helps an organization and its publics adapt mutually to each other."*

Scott M. Cutlip, a leading scholar in the field, developed this oft-quoted definition: "Public relations is the planned effort to influence public opinion through good character and responsible performance, based upon mutually satisfactory two-way communication." But he adds, "The world knows the public relations function more by what practitioners DO than what practitioners aspire to BE."[1]

What is it, then, that public relations people do? According to the *Public Relations Society of America* (PRSA), most public relations positions involve work in one or more of these areas:[2]

1 *Programming/issues management:* sizing up opportunities and potential problems, setting goals, and recommending a systematic agenda of activities. This might require planning public relations missions for the organization's chief executive officer as well as for members of the public relations staff.

2 *Relationships.* Information from both inside and outside the organization must be gathered and evaluated, and recommendations for management formulated. Public relations staff members often represent their organizations in communications with the press, government agencies, and the public at large.

3 *Writing and editing.* The output includes news releases, reports, booklets, speeches, film and slide presentation scripts, trade magazine articles, production information and technical material, newsletters, shareholder reports, and other management communications for both internal and external audiences. An effective, understandable style of writing is a necessity. *There is almost no such thing as a successful public relations person who cannot write clearly.*

On the campaign trail. Political public relations people arrange for "photo opportunities" to showcase their candidate in the most favorable light. Here, Speaker Newt Gingrich of the U.S. House of Representatives and friends.

4 *Information.* Of importance here is establishing and maintaining channels to disseminate material to newspaper, broadcast, and general and trade publications editors, as well as cultivating media contacts to encourage publication of an organization's news and feature story ideas. This requires a keen understanding of how all media, and especially newspapers, work. Editors and broadcast news directors are pressed for column space and air time, and many voices clamor to be heard. Gaining confidence and developing a spirit of cooperation and mutual respect are essential to both the public relations professional and the journalist.

5 *Production.* The public relations staff may have to produce reports, brochures, company newspapers and magazines, even video news release (VNR) videotapes and multimedia programs. Individual practitioners need not have the skills of a specialist in commercial art, layout, typography, computer-generated graphics, and photography, but a background understanding of these techniques is essential for their effective utilization and for working with true production specialists.

6 *Special events.* Organizations plan conventions, news conferences, exhibits, plant tours and open houses, anniversary celebrations, contest and award programs, and special meetings to obtain public recognition. Often handled by the public relations staff, these events involve careful planning, coordination, and rigorous concern with detail.

A Press Secretary's Job

[Lloyd] Bentsen was about to make his television debut as Treasury Secretary . . . on NBC's "Meet the Press." As a spokesman for the administration, he wanted to make sure what he planned to say would fit with White House plans. Bentsen brought along his press secretary of two decades, Jack R. DeVore, 54, a cagey, cigar-smoking Texan who believed in giving the media the truth but not too much of it. DeVore once said that a press secretary's job was to manufacture a steady stream of doggie biscuits for the press, who would gleefully lick the hand that fed them, thumping their tails as long as there was news. But, DeVore said, if you ran out of treats or news, the press would eat your arm and try for more.

Bob Woodward, *The Agenda: Inside the Clinton White House* (Simon & Schuster, 1994).

7 *Speaking.* This might consist of presenting material at conferences, delivering public speeches, or preparing speeches for others. Not every public relations person is an accomplished platform speaker, but the man or woman who can effectively address individuals and groups does have an advantage.

8 *Employee/member relations:* responding to concerns and informing and motivating an organization's employees or members and their families.

9 *Research and evaluation.* The ability to gather information accurately, thoroughly, and promptly is essential. Besides personal interviews and library research, this may involve using survey techniques and designing and conducting public opinion polls. To an increasing degree, top managements expect research and evaluation proficiency from their public relations advisers.

These functions describe a demanding and sophisticated industry. Few public relations people would claim to be experts in all of these areas. Nevertheless, extensive training and preparation are required for top performance in the public relations field. Professionals cringe when they hear a job applicant say, "I think I would be good in public relations because I like people." Liking people, while a commendable trait, in and of itself rarely assures a successful career in public relations.

Public relations research: an opinion pollster at work.

Historical Developments

The art of public relations is as old as humanity. Few of history's great leaders rose to power without possessing a well-developed sense of drama as well as skills in communication, persuasion, and other elements now known to be essential for public relations practice.

Systematic public relations, as a business procedure and career field, is a much more recent development that began in this country during the latter years of the nineteenth century. Huge private fortunes were being amassed to finance such projects as the creation of the iron and steel industries and construction of railroads from coast to coast. Far more than a mere extension of democratic capitalism, this was in fact a change in the nature and outlook of U.S. society. The population was shifting from the farms to the cities; the United States was no longer a nation comprised, as Thomas Jefferson had seen it, of shopkeepers and small farmers. Instead it was caught up in the dramatic rise of big business, of industrialization, urbanization, and concentrations of wealth and economic might.

Not all the growth was admirably achieved. Certain captains of industry, scornfully referred to as Robber Barons, were men who catapulted their way to fame and fortune by cheating their competitors and exploiting their customers. Reform groups and a small, determined band of investigative journalists writing for national magazines exposed some of these abuses. These *muckraking* articles, appearing in *McClure's* and other influential publications of the day, threatened to create a hostile climate for big business, the just as well as the unjust. Corporations sensed the need to defend their positions to the general public and the government but were not sure how to go about doing so.

Ivy Lee

At this point, a handful of men who offered advice to top management arrived on the scene. These consultants came from newspaper backgrounds and knew how the press operated. For a fee, they attempted to counter the bad publicity with positive

Teaching Idea

Invite a public relations professional (or a colleague who teaches PR) to discuss each of the functions outlined in the text.

P. T. Barnum (shown here with Tom Thumb) was one of the most successful publicists of all time.

Suggested Audiovisual Aid

PBS Video has a Bill Moyers videotape which shows some of Ivy Lee's early PR work, plus interviews with Ed Bernays.

Background

Newsreels and movies in 1917–18 were used to influence public opinion against the Central Powers. Movie stars peddled Liberty Bonds in public rallies.

news. The most famous of these early practitioners was Ivy Ledbetter Lee. He announced his intentions this way: "Our plan is, frankly and openly, on behalf of business concerns and public institutions, to supply to the press and public . . . prompt and accurate information concerning subjects of value and interest to the public to know about."[3]

The material Lee and his associates distributed was not advertising, which companies could have bought. It was in the form of **press releases,** articles written in accepted journalistic style and designed to fit into the *news* columns of the nation's papers to present a company's interests in a favorable light. Because these press releases would appear in the news columns, if at all, they had a certain legitimacy.

Editors were free to crumple these press releases and throw them away, and many did. More than a few editors, however, found parts or all of the press releases newsworthy, and some even applauded business leaders for their efforts to tell their side of the story. Lee's strategy began to work. His clients, including the Pennsylvania Railroad, John D. Rockefeller, Jr. (then under attack in the press for the strike-breaking activities of a family-owned subsidiary), and the Colorado Fuel and Iron Company, soon came to admire Lee's skill at cultivating favorable publicity. Other beleaguered corporate executives joined in, employing publicists of their own.

Some years later, Ivy Lee and others like him came to realize that mere press agentry was not enough; favorable publicity was not effective unless it was supported by good works. Or, as today's public relations people might warn, "you can't sell an empty box."

Edward L. Bernays

In 1923 another pioneer, Edward L. Bernays, set forth a two-way interpretive concept that was to become the basis for modern-day practice. Public relations, he insisted, involves (1) advising clients on how to present a favorable image to the public to gain popular support and (2) directing messages to the public through the press. Thus, public relations took on a positive, rather than a purely negative, reason for being. Some experts argue that, in terms of influence, Bernays far outweighed Ivy Lee, who was a brilliant publicist but lacked Bernays's vision. Bernays originated the occupation of public affairs consultant[4] and went on to contribute greatly, through his long career and voluminous writing, to the advancement of the field.

The Creel Committee

A major turning point for the emerging industry came with World War I. The federal government, desperate to arouse the nation into fighting a remote and unpopular war, moved into the public relations arena. Spearheading the effort was the government's Committee on Public Information (CPI), established by President Woodrow Wilson and directed by George Creel. The Creel Committee, as it came to be known, successfully mobilized public opinion behind the war effort. At the same time, related public relations campaigns proved effective at promoting the sale of Liberty Bonds and raising money for the Red Cross and other service agencies. Such patriotic successes deeply impressed business leaders with the possibilities inherent in coordinated, systematic, positive public relations programs.

The Creel Committee trained dozens of men and women in the latest public relations and propaganda techniques. After the war, these increasingly sophisticated public relations experts turned their attention to various subgroups (publics) such as investors, government agencies, employees, and customers. Separate means and skills were developed for communicating with each of them. Improved research methodology suggested what would and would not work in terms of message clarity and credibility, problem spotting, an audience's self-interests, and so on. The techniques are still far from perfect, but they have come a long way in a short time.

New Activism

In the early 1970s, the Mobil Oil Corporation launched an aggressive, high-profile public relations campaign that marked a sharp departure from the traditional pattern. Armed with top management support and a budget that at one time averaged $20 million or more a year, Mobil's vice-president for public affairs, Herbert Schmertz, boldly initiated a strategy of fierce corporate activism. While in the past many large companies had passively absorbed consumer group and mass media criticism, Schmertz and Mobil chose to respond immediately and directly. They complained, at full volume, when they thought media coverage was inaccurate or unfair. The moment Mobil—or the entire oil industry, for that matter—came under fire, Mobil executives launched fierce counterattacks, blitzing the media with news conferences, letters, and telephone calls to editors and demanding appearances on talk shows.

One of the most formidable weapons in Mobil's arsenal has become issue, or **advocacy, advertising.** Buying ad space in the New York *Times* and other publications, Mobil stated the company's positions on national energy and economic policy and environmental matters, pointing out perceived flaws in media coverage of the oil business. The campaigns were expensive—an estimated $6 million a year in advocacy ads alone—but helped the company emerge as a spokesperson for the commercial world. In addition, claimed Rawleigh Warner, Jr., then chief executive at Mobil, the company "gained the respect of many people, both in and outside the media. People know that if they take a swipe at us, we will fight back."[5]

The Mobil campaign had its detractors. Some observers feared that Schmertz was using his multimillion-dollar budget in "an ominously brazen attempt to manipulate public opinion."[6] Supporters of the Mobil strategy contended that it helped take business off the defensive and ramrodded passage of legislation favorable to the oil business, such as loosening oil price controls. At the same time, it dramatically spruced up the company's image with the public and with stockholders. For good or ill, Mobil had introduced a new activism to the public relations field, an aggressive strategy defined by immediate responses to attacks and by "spin doctors" that place potentially troubling situations in the best light. The political campaigns of the 1990s often reflected this approach.

Crisis Management

In the 1990s, public relations people became more and more concerned about planning for, and dealing with, corporate disasters. An oil spill (Exxon), charges that a surgical breast implant caused desperate medical problems (Dow Corning), reports that an airline's pilot and crew had been drinking heavily just before a flight (Northwest Orient), charges that some soft drink cans contained syringes (Pepsi-Cola), accusations of bogus charges and installation of unnecessary auto parts (Sears), and reports of dangerously designed pickup trucks (General Motors) created public relations problems of gigantic proportions. How well, or how poorly, corporate spokespersons react to such crises directly affects the extent of the damage, for a public relations disaster can bring an organization to its knees just as surely as any financial reversal.

Teaching Idea

As of late 1994, Mobil was still running ads on the op-ed page of the N.Y. *Times.* Assign students to get copies of several ads from papers or microfilm in the library and discuss them in class.

During such crises, top managements may receive conflicting advice. The company's lawyers, for example, may warn top management to say nothing, on the grounds that admissions of any kind might later prove damaging in court. But public relations people often argue that media coverage, which is inevitable, will be less damaging if all sides of the story are told.

The 1993 syringes-in-the-Pepsi-cans scare was quickly exposed as a hoax, but other public relations crises have been more difficult to resolve. When the issue is less clear cut, and the company is at least to some degree at fault, the most successful crisis management seems to come when the company acknowledges its mistakes, apologizes, and demonstrates that the problem is being corrected.

Shrewd public relations people develop plans to anticipate a worst-possible-case scenario. Such strategies call for designated spokespersons, crisis communications workshops, and plans to assist victims and families should the worst happen. The objectives include helping the mass media (1) report responsibly and (2) avoid distorting the story.[7]

The Industry Today

According to current estimates, more than 400,000 men and women hold full-time positions in public relations work,[8] and the numbers are increasing. Public relations people are employed by

1 *Business corporations.* This is where the practice of public relations began, and corporations presumably remain the largest segment of the industry today. (The point is in some dispute, for the figures are imprecise, as is the definition of "full-time position in public relations." It is possible that government, with its intensified interest in this area, may have overtaken the private sector in terms of PR hirings.)

Most companies of any size engage one or more persons to assist in handling public relations responsibilities. The duties vary with corporate orientation. In a manufacturing concern, for example, the public relations department may focus chiefly on employee relations and company publications, while in a retailing firm the public relations staff might deal extensively with external matters, such as customer and media contacts. Most business PR departments are fairly small, six persons or fewer, although a corporate giant may boast a public relations staff numbering one hundred or more. Some company PR departments also handle **institutional advertising**—advertising that enhances the image of the company itself, as contrasted with advertising designed to sell specific goods or services. In many cases, the company merges the public relations department into a larger operation known as *integrated marketing communications,* wherein advertising, PR, and sales forces combine their energies and resources to present the communications/selling messages under a common umbrella.

2 *Associations,* created to develop favorable operating environments for a trade or an industry, provide thousands of jobs for public relations people. This category includes such diverse groups as the Chamber of Commerce, the Distilled Spirits Council of America, National Association of Broadcasters, the American Bankers Association, and many more—an estimated 14,000 associations exist throughout the country. Most have main offices situated in or near major media centers such as New York, Washington, Chicago, or Los Angeles. Association PR people plan conventions and workshops for their affiliates, lobby, and provide information to the press and public to cast their industry in the most favorable light.

3 *Labor unions* employ public relations staffs to develop news bureaus and publications for communicating with their members and the general public. They also arrange for speakers to visit civic, government, scholastic, and other groups and lobby government at all levels for legislation favorable to labor. In the event of a strike or another labor dispute, public relations specialists from the union's international headquarters may be deployed to the scene to present the local's side of the story through the media to the public.

4 *Nonprofit service agencies,* including the Red Cross, Girl Scouts of America, the Easter Seal Society, Arthritis Foundation, church groups, and thousands of other agencies employ public relations staffs to assist with fundraising and to enlist local support.

5 *Government* units—perhaps 80,000 of them, at all echelons—are heavy utilizers of public relations people. These "public information" or "public affairs" personnel attempt to develop and maintain good communication with the public and to present information about the activities of the organizations they represent. Often a PIO (public information officer) can assist a news reporter by skillfully cutting through bureaucratic red tape to gain prompt access to an official needed for an interview.

Military public information personnel, who produce broadcasts and publications for troops as well as background material for the press and general public, are trained at the Defense Information School. The job of a military PIO is seldom easy. Within the military—as, indeed, is true throughout much of government—there is widespread distrust of the media of mass communications. The PIO is often caught between a commanding general's penchant for secrecy and journalists' demands that everything be made public.

A particularly acute example of this conflict occurred in October 1983 when an assault force of Army Rangers and U.S. Marines invaded the small island of Grenada. The troops were to rescue several hundred Americans believed to be at risk and to neutralize forces thought to be planning terrorist missions in the West Indies and Latin America. The U.S. government barred the press from the scene for the first few days of the operation. Angry editorials in both broadcast and print media ensued, and military credibility, still smarting from the war in Vietnam, faced sharp criticism once again. Then, in 1991, as journalists attempted to report on the war in the Persian Gulf, they ran into tight military restrictions. "From the White House on down," one angry critic wrote, "the idea was to beat the Vietnam syndrome with a winning war, blame the messenger [the mass media] for any bad news, and keep the American press under control and the public in the dark."[9] The Defense Information School philosophy, which top generals and admirals do not always find persuasive, is "Maximum Disclosure, Minimum Delay."

This same outlook guides the United States Information Agency (USIA), a direct descendant of World War I's Creel Committee, which has become in effect this country's public relations bureau throughout the rest of the world. Severely underfunded for much of its history, and required by law to limit its activities to foreign countries—Congress is concerned lest a national propaganda apparatus might be employed for domestic political purposes— the USIA operates the Voice of America shortwave radio network, which spans the globe, and, as of 1994, was maintaining 205 posts in 128 countries around the globe.

In the 1980s, the USIA also began a worldwide satellite television operation. Worldnet, as the service is called, transmits news programming, public affairs, sports, interview shows, and service features about the United

Teaching Idea
Students may want to see if your institution's library has back copies of the *Columbia Journalism Review* or the *Washington* (later *American*) *Journalism Review*. If so, have them review critical articles written about the Gulf war in 1991, 1992, or 1993.

Background
Voice of America broadcasts may be picked up on almost any shortwave receiver that covers all or parts of the 3 to 30 MHz shortwave spectrum. Other countries also broadcast news and information on shortwave. If you or any of your students have shortwave receivers, listen to a broadcast in class. Many newsstands carry magazines with information on current station frequencies and operating hours.

Promotional material from Ruder Finn, Inc., a public relations counseling firm.

States by earth satellite via 214 satellites to some 189 cities in 126 countries. In addition, the USIA maintains overseas libraries to inform people of other nations about the ideals and workings of the American system.

Fair-minded observers give the USIA high marks for its honesty in presenting a solid diet of news, often reporting stories on racial disturbances, economic downturns, unemployment figures, and political scandals that may not always show the country in its most favorable light. The propaganda agencies of most other countries are rarely so candid.

Public Relations Counseling Firms

There are about four thousand separate public relations agencies which, like law firms, certified public accountants, and advertising agencies, are available for hire by a variety of clients. Counseling firms, as many are called, may be especially skilled in government negotiations, issues management, or both. Many businesses are too small to maintain their own PR departments and find it more efficient to utilize the services of a public relations counseling firm, on retainer or on an hourly basis as needed. Other companies that do have their own PR staffs often discover they need an outside counselor to handle a specific project, such as staging a big anniversary celebration or lobbying for a bill pending before Congress.

Morale within a company or an organization often depends on successful communication with employees. This newsletter, prepared by the public relations department for employees, helps them better understand their role in achieving the organization's goals.

Men and women employed by PR counseling firms tend to be self-starting, versatile individuals able to grasp quickly the central issue of a situation and deal with it effectively—and then, minutes later, dig into another client's problems, which may demand a whole different set of skills. One medium-sized public relations agency in a Southwestern city not long ago served about thirty clients, including:

- An industrial equipment manufacturer who was planning to open two new plants that year in different regions of the country. The PR agency was hired to coordinate details of the openings with local officials, prepare publicity kits for media people in the area, and plan the ribbon-cutting ceremonies. The PR firm also, for an hourly fee, produced the manufacturer's employee newsletter each month.
- A prominent physician who was raising money to build a unique clinic and treatment facility. The PR agency successfully campaigned to give the physician and his cause wide, positive exposure by ghostwriting magazine articles to go out over his byline, arranging for his appearance on regional and national interview programs, and suggesting new angles to magazine editors for developing profile articles on the client.
- Several political campaigns, one a wet/dry liquor referendum in a neighboring community, and another involving regional fundraising for a national political party.
- A wealthy oil entrepreneur, who retained the firm to write occasional speeches for him and to provide discrete advice about worthy philanthropic activities.
- A Protestant church that had found itself with a disproportionately large number of elderly members on the rolls. Worried about its future, the congregation hired the public relations agency to develop campaign strategies for attracting more young people.

This agency served more than two dozen other clients as well, but this brief list suggests the kinds of tasks counseling firms perform and why various individuals and organizations make use of a counselor's expertise and independent judgment.

Career Opportunities

If current projections are accurate, the public relations field seems destined for astonishing growth in the years ahead. One authority, Robert Kendall, predicts that public relations people will account for *one million jobs by the end of the century*. That would mean the field will have more than doubled in size between the mid-1980s and the year 2000. Related occupations that include public relations functions—lobbyist, fundraiser, and some communication, promotion, and advertising professionals—will account for another two million positions.[10] While these predictions may be overly optimistic, the fact remains that thousands of additional public relations positions open up each year.

U.S. Bureau of Labor Statistics projections indicate a somewhat more conservative, but still impressive, growth pattern—a 27 to 32 percent increase in the number of public relations specialists needed during the 1990s. Labor experts also predict significant hiring increases in fields closely connected to public relations, including a

- 17 to 24 percent increase in community organization workers.
- 25 to 31 percent increase in technical sales representatives.
- 23 to 27 percent increase in personnel and labor relations specialists.
- 34 to 38 percent increase in writers and editors.
- 25 to 27 percent increase in commercial and graphic artists.
- 38 to 44 percent increase in designers.[11]

What a PR Student Intern Does

Many public relations departments for corporate and nonprofit agencies take on college students as interns—partially to help the student bridge the gap between formal classroom education and the professional world. At Dow Chemical, which maintains one of the more structured public relations intern programs, students are usually offered three assignments, each lasting four to six months. Here are some of the projects Dow interns typically perform:

Corporate or Manufacturing Communications

1. Research and write news releases and articles for various internal newsletters.
2. Produce a newsletter for an employee Political Action Committee.
3. Communicate and implement a community environmental awareness program.
4. Plan and produce a multimedia program to introduce a new employee benefits plan.

5. Write a speech on an environmental topic for a Dow executive to present.
6. Assist with the writing and production of the Dow Annual Report to stockholders.

Product Department Communication

1. Plan and implement a seminar on Dow products for trade publication editors.
2. Work with a communications agency to plan and produce a video on safe product handling techniques.
3. Assist in the strategic planning and implementation of a Dow exhibit or hospitality event at a major trade show.
4. Write or revise and produce a sale brochure describing a Dow product's uses and capabilities.
5. Prepare a status report to customers on a current product-related issue.

The economic recession of 1991 and 1992 may well have affected these long-term projections somewhat. While total PR employment increased by 26 percent between 1980 and 1990, the recession prompted widespread, and sometimes severe, cutbacks. Agencies overstaffed in anticipation of attracting more new business were obliged to retrench. Moreover, there was repositioning within the industry—not necessarily a bad thing, said some top PR executives. "It [the recession] has enabled us to become fully integrated into the marketing function," wrote Carol Gies, public relations director for Bloomingdale's. "The positive outcome is that practitioners have actually been elevated to professionals because we are no longer perceived as strictly publicists but as members of a marketing team that has a direct, measurable impact on our organization's bottom line."[12]

So what kind of public relations person will be needed for the years ahead? According to one experienced set of corporate recruiters, the best prospects for entry-level jobs in the field will be college graduates who

1 *Can demonstrate writing skill and experience.* Work on the student newspaper, they advise. String for local papers, do volunteer publicity work for the Big Brothers, the Red Cross, or any other organization that gives you a chance to *write*. As your work improves, be sure to keep a collection of writing samples. They'll help sell you.

2 *Have taken a wide range of courses.* Many graduates complete classes in journalism and public relations but neglect business administration, sociology, psychology, economics, and marketing—subjects that deal with matters important to public relations and that help provide a broad intellectual and professional base.

3 *Are good at conceptualizing.* Successful PR candidates see what needs to be done and do it, often without having management spell out detailed instructions.

Teaching Idea

Find out whether any of the students are now doing, or have ever done, volunteer writing. If so, ask them to explain their work.

Teaching Idea

Mention also that, with the increasing number of foreign companies with offices or plants in this country, fluency in a foreign language can be a great plus when looking for a PR job.

The PR Job Interview

Here are some likely questions:

1. "Why have you chosen a career in public relations?" If you say, "Because I like people," you've just stumbled.
2. "How would you define 'public relations'?"
3. "How would you differentiate between 'public relations' and 'public affairs'?"
4. "Do you have any strong geographic preferences?" If you can't stand the East or West, say so.
5. "Do you have any limitations on the amount of travel you will do?" Few PR people can function well by never leaving corporate headquarters, so some travel is required—and desirable. If you won't travel, say so.
6. "Please tell me how you go about solving a business problem." In other words, tell me about your style.
7. "How do you handle conflict situations?" A skillful negotiator will go further than a nose-breaker. PR people often deal with adversaries. Honey or vinegar?
8. You should be aware of public issues involving the company and the industry you are interviewing. If it is a chemical company, questions might cover environmental, energy, or regulatory matters.

Finding That First Job in Public Relations, published by the Dow Chemical Company, 1985.

4 *Demonstrate teachability.* Public relations people need to be versatile and flexible; able to profit from constructive criticism; and have a capacity for growth and change.

During placement interviews, recruiters or corporate "headhunters" typically try to evaluate the public relations job prospect in each of fifteen categories: confidence; drive/self-motivation; enthusiasm; verbal skills; listening and comprehension; persuasiveness; human relations skills; credibility; technical competence; conceptual skills; organizational skills; growth potential (supervisory versus specialization); functional interests; geographical preferences/limitations; overall applicant/job match.[13]

Public relations salaries in the early 1990s averaged $46,556 for established professionals, according to the annual survey conducted by the **Public Relations Society of America.** Public relations executives working with utility companies enjoyed a median salary of $52,216, toward the higher end of the scale, while PR practitioners with nonprofit organizations earned a median salary of $34,419. These figures, representing the incomes of PRSA members, tend to reflect higher averages than those for PR practitioners generally. Overall, the salary levels have remained fairly steady in recent years, showing little total growth. Industry observers attribute this to (1) further "feminization" of the work force—inequities in women's salaries, compared to those of men, persist—and (2) a younger professional work force. Women comprise about half of the respondents in the 1992 PRSA salary survey, but more than 60 percent of practitioners in the 25-to-29 age group are women. The median salary for heads of public relations counseling firms was $52,216.

Accreditation

More than 15,000 public relations professionals are members of the Public Relations Society of America. About one-third of these are *accredited* by PRSA, which means they have five years or more of professional experience, have passed rigorous written and oral examinations, and have pledged to adhere to a tough code of professional ethics. PRSA members, though only a tiny percentage of all public relations practitioners, have done much to upgrade their profession through competency testing, seminars, conferences, publications, and other means. PRSA has more than one hundred professional chapters throughout the United States, and the society's concern for professional development is exemplified by its sponsorship of the Public Relations Student Society of America (PRSSA), which has about 5,700 members and

Teaching Idea

Ask several students to call local PR agencies to see what average starting salaries are for a typical college graduate.

Teaching Idea

If your institution has a PRSSA chapter, invite one of the officers to explain what it does.

172 campus chapters. PRSSA fosters competitions and a student internship program designed to provide professional experience to qualified undergraduates who aspire to public relations careers.

Another organization devoted to increased professionalism in public relations is the **International Association of Business Communicators (IABC),** which has virtually tripled in size during the past decade and now boasts about 12,000 members in 120 chapters in the United States, Canada, the United Kingdom, and the Far East, more than forty different countries in all. IABC has set forth a code of ethics, created an ethics review committee to enforce it, and formulated standards of excellence in business communications practice. IABC members compete in more than eighty awards categories each year, and the society's monthly magazine, *Communications World,* provides news and guidance. Like PRSA, IABC supports student involvement and has a foundation to encourage research and publication in the public relations field.

The professionalism of PRSA and IABC has not only brought increased respect for the industry, but financial rewards for those involved: Research reported in 1992 by IABC, for example, indicated that accredited members earned an average of $11,000 more a year than nonaccredited members.[14]

A Day at the Office

Whether at a counseling firm or in an internal department, the public relations staff stays busy. A spokesperson for the Public Relations Society of America describes a day's activities:

> Work schedules are choppy and frequently interrupted. The junior employees will answer calls for information from the press and public, work on invitation lists and details for a press conference, escort visitors and clients, help with research, write brochures, deliver releases to editorial offices, work on contact and distribution lists, scan newspapers and journals, paste scrapbooks of clippings. . . .
>
> The employee will brief his or her superior on forthcoming meetings, help write research reports, speeches, presentations, and letters, research case histories, help produce displays and other audiovisual materials, proofread, select photographs for publication, arrange for meetings, perform liaison jobs with advertising and other departments, arrange for holiday and other remembrances, conduct surveys and tabulate questionnaires, work with letter shops and printers. The telephone, typewriter, photocopier, postage meter, fax, postal systems, and messenger services are communications tools. All are familiar in the public relations office. . . .
>
> Not infrequently public relations programs operate against deadlines. Under such high-pressure conditions, nine-to-five schedules go out the window. While the public relations executive will not be tied to his desk for long periods, meetings, community functions, business lunches, travel assignments, special speaking and writing commitments, and unscheduled work on "crisis" situations often mean long hours—sometimes creating envy of those engaged in occupations with more settled routines.[15]

Planning for the Future

"By the year 2000," an optimistic public relations agency head predicted as the 1990s began, "we will have nothing to complain about—except the heavy burden of work."[16] That rosy forecast is based to a great extent on the dramatic growth in international public relations, made possible in part because:

1 *Massive political and economic restructuring have occurred across the globe.* The former Soviet Union and the Eastern European nations, once largely closed to western commerce, now are transforming themselves into active players on the world stage. The dynamic economic growth of the Pacific Rim nations promises to continue unabated in the years ahead.

2 *Acquisitions and mergers across international boundaries have intensified demand for global public relations efforts.*

3 *Advances in telecommunications media have facilitated interaction among nations.* The video news release (VNR), so successful in the United States, showed promise of comparable success in fast-growing European markets. Though there are only about 150 television stations in Europe, compared to more than 700 in the United States, European news directors in 1993 manifested keen interest in U.S. business news, prompting VNR producers and distributors, such as Medialink in New York, to be highly optimistic about the long-term prospects for international video public relations activities.[17]

In all of these areas, the "PRF"—or public relations factor—will be a basic element in the strategic and tactical business decisions of the future.[18] And, as a top PR agency head predicted, sophisticated public relations efforts will be required to develop and enhance organizational images in what he described as "the age of Transnational Identity."[19]

Another aspect of international public relations is the representation of foreign governments and causes in this country. Japan, Saudi Arabia, and other nations, as well as foreign industrialists and other commercial interests, retain U.S. public relations agencies to serve as listening posts and lobbyists.[20]

International growth factors, plus the increased reliance organizations place upon communications among all their local and national publics, persuade public relations executives that the field's future is a rosy one.

Background

A video news release (VNR) is a videotape of an alleged news event produced by a private or government agency with a stake in how the story is presented. Many TV news directors use them to substitute for their own coverage. Some edit the PR material; some don't edit but identify the source of the tape; others just run them verbatim.

Criticisms and Challenges

Despite the enormous expansion of the public relations field, both in the size of it and in contemporary society's acceptance of it, there remains a basic, and largely unresolved, adversarial relationship between the PR person and the journalist. Their fundamental interests are different. The public relations practitioner works for a particular organization or client, while the journalist supposedly serves *all* members of the audience, not just some. A company's publicity release may be of vital

In Defense of PR: The Industry Makes Its Case

Spin doctors? Flacks? Charlatans? Some public relations practitioners have been called these things, and worse, by critics who fear society is somehow being hoodwinked by slick PR tactics. But PR professionals can argue that what they do can, and does, bring a number of social benefits as well, among them:

• Public relations is a means for the public to have its desires and interests felt by institutions in society. It speaks for the public to otherwise unresponsive organizations, as well as speaking for those organizations to the public.

• Public relations helps achieve mutual adjustment between institutions and groups, establishing smoother relationships that benefit the public.

• Public relations can be a safety valve for freedom. By providing means of working out accommodations, it makes arbitrary action or coercion less likely.

• Public relations is an essential element in the communications system that enables individuals to be informed on many aspects of subjects that affect their lives.

• Public relations can help activate organizations' social conscience.

• Public relations is a universal activity. Everyone practices principles of public relations in seeking acceptance, cooperation, or affection of others. Public relations professionals only practice it in a more professional way.

Report of PRSA's Task Force on the Status and Role of Public Relations, 1991.

importance to the public relations executive who's trying to obtain favorable press coverage for a corporation; a journalist, on the other hand, may well regard that same release as self-serving propaganda that has no general news value. Yet Lillian Lodge Kopenhaver found that public relations practitioners and newspaper editors do, intellectually, at least, hold remarkably similar news judgment priorities.[21] Perhaps the nature of their respective jobs requires members of each group to *act* upon press releases differently.

Frequently, however, their interests will coincide. A company's press release might have both community and corporate news value. Or a helpful PR executive can provide excellent background information to a reporter who's digging into a complicated news or feature story. Virtually every journalist will at some point work closely with public relations people, often in a businesslike, mutually beneficial way. A 1992 study suggests that daily newspapers publish press releases at a significantly higher rate than previous research indicated; the authors conclude that public relations people are now preparing timelier, better-targeted press releases and that editors place more confidence in the releases that come into the newsroom.[22]

But at times the PR-journalist relationship can be uneasy. In stern language that expressed the sentiment of many journalists, an Associated Press Managing Editors guidebook warned reporters and editors to beware of publicity-seeking PR people, or **flacks:**

> A flack is a person who makes all or part of his income obtaining space in newspapers without cost to himself or his clients. . . . They are known formally as public relations men. The flack is the modern equivalent of the cavalier highwayman of old. . . . A flack is a flack. His job is to say kind things about his client. He will not lie very often, but much of the time he tells less than the whole story. You do not owe the PR man anything. The owner of the newspaper, not the flack, pays your salary. Your job is to serve the readers, not the man who would raid your columns.[23]

More specifically, journalists over the years have accused public relations practitioners of:

1 Trying to manage or control the news, especially news that reflects adversely on the companies or organizations they represent.

2 Attempting to finagle space in the news columns for purposes of praising their clients. Not only does this practice trivialize the news columns, it drains away income the paper might have obtained through the sale of advertising.

3 Employing pressure, often at the highest level, to affect editorial policy, to slip a story or an editorial into the paper or into a newscast, or, more commonly, pressing to have a story written a certain way—or kept out of the paper altogether. This goes beyond "spin control," which simply means attempting to place a certain event in the best possible light. Most journalists understand and accept the role of spin doctors, who try to influence the way the media presents a story by describing the event or its outcome in ways that benefit their clients. In the 1990s, spin controllers became a fact of political life. Journalists could accept, or dismiss, efforts at spin control accordingly. High-level pressure is more direct, and far more sinister.

4 Being uninformed or indifferent to the media's editorial requirements: what news is, how it should be presented, the harsh reality of deadlines.

5 Hiring away talented reporters from the media for better-paying jobs as public relations executives.

Public relations practitioners, on the other hand, can present some complaints of their own. They charge that reporters and editors frequently are guilty of:

1 Neglecting to cover many types of important and worthy news, especially news from the business community, education, the health care field, and so on.

Teaching Idea

Assign students to examine nonwire service news stories in your local or regional daily paper to see whether any are obviously PR releases. One good place to look is the food section. If a brand name for a food product appears in a recipe, you can be fairly sure the origin was a press release. (As an alternative, ask your local paper for samples of press releases.)

Teaching Idea

If a national or local crisis occurs during the class term, ask students to detect and analyze any spin.

2 Lumping all public relations people together—the incompetents and the skilled, honest practitioners—in a stereotypical and unfair way.

3 Failing to realize that a good story is a good story, even if it does reach the editor's desk in the form of a press release with a corporate letterhead.

4 Continuing to overemphasize negative news of strife and conflict, while ignoring many upbeat, constructive stories.

Scott M. Cutlip, who has trained many of the country's leading public relations practitioners, compiled these critical themes. He offers this cogent advice to PR people who want to improve their effectiveness with the media: (1) shoot squarely, (2) give service, (3) don't beg or carp, (4) don't ask for kills (to "kill" a story is to keep it out of the newspaper, off the wire, or off the air), (5) don't flood the media (with too many press releases), and (6) keep updated lists of media contact people. "Good press relationships," he warns, "must be earned."[24]

Since 1950, the Public Relations Society of America has had its own code of professional ethics. The revised version of it, the *Code of Professional Standards for the Practice of Public Relations,* adopted in 1988, says, in part, that each PRSA member shall:

- Exemplify high standards of honesty and integrity while carrying out dual obligations to a client or an employer and to the democratic process.
- Adhere to the highest standards of accuracy and truth, avoiding extravagant claims or unfair comparisons and giving credit for ideas and words borrowed from others.
- Not knowingly disseminate false or misleading information and act promptly to correct erroneous communications for which he or she is responsible.
- Not engage in any practice which has the purpose of corrupting the integrity of communications channels or government processes.
- Not represent conflicting or competing interests without the express consent of those concerned, given after a full disclosure of the facts.
- Not accept fees, commissions, gifts, or any other consideration from anyone except clients or employers for whom services are performed without their express consent, given after full disclosure of the facts. (Used with permission of the Public Relations Society of America.)

Despite their differences, public relations people and media people do have a lot in common. More to the point, circumstances dictate that they coexist. The PRSA's Declaration of Principles affirms the organization's belief that "the fundamental value and dignity of the individual, holding that the free exercise of human rights, especially the freedom of speech, freedom of assembly, and freedom of the press, is essential to the practice of public relations." And to all of mass communications.

summary

Public relations is a large, complex field designed to help an organization and its various constituencies—employees, suppliers, customers, stockholders, and so on—adapt to each other. Public relations practitioners are involved with writing and editing, programming and issues management, relationships, providing information through various channels, producing informational materials, handling employee relations, and performing research that helps define an organization's objectives and evaluate its progress toward meeting them.

An estimated 400,000 persons hold full-time positions in public relations, working with corporations, associations, governmental agencies, labor unions, and nonprofit service organizations. Others are members of public relations counseling firms which, like law and accounting firms, serve a variety of clients.

Continued growth is expected in the PR field, and the men and women hired for public relations positions are likely to be able to grow and change with economic and social conditions as well as be skilled at writing, editing, and conceptualizing.

Throughout much of their history, public relations practitioners and journalists have often seemed to work at cross purposes; a press release issued by a public relations person to create favorable publicity for an organization might seem to the journalist to be mere self-serving propaganda. But in recent years, with the heightened degree of professionalism in the public relations field, journalists have come to depend on skilled PR practitioners as important—and, in many cases, indispensable—sources of news and information. Media people and public relations practitioners now have much in common—including the need for the other to succeed.

? questions and cases

1. You have been appointed public relations director of a small, high-quality liberal arts college. The college's attractions include a good teaching faculty and a beautiful campus. However, the administration of the college has detected a small decline in the applications for admission for next year. "We aren't worried yet," the college president tells you, "but even a little slippage in the size of our student body could have serious implications." She asks you to prepare some recommendations for sprucing up the college's image. How do you go about developing your report?

2. What priorities of allegiance should public relations people give to the companies or clients that employ them and to the public, which they also serve? Can they serve both constituencies equally? Consider the following case. You are public relations adviser and press liaison for a political candidate who is seeking the governorship of your state. The candidate, ostensibly a happily married man, is running on a campaign that strongly emphasizes family values. Two weeks before the election, however, rumors surface that the candidate has engaged in several steamy affairs with younger women on his staff and, in addition, has for the past six months secretly maintained an adulterous relationship with a go-go dancer in a capital city night club. You warn the candidate that reporters are sure to hear the rumors and raise sharp questions about them. "Deny everything," he orders you. "My election is too important to this state for me to be brought down by scandal. My private life is not the issue here, anyway." What do you tell your boss? What do you tell the press?

3. Though by definition they are concerned with the image of others, public relations people often find they have an image problem of their own. Why does this problem exist? What, if anything, can they do about it?

4. Take a personal inventory: What traits and/or skills do you have that would make you an effective public relations practitioner? What weaknesses might give you difficulties in this field?

5. In this same vein, discuss the public relations *work* you have observed. This can range from political spin control, to publicity programs press agents developed, to communications materials an organization you are familiar with prepared. What sorts of things make you trust—or distrust—such efforts? What kinds of public relations techniques are most successful in terms of persuading *you?* Explain.

chapter glossary

advocacy advertising Advertising that presents an organization's point of view on social or political issues, as compared with advertising designed to sell goods or services, or with institutional advertising, which aims to enhance an image.

flack A press agent. The term is often used pejoratively.

institutional advertising Advertising messages promoting a company's image and seeking public goodwill rather than the sale of a specific product or service.

International Association of Business Communicators (IABC) A professional society composed of some 12,000 communications managers, industrial editors, and others engaged in various aspects of public relations work.

press release Publicity article prepared by an individual or organization (often the public relations staff) and distributed to the news media.

Public Relations Society of America (PRSA) Association advocating high professional and ethical standards within the public relations field.

notes

1 Scott M. Cutlip, Allen H. Center, and Glen M. Broom, *Effective Public Relations,* 6th ed. (Englewood Cliffs, N.J.: Prentice-Hall, 1985), 1–21.

2 From *Careers in Public Relations* and other background materials provided by the Public Relations Society of America.

3 Quoted in Cutlip, Center, and Broom, *Effective Public Relations,* 35.

4 Edward L. Bernays, "The Psychology of Public Relations," *Propaganda* (New York: Liveright, 1928), 47.

5 Irwin Ross, "Public Relations Isn't Kid Stuff at Mobil," *Fortune,* September 1976, 31.

6 Linda Charlton, "Upwardly Mobil," *Channels,* August/September 1981, 28.

7 Background materials furnished to the author from various public relations firms, notably Ruder Finn of New York.

8 U.S. Census Bureau figures, quoted in Robert Kendall, "Public Relations Employment: Huge Growth Expected," *Public Relations Review,* Fall 1984, 13. The classifications and duties that appear here are based on PRSA industry analyses.

9 John R. MacArthur, *Censorship and Propaganda in the Gulf War,* (New York: Hill & Wang, 1992), 23.

10 Kendall, "Public Relations Employment."

11 Gay Wakefield and Laura Perkins Cottone, "Education for the '80s and Beyond," *Public Relations Review,* Summer 1986, 37.

12 Janis Brett-Elspas, "Recession Teaches Practitioners Hard Lessons," *Public Relations Journal,* June 1992, 25.

13 "Finding That First Job in Public Relations," booklet published by the Dow Chemical Company, 1985.

14 "Your Business Partner for Life," booklet published by the International Association of Business Communicators, 1992.

15 *Careers in Public Relations,* published by the Public Relations Society of America, undated.

16 James H. Dowling, "Public Relations in the Year 2000," *Public Relations Journal,* January 1990, 6.

17 "Will Europe Be the Next Frontier?" *Public Relations Journal,* December 1991, 10.

18 Dowling, "Public Relations in the Year 2000."

19 Murray J. Lubliner, "The Age of Transnational Identity," *Public Relations Quarterly,* Winter 1992, 23.

20 See especially Dr. Kathy Bloomgarden, "The Communication Function in a Global Market," brochure published by Ruder Finn, New York, 1992. It should be added that PR counselors who serve foreign interests must register under the Foreign Agents Registration Act, whether they are lobbyists or not.

21 Lillian Lodge Kopenhaver, "Aligning Values of Practitioners and Journalists," *Public Relations Review,* Summer 1985, 34.

22 Lynne Masel Walters and Timothy N. Walters, "Environment of Confidence: Daily Newspaper Use of Press Releases," *Public Relations Review,* 18:1 (1992), 31.

23 Quoted in Cutlip, Center, and Broom, *Effective Public Relations,* 430.

24 Ibid.

chapter

0

Advertising

The scene: a modern supermarket, small by urban standards, but much the largest grocery store in this dusty southwestern town. It is Monday morning, and inside the manager's office

Objectives

When you have finished studying this chapter, you should be able to:

@ Define various forms that advertising takes and explain the differences among them

@ Describe how the creative response to a marketing problem may be developed

@ Apply such measurements as cost per thousand, reach, frequency, and gross rating points to the development of a simple media-buying plan

@ Discuss current criticisms of the advertising field as well as industry responses to such criticisms

The scene: a modern supermarket, small by urban standards, but much the largest grocery store in this dusty southwestern town. It is Monday morning, and inside the manager's office store executives huddle around a small conference table, drawing up a list of goods to be featured in this week's full-page ad in the community newspaper. For more than an hour, the manager and his assistants have been poring over recent orders and cost figures, searching for items that could be marked down, if only slightly, to lure shoppers into the store. Since the management prides itself on razor-thin profit margins anyway, further price cuts are not easily arrived at. Some products are already priced below actual cost—tempting bargains, the losses from which, with luck, the store can recoup through profits on impulse items a customer may buy on the same shopping errand. An item sold below cost to attract customers is called a loss leader.

"At least we know what our loss leader will be this week," the store manager says. "Yes," an assistant agrees. "Let me make sure I have the copy right: COLAS: $1 A CASE (Limit 1) with Coupon and $10 Purchase."

Through the glass partition, the manager can observe most of the supermarket's main floor. Across one entire wall, stock clerks are relocating canned goods and replacing them, for this week only, with hundreds of cases of soft drinks. "Those cases are heavy," the manager remarks. "Customers will need help getting 'em out to their cars. We'd better hire plenty of extra sackers Thursday through Saturday. If this ad works, we're gonna need 'em."

The newspaper rolls off the press and goes into the mail and on the newsracks Wednesday night. Early Thursday morning, it becomes apparent that the supermarket's advertisement is indeed going to "work." Hundreds of customers, nearly all clutching coupons, flow into the store. Throughout the day, sackers lug case after case of soft drinks outside to waiting cars, station wagons, and pickup trucks. The wall of colas melts away. By Friday night, the soft drinks are gone altogether, and the store management happily issues "rain checks" promising to make good the same terms to disappointed shoppers. Business has been brisk and, the loss leader notwithstanding, profitable.

This little story, true but by no means unusual, helps illustrate the vital role advertising has come to play in American life. An offer to sell a case of soft drinks for one dollar is clearly a bargain; those cases would have sold anyway, without advertising. *But they almost certainly would not have sold within forty-eight hours.* And this, in its simplest and most direct form, reflects what advertising does best for the economy—it speeds up the marketing process. Advertising provides consumers information to trigger buying decisions, decisions that move goods off shelves, prompting manufacturers to produce more, thereby increasing jobs and payrolls. Not often are the results as clear-cut and dramatic as the soft drink example suggests. Much advertising, in fact, does not lead directly to a sale at all; instead it attempts to develop

Teaching Idea

Ask students to bring in the local paper's grocery ads. Do the ads feature loss leaders and bargains? Does there seem to be a lot of competition? How many and what types of coupons are offered?

Write It Down: Advertising Works!

A rather meaningless debate has gone on for some time as to who said (or first said), "I know half of my advertising is wasted; the problem is I don't know which half."

Was it John Wanamaker or Lord Leverhulme?

More to the point, would either admit to authorship today?

For to announce, in the 1990s, that one is wasting half of one's advertising budget would be grounds for dismissal. To imply that one didn't know what part of the investment wasn't producing would be evidence of incompetence.

We know that advertising works. We know that the brand that advertises more than its competitors increases its share of the market and, as a result, its return on investment. This is not self-serving speculation; it is documented fact.

John O'Toole, President and CEO, American Association of Advertising Agencies.

or enhance an image, or to reposition a product in the minds of consumers. The sales, advertisers hope, will then follow. In any case, advertising helps grease the skids, making business move faster.

Additionally, advertising helps bankroll the media of mass communications. Today's 25-to-75-cent newspaper would cost two dollars or more without advertising. Network television, if it could exist at all, would entail a heavy tax on each TV receiver—either that, or government would own and control the television industry and might or might not permit journalists full freedom to report and comment upon the news. Governments do not tend to produce courageous newspaper editors or broadcast news directors. The media of mass communications are expensive to establish and maintain. The expense must be borne chiefly by (1) the audiences themselves, at greatly increased costs for individuals and families; (2) the government, through increased taxation—and probably tighter restrictions; or (3) the private economy, through revenue generated by advertising. Advertising has kept U.S. communications media essentially in private hands. Our society is almost certainly better off, and better informed, as a result.

Advertising also provides consumers with the information they need to make purchasing decisions. Indeed, with the trend in recent years toward *direct marketing*—selling to consumers at home through catalogues and other means, bypassing retail stores altogether—advertising may supply consumers with the *only* information they obtain before making a purchasing decision. Finally, advertising is important as a career field, one in which creative and communications skills may be, and often are, richly rewarded.

Terminology

During the early years of this century, well before the broadcast media came along, advertising was defined as "salesmanship in print."[1] That snappy phrase, though out of date, makes a point: Advertising does utilize the mass media, and most advertising exists purely and simply to sell. A better definition of today's advertising might be *paid communication by identified individuals or organizations attempting to inform or influence an audience.*

In distinguishing advertising from other types of communications, it is important to note that true advertising is indeed paid for—as opposed to publicity, which might be published or broadcast for free. Advertising messages identify their sponsor; publicity, propaganda, or promotional materials may not.

Advertising is classified by type:

1 *National* or *regional* advertising is designed to establish the value of a product or service in the mind of the consumer, who is then encouraged to buy it wherever it is sold.

Background

Newspapers have experimented with obtaining support entirely from subscribers, but without much success. The most famous was *PM*, a New York tabloid published in the 1940s.

Teaching Idea

Have the class compare this definition with the one for propaganda in the previous chapter, discussing the similarities and differences.

Background

Some advertising is "co-op"—that is, a national advertiser sends copy to its local outlet, which adds the local information and places the ad in the paper. The national advertiser and local dealer split the cost. TV and radio advertisers use the same method.

Aiming at Your Mind: How Many Ads Each Day?

The controversy has been raging for many years: How many advertising messages does a person really see in a day?

A hypothetical family of four is exposed to advertising 1,518 times a day, according to a 1957 speech by Edwin Ebel, then vice president/advertising at General Foods.

Exposures noticed by people per day: 76, according to a 1968 report, "Advertising in America: The Consumer View," in which 750 people were asked to count the number of ad messages they saw throughout the day.

TV Dimensions said in 1989 that there are 139 actual exposures and 255 potential ones in a day. The difference is the amount of attention given to each ad.

Agency magazine, fall 1990.

2 *Local,* or *retail,* advertising encourages a consumer to trade at a particular store.

3 *Direct response* advertising encourages the consumer to buy directly from the manufacturer or distributor. While national or retail advertising may simply hope to arouse a spark of interest in the product, perhaps enough to inspire customers to consult salespeople in the nearest store, direct response advertising attempts to sell the product outright without benefit of intermediaries.

4 *Trade,* or *business-to-business,* advertising, much of which the general public does not see, includes messages to wholesalers and dealers urging them to stock items in their stores so that consumers have access to them. Suppose the Pearly Toothpaste Company has developed a new formula that will dramatically reduce tooth and gum deterioration. A major advertising campaign is planned for September, utilizing network television and consumer magazines. Well before September, the Pearly people will launch another, equally essential, advertising campaign through trade journals to alert drug store and supermarket buying executives so they can have the product *in stock* when consumers first hear about it.

5 *Professional* advertising targets physicians, dentists, architects, interior decorators, and others who are not themselves customers but who might influence the purchasing decisions of others.

6 *Institutional* advertising is designed to sell an entire company, or even an idea, rather than a specific product. These messages are especially targeted at stockholders, employees, and the general public. An ad exhorting consumers to buy a new-model Acme personal computer would obviously be a product ad; if, on the other hand, the ad copy described Acme as a responsible, innovative, caring company that practiced good corporate citizenship, then the ad would be classified as institutional.

Extra Information
One example of direct response advertising is the "have-your-credit-card-ready-and-call-this-800-number" ad on TV. Some of these ads are billed "PI" or "per inquiry," meaning that the station is paid according to the number of responses.

Teaching Idea
Assign students to find and bring to class examples of trade, professional, and institutional advertising.

How the Industry Evolved

Advertising is as old as trade, which is to say that the first advertising came the moment some primitive human decided to announce publicly that he or she had something of value and was prepared to barter for something else.[2] As labor became more specialized, those who produced bread, shoes, and other products walked through the streets hawking their wares. Later, places of business adopted symbols to advertise: A green branch displayed over a shop door indicated that new wine was available; a striped pole announced the presence of a barber, who was probably a part-time surgeon as well; a coat of arms signified an inn. **Trade marks,** which conferred prestige on certain businesses and assisted customers who could not read, stem from the Middle Ages.

Advertising's pace, like that of civilization itself, kicked into a much higher gear about halfway through the fifteenth century with the invention of movable type, which gave rise to printing on a mass scale. John Campbell, whose Boston *News-Letter* was this country's first continuously published newspaper, printed the first colonial ad in 1704; it was a lost-and-found notice from a man who had inexplicably misplaced two anvils.[3]

Benjamin Franklin, associated with so many attainments in early American life—he is affectionately remembered by the industry as the first person in this country ever to make a fortune in the mass communications business—published the first magazine advertisement.[4] Indeed, some scholars today consider Ben Franklin the father of American advertising. Certainly he was a gifted copywriter. Consider the fol-

Teaching Idea
For fun, have students look through the lost-and-found classified ads in the local or regional daily. Are there any "oddball" ads?

lowing, which he penned to sell another invention of his, the Pennsylvania Fire-place—or, as it became better known, the Franklin Stove:

> Fireplaces with small openings cause draughts of cold air to rush in at every crevice, and 'tis very uncomfortable as well as dangerous to sit against any such crevice. . . . Women, particularly from this cause (as they sit so much in the house) get cold in the head, rheums and deflexions which fall into their jaws and gums, and have destroyed early, many a fine set of teeth in these northern colonies.[5]

But it was the Penny Press publishers, beginning in the 1830s with Benjamin Day and James Gordon Bennett, who truly grasped the possibilities advertising could offer to the newspaper field. They courted the mass audience, knowing that if a newspaper attracted a substantial number of customers, the advertisers would pay to reach them. A few years later, enough railroads had been built to create national markets, and thus the demand for national brands. National magazines then emerged to serve them.

Until then, businesspeople who had wanted to place advertising with news-papers and magazines had to deal directly with the publishers—not an easy task, given the bewildering differences among publications in page sizes, column widths, space rates, publication deadlines, and mechanical requirements. It was at this point that America's first *advertising agent,* Volney B. Palmer, arrived on the scene. Initially at least, Palmer did not provide creative assistance. Instead, he was a broker who contracted for large blocks of space in newspapers and magazines, then sold the space to businesses that had advertising messages to run. Palmer bought the space at volume discounts and made his profit by selling to advertisers full price, which the businesses would have had to pay anyway. In effect, they got Palmer's services for nothing.

Soon clients came to rely upon the agencies to prepare their advertising as well as place it in appropriate media. F. Wayland Ayer founded what would become the first full-service agency in 1869. All of twenty years old at the time, and fearful that no one would want to spend important dollars with someone so young, he de-cided to name the agency N. W. Ayer & Son, though his father was never involved in the business except symbolically. Other pioneers of the modern agency include Al-bert Lasker, whose hard-driving sales techniques moved goods off the shelves and convinced business leaders of the value of big-time advertising budgets, and Claude Hopkins, a talented copywriter who could explain a product's benefits to consumers in ways that made buying it easier. Hopkins and another early copywriter, John E. Powers, relied upon simple, direct, sincere language. Their style flew in the face of the overblown, boastful claims noised about at the time and helped elevate the advertising industry to a new plateau.

World War I, initially an unpopular cause, provided a massive challenge for the advertising industry as government mounted an all-out effort to shore up morale and mobilize the country. Patriotic themes, employed by the Committee on Public Information as well as by private corporations, rang out across the country.[6] News-papers and national magazines dramatically increased their circulations during this period. By the time the first radio advertising appeared in 1922, the country had come to accept advertising messages as inevitable.

While the depression of the 1930s affected all businesses in different ways, nearly all of them bad, it did force advertisers to become more selective. Market re-search received a strong boost during this period, since clients required more specific information before authorizing big advertising campaigns. Audience rating services measured people's taste in publications and radio programs, while consumer and product research probed the mysteries of sales resistance, and why a customer might choose one brand over another. By the time the economy pulled back up to speed, advertisers knew far more about their markets and the media they depended upon to reach them. They allocated advertising dollars much more shrewdly.

Background

For there to be a mass market, there had to be a rapid and dependable way for ads to reach customers and for customers to obtain the goods advertised. For over a century the railroads provided this service. Remember, Sears of Sears and Roebuck got his start as a railroad station agent who advertised.

Teaching Idea

Ask students to copy old ads from back copies of magazines in your institution's library and compare them with today's magazine ads.

Television advertising appeared as early as 1939, but World War II delayed its development. By the late 1940s, however, television's unique ability to combine words and pictures, sights and sounds, was already making it an integral part of American culture.

Why Advertising Has Grown

No single, simplistic explanation exists as to why advertising has developed into so potent a force in our lives. Many factors are involved, among them:

1 *A psychological maturing.* Americans have become a nation of cash customers willing to, as the carnival barkers put it, "pays your money and takes your choice." Political scientists tell us that expressing opinions is a rather new concept for much of the world. Many people, especially those who live in developing nations, require strong, personal leadership. Not so in the United States, where self-starting individuals are willing to seek out information and act accordingly.

2 *Prosperity and the rise of a middle class.* Dramatic increases in disposable income make it possible for Americans to buy far more than the basic necessities. Millions of us have at least some extra money to spend, and advertising is the product of a tireless, ever-present sales staff trying to help us reach buying decisions.

3 *Improved transportation.* More products and more regional distribution centers put us within reach of far more shopping facilities. This has led to wider choices, increased competition, and expanded advertising campaigns.

4 *More credit.* Dramatic increases in the availability and acceptance of personal credit have stimulated consumer demand and boosted sales.

5 *Less personal selling.* Not so many years ago, a homemaker intent on buying groceries would be met at the door of the market by the store owner, who would grab a shopping basket and accompany her on her rounds. Often he would discuss with her the relative merits of a particular brand of coffee or an improved laundry detergent. No more. Today's shopper is likely to arrive at the market armed with a prepared list, usually mentioning specific brand names. *The customer, in other words, has been pre-sold before entering the store.* The store manager most probably will be nowhere in sight, and the only employee the shopper may encounter will be at the checkout stand. For thousands of retailers, advertising has replaced the personal salesclerk.

6 *Better media.* If advertising has strengthened the media of mass communications, so stronger and more diversified media have enhanced advertising's ability to reach specific audiences. This effectiveness in pinpointing markets has prompted many more businesses to adopt and enlarge advertising commitments.

7 *Better advertising.* Today's commercial messages, for the most part, are creative and handsomely produced. They reflect better research, testing, and marketing techniques than ever before. The industry has grown because it has continued to improve in quality and effectiveness.

One of the most successful advertisements, published early in the twentieth century, helped change U.S. eating habits.

The Industry Today

Advertising in the 1990s has become a $132-billion-a-year business, employing perhaps as many as 400,000 persons.

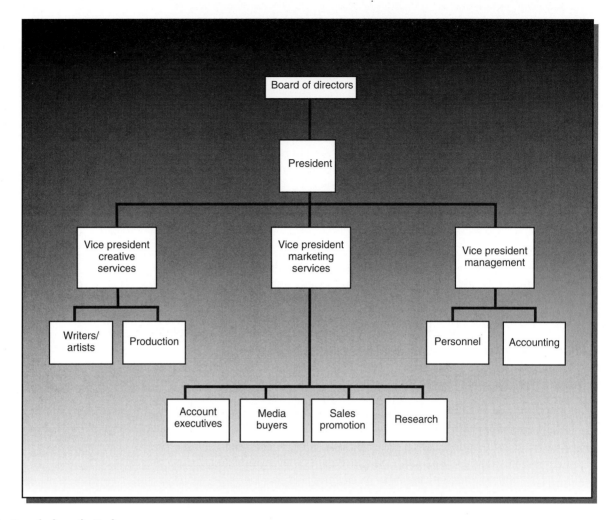

Basic organization of a hypothetical full-service agency.

Advertising Agencies

Full-service agencies provide market research, creative services, media planning (advertising placement), and *sales promotion,* which might include coupons, contests, and premiums, as well as a variety of additional types of support for their clients. Often agencies also provide public relations services—a comprehensive plan of *integrated marketing communications.* Some agencies, called **boutiques** or **creative boutiques,** do message preparation only. Others, often referred to as **media buying houses,** specialize in recommending media strategies and in placing advertisements in various print and broadcast media.

Census figures indicate there are more than ten thousand advertising agencies in the United States. While most of them remain fairly small, the largest agencies are very large indeed, with hundreds of employees and sales—as measured by their *billings,* the advertising they process—that may run into hundreds of millions of dollars a year.

Agencies make their money from commissions, fees, and percentage charges on services and materials they purchase for their clients. Commission income, the biggest source of revenue for most larger agencies, comes in the form of a discount the media provide to "recognized" advertising agencies. Discounts work this way: Assume that the rate for a full-page ad in a given magazine is $40,000. A recognized agency might be awarded a 15 percent discount of $6,000. The net amount the agency would pay for the page is thus $34,000. Since the client would have to pay $40,000 in any case, it makes sense to use the advertising agency, which will develop the advertisement with more expertise and polish than the client could do alone.

Agency compensation is far more complicated than this simple example suggests. For one thing, an agency that pays the media in cash normally receives an additional 2 percent cash discount. And the agency, in preparing the ad, may well incur research and production costs it will charge the client for, along with a price markup for its services. Both agency leaders and clients have roundly criticized the commission system in recent years. And a number of agencies have negotiated commissions at rates other than 15 percent. The agency people argue that it may take as much creative time and talent to prepare an ad for a tiny trade journal as for a lavish national magazine, yet the trade journal ad may bring in only one-tenth the commission. But the majority of advertising income remains commission-based; only a fraction of ad agencies operate purely on a fee basis.

Advertising Departments

Most businesses engage in some sort of advertising or promotion. In smaller firms, the advertising department develops and places the advertising itself; local media may well refuse to grant the 15 percent commission to purely local advertising. Some companies deal with this problem by creating their own **house agency.** In larger concerns, the advertising department will serve as liaison with the company's advertising agency, recommending which agency to choose and evaluating the agency's creative and marketing performance.

Media Advertising Staffs

Newspapers, magazines, and radio and television station advertising staffs are actually sales departments. A media sales representative, or "rep," often becomes a one-person ad agency, responsible for developing an idea, presenting it to the client, securing the order, and producing the advertisement. This is valuable training. Many young people enter the advertising field via the media route.

Thousands of other persons in related jobs also earn their living directly from the advertising field in art studios, graphic design houses, film production companies, direct mail operations, commercial photography and recording studios, and supply companies.

Creating and Delivering the Advertising Message

Advertising is not an end in itself, though many advertisements may be, in their own ways, works of art. The important thing is for the potential customer to remember the theme of the ad, not merely the ad itself. Thus, a creative and otherwise brilliant advertising message might prove useless ("Cute ad, but what was it selling?"), while other ads, duller and homelier, seem to endure forever, for the very sensible reason that they move goods off the shelves.

In this section we will look at how advertising messages are developed and distributed. We will see that the typical ad campaign does not erupt from one sublime burst of spontaneous fervor, but instead evolves through a series of strategic and tactical plans designed to reach the right people at the right time with a carefully crafted message that will trigger the "right" response.

Campaign Research

An advertising campaign is a planned effort that extends for a specified period of time in behalf of a given product or service. It begins with an attempt to find the best answers to a number of questions that help define the marketing problem. Some of the things an advertiser will want to know are

Extra Information

Radio and TV advertising time sales and newspaper advertising space sales can be very profitable. Many stations and papers pay up to 15 percent commission. Students sometimes overlook sales careers, particularly if they consider themselves shy. While not as glamorous as creating ads, ad sales can be more profitable.

- Who uses the product and why?
- What are the buying habits of the potential customers?
- Who makes the buying decisions?
- Which media are these decision makers most likely to rely upon?
- Which sales appeals are strongest and most persuasive?
- What attitude problems, if any, must be dealt with?
- What is our competitive situation? What can we do to improve it?

One phase of the research will focus on *consumer* opinions and attitudes toward the product or service itself—how the person who buys it perceives it, or, perhaps more accurately, the person who logically should buy but doesn't. Such research may suggest the need change packaging, for instance; with the increase in customer self-service and self-selection, packaging has taken on dramatic new prominence.

Can Advertising Change Attitudes?

One case study suggests that it very well might. The Partnership for a Drug-Free America formed in 1986 in response to growing national alarm over drug abuse. Using both print and broadcast media, the Partnership launched a vigorous campaign to "unsell" drugs. An estimated billion dollars worth of advertising—the creative talent, media space, and time were

Advertising techniques can successfully address social problems. Agencies often donate creative services as well as media presentations to produce public service announcements.

donated—attacked the use of drugs. The Partnership's campaign was based on the theory that attitudinal change is a precondition for reducing the demand for illegal drugs, particularly marijuana, cocaine, and crack.

A five-year tracking study, concluded in 1991, reported these findings:

- The attitudes of children (ages 9–12) toward drug use are becoming more negative over time.

- More parents are talking to their children about using drugs now than in 1987.

- Fewer children report that their siblings use marijuana now than in 1987. In addition, 48 percent of children report that siblings have warned them not to try drugs.

- Children report that marijuana is becoming more difficult to obtain.

Where adults (18 and older) are concerned, strong evidence suggested that exposure to, and recall of, Partnership advertising messages did in fact produce behavior change:

Recall of Partnership Messages (Television and Radio)

Affirmative Response to:	Adults Who Recalled Less Than 2 Ads (%)	Adults Who Recalled 5 or More Ads (%)
To what extent are you less likely to use cocaine in the future?	48%	59%
To what extent are you less likely to use marijuana in the future?	35	45
In the past twelve months have you disapproved of pot at a party?	19	39
In the past twelve months have you discussed the dangers of drugs with your kids?	35	56

Source: Partnership for a Drug-Free America, Five-Year Tracking Study conducted by the Gordon S. Black Corporation, 1991.

Market research. Dana Point, California, children sample and evaluate a local resort hotel restaurant's fare to aid in compiling a children's menu.

Positioning the product in the mind of the consumer. In this case, a soft drink company reassures a new generation.

One snack food manufacturer proudly advertised that its foil liner kept the munchies fresher longer; research revealed, however, that many customers resented the foil liner, believing it made the snacks more expensive than they would be otherwise. Besides, as the customers pointed out, the snacks, once opened, never lasted long enough to grow stale anyway. The package was changed, with profitable results.

Consumer Research

Consumer research helps the advertiser target specific audiences, or **target markets,** in various ways. Among the most common types are

1 ***Demographic*** *profiles.* Age, sex, income level, educational level, occupation, size of the family, stage in the family life cycle, religion, and race influence reception of advertising messages and buying decisions. African American families, for example, tend to save a higher percentage of their income than white families; they buy more milk and soft drinks, but less coffee and tea.[7] A family's life cycle will obviously affect its buying patterns; a "full nest" household shops differently from an "empty nest" home, for

Extra Information

Much demographic information comes from U.S. Census Bureau reports, available to ad agencies in computer formats. Also, warranty cards for many products ask that the consumer include demographic information before returning them, and magazines sometimes sell subscribers' names and addresses to other publications or direct mail marketers.

Advertising's Environment for the 1990s

In a speech to newspaper advertising executives, Owen Landon, Jr., who heads a leading newspaper advertising sales firm, predicted these economic conditions for the years ahead:

- The 50-and-older age group will grow by 18.5 percent, to 76 million. By comparison, the group under age 50 will grow by only 3.5 percent.

- Advertising to "mature market" consumers will reflect at least these seven concerns: (1) the home; (2) health care; (3) leisure time; (4) personal and business counseling; (5) educational services; (6) financial products and services; and (7) products that combat aging.

- By the end of the 1990s, 80 percent of all Americans will live in metropolitan areas. Half of that 80 percent will live in suburbia.

- The changing markets will result in an influx of retail chains in suburbia, creating a glut of consumer options and—through intense competition—diminished retail profit opportunities. This will force advertisers to target more tightly, more intelligently, and more cost-efficiently than ever before.

Bulletin of the Southern Newspaper Publishers Association, 1991.

example. Sexual stereotypes, which advertisers at one time thought were easy to identify, now are blurring—as more and more women enter the work force, their buying habits no longer fit conventional molds. Old appeals, based largely on emotion, are being replaced by an emphasis on value, ability to pay, and increased wants and needs.

2 *Geographic profiles* may also need to be taken into account. Southerners consume more soft drinks per capita than New Englanders. Coffee and alcohol don't sell well in Utah because Mormons disapprove of these products. Urban audiences respond better to some advertising appeals, worse to others, than their small-town counterparts.

3 **Psychographics** analyze potential customers by their lifestyles and the sociopsychological factors that influence them. Two young professionals may share the same office, for example; each has a bachelor's degree, and each earns a yearly salary of $35,000. But one hopes in time to buy a house; he is saving as much of his income as he can. When he does spend money, he invests in furniture and appliances, big-ticket items that fit into his long-term plans. Meanwhile, his friend at the next desk enjoys travel and leisure. Her disposable income goes for vacations, entertainment, trendy clothes, and sports equipment. An advertiser attempting to sell a pricey new workout suit has an excellent prospect in the second but is wasting time with the other.

Psychographic classifications are developed through careful interviews with a small but representative sample, then projected to national proportions. One example is the Media and Market Study questionnaire used by the Simmons Market Research Bureau. Advertisers find these services invaluable as they attempt to discover who their customers are, where they can be reached, and what types of selling appeals are most likely to succeed.

The Creative Response[8]

At times, especially in smaller agencies, one person will conceive, develop, polish, present, and execute an advertising campaign. More commonly, however, a creative team of copywriters, artists, and production people accomplish these tasks. An **account executive** oversees the team's labors and ultimately presents their recommendations to the client for approval. By now, the agency's research staff will have provided solid information about the product or service and the primary prospects for buying it. After much discussion, in which they consider numerous approaches, the copywriter and artist can begin developing their ideas.

Suppose the creative team is assigned to produce an advertising campaign for Affordable Rent-a-Car, an up-and-coming automobile rental company offering lower prices in an attempt to compete with the larger and more established industry leaders. The copywriter might first set down key strategic points that the finished advertisements must address. Early on, he or she would develop answers to these questions:

- *What is our target audience?* In this case, it may be working men and women between ages twenty-five and sixty, or business executives whose jobs entail considerable air travel.
- *What is the most important idea of the ad?* Affordable has arrived as a major competitor in the car rental field.
- *What is the most important selling feature?* Equal service at lower cost.
- *What other important sales features should we stress?* Convenient locations at most major airports; courteous service; prompt, simplified processing; excellent maintenance standards.

- *What do we want the reader/viewer to do?* Be convinced that we offer the same quality for less money.

Bearing these essentials firmly in mind, the copywriter then begins to develop the text. There are some similarities between writing news and writing ad copy; in both cases, the copy should be interesting, lean, and to the point. But there are differences as well. While the news reporter rarely writes his or her own headlines, the ad copywriter or art director always does. And while the elements of a news story may be presented in order of descending importance—the inverted pyramid—ad copy might be organized this way:[9]

- *A headline.* To capture the reader's attention and to select prospects for the ad.
- *Development of the headline.* Perhaps answering a question the headline poses.
- *Explanation of benefits.* Where the serious selling is done.
- *Proof of unusual claims.* Nailing down credibility.
- *Further advantages.* Secondary benefits.
- *The closing.* Where the ad "asks for the order," that is, tells the reader/viewer what action to take.

Not every ad embodies each of these elements. Nor are ad copywriters given the opportunity—or space or time—to explain any of the elements at length. Often the finished copy of an advertisement may run well under fifty words.

The artist, meanwhile, is sketching a layout for the ad—while remaining in close touch with the copywriter. At one time, a lordly copywriter might have thrust a text at an artist and said, "Here's the copy, now illustrate it." Or an artist might have insisted, "Here's how I want the ad to look. Please write me some words to fit this copy block." Not so now. Teamwork between copywriter and artist dictates that text and visual ideas develop together. As the writer searches for just the right phrases, the artist strives for a design that presents the idea most effectively.

Creating Commercials for Television

Up to now we have been thinking in terms of a creative campaign for the print media, and most of the ads for Affordable Rent-a-Car will be placed in such publications as in-flight magazines and business journals. The electronic media, however, pose a very different set of creative challenges.

Those Fleeting Ad Images

If you think the world moves fast, try watching commercials.

A 60-second Pepsi-Cola ad takes a boy from age 12 to retirement. A 90-second Nike spot sends Michael Jordan to Mars and back. A 30-second Little Caesar's commercial follows a speeding gurney as it races through a hospital corridor and cuts through five different story lines.

Advertising is picking up speed. After more than 45 years of watching television commercials, after more than a decade of MTV and video games, viewers are used to a barrage of visual stimuli. In fact, younger viewers demand it. So television commercials move blindingly fast: Sometimes hundreds of images are crammed into 30 seconds. To follow the story in Nike's 1993 Super Bowl ad, in which Jordan and Bugs Bunny battle Marvin the Martian and his flock of giant green chickens, you probably needed super-slow motion on your VCR.

Martha T. Moore in *USA Today*, 15 June 1993.

Teaching Idea

Assign students to count the number of commercials on a particular channel during a one-hour period. Did any ads for *competitive* products appear close together? How much of the hour did commercials take up?

Looming large among these is the sheer magnitude, in terms of numbers, of commercial messages telecast around the clock. The typical American family, which may watch several hours of television each day, may be exposed to a hundred or more commercials during that time. Most they ignore outright or else soon forget. The truly memorable commercial is hard to come by. Those that do succeed—through some mysterious combination of sights and sounds, words and music, hard sell and soft sell, common sense as well as deep emotional appeals—become a part of our lives.

Making a TV commercial requires close and continuous cooperation among members of a creative team which includes, at a minimum, a copywriter and an art director/producer. Their objective is to communicate a single, powerful selling message within a rigid time span. Most commercials run 15, 20, or 30 seconds; few are longer. The brevity still permits the resourceful advertiser a certain amount of flexibility in approach and style. The creative team might decide upon a *testimonial* format, or a *standup* "presenter" talking directly into the camera. They might stage a miniature drama, or *vignette,* complete with setting, conflict, and happy resolution. If the product lends itself to one, they might choose a *demonstration;* television affords ideal opportunities to show how a product works, and why. Or the creative team might opt for a full-blown *song-and-dance production number,* or even an *animated cartoon.*

Once the format is agreed upon, the **storyboard,** comparable to the layout in a print ad, can begin taking shape. Sets of sketches not unlike comic strips, the "boards" describe the setting for each scene and include script copy, music, and special effects. A shooting script containing precise instructions may eventually accompany some storyboards. The client must approve both the storyboard and the script. After that, the agency will contact production houses for competitive bidding on shooting the commercial.

The shooting script, meanwhile, will pass on to the agency's legal department and various other authorities, such as the acceptability offices of the television networks for approval. What are these "censors" looking for? Any trace of fraud or deception, intentional or otherwise; claims the advertiser cannot verify; copy that may be in poor taste, suggestive, or even faintly misleading; ideas that may promote illegal activity or defame a competitor.

Once the script clears these legal hurdles and the advertiser chooses a production house, the actual making of the commercial can begin. Talent casting, all important, is now often a matter of screening actors and actresses via videotape; no longer does each major commercial require a casting trip to the West Coast or New York. The production house provides the director, assistant director, camera and sound crews, set designers, makeup experts, and hair stylists. The storyboard becomes a kind of road map for the actual shooting. Music comes later. None of this is cheap. In 1993, a 30-second TV commercial could cost several hundred thousand dollars just to produce. Showing it with any frequency, especially during network prime time, could cost millions more.

Developing the Media Plan

No matter how brilliant the finished advertisements are, the entire campaign will go for naught unless the proper audiences see or hear the ads. While the agency's creative staff is writing and producing the messages, the media department is cranking out a plan for delivering them effectively. The task won't be easy; in the United States there are nearly 1,600 daily newspapers and 7,500 weeklies, 1,128 television stations and 11,253 AM and FM radio stations, 11,556 consumer and farm magazines

1. (MUSIC: UNDER THROUGHOUT)

2. KID: What'cha doin?

3. MOTHER: The dishes.

4. KID: I thought the dishwasher does the dishes.

5. MOTHER: It does.

6. (MUSIC)

7. (AVO): It does...

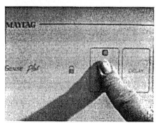

8. if it's a Maytag Jetclean Dishwasher.

9. It cleans with 43 powerful jets...

10. that way you never have to...

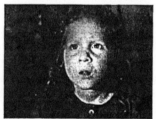

11. wash all the dishes...

12. before you wash all the dishes.

13. GORDON: Unless, of course, you're looking for something to do.

14. (AVO): Maytag. The Dependability People.

15. (:05 TAG)

A storyboard from the "Lonely Repairman" commercial from Maytag.

and trade journals as well as several hundred thousand billboards—not to mention millions of car cards (posters inside mass transit vehicles) and specialty and premium advertising media. No one client can buy into them all, so the media people must make some choices.

Each media plan will reflect the agency's best research findings as to which audiences should be targeted. No two media plans will be exactly alike. Similarly, each medium of mass communications has strengths and weaknesses insofar as delivering audiences. Table 1 describes some pertinent considerations.

Costs

The mass media base their advertising charges to a very great extent on the size of the audience they expect to reach. The more people that will be exposed to a 30-second spot or a half-page ad, the more money advertisers are willing to pay. This helps explain why newspapers and magazines constantly seem to be hustling new subscribers, and why TV networks worry so much about the "ratings" such firms as Nielsen and Arbitron report. Bigger audiences represent convincing arguments for high ad rates; declining audiences make advertising buyers suspicious.

But precise unit costs, on a comparative basis, may be difficult to fathom. A media planner attempting to buy space or time across various media runs headlong into an array of numbers and terms that can seem bewildering. One yardstick, useful for comparing the efficiency of advertising media, is the **cost per thousand.** CPMs, as they are called, represent the cost to an advertiser of delivering an advertising

table 1   Advantages and Disadvantages of Different Media

Medium	Advantages	Disadvantages
Newspapers	Flexible, fast (late deadlines make last-minute changes possible). Readers *like* newspaper ads; couponing available; precise geographic targeting capability; good audience measuring data.	Short life span; easy for ads to get lost in bigger editions; poor-quality reproduction on many papers; color uneven; lack of selectivity.
Magazines	Reach more selective audiences; long life span means many chances for ad to be seen; excellent color; readers control ad exposure; many magazines enjoy high prestige; high pass-along readership.	Slow closings (several weeks, usually) make it impossible to change ads at last minute. Zoned editions may not be available to cover specific geographic regions desired.
Radio	Immediate; mobile; highly flexible; possible to target specific audiences, both geographically and psychographically.	Fleeting quality affects attention intensity; fragmented audiences; precise measurement data for audiences difficult to get.
Television	Powerful impact; mass coverage; flexibility.	Mass audiences that must be paid for necessarily include many who are not good prospects; high costs; "commercial clutter" affects viewer attention span.
Outdoor	High impact (larger-than-life image); high reach and frequency (assuming the billboard is on a busy route).	Limited copy message (6–8 words, usually); landscape clutter.

message to a thousand readers, viewers, or listeners. CPMs are computed by multiplying the unit cost by 1,000, then dividing by the number of prospects reached. Suppose the black-and-white full-page ad rate is $7,500 for a farm magazine with a circulation of 468,000. The cost per thousand would be

$$\frac{\$7,500 \times 1,000}{458,000} = \$16.37 \text{ CPM}$$

The advertiser can compare this with the CPM for a 30-second network commercial costing $220,000 and shown on a prime-time show with an estimated audience of 24 million:

$$\frac{\$220,000 \times 1,000}{24,000,000} = \$9.16 \text{ CPM}$$

But the CPM reveals only part of the story. If the product to be sold is a piece of agricultural equipment, there may be more genuine prospects among the 458,000 farm magazine readers than among the 24 million viewers of the TV message. So despite its higher CPM, the farm publication may present the better buy.

Just to complicate the picture further, consider that each medium's advertising rate may vary, depending on the volume purchased and the services required. A newspaper's **open rate** is for one-time-only clients, or for advertisers who don't buy much space. More frequent customers receive a volume discount, called an **earned rate,** which often scales down the unit costs considerably. Often advertisers placing ads requiring the use of color, or ads with **preferred position**—on a specific page or, with a magazine, on the inside back cover—can expect extra charges. Otherwise, the ad may appear **ROP**—run of the paper—that is, anyplace. Television charges have become so complex and diverse that each purchase often amounts to a separate deal; a commercial on a prime-time situation comedy may cost $175,000—unless that sit-com has become enormously popular, in which case the price may run far higher.

Still More Measurements

An editor may think lovingly of his or her publication in terms of its journalistic soul, its courageous investigative reporting achievements, the literary quality of its writing, its daring graphic design, or its proud tradition of public or intellectual service. Advertising media planners do take into account the quality of the audience and the environment in which their ads will appear. But in essence, the media vehicle, as it's called, must be counted upon to deliver a certain audience. The media buyer's job is to reach as many target prospects for a client as possible, given the limited funds available. The media buyer might personally subscribe to, and admire, Magazine A. But if a particular client's best prospects are among the readers of Magazine B, then that's where the media buyer will spend advertising dollars for this client.

Two of the concepts a media buyer uses in deciding where the client's advertising funds will be spent are **reach** and **frequency.** Reach is the term used to describe the total *number of persons*—or, in the case of television, households—that will be exposed to an advertising message over a given period, usually four weeks.

Frequency refers to the *number of exposures* to the message that same person or household can be expected to receive during that period. Each household's reading/viewing/listening habits vary. Suppose that in a sample of 100 households we find that 45 of them, in any particular month, will view at least one episode of "The Joe Gadget Show" on the XYZ network. The show would then have a "reach" of 45. But not every household watches the show every week. We find that within our sample of 100, persons living in the 45 homes that did view "Gadget" at least once saw an average of 3 episodes during the month. Thus the program, with a reach of 45, also has an "average frequency" of 3. This gives us the information we need to compute the gross rating points, or the media weight, of the program:[10]

$$\text{Reach} \times \text{average frequency} = \text{gross rating points (GRPs)}$$
$$45 \quad \times \quad 3 \quad = 135 \text{ GRPs}$$

Gross rating points (GRPs) are useful in comparing the relative impacts of various television programs. GRPs can also be used to ascertain the impact of magazine ads, billboard exposures, radio commercials, newspaper ads, and so on. A finished media plan usually reflects the number of GRPs that will be purchased in various media, letting the client know the approximate size of the audience that the message should reach.

Media Selection

However helpful CPM, GRPs, earned rate, and other indicators may be, they still don't tell us much about the interests of the specific media audiences we are trying to influence. This means we need still more information before we can recommend a detailed media plan for our client, Affordable Rent-a-Car. Our task now is to find out which media can communicate with the most and best prospects for our client's money. Fortunately, much information is available to help us arrive at these important buying decisions.

The Simmons Market Research Bureau, among other companies in the field, each year publishes a massive study of media and markets, more than forty volumes of data in all. Thirteen or so of these volumes deal with the measurement of media audiences—newspapers, magazines, television, radio, cable, outdoor, even the Yellow Pages. The population, based on projections from a sample of 19,000 different households, is divided into twenty-seven different categories, including age, sex, income, education, occupation, marital status, number of children, geographic region, county size, and value of residence. Consumption and purchasing information for more than 800 product categories and some 3,900 brands includes, among other correlations, intermedia comparisons of heavy, medium, and light readers, viewers, and listeners by various demographic classifications. We can compare both the media and the product/brand usage data with information in other databases, such as Mediamark Research, Inc. (MRI). So, in other words, if we want to, we can find out for Affordable about how many businessmen and women between the ages of 25 and 60 who expect to rent a car within the next year will likely watch the "CBS Evening News" tomorrow night. We can also get a fair insight, assuming we want one, into the kind of coffee preferences they have and how often they buy peanut butter.

The media reps themselves can add a great deal of data about their own companies and about their competition. A salesperson, or rep, from *Better Homes and Gardens* could tell us about "Super Spot," a high-income edition of the magazine which reaches more personal computer owners than *Newsweek* or *People*. A rep from *National Geographic* could cite a recent study showing it has three times as many readers as *Playboy* with a net worth of $1 million or more.[11]

Affordable Rent-a-Car's advertising budget, not lavish, dictates that we forego network television. It's too expensive, in this situation; we'd be buying a huge audience, but one with lots of **waste circulation**—large numbers with little likelihood of response insofar as car rental prospects are concerned. The same goes for newspapers; again, that would get us an across-the-board audience; we must target better. Radio and most consumer magazines likewise aren't focused tightly enough for our purposes. Probably we'll concentrate on in-flight magazines, with perhaps some space in *USA Today,* which is popular with airline passengers, and business publications that we know are read by executives who do a great deal of commercial traveling. We might rent some outdoor space, too, for supplementary purposes, provided we can clear good billboard sites on high-traffic thoroughfares near major airports.

Our finished media plan would include our major objectives and strategies, how we defined primary target audiences, our selection of *media types* (for example, business publications and in-flight magazines), *media vehicles* (such as *Forbes* and *The Wall Street Journal*), how much volume for each, how much exposure (GRPs) this would represent, and a specific schedule, or *continuity,* and cost breakdown. This won't guarantee that Affordable's advertising campaign will be a roaring success, but it should go a long way toward assuring that the most promising prospects will receive the messages our creative people have devised, and that the client's dollars will be wisely expended.

Larger ad agencies have developed their own mathematical models for assistance in media planning, and computers now help ascertain the proper media mix for a given client. This furious number crunching can be disquieting to a journalist or television producer, for it suggests that these talented, dedicated people are not creating works of intellectual or artistic merit, but merely "audience delivery vehicles." Such an assessment oversimplifies and can be unfair. Besides, artistic quality and commercial success do not have to be mutually exclusive. In the 1990s, one of television's most consistent audience leaders continues to be "60 Minutes," a hard-hitting investigative reporting series that has won professional acclaim as well as vast popular appeal and advertising support.

Media planning is already a fact of advertising life and, given the rising costs of advertising and the proliferation of new media into the marketplace, is certain to become more intense and sophisticated in the years ahead. Editors and broadcast producers must become even more aware of and familiar with the particular audiences they serve, the people who read their publications and watch their TV programs. Advertising media buyers and research people know a lot about them already.

Advertising Under Fire

Because it is such a big, noisy business, and by definition highly visible, advertising comes in for heavy barrages of criticism. While some of the attacks are well deserved—there are charlatans in advertising as in any other endeavor—the industry nevertheless can mount a spirited defense of its role and its performance. See table 2 for some of the most common critical themes, as they have evolved over the years, and some of the arguments the industry has used by way of reply.[12]

More difficult to deal with are suggestions that advertising somehow manipulates our lives, creates unrealistic expectations, and distorts our values. Many critics argue that advertising transports us into an unreal and wholly materialistic world where life's problems can be happily resolved within the context of a 30-second

And Now for the Bad News . . .

The bad news is that advertising has a credibility gap. It isn't just late-night infomercials or the 900-numbers for adult services. It isn't just the back-of-the-book health cures that you see in the supermarket tabloids. Unfortunately, we now are going through a period where ads by Joe Isuzu, the Energizer Bunny, and movies like *Crazy People* reinforce the notion that ads are banal and untruthful and that only crazy people would tell the truth in an ad.

Barry Cutler, Director of the Bureau of Consumer Protection, Federal Trade Commission, 1992.

table 2   Criticisms of Advertising and the Industry's Response

Allegation	Response
Advertising causes us to buy things we don't need and can't afford.	Who's forcing you? This is a country where people make choices. Advertising presents choices. Would you prefer to outlaw advertising and let government tell you how to spend your money? The problem calls for individual self-control and common sense—not the broadaxe of government control.
Advertising appeals too much to our emotions, and not enough to intellect and reason.	Much buying *is* emotional. After all, what in this world do you really need? Food (plain food), clothing (but not designer fashions), shelter. Beyond that, you can pick and choose, and your decisions reflect emotional as well as rational drives. Advertising can help confer a value not inherent in the product; you may be buying—or believe you are buying—a look or an effect in addition to a specific product. If this helps your confidence and makes you feel better, fine. After all, it's your money.
Advertising is too obtrusive and needlessly repetitious.	Consumers are constantly moving in and out of the market. We can never be sure which advertising message triggers the actual buying decision. Besides, the additional repetitions help confirm the choices our customers have made. Retention is an important factor as well. We do monitor ad campaigns, and usually modify them when our research shows they are ineffective. So if you see a particular ad repeated again and again, you can assume it's continuing to work.
Too much advertising is false, deceptive, and in bad taste.	Falsity and deception are two of the greatest problems that responsible advertisers face. The Federal Trade Commission does have the power to halt false advertising and punish those who perpetuate it. Advertisers should be able to prove any specific claims they make. Bad taste is less serious, but far more common, and made worse because many advertisements, notably on broadcast media, cannot easily be ignored. Most advertisers, fortunately, employ tasteful appeals and high professional standards.
Advertising is expensive and wasteful. Wouldn't it be better for everybody if manufacturers cancelled advertising expenditures and simply cut prices instead?	Consumers *do* have to bear all the expense of a product, including advertising costs. However, in many instances advertising has actually brought about savings to consumers by stimulating demand to the extent that increased production has made possible decreased costs per unit. The fact that a consumer has to pay for advertising does not mean, necessarily, that he or she paid *more* because of the advertising. The real test of advertising efficiency is whether it costs less than other forms of selling.

commercial. In a media-dominated society, where other influences—the churches, synagogues, and other religious institutions, the schools, the family—are possibly in decline, concerns about the power of advertising can be legitimate. At the same time, we can argue that the competitive nature of advertising—and all commerce, for that matter—dictates that the producer of goods and services be in the business of attempting to satisfy the customer. If advertising has become powerful, it is because advertising continues to strike a responsive chord with the buying public.

That may or may not be a satisfactory defense, but burying all advertising under a mass of oppressive government or social regulation is hardly a reasonable solution, either. Advertising has become inevitable in American life—as inevitable, and almost as essential, as the highways. There are good roads and bad roads, and advertising's qualities are similarly uneven. The hope is that in the long run consumers will become more discriminating in how they respond to advertising messages, to the extent that only the most tasteful and informative advertisements will succeed. In the short term, it might be useful to keep advertising in perspective, and not attribute to it more sinister control over our collective destinies than it actually has.

Career Opportunities

Some 20,000 newcomers enter the advertising field each year, filling jobs as account executives, trainees, copywriters, artists, graphic designers, production assistants, sales representatives, and the like. There is no one educational path to follow. Highly successful advertising people have majored in business, where they learned marketing; in English, where they studied writing; in fine arts, where they were exposed to creative concepts; and in psychology, where they learned behavior patterns.

About seventy-five of the country's schools of journalism and mass communications have accredited programs in advertising. Students enrolled in these sequences are exposed to a wide range of cultural as well as professional courses, on the theory that the successful advertising executive should be a well-rounded person as well as someone fully grounded in the specific discipline. Ad majors are advised to learn something about marketing, public relations, psychology, sociology, anthropology, economics, and other social and behavioral sciences.

What kinds of persons are best suited for advertising work? A career guide published by the American Association of Advertising Agencies puts it this way: "If you're looking for a career at the core of business . . . if you enjoy working with quick, imaginative people . . . if the challenge of winning the public's attention and trust through bright, effective communication excites you . . . if you're resilient and have a knack for solving problems under pressure . . . if you're not afraid of assuming responsibility and making decisions—then consider advertising." [13]

Discussion
Can a local advertiser get away with more deceptive ads merely because it won't receive regional or national scrutiny?

Teaching Idea
Consumer Reports, the monthly publication from Consumers Union, has a section exposing some of the more flagrantly deceptive advertising. Students might enjoy reading it.

Class Project
Pick out a display ad from a newspaper or magazine, and ask small groups of students to devise a better way to present the product. (Perhaps offer a prize for the best presentation.)

summary

Advertising, paid communication by individuals or organizations attempting to influence or inform an audience, speeds up the marketing process and is an important career field in and of itself. Advertising revenue supports much mass communications activity, and has permitted U.S. communications media to remain chiefly in private hands.

The primary types of advertising include national, retail, business-to-business, direct response, professional, and institutional advertising. Advertising has grown in this country because of a number of factors, including a decline in personal selling, a psychological maturity on the part of customers, and improved transportation, communications, and credit services.

As many as 400,000 persons are employed by advertising agencies, which provide creative and media buying services for their clients. Thousands more work in other areas of the field, such as advertising departments, media advertising staffs, and in supply and production houses connected to the advertising industry.

Several steps are involved in the preparation and delivery of advertising messages. These include performing market and product research to define the particular marketing problems ahead, developing the creative response to the marketing problems, composing the specific messages, then selecting—from the many choices available—the appropriate mass media vehicles to transmit the messages to the target audiences.

Because it is a big and noisy business, advertising has come in for its share of criticism from consumers and social critics. In a media-dominated society, where other influences—religious institutions, schools, the family—seem to be in decline, concerns about the power of advertising can be legitimate. But if advertising has become powerful, it is because it continues to strike a responsive chord with the buying public. Consumers have come to look to advertising for the information they need to make buying decisions—a trend that shows no sign of changing course in the years ahead.

? questions and cases

1. Suppose you are employed by an advertising agency. You are assigned to work as a copywriter on a major cigarette account. Given the medical community's concerns about the harmful effects smoking can have on human health, would you accept or refuse the assignment? Why?

2. A hypothetical client, Affordable Rent-a-Car, was used in this chapter to illustrate campaign strategy development. What creative appeals do you believe would succeed with this account? Provide four separate strategies, listing strengths and weaknesses of each.

3. Identify some advertising messages you find especially (a) appealing and (b) revolting. Explain your choices.

4. Describe your own "psychographic" profile and how it influences your buying behavior. What types of advertising messages are most likely to influence your buying decisions? Would you characterize your responses as being typical of your peers? Why or why not?

chapter glossary

account executive Member of an advertising agency staff who supervises servicing of one or more clients; operates as a liaison between the client and the agency.

boutique, or creative boutique An independent company that specializes in creating advertising messages, as opposed to a *media buying house,* which concentrates on placing the finished advertising with the media, or a *full-service agency,* which can handle both creative and placement responsibilities.

cost per thousand (CPM) Measurement utilized to compare media costs of reaching one thousand prospects (or viewers or readers) with an advertising message.

demographics A statistical description of a group's social and economic characteristics, reflecting such data as age, sex, marital status, income and educational levels, and so on.

earned rate A volume discount for frequent advertisers.

frequency In advertising, the number of times a person or household is exposed to a particular message during a given time period.

gross rating point (GRP) Unit that measures total impact (*reach* times *frequency*) of an advertising message.

house agency An advertising agency owned and operated by the advertiser.

media buying houses Agencies that specialize in developing strategies for advertising placement.

open rate Refers to the highest rate charged for advertising by a medium of mass communications. Usually paid by one-time-only advertisers, the open rate is the basis for the volume discounts (the earned rate).

positioning An advertising/marketing strategy designed to influence the consumer's perception of the product in relation to its competition.

preferred position A special, desired location in a publication for which the advertiser must usually pay a premium. Otherwise, the message will be published *ROP* (run-of-paper)—that is, wherever the publisher wants to put it.

psychographics Study of a target audience with special emphasis on lifestyles, interests, and values.

reach The total number of households (or persons) exposed to a given advertising message or program during a specified time period. See *frequency* and *gross rating point.*

ROP (run-of-paper)   In the position in the paper that the publisher chooses. (Compare to *preferred position*.) ROP may also be used to describe production capabilities; a publication offering ROP color is able to produce color printing on every page.

storyboard   The layout for a projected TV commercial, including pictures, action, and narration copy.

target market   A specific segment of the total audience (young professionals, new mothers, retired persons) at which an advertising campaign might be directed.

trade mark   Any device or word that identifies who made or sold a certain product. Laws may protect trade marks from competitors' imitations.

waste circulation   Generally refers to portions of an audience who are not likely prospects for that medium's advertising messages. Newspaper readers who live far beyond the paper's retail trade zone may be in this category.

··

notes

1 Attributed in 1905 to John E. Kennedy, a pioneering marketing theorist, this statement is reprinted in *Advertising: A Guide to Careers* (American Association of Advertising Agencies, 1975), 1.

2 This passage on advertising history is drawn largely from J. Thomas Russell and Ronald Lane, *Kleppner's Advertising Procedure,* 11th ed. (Prentice-Hall, 1990), 3–20, and S. Watson Dunn and Arnold M. Barban, *Advertising: Its Role in Modern Marketing,* 6th ed. (Chicago: Dryden, 1986), 21–46.

3 Frank Luther Mott, *American Journalism* (Macmillan, 1962), 58.

4 John Tebbel, *The Compact History of the American Newspaper* (Hawthorn, 1969), 17.

5 Quoted in Dunn and Barban, *Advertising,* 25.

6 See especially Scott M. Cutlip, Allen H. Center, and Glen M. Broom, *Effective Public Relations,* 6th ed. (Englewood Cliffs, N.J.: Prentice-Hall; 1985), 22–58.

7 Dunn and Barban, *Advertising,* 299.

8 The author is grateful to the late Theodore Schulte, former senior creative director of the J. Walter Thompson agency, and colleagues A. Jerome Jewler, Ralph Morgan, and Bonnie Drewniany for reviewing this passage.

9 Kleppner, *Advertising Procedure,* 51–88.

10 Dunn and Barban, *Advertising,* 366–97. Also, Donald W. Jugenheimer and Gorden E. White, *Basic Advertising* (Grid, 1980), 229–343.

11 Sales promotion materials furnished by *Better Homes & Gardens* and *National Geographic.*

12 For a fuller treatment of this topic—and a ringing defense of the advertising business—see "The Economic and Social Aspects of Advertising" in Kleppner, *Advertising Procedure,* 568–83.

13 *Advertising: A Guide to Careers,* 17.

chapter P

The story is old and more than a little shopworn, but it makes a point: A man was arrested for swinging his arm in a crowd of people and, in the process, accidentally bashing another fellow on the nose, facing an assault

Mass Communications and the Law

Free Speech: How Free Is Too Free?

The answer to bigotry on campus, say critics of speech codes ranging from the liberal American Civil Liberties Union to Chester
Finn, an Education Department official in the Reagan Administration, is not censorship, but rather more and better speech aimed
to open closed minds, rebut ignorance, and increase tolerance.

But proponents of campus codes, including representatives of
many women's and minority groups, counter that true learning
cannot go on in an environment poisoned by hate. In the absence
of minimum standards of civil and respectful behavior on campus,

they say, many victims of bigotry will feel intimidated and will
withdraw from the intellectual and social life of the school.

Advocates of curbs on bigoted expression say that as America
becomes a more multiethnic and urbanized society, the potential
for incendiary social friction grows apace. A society has a right to
defend itself from verbal arsonists and bomb throwers, they insist,
even if the cost is some restraint on free speech. . . .

Can America no longer afford the First Amendment? Or is the
First Amendment more important today than ever?

James H. Andrews, writing in *The Christian Science Monitor,* 12 November 1991.

The story is old and more than a little shopworn, but it makes a point: A man
was arrested for swinging his arm in a crowd of people and, in the process, accidentally bashing another fellow on the nose. Facing an assault charge, the prisoner
huffily asked the judge, "Why, this is a free country, isn't it? Don't I have the right to
swing my arm in a free country?" The judge replied, "Your right to swing your arm,
sir, ends where the other fellow's nose begins. Twenty-five dollars and costs."

The First Amendment to the Constitution, much referred to in these pages, declares that Congress "shall make no law . . . abridging the freedom of speech, or of
the press." That sounds absolute. It isn't. A journalist might criticize the government,
but had better not advocate violent overthrow of it; a citizen is privileged to yell
"Phooey!" or worse at a political rally, but not "Fire! Fire!" in a packed movie theater.
The mass media have extensive liberty to print and broadcast news and commentary, but not to falsely and unfairly damage an individual's or a group's good name.
The Supreme Court has described the limits this way:

> All men have a right to print and publish whatever they deem proper unless by doing so they
> infringe upon the rights of another. For any injury they may commit against the public or an
> individual, they may be punished. . . . The freedom of speech and the press does not permit
> the publication of libels . . . or other indecent articles injurious to morals or private
> reputations.[1]

Libel is the most common, and perhaps the most serious, legal problem facing today's journalist. Because of that, and because all of society, and not just the
press, has a profound stake in freedom of expression, we will examine the subject of libel in some detail. Our purpose in this chapter will not be to provide a
definitive treatment of this complex topic, but rather to suggest some of the legal
dilemmas journalists encounter while reporting the news. We will also see how
the courts, when forced to make tough choices in this area, either to uphold the
public's interest in information or to protect a private reputation, have reacted.
Afterward, we shall look briefly at other legal problems facing the journalist,
among them invasions of privacy, obscenity, and the difficulties of shielding
sources of information from disclosure.

Terminology

Defamation is traditionally defined as that which *exposes a person to hatred or contempt, lowers him in the esteem of his fellows, causes him to be shunned, or injures
him in his business or calling.* Printed defamation is referred to as *libel.* Spoken
defamation is called *slander.*

Background

It is sometimes difficult to find
out about libel suits brought
against the local or regional
daily paper. Most papers will not
print stories about such suits for
fear of encouraging others to sue.
Your state's press association
may be able to furnish
information about past and
present cases.

Hustler magazine publisher Larry Flynt and the parody advertisement in his magazine that prompted evangelist Jerry Falwell to sue for invasion of privacy, intentional infliction of emotional distress, and defamation. The jury found in Reverend Falwell's favor, but the Supreme Court overturned the judgment, holding that the advertisement was an opinion protected by the First Amendment.

Which of these terms describes broadcast defamation? If the offending remarks came from a script, they would likely be regarded as libel. If they were live, spontaneous comments—ad libs—they would probably be classified as slander. Courts tend to regard libel as more serious than slander.

While penal laws against defamation are on the books in every state, the overwhelming majority of libel and slander cases are handled as civil wrongs, or *torts;* matters in which individuals can file suit, as they do in contract disputes, determinations of negligence in medical malpractice cases, and so on. *Criminal libel,* in which the police and the prosecuting attorney get involved, is rare. Thus, one who loses a libel case is not "found guilty" of libel.

Nearly every news article, feature, or editorial carries with it the potential for a libel suit. While a number of libel actions have arisen from momentous news stories, most libel suits are prompted by small items that seem of little importance and are, for that reason, carelessly handled.

A libel suit is an expensive, time-consuming, and fatiguing affair. The person instigating the action, the *plaintiff,* seeks *damages*—that is, a monetary award—to pay for restoring what he or she believes to be a sullied reputation. Judges and juries are hard-pressed to place precise dollar values on an individual's reputation, much less on the depreciation of it caused by a defamatory remark, and as a result, libel suits often end in frustration for everyone concerned. Many who bring suit for libel may be less interested in obtaining money than in moral vindication—having some official organization, such as a court of law, proclaim to one and all that a wrong has been committed. But when plaintiffs win, they usually are awarded a sum of money. This may seem a crude and inappropriate means of restoring so intangible a thing as one's reputation, but it appears to have worked over time. If nothing else, cash does translate the harm into a language everybody can understand.

For the Press: "A Litigation Time Bomb"

The million-dollar libel suit has become the newest American status symbol. It seems that everybody who's anybody has a libel suit going on the side. The awards many juries are willing to return indicate that the American public is not shocked by the size of the judgments these plaintiffs are seeking. A Washington, D.C., jury awarded Mobil Oil President William Tavoulareas $2 million in his suit against the Washington *Post;* writer Jackie Collins was awarded $40 million against a Larry Flynt distributing company; Kimberli Jane Pring, Miss Wyoming of 1978, was awarded $26 million by a Wyoming federal court jury in a suit against *Penthouse* magazine; and even E. Howard Hunt of Watergate infamy managed to win a $650,000 award from a federal jury in Miami. . . . Most of these jury awards ultimately get reduced or eliminated altogether by the trial judge or on appeal, but the uninhibited willingness of juries to shower plaintiffs with gigantic awards indicates that something very new has infiltrated the popular mood, and the mere *threat* . . . hangs like a litigation time bomb over writers, publishers, and broadcasters of every variety from *Penthouse* to the New York *Times.*

Rodney A. Smolla, in *Suing the Press* (Oxford University Press, 1986).

Before a plaintiff can expect to win a libel suit, he or she must establish at the outset that:

1 The offending statement has been published.

2 The *plaintiff,* or person bringing the action, has been identified in the statement.

3 The statement is defamatory.

4 It appeared because the *defendant*—the one being sued, in this case the publication or broadcaster—was somehow at *fault.*

Let us examine each of these points in turn.

Publication

Technically, publication can occur the moment a third person has seen the communication. The Alton, Illinois, *Telegraph* in 1982 was hit with a $9.2 million libel judgment, enough to force the paper into bankruptcy, even though the suit was eventually settled for $1.4 million. The suit stemmed from a note *that was never even published in the paper.* It was an internal memorandum written by two of the paper's reporters who accused a local contractor of having ties with a savings and loan institution that seemed, to the reporters, at least, connected to organized crime. If a communication circulates, publication has occurred.

Incidentally, the publisher is responsible for everything that appears in the paper—even letters to the editor, advertisements written by nonstaff, guest columns, and editorials. The publisher is not *required* to print everything—or anything—that crosses her desk, certainly; she is free to control what goes into the publication. But once the material is printed, the publisher must be prepared to defend it, in court if necessary.

In the eyes of the law, "tale bearers are as bad as tale tellers." Put another way, anyone who passes along a defamatory statement is as answerable to the court as the person who originated it. Suppose a reporter quotes a county sheriff who claims that a local businessman embezzled funds. Attributing the story to the sheriff does not provide immunity to the reporter or the publisher. Nor would such qualifying terms as "the *alleged* killer," "the *reported* jewel thief," and so on. These could republish a libel.[2]

Actress-comedienne Carol Burnett, photographed during her lawsuit against the *National Enquirer.*

Background

The reason most newspaper libel suits are brought against the publisher rather than the reporter is money. Reporters, believe it or not, seldom have deep pockets.

Blood Libel

In 1982, hundreds of Palestinian civilians were slaughtered in a refugee compound in Lebanon. An official investigation followed, and when it issued its report four months later, *Time* magazine published a cover story about it, "Verdict on a Massacre." The piece implied that Israel's controversial former defense minister, Ariel Sharon, had encouraged the murderous intentions of the Lebanese extremists.

Describing the story as a "blood libel," Sharon sued *Time* for $50 million. The lengthy courtroom drama, played out in New York in 1985, came to a climax when the jury was asked to decide, one at a time, the key questions:

1. Was the article capable of defamatory meaning? The jury said it was.
2. Was the story false (regarding Sharon's role)? The jury said yes; the story was both untrue and defamatory.
3. Did *Time* believe the story to be true? Again, the jury said yes.

The jury issued a statement criticizing *Time* for handling the story "negligently and carelessly"—but not maliciously. The magazine did not knowingly and deliberately publish a lie, in the jury's view, and as a result, *Time* won the lawsuit.

Identification

If the audience, or even a tiny portion of it, believes that the story referred to the plaintiff, the story identifies that plaintiff. Identification need not be by name; veiled references may be enough for readers to know, or think they know, whom the story concerned. Identification of group members for libel purposes is more difficult. A statement such as "students at Siwash State are deep into drugs and booze" may be hurtful to you if you are enrolled at Siwash State, but the courts would almost certainly decide that the student body is too large for any single member of it to suffer extensive damages from a defamatory publication. Those who belong to small groups—about twenty-five members—may sue and collect, however, even if they are not personally identified in a defamatory publication. Two racy paragraphs from a 1952 book, *U.S.A. Confidential,* by Jack Lait and Lee Mortimer, illustrate this point. Breathlessly revealing "inside" information turned up in their travels, the two writers had this to say about employees of a chic specialty store in Dallas:

> He [Stanley Marcus, president of the Nieman-Marcus Company] may not know that some Nieman models are call girls—the top babes in town. The guy who escorts one feels in the same league with the playboys who took out Ziegfeld's glorified. Price: a hundred bucks a night.
> The sales girls are good, too—pretty, and often much cheaper—twenty bucks on the average. They're more fun, too, not as snooty as the models. We got this confidential, from a Dallas wolf.[3]

In the inevitable lawsuits that followed, the court found that the models—there were only nine—had indeed been identified. But 30 sales girls, who acted on behalf of the 382 then working at Nieman-Marcus, had not been; this group, the court held, was too large to permit individual identification.

Defamation

Here the plaintiff must show that the words did in fact hurt business or a reputation. Some words may be libelous *per se*—that is, in and of themselves. Swindler, cheat, blackmailer, prostitute, forger, criminal, murderer—these words and many others can cause a jury to believe that an individual so described is diminished in the eyes of fellow citizens. Libel *per quod* means the words themselves might not be libelous, but the way they are used makes them so. Suppose a paper reports that "Mr. and Mrs. L. Q. C. Lamar III last week became the parents of twins." The item is incorrect. The paper misidentified the new parents. Have the Lamars been defamed? Quite possibly, if some readers knew that the couple got married only a month ago. In this situation, what the readers knew—*extrinsic circumstances*—made the item defamatory. Satire, irony, and parody can also turn innocent phrases into libels. Attitudes and circumstances change. No hard-and-fast rules determine whether the words, in

Very, Very Angry

Most celebrities are reluctant to bring libel suits, perhaps on the theory that the attendant publicity and the staggering legal fees make it impossible, in any real sense, to win. Carol Burnett proved an exception.

A gossipy item the *National Enquirer* published in 1976 falsely implied that Burnett had been drunk and boisterous at a restaurant in Washington. Declaring that the piece made her "very, very angry," she sued the *Enquirer* for libel.

When the paper conceded that it had no proof for its story, a sympathetic jury awarded Burnett $1.3 million in punitive damages and $300,000 in actual damages. An appeals court reduced these amounts, and she later settled with the *Enquirer* for an undisclosed sum, using the proceeds to establish a fund to promote discussion of higher ethical standards in media performance.

themselves or in how they are used, convey a defamatory meaning. If jurors believe that people in the community will think less of someone because of the communication, the communication probably is defamatory.

Defendant Fault

In addition to publication, identification, and defamation, the person bringing the libel suit must show that the defendant—for our purposes, a magazine, a newspaper, or some other medium of mass communications—was in some way *negligent* in publishing or broadcasting the offending material. The extent of the negligence that must be shown depends on whether the person bringing the suit is, according to the court, a "private" or a "public" figure. Current libel law is far more protective of private citizens. **Public figures**—people who hold elective office or who attempt to influence public issues—according to the law to a considerable degree must fend for themselves.

Private persons often need only show that the material was published because the defendant was careless. Thus, an accidental mistake—sloppy editing, for example—may constitute fault where a private person is concerned. There is no national standard for determining negligence in matters such as this; each state can establish its own level of required proof. But the reputations of private individuals are fragile indeed, and current libel law affords them protection by making it easier to establish a libel case against a media defendant.

Public persons, on the other hand, have a much tougher task. They must establish that the defamatory passages were published with *actual malice;* in other words, that the defendant published a *deliberate lie* or, alternatively, showed a *reckless disregard for the truth* in handling the story. Where libel is concerned, the term **malice** does not refer to hatred or spite in the usual way; malice against individuals is demonstrated by deliberately or recklessly publishing untruths about them.

Actual malice is hard to prove, and as a result, most public figures who bring libel suits ultimately lose. The media lawyers need not show that the offending statements are true, only that their clients *believed* they were true at the time they were published or broadcast. To determine what reporters and editors believed before publishing a controversial story, libel lawyers try to probe the journalist's "state of mind" as reflected in private conversations, reporters' notebooks, internal memoranda, and other records. For the most part, such inquiries have not turned up widespread, pervasive evidence of a reckless disregard for the truth, much less a tendency on the part of reporters and editors to print deliberate lies. So unless journalists have been flagrantly unprofessional and reckless in handling a story about a public person, they will find sympathetic treatment from the courts—at the appeals level, at least—where libel is concerned. Such has been the letter and spirit of defamation law since 1964, when the Supreme Court handed down its far-reaching judgment in New York *Times v.* Sullivan.

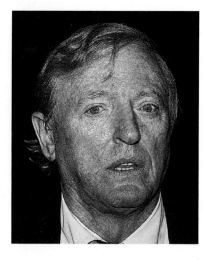

A court has held that William F. Buckley, Jr., a syndicated conservative columnist, magazine editor, and novelist, is an "all-purpose public figure" for purposes of a libel suit.

Background

Libel cases have been brought against newspapers that unwittingly printed false obituaries and engagement or wedding announcements. Most papers now require solid verification before they will print such items.

An Absence of Malice

General William Westmoreland, chief of the U.S. armed forces in Vietnam, contended he was defamed in a documentary, "The Uncounted Enemy: A Viet Nam Deception," first telecast in 1982. The program reported that the general and his aides manipulated the estimates of enemy strength during the war, apparently for political effect.

The CBS coverage was flawed, as it turned out, but the errors did not amount to actual malice—knowingly publishing or broadcasting deliberate lies. After weeks of testimony, and shortly before the case was to go to the jury, General Westmoreland withdrew his suit. His legal fees, like those for the CBS attorneys, were estimated to total $4 million.

"Perhaps the most significant lesson I have learned," he said later, "is this: A court of law is not the proper place for deciding motives of those who played important roles in history."

New York *Times* v. Sullivan

Teaching Idea

If your institution's library has microfilm copies of the N.Y. *Times*, assign students to make copies of the original ad and pertinent sections of the Supreme Court decision later printed in the *Times*.

This controversy arose out of a full-page advertisement that appeared in the *Times* on 29 March 1960. The ad was an attempt to raise money to support civil rights crusades in the South. The copy called attention to the leadership of a dynamic young minister, Dr. Martin Luther King, who was resisting racial segregation policies in Montgomery, Alabama. Sixty-four celebrities including Marlon Brando; Sidney Poitier; Sammy Davis, Jr.; Nat King Cole; and Mrs. Eleanor Roosevelt signed the advertisement and paid to have it published.

The ad copy contained harsh statements, many of which later proved untrue, about the treatment accorded black leaders and white sympathizers—for example:

> In Montgomery, Alabama, after students sang "My Country, 'Tis of Thee," on the state capitol steps, their leaders were expelled from school, and truckloads of police armed with shotguns and tear gas ringed the Alabama State College campus. When the entire student body protested to state authorities by refusing to register, their dining hall was padlocked in an attempt to starve them into submission. . . .
>
> Again and again Southern violators have answered Dr. King's peaceful protests with intimidation and violence. They have bombed his home, almost killing his wife and child. They have assaulted his person. They have arrested him seven times—for "speeding," "loitering," and similar "offenses." And now they have charged him with "perjury," a *felony* under which they could imprison him for ten years.[4]

These simply were not accurate accounts of events that had transpired in Montgomery. The city had used no padlocks and no tear gas, and Dr. King had a far milder arrest record. Thus, when Montgomery city officials sued, the *Times*—which, to its embarrassment, had not verified the assertions in the ad—could not plead that it was printing truth. The first of eleven lawsuits against the *Times* was filed by L. B. Sullivan, the elected city commissioner of Montgomery who was responsible for operating the police department. The trial judge instructed the jury that the statements were libelous *per se,* and the jury awarded Sullivan $500,000. After the state supreme court upheld this judgment, the *Times* carried its appeal to the U.S. Supreme Court.

On 9 March 1964, in a unanimous ruling, the Supreme Court reversed the judgment against the *Times,* and in the process pronounced a new method for determining the extent and character of the libel of a public official. The newspaper had published the advertisement without malice, the Court held, and in effect was attempting to do a job the press is supposed to do—discuss public officials in the common interest. Justice William J. Brennan wrote the majority opinion:

> Thus we consider this case against the background of a profound national commitment to the principle that debate on public issues should be uninhibited, robust, and wide open, and that it may well include sharp attacks on public officials.[5]

Though acknowledging errors in the ad copy, the Court rejected the argument that the newspaper had published the errors intentionally. The opinion quoted John Stuart Mill's treatise, *On Liberty:*

> Even a false statement may be deemed to make a valuable contribution to public debate, since it brings out "the clearer perception and livelier impression of truth, produced by its collision with error."[6]

The Court was emphatic in reasserting the right of the press to criticize the government—all aspects of it, down to and including the conduct of the police department in Montgomery, Alabama—so long as the criticism is genuinely meant, and not laced with intentional lies. To limit such criticism would diminish what the Court described as "the unfettered interchange of ideas for the bringing about of social changes desired by our people." It also noted that Sullivan, a public official, was not helpless: He had the means to dish out criticism as well as to take it. Public officials *seek* attention by running for office, and heated attacks from the citizenry come with the territory. *Times v.* Sullivan was, in short, a significant victory for freedom of expression.

Later Supreme Court decisions expanded the *Times v.* Sullivan doctrine to include "public figures" as well as public officials. A public figure, in the view of the court, was an individual well known as an outspoken participant in civic matters. Consumer advocate Ralph Nader could be such a person, as might the Reverend Jesse Jackson, a nationally known political activist, or Jay Leno, the comedian, whose monologues often concern politicians and political issues. Or an individual might *become* a public figure *in certain limited areas of interest.*[7] If a person *voluntarily* stepped into the spotlight in a public debate concerning the legalization of cocaine or some comparable issue, and while doing so attempted to influence the outcome of it, then he or she might well be considered a *limited public figure* for purposes of any libel action arising out of that particular controversy.

The court must decide in each case whether the person who brings the libel action is a public or private figure. Much depends on this decision; one is far more likely to win a libel suit as a private person than as a public figure because the fault requirement is easier to establish. Any journalist can make a mistake and handle a story negligently, but responsible media of mass communications seldom publish or broadcast deliberate lies or, for that matter, act with extreme recklessness in reporting the news.

Common Law Defenses

Once a libel plaintiff has made a case—that is, established publication, identification, defamation, and fault—it is time for the other side to put on a *defense,* or argument used in vindication. The traditional, or common law, defenses that have evolved over time include truth, conditional privilege, and fair comment.

Truth

This is now regarded as a complete defense, under the rationale that no one's reputation is harmed when the simple truth is told about it. But truth is often hard to prove. In reality, it often boils down to one person's word against another's. Thus a journalist may know, deep inside, that a news story is true but still face enormous difficulty proving it before a judge and jury. News sources who speak fearlessly to reporters while a story is being developed have been known to lose their voices, or their memories, while under oath on the witness stand. But when truth can be proven, it will prevail.

Privilege

In this respect, privilege means the freedom to discuss certain aspects of the public's business with impunity. *Absolute privilege* is conferred on members of Congress during debates and hearings, for example. On these occasions, Congressional representatives are accountable to no court for any statement they may make while pursuing their official duties. Prosecuting attorneys, judges, mayors, city council members, members of the school board, zoning commissioners—all must be able to comment fully and freely while performing their official duties. If they had to worry about full legal justification for everything they said, they would become too inhibited to get their work done. Outside the official arena, however, privilege can disappear. During a court trial, a prosecuting attorney might accuse a witness in a criminal case of being a "chronic liar," and that witness can do nothing about it. If the prosecutor makes the same accusation at a cocktail party, however, he or she has no special privilege and might be sued just as any ordinary citizen could be.

A journalist enjoys a similar immunity, called **conditional** or **qualified privilege,** to report information stemming from someone who has absolute privilege. Suppose Senator McNoise, on the floor of the state legislature, delivers an angry

Background

Both cable channels C-SPAN and C-SPAN II carry gavel-to-gavel coverage of the U.S. House and Senate. Some of the debates and speeches may contain material of a libelous nature, particularly during heated debates and special orders.

Teaching Idea

Ask students to check the media for negative reviews of movies, plays, or concerts. If the reviews were not protected as fair comment, would any of the material be potentially libelous?

speech in which he refers to several prominent bankers by name and accuses them of being "loan sharks who gouge their customers with illegal interest rates." So long as he makes his comments in the course of performing his official duties, Senator McNoise enjoys absolute privilege. The journalist covering the legislative session can report what the senator has said, provided that she writes a fair and accurate account of it, because at that moment the journalist enjoys conditional privilege. This is an important freedom, for it lets journalists tell society what public servants such as Senator McNoise are saying. The journalist is not personally agreeing with the assertion that these bankers are loan sharks; that is beside the point. The immediate concern is to keep voters informed about what goes on in government meetings.

The journalist's conditional, or qualified, privilege extends to many—but by no means all—*public records* as well. Journalists can quote from privileged public documents without fear of libel suits or criminal prosecutions—again, so long as the published or broadcast accounts remain essentially fair and accurate.

Fair Comment

This gives journalists the right to express opinions about anything offered to the public for acceptance or rejection. A politician's performance record, a concert pianist's keyboard technique, an actor's stage presence, an architect's creativity—all of these are acceptable targets for public discussion under the protection of fair comment, even when such adverse criticisms might hurt the "business" of the individual. The classic example is a review written in 1901 for a Des Moines newspaper about a vaudeville act, the Cherry Sisters:

> Effie is an old jade of 50 summers, Jessie a frisky filly of 40, and Addie, the flower of the family, a capering monstrosity of 35. Their long, skinny arms, equipped with talons at the extremities, swing mechanically, and anon waved frantically at the suffering audience. The mouths of their rancid features opened like caverns, and sounds like the wailings of damned souls issued therefrom. They pranced around the stage with a motion that suggested a cross between the *danse du ventre* [belly dance] and the fox trot—strange creatures with painted faces and hideous mien. Effie is spavined, Addie is stringhalt, and Jessie, the only one who showed her stockings, has legs with calves as classic in their outlines as the curves on a broom handle.[8]

Such withering prose must have severely tested the outer limits of fair comment. But when the outraged Cherry Sisters sued, the judge held that the review was not libelous. "Fitting strictures, sarcasm, or ridicule, even, may be used," he wrote, "if based on facts, without liability, in the absence of malice or wicked purpose."[9] This meant that so long as the writer confined the remarks to that portion of the Cherry Sisters that was offered to the public—the performance, not their private lives—then the comments were defensible.

More recently, the courts have gone even further. In another famous libel case, Gertz *v.* Welch, the Supreme Court held in 1974:

> We begin with the common ground. Under the First Amendment there is no such thing as a false idea. However pernicious an opinion may seem, we depend for its correction not on the conscience of judges and juries, but on the competition of other ideas.[10]

Opinions, then, are protected by law. But when opinions are bolstered by "facts," or dubious assertions presented as facts, problems can arise. A music critic might write that the conductor of the local philharmonic is a worthless musician, and that would be fair comment (harsh, but, within the bounds of fair comment). But if the critic writes, "He is a worthless musician and none of his own musicians can stand him," then the statement takes on a different character. The attitude of his musicians toward him might be proven or disproven. In general, the courts have given wide latitude in the area of fair comment, and journalists find it a valuable defense as they attempt to interpret events for their audiences.

Other Defenses

In addition to truth, privilege, and fair comment, there are *secondary defenses,* often called *defenses in mitigation.* One of these is *retraction.* A voluntary retraction can show good faith on the part of the communicator, an attempt to set the record straight and atone for a wrongful statement. For the court to find it persuasive, the retraction should be timely, prominently displayed, and complete. (Your paper mistakenly accuses a local physician, Dr. Needle, of practicing medicine without a license. To be effective, the retraction should not say, "We are sorry that we said Dr. Needle practices medicine without a license," but rather, "Dr. Needle is *not* guilty of practicing medicine without a license.") Another secondary defense is to offer the offended persons the **right of reply,** that is to provide space to let those who have been wronged, or think they have been, to tell their side of the story.

Neither a retraction nor a right of reply can be *imposed* on the publisher of a newspaper or magazine. The courts recognize the rights of publishers to control the content of their publications. Corrections, retractions, and rights of reply are all provided voluntarily, when they are provided at all. Even then, secondary defenses do not afford full protection. But they can lessen the blow of an adverse libel judgment by lowering the damages a court might award.

"I'm Winning Myself Broke"

Since *Times v.* Sullivan, the press has been victorious most of the time in libel actions. Well over half of the libel actions against publications are dismissed before trial in summary judgment motions. This means that the person bringing the suit was not convincing in efforts to establish publication, identification, defamation, and fault. Of the lawsuits that have reached juries in recent years, 62 percent were decided *against* media defendants—not a comforting measure of juries' respect for the press. However, almost 78 percent of these judgments were modified or reversed on appeal by judges familiar with the technical and constitutional safeguards of freedom of expression.[11]

But such victories are expensive. In recent years, the cost of defending a libel suit in a major city, when the case actually went to trial, averaged $150,000 or more.[12] Many publications carry libel insurance, but premiums have risen sharply in recent years and several libel insurers have been reporting substantial operating deficits. Many libel policies now carry a coinsurance clause, requiring the media client to pay a portion of the costs, typically 20 percent, of defending the libel suit. Legal fees, running several hundred dollars an hour in some localities, can create a heavy drain on media resources. Many publishers would share the grim assessment of an embattled weekly newspaper editor in Kentucky, Homer Marcum, whose gutsy editorials and aggressive reporting at one time brought him several libel suits a year. The courts vindicated Marcum most of the time, but, as he remarked ruefully to a friend, "I'm winning myself broke."

Other ominous signs come from within the Supreme Court, where at least one justice has publicly asserted that, in his view, the preferred position granted the press in *Times v.* Sullivan "ought to be reexamined." In a 1985 libel case, Dun & Bradstreet *v.* Greenmoss Builders, Justice Byron White questioned the actual malice standard set forth in *Times v.* Sullivan and commented, "I came to have increasing doubts about the soundness of the court's approach and about some of the assumptions underlying it." Former Chief Justice Burger agreed, adding that "the great rights guaranteed by the First Amendment carry with them certain responsibilities as well."[13] The former chief justice did not elaborate as to what he meant by "certain responsibilities," but clearly he favored a harsher fault requirement than *Times v.* Sullivan and its offspring cases have thus far afforded.

So might much of the general public. Juries are awarding massive amounts in damages to plaintiffs suing media defendants for libel. Although these judgments are often reduced or thrown out altogether as the cases are appealed to higher courts, the antipress sentiment demonstrated by jurors, who ostensibly reflect the community at large, is disturbing to editors and broadcasters. Attitude studies, revealing that Americans are reading and trusting newspapers less, are likewise not reassuring.[14]

While many journalists concede that criticism of the mass communications field is justified, they warn that the cure for it might be far worse. Editors and broadcasters could choose to impose a certain self-censorship on their own operations—tone down an outspoken editorial page, authorize fewer and fewer investigative probes into sensitive issues, back off from criticizing inept officials and questionable government policies—and concentrate on producing newspapers, magazines, newscasts, and documentaries that are safe and bland and empty. Such a policy would surely result in fewer lawsuits against the media, but whether the public would be better served is an open question. These are perilous, complex times, and an intimidated press is unlikely to give the country the information it needs to sustain itself through them. Thus, the subject of libel, which appears at first glance to be a technical matter of interest only to lawyers and journalists, has powerful implications for the rest of society as well. The language and subtle changes in libel rulings are not always easy to understand, but we are all affected by them, whether we want to be or not.

Other Areas of Legal Concern

The legal system is designed to guide a society's conduct, while the mass communications system aspires to keep society informed. These are both ambitious tasks, and practitioners in each field often find their respective paths crossing. Head-on collisions are not uncommon. At any given moment, a journalist attempting to develop an important story may run afoul of laws that prevent access to newsworthy government information or that jeopardize a delicate and confidential relationship with a news source. In the passage that follows, we will look briefly at these problems as well as the mass media's concern with obscenity law. But first let us explore another important concern—the murky, elusive, yet important realm of individual privacy—and discuss how the media of mass communications can find themselves in direct conflict with it.

Privacy and the Mass Media

The right to privacy was first defined as the right to be let alone. A more modern definition might be *the right of individuals to keep certain information about themselves from the general public*. While libel law deals with the damage untruthful and defamatory statements can do to one's *reputation,* privacy law protects against the damage unwarranted publicity can do to one's feelings, even if the publicity happens to involve facts. While truth is virtually a complete defense in libel, it may prove of no help whatever in a privacy action.

In the last years of the twentieth century, individuals find it difficult to live their lives in isolation. Our culture bristles with computers, databanks, electronic eavesdropping devices, powerful telephoto lenses, and a whole arsenal of high-tech equipment for gathering, storing, and retrieving information about our private lives. If all the federal government's databanks were linked to pool tax return information with military, census, Social Security, and other data, it has been estimated that a dossier of twenty pages or more could be compiled on every man, woman, and child in the United States. Commercial databanks possess salary, employment, credit, home mortgage, and other personal information that may be even more sensitive.

Few celebrities have had their privacy threatened more than the late Jacqueline Kennedy Onassis. She once won an invasion of privacy lawsuit in an attempt to get some "breathing room" for herself and her children as photographers crowded them to get pictures.

And the ever-present media of mass communications are capable of disseminating a great deal of material about us, including our photographs, even though we may urgently wish they wouldn't.[15]

While only a portion of today's *invasions of privacy* concern the media of mass communications, the excessive, sensational press coverage of a century ago first prompted legal scholars to advocate enactment of privacy laws. The lurid era of yellow journalism found journalists prying feverishly into the private affairs of the rich and famous. In 1890, two attorneys, Louis D. Brandeis and Samuel Warren, wrote an article for a distinguished law journal in which they contended that the shrillness of contemporary journalism subjected certain readers to "mental pain and distress, far greater than could be inflicted by mere bodily injury." The press, they asserted, was "overstepping in every direction the obvious bounds of propriety and of decency." [16] Eventually legislatures and the courts began to recognize the merits of the Brandeis-Warren argument, and privacy law has been evolving, in fits and starts, ever since. Currently, the courts acknowledge that an individual's privacy can be violated in four distinct ways:

1 *Unreasonable intrusion upon one's physical solitude.* "For a man's house is his castle," wrote John Dryden, a seventeenth-century English poet, dramatist, and critic, "and one's home is the safest refuge to everyone." A 1971 case, Dietemann *v.* Time, Inc., illustrates this point insofar as mass media coverage is concerned. Two staff members of *Life* magazine posed as patients and entered the home of an herb doctor. They secretly tape recorded his "treatment" and photographed him without his knowledge, then published their findings in an exposé of medical quackery. The "doctor" sued for invasion of privacy and won. "The First Amendment is not a license to trespass, to steal, or to intrude by electronic means into the precincts of another's home or office," the judge ruled. "It does not become a license simply because the person subjected to the intrusion is reasonably expected of committing a crime."[17]

2 *Unauthorized appropriation of a person's name or likeness for commercial purposes.* An individual has the right to prevent others from using his or her reputation or photograph, without permission, to help sell goods or services.

This protection was officially recognized for the first time in 1905, when an Atlanta resident discovered an insurance company displaying his photograph, along with a statement depicting him as a satisfied insurance policy holder. The victim, Paul Pavesich, sued for $25,000 and won his case. "The form and features [of Mr. Pavesich] are his own," the Georgia court said. "The defendant insurance company had no more authority to display them in public for the purpose of advertising the business . . . than they would have to compel the plaintiff to place himself upon exhibition for that purpose."[18]

3 *Unreasonably placing an individual in a false light before the public.* This is a form of fictionalization. Poetic license—deviating from what actually happened or enhancing the facts to produce a desired effect—is risky journalism. In 1967, a reporter wrote an award-winning article about the collapse of a bridge which killed forty-three persons. Some months later, he returned to the scene for a follow-up story explaining how family members had coped with the tragedy. He reported that one widow would "talk neither about what happened nor about how they are doing. She wears the same mask of nonexpression she wore at the funeral; she is a proud woman. Her world has changed. She says that after it (the tragedy) happened, the people in town offered to help them out with money and they refused to take it." There were several misrepresentations in the piece, including the writer's assessment of the family's poverty. Actually, the reporter did not see the woman before writing the follow-up story. When she sued, the Supreme Court agreed with her that the First Amendment did not protect reporting that contained calculated or reckless falsity.[19]

4 *Unjustified publication of embarrassing facts.* This includes material showing individuals "violating the ordinary decencies," as the courts have put it. All of us undergo moments and situations that we would prefer to keep private, occasions when we emphatically do not wish to be written about or photographed, *even if the descriptions and illustrations are true. Time* magazine overstepped the bounds in a 1942 article about a young woman who suffered from a rare pancreatic condition that caused her to lose weight even though she ate frequently. Headlined "Starving Glutton," the *Time* piece named the woman and featured photos of her captioned "Insatiable Eater" and "She Eats for Ten." When she sued, the court awarded her damages: "While the plaintiff's ailment may have been a matter of some public interest because unusual, certainly the identity of the person who suffered this ailment was not."[20]

Under certain circumstances, an individual's right to privacy becomes secondary to a larger consideration—that is, a legitimate public concern in the person or situation. This defense, *newsworthiness,* allows the media of mass communications to be protected while publishing or broadcasting truthful accounts of events of public interest. Suppose that Jones slips away from his office one afternoon to attend a baseball game. A news photographer snaps crowd shots, one of which includes Jones among the spectators. The photo appears in the next morning's newspaper. This causes Jones considerable embarrassment and perhaps even his job, since he wasn't supposed to be attending a ball game during working hours. Has his privacy been invaded? Was the photographer required to have sought Jones's permission before snapping the picture? No, in both instances. Whether he intended to be or not, Jones was in a newsworthy situation, and the courts have been lenient with the media in their sympathetic understanding of "the public interest."

But suppose the photo of Jones had been used, again without his permission, in an advertisement promoting ticket sales for the baseball club. Does *this* use of the picture constitute an invasion of privacy? Probably it does. In the first situation, the photograph was used to inform and entertain the community audience; in the latter case, the motive for using the photo was commercial gain.

Other defenses in privacy actions include *privilege* and *consent*. The mass media may indeed publish embarrassing and private information that surfaces in an official proceeding, such as a court of law or a legislative hearing. As a general rule, readers are entitled to know what goes on in public meetings—thus the defense of conditional or qualified privilege applies in privacy matters, even as it does in defamation cases. The safest and most obvious defense, of course, is *consent*—securing permission to use one's photograph or testimonial. The consent should be in writing and be highly specific. Photographers, especially those on advertising shoots, routinely carry blank consent forms for recording signed permissions from individuals whose photos may be used for commercial purposes. *News* photographers and reporters need not worry about obtaining consent to write about or photograph persons in newsworthy situations.

Still in its relative infancy, privacy law continues to develop, its progress much affected by each new generation of technology. The all-seeing camera and the all-knowing computer have provoked indignant citizens to demand more control over their lives. For the media of mass communications, the challenge lies in understanding and respecting an individual's right of privacy while at the same time providing society with the information it needs to function.

Teaching Idea

Invite a photographer from a local or regional newspaper to visit the class, bringing sample releases and consent forms. Ask him or her to discuss the privacy aspect of photojournalism.

Access to Government Information

While our Constitution provides great protection from government censorship and permits the mass media wide latitude to discuss and criticize individuals and policies in the public interest, its First Amendment does not guarantee journalists unlimited access to the *information* they need to develop their stories. There are many meetings reporters are not allowed to attend, and many documents they cannot examine. No laws *compel* individuals to talk with reporters. Secrecy in government, in other words, is a troublesome issue for the mass media—and, far more important, for society at large.

While journalists and public officials are not necessarily natural enemies, members of the two camps often distrust each other. Government officials tend to prefer private conditions when they formulate policy so that discussions can be frank and differences can be reconciled smoothly. Once they reach a consensus, settle the arguments, and iron out appropriate compromises, they can present the policy behind a united front to press and public. Journalists, on the other hand, worry when officials reach decisions in secret. Unless there is open debate, they argue, citizens get little chance to make their views known in time to influence the bureaucratic decision-making process. Public officials fear that premature, fragmentary disclosure in the press can disrupt orderly planning and weaken government's effectiveness. Journalists disagree, contending that if the people receive full information the moment it becomes available, they will know what to do about it.

Neither position is wholly right or wrong, of course, but many public officials and many journalists remain convinced that an adversarial relationship exists between government and the press. The debate is older than the republic. The U.S. Constitution was drafted in secret; despite the bitter objections of journalists of the day, the fifty-five distinguished framers held fast in their determination to work behind closed doors. Only when the document was in final form, signed, and ready to present to the voters for ratification were journalists allowed to see it. Officialdom has continued to close meetings and files since that time, and journalists have continued to complain about it.

A major attempt at resolving the access problem came in 1966 when Congress passed the **Freedom of Information Act (FOIA)** and opened up files and reports that previously had been closed to public inspection. Under this act, all federal government records are presumed to be available to the public *unless specifically excluded.* There are nine exempt categories, classifications of materials that the government can legally close to the media and the public. These include certain national defense and foreign policy files, income tax and other private information, certain intra-agency memos, and investigative files. Apart from these excluded categories, federal records are presumed to be open to the press and public.

In that same vein, most states now have on the books open meetings/open records statutes. These *government in the sunshine* laws—so-called to symbolize the mandate to conduct the public's business out in the open, not inside smoke-filled rooms—basically clarify and encourage the public's rights to access official proceedings and state and local records. Again, there are exceptions. The open meeting laws will not permit unauthorized spectators at jury deliberations, for example, or at board meetings when a personnel matter—such as a proposed salary raise or a decision to hire or discharge a public employee—is being discussed. Many public records generated at the local and state levels also remain secret.

By and large, experts seem to agree that sunshine laws have resulted in more freedom to gather news and, inevitably, more authoritative and effective media reporting in the realm of public affairs. Among individual journalists, however, many problems remain; they must win some of the same gains again and again. The Washington press corps wages the biggest and noisiest freedom of information battles, but state and local journalists fight far more numerous and equally important skirmishes in the state capitol buildings, county court houses, and city halls throughout the land. Many government officials are indignant about a working environment that seems to resemble a fishbowl. But given the enormous growth in the government's size and complexity at every level, today's mass media, and the audiences they serve, need all the help they can get.

Confidentiality of News Sources

Another conflict between the media and the law can result when journalists attempt to shield the identity of confidential news sources from public disclosure. Reporters and editors need this protection, often called *journalist's privilege,* and many investigative reporting efforts are seriously impaired without it.

The courts have long accepted privileged relationships in certain areas. A physician, for example, usually cannot be forced to reveal on the witness stand information a patient provided in confidence—even if the patient, during the consultation, admitted to having committed a crime. In recognizing the special bond between

Teaching Idea

Your state's press association is a good source of copies of both federal and state FOI acts, plus information about any FOI cases local or regional media have brought.

Discussion

Designate students to represent a local school board, and other students to represent the local press. The board wants to go into executive session to discuss censorship of books in the high school library. This should insure some lively debate.

Confidentiality: The Courts and the Press

All too often, the journalist's desire to protect the confidentiality of news sources directly conflicts with the judicial system. The following, excerpted from a New York *Times* report (2 July 1992), is a case in point:

> MIDDLEBURY, VT., Aug. 1—A Vermont newspaper reporter faces the likelihood of jail and fines on Tuesday if she persists in refusing to answer questions about three telephone interviews that she conducted with a prisoner. The reporter, Susan Smallheer of The Rutland *Daily Herald,* will appear before Judge George F. Ellison of Vermont District Court in White River Junction, 40 miles east of here.

Last Monday, she declined to give information in a deposition sought by both the prosecution and the defense in a case involving the prisoner's escape from jail last year. . . .

Ms. Smallheer and *The Herald* contend that compelling her testimony would have a chilling effect on the gathering of news and that the fact of the escape is well-known in any case.

"For me to take the stand," Ms. Smallheer said, "is to send the wrong message: that reporters can be made part of the prosecution. That has the effect of trampling on the privileges of reporters and of the people they talk to."

doctor and patient, the courts in effect say that society as a whole benefits when patients know they can talk openly and confidentially to their physicians, that open disclosure would cause such candid communications to cease. Society would in the long run be worse off if patients suspected that their physicians might later testify against them in a court of law. Attorneys are granted this same privileged relationship with their clients. Husbands and wives cannot be compelled to testify against each other in court, and members of the clergy are usually protected from having to reveal what their parishioners have said to them in confessionals or other private interviews.

Journalists want, but don't always get, this protection, or *shield,* for their confidential informants. While many news sources deal openly with the media, a substantial number prefer to pass along their information in private. Consider the following situation: An employee in a state-operated mental hospital was shocked to learn that some orderlies and nurses used canes and other instruments to thrash patients who were slow in responding to directions. When she learned that her superiors in the hospital tacitly approved of such abusive practices, the employee asked the local newspaper to investigate, urging that they withhold her name. The paper assigned a reporter to look into the matter, and his research convinced him that physical abuse of the more retarded patients was severe and widespread. He wrote an article exposing conditions at the hospital.

In the outcry that followed, a state agency charged with regulating the hospital subpoenaed the reporter, demanding to know who inside the hospital had been the source for the story, then threatened the reporter with jail for contempt by disobeying when he refused to reveal the name of the informant. The reporter felt that the employee would lose her job—or worse—if her identity became known. This type of situation, from an actual case, is not uncommon when the media delve into controversial matters. The journalist in this instance did not go to jail, but others in similar circumstances have, and such a prospect can create a chilling effect on investigative reporting efforts.

More than half the state legislatures have attempted to deal with the problem by passing **shield laws** that provide source protection. Typical of these is the Kentucky statute:

> No person shall be compelled to disclose in any legal proceeding or trial before any court, or before any grand or petit jury, or before the presiding officer of any tribunal . . . or before the General Assembly, or any committee thereof, or before any city or county legislative body, or any committee thereof, or elsewhere, the source of any information procured or obtained by him, and published in a newspaper or by a radio or television broadcasting station by which he is engaged or employed, or with which he is connected.[21]

State shield laws are limited and uncertain, however, because they must be interpreted by judges who may be more interested in full disclosure than in protecting source confidentiality. *No journalistic shield is officially recognized in the federal court system.* The Supreme Court held in 1972 that the First Amendment does not provide immunity for journalists who may be called to testify before a grand jury or in court.[22] Reporters are therefore like any other citizens who must reveal all information, including the names of sources, the federal courts demand. More recent decisions, however, have given journalists limited protection in this sensitive area. Current practice in many jurisdictions says that journalists should not be compelled to testify merely on wide-ranging "fishing expeditions." But when a reporter does have information directly pertinent to the central issues of a case, and when the information is not available through other means, then the journalist can be compelled to testify.

This position still leaves many journalists worried, because they cannot promise complete protection to their informants. Inside news sources often turn up leads to important stories that might otherwise go unreported. Without shield protection, journalists are concerned that such sources would simply disappear. Too,

New York *Times* reporter Earl Caldwell faced jail for refusing to reveal his sources for a series of articles he did in 1970 on urban gangs. He contended that he had obtained the information in confidence and would not break his promise to protect the identity of his informants by revealing it to the court.

Teaching Idea

Ask students to see if your state has any shield laws protecting reporters. (Again, a good source for this information would be your state's press association.)

reporters and editors fear they might find themselves being used to provide information for government and judicial purposes. Journalistic credibility requires a certain independence, and making the media a quasi-official arm of the government—or even appearing to do so—is hardly a step in that direction.

Obscenity and Pornography

Obscenity is material considered offensive enough to threaten the public morality. *Pornography* is printed or pictorial matter primarily aimed at sexual stimulation. Often the two terms are used interchangeably, though obscenity covers more ground; some persons would consider violence, dishonesty, and profane language obscene. Most cities and states have laws against publishing, selling, or distributing obscene materials, but these laws are hard to enforce because judges and juries interpret them in different ways.

The problem is not of much direct concern to mainstream journalists, most of whose publications and newscasts present no problem to would-be censors. But others in the media—notably radio station managers and disc jockeys, television station and cable system operators, and people in the movie business—are increasingly fearful of reform groups and cleanup campaigns which could, they feel, inhibit creative expression and pose a serious threat to artistic freedom.

Federal laws against obscenity have been on the books since 1842, when Congress, in passing the Tariff Act, made it illegal to import "indecent and obscene" materials into the United States. After the Civil War, an ardent reformer, Anthony Comstock, persuaded Congress to ban "every vile article, matter, thing, device or substance" from the mails. The Comstock Law of 1873 led to the enactment of obscenity statutes and ordinances at the state and local levels.

But legislating against obscenity proved easier than defining and controlling it. In certain jurisdictions, works of acknowledged literary merit, including James Joyce's *Ulysses* and Ernest Hemingway's *For Whom the Bell Tolls,* were adjudged obscene and banned. Those rulings were later overturned, but troublesome problems remained as government and the courts struggled to protect the public morality without violating the rights of free press and free speech in the process.

Since 1973, the Supreme Court has held that material is obscene if:

1 An average person, applying contemporary community standards, finds that the work, taken as a whole, appeals to prurient (sexually arousing) interests.

2 The work depicts, in a patently offensive way, sexual conduct specifically prohibited by applicable state law.

3 The work lacks serious literary, artistic, political, or scientific value.[23]

Discussion

Have the class discuss their interpretations of "contemporary community standards" and "patently offensive."

But there are elusive elements among these criteria, such as "contemporary community standards" (as opposed to a consistent national standard), "patently offensive" (To whom? What one person looks upon as trash another may regard as pure art), and "serious value."

One consistent theme running through the obscenity debate is the need to protect children from obscene material. But even here there is substantial disagreement. A national Commission on Obscenity and Pornography, convened by Congress in 1967, reported after three years of intensive research that it could find no convincing evidence that pornography caused crime among adults or delinquency among young people. In 1985, the Attorney General's Commission on Pornography did conclude that certain types of sexually explicit materials could be harmful, especially materials depicting violent sex, but even here the opinions were divided. The Meese Commission, as it came to be known, recommended no new laws, only tougher enforcement of statutes already on the books. The commission's research methodologies were sharply questioned, and its findings dismissed by many as inconclusive.[24]

Do "adult films" possess "redeeming social value"? The only crime they can commit—and which is difficult to prove—is in influencing immoral or illegal behavior.

But a fearsome increase in the number of rape cases, a heightened awareness of the extent of sexual abuse and ignorance in society, and the ravages of acquired immune deficiency syndrome (AIDS) combine to make the obscenity problem hard to ignore. Various pressure groups, some of them nationally powerful, continue to demand tougher standards for controlling lewd and violent lyrics of popular songs played on radio and in videos, and in defining the ratings awarded feature films, particularly those shown on television.

In the summer of 1993, under heavy pressure from Congress, the four major broadcast networks—NBC, ABC, CBS, and Fox—announced they would instigate warnings on programs they think are violent: "Due to some violent content, parental discretion advised." This step, designed to head off possible creative controls on network TV programming, did not satisfy some critics, who charged that the networks would run just as many violent shows, but use the advisory as an excuse.

Many journalists, though they would not be affected by the new ratings systems or other crackdown measures, still instinctively resist any additional limitations on freedom of expression. If publication of "obscenity" can be regulated today, the argument runs, then perhaps publication of other, worthier material might be regulated tomorrow. It is an important if somewhat obscure point, one easily drowned out in the noisy protest over erotic movies and heavy-metal rock lyrics.

Extra Information
The cable industry, under pressure from Congress, also agreed to begin using warning labels.

Teaching Idea
Ask your students to watch for "warning" labels on TV shows they watch and discuss whether labels were justified in terms of content. Also discuss whether such labels really "protect."

summary

The First Amendment does not provide unlimited protection for all forms of expression. There are limits, and for journalists perhaps the most serious is the risk of defamation—any publication which unfairly injures a person's reputation or hurts his or her business. Before an injured party can expect to win a libel suit, he or she must establish at the outset that:

1 The offending statement has been published.

2 The injured person was identified in the statement.

3 The statement is defamatory—that is, harmful to reputation—and

4 The statement appeared because the person publishing it was somehow at fault.

The degree of fault that must be proven depends on whether the injured person is found to be a public figure or a private person. Private persons have more protection under current libel law. Public figures generally must prove that the statement was a lie, deliberately or recklessly published.

Journalists may also risk legal action if they invade the privacy of another, either by intruding in that person's solitude, casting him or her in a false light, unfairly using some aspect of that individual's personality for commercial gain, or disclosing needlessly offensive private information about that individual.

Other pertinent areas of communications law involve access to official information—freedom of information, or "sunshine" laws, are designed to assure that the public's business is not conducted in secret, and shield laws allow journalists to attempt to protect the confidentiality of certain news sources.

? questions and cases

1. Assume you are a *Daily Clarion* reporter, primarily assigned to cover business and financial matters. Late one night you receive a telephone call at home from a woman who tells you that the city's largest bank is covering up a major scandal. Two highly placed executives of the bank, she says, have been caught embezzling funds—but the story is being hushed up. "I know what's been going on and will give you the details—on the condition that you never, never tell anyone where you got your information." What is your response? Are you prepared to offer this source full protection? Would you go to jail, if necessary, to assure her confidentiality? Explain.

2. Do you agree that "public figures" deserve less protection than private individuals under libel laws? Explain.

3. In this regard, does the "robust" discussion of public officials, permitted by *Times v.* Sullivan and similar cases, tend to discourage otherwise qualified citizens from seeking high elective office? Consider the case of recent presidential candidates, among

others, who have been subjected to intense media questioning about their morals and judgment. How free *should* the media of mass communications be to examine and discuss public personalities?

4. Does the fair comment libel defense present problems to you? Suppose you were in the audience for the Cherry Sisters performance that prompted so harsh a critical reaction. Reading the review the following day, you react angrily. "That critic is a bully!" you exclaim. "The performance wasn't *that* bad. The critic is just having fun hurting people!" What recourse, if any, do performers have when they are hurt by scathing press reviews?

5. To many persons, the following argument is persuasive: (a) In recent years more and more erotic material has been presented to our society via movies, magazines, rock and rap music, and suggestive books. (b) Massive increases are being reported in numbers of rapes and cases of spouse abuse. Therefore, (a) and (b) are related. Do you agree? Discuss.

chapter glossary

conditional privilege A journalist may accurately report statements uttered in public forums (such as the Congress, legislature, school board meeting, and so on)—even defamatory statements—with immunity from libel actions. Certain public records may also be privileged, meaning the journalist can safely quote from them.

defamation Communication which exposes individuals to ridicule or contempt, or which hurts business. Written defamation is called *libel,* spoken defamation is *slander.*

fair comment A defense in libel that permits publication of critical commentary on matters offered to the public—a harsh review of an actor's performance, for example.

FOIA (Freedom of Information Act) Adopted in 1966 and subsequently modified, the Act opened many federal records to press and public. Most states have enacted FOI statutes, often called "sunshine laws," also.

malice As defined in libel actions, publication of a deliberate lie or publishing with reckless disregard for the truth.

public figure In libel actions, an individual who has become involved in a public issue and attempted to influence its outcome. Public figures generally enjoy less protection from mass media scrutiny than private persons.

right of reply Though not required of print media in the United States, the right of reply in some countries gives individuals or governments the right to present their side of the story when they believe a false or misleading impression has been created.

shield law Legal protection allowing journalists in certain circumstances to keep confidential the identities of their news sources. Most states have shield laws on the books, and in recent years the federal courts have recognized limited shield rights.

notes

1 Near *v.* Minnesota, 283 U.S. 697 (1931).

2 This is admirably discussed in Don R. Pember, *Mass Media Law,* 5th ed. (Dubuque, Ia.: Wm. C. Brown, 1990), 120.

3 Neiman-Marcus *v.* Lait, 13 F.R.D. 311 (1952).

4 New York *Times v.* Sullivan, 376 U.S. 254 (1964).

5 Ibid.

6 Ibid.

7 Gertz *v.* Welch, 94 U.S. 2997 (1974).

8 Cherry *v.* Des Moines *Leader,* 86 N.W. 323 (1901).

9 Ibid.

10 Gertz *v.* Welch, 94 S. Ct. 2997 (1974).

11 Ronald Farrar, "News Councils and Libel Actions," *Journalism Quarterly,* Winter 1986, 509.

12 Floyd Abrams, "Why We Should Change Libel Law," *New York Times Magazine,* 29 September 1985, 34.

13 Dun & Bradstreet, Inc. *v.* Greenmoss Builders, Inc., 105 S. Ct. 2939 (1985).

14 Tony Case, "Hodding (Carter) Hammers the Press," *Editor & Publisher,* 16 November 1991, 10.

15 For a full discussion of the entire privacy area, especially insofar as implications for the mass media are concerned, see Arthur Miller, *The Assault on Privacy* (Ann Arbor: University of Michigan Press, 1971), and Don R. Pember, *Privacy and the Press* (Seattle: University of Washington Press, 1972).

16 Samuel D. Warren and Louis D. Brandeis, "The Right to Privacy," 4 *Harvard Law Review* (1890), 196.

17 Dietemann *v.* Time, Inc., 499 F. ed. 245 (1971).

18 Pavesich *v.* New England Mutual Life Insurance Co., 95 S.Ct. 465 (1905).

19 Cantrell *v.* Forest City Publishing Co., 95 S.Ct. 465 (1974).

20 Barber *v.* Time, Inc., 159 S. W. 2d 291 (1942).

21 Kentucky Revised Statutes, 421.100

22 Branzburg *v.* Hayes, 408 U.S. 655 (1972).

23 Miller *v.* California, 413 U.S. 15 (1973).

24 A good perspective on the Meese Commission may be found in Pember, *Mass Media Law,* 423.

chapter

Q

To Walter Williams, who founded the world's first school of journalism early in this century, there was a golden rule for resolving ethical problems within the field of mass communications. "No one should write as a journalist," he

Ethics and Self-Regulation

Objectives

When you have finished studying this chapter, you should be able to:

- Describe some of the difficulties journalists face in their relationships with news sources, conflicts of interest, gifts and subsidies, and confidentiality

- Discuss contemporary issues in the field, such as reporting about AIDS victims, checkbook journalism, news leaks, staged media events, and "outing" homosexuals

- Outline various means of self-regulation in the fields of advertising and public relations, including acceptability codes, creative codes, and the National Advertising Review Board

- Explain why industrywide attempts at mass media self-regulation can clash with constitutional guarantees of freedom of expression

To Walter Williams, who founded the world's first school of journalism early in this century, there was a golden rule for resolving ethical problems within the field of mass communications. "No one should write as a journalist," he proclaimed, "that which he cannot say as a gentleman."[1]

That advice, from a milder era, remains sound, but it grandly oversimplifies the raft of gritty moral dilemmas facing today's reporters, editors, photographers, broadcasters, and advertising and public relations people—problems ranging from conflicts of interest to puffery, from gifts and free trips to handling information delivered off the record, from disclosure of intimate information about a presidential candidate to the computer doctoring of a news picture. "The law's made to take care of raskills," wrote George Eliot in *The Mill on the Floss*. But laws affecting mass communications, overwhelming as they sometimes seem, in truth can be applied to only a fraction of contemporary journalistic situations. In this chapter, we will look at industry self-regulation and voluntarily developed ethical policies that pick up where lawmakers, judges, and juries leave off.

Reporters and Editors

Faking a story. "NBC News" in 1993 produced a controversial segment showing a General Motors pickup truck bursting into flames when struck by another vehicle. Later it was revealed that NBC had planted detonating devices in the truck to ignite a fire upon impact.

The term *professional ethics* strikes many journalists as high-flown and pretentious, a topic better suited to academicians and seminarians than journalists facing the harsh realities of newsgathering in a competitive society. Yet within the newsroom exist rigorous standards—understood, if not always spelled out—of honesty, integrity, and professional behavior: Verify facts; avoid blatant promotional material, which does not often qualify as legitimate news; avoid sensationalism, especially in treating science and crime news; never go to press with only one side of a story if another side exists and can be obtained; do not perpetuate racial and other stereotypes; keep repellent photographs and gratuitous profanity out of the newscast and/or the paper. These and a hundred other considerations guide the on-the-job conduct of reporters and editors.

Journalistic right and wrong, however, may not always be so easy to discern. Suppose a reporter needs the direct quotes of an eyewitness who happens to have used incorrect grammar. Some journalists would print the words exactly as they were spoken—in the name of accuracy and authenticity. Other reporters might tactfully change the quotes into proper English, on the grounds that decency forbids making the person appear illiterate. Both sides can muster persuasive arguments to support their position. The decision in this instance would probably be made on the basis of taste, and the news value would not be much affected

Discussion

Should reporters always quote verbatim, even when interviewees use offensive language? When should reporters paraphrase?

Cops, Killers, and Crispy Critters

At the moment you begin reading this, some poor bastard three years out of journalism school is sitting at a video-display terminal in a newspaper office somewhere in these United States, fingers darting on a keyboard:

"A seventeen-year-old West Baltimore youth was shot to death yesterday in a murder that police say is related to drugs. . . ."

Or, perhaps: "The battered body of a 25-year-old Queens resident was found by police along the shoulder of a Long Island expressway. . . ."

Or: "A 43-year-old East Los Angeles man was found stabbed to death in the trunk of his car. . . ."

Behold the entrails of any large American newspaper's metro section—misdemeanor homicides, casualties that will for the most part be interred in four paragraphs or less. . . . Oh sure, if someone is unfortunate enough to be killed in the right zip code, if the victim happens to be famous, if he or she is killed for some unusual motive or in some unusual way ("Police said it was the first slaying involving a staple gun in more than a decade."), then chances are a good newspaper will give it some space. But most violence, when it first crosses a city editor's path, looks decidedly similar: drug murder, drug murder, robbery murder, drug murder.

As a result much of a city's pain is recorded in that tried-and-true four-paragraph formula, then used as filler on page D17. . . .

It's bad journalism. In fact, it's the very essence of what journalism should not be: writing and reporting that anesthetizes readers, that cleans and simplifies the violence and cruelty of a dirty, complex world, that time and again manages to reduce life-size tragedies to easily digestible pieces.

David Simon, in *Media Studies Journal* (Winter 1992).

whichever position is adopted. But in other, more complex situations, the journalist's ethical behavior *can* influence the way news is presented. Following are four categories of ethical problems that reporters and editors find especially troublesome.

Relationships with Sources

Rarely will a reporter develop a news story based exclusively on personal observation; almost always the piece requires interviews with one or more sources—the governor, an eyewitness, the arresting officer, the attending physician, the winning coach. The reporter will inevitably take a liking to some sources, while others may provoke negative feelings. Either reaction could prompt the reporter to select words for the story which subtly, or not so subtly, inject a degree of bias. The problem is compounded when the source does the reporter a favor—provides a useful tip, arranges an invitation to a social event, offers transportation or some other free service. The source may call in such "debts," asking for favored news treatment at some critical point down the line. In any case, the debts exist.

Most reporters, especially those on regular beats, are careful to cultivate their news sources on the theory, often expressed in newsrooms, that a reporter "is only as good as his or her contacts." Other journalists prefer to keep their sources at arm's length for fear of incurring professional obligations that could become awkward to repay. Reporters who are too aloof, however, often find themselves scooped by their more affable competitors. The American Society of Newspaper Editors *Statement of Principles* simply warns reporters to "*be vigilant against all who would exploit the press for selfish reasons.*"

Young reporters soon learn that they will often need specific information that only cooperative news sources can provide. They also learn that these sources care a great deal about the subject matter and tone of each article written about them. Reporters are, in short, expected to use their news sources while attempting at the same time to make sure their news sources don't unduly use them in return. The credibility of the publication or broadcaster depends in large measure on how skillfully its reporters manage their delicate relationships with key news sources.

Discussion

Reporters are human beings. Ask the class how a reporter—in print or electronic media—can avoid bias when covering stories.

The Society of Professional Journalists Code of Ethics

The Society of Professional Journalists, Sigma Delta Chi, believes the duty of journalists is to serve the truth.

We believe the agencies of mass communications are carriers of public discussion and information, acting on their Constitutional mandate and freedom to learn and report the facts.

We believe in public enlightenment as the forerunner of justice, and in our Constitutional role to seek the truth as part of the public's right to know the truth.

We believe those responsibilities carry obligations that require journalists to perform with intelligence, objectivity, accuracy, and fairness.

To these ends, we declare acceptance of the standards of practice here set forth:

I. RESPONSIBILITY: The public's right to know of events of public importance and interest is the overriding mission of the mass media. The purpose of distributing news and enlightened opinion is to serve the general welfare. Journalists who use their professional status as representatives of the public for selfish or other unworthy motives violate a high trust.

II. FREEDOM OF THE PRESS: Freedom of the press is to be guarded as an inalienable right of people in a free society. It carries with it the freedom and the responsibility to discuss, question, and challenge actions and utterances of our government and of our public and private institutions. Journalists uphold the right to speak unpopular opinions and the privilege to agree with the majority.

III. ETHICS: Journalists must be free of obligations to any interest other than the public's right to know the truth.
   1. Gifts, favors, free travel, special treatment or privileges can compromise the integrity of journalists and their employers. Nothing of value should be accepted.
   2. Secondary employment, political involvement, holding public office, and service in community organizations should be avoided if it compromises the integrity of journalists and their employers. Journalists and their employers should conduct their personal lives in a manner that protects them from conflict of interest, real or apparent. Their responsibilities to the public are paramount. That is the nature of their profession.
   3. So-called news communications from private sources should not be published or broadcast without substantiation of their claims to news values.
   4. Journalists will seek news that serves the public interest, despite the obstacles. They will make constant efforts to assure that the public's business is conducted in public and that public records are open to public inspection.
   5. Journalists acknowledge the ethic of protecting confidential sources of information.
   6. Plagiarism is dishonest and unacceptable.

IV. ACCURACY AND OBJECTIVITY: Good faith with the public is the foundation of all worthy journalism.
   1. Truth is our ultimate goal.
   2. Objectivity in reporting the news is another goal that serves as the mark of an experienced professional. It is a standard of performance toward which we strive. We honor those who achieve it.
   3. There is no excuse for inaccuracies or lack of thoroughness.
   4. Newspaper headlines should be fully warranted by the contents of the articles they accompany. Photographs and telecasts should give an accurate picture of an event and not highlight an incident out of context.
   5. Sound practice makes clear distinction between news reports and expressions of opinion. News reports should be free of opinion or bias and represent all sides of an issue.
   6. Partisanship in editorial comment that knowingly departs from the truth violates the spirit of American journalism.
   7. Journalists recognize their responsibility for offering informed analysis, comment, and editorial opinion on public events and issues. They accept the obligation to present such material by individuals whose competence, experience, and judgment qualify them for it.
   8. Special articles or presentations devoted to advocacy or the writer's own conclusions and interpretations should be labeled as such.

V. FAIR PLAY: Journalists at all times will show respect for the dignity, privacy, rights, and well-being of people encountered in the course of gathering and presenting the news.
   1. The news media should not communicate unofficial charges affecting reputation or moral character without giving the accused a chance to reply.
   2. The news media must guard against invading a person's right to privacy.
   3. The media should not pander to morbid curiosity about details of vice and crime.
   4. It is the duty of news media to make prompt and complete correction of their errors.
   5. Journalists should be accountable to the public for their reports and the public should be encouraged to voice its grievances against the media. Open dialogue with our readers, viewers, and listeners should be fostered.

VI. PLEDGE: Adherence to this code is intended to preserve and strengthen the bond of mutual trust and respect between American journalists and the American people. The Society shall—by programs of education and other means—encourage individual journalists to adhere to these tenets, and shall encourage journalistic publications and broadcasters to recognize their responsibility to frame codes of ethics in concert with their employers to serve as guidelines in furthering these goals.

Conflicts of Interest

In certain Third World nations a few years ago, it was not uncommon for a reporter assigned to a government agency such as the Ministry of Defense to be approached, perhaps by the minister himself, with a proposition: "Since you will be gathering news from here anyway, possibly you could help us by also writing publicity releases for our agency, to ensure that we keep all the people informed. You could save us the expense of hiring a publicity staff, and of course we would be prepared to pay you handsomely for your efforts. You can do us a splendid service and enrich your own income at the same time." Obviously a journalist who accepted such an offer would find it difficult, if not impossible, to report anything unkind about the Ministry of Defense.

Most journalistic conflicts of interest are not so flagrant, but they can be equally debilitating. A reporter is not exclusively a reporter; he or she is also a member of a racial group and a residential community, perhaps involved with a religious denomination, sympathetic to a political point of view, and probably a member of half a dozen civic, fraternal, or social organizations. Divided loyalties in journalism are as numerous as they can be painful. Consider the following:

1 A sportswriter, also an alumnus of Siwash State, unearths evidence of NCAA recruiting violations committed by Siwash State coaches and boosters. The story, *if it is published,* will almost certainly bring the school stiff penalties which might cripple its sports program for years.

2 A managing editor learns that the board chair of the city's largest department store—and the paper's most consistent advertising customer—is among those arrested by federal narcotics agents on charges of trafficking in cocaine. The story, *if it is published,* could cost the paper badly needed advertising revenue.

3 A city hall reporter assigned to cover the mayor's important dinner speech finds the mayor too intoxicated to do more than utter a few slurred platitudes and then stagger away, protected by trusted aides. The reporter has observed the mayor in what appeared to be a drunken condition on several occasions previously, but refrained from writing about it because the mayor is otherwise progressive and highly effective in office, and the reporter admires him and his program for the city. The reporter's story, *if it is published,* could lead to the mayor's defeat—by a far less able opponent—in next month's election.

These examples, taken from actual cases, typify the kinds of ethical dilemmas editors and broadcast news directors encounter regularly. Should these particular stories have been published? The first two were, the third was not. Each decision is arguable, and was argued. The editors who made them might well have envied Charles A. Dana, the cavalier, cynical editor of the New York *Sun* a century ago: "I have always felt," he announced piously, "that whatever the Divine Providence permitted to occur I was not too proud to report."[2] Today's journalists can seldom resolve conflicts of interest on matters of professional right and wrong quite so glibly.

Gifts and Subsidies

At one time, newsrooms abounded with "freebies"—complimentary tickets to films, sporting events, and concerts. Just before Christmas, messengers hauled in cases of whiskey, cartons of chocolates, baskets of fruit, and dozens of similar "expressions of friendship" from politicians, utility executives, entertainment and sports promoters, and others who benefited from friendly press coverage. Opportunities for free travel (**junkets**) came from Hollywood film studios, sports teams, public officials, high-ranking military commanders, and even foreign governments to receptive journalists who often came to regard gifts and subsidies as an attractive fringe benefit.

Freebies to journalists are much less in evidence today, owing to the rigid new "**purity codes**" many publications and broadcasters have adopted. The **Society of Professional Journalists** holds in its *Code of Ethics* that "gifts, favors, free travel, special treatment or privileges can compromise the integrity of journalists and their employers. *Nothing of value should be accepted.*"

Purity codes can be expensive to enforce. The sportswriter who once traveled free with the team on road trips must now get the publisher to provide airfare. The film critic who previously had free passes to all the theaters in town must now buy a ticket for every film to be reviewed, then request reimbursement from the paper or television station. The political reporter who was a nonpaying guest along the campaign trail now expects to pay, or have the publication pay, his or her costs. A city hall reporter who schedules an interview over lunch with the mayor must now pick up his or her share of the restaurant tab.

These policies often go against the grain. Some reporters argue that (1) they cannot be bought for a free ticket or a free meal, anyway, and (2) the money used to support the purity code might be better allocated to something else—the salary fund, for example. The ban on free travel, especially travel overseas, may mean that some journalists obtain far less firsthand knowledge than they otherwise might. A number of foreign governments—Israel, Japan, Germany, Taiwan, and South Africa among them—have invited various journalists to visit their countries on paid or heavily subsidized trips. Would a journalist who accepted such a junket be compromised? Would he or she automatically provide favorable coverage in return for the trip?

Most publications and broadcasters cannot afford to pay the costs of extensive foreign travel for their reporters. Is it better for the journalists to remain at home, and write their articles and editorials from secondhand sources? Possibly not, but purity codes are here to stay. Journalistic credibility depends to a great extent on independence. And independence, in the view of many editors and broadcasters, dictates that gifts and subsidized travel offers be declined.

Confidentiality

Many news sources will agree to talk with reporters only if the interview is kept in confidence, or "off the record." "I'll give you the information you're after," the source says, "but in return you must promise you won't say where you got it." Such a bargain poses real problems for reporters, who realize that unattributed or anonymous quotes can undercut a story's credibility. Many journalists will accept off-the-record information from one source, then confront a different source with the information in an attempt to obtain an "on-the-record" confirmation—in other words, a statement freely publishable without conditions. Some editors order their reporters not to take *any* information off the record; keep digging, they advise, and eventually you'll turn up the facts you need, no strings attached.

Off-the-record background briefings can be helpful in gaining a better perspective on sensitive stories. But reporters may encounter pitfalls. Reporters who accept off-the-record conditions can find themselves trapped into suppressing important news developments. If a reporter does give his or her word to protect the confidentiality of a news source, he or she must keep that promise, even if it leads on occasion to a kind of self-imposed censorship.

A bizarre twist to a shield story developed in the late 1980s in the Twin Cities of Minnesota. Reporters for the St. Paul *Pioneer Press* and the Minneapolis *Star and Tribune* promised confidentiality to a news source in return for a juicy bit of information about a political candidate. But, as the reporters began to write their articles, their editors overruled the pledge of confidentiality. The editors argued that the

Teaching Idea

Assign students to find out from the local or regional daily newspaper if it has a "purity code," and if so, discuss it in class.

Background

For excellent examples of beat reporting, off-the-record, and confirmation of information, read *All the President's Men* (Woodward and Bernstein), or see the movie of the same name.

A new ethical concern: digitally altering photographic images. Woody Allen, in *Zelig*, moves back sixty years in time to appear with Presidents Calvin Coolidge and Herbert Hoover.

source, himself involved in the political campaign, was using the reporters for political purposes. Over the objections of the reporters, the identity of the source was published. The source, who was fired from his public relations position as a result of the disclosure, sued the newspapers for damages. After a prolonged legal battle, the Supreme Court in June 1991 decided against the newspapers, holding that the reporters' pledge of confidentiality was a contract the editors had broken.[3]

Contemporary Issues

In the 1990s, journalists were facing new ethical problems, or old problems with dramatic new dimensions.

Computer Imaging of Photographs

Advanced technology has made it possible to alter photographs electronically—changing colors; adding or moving or eliminating elements, including faces; subtly or radically changing the photographic image. Further, these changes are all but impossible to detect. Such manipulation opens up endless possibilities for journalistic malpractice by distorting the integrity and meaning of a photograph. Electronic imaging means that the old phrase, "pictures don't lie," must now be qualified. Pictures *can* lie—or be made to appear to lie. The consumer's best, and perhaps only, protection: high ethical standards on the part of photojournalists and editors.

Reporting About AIDS Victims

Is it newsworthy that a celebrity has AIDS? *USA Today* clearly thought so in April 1992, when it notified Arthur Ashe, a barrier-breaking African American tennis star and former champion, that it was pursuing a story for publication that he had AIDS. Ashe confirmed he had contracted the disease from a blood transfusion. Before the *USA Today* story could be published, Ashe called a news conference, then in emotionally charged language blamed the publication for what he regarded as a devastating invasion of his, and his family's, privacy. Though internationally prominent, Ashe at the time of the disclosure held no public office and argued that his illness was a private matter. In the trade-press discussion that followed, most editors seemed to agree that Ashe's prominence warranted publication of the story. But, as one editor put it, was this a real public issue—or just titillating the public?[4]

"Outing" Homosexuals

Is disclosure of a person's sexual preference newsworthy? Most editors historically have argued that it isn't. But policies that discriminate against gays and lesbians, especially those serving in the military, have brought the matter to the forefront of public discussion. In August 1991, the *Advocate,* a gay magazine published in Los Angeles, published an article "outing" (bringing out of the closet, making public) a prominent official in the Defense Department. The magazine said it did so to point out the hypocrisy of the Pentagon's policy on gays. A number of "straight" publications picked up the *Advocate* story. "Outing," in view of many members of the gay and lesbian community, is essential in removing the stigma much of society attaches to homosexuality and in underscoring the magnitude of the gay and lesbian community in terms of numbers of voters. "Outing" stories can trap editors and broadcasters between protecting personal privacy and reporting stories of strong reader interest. But, as William A. Henry of *Time* magazine put it, "If news organizations, in the zeal to keep up with competitors, compromise their standards and let themselves be manipulated, they imperil their credibility and integrity—and ultimately everybody loses."[5]

Checkbook Journalism

Early in the 1992 presidential campaign, a supermarket tabloid, *The Star,* alleged that the man who would become the Democratic nominee, Governor Bill Clinton of Arkansas, had engaged in multiple adulterous affairs, among them a twelve-year liaison with a woman named Gennifer Flowers. It was disclosed that *The Star* had paid Flowers, whose interview was a primary source for the report, between $130,000 and $175,000 (money easily recovered; *The Star* reportedly sold $800,000 in additional copies that week). Was the paid-for disclosure tainted? Was it nevertheless newsworthy? Most editors, perhaps through clenched teeth, answered yes to both questions.

Checkbook journalism. Should the mass media pay news sources for revealing their secrets? *The Star* seems to think so, reportedly shelling out between $130,000 and $175,000 to Gennifer Flowers, who claimed she had carried on an adulterous affair with President Bill Clinton.

Media Events

In July 1992, a gunman opened fire inside a Fort Worth, Texas, courtroom, killing two attorneys and wounding three other persons. Later the man turned himself in—at a Dallas television station—and announced he meant the shooting to call attention to a court case in which he had lost custody of his young son. In January 1987, a prominent state official in Pennsylvania under investigation for fraud called a news conference to tell his side of a story, then, while the television cameras rolled, whipped out a loaded pistol, put it to his mouth, and pulled the trigger. Videotape and still photos of the event were widely shown across the country. Staging events to attract notoriety is not new—the Boston Tea Party was a publicity stunt—but in the 1990s, media-staged tragedies seemed to be increasing. Should the media show pictures of such morbid events? How can news organizations avoid being used by those who would go to any lengths to obtain publicity? In a media-driven society, the answers to such questions do not come easily.

News Leaks

Closely related to media events are news leaks—confidential and often anonymous disclosures of sensitive information to news media. A spectacular example in this regard occurred in July 1991 during the confirmation hearing of Judge Clarence Thomas for the Supreme Court. An outspoken conservative, Thomas faced opposition from many liberals and civil rights groups. The Senate Judiciary Committee, which was conducting the hearing, had heard in a closed-door session allegations from a University of Oklahoma law professor, Anita F. Hill, that Thomas had sexually harassed her ten years previously when she was his assistant at the Department of Education and the Equal Employment Opportunity Commission. Some time later, these allegations were leaked to the press, prompting a huge public outcry and pressure for a public hearing. This televised proceeding held the nation spellbound for nearly a week. Eventually Thomas was confirmed, but sharp questions remained—not only about the nominee's suitability for the Court, but about the confirmation process in the Senate.

In a spectacular criminal proceeding during 1994, the Los Angeles police department's news leaks regarding evidence being assembled against celebrity O. J. Simpson threatened to undermine his chances for a fair trial.

News leaks are an accepted, if not always satisfactory, means of doing business in Washington. While many Americans deplore such leaks as divisive, others applaud them for allowing the media of mass communications to push an important question onto the public agenda. Ethical codes in mass communications do not forbid the use of leaked information—nor should they, for published reports resulting from news leaks are often directly in the public interest. Leaked information, like any other type of disclosure, should be handled fairly and responsibly. As the Society of Professional Journalists *Code* puts it: "The news media should not communicate unofficial charges affecting reputation or moral character without giving the accused a chance to reply."

News Councils

A more comprehensive attempt at journalistic self-regulation is the **news council.**[6] A news council is an independent, nongovernmental, nonprofit, voluntary organization that serves as a forum through which individuals and organizations can present

How much violence should TV news viewers see? In 1987, Pennsylvania State Treasurer R. Budd Dwyer, at a news conference he had called, pulled out a pistol and committed suicide while the cameras were rolling. Some news media showed the entire tragedy; most did not.

Background

An unbalanced man called a TV station and announced he was going to set himself on fire at a certain time and place. A camera crew taped it, and the station showed clips on the air. Many criticized the reporters for not stopping the man.

Extra Information

On the other hand, Washington news leaks are sometimes deliberately launched trial balloons to see which way the political winds are blowing. Officials can always confirm or deny them later.

a complaint when they feel an injustice has occurred because of inaccurate or unfair news reporting. A news council has no legal power; there would be a direct conflict with the First Amendment if it did. A news council hears a complaint, discusses it, and then gives its opinion as to whether the complaint was justified. Newspapers, radio, and television stations receive copies of news council opinions; they may or may not choose to publish or broadcast them. Publicity is the only "power" a news council has.

This concept originated in Sweden as early as 1916, and news councils today enjoy considerable success in Great Britain, Canada, South Africa, and a number of other countries. In the United States, however, the news council has for the most part been rejected. The National News Council, a well-financed organization head-quartered in New York, never won the confidence of the national media nor the general public; in 1984, after a decade in which its efforts were hugely ignored, it went out of business. Proposals to establish statewide news councils have met with defeat in every state except one—Minnesota—that has introduced them.

Nevertheless, various journalistic groups doggedly continue to pursue dreams of establishing press review boards, or news councils, to monitor their members and serve their publics. In June 1992, as an example, the Northwest News Council, with a handful of member newspapers in Washington and Oregon, was formed to deal with media complaints from that region.[7] But there, as elsewhere, the Society of Professional Journalists and others who favor news councils must contend with the determined opposition of more vocal publishers and their lawyers, who regard news councils as something to be deplored—or feared.

Proponents assert that news councils demonstrate to the public that the press, which demands accountability from others, is willing to subject its own performance to outside scrutiny. These individuals see a news council as a vehicle for enhancing credibility and good faith with the public, and as a deterrent to libel suits by providing a means by which individuals can air grievances without undergoing the trauma and expense of a formal legal action.

Opponents argue that news councils are cumbersome, unnecessary, and a real or implied threat to press freedom. Some fear that a news council might evolve into a judicial body which would threaten free expression as we know it. These individuals fear that news council decisions would be compiled into a body of quasi-official case law and used as yardsticks of journalistic performance to measure negligence or reckless disregard for truth in libel actions. For all these reasons, many editors and broadcasters are reluctant to submit voluntarily to an outside agency's review, even though the agency's findings would not carry the force of law.

The Minnesota News Council, on the other hand, has been regarded as a successful venture. Since its founding in 1971, the Council has handled several hundred complaints against the mass media of that state. The great majority of these were resolved early on, with the news council officials serving as mediators while the complainant and the publication or broadcaster talked out the problem. Only about one hundred complaints have gone to a full hearing, and a number of these were found to be without merit, that is, the news council determined that the newspaper or broadcaster had not handled the story unfairly. Most Minnesota newspapers report the news council's decisions, even if they fault the paper's own performance, and the council seems to enjoy widespread support among media groups and the general public.

At the local level, only a handful of news councils continue to function. The Honolulu Community-Media Council, as an example, has worked for improvements in news policies of city council and city police, lobbied successfully for passage of state open meetings/open records laws, and conducted forums on controversial issues involving public understanding of news operations. News councils in Canadian provinces have been instrumental forces in protecting press freedoms against government restrictions.

Teaching Idea

Assign some members of your class to be "public" members of a news council with several different occupations; assign others to be media representatives. Have them discuss the suitability of a controversial news story or TV program.

Several dozen U.S. dailies employ **ombudsmen,** or readers' advocates. The concept originated in Scandinavia: In 1713, the Swedish government hired a *hogsta ombudsman*—supreme commissioner—to protect citizens against wrongs *committed by the government itself.*[8] The term *ombudsman* now is used to describe a people's advocate. The newspaper ombudsman receives complaints from readers about unfairness and inaccuracies in news reports, and then conducts an internal investigation, with management's blessing, to see which complaints are justified. When one is found to be, the newspaper will likely issue a public correction and/or apology. Though small, the Organization of News Ombudsmen (ONO, or, as its members refer to it, Oh! No!) has become a respected force for informed criticism of press performance in the United States.

Broadcasting Self-Regulation

Because the federal government licenses radio and television to perform "in the public interest, convenience, and necessity," they have relatively less freedom than the print media. While the Federal Communications Commission has no authority to impose *prior restraint* on most broadcast activities, it does have broad regulatory powers. The six hundred sections of the FCC Code spell out acceptable behavior in many situations involving broadcast operation and program content.

Beyond government regulation, broadcasters have adopted voluntary codes to provide guidance to radio and television stations in dealing with programming policies and ethical conduct. Since its founding in 1946, the Radio-Television News Directors Association (RTNDA) has devoted much energy toward fostering professionalism in the field of electronic journalism. Article Three of the RTNDA Code of Ethics holds that

> broadcast journalists shall seek to select materials for newscasts solely on their evaluation of its merits as news. . . . This standard means that news will be selected on the criteria of significance, community and regional relevance, appropriate human interest, service to defined audiences. It excludes sensationalism or misleading emphasis in any form; subservience to external or "interested" efforts to influence news selection and presentation, whether from within the broadcasting industry or from without. It requires that such terms as "bulletin" and "flash" can be used only when the character of the news justifies them; that bombastic or misleading descriptions of newsroom facilities be rejected, along with undue use of sound and visual effects; and that promotional or publicity material be sharply scrutinized before use and identified by source or otherwise when broadcast.

For years, the National Association of Broadcasters (NAB) closely monitored the performance of its members, who had voluntarily agreed to submit to self-regulatory procedures within the industry. The NAB Seal of Approval, which member stations proudly displayed, could be revoked or suspended if the Television Code Review Board or the Radio Code Review Board found evidence of ethical or performance violations. The NAB codes dealt extensively with the amount of advertising allowed per time period, standards of acceptable taste in advertising and programming, and literally hundreds of related matters. The NAB's diligent efforts met with only partial success; in 1982, when the courts found some sections of the codes conflicted with federal antitrust laws, the NAB decided to put an end to its broadcasting code enforcement activities.

The NAB experience reflects the difficulty the entire mass media field faces in attempting to police itself. If industry codes are too broad and vague, they have little meaning. On the other hand, codes that become too specific create possible violations of the First Amendment and federal statutes involving restraint of trade. The regulatory cure, in short, may be worse than the disease.

The Society of Professional Journalists encountered much the same problem in attempting to enforce ethical code provisions. In 1973, the Society adopted a "pledge" which called upon journalists to "actively censure and try to prevent violations" of the ethical code. Shortly thereafter, a split developed within the Society; those who opposed the pledge asserted that it would have a chilling effect on the First Amendment. By 1985, the pledge had been rescinded. Thus the Society, like other mass media organizations, was in the unenviable position of clamoring for tough ethical standards, knowing there was no effective way to enforce them.

Internal Criticism

In spite of, or perhaps because of, self-regulation, the journalism field has no shortage of self-criticism. Indeed, few professions are more self-critical. A leading vehicle in this regard is the *Columbia Journalism Review,* which has made good the pledge it carried in its 1961 founding issue, "to assess the performance of journalism in all its forms, to call attention to its shortcomings and strengths, and to help define—or re-define—standards of honest, responsible service . . . to help stimulate continuing improvements in the profession and to speak out for what is right, fair, and decent." The *American Journalism Review* is another forthright critic of media performance.

Quill, the official magazine of the Society of Professional Journalists, also carries numerous articles that evaluate press performance, often sternly. *Nieman Reports,* published by the Nieman Foundation at Harvard, contains thoughtful appraisals of media coverage, particularly coverage of major stories and trends. Local and regional journalism reviews are published in several localities. Various professional groups, notably the American Society of News Editors, the Associated Press Managing Editors, and the National Conference of Editorial Writers, publish well-researched studies monitoring patterns and behavior in the mass media field. Shortcomings are aired regularly at conferences and conventions of professional societies.

Does the internal criticism work? There is no way to know for certain, because it is impossible to consider articles journalists did *not* write for fear of provoking a scathing comment in a journalism review. Most editors will not admit that outside criticism influences them; that admission would suggest that they were not making judicious decisions based on the value of the story. Self-criticism has, however, evidently raised the journalistic conscience in a number of areas, such as the handling of racial and sexist stereotypes, biased reporting, and advertiser influence in news columns and broadcast programming. Among journalists, perhaps more than other professionals, the respect of one's peers is of the first importance. Journalists do not take internal criticism lightly.

External Criticism

Because of the power the media have come to wield in modern society, a number of "watchdog" groups have mobilized members who call prominent attention to what they consider improper media performance. These groups include:

- The Office of Communications, United Churches of Christ, which monitors television coverage and on occasion spearheads efforts to challenge a local station's license to operate "in the public interest, convenience, and necessity." As an example, this group took to task the management of a Jackson, Mississippi, television station widely perceived as racist in its news and programming policies. The station later lost its license. This group has mounted or threatened similar license challenges elsewhere, often with salutary results.

Background

Many media outlets are afraid to post any ethical codes in their newsrooms. They fear that courts could require them to enforce the codes, and hold them liable for damages if they don't.

Teaching Idea

If you, your colleagues, or your institution's library have copies of these magazines, assign students to review them and discuss any ethical problems they read about.

The media and society. Do editorial decisions influence community values and behavior?

- **Accuracy in Media (AIM)** is funded by, and supportive of, conservative interests. AIM calls attention to coverage it deems biased, especially coverage of business and government.
- Action for Children's Television (ACT) and the Coalition for Better Television (CBT), among other groups, protest television programming they think is unduly violent or objectionable on moral grounds. These organizations have used a number of strategies, including pressure campaigns directed at commercial sponsors of controversial telecasts, to emphasize their concerns.

Many other such groups operate at the local, state, and national levels—enough, in fact, to convince many journalists that "bash the media" feelings are rampant throughout the land. Such fears may be exaggerated, and certainly they are not new. When George Washington retired to Mount Vernon after serving out his presidency, one of his very first acts—performed, friends said, with considerable relish—was to cancel all his newspaper subscriptions.[9] A vigilant press is bound to make enemies. "The press is less cozy with officials," a New York *Times* analyst observed in June 1992, "but so aggressive that it may be as disliked as those it covers."[10] Many journalists believe their most urgent ethical consideration is to report the news; thus, anything that would diminish full disclosure of the news has to take a back seat. That is a hard-line position, but those who hold that view believe that an aggressive press has served the country well. Few dedicated journalists are willing to sacrifice respect for popularity, to duck controversial issues merely to court public favor. But the fact remains that many Americans harbor at least some degree of antipress sentiment. The First Amendment provides protection for the press, but hardly guarantees it public affection as well.

Advertising

Americans traditionally have prided themselves on their *laissez-faire* individualism and their shrewdness as horse traders. Largely because of these attitudes, government regulation of advertising was relatively slow in coming. The first attempt to outlaw fraudulent advertising, the *Printer's Ink* statute, named for the trade journal that sponsored it, was not established until 1911. The **Federal Trade Commission,** the agency primarily responsible for monitoring the advertising industry, was created in 1914 but did not move massively into the field of competitive practices, where most advertising violations occur, until passage of the Wheeler-Lea Act in 1938. Since that time, advertising regulations have come thick and fast, many brought on by the consumerism movement which swept the nation in the late 1960s.

Advertising Ethics and Target Marketing

Camel cigarette advertisements have been heavily criticized and even lampooned by Doonesbury for the "Joe Camel" figure. Critics claim the ads target children. Research shows that Camels are indeed the leading cigarette used by underage smokers. However, R. J. Reynolds, manufacturer of Camel cigarettes, denies the ads are targeted at children.

Sometimes it's clear to see how advertising insults and stereotypes ethnic audiences. Other times, the offense is more subtle.

Because the lines are unclear and because of the potential for bad publicity in response to a perceived racial slur, some advertisers opt to ignore ethnic consumers altogether. Others hire ethnic advertising agencies and consultants to help them develop campaigns. Others venture into known territory, only to find themselves surrounded by controversy and consumer backlash.

Philip Patterson and Lee Wilkins, *Media Ethics* (Brown, 1994).

Even today, advertising regulation remains controversial. Many critics, both inside and outside the government, complain about advertising's power and its excesses. They would prefer much tighter controls. Those within the industry express grave concern that stronger laws would impair advertising's effectiveness and sap its vitality. As one industry leader put it, "Advertising cannot live with too many rules."

Recent court decisions have reinforced the point, welcome to advertising people, that "commercial speech" does indeed enjoy First Amendment protection.[11] At the same time, individual advertisements are subject to the usual restrictions posed by the libel, privacy, obscenity, and copyright laws that pertain to all published communications. Beyond this, advertising must not be false, unfairly deceptive, or even misleading. Specific claims should be provable. The Federal Trade Commission has an arsenal of weapons available, including fines and **cease-and-desist orders,** to deploy against advertisements that stray out of bounds. Other government agencies, such as the Food and Drug Administration, Federal Communication, Bureau of Alcohol, Tobacco and Firearms, and the Postal Service, possess enforcement powers that can extend into the advertising field. New consumer protection laws that require warning notices on cigarette advertising, full financial terms and disclosure (truth in lending) on financial instruments, and more extensive labeling on consumer goods also affect the ways in which products and services can be advertised.

In the 1980s, a trend toward *deregulation* diminished the impact of these governmental controls somewhat. This trend included a rollback of some laws considered unduly cumbersome, and for which compliance is expensive and fraught with paperwork, in an attempt to let market forces rather than government officials exert more control over advertising and marketing. Even so, advertising people have turned increasingly to self-regulation on the theory that voluntary codes and reform policies are preferable to harsh new laws the government, in some renewed burst of consumerism, might enact.

Acceptability Codes

National Geographic magazine will publish no advertising for tobacco or alcoholic beverages in its U.S. editions. The Louisville *Courier-Journal* bans advertisements that offer to introduce persons to members of the opposite sex. A number of college and university newspapers refuse ads from organizations that sell ghost-written term papers. Most publishers and broadcasters have detailed acceptability codes outlining not only the types of ads they will reject, but how advertised goods or services must be presented. Some codes go so far as to outlaw certain superlatives; ad copy that boasts "the finest suit in town," for example, might be modified to "the finest suit in our store." Often an acceptability code requires advertisers to substantiate specific claims in the advertisement. Some publications will actually test products ahead of time, making sure they perform as promised before accepting advertisements for them.

Television networks maintain staffs to prescreen commercial messages before they are aired. The Program Practices offices often reject advertisements that make unproven claims, are in bad taste, or that might be misleading. They frequently send scripts back to the advertising agency for modification—to tone down **puffery** or revise a needlessly offensive scene.

Acceptability codes and program practices offices may anger some advertisers who resent submitting their creative efforts to media censorship. But the media people are well within their rights; recent court decisions, notably the Supreme Court's majority opinion in Miami *Herald v.* Tornillo,[12] reaffirm the principle that mass media owners should have great control over their content.

Teaching Idea
Have students check with the local or regional newspaper's advertising department to see if it imposes any restrictions. If so, discuss these restrictions in class. Are they reasonable? Why or why not?

Creative Codes

Throughout the industry, advertising agencies and professional associations can draw upon creative codes for ethical guidance. The American Advertising Federation (AAF), with a long history of concern for exemplary professional conduct, adopted in 1984 a revised statement of principles which condemn "bait and switch" advertising (offering a low-priced item to attract customers into a store, so that the sales staff can then "switch" them to a much more expensive product), misuse of testimonial statements, and misleading comparative advertising claims.

The American Association of Advertising Agencies, a prestigious group of agencies that industry leaders have nationally accredited, can deny membership to agencies judged ethically unqualified. The 4 A's Creative Code forbids unfair comparisons, falsity, deception, and advertising that offends public decency.

The Council of Better Business Bureaus serves as a clearinghouse for advertising complaints, especially those dealing with bait and switch tactics. Funded entirely by the private sector, Better Business Bureaus are helpful in calling attention to all types of corporate malpractice, including that in the advertising field.

Standards of Practice of the American Association of Advertising Agencies

We hold that a responsibility of advertising is to be a constructive force in business.

We hold that, to discharge this responsibility, advertising agencies must recognize an obligation, not only to their clients, but to the public, the media they employ, and to each other. As a business, the advertising agency must operate within the framework of competition. It is recognized that keen and vigorous competition, honestly conducted, is necessary to the growth and health of American business. However, unethical competitive practices in the advertising agency business lead to financial waste, dilution of service, diversion of manpower, loss of prestige, and tend to weaken public confidence both in advertisements and in the institutions of advertising.

We hold that the advertising agency should compete on merit and not by attempts at discrediting or disparaging a competitor agency, or its work, directly or by inference, or by circulating harmful rumors about another agency, or by making unwarranted claims of particular skill in judging or prejudging advertising copy.

To these ends, the American Association of Advertising Agencies has adopted the following *Creative Code* as being in the best interests of the public, the advertisers, the media, and the agencies themselves. The A.A.A.A. believes the Code's provisions serve as a guide to the kind of agency conduct that experience has shown to be wise, foresighted, and constructive. In accepting membership, an agency agrees to follow it.

Creative Code
We, the members of the American Association of Advertising Agencies, in addition to supporting and obeying the laws and legal regulations pertaining to advertising, undertake to extend and broaden the application of high ethical standards. Specifically, we will not knowingly create advertising that contains:

a. False or misleading statements or exaggerations, visual or verbal.
b. Testimonials which do not reflect the real opinion of the individual(s) involved.
c. Price claims which are misleading.
d. Claims insufficiently supported or that distort the true meaning or practicable application of statements made by professional or scientific authority.
e. Statements, suggestions, or pictures offensive to public decency or minority segments of the population.

We recognize that there are areas which are subject to honestly different interpretations and judgment. Nevertheless, we agree not to recommend to an advertiser, and to discourage the use of, advertising that is in poor or questionable taste or that is deliberately irritating through aural or visual content or presentation.

Comparative advertising shall be governed by the same standards of truthfulness, claim substantiation, tastefulness, etc., as apply to other types of advertising.

These Standards of Practice of the American Association of Advertising Agencies come from the belief that sound and ethical practice is good business. Confidence and respect are indispensable to success in a business embracing the many intangibles of agency service and involving relationships so dependent on good faith.

Clear and willful violations of this Code shall be referred to the Board of Directors of the American Association of Advertising Agencies for appropriate action, including possible annulment of membership as provided in Article IV, Section 5, of the Constitution and By-laws.

The National Advertising Review Board

The advertising industry's most far-reaching attempt at self-regulation is represented by the National Advertising Review Board. Begun in 1971, the NARB investigates the complaints of consumers, business competitors, and local Better Business Bureaus. When the Board cannot resolve a complaint by preliminary mediation, it goes on to a formal hearing where an NARB panel can uphold the complaint, dismiss it, or request that an advertisement be modified. These deliberations take place in private. If a complaint is found to be justified, however, and if the advertiser refuses to accept the NARB's recommendation to correct the abuse, then the NARB publicly identifies the advertiser and the facts of the case and turns over the file to the appropriate government agency, usually the Federal Trade Commission.

The NARB maintains a low profile, and recent studies suggest that most consumers are unaware the organization exists. The NARB adjudicates only a few dozen cases a year; given the present small staff and modest level of financial support, it might be hard-pressed to handle a heavier load.[13] But industry leaders, both inside and outside the advertising field, give the NARB high marks for its judgment and quiet diplomacy.

Public Relations

The two largest professional organizations in the public relations field, the Public Relations Society of America (PRSA) and the International Association of Business Communicators (IABC), attempt to guide industry ethics by monitoring the professional conduct of individual practitioners. Both PRSA and IABC require their members to adhere to principles of their respective ethical codes, which call for strict concern for accuracy, truth, fairness, and responsibility to the public. The codes specifically prohibit conflicts of interest—for example, representing competing clients without full disclosure. The subject of professional ethics consumes a substantial portion of the convention programs and the regular meetings of these two high-minded groups, which have done much to shore up the oft-beleaguered image of the public relations field.

This is an especially difficult area because public relations people must take into account the ethics of their clients. Indeed, the ethics files in the PRSA library in New York contain far more materials on business ethics in general than on public relations ethics in particular.

Another problem is that PRSA and IABC members comprise only a small fraction of the total number of men and women engaged in public relations work. The "good guys" probably don't need a rigid regulatory code, while the "bad guys" probably wouldn't pay much attention to one, anyhow. Thus, self-regulation in public relations, as throughout the mass media field, is at best uneven.

Spin Doctors

Does a spin doctor have the right to remake a candidate, to revise the meaning of the office seeker's message, to add meanings not present in the candidate's personal appearances, to create a mirage candidate based on possibility and potential but disconnected nonetheless from Mr. Mayor himself?

No. Reporting based on such a massage of the candidate invariably deceives; it is tantamount to seeing a different face while looking in a mirror. Citizens of the city have a right to know the candidate herself, not a mannequin image of her. Virtue demands that a public relations specialist interpret her subject in terms consistent with her subject, so that the real person, not a shadow image, achieves clarity and distinction in the public mind.

Clifford G. Christians, Kim B. Rotzoll, and Mark Fackler, *Media Ethics* (Longman, 1991).

Should a Rape Victim's Name Be Made Public?

Editorial judgment or censorship? That seems to be the question surrounding the Associated Press' decision not to identify the woman who accused William Kennedy Smith of raping her. . . .

"I firmly believe that AP, as a subscriber service, should make the name available to editors who want it," wrote Irene Nolan, managing editor of the Louisville *Courier-Journal,* in a letter to AP President Lou Boccardi the day after the alleged rape was reported. ". . . It's simply unrealistic that, in a situation like this, AP has the option of a no-blood-on-my-hands approach that just puts the name out there with no editorial responsibility for that step accruing to us. . . ."

Gannett News Service, which supplies wire copy only to Gannett newspapers, moved the name only in an advisory. However, GNS editor Bob Ritter says the general policy is not to identify rape victims or alleged victims in stories ready for publication.

"There may someday be a compelling reason to break that very strong guideline," he says. "But for now I think this is a situation where I would err on the side of protection and privacy."

Traci Bauer in *Quill,* October 1991.

Drawing the Line—but Where?

Mass communications is by necessity an unwieldy profession, mostly because it must deal with the presentation of information and ideas, themselves unwieldy, to an unwieldy society. Often the process misfires, and the public clamors to restrict the practice of mass communications to those who can pass competency tests and who will swear to abide by all the rules. This complaint, like much else said and written on the subject, may oversimplify. The clamor for public regulation of the mass media often has more complicated origins than mere frustration over performance. For example, a great many critics demanded regulation of the press during the 1930s because the press did not appear to be politically correct at that moment— that is, in sympathy with the New Deal. That particular problem was not connected to "misfiring" so much as to partisan politics.

Licensing and quality control standards might result in some temporary "upgrading" of the mass communications industry. They almost certainly would also preclude journalists like William Lloyd Garrison—whose impassioned *Liberator* broke all of journalism's known ethical guidelines when it first appeared in 1831—from entering the field. The *Liberator* also awakened the conscience of a nation to the wretchedness of slavery. There have been others like William Lloyd Garrison in the American experience—not a great many, perhaps, but more than enough to keep Congress from rewriting the First Amendment. Journalism is uncomfortable with and can be hampered by regulation, even regulation that the industry attempts to impose upon itself.

Discussion

Lead a class discussion on "political correctness" in the media, both local and national. Do students support or reject the concept?

summary

This chapter provides an overview of industry self-regulation and voluntarily developed ethical policies that pick up where the lawmakers and courts leave off. Journalists must deal with many sensitive situations that could pose ethical problems: relationships with news sources, conflicts of interest, gifts and subsidies, and protecting the confidentiality of news informants. More specific contemporary ethical problems include news leaks, digital altering of photographs, excessive investigations into the private lives of public figures, reporting about AIDS victims, "outing" homosexuals, and reporting on staged media events—among many others.

Throughout the mass communications industry, organizations have developed voluntary policy statements in an attempt at self-regulation. These include codes of ethics for journalists, public relations practitioners, and advertising people; acceptability and creative codes, to insure that advertising meets accepted standards; and quasi-official bodies, such as the National Advertising Review Board and various state and local news councils, which call attention to unethical or unprofessional behavior. Internal criticism from journalism reviews and other publications and media ombudsmen also can have a positive effect in dealing with substandard media performance. External criticism comes from Action for Children's Television, Accuracy in Media, and other watchdog groups.

Because the Constitution guarantees freedom of expression, government cannot officially control mass media content. Thus, self-regulation and voluntary compliance with professional ethics are highly important not only to the mass media, but to the general public as well.

? questions and cases

1. In medicine and law, among other professions, disciplinary committees have powerful weapons—including the authority to recommend revoking the license of a physician or disbarring an attorney—to punish those judged guilty of professional malpractice. Why does journalism have no comparable disciplinary bodies? Do you think it should? Discuss.

2. Do you favor printing (or broadcasting) the names of local citizens convicted of drunk driving? the names of rape victims? juvenile offenders? Explain what policy you would adopt to cover each of these sensitive categories of news.

3. Assume you have been named news director at a television station in a medium-sized city. The station at present has no "purity code" to provide ethical guidance to the news staff, and the general manager asks you for your thoughts as to (1) whether a purity code is needed and (2) if so, what it should contain. In general terms, how do you respond?

4. Do you agree that a "bash the media" sentiment exists throughout the country? If so, why? Are the ethical standards of journalists, as the public perceives them, cause for concern? If so, what, if anything, can be done?

5. Earlier in this chapter, a leading industry spokesperson was quoted as saying, "Advertising cannot live with too many rules." Interpret what you think he meant. Explain why you agree, or disagree, with his assertion. As a consumer, would you prefer that government regulate advertising more, or less, closely? Explain.

chapter glossary

Accuracy in Media (AIM) Politically conservative private agency which monitors media performance and calls attention to what it regards as unfair or inaccurate reporting.

cease-and-desist order A directive issued by a court or regulatory agency, such as the Federal Trade Commission, requiring that a certain practice (such as advertising a product in a deceptive way) halt.

Federal Trade Commission Government agency charged with the regulation of unfair business competition. Complaints about deceptive advertising practices may end up here.

junket Expenses-paid travel offered to journalists, public officials, and others, usually in an attempt to develop favorable news coverage for a given company or situation.

news council A nonjudicial body which hears complaints about media performance. News councils have no legal authority, but can draw attention to problem areas.

ombudsman A "people's advocate," the ombudsman is an executive of an organization whose job is to investigate complaints of unfairness, inaccuracy, or omission and to call attention to mistakes.

puffery Exaggerated, self-serving praise of a product or service. So long as an advertiser makes no specifically false claims, puffery usually is not actionable.

purity codes Term frequently applied to codes of ethics.

Society of Professional Journalists (SPJ) Encourages high professional and ethical standards for print and broadcast journalists, has chapters for both student and professional members, and publishes an important magazine, *Quill*, dealing with industry problems.

notes

1 Sara Lockwood Williams, *Twenty Years of Education for Journalism* (Columbia, Mo.: Stephens, 1929) frontispiece.

2 Quoted in Frank Luther Mott and Ralph D. Casey, eds., *Interpretations of Journalism* (New York: Crofts, 1937), 159.

3 Debra Gersh, "Implied Contract with Sources Upheld," *Editor & Publisher,* 29 June 1991, 9.

4 Quoted by Alex S. Jones, "Reports of Ashe's Illness Raise Old Issue for Newspaper Editors," New York *Times,* 10 April 1992.

5 William A. Henry, "To 'Out' or Not to 'Out,'" *Time,* 19 August 1991, 17.

6 Ronald T. Farrar, "News Councils and Libel Actions," *Journalism Quarterly,* Winter 1986, 509.

7 M. L. Stein, "Regional Revival," *Editor & Publisher,* 20 June 1992, 15.

8 See Robert D. Murphy, *Mass Communication and Human Interaction* (Boston: Houghton Mifflin, 1977), 392.

9 James E. Pollard, *The Presidents and the Press* (New York: Macmillan, 1947), 26.

10 Adam Clymer, "Watergate's Shadow Lays Across the Land," New York *Times,* 14 June 1992.

11 For a good discussion of specific cases defining the constitutional protection afforded commercial speech, see Ralph L. Holsinger, *Media Law,* 2d. ed. (New York: Random House, 1991), 438–67.

12 Miami *Herald v.* Tornillo, 418 U.S. 241 (1974).

13 See S. Watson Dunn and Arnold M. Barban, *Advertising: Its Role in Modern Marketing,* 6th ed. (Chicago: Dryden Press, 1986), 133–36.

When prehistoric man returned home from a hunt, he was almost certainly asked the question you and I would ask today: "What happened?" Quite possibly he replied in a factual manner, providing a terse news report of the terrain

chapter R

Communications Theory and Research

Objectives

When you have finished studying this chapter, you should be able to:

- Give working definitions of terms communications scholars commonly use—feedback, semantic noise, channels, encoders, decoders
- Describe approaches researchers use to find out more about how the process works, and discuss theories of mass society, of diffusion, and of mass media processes and effects, as well as various subcategories such as agenda setting and dependency theory
- Describe such research techniques as semantic differential studies, surveys, focus groups, laboratory experiments, readership studies, and content analysis
- Explain how the findings of communications researchers can help improve mass media performance and effectiveness

When prehistoric man returned home from a hunt, he was almost certainly asked the question you and I would ask today: "What happened?" Quite possibly he replied in a factual manner, providing a terse news report of the terrain covered, the number of animals spotted, and the results. Or perhaps he chose a more dramatic approach, lacing his narrative with elements of humor and suspense. In either case, he was attempting to communicate, *to transmit information, attitudes, or ideas*—or, as others have defined the process, *to enable two minds to share the same thought.*

The caveman's task, though no doubt difficult, was made easier by the fact that his audience was close at hand. Face-to-face communication offers excellent opportunities for listeners to provide **feedback** signals as to how well the messages are getting through. One can pose a question, or ask for clarification or more detail. The speaker can *see* the faces in the audience and get some sense of how well the talk is going; too many blank looks and the speaker instinctively knows to retreat, then go over the same point in a different way.

The abundance of feedback, both spoken and observed—and sometimes, with a perceptive person, sensed—makes face-to-face communication potentially very effective. But it is also severely limited; only those within sight and sound of the speaker can receive the message. Because of this, and perhaps because he thought his communication should be recorded in more permanent form, the caveman eventually wearied of mere face-to-face communication. He began to draw his message, the report of his latest adventurous hunt, on the wall of the cave. This opened up a whole new range of possibilities: The wall was *there* twenty-four hours a day, seven days a week. The caveman could go about his other business, whatever that may have been, and still know that his message could be communicated, for the audience was communicating not with the caveman himself, but with the wall. This was *mass communication—impersonal communication with a diverse audience with limited opportunity to respond*—and early humans gained much from it.

But there was a downside also. Perhaps the caveman couldn't draw very well. Since there were fewer opportunities for feedback, there was no quick way to clarify a confusing message. Too, there may have been some interference, or **channel noise** a term applied to almost anything that inhibits the communication process (static on the radio is an example). In our caveman's time, perhaps some moisture collected on the wall of the cave, blurring the drawings and making them partly or wholly illegible. The process was vastly imperfect.

It remains so today. In modern mass communications theory models, a communicator (often referred to as an *encoder*) devises a *message* (a news story, perhaps, or an advertisement) and launches it through a *channel* (newspaper, radio or television station, magazine) to *decoders* (audiences).[1] The perils of channel noise lurk at every turn. In addition to the more or less obvious types of noise, scholars have warned us darkly about the other, equally ruinous barriers to effective communication. There is *psychological noise,* such as worrying or daydreaming; **semantic noise,** when the audience and the encoder define certain words differently; and *psychological block,* such as the refusal to listen to a TV newscaster because we don't like her hairstyle or his necktie.[2] The possibilities for garbling a message seem endless. Moreover, feedback is difficult to obtain. A magazine editor may not know whether a message got through until weeks later, when a readership study is completed, and a television producer must wait for audience ratings books to come out before finding out how many persons were even watching a program, much less liking and understanding it.

Mass communications is a delicate business, fraught with hazards. We know a great deal about how communication does *not* work; we have learned relatively little about how it does, when it does, and why it does. Researchers, however, are making massive efforts to do so. Communications theorists are energetically searching for

Background

Although many students may find theory and research theory boring, they are actually vital to all areas of mass communication. Explain the two major forms of research—pure research, which may have no predetermined objectives or limits and applied research, which is designed to answer practical questions such as how *many* are reading, *what* are they reading, *why* are they reading, and so on.

Teaching Idea

Ask students to think about and discuss the "coding" processes they use every day to communicate with others. For example, how would they ask for a date?

Teaching Idea

Survey the class to see if any students refuse to watch a TV program or commercial because of a psychological block.

Kathleen Hall Jamieson and Karlyn Kohrs Campbell, *The Interplay of Influence* (Wadsworth, 1992).

ways to make the process function better. Their studies examine the mass media vehicles, the messages transmitted, and the audiences targeted to receive the messages. In this chapter, we will look at what this research is beginning to tell us. One thing we know already: The findings are directly linked to past and current media practices and effectiveness. That alone should make the study of communications theory and research important to mass media consumers.

Creating a Hybrid Discipline

The field of mass communications theory has had to develop without clear-cut, comprehensive underpinnings. As new beliefs have evolved concerning the process, effects, and role of the media of mass communications, researchers have borrowed, modified, and reformulated theories to deal with changing conditions and levels of understanding. The mass communications scholar owes much to colleagues in anthropology, sociology, psychology, and related social and behavioral sciences—the study of people and how they react to ideas and to each other. Much research concerns the *interpersonal communication* process—communication between individuals—which is important work, but outside our immediate scope. Also beyond our focus is the fascinating realm of *intrapersonal communication,* the thinking process which occurs *before* one actually talks to others—the creative, critical moments when one forms impressions, contemplates strategies, and sizes up the actions of those nearby. We will focus instead on *mass communication*—the process of transmitting material to a varied and often large audience through channels (media) specifically developed for that purpose. Research in this area has produced theories in a number of broad categories.

Theories of Mass Society

This type of research presupposes that the vast general public is affected as a whole by mass communications, and especially by technology. A leading exponent of mass society theory was Marshall McLuhan, who told the world that "the medium is the message," that lives were profoundly changed as communications media evolved technologically. McLuhan regarded the introduction in Johann Gutenberg's day of printing on a mass scale, for example, as a turning point in human's thought processes; printing institutionalized a logical, linear progression in the development of ideas; words became sentences, which became paragraphs, then pages, neatly packaging ideas and images in a context with a beginning, a middle, and an end. These printed words, requiring a systematic intellectual process to turn them into rational thoughts, eventually displaced the old tribal leaders who had heretofore preserved the tribe's history and culture and passed it along to later generations through

Teaching Idea

Assign two students to each read one of the McLuhan books mentioned in the chapter notes. Ask them to report back to the class, presenting the theories and discussing their reactions.

It is now commonplace to say that human behavior is more complex than the phenomena of physical and biological science. But there is another complication making broad communication inquiry difficult and historical sensitivity essential. In mass communication the present is always moving!

While the forces of gravity or molecules of basic elements are little changed over recent millennia, the mass media of the 1990s are vastly different from those of our childhood. If there is

to be a mass communication science, it must be cumulative in two senses. First, it should be conceptually and intellectually cumulative just as all science is. But it also must be historically cumulative. . . . The constantly shifting nature of mass communications, technologically, socially, and behaviorally, most likely means that the marketplace of ideas in mass communication research will remain a mixture of contributors from many intellectual disciplines.

Shearon Lowery and Melvin L. De Fleur, *Milestones in Mass Communications Research* (Longman, 1983).

tales told around a campfire. Television, warned McLuhan, would ultimately reverse the effects of the cold, intellectual printed page and, in effect, "retribalize" us into what he called a "global village." In the process, new media would reawaken our senses, involving more of our feelings in deeper reactions to the world around us. The medium would not only be the message, but the *massage* as well.[3]

Other scholars less flamboyant and controversial than McLuhan also regard the mass society as composed of reactive individuals who absorb media messages and then adjust their behavior accordingly. Harold Lasswell, author of the simplest, clearest, and most pervasive model of mass communications process *("Who says what, through what channels, to whom, and with what effect?")* also gave us the "bullet theory" or "hypodermic needle theory" of mass communications. This theory views audiences as essentially defenseless and passive; the media of mass communications blast messages into them, much as an electric current turns on a light bulb.[4] But the bullet theory, as Wilbur Schramm and others have pointed out, can on occasion be shot full of holes.[5] Some studies have shown that the bullet may ricochet; in one study, researchers found that bigoted individuals, when subjected to antiprejudice propaganda, actually used those messages to reinforce and intensify their prejudices. People respond to communication in different ways.

Theories of Diffusion

These theories are predicated on the notion that the media audience is not a homogeneous mass but rather a complex of small subgroups, each with its own system for handling information and change.

The Two-Step Flow Theory

This theory contends that the mass media do not influence individuals directly; instead, an intermediary of sorts, a person in some formal or informal leadership capacity, is influenced by the mass media and passes along information and ideas in a personal way to the other members of a subgroup. Originating about 1940 with Paul Lazarsfeld, the two-step flow theory has been employed to explain any number of successful communications efforts.

One study, performed in a Third World country some years ago, found the government media, chiefly radio, repeatedly urging farmers to adopt a new seed planting procedure. The farmers ignored the advice altogether. Exasperated government leaders then tried a new approach. Instead of telling the farmers how to plant their seed, they chose a roundabout path, using the state-owned media to sing the praises of the district agricultural extension agent. Fulsome announcements were

Teaching Idea

Ask the class whether satellite and television terminology, with instantaneous international communication, have actually brought the world closer together. Are we truly a global village?

Teaching Idea

Ask students where they *first* heard or read information about a major news item of the day—directly from a mass medium, or from some intermediary source.

Background

Governments of developing countries typically use radio to communicate with their people. It is cheap and effective in areas with low literacy and poor transportation. The Soviets used radio extensively in the 1920s, 1930s, and 1940s as a propaganda medium.

broadcast whenever each agent had completed an advanced training course or attended a high-level agricultural conference. After some months of this publicity buildup, referred to as *status conferral,*[6] each agent went on a farm-by-farm tour of the district, explaining in person how the new seed-planting techniques could increase crop yields. Impressed, the farmers responded in overwhelming numbers, and the procedure proved to be a great success.

Later research has shown that sometimes the mass media can influence audiences directly, with or without the intermediary, depending on the type of information involved and how strongly individual and collective views are held on a given subject. As a general guide, the deeper a person feels about a subject, the less the mass media will influence his or her opinion about it. The mass media, in other words, are highly unlikely to cause people to do things they *really* don't want to do. While some scholars prefer to dismiss the two-step flow theory as simplistic, the fact remains that certain individuals do hold some degree of influence over various constituencies. Shrewd communicators—advertising people, politicians, and public relations experts among them—know the value of "teaching the teachers," that is, of persuading peer group leaders who can, in turn, persuade others.

Diffusion of Innovations Theory

Teaching Idea
Remind the students that *you* are the opinion leader for this class. Can they identify any peer group leaders?

This theory outlines the combined role of the mass media and interpersonal communication in spreading new information through specific channels of communication over time through a given social structure—or describes how the media report information to individuals, who then pass it along to others. This particular theory, first put forth in the 1950s by Everett Rogers and other scholars, has proven useful in tracking the processes by which new ideas enter the social system, and in determining just which members of the audience provide leadership in accepting and adopting new ways of doing things or buying new products. Diffusion of innovations theory has proven useful, especially among rural sociologists, in suggesting what the media of mass communications can and cannot achieve in implementing rapid technical and social change.

Theories of Mass Media Processes and Effects

A pathbreaking study, *The Mathematical Theory of Communication,* published by Claude E. Shannon and Warren Weaver in 1949, in an early moment in the brief history of the discipline, regarded mass communications as largely a matter of arithmetic.[7] Information theorists attempted to calibrate the number of messages that could be transmitted via such media as telephones and radios. The engineering models they developed were useful in describing systems and parameters, much as a cartographer develops a map. But a map only points out cities and rivers with dots and lines; it says nothing about beautiful scenery in a given valley, much less about the people who live there. The engineer who designs a telephone system, as Leon Brillouin pointed out, does not much care whether this link will be used for transmission of gossip, for stock exchange quotations, or for diplomatic messages. The technical problem is always the same: to transmit the information correctly.[8] Later research has begun to focus on the type of message and on value judgments and other human frailties within the mass media audience.

Reinforcement Theory

Background
Much of the terminology used in communications theory derives from electronics: *channel, noise,* and *feedback,* for example.

Largely associated with Joseph Klapper, this theory contends that the media of mass communications rarely can bring about attitude change because members of the audience tend to seek out only those media and messages that support their existing beliefs.[9] Implicit in this rationale are such concepts as the following.

Selectivity in Action

Selective exposure is the tendency of an individual to avoid disagreeable messages. A heavy smoker probably will turn away from or tune out commercials warning of lung cancer and emphysema; a Chicago Cubs baseball fan may read all that is written about the Cubs, even on those occasions when they lose, but skim lightly over the National League news and ignore the American League altogether.

Selective perception assumes that since individuals cannot process all the messages that come in, they perceive some and not others. Oftentimes they choose what to receive based on the novelty of the presentation and, perhaps more important, on how welcome the message is likely to be. Returning to the Cubs fan: Suppose a Cub runner is called out on a close play at third base. Diehard Cub fans will perceive that part of the scene in which the runner's foot touches the base, but may not perceive the sight of the infielder making the tag. And the fans in the bleachers will accuse the umpire of selective perception—though the outraged Cubs fans may describe the condition in somewhat more colorful terms than this.

Selective retention takes this a step further; of those messages perceived, only a portion is retained. Individuals sort through the various stimuli available and choose—sometimes consciously, more often unconsciously—what to store.

In short, people tend to read what they want to read, see what they want to see, and remember what they want to remember. Like much else in communications theory, that generalization seems to belabor the obvious, but anyone who would communicate through the mass media forgets this at his or her peril. *The task of the individual communicator is to arouse sufficient curiosity within an audience to permit a message to be perceived, accepted, and remembered.*

Repetition, as advertisers and politicians discovered long ago, is a powerful ally in this regard. Group norms are likewise influential; the urge to conform seems to run deep. Mass communicators, and especially creative experts in advertising, know full well that selling is easiest when product and service appeals flow with, and not against, the prevailing tide of public opinion.[10] Such sensitivity is not a legitimate excuse for condoning timid news reports, empty editorials, and mindless television programming. But leaders who disregard the beliefs of their followers usually don't remain leaders for long. An elected official who loses touch with her constituents probably won't survive the next election, and an editor who loses touch with his readers is likewise apt to become uninfluential, unread, and unemployed.

Agenda Setting Theory

The real power of the press, some theorists contend, is **agenda setting**—*simply in calling our attention to events* and placing them on the public agenda for discussion. Or, as Bernard Cohen put it, "The press may not be successful in telling people what to think, but it is stunningly successful in telling its readers what to think *about*."[11] This theory is not new; Walter Lippmann, the brilliant newspaper columnist and

Teaching Idea

Bring the three "selectives" outlined here to life by asking students related questions—for example, what do students remember about a commercial they watched recently? What do they remember from this morning's newspapers?

author, suggested the implications of agenda setting more than half a century ago.[12] Much current scholarship is now devoted to examining how the media of mass communications shape our lives and thoughts simply by establishing what is news, and thus what is important. Other research has analyzed **gatekeepers,** the men and women who edit newspapers and newscasts and decide what we as audiences will be exposed to, and why.[13] If the mass media do influence control of the public agenda, then those who make key decisions within the media wield great power. Thus, research that helps us know more about them is important.

Uses and Gratifications Theory

This approach focuses less on the media than on the audience, on why people select specific mass media and what they expect to get when they do. Scholars have identified a number of categories of **uses and gratifications** that certain mass media provide, including:

1 *Cognition*. Many persons read news reports to heighten their awareness of the world about them, to gain new ideas, to placate a restless, curious mind. As Frank Luther Mott asserted more than a generation ago: "News hunger is fundamental in human nature. It is characteristic of social man, whether he is conscious of it or not. The basic desires are those for food, shelter, and sex expression; after these are satisfied, other desires crowd forward—for social life, for recognition among one's fellows, for new experience and adventure. These latter desires are greatly stimulated by information, or news, about others."[14]

2 *Diversion*. Mass media can provide stimulation to relieve boredom ("I really got a kick out of that movie"), relaxation ("I'm still keyed up from the office; all I want to do tonight is watch a little TV and unwind"), and emotional release or escape. Aristotle wrote in his *Poetics* of the value of drama in helping audiences rid themselves of pent-up energies and frustrations, "wherewith to accomplish its catharsis of such emotions."[15]

3 *Socialization*. Mass media permit us to interact better with friends and the rest of our culture. As Wilbur Schramm and William Porter put it, "All television is educational TV; the only difference is what it is teaching."[16] The same can be said for other media as well; they explain to us what clothes are being worn, how some persons succeed in business, government, or the arts, what others think is important, or how certain individuals handle situations and relationships. There is conversational value, too, in having seen an important new film, in having read the latest bestseller, in knowing the most recent plot twist in a soap opera, or in being able to analyze the sports columnists' Super Bowl predictions.

Many persons seem to use the mass media to head off loneliness; radio is an especially welcome companion for millions of solitary individuals. A television comedy star, a late-night radio disc jockey, a folksy newspaper columnist—people often react to them as personal friends rather than distant media personalities. Walter Cronkite, who anchored the "CBS Evening News" from 1962 to 1981, was voted Most Admired Person in America in a popularity poll where the ballot included the president, former presidents, religious leaders, sports idols, and giants of industry.

Still other viewers and readers use the media of mass communications to help achieve the opposite effect—to withdraw, if only for a moment, from society. These individuals may use the media to put off doing a chore ("Don't bother me now. I've got to see the end of this program") or to establish a buffer between themselves and

Teaching Idea

Using the text as background, ask students *why* they read newspapers, listen to radio, and watch TV. Is it for cognitive, diversion, or social purposes? A discussion should bring out different reasons people use the media.

the world. An airplane passenger who sits quietly with her nose deep in a book may be making it clear she does not want to engage in conversation with fellow passengers during the flight.

Uses and gratifications theory is valuable in examining the extraordinarily complicated relationships that can exist among audiences and the media of mass communications they choose. Such research can also help editors and broadcasters compete better by helping them know why certain persons select their products, and what they hope those products will provide.

Dependency Theory

As you may have gathered by now, anyone who attempts to assess the impact of mass communications runs head-on into a barrage of contradictions. Some social scientists can argue persuasively that the media have little effect on human behavior, that mass communications cannot compel people to do things they wouldn't ordinarily do anyway. Others can make a stout case that the media exert considerable effect on our lives, and that these effects, though massive, come about in cumulative, often subtle, ways. Melvin H. De Fleur and Sandra Ball-Rokeach attempt to reconcile these two seemingly conflicting viewpoints by exploring the premise that people become dependent on the mass media when informal channels beyond their immediate groups are disrupted or inadequate.[17] Dependency theory, they contend, can identify and predict certain kinds of changes in people resulting from exposure to the media of mass communications. The effects may be

1 *Cognitive,* helping individuals learn more about a situation when information from other sources is inadequate. An individual who is puzzled about a forthcoming bond issue or a new tax increase would turn to, and perhaps depend upon, newspapers and newscasts for assistance. An additional cognitive effect might include *attitude formation*—preliminary impressions from the media about political figures, new products, sports teams, celebrities, restaurants, entertainments, and tourist attractions. As a number of readership studies of newspapers and magazines have revealed, audiences want help in coping with the world around them. *Service journalism,* practiced by many magazines and newspapers, and especially *USA Today,* may be considered a response to this type of audience need.

2 *Affective,* in the sense that the mass media may evoke in their audiences such emotions as anger (at pictures and stories depicting racism, brutality, injustice), anxiety (about crime, national security, the economy), love (human interest stories), joy, laughter, and so on. Some social critics fear that excessive violence on television and in the movies may numb us into insensitivity, a condition where we accept violence and bloodshed as a matter of course. Other theorists, agreeing with Aristotle's catharsis theory, argue that vicarious violence presented via the media (bloody Western movies, boxing matches, and pro football games) provides a healthy substitute, allowing us to get the *real* violence out of our systems without hurting others or ourselves. Seymour Feshbach, among other catharsis theorists, argues that exposure to violent television content can *decrease* the probability of violent behavior among TV viewers, though the effects seem to differ according to socioeconomic level: Wealthier viewers seem relatively less affected by TV violence.

3 *Behavioral,* wherein some direct action may result from exposure to mass media messages. A weatherman's warning that snow is on the way may trigger an immediate dash to buy some antifreeze, while a gloomy stock market forecast could prompt a decision to sell.

Teaching Idea

To illustrate this section, ask the class where they got their weather information this morning. Did it affect how they felt about the upcoming day? Did it affect any of their actions?

Dependency theory, as De Fleur and Ball-Rokeach point out, is difficult to integrate into a clear and persuasive model. The variables are overwhelmingly complex; given our present primitive level of understanding, any proposition that somehow encompasses them all is almost certain to be so vague and general as to be useless. Still, the work continues by scholars now convinced that the media of mass communications are not omnipotent forces in modern society, but that they can and do exert influence and change in certain limited ways. Meanwhile, much depends on how actively members of the society *involve themselves* with the mass media (audience motives, needs, desires, perceived rewards).[18] Successful communication, it should be obvious by now, requires effort at both ends of the pipeline.

Theoretical Evolution: Emergence and Eclipse

Mass communications theories, like theories about teaching mathematics and raising children, are constantly evolving. As new concepts are presented, older theories may become less persuasive. The "powerful versus the weak" media effects controversy among mass communications theorists is a case in point.

Walter Lippmann's *Public Opinion,* a brilliant, seminal work which appeared in 1922, contended that the media burned stereotypes into the collective mind. That book and subsequent studies gave rise to the widespread belief that media power was vast and pervasive. But a new generation of scholars, writing in the years following World War II, took a much milder view. They decided that the media of mass communications are only one of many forces tugging at individuals and societies. Media power, one step removed from face-to-face contact, is secondary, therefore limited, therefore weak.

In more recent years, a new crop of "powerful effects" theorists has emerged.[19] *On certain matters and issues,* these scholars argue, the media of mass communications can indeed exert considerable influence. While the media may not bring about attitude change directly, they can and do affect decisions through agenda setting and rewards (uses and gratifications, information seeking), among other ways.

And so it goes. Much of the early theoretical work is now all but obsolete; the "bullet theory," as an example, has long since gone out of fashion. Marshall McLuhan in the 1960s was glibly forecasting the end of the print media, a prediction that later must have seemed premature to organizations such as the New York *Times* Company, which shelled out $1.1 billion in 1993 to buy the Boston *Globe.* But the early theories were useful at the time, if for no other reason than they were provocative, and they helped identify fertile terrain for other scholars to cultivate productively later.

The media must compete, with each other as well as with other sources of information and entertainment, for audience time and attention. Communications theory research can help editors and broadcasters compete more effectively. For the

Mass Communication and Social Change

What is needed in the years ahead is a new conception of public communication as the crucial instrument which can promote psychic mobility, political stability under conditions of societal equilibrium. The mass media can be used to mobilize the energies of living persons (without creating insatiable expectations) by the rational articulation of new interests. Flanked by the schools and community leaders, the mass media can simultaneously induce a new process of socialization among the rising generation that will, among other effects, recruit new participants into political life. These two processes—short-run mobilization and long-run socialization—can then converge a generation later, in new aggregations of private interests which are the stuff of democratic wisdom.

Daniel Lerner, in *Communications and Political Development* (Princeton University Press, 1963).

general public, theory research is shedding new light (if only a few rays at a time; the progress seems maddeningly slow and the questions are big ones) on the world we live in, helping us gain a better understanding of the role and influence of the mass media in contemporary society. Necessarily, because they involve rigorous study of human behavior, communications theory studies are also telling us more about ourselves, and that is no small thing.

Mass Communications Research

At one time, more than a few journalists were wary of communications research. "I don't need a market survey," thundered one particularly pugnacious editor, "to tell me what my convictions are."[20] Communications research has far more support today. Editors and broadcasters know that modern audiences have ready access to many more media of mass communications than ever before. In the face of such withering competition, editors and broadcasters are turning to research for guidance in story selection, graphic design, tone, content, and presentation style. There will always be a prominent place for art and intuition in the communications field; editing and programming are never likely to be reduced to a pure science. But shrewd editors know that public tastes change rapidly, and a constant, careful research program can provide the data for sound editorial and business decisions in a highly competitive and often turbulent media society.

There are two primary reasons for doing research of any kind: (1) to find out more about the basic laws of nature and (2) to apply this basic knowledge to solve practical problems. The first type is called *basic or pure research,* the second is *applied research.* Basic research aims at solving fundamental questions about the universe and about human behavior. Basic research in the mass communications field might tackle such questions as "How do we process and absorb information?" or "Why do we choose certain individuals to be our opinion leaders?" Basic research is simply an effort to explore the unknown, to advance knowledge. Applied research,

Political pollsters can help candidates focus on issues that are most important to voters.

on the other hand, aims at some specific objective. Instead of asking, "How do we process and absorb information?" the applied researcher might test two versions of the same advertising message to see which works better with a specific audience at that particular moment. Instead of asking, "Why do we choose certain individuals to be opinion leaders?" the applied researcher might convene a focus group to explore perceived strengths and vulnerabilities of a single congressional candidate in an up-coming race. Because of its immediate and direct importance to the mass communications industry, by far the larger portion of all communications research is in the realm of applied research.

Mass communications research may be further classified in a variety of ways. We will consider three broad groupings: Audience analysis, product analysis, and market research.

Audience Analysis

A logical first step is to understand the intended reader or viewer by gathering as much information as possible about his or her background, interests, needs, and ex-pectations. Audience research can be as simple as developing a *demographic* pro-file—a compilation, using Census Bureau data, of the age, sex, educational and income levels, racial and ethnic composition, religious preference, marital status, and family size in a given region. Or it might be as complex as a study of cultural and social factors, or *psychographics*—personality characteristics such as conformity, leadership, independence, aggressiveness, and gregariousness—that influence behavior and choices.

Product Analysis

In this context, the product is the communications medium (a newspaper, maga-zine, radio station) or, within that, a communications message (article, advertise-ment, program). What are the perceived characteristics of the product? How might the audience use it? What image does the product present to the reader or viewer? Or, as the term is widely used today, how is the product "positioned" in the mind of the consumer?

Audience Analysis: Nielsen on TV Ratings

Why have TV ratings at all?

Simply because the networks, stations, program producers and cable people are in the business of entertainment. They couldn't survive very long without being responsive to people's likes and dislikes. You'll find all kinds of parallels to this: the theatre which keeps tabs on its box office receipts; the newspaper which closely follows circulation trends; the manufacturer who can tell from his sales figures if his product is acceptable; and on a very small scale, the hostess who gives some thought to what her guests might like to have for dinner. The act of tuning in and watching a TV program is, quite literally, a *vote* for that program. A vote in preference to other programs being aired at the same hour. Ratings represent a tally of these votes. . . .

Quality is an elusive thing. One man's treasure is another man's trash, and so it will always be. Since there are just so many hours in a day for TV broadcasting, no one has yet come up with a proposal that makes as much sense as *counting the votes.*

Nielsen Media Research, *What TV Ratings Really Mean,* 1991.

Product research can measure the way the product's message is received and understood; it can compare alternative approaches to achieve the same result, and it can suggest which type of presentation technique might be more effective in a given situation. Restyling a publication's graphic design, reformatting a radio station, simplifying a complex news story, redesigning a television news set—all may be decisions stemming from data gathered in product analysis studies.

As an example, let us consider research in just one subgrouping of particular interest to television people, *nonverbal communication.* Scholars probing this area contend that as much as 65 percent of what we communicate is nonverbal, through actions rather than words. To aid in navigating these murky waters, researchers have coined several terms:

- *Kinesics,* or body movements, are gestures, facial expressions, and postures that communicators and audiences employ.
- *Proxemics,* or spatial behavior, is how we position ourselves in relation to others during conversations.
- *Paralinguistics* are all that go along with verbal communication: volume, pitch, rate, and so on.[21]

Nonverbal messages, or cues, can reinforce verbal messages, contradict them, or replace them altogether. Mere words pronounced by a television anchor might convey one message, but the way she says them might convey another meaning entirely. Product research, then, involves the message itself, as well as who is delivering it, and how.

Teaching Idea

Ask a student (or students) to send a message using *only* kinesics and proxemics.

Market Research

An editor soon finds that the marketplace will to a great extent dictate her publishing strategies. There's no need to plan on adding a world news section to the paper if the local economy will never generate enough readers or advertisers to justify it, or to develop a local television morning talk show if a competing station already has a similar program that appears unbeatable. Market research, whether comprised of systematic studies or informal observation, can tell publishers and broadcasters a great deal about what they might reasonably do, and what they clearly cannot do with a reading or viewing audience.

Well before going into the field, market researchers undergo training in how to conduct thorough and reliable interviews.

Research Methods: Pretesting and Posttesting

It has been estimated that more than half of *all* research in the field of human communication has occurred since the early 1950s. Obviously the techniques are still emerging. For our purposes, we will classify various procedures into two broad groupings, pretesting and posttesting.

Pretesting

Pretesting tries out an idea, a program, or a presentation ahead of time, on a reduced scale, in an attempt to predict which approach might work best.

Attitude and Opinion Surveys

Each of you probably has been asked in a personal interview or via a written questionnaire about your feelings toward a product, political figure, campaign issue, radio format, new movie, television commercial, or magazine design. Possibly you saw several similar presentations or concepts and were asked to rank-order them. If so, you were likely participating in a pretest, in which someone was trying to find out what members of the public would find appealing.

It may be that you were part of a statistical *sample,* a small group that will presumably reflect a given **universe.** This term is not as all-inclusive as it sounds; a universe, where samples are concerned, refers to the larger group the samples represent. The universe for a study of student attitudes at Siwash University would consist of all the students enrolled there at that particular time. A **random sample** could be obtained by interviewing every fiftieth student, or some other number chosen purely at random. Researchers rely on mathematical laws of probability to determine just how closely that sample is likely to represent the population as a whole. A **quota sample,** on the other hand, requires the researcher to divide the universe into subgroups such as age, sex, race, geographic location, and economic level and to assign each subgroup its proper share in the final sample, thus making it representative.

Relatively small samples can yield accurate results if they are carefully drawn. Professional polling organizations often conduct nationwide samples using fifteen hundred persons, sometimes even fewer. They must also draft questions with care, lest the respondents misunderstand them or, more likely, respond to "loaded" words that can produce biased answers.

The Semantic Differential Technique

This technique is frequently used in questionnaires and interviews to evaluate attitudes.[22] For example, a respondent might look at a series of page layouts from a magazine and then rate different concepts on a scale:

	+2	+1	0	-1	-2	
Modern	——	——	——	——	——	Old-fashioned
Warm	——	——	——	——	——	Cold
Expensive	——	——	——	——	——	Cheap
Clean	——	——	——	——	——	Dirty

The numerical values permit the researcher to quantify the results (median, mode, standard deviation, and so on) as well as to develop *inferences* from the data: Which types of persons liked which types of layouts? Which traits evoke the strongest responses?

Teaching Idea

Ask your students if they have recently been surveyed on any subject. If so, what was the aim of the survey? What types of questions were asked?

Background

Questions on a questionnaire should be viewed with some skepticism. If you or any of your class have recently received questionnaires, discuss the questions and the placement of questions to see if they indicate bias or predetermined outcomes.

Focus Groups, or Consumer Juries

Focus groups are another means of pretesting. Small groups of consumers are seated around a table and asked to speak freely while a trained moderator guides the discussion across a number of pertinent topics and analyzes what is said.

Laboratory Experiments

Since the introduction in 1930 of the eye camera, which photographs the movements of a person's eyes while he or she is reading, mass communications researchers have been attempting to measure the responses of a consumer to a news story, a page layout, or an advertisement. Various such contraptions are in use today. The *tachistoscope,* for example, controls and times exposure to a message so that the tester can observe when that message is being received; one can learn which of two headlines is understood more quickly, or how long it takes to pick up the meaning of an illustration. Other devices can detect changes in blood pressure, perspiration, brain wave patterns, eye pupil dilations, and so on as a respondent is receiving a communications message. Indications of interest, if not learning, can thus be calibrated.[23]

1949
MAILABLE AUDIMETER
(Kenyon Instrument Co.)

An early audience measurement device. The Nielsen organization in 1936 was using its first Audimeters, which kept a 24-hour record of radio listening and depicted the results on tapes. The information was forwarded to Nielsen headquarters, where it was tabulated, and the results were reported to clients.

Depth Interviews

Some researchers believe it is more useful to gather a great deal of information from a few persons rather than superficial data from a large sample. Depth interviews can probe a respondent's innermost thoughts about a communications medium or a message and allow that person to project his or her feelings about it. Interviewers may use word association and sentence completion techniques. Though an expensive procedure, and one that only well-trained interviewers or psychologists should attempt, this method can be very valuable. Many important media decisions, especially those involving advertising strategies, have resulted from ideas developed through depth interviews. **Motivational research,** the attempt to discover how consumers perceive their needs and how buying specific brands and products enhances their self-images, relies heavily on this type of projective technique.

Field Tests

Often the best way to pretest an idea is to run small-scale experiments with actual audiences, adjusting certain variables—graphic design, message content, timing, frequency of message appearance, and so on—with different subgroups. **Split-run** tests are used by publications and advertisers to test various themes or approaches. Many newspapers and magazines can divide their press runs and permit an editor or advertiser to use a different piece of copy in each *split.* The tester prepares two messages of the same size; each contains a coupon or an invitation to order or send in for something. The publication prints half the press run with one message, half with the other. They can then compare the responses. *Test markets* are also often used. Before risking huge sums of money on a national campaign, an advertiser may choose to experiment with one or more variables in seeking out the strongest audience appeals in individual cities.

Posttesting

Posttesting is designed to help judge the total effectiveness of the messages—how well they are received and accepted—and probes for trends.

Extra Information

Compare this means of testing with a polygraph (lie detector).

Background

One survey method had well-dressed interviewers go to the *front* door and ask what magazines the residents read. Next day, a scruffy guy in a pickup went to the *back* door and bought all the used magazines. There were a number of differences between the magazines people reported reading to the front door interviewers and the magazines they gave to the back-door visitor. This is an example of "unobtrusive" research.

Audience Analysis: Starch Impression Studies

One of the venerable media research companies is Starch INRA Hooper, Inc., which Harvard psychologist Daniel Starch began in 1923. *Starch Reports,* especially associated with magazine advertising, provides a great deal of information about which ads readers notice, associate with a particular sponsor, and most thoroughly read. Here, from material provided by the New York-based firm, is how a Starch INRA Hooper impression study is conducted.

The standard Impression interviewing procedures progressively focus the reader's attention on:

- Ad as a whole
- Product, service, or company advertised
- Illustrations
- Copy ideas

The standard Impression interview is an integrated series of neutral questions and probes designed to ascertain the personal meanings readers find in your advertisement. This carefully developed procedure encourages readers to respond as ad readers and consumers and not as advertising experts. In questioning the respondent, the interviewer probes in four key areas:

1. "When you first looked at this advertisement, what was outstanding to you? Tell me more about it. What does that mean to YOU?"
2. "In your own words, what did the advertisement tell you about the (product, service, company)? Tell me more about it. What does that mean to YOU?"
3. "What did the pictures tell you? Tell me more about it. What does that mean to YOU?"
4. "In your own words, what did the written material tell you? Tell me more about it. What does that mean to YOU?"

Hence, the Impression questions and probes provide an opportunity for the reader to show degree of involvement with the advertisement through spontaneous comments.

Readership Studies

These tell editors how many and what types of persons have read a given article or story. Often the information is highly specific. *Starch Reports,* the Starch INRA Hooper firm's reports, on selected magazines, can project how many persons read enough to get the gist of an article or ad (in an advertisement, this means associating the ad with a certain advertiser) and how many read most of it. A newspaper editor may take the latest readership study figures into account in planning how much international news to place on page one, how much feature material, how many photos and how large to play them, how much sports news, and so on. Readership studies also help editors determine which comics or syndicated columnists to retain. Radio and television stations draw upon comparable research to find out how many persons are in the audience at a particular time.

Readership studies also provide yardsticks for measuring shifts in consumer patterns and interests. While readership studies do generate a great deal of valuable information, they have drawbacks as well; the most important is the underlying assumption, risky at best, that just because an individual reads a message, he or she understands and accepts it. Another limitation is that a particular reader might be misled or confused; the individual probably has been exposed to many messages from a variety of mass media, and may not remember correctly whether the message appeared in this publication or that. Also, readers often claim to have read a particular publication merely to impress the researcher; many persons think they *should* read the paper or magazine and can't bring themselves to admit they don't.

Content Analysis

As the name indicates, **content analysis** is a procedure for the careful, systematic study of a publication or broadcast. Each article or advertisement is examined in detail. Individual assertions are then categorized according to subject matter and perhaps according to the tone—favorable, neutral, or unfavorable—that is struck. These are delicate judgments, but they can yield a great deal of useful information. An editor might believe she is devoting a great deal of space to international news,

Promoting market research. This advertisement, placed in a trade journal serving the advertising field, is designed to inform media buyers of the advantages of one company's magazines in targeting the Hispanic market.

for example, when a content analysis may reveal she is using far less than she thinks. Content analysis of television situation comedies or commercials might show that racial and sex stereotypes are indeed being perpetuated, if unintentionally. Content analysis of a foreign government's propaganda messages might penetrate the rhetoric and bring to light issues and themes that are truly important.

Process and Effects Studies

Research in this vast realm may range from an examination of editorial decision making by so-called *gatekeepers,* studies of which stories are chosen to run in the paper or on the air, to public opinion surveys showing whether awareness levels have changed following a media campaign. These studies employ many techniques and procedures that measure such indicators as recognition of a previously seen message, **aided recall** (remembering the message, with prompting), and **unaided recall** (remembering the message without prompting).

Process and effects studies also attempt to measure specific and cumulative impacts on given audiences—television violence on children, for example—and to assess how mass media may be helpful in the larger socialization process, or how information and ideas are diffused throughout the community.

Career Opportunities in Communications Research

About 80 percent of all U.S. companies of any size have a department devoted to market research. Most larger newspapers, magazines, and broadcasters use research departments to provide market, readership, and public opinion data. Advertising agencies, among the heaviest consumers of research, perform many studies in-house and retain independent research firms for additional data. At many colleges and universities, professors in mass communications and the social and behavioral science disciplines engage in mass communications research as part of their professional duties. Much of the basic research in mass communications, in fact, comes from faculty members. Their research output, as measured by numbers of articles in scholarly and professional journals as well as research-oriented books, continues to increase rapidly.

Most people who go to work in media positions will of necessity be affected by communications research findings. Because so much communications research is quantitative, some rudimentary knowledge of statistics proves invaluable in understanding and interpreting research data. Previous experience in mass communications is not an absolute requirement for performing mass communications research, but a good understanding of industry techniques and practices is helpful in designing realistic, useful communications research projects. As editors, media owners, and advertisers can attest, there is much work to do.

summary

Mass communications is a delicate business, fraught with hazards. We know a great deal about why communication does *not* work; we have learned relatively little about how, when, and why it does. Researchers, however, are making massive efforts to do so. Communications theorists are studying the mass media vehicles, the messages transmitted, and the audiences targeted to receive the messages.

Their studies have produced theories in a number of broad categories: theories of mass society; theories of diffusion; theories of communications processes and effects; uses and gratifications theories; and agenda setting and dependency theories, among others. These theories help us gain a better understanding of the role and influence of the mass media in modern society; they also provide insights into human behavior.

Less concerned with broad theory than with finding solutions to immediate problems, applied research studies in mass communications typically deal with such matters as audience analysis and product analysis. Research methods include attitude surveys, polls, and samples; focus groups and consumer juries; laboratory experiments; depth interviews; field tests; readership studies; content analysis, and process and effects studies.

About 80 percent of all U.S. companies of any size have a department devoted to market research, and most larger newspapers, magazines, and broadcasters use research departments to provide market, readership, and public opinion data. Advertising agencies and universities also generate many research studies in the field of mass communications.

? questions and cases

1. Suppose a political leader who wants to start a new, and highly opinionated, monthly publication aimed at young voters in your state approaches you for help. The publication would feature articles and commentary on such controversial issues as abortion, drug legalization, gun control, and economic support for higher education. "I want you to explore this idea," she tells you, "and let me know if there's a demand for it. I will pay any reasonable research costs involved." What procedures would you follow in attempting to obtain reliable market information for your client?

2. Comment on the media's agenda setting role. Who sets the agenda in your community? among your circle of friends? Suppose you, as editor of the local newspaper, are determined to stamp out any lingering traces of racial prejudice in the town; day after day, your paper calls attention to racial discrimination and editorially deplores it. Would this campaign likely succeed? If so, to what extent? Explain.

3. Discuss Aristotle's catharsis concept in light of today's movies and television programming. Does violence on the screen lead to more violence in real life? Or is screen violence merely a healthy substitute into which antisocial behavior can be channeled? Are there other possible explanations? Discuss.

4. What influences have been most powerful in determining your own attitudes? What role, if any, have the media of mass communications played in forming your opinions and beliefs? Cite specific examples. Have any of your beliefs changed because of something you read or saw in the media? Explain.

chapter glossary

agenda setting   The mass media's function of calling attention to certain events, thereby prompting public discussion and action on them. The ability to influence the public agenda, many believe, is one of the most significant aspects of media power in modern society.

aided recall   A method of testing advertising impact. Respondents are given cues (mention of a campaign theme, perhaps) to refresh their memories. In *unaided recall,* by comparison, respondents are tested without assistance.

channel noise   Term used in communications theory to describe anything that impedes the successful transmission of a message.

content analysis   A research methodology for systematic study of media content to determine major themes, literary and other devices employed, the amount of coverage given topics, political figures, and so on.

feedback   Response of an individual or an audience to a communications message.

focus group   A research technique in which small groups of consumers are interviewed in an attempt to obtain qualitative information about a product or service.

gatekeeper   An individual, usually an editor, who has the power to transmit or withhold material through one or more of the media of mass communications.

motivational research   In-depth interviews conducted by highly trained professionals who attempt to probe a consumer's interests and reactions.

quota sample   A relatively small group to be studied for characteristics and attitudes of the larger audience. In a quota, or stratified, sample, every effort is made to develop a small replica, in terms of age, race, sex, and other factors, as the entire market. Compare with *random sample.*

random sample   One in which every member of the audience has an equal opportunity to be included. Statistical probabilities indicate the point at which the random sample is large enough to resemble the total market.

semantic noise   Interference with a communications message arising from a misunderstanding of the words used, even though they were transmitted accurately. Compare with *channel noise.*

split run   Production capability offered by some newspapers and magazines to compare two or more messages by printing both simultaneously among different portions of a single press run.

unaided recall   A method of testing advertised impact, in which respondents are tested without receiving assistance.

universe   For our purposes, all the persons in a specific area to be studied; the basis from which random or quota samples are drawn.

uses and gratifications research   Studies which examine ways and motives by which members of audiences utilize the media of mass communications.

notes

1 For a discussion of these and other approaches, see Bruce H. Westley and Malcolm S. McLean, Jr., "A Conceptual Model for Communications Research," *Journalism Quarterly,* spring 1957, 31.

2 A useful discussion of noise may be found in Werner J. Severin and James W. Tankard, Jr., *Communications Theories* (New York: Hastings House, 1979), 47.

3 These themes are stressed throughout McLuhan's writings, especially in his *Understanding Media: The Extensions of Man* (New York: McGraw Hill, 1964) and *The Medium Is the Message* (New York: Bantam Books, 1967).

4 Harold Lasswell, "The Structure and Function of Communication in Society," published in Lyman Bryson, ed., *The Communication of Ideas* (New York: Harper, 1948).

5 Wilbur Schramm, "Media as Communication Institutions," in Wilbur Schramm and Donald F. Roberts, eds., *The Process and Effects of Mass Communication,* 2d ed. (Champaign: University of Illinois Press, 1971), 10.

6 Donald F. Roberts, "Nature of Communication Effects," in Schramm and Roberts, *Process and Effects,* 379.

7 Claude E. Shannon and Warren Weaver, *The Mathematical Theory of Communication* (Champaign: University of Illinois Press, 1949).

8 Leon Brillouin, *Science and Information Theory,* 2d ed. (Paris: Academic Press, 1960), xi.

9 See especially Joseph T. Klapper, *The Effects of Mass Communication* (New York: Free Press, 1960).

10 An able treatment of the marketing communication environment may be found in S. Watson Dunn and Arnold M. Barban, *Advertising: Its Role in Modern Marketing,* 6th ed. (Chicago: Dryden, 1986), 51–75.

11 Bernard C. Cohen, *The Press and Foreign Policy* (Princeton, N.J.: Princeton University Press, 1963), 13.

12 Walter Lippmann, *Public Opinion* (New York: Macmillan, 1922).

13 A seminal work in this regard is David Manning White, "The Gate Keeper: A Case Study in the Selection of News," *Journalism Quarterly,* fall 1950, 383.

14 Frank Luther Mott, *The News in America* (Cambridge, Mass.: Harvard University Press, 1952), 1.

15 Aristotle, "The Nature of Tragedy," from *Poetics* (VI), *c.* 350 B.C., translated by S. G. Butcher (New York: Macmillan, 1938). Seymour Feshbach's views on symbolic catharsis and its relative effects on viewers—the impact tends to vary somewhat according to income level—are well explained in Melvin L. De Fleur and Sandra Ball-Rokeach, *Theories of Mass Communications,* 4th ed. (White Plains, N.Y.: Longman, 1982), 201 ff.

16 Wilbur Schramm and William E. Porter, *Men, Women, Messages, and Media,* 2d ed. (New York: Harper & Row, 1982), 225.

17 De Fleur and Ball-Rokeach, *Theories of Mass Communication,* 236–51.

18 Ibid.

19 For a detailed discussion of limited, moderate, and powerful effects, see Severin and Tankard, *Communications Theories,* 246.

20 Eugene Pulliam, late editor and publisher of the Indianapolis *Star* and other newspapers.

21 A good overview of nonverbal communication may be found in Nan Lin, *The Study of Human Communication* (Indianapolis: Bobbs-Merrill, 1973), 68–89.

22 Described fully in Charles E. Osgood, George J. Suci, and Percy H. Tannenbaum, *The Measurement of Meaning* (Champaign: University of Illinois Press, 1957).

23 These and other measuring devices are explained in more detail in Dunn and Barban, *Advertising,* 407.

chapter S

Education and Professional Development

It is humbling experience for mass communications educators to realize that many of the industry's most brilliant successes never saw the inside of a school of mass communications

Lincoln Steffens

Objectives

When you have finished studying this chapter, you should be able to:

◉ Explain how schools of journalism developed, and why they were so long in coming

◉ Discuss the policies and procedures of the Accrediting Council on Education in Journalism and Mass Communications

◉ Describe career opportunities in journalism education at the scholastic, community college, and four-year college and university levels

◉ List the various trade journals serving the journalism/mass communications field, and describe the kinds of content one can expect to find in each publication

It is a humbling experience for mass communications educators to realize that many of the industry's most brilliant successes never saw the inside of a school of mass communications. Lincoln Steffens, widely regarded as one of the greatest reporters of all time, never took a course in news writing, and Horace Greeley's professional credentials did not include completing Editing I. David Sarnoff, who founded the Radio Corporation of America, which became the parent company of the National Broadcasting Company, never completed a course in media management, nor did Ivy Ledbetter Lee ever sit through a college class in public relations. While it is unlikely we shall ever encounter a self-taught brain surgeon or meet a Supreme Court justice who never studied law, plenty of people in the mass communications field, including many of today's top-of-the-line stars, have yet to undergo an hour of formal study in their chosen profession.

It was ever thus. Throughout much of American history, mass communications was not regarded seriously as a career field, much less a subject worth intensive investigation at a college or university. The earliest publishers were, in fact, postmasters who produced newspapers primarily as a service to their constituents. Later newspapers were published by printing-house proprietors as a sideline to their larger and more lucrative printing businesses. During the formative years of the republic, politicians often operated newspapers by and for themselves. While some editors of this period wrote brilliantly, they did so almost as an afterthought. The main goal was to perpetuate a philosophical point of view and to root for a political party; journalistic techniques remained pretty far down on the editor's list of priorities.

During the 1830s, when newspapers first began to break away from narrow partisanship in quest of the mass audience, publishers tended to be promoters bent on making profits. For these cold-eyed individuals, staffing was easy; there was almost always a bright young person around with a literary flair and an eagerness to become a reporter or an editor.

Some publishers of this period were splendid teachers as well, and they were able to train their staffs to perform outstanding work. Many would share the view of an early press historian, Frederic Hudson, who proclaimed that the office of a daily newspaper "is the one true college for newspaper students. Professor James Gordon Bennett or Professor Horace Greeley would turn out more genuine journalists in one year than the Harvards, the Yales, and the Dartmouths could produce in a generation."[1]

But only a privileged few would ever work for Bennett's New York *Herald* or Greeley's *Tribune,* and as events grew more complex the uneven quality of news reporting became embarrassingly apparent. General Robert E. Lee's experience with reporters covering his headquarters during the Civil War convinced him that formal education in the journalism field was plainly necessary. In 1869, he initiated the practice of offering full-tuition scholarships to Washington College in Virginia, now Washington and Lee University, to a selected number of students on the condition that each student would "labor one hour a day in his profession of journalism" and spend considerable time studying with an outstanding editor, much as a would-be lawyer of the period would study in the office of a good attorney. General Lee's program did not work as well as he had hoped, but this idea was well publicized; other institutions soon began, in one way or another, to consider providing some systematic instruction in journalism.

In 1877, a young professor of English at the University of Missouri, David R. McAnally, Jr., inaugurated a course in the history of journalism and a series of tutorials for students interested in learning newspaper-style composition. McAnally's work gained enthusiastic approval, both from students and the university administration; if he had remained at Missouri, he very probably would have gone on to establish a school, or at least a department, of journalism there.[2] But McAnally grew weary of

Background

The Civil War marked the first time reporters sent immediate battlefield reports by telegraph back to their newspapers. The military on both sides, somewhat like the U.S. military in recent years, complained that reporters not only exaggerated and fabricated, but also gave away military secrets.

vicarious journalism and left the teaching field to become an editorial writer for the St. Louis *Globe-Democrat*. While the university did not replace him—professors of his caliber, enthusiasm, and range of interests must have been hard to find then, as they are today—the feeling persisted at Missouri that journalism should have a place in the curriculum of the state university.

In New York, meanwhile, the celebrated newspaper publisher Joseph Pulitzer had been urging Columbia University to establish, with funds he himself would donate, a school of journalism. Fearing its dignity would suffer if it appeared to endorse the concept of purely vocational training, Columbia turned down Pulitzer's multimillion-dollar offer. But Pulitzer had in mind far more than a trade school. He wished to bring to the newspaper field an enlightenment, a sense of social responsibility, and national prestige comparable to that of the attorney or physician. "My idea," he wrote, "is to raise the character of the profession to a higher level."[3]

Part of Pulitzer's motivation may have been remorse over his own excessive behavior during the sordid yellow journalism circulation battles he had waged with William Randolph Hearst. He wanted future journalists to know better. "One of the chief difficulties with journalism," Pulitzer wrote, "is to keep the news instinct from running rampant over the restraints of accuracy and conscience."[4] He was convinced that a well-conceived school of journalism would instill in young reporters high ethical purpose, and would soon benefit society as a whole. Columbia's trustees eventually came around to Pulitzer's point of view, but it was not until 1912 that the Columbia school of journalism opened.

While Columbia's distinguished president, Nicholas Murray Butler, remained dubious about the value of a formal journalism education, presidents of other institutions did not. The University of Illinois as early as 1904 developed a series of courses in the field. At the University of Kentucky in 1907, Dr. James K. Patterson told his trustees that "the time, I think, is opportune for the establishment of schools of journalism in the great American colleges and universities . . . to prepare young journalists to handle intelligently and profitably the great questions with which the American citizen has to deal . . . to furnish the necessary information to the general public, and to become an intelligent leader of thought, giving thought definite and consistent shape for the realization of great and noble ends."[5] Patterson's proposal came during lean budget times, however, and Kentucky's journalism program was not to begin until 1914.

Success came more quickly at Missouri, where the memory of McAnally's lectures and tutorials in journalism still burned brightly. Given direction by an ambitious, determined, self-educated weekly newspaper publisher, Walter Williams, the state press association brought pressure to bear on the University of Missouri Board of Curators to create a school of journalism. They overcame the initial resistance of the faculty—again, the trade school question—but curators delayed establishment of the school for more than a year while they searched for a competent person to direct the new and experimental program. Several prominent newspaper executives turned down offers for the deanship, regarding it as too speculative. In time, Williams himself was invited to take the position. He accepted eagerly, and in 1908 the first classes began. The university's president, A. Ross Hill, set what he hoped would be the keynote for the new school in a thoughtful talk to the students and faculty:

> I believe it is possible for this School to give dignity to the profession of journalism, to anticipate to some extent the difficulties that journalism must meet and to prepare its graduates to overcome them; to give prospective journalists and professionals spirit and high ideals of service; to discover those with real talent for the work in the profession, and to discourage those who are likely to prove failures in the profession, and to give the state better newspapers and a better citizenship.[6]

Background

The Columbia school is still in operation, but primarily for graduate students. It publishes the *Columbia Journalism Review*.

From Early Journalism Education: A Statement of Beliefs

One of the first professional codes of ethics in the mass communications field was *The Journalist's Creed,* written in the early 1920s by Walter Williams, who had founded the world's original journalism school.

Widely translated and adopted by professional groups around the world at the time, the *Creed* was written at a time when there were no broadcast news media and no satellites and when life seemed simpler. Thousands of journalism students in earlier generations were required to memorize *The Journalist's Creed.* The flowery language and simplicity of its declarations are badly dated today, though perhaps the idealism the *Creed* represents is not.

The Journalist's Creed

I believe in the profession of journalism.

I believe that the public journal is a public trust; that all connected with it are, to the full measure of their responsibility, trustees for the public; that acceptance of lesser service than the public service is betrayal of this trust.

I believe that clear thinking and clear statement, accuracy and fairness, are fundamental to good journalism.

I believe that the journalist should write only what he holds in his heart to be true.

I believe that suppression of the news, for any consideration other than the welfare of society, is indefensible.

I believe that no one should write as a journalist what he would not say as a gentleman; that bribery by one's own pocketbook is as much to be avoided as bribery by the pocketbook of another; that individual responsibility may not be escaped by pleading another's instructions or another's dividends.

I believe that advertising, news and editorial columns should alike service the best interests of readers; that a single standard of helpful truth and cleanliness should prevail for all; that the supreme test of good journalism is the measure of public service.

I believe that journalism which succeeds best—and best deserves success—fears God and honors man; is stoutly independent, unmoved by pride of opinion or greed of power; constructive, tolerant but never careless, self-controlled, patient, always respectful of its readers but always unafraid; is quickly indignant at injustice; is unswayed by the appeal of privilege or clamor of the mob; seeks to give every man a chance and, as far as law and honest wage and recognition of human brotherhood can make it so, an equal chance; is profoundly patriotic while sincerely promoting international good will and cementing world-comradeship; is a journalism of humanity, of and for today's world.

Walter Williams

The curriculum Williams devised focused on the nuts-and-bolts aspects of newspaper work. Never having attended college himself, Williams was far more impressed with practice than theory. He launched a five-day-a-week community newspaper at the school of journalism and organized his academic program around it. Students were required to work on the paper, and faculty members who doubled as editors closely monitored their performances. All students had to sign up for a four-credit course in newspaper making as well as a five-credit course in journalism history, but the thrust of the program was intensively pragmatic. Ninety-seven students, far more than expected, decided to cast their lots with the new school at registration that September. Journalism education was off and running.

By 1912, at least thirty-three colleges and universities were offering journalism instruction. In Chicago that autumn, the American Association of Teachers of Journalism was organized, with seventeen professors as charter members. Journalism students formed their own fraternity, Sigma Delta Chi—it would later become the Society of Professional Journalists—on the campus of DePauw University in Greencastle, Indiana; by the time it convened its first national meeting in 1912, Sigma Delta Chi had twelve chapters and was growing rapidly.[7]

Philosophical Problems

As the number of journalism programs around the country proliferated, journalism teachers felt the need to develop academic and professional standards and to recognize the schools that had attained them. In 1924, the newly created Council on

Criticism of the university by media practitioners often is ignorant, offensive, and anti-intellectual in tone.

But the critics are not always wrong. The university frequently treats enlightenment like a monopoly. Higher education protects its authority with acute specialization, devising arcane codes of language that turn academic departments into occult knowledge sects. Expertise often is cultivated to customize individual careers, challenging what Wendell Berry has described as the university's core mission of making humanity. Journalism educators should keep a watchful distance from both institutions.

Douglas Birkhead, in *Gannett Center Journal,* Summer 1991.

Education for Journalism issued a statement of Principles and Standards of Education for Journalism. Under this code, a proper journalism curriculum had to "be sufficiently broad in scope to familiarize the future journalist with the important fields of knowledge, and sufficiently practical to show the application of the knowledge to the practice of journalism." The statement also called for a heavy emphasis in such areas outside journalism as economics, history, sociology, political science, literature and language, psychology, natural science, and philosophy. It warned that within the journalism classroom "the aims and methods of instruction should not be those of trade schools, but should be of the same standard as those of other professional schools and colleges."[8]

Those high-minded aims proved easier to assert than to achieve. The newspaper industry preferred instructors with extensive practical experience who would ground the students thoroughly in reporting and editing techniques. University administrators, on the other hand, were more comfortable with traditional academic approaches; they wanted professors with doctorates to examine the societal aspects of the press rather than teach students merely how to write obituaries, headlines, and reports of armed robberies.

While editors disdained the ivory tower approach, college presidents and faculties resented the trade school viewpoint at many journalism schools, regarding the faculty as cheerleaders for the newspaper industry rather than as independent scholars. One social historian of the period, Alfred McClung Lee, dismissed journalism schools as "a means devised by publishers to maintain an oversupply of potential reporters with which to minimize wages."[9] This characterization, like the hardline, polar positions of some college presidents and newspaper editors, oversimplified the case and was unfair. Even so, the fledgling journalism schools attempted to strike middle ground between a theoretical and a practical curriculum; as a result they were often criticized from both within and without the academic community.

Despite these obstacles, journalism schools continued to grow in numbers and improve in quality. The theory-versus-practice issue has never been ironed out. Some journalism faculties stuck with a heavily professional approach that stressed technique; other faculties emphasized communications theory and the social and ethical responsibilities of the press. Most faculties attempted, with varying degrees of success, to balance the two points of view. National accreditation standards, as they evolved over time, wisely reflected an understanding that more than one approach to teaching mass communications can be valid.

Background

These two approaches, which still exist today, are usually characterized as "green eyeshade" (nuts-and-bolts writing and editing), and "chi square" (theory and research). Most journalism schools have both sides represented on the faculty.

Accreditation

As many as one thousand U.S. colleges and universities, possibly even more, offer some instruction in the field of journalism. Only about one hundred of these institutions, however, maintain programs accredited by the Accrediting Council on Education in Journalism and Mass Communications. The decision to apply for

accreditation is purely voluntary, and many sound, well-run mass communications programs never seek formal accreditation, which requires considerable effort, money, and time. Some institutions oppose accreditation as a matter of principle, regarding it as a threat to academic freedom and local autonomy. The schools that have gained accreditation, on the other hand, did so largely because of the opportunity accreditation presents to open up their mass communications program to outside scrutiny. They see this as an opportunity to show that the program is performing at a nationally acceptable and competitive level. The Accrediting Council made its case this way:

> Accreditation serves students, parents, faculty, employers, universities, and the public at large. It seeks to ensure continued improvement in the quality of instruction of journalism and mass communications through re-evaluation, including a thorough and useful self-study, at six-year intervals. Further, accreditation provides administrators and faculty with the stimulation that comes from exchanging viewpoints with persons outside their own institutions and outside the academy. The accreditation process provides a forum for hearing and acting on complaints by students, faculty, and the public. Finally, it ensures that journalism and mass communications education continues to provide both breadth and depth of exposure to the liberal arts and sciences.[10]

The accreditation process in the mass communications field began, informally, at least, as early as 1917 when a group of the larger schools formed the American Association of Schools and Departments of Journalism. Before a program could qualify, its dean or chair had to fill out a lengthy questionnaire describing that unit's educational philosophy, faculty, curriculum, budget, and physical facilities. If the Association adjudged the answers satisfactory, then that unit was permitted to join the ranks. Currently, the much-intensified procedure calls for accreditation only after a mass communications program has undergone extensive self-study and compiled a great deal of information about its faculty, students, alumni, library holdings, equipment and other institutional resources, and so on. After carefully studying this pre-visit data, the Association sends an outside team composed of representatives of the communications field as well as educators to conduct an on-site inspection of the unit and talk at length with students, faculty, administrators, and outside professionals in the region who are familiar with the program and its graduates. The team then makes a recommendation (for full accreditation, provisional accreditation, or no accreditation), which the Accrediting Council later acts upon.

This group, which usually meets twice a year, consists of more than thirty members representing newspapers, magazines, broadcasting, business communications, advertising, photography, public relations, various professional societies, journalism educators, and other interests. If they grant accreditation, it extends for six years, after which the program must be evaluated again.

Just as the Accrediting Council's membership is diverse, so are its views on what makes a successful school of mass communications. The Council makes no real attempt to decree a national curriculum for accreditation purposes, nor does it require or expect mass communications professors to teach their courses in lockstep. There are a few rigid standards; one is the 15:1 ratio in skills courses. This rule requires that in the intensive, individualized laboratory courses such as reporting and editing, there must be no more than 15 students per instructor. Another rule, rather more controversial, requires that mass communications classes consume only about 30 percent or less of the student's total academic program. The remaining 70 to 75 percent must be in liberal arts and other areas outside the mass communications school. Apart from these and a few other specific standards, however, the Council permits considerable flexibility. Accreditation thus depends to a large degree on the inspection team's and the Accrediting Council's subjective assessment of the overall worth of the individual program. If the unit seems to be doing its job, as measured in the quality of students and faculty and success of its recent graduates, then that program will likely gain accreditation.

Teaching Idea

If your institution is ACEJMC-accredited, obtain a copy of the latest self-study and demonstrate to your class the preparation necessary to become accredited.

Teaching Idea

Have the class discuss the 30/70 percent division the accreditation standards call for. Do they agree or disagree with this philosophy? What reasons can students give for wanting more journalism classes?

The accreditation process is far from perfect—again, many good mass communications schools and departments are not accredited—but most mass communications educators would probably agree that accreditation has had a positive effect, helping to shore up weaknesses in teaching and administrative support, and in general giving the discipline higher standards.

Mass Communications Schools Today

The 1991–92 annual enrollment survey for the field found 151,740 journalism/mass communications majors in the 347 largest programs alone.[11] Add to that majors in schools not participating in the survey, and the total could include several thousand more. This total—somewhat greater than in the nation's accredited law schools but far below enrollment in the business schools—represents massive growth over the past generation.

In 1963, the national headcount of journalism/mass communications majors was around 15,000. In the late 1960s, the surge began. It continued unabated until 1982, reaching a peak estimated at 110,000, with 91,016 in the top 200 schools alone. Enrollments tapered off a bit for two years after that, then started rising again at a rate exceeding higher education enrollments generally. More than 60 percent of the majors are women.

In most of the larger mass communications programs, students may enroll in one aspect, or sequence, of concentration. The news-editorial sequence, the oldest and the one most associated with traditional reporting and editing skills, is no longer the largest in terms of enrollment. The advertising sequence, which has grown dramatically in recent years, now leads, followed by public relations, radio and television, and broadcast news. Some schools also have photojournalism, magazine, agricultural journalism, and media management sequences available. Because some institutions offer more sequences than others, and schools keep records by different systems, the enrollment figures are imprecise. The trend, however, is for continued growth in the "nontraditional" sequences of advertising, public relations, and broadcasting at the expense of news-editorial. Minorities remain underrepresented in mass communications schools. African Americans comprise only about 7.4 percent of the total and Hispanics about 4 percent.[12]

Mass communications faculties, once made up almost exclusively of former newspaper people, now reflect a blend of academic and professional backgrounds. Today's typical mass communications professor brings to the classroom several

Background

Some believe that Woodward and Bernstein's Watergate reporting for the *Washington Post*, plus the book and movie *All the President's Men*, was a great recruiting tool for journalism schools. (If you can, show the movie and ask students for their reaction.)

Teaching Idea

Survey your students to find out which sequences they are pursuing and why. Are minorities well represented? Do women make up more or less than 60 percent of the class?

An interview conducted by students in a television communications department studio at a Boston-area college.

Mass Comm Professors: A Composite Profile

The composite faculty member promoted to associate professor with tenure in an accredited school of journalism and mass communication during the 1990–91 academic year was a white male in his middle forties. He held a Ph.D. and averaged seven years of professional media experience. According to his unit head, his strength was a balance of superior teaching and research activity. He generally had a good [professional and institutional] service record as well. . . .

The composite faculty member promoted to full professor at an accredited school of journalism and mass communication during the 1990–91 year was a white male in his late forties. He held a Ph.D. and averaged eight years of professional media experience. His strength was described by his unit head as a balance of superior teaching and research, although his publication record was more likely to have been recognized. . . .

Frederic A. Leigh and Douglas A. Anderson in *Journalism Educator,* Spring 1992.

years of professional experience—as a reporter, an editor, a television news anchor or producer, an advertising account executive, or a public relations practitioner—as well as one or more advanced degrees. Like their colleagues in other departments on campus, mass communications professors are hired, retained, promoted, and awarded tenure on the basis of their teaching, service, and writing and research. Service reflects the individual's work outside the classroom in behalf of the college or university or the industry.

Mass communications teachers are frequently called upon to judge professional news, editorial, and advertising competitions, speak to scholastic and professional groups, conduct in-service training programs for an industry association, or perhaps act as a writing coach or consultant to a publication or broadcast operation. Research involves developing new knowledge. A mass communications professor might conduct a study involving mass media process and effects, for example, and develop from it a book or an article for a scholarly publication such as the *Journalism Quarterly.* Some campuses stress research performance far more than others, but in recent years most administrations increasingly expect mass communications professors to study new methods or to develop improved interpretations of existing knowledge, and to share their findings with the academic and professional communities through their scholarly writing.

Criticisms and Challenges

By the mid-1990s, mass communications schools appeared to be generally holding their own in an era of academic downsizing and fierce competition for funding, though a few programs had been reorganized or severely cut back. Enrollments continued at near-record levels; outside financial support from foundations, wealthy alumni, and media companies came at an unprecedented rate. Mass communications and journalism graduates were actively recruited by hundreds of newspapers, broadcasters, advertising and public relations firms, nonprofit organizations, and business concerns. Many schools of mass communications occupied handsome new buildings.

Despite these attainments, some of the old problems remain, and mass communications education continues to collect a measure of criticism, especially from editors and broadcast executives. Some specific charges are that too many mass communications schools:

- *Refuse to renovate a curriculum that is unimaginative and too heavily oriented toward the print media.* Since the days of Walter Williams, mass communications professors have come predominantly from newspaper backgrounds, and their teaching has tended to be geared toward the

Teaching Idea

Consider explaining the "publish or perish" imperative to students, if your institution emphasizes it as a criterion for promotion and tenure.

A professor working with a student who is preparing a computer-assisted page layout.

Teaching Idea

Review your school's journalism curriculum with your students. Do they perceive the print-oriented criticism as valid?

Teaching Idea

If your school's journalism curriculum includes required economics, statistics, or management courses, this might be a good time to emphasize them.

newspaper field. Accordingly, other media can be neglected or ignored.[13] Traditionalists accurately point out that more graduates are likely to go to work for newspapers than for broadcasters, and that every mass communications student can benefit from the discipline of learning to write crisp, lean, accurate, newspaper-style copy.

While these arguments are persuasive, in truth only about 20 percent or less of all mass communications graduates actually choose newspaper careers, and those critics who clamor for more attention to be given to the other media seem to have a point. A blue-ribbon panel of scholars who conducted a recent examination of journalism education concluded that the typical mass communications curriculum did not reflect enough concern for broadcast news, cable television, newsletters, and a variety of other media that well-prepared mass communications graduates will need to know about in the years to come.[14]

- *Aren't putting enough emphasis on leadership training.* Typical mass communications graduates, this argument contends, think only in terms of filling entry-level positions. Such young men and women may not be intellectually or professionally prepared to grow into management roles. As a result, the leadership of tomorrow's newspapers, magazines, radio, and television operations will ultimately go by default to "outsiders"— lawyers, accountants, graduates of business or engineering schools. Executives chosen from among these ranks may not concern themselves much with freedom of expression and the public's right to know— concepts most graduates of mass communications schools understand well and believe in deeply.

The mass communications schools' response, slow in coming, has been to add courses in media management and media economics and to incorporate more leadership training in editing courses and at other key spots in the curriculum. Effective management preparation is not easy to provide, especially at the undergraduate level, but certainly more mass communications educators are aware of the need than in the past.

- *Are turning out graduates who have a poor command of the language.* With increasing frequency, as well as a certain stridency, editors are complaining about mass communications graduates who can't write well or spell properly. Schools are not devoting enough instruction to language fundamentals, critics charge, because too many mass communications faculties are dominated by theoreticians who lack solid professional experience themselves and who seem more interested in scholarly research than in teaching students how to write clearly and report accurately. Sensitive to this charge, a number of mass communications schools have established or toughened admissions requirements, and instructors are bearing down harder in the classrooms and the reporting labs.

Such criticisms, along with others directed at schools of journalism and mass communications, no doubt have some validity. At the same time, it might well be argued that critics of mass communications education may be expecting more than schools can reasonably provide, given the present philosophy, structure, and organization of the education establishment. After all, medical schools require four years of postgraduate training, plus a lengthy residency, to turn out a physician, and law schools take three years of intensive postgraduate instruction to develop an attorney. Theological seminaries and dental colleges consider three postgraduate years a minimum for preparing their young professionals.

The schools of mass communications, on the other hand, are limited to about one-fourth of a student's undergraduate education. The remaining three-fourths, by accreditation rules (which are, to a great extent, followed closely, even in unaccredited programs) must be devoted to liberal arts and other fields quite apart from mass communications. The typical student in mass communications takes only about ten to twelve semester-long courses in his or her major field, and half or more of these are introductory classes or courses in reporting, editing, communications law, media history, and perhaps an ethics course as part of a core curriculum. This leaves only a few classes for exploring the myriad electives, such as magazines, advertising, public relations, photojournalism, broadcast news, science writing, business writing, media management, international communications, and others that represent the rich diversity of the field. The wonder is that mass communications schools accomplish as much with their students as they do.

Despite curricular restrictions, the graduate of a good mass communications program gains useful and highly marketable skills as well as a solid liberal arts education, and few undergraduate majors offer so promising a combination. This type of background enables many mass communications majors to perform well in fields

Teaching Idea
Ask students what they have learned from their required writing courses. As an alternate, invite an editor or a news director to help emphasize the importance of good writing.

Hitting the top. Dallas *Morning News* writers and photographers react to news they had just won a Pulitzer prize. Their award, presented in 1994, was for a series on violence against women.

Professional Development

As economic trends change and technologies develop, so does the need for more on-the-job and midcareer training in the mass communications field. While industry associations and media groups, along with many schools of mass communications, have for some time operated training programs to help practicing professionals adjust to changing circumstances and handle new responsibilities, recent years have seen these efforts greatly intensified. Literally hundreds of midcareer classes are offered each year throughout the industry. The American Newspaper Publishers Association, the Southern Newspaper Publishers Association, the Knight-Ridder and Gannett newspaper chains, the Poynter Institute, and a number of other associations regularly conduct seminars in management, executive development, technology updates, improving job knowledge, sharpening interpersonal and leadership skills. A number of mass communications schools provide on-the-job and midcareer instructional pro-grams, and dozens of mass communications professors serve as writing and editing coaches each year to professional newspaper staffs.

The midcareer classes cited here have come primarily from the newspaper field, but broadcasters and advertising and public relations people also have comparable career development opportunities available. The Television Bureau of Advertising and the National Association of Broadcasters host conferences and workshops each year, as does the Magazine Publishers Association. Advertising executives can choose from among a rich selection of creative workshops and media planning seminars that various trade associations and private groups offer. The International Association of Business Communicators and the Public Relations Society of America arrange intensive training sessions for individuals seeking professional accreditation, as well as special topics conferences, particularly dealing with ethical matters, for practitioners.

besides their own. In any given year, thousands of mass communications graduates move into positions with business and industry. Those who seek communications-related jobs find that their writing and editing abilities and their knowledge of media operations often give them a competitive edge over students whose educational backgrounds are limited to purely liberal arts subjects. Many editors and broadcasters schedule hiring interviews primarily or exclusively with mass communications graduates, on the theory that applicants truly interested in entering the mass communications field will have explored the subject in college.

In addition, schools of mass communications have helped foster a feeling of professionalism among students. Beyond that, the teaching, research, and critical analysis of media performance taking place within journalism schools has been a healthy development for the industry as a whole. The late Frank Luther Mott, a Pulitzer prize–winning author and journalism educator, asserted:

> Newspapers, radio, and television will surely benefit in the years to come from a growing sense of professionalism in the field of communication. Journalists are far better educated than they were a generation or two ago; they have better backgrounds in the social sciences and in the knowledge necessary to anyone working with news. Schools of journalism, at first misunderstood, sometimes stumbling, are now generally accepted by the better minds in both educational and journalistic circles. Many of them have been working away faithfully for years, so that thousands of their graduates are now prominent in practical communications work. The new generation of journalists gives us encouragement for the progress and development of our news system in the ensuing decades.[15]

Career Opportunities Teaching Mass Communications

Four-Year Colleges and Universities

It is a privilege to be asked to teach in one's chosen field. Mass communications professors, like their colleagues in other departments across the campus, work very hard to win their positions on the faculty. About half of the professors in the country's largest three hundred mass communications programs hold earned doctorates. Most of the others were hired to teach only after they had put in years of solid professional media experience. The typical mass communications professor has both media experience and one or more advanced degrees. Many are members of the professional organization known as the **Association for Education in Journalism and Mass Communications (AEJMC).**

Young people who aspire to careers as mass communications educators should plan on a lengthy preparation period that will include both graduate school and substantial on-the-job training as a reporter, copyeditor, broadcast journalist, or advertising or public relations professional. About twenty-five U.S. colleges and universities presently offer doctorates in mass communications. It is possible to obtain a doctorate in a related field such as political science, history, English, law, or American studies and combine it with a strong academic background in mass communications (or considerable media experience) to land a teaching position. Many excellent mass communications teachers do not hold doctorates, of course. But a young person facing today's highly competitive teaching job market will need as many credentials as possible, and the youthful applicant without a Ph.D. will likely be at a marked disadvantage.

The media experience should lead to areas of teaching expertise. Most mass communications curricula include courses in reporting, editing, media law, communications history, magazine writing and editing, broadcast news, graphics, production, programming, photojournalism, media management, and a full range of classes in advertising and public relations. Graduate-level seminars are offered in nearly a hundred mass communications programs.

Except in the largest schools of mass communications, professors are rarely able to confine themselves to a narrow teaching specialty. Most faculty members must be able to handle a reporting lab as well as a lecture course, and to work with incoming freshmen as well as graduating seniors.

Just as the professional media experience strengthens teaching qualifications, postgraduate study leading to a master's degree and Ph.D. opens up opportunities in both teaching and research. Graduate seminars in mass communications examine international news flow, research methods, mass media and public policy, communications theory, and a variety of other complex topics. At the end of the course work, each doctoral candidate must produce a dissertation, an extensive and original study of a significant issue. While the dissertation is important in and of itself—many dissertations later appear in book form—it is particularly useful in launching the doctoral candidate on a long-term research program. This is vital, for many colleges and universities expect mass communications faculty to engage in more or less continuous research as well as work with the media in service activities and handle a teaching load. There is a brisk demand in the teaching marketplace for those who have both media experience and a Ph.D. Broadcast news and advertising professors tend to be in especially short supply.

Community Colleges

Most community colleges offer at least some mass communications instruction, and opportunities for teaching in this area continue to expand. Typically, the community college curriculum in mass communications includes the introductory course, one or two classes in reporting and photojournalism, and perhaps preliminary instruction in editing. Often these classes use the student newspaper as a working laboratory; many times, the community college mass communications teacher is the publications adviser as well. In a great many cases, the community college mass communications teacher has the additional responsibility of handling public relations duties

Publications advisor Calvin Hall, left, of Asheville (North Carolina) High School, critiquing the latest edition of the school newspaper with editor Stefan Weir.

for the institution. This work places the teacher in close and direct working proximity to the president of the college and, not infrequently, community college mass communications faculty later move into the central administration.

About three-fourths of the community college mass communications faculty hold the M.A. degree, and an increasing number have doctorates. Most community colleges do not expect mass communications teachers to perform scholarly research, though a number do. Teaching loads, however, are normally much heavier in community college programs than in four-year colleges and universities. The Community College Journalism Association has been helpful in focusing attention on the special problems and unique teaching opportunities in this important field.

Secondary Schools

Somewhere between forty and fifty thousand regularly issued publications come from the country's junior and senior high schools, and about five thousand secondary schools currently offer one or more classes in journalism. Secondary school teaching, in other words, offers many job opportunities for mass communications graduates.

Those interested in scholastic communications teaching need to coordinate their class schedules with pertinent offerings in the department of secondary educa-

Academic Freedom *v.* Administrative Authority

What is educationally significant about [high school] journalism education is its ability to teach students how to handle freedom, not how to handle publishers. The attractive argument that censorship is good preparation for a life in which reporters are subject to private editorial censorship misses the point. High School students in journalism are not being trained for jobs. No high school graduate is close to being employable as a journalist. But every high school graduate should be prepared to be a citizen, one who understands how and why his thoughts and opinions, letters, and comments are not subject to government censorship.

Jack Dvorak and Jon Paul Dilts in *Journalism Educator*, Autumn 1992.

Thirty years ago most student newspapers were filled with gossip columns and editorials about school spirit. Today, student journalists are writing about gangs, suicide, homosexuality, drug use, teen pregnancy—the issues of their age. The best of student newspapers inform and influence the entire school community, including adults. As their newspapers have become more professional, there is a greater need for better qualified journalism teachers and advisers. . . . High school newspapers strive for professionalism. Students need a knowledgeable and certified teacher to guide them.

Mary Anne Siefkes, journalism teacher at Newton High School, Newton, Kansas, writing in *Death by Cheeseburger: High School Journalism in the 1990s and Beyond* (Freedom Forum, 1994).

tion to properly prepare for state teaching certification. Scholastic communications teaching is rarely a full-time specialty; usually the teaching load includes one or more English or social studies classes as well. Almost always, the scholastic journalism teacher also serves as adviser to the school newspaper or yearbook, or both. Many high schools offer radio and television classes, and some high school students produce newscasts and other programs for local cable television systems. With increasing frequency, high school journalism classes are asked to operate news bureaus for their schools, providing opportunities for students to write press releases for professional media.

Scholastic mass communications teaching is challenging work, especially in the wake of recent court decisions which, perhaps to the consternation of some principals and superintendents, have resoundingly affirmed the rights of student journalists to express themselves more freely, under certain conditions, on controversial issues. In one landmark case, Tinker *v.* Des Moines Independent School District, the Supreme Court held that "it can hardly be argued that either students or teachers shed their Constitutional rights to freedom of expression at the schoolhouse gate."[16]

While other decisions have given school administrators authority to suppress a student publication if it might pose a substantial threat to order and discipline within a school, or perhaps invade the privacy of a student,[17] the fact remains that today's high school publications staffers are at considerable liberty to report and comment in print. As a result, scholastic communications teachers are faced with more demanding responsibilities: Instead of controlling student newspapers and yearbooks via heavy-handed censorship, teachers now must rely more on counseling and persuasion—as many have been doing all along. Most scholastic publications are socially responsible due, in no small measure, to the sensitivity and thoughtful advice high school mass communications teachers provide. Such labors, though difficult, can be highly satisfying. Another reward is that scholastic journalism and mass communications teachers have the opportunity of working with some of the brightest and most promising students in their schools.

Dramatic improvement over the years in the quality of scholastic publications advising is one of the leading factors contributing to the general increase in mass communications enrollments at the nation's colleges and universities.

The Journals

Indispensable to professional development are the trade journals and **journalism reviews,** which promptly and faithfully chronicle events taking place throughout the industry. Any individual who seriously aspires to a career in the mass communications field should become thoroughly familiar with the publications that report on his or her areas of special interest. Here is a partial listing:

- *Editor & Publisher.* Weekly magazine covering the newspaper business, filled with news and comment on industry trends and personnel and

Background

Most states have a Scholastic Press Association or equivalent association which can furnish information about this area. Also, many of your students probably worked on student newspapers, magazines, yearbooks, and TV programs in high school. They can be good sources of information about what secondary schools are doing in mass communications education.

ownership changes. Like many of the trade publications listed here, *Editor & Publisher* carries in each issue a large classified advertising section, which invariably includes dozens of "Help Wanted" notices for persons seeking newspaper jobs.

- *Publisher's Auxiliary.* Biweekly serving the community press field. This journal reports on trends affecting the press generally but has special import for persons interested in weeklies and small dailies.
- *Quill.* Monthly magazine published by the Society of Professional Journalists. *Quill* carries many articles by, and about, younger journalists. It tackles issues of concern to radio and television newspeople as well as print journalists.
- *Columbia Journalism Review.* Topical, specific, candid criticisms of press performance. This prestigious magazine, published six times a year, is widely read by leaders of government and business as well as those inside the media field. Other local, regional, and national journalism reviews also analyze media performance. Of these, the *American Journalism Review* is the best known. Begun as the *Washington Journalism Review,* the *American Journalism Review* in 1993 changed its name to reflect its national focus. Many media leaders not only read it, but write for it as well.
- *Nieman Reports.* Thoughtful commentaries on mass media treatment of social and political issues written mostly by former Nieman Fellows.
- *Presstime.* Management-oriented (published by the American Newspaper Publishers Association) examination of all aspects of the newspaper field. Excellent at detecting problems and emerging trends inside the industry.
- *World Press Review.* Contains translated summaries of key articles from leading newspapers and magazines around the globe.
- *Journalism Quarterly.* Scholarly research pieces dealing with all aspects of journalism and mass communications. Though much of *JQ*'s content can be heavy going for anyone but a communications specialist, the articles are well researched and judiciously chosen. Some studies reported in *JQ*, especially those involving audience analysis and research design, have valuable practical as well as theoretical application. Other scholarly journals serving the field include *Public Opinion, Public Opinion Quarterly, Human Communications Research, Mass Comm Review, Journalism Monographs, Journalism History, Communications Research, Gazette, Quarterly Journal of Speech,* and the *Journal of Communication.*

- *Broadcasting.* Comprehensive weekly filled with brisk, savvy reporting. *Broadcasting* is invaluable for keeping tabs on the world of radio and television, as is *Electronic Media.*
- *Journal of Broadcasting.* Reports scholarly research in the electronic media field.
- *Cablevision.* As the name suggests, reports on cable programming trends, industry news, advertising to and for the cable industry.
- *Radio and Records.* Popular with broadcast station staff and managements.
- *Advertising Age.* Covers the advertising field in great—and sometimes spicy—detail. This magazine is valuable, too, for what it carries each week about the mass media and about business generally, and for voluminous, facts-and-figure-oriented special reports on advertising expenditures and consumer behavior.
- *AdWeek.* Well-written, nicely presented profile of a lively industry. *Adweek* gets high marks from top advertising professionals for its analytical reports, especially those dealing with creative problems. *BrandWeek* authoritatively describes marketing trends.
- *Folio.* Monthly for the magazine field. Besides reporting fully and authoritatively on the industry, *Folio* provides excellent advice to magazine executives, especially in the areas of publication management and graphic design.
- *Publishers Weekly.* An invaluable guide to the book business. *PW* spots themes and trends early. It provides hard news, particularly about newly released books, personnel changes, and marketing.
- *Billboard.* Weekly guide to the recording field. *Billboard* contains much news about industry people, programming trends, merchandising of new recordings, concert reviews, and profiles of outstanding artists.
- *Variety.* Venerable guide to show business in general, and the movie industry in particular. This piece is famous for its spirited, unique writing style.
- *Public Relations News.* One of several media for public relations professionals and for students who hope to become public relations professionals. Similar publications include *pr reporter, Jack O'Dwyer's Newsletter* (weekly), and *O'Dwyer's PR Services Report* (monthly). Also available and useful are *Public Relations Journal* and *Public Relations Quarterly,* both featuring essays, trend articles, and how-to pieces; and *Public Relations Review,* with its research findings and commentary.

Many of these publications can be found in a mass communications reading room, in the general library of a college or university, and in many public libraries. Professionals in mass communications rely heavily on the trade press for current, accurate information about a fast-moving industry. Students can also—and they should.

summary

Journalism schools are a relatively recent development in higher education, entering the field in the twentieth century. Hundreds of U.S. colleges and universities offer courses in mass communications. About one hundred institutions of higher learning have mass communications programs nationally accredited by the Accrediting Council on Education in Journalism and Mass Communications, though good mass communications instruction can be found at many programs which have not undergone formal accreditation procedures. In the early nineties, more than 150,000 journalism/mass communications majors were enrolled in the 347 largest college and university programs alone. This total represents massive growth over the past generation.

Many opportunities exist for teaching mass communications at the scholastic, community college, and four-year college and university levels. Most journalism teachers, especially at the college level, have several years of professional media experience as well as academic credentials.

Continuing education for professionals in media and media-related positions comes through conferences, workshops, retraining programs, and numerous other activities sponsored by industry associations, university schools and colleges of mass communications, and many private and corporate-sponsored in-service agencies. Beyond that, a rich variety of trade journals serves virtually every segment of the mass communications field, providing up-to-the-minute news and industry trend articles.

? questions and cases

1. In his remarks prior to the opening of the first school of journalism in 1908, President A. Ross Hill of the University of Missouri asserted that one of the journalism faculty's duties would be "to discourage those who are likely to prove failures in the profession." Do you agree or disagree with this philosophy? Explain.

2. National accrediting policy in mass communications limits the amount of course work a journalism/mass communications major can take in the major field to 30 percent or less of the undergraduate total. Does this limit trouble you? Why or why not? What additional subjects, beyond those required as part of your degree plan, do you think would make you more effective in the mass communications field?

3. Evaluate the school newspaper and yearbook as you remember them from high school. What were the strengths of these publications? What were their weaknesses? If you were the high school principal, what improvements would you attempt to implement in the journalism/publications program? Would your priorities be different if you were the school publications adviser? What if you were the student editor? Discuss.

4. From what you have studied and learned in this course thus far, comment on the training that U.S. journalists receive. Is it adequate to meet the information needs of our society? As a mass media consumer, are you comfortable with the skills and professionalism of journalists whose work you read or watch? Discuss.

chapter glossary

accreditation   Official authorization by a recognized professional body, indicating that the program has met industry or academic standards.

Association for Education in Journalism and Mass Communications (AEJMC)   Professional organization for college and university teachers in the field.

journalism review   For our purposes, a publication devoted to internal and external criticism of mass media performance.

notes

1 Frederic Hudson, *Journalism in the United States, 1690–1872* (New York: Harper, 1873), 713.

2 Ronald Farrar, *Reluctant Servant: The Story of Charles G. Ross* (Columbia: University of Missouri Press, 1968), 31–60.

3 William A. Swanberg, *Pulitzer* (New York: Scribner's, 1967), 378.

4 Ibid.

5 Annual report to the University of Kentucky Board of Trustees, 1908. The manuscript is housed at the King Library, University of Kentucky, Lexington.

6 Farrar, *Reluctant Servant,* 43.

7 Alfred McClung Lee, *The Daily Newspaper in America* (New York: Macmillan, 1937), 662.

8 Ibid., 658. Also, Willard G. Bleyer, *Main Currents in the History of American Journalism* (Boston: Houghton Mifflin, 1927), 427, and Frank Luther Mott, *American Journalism* (New York: Macmillan, 1962), 727. Bleyer and his colleagues at Wisconsin became key players in accreditation and in the acceptance of journalism programs within the academic community.

9 Lee, *Daily Newspaper in America,* 659.

10 Policy statement issued by the Accrediting Council on Education in Journalism and Mass Communications, in effect in 1993.

11 Gerald M. Kosicki and Lee B. Becker, "Annual Census and Analysis of Enrollment and Graduation," *Journalism Educator,* Autumn 1992, 61.

12 Ibid.

13 See especially John W. Whelen, "Second Class Citizens," *Quill,* July 1984, 14.

14 *Planning for Curricular Change: A Report of the Project on the Future of Journalism and Mass Communications Education* (Eugene: University of Oregon School of Journalism, 1984).

15 Frank Luther Mott, *The News in America* (Harvard University Press, 1952), 217.

16 Tinker *v.* Des Moines Independent School District, 393 U.S. 503 (1969).

17 See especially Hazelwood School District *v.* Kuhlmeier, 484 U.S. 260 (1988).

chapter

T

Despite a barrage of affirmative action legislation, court decisions striking down barriers of racial discrimination and the genuine good intentions of mass media executives, we continue to live in a time when:

Minorities, Women, and the Media

Objectives

When you have finished studying this chapter, you should be able to:

◉ Discuss the relationship between media content and the hiring of minorities and women for mass media positions

◉ Trace the history of the African American press in the United States

◉ Analyze some of the problems affecting African Americans, Latinos, Asian Americans, and Native Americans in integrating the mass media industry as well as in developing their own media outlets

◉ Recount major contributions of certain women leaders in U.S. media history

◉ Describe the progress and the difficulties of minorities and women in attaining media management positions

Despite a barrage of affirmative action legislation, court decisions striking down barriers of racial discrimination, and the genuine good intentions of mass media executives, we continue to live in a time when:

- Well over half of the nation's daily newspapers employ no African American journalists.
- The representation of minorities in professional categories of the broadcasting industry stands at about 13 percent in television, 10 percent in radio—about the same as it has been for over a decade.
- African Americans represent 11.8 percent of the 53,980 actors holding membership in the Screen Actors Guild, yet account for only 8.8 percent of all lead players and log only 5.9 percent of all the time worked by SAG members.
- Other minorities—Latinos, Asian Americans, Native Americans—fare even worse.[1]

These figures describe a situation that minorities find doubly depressing: Not only are employment opportunities sorely lacking, but so are the chances to educate the white majority about minorities in the United States. Minorities and women are likewise concerned about their images as depicted in prime-time culture—the role models offered to viewing audiences. Nolan A. Bowie, summarizing an Aspen Institute for Humanistic Studies conference, put it this way:

> The mass media are as much power molders of beliefs, images, and myths as they are vehicles for presenting facts and other information. They constitute the crucial distribution system of messages to and among members of the American public. They help to shape opinion and political, social, and cultural affairs, and, not least, attitudes toward minorities, about whom the white majority may have little first-hand knowledge.[2]

In fairness, a number of mass media organizations have made impressive gains. Whether through their own initiatives or because of pressure from courts and the government, many publications and broadcasters are aggressively attempting to recruit, retain, and promote minority staff members. But these efforts, well intentioned

Success Story: Wanda Jacobs

The first African American woman ever to head a daily newspaper in the American South is Wanda Jacobs. Jacobs, publisher of the *Mississippi Press-Register* in Pascagoula, said in a letter to the author that she does not feel any pressure because of her race:

"What I do feel is a responsibility as a role model regardless of gender and race," she said. "My responsibility as an adult is to live in a wholesome, upright manner, and to conduct my business in the best possible and most professional manner I can."

Conceding that she may be a role model to females of color, Jacobs added that "I want to be a role model to young people whether they be black or white and to the employees here. I want to display the best ethics I can and in turn inspire the same in my employees."

Wanda Jacobs, the first African American woman to be named publisher of a daily newspaper in Mississippi.

as they are, do not yet represent a total, industrywide commitment to a mass media system that fully reflects the country's pluralistic culture. The American Society of Newspaper Editors has set as its goal the thorough integration of the newspaper industry—that is, to attain in the newspaper field the same percentage of minority staff members as in the population as a whole—by the year 2000. Other media organizations have adopted similar objectives. As publisher David Lawrence of the Miami *Herald* put it in a task force report on minorities in the newspaper business:

> Minorities on a news editorial staff can provide meaningful coverage beyond negative news stories on crime and poverty. Minority executives and managers in the business office, as well as in the newsroom and on the editorial page, can send significant signals to readers and advertisers that the newspaper cares about representing all segments of its market. . . . [3]

How much racial progress is the mass media industry making today? What successes can we reasonably expect minorities to achieve in the years ahead? These are the questions that concern us in the pages that follow. We study these issues not to isolate the problems of minorities and women into a separate ghetto, but to focus special attention on matters that affect the entire mass communications industry and the society it serves.

Development of the African American Press

Clearly precluded from mention in the white press, African Americans early on began producing newspapers for themselves. The effort was arduous, but in the face of overwhelming odds, African Americans published some forty newspapers in the United States prior to the Civil War.[4] This occurred despite the fact that southern African Americans were slaves, penniless, and forbidden by state laws to receive any formal schooling. Northern Negroes were politically freer, but two-thirds of them were illiterate and nearly all were deprived socially and economically. African American newspapers nevertheless did appear. In nearly all cases, they were established primarily to crusade for an end to slavery. The first was *Freedom's Journal,* printed in New York in 1827 and bearing the motto "Righteousness Exalteth a Nation." Aggressive and outspoken, *Freedom's Journal* promoted the cause of abolition and answered racist articles and editorials that appeared in other New York newspapers. The *Journal* served as a forum for African American writers and educators during its three-year history.

The most famous African American newspaper was the *North Star,* launched in Rochester, New York, in 1848. Its proprietor was Frederick Douglass, who would achieve world renown as a leading spokesman for racial equality during the nineteenth century. Born a slave, Douglass educated himself, fled from Maryland to New England, and developed into a powerful orator and writer. In 1845, he finished his autobiography, *Narrative of the Life of Frederick Douglass*. Fearing that his identity as a runaway slave would make him a target when the book was published, Douglass left for England that same year. Speaking against slavery overseas, he attracted the support of friends who raised enough money to buy his freedom. In 1847, he safely returned to the United States and a few months later announced his plan to publish a newspaper. The notice read:

> PROSPECTUS for an anti-slavery paper; to be entitled *North Star*. Frederick Douglass proposes to publish in Rochester a weekly Anti-slavery paper with the above title. The object of the *North Star* will be to attack Slavery in all its forms and aspects; Advocate Universal Emancipation; exalt the standard of Public Morality; promote the Moral and Intellectual improvement of the COLORED PEOPLE; and hasten the day of FREEDOM to the Three Millions of our Enslaved Fellow Countrymen.[5]

The *North Star*, eventually renamed *Frederick Douglass' Paper*, crusaded not only against slavery but against job discrimination in the North. "Every hour," Douglass wrote, "sees the black man elbowed out of employment by some newly arrived immigrant whose hunger and whose color are thought to give him a better title to the place."[6] Douglass also spearheaded a successful crusade against segregated schools in his adopted hometown of Rochester. His fiery editorials insured him plenty of enemies: The powerful New York *Herald,* among others, accused Douglass of fomenting rebellion and urged the people of Rochester to banish him to Canada and throw his press into Lake Ontario. But he also attracted a wide following, including President Abraham Lincoln, with whom he discussed the slavery question. Thousands of other Americans, white and of color, admired his eloquence and conviction.

The first African American newspaper in the South is believed to have been *L'Union,* published in New Orleans in 1862. Half its text was in English, the other half in French, and the paper existed largely to explain to newly free African Americans their rights and responsibilities under the Constitution.

Research by Armistead Pride of Lincoln University indicates that more than 2,700 black newspapers have been founded, 70 percent of them in the South. Other scholars contend that the figure may be nearer 3,000.[7] Only about 190 survive today, though they have a combined circulation of several million. The leaders include the *Indiana Herald* of Indianapolis; New York's *Amsterdam News;* the New York *Black American* and *Daily Challenge;* the Philadelphia *Tribune;* the Los Angeles *Sentinel;* the Baltimore *Afro-American;* the Chicago *Defender;* and the Pittsburgh *Courier*. Most have circulations of 60,000 or less. Some special interest, religious, and free distribution papers also command large audiences. The Central-News Wave group, based in Los Angeles, has a consolidated circulation of more than a quarter of a million, and the Philadelphia *Tribune*'s free circulation each week runs in excess of a million.[8]

The African American Press Today

The African American press has a long tradition in both newspaper and magazine production. Each offers distinct opportunities and challenges to publishers.

Newspapers

Circulation of African American newspapers rose dramatically following World War II and neared a peak in 1949. During that year, a prominent African American publisher described the modern day role, as he saw it, of his newspaper:

> First, to report the news, good and bad, about or peculiarly concerning our race, much of which is ignored, incompletely reported, or sometimes distorted by the general press. Second, we aim to attack, to oppose, to marshal public opinion, against all wrongs and injustices, all

discrimination and inequalities, but especially those adversely affecting the aspirations of the Negro. And, third, to inspire members of this minority group to higher aims and to greater deeds by heralding the accomplishments of Negro individuals, groups, and institutions.[9]

Additionally, this press is characterized by a more personal approach to the news, limited advertising, and a need for more professional news staffs.

A More Personal Approach to the News

A teenager's tragedy in a southern city provides this example: Virginia Jones (her name has been changed here), a popular but deeply troubled African American senior in high school, threw herself off a river bridge and drowned. The following morning, the city's leading daily newspaper carried a brief, routine account of the incident, three paragraphs on an inside page. A few days later, however, when the city's African American weekly newspaper appeared, the girl's death was the leading story on page one. Bearing the headline, VIRGINIA JONES COMMITS SUICIDE . . . AND THE BLACK COMMUNITY WONDERS WHY, the article was a long, sensitive profile of Virginia Jones and the conflicts and despair she had faced growing up as an African American girl in a city where strong racial prejudices had not died out. It was a moving narrative, sometimes bitter, and contained far more commentary than would normally appear in metropolitan daily journalism. The story of Virginia Jones illustrates the more personalized treatment of the news the minority press offers.

Limited Advertising

The combined buying power of African Americans is enormous—an estimated $200 billion a year, roughly that of Canada and far more than most nations of the world— but black newspapers have not captured a proportionate share of advertising dollars. The African American press is a secondary press, supported almost entirely by African Americans. Yet few African Americans read only African American newspapers. Advertisers believe they can reach this audience through other media. As a result, the vast majority of African American newspapers have not generated the solid economic base necessary to ensure growth and to develop stronger news and editorial products.

A Need for More Professional News Staffs

While the black press has developed more than a few truly distinguished journalists, many of these newspapers are produced by physicians, educators, lawyers, members of the clergy, and others whose professional training is in fields other than journalism.

For years, the typical African American newspaper, in outward appearance, resembled the weakest of the general press. This situation is improving as more minority students choose journalism as a field of study and more trained professionals are added to African American newspaper staffs. The personnel pool, as we shall see, is not a large one, and increased competition for qualified minority reporters and editors from the general press has prevented many minority-oriented newspapers from recruiting as many trained professionals as they would like.

Magazines

The first magazine for persons of color was *Mirror of Liberty,* begun in 1837 and, like the African American newspapers of its day, devoted to the abolition of slavery. That civil rights tradition was maintained by *Crisis,* established in 1910 by W. E. B. Du Bois, who helped found the National Association for the Advancement of Colored People. Du Bois continued to edit *Crisis* for a quarter of a century, firmly establishing the magazine as a forum for civil rights and race relations leaders, black and white. *Crisis* remained the official publication of the NAACP and currently has a circulation of more than 300,000, including influential leaders of the African American community as well as other political and social leaders of all races.

John H. Johnson of Chicago publishes the largest and most successful commercial magazines for African Americans. Beginning in the 1930s with $500 in borrowed money, Johnson launched *Negro Digest,* which lasted several years and led to his next venture, *Ebony,* a magazine he promised "would mirror the happier side of Negro life—the positive, everyday achievements from Harlem to Hollywood." Drawing heavily on format and content ideas developed by his friend Henry R. Luce, publisher of *Life,* Johnson filled the pages of *Ebony* with picture stories and slickly written articles, surrounding them with handsome advertising messages. Shrewdly positioning *Ebony* to appeal to a growing black middle class, Johnson soon made the magazine, in William H. Taft's phrase, "a pictorial *Who's Who* in black America."[10]

Though far less angry than *Crisis* and other magazines that deal extensively with civil rights, *Ebony* can get tough on the subject. Johnson has decreed that *Ebony* will be "the spokesman for the full and equal treatment of all Negroes of this day and age."[11] *Ebony* has succeeded as an advertising medium as well, reaching more upwardly mobile black families than any other publication. The Johnson empire also includes *Jet,* a pocket-sized weekly with more than 849,000 circulation—*Ebony,* clearly the leader in the field, has 1,745,166—along with a number of other enterprises, including broadcast properties and a cosmetics firm. With annual gross revenues approaching $300 million, Johnson in the early 1990s presided over the second largest African American–owned business in the United States, trailing only TLC Beatrice International Holdings, a multinational food products conglomerate.[12]

Another African American–oriented magazine is *Essence,* begun in 1970 to, in the words of its publisher, Edward Lewis, "make black women feel good about themselves." *Essence* was an immediate success. Each year it has expanded its audience, and for a time in the 1970s it was the fastest-growing women's magazine in the country. In 1992, it had a paid circulation of 850,607 and a readership estimated at 3.7 million. "We look beyond the numbers and to the reader's mind set," said its editor, Susan L. Taylor, in an interview with the New York *Times* when *Essence* observed its fifteenth anniversary. "We're editing this book for black women whether they're doctors or lawyers, secretaries, nurses, college students, single mothers, women struggling to get off welfare. The thread that connects us is that we're all interested in moving forward."[13]

Black Enterprise, aimed at the growing numbers of black men and women moving into management and ownership positions, also began in 1970. Often compared to *Fortune* and *Business Week, Black Enterprise* speaks for the minority commercial community. Its relatively small but influential and affluent circulation—251,983 in the early 1990s—has attracted a number of large corporate advertisers.

Black Collegian, slanted toward the minority student population, has developed an editorial formula calling for special sections on careers, money management, and other service-related topics. Much like *Black Enterprise, Essence,* and the Johnson publications, *Black Collegian* is less concerned with political ideology than with pragmatic advice on how to move forward in a competitive, business-oriented society.

African Americans in Broadcasting

Despite individual success stories in major markets and at the network level, in the early 1990s the overall situation for blacks in professional broadcasting had changed little in a decade. The professional job classification includes on-the-air talent visible to the general public, and advertising sales, the surest and most direct route to station management. The Radio-Television News Directors Association (RTNDA) is on record as committed to taking a leading part in breaking down racial and gender barriers in broadcasting employment, but these efforts have been impaired, RTNDA members say, by a shortage of qualified minority applicants. The

Teaching Idea

Ask students to bring minority-owned or -oriented magazines to class and compare them with the closest equivalents among nonminority magazines. What similarities and differences do students see in advertising as well as editorial matter?

National Association of Broadcasters, through its Minority and Special Services office, has developed a hiring database and a jobs information clearinghouse to assist in recruiting minorities into the field. But industry leaders agree that too many minority members in the electronic media are stuck in entry-level positions.

Minority ownership of broadcast properties is a key toward fully integrating the industry, but progress in that direction comes slowly. By the mid-1990s, African American interests owned only about 200 of the 9,505 commercial radio stations and an even smaller share, less than 2 percent, of the 1,128 licensed commercial television stations. A number of these minority ownerships were in financial straits because of a sluggish economy which intensified the difficulty of establishing and sustaining an adequate advertising base. In an attempt to increase minority ownership in broadcasting, the Federal Communications Commission in recent years has authorized several incentives that give special preference to minority applicants for new broadcast licenses as well as unusually favorable terms to minority interests attempting to purchase existing broadcast properties. Despite these difficulties, preparing other minority members for positions of management and ownership must become a top priority, according to industry leaders who have urged specific action programs, including:

- Putting minority employees onto the "fast track," or into accelerated skills development or training programs leading to editorial and other decision-making positions affecting media content, hiring, promotions, personnel assignments, marketing, and sales.
- Training managers and editors to be more sensitive to the nexus between employment policy and media content, particularly the danger of negative portrayals and racist stereotyping originating from a work force composed of and directed almost entirely by white males.
- Recognizing that effective Equal Opportunity policies and practices are simply good business.
- Linking managers' bonuses and advancement opportunities to their success in meeting minority hiring and promotion goals.
- Encouraging minority members to assume a greater diversity of roles, responsibilities, and situations.[14]

Latinos

In April 1984, the **National Association of Hispanic Journalists (NAHJ)** was organized, reflecting the desires of Hispanic reporters and editors, most of them Latinos, for improved employment opportunities and for wider recognition of their talents and professional skills. Formation of the NAHJ also served to symbolize the dramatic increase in Latino numbers and influence in U.S. society. This country's Latino population in the 1990 census was estimated at some 22.4 million, compared to just 14.6 million a decade earlier. While most are fluent in English, an estimated 8 million speak fluently only in Spanish. To serve these individuals, and to reflect the social and cultural interests of the others, a lively Hispanic mass media system has evolved.

It began in 1808 with *El Misisipi* of New Orleans, the first Spanish-language newspaper published in the United States. More than one hundred other Spanish newspapers appeared, some only briefly, before 1900.[15] Most of these were in California, Texas, Arizona, and New Mexico. Besides reporting news of particular interest to their readers, they editorialized against racial intolerance and employment discrimination.

With the surge of Latino population growth in recent years, additional Spanish-language newspapers appeared on the scene. Now there are more than fifty, including several dailies. The largest of these include *El Diario-La Prensa,* published in

Teaching Idea

If a minority-owned or -operated radio station airs in your area, invite the owner or manager to visit your class and discuss his or her operation.

Success Story: Don Flores

Dionico (Don) Flores, president and publisher of the Iowa City *Press-Citizen,* was also 1993 president of the National Association of Hispanic Journalists.

A 1973 graduate of Southwest Texas State University in San Marcos, Flores held editing and management positions with newspapers in Texas, Arizona, and New Mexico before the Gannett Company named him as publisher of the *Press-Citizen.* In a statement written for this book, he summarized his work ethic:

I have been very fortunate to be at the right place at the right time. This timing, however, has been accompanied by my willingness to take chances in the pursuit of my chosen career—journalism. Whether it was writing for my junior high newsletter or my high school newspaper or my college newspaper, journalism has been a big part of my life. This passion for reporting and editing has been rewarded many times, in many ways.

The most visible rewards have been in the form of promotions. When I was a beginning reporter on a small daily newspaper in

West Texas, I had no idea I would become an assigning editor, a top editor, or a publisher. This is not to say that I saw career limitations. Instead, I saw challenges that made me a good reporter and prepared me for other opportunities. I knew if I wanted to be successful, I had to be prepared and committed to do the work that others did not want to do.

Don Flores, publisher of the Iowa City *Press Citizen* and president of the National Association of Hispanic Journalists.

New York, and *Diario de las Americas* of Miami, *El Mañana Daily News* of Chicago and *La Opinion* of Los Angeles, each with a circulation ranging from 45,000 to 75,000.

The magazine field serving this audience includes more than one hundred titles. A leader is *Hispanic Business Magazine,* which targets professional and managerial readers. Audience studies suggest that the largely bilingual Latino market seems to prefer listening to Spanish-speaking radio and, to a lesser extent, watching television programs broadcast in Spanish. Many Hispanic audiences read, however, predominantly in English.[16]

Spanish-language broadcasting has enjoyed a strong surge of popularity—this after long years when it was little more than a stepchild of the industry. As late as 1985, Spanish-language stations captured less than 1 percent of television's advertising dollars, though Latinos then represented 8 percent of the U.S. population. More recently, however, that gap has begun to close in dramatic fashion. Latinos continue to increase their financial income and buying power at a rate higher than the national average. The relatively larger household size (3.7 persons, as opposed to the national average of 2.7) and their proven brand loyalty make Latinos promising advertising targets. Market research studies indicate that 88 percent of all Latino adults speak fluent Spanish and that 75 percent of urban Latinos watch Spanish-language television programs at least once each week.

Much of the programming originated with Univision, a vast media empire headquartered in Miami which reaches 90 percent of Latino households in the United States, and Telemundo of Miami and New York, which claims to reach 84 percent of the Latino households in forty-four U.S. markets.[17] Industry forecasters expect more American-made productions for this market to be forthcoming, especially as the rival networks continue to grow, but high production costs probably dictate that the bulk of the programs continue to be imports.

Few Latinos have penetrated the upper echelons of the broadcasting industry as a whole. FCC figures indicate that only about 1 percent of all broadcast professionals, and about 1.2 percent of all senior broadcast officials and station managers, are Latinos. Unity '94, a recent convention of minority journalists held in Atlanta, attracted several thousand participants, including more than 600 from the NAHJ.

Native Americans

There are more than 450 Native American media organizations and about 700 Native American journalists in the United States and Canada. Relatively few of these journalists work for publications and radio and TV stations which serve the general public, though the Gannett group claims to have about two hundred Native American journalists working on the payrolls of its affiliated newspapers. Many newspapers for Native Americans are owned by various Indian reservations, supported with federal funds, and often under the control of public officials who have little interest in journalistic excellence. Even so, when the **Native American Journalists Association** was formed in 1984, its members took as their motto "Pursuing Excellence in Journalism." Their primary goal was to provide greater access to news of the affairs of U.S. and Canadian Indian nations. Most such news at present comes from government agencies such as the U.S. Bureau of Indian Affairs.[18]

"The papers are run by people who have no newspaper experience, yet their word is law," charged a former president of the NAJA, Tom Giago, in a 1992 interview with *Editor & Publisher*. "If a story upsets a tribal council, it's often deleted. The newspaper is expected to be a propaganda tool for the tribal administration. It's that simple."[19] Despite these and other handicaps (including economic adversity—unemployment on some reservations runs in excess of 80 percent), the Native American Journalists Association attempts to strengthen its member publications through workshops, idea exchanges, and other programs aimed at improving communication between Native Americans and the general public. In 1991, the Native Communications Group was formed as an umbrella organization to promote a national agenda for Native communications, both print and broadcast.

The painstaking research of James P. Danky and Maureen B. Hady of the Wisconsin State Historical Society turned up a list of 1,164 periodicals and newspapers by and about Native Americans: Aleuts, Eskimos, Indians, and Native Hawaiians.[20] Only a handful are still published today. New publications have been launched, however; most NAJA member publications are less than twenty-five years old. A leader in this regard is *The Lakota Times,* which in 1993 had a circulation of more than 12,000, making it the largest independently owned Indian newspaper in the United States as well as the largest weekly of any kind published in South Dakota. Native Americans also own about a dozen radio and five television stations.

Asian Americans

The fastest-growing minority in the United States—their numbers have doubled since 1970—Asian Americans remain notably underrepresented in a variety of fields, including journalism. The **Asian American Journalists Association,** founded in 1981 and headquartered in San Francisco, provides a job network system through its thirteen local chapters and has established scholarship funds to assist Asian Americans moving into the mass communications industry. More than twenty-five newspapers, including a dozen or more in Chinese, ten in Japanese, and three in Korean, are published in the United States. Asian Americans own at least twelve radio and television stations, though other broadcast and cable outlets do offer programming in Asian languages on a regular basis. The Asian American

The following addresses may be useful to minority students interested in mass communications careers:

National Association of Black Journalists
Box 17212
Washington, D.C. 20041   (703) 648–1270

National Association of Hispanic Journalists
1193 National Press Building
Washington, D.C. 20045   (202) 662–7145

Asian American Journalists Association
1765 Sutter Street, Room 1000
San Francisco, Calif. 94115   (415) 346–2051

Native American Journalists Association
P.O. Box 287
Boulder, Colo. 80309   (303) 492–7397

Dow Jones Newspaper Fund
P.O. Box 300
Princeton, N.J. 08543–0300   (609) 520–5804

Women in Communications, Inc.
2101 Wilson Boulevard, Suite 417
Arlington, Va. 22201–3008   (703) 528–4200

Women's Institute for Freedom of the Press
3306 Ross Place, N.W.
Washington, D.C. 20008–3332   (202) 966–7783

Minority Affairs Office
American Society of Newspaper Editors
11600 Sunrise Drive
Reston, Va. 22901   (703) 648–1144

Minority Affairs Office
National Association of Broadcasters
1771 N Street, N.W.
Washington, D.C. 20036–2891   (202) 429–5410

Minority Internship Program
American Association of Advertising Agencies
666 Third Avenue
New York, N.Y. 10017–4056   (212) 682–2500

Journalists Association not only provides assistance and opportunities to its eleven hundred active members but also encourages fair, sensitive, and accurate news coverage of Asian American issues.[21]

Training and Networking

"If schools and other government agencies desegregated as slowly as America's newsrooms," asserted Loren F. Ghiglione, a Massachusetts publisher and former chairman of the American Society of Newspaper Editors Minorities Committee, "many of us would label them dawdling defenders of the status quo."[22] As previously suggested, there does appear to be substantial interest in hiring qualified minority applicants for mass media positions. Now the challenges are (1) to demonstrate publicly that the mass communications field is indeed attempting to integrate all segments of the population and (2) to provide encouragement and educational opportunities for minority students interested in journalism as a vocation. For those students, a number of programs are available:

- *Minority scholarships.* Many schools and departments of mass communications actively recruit minority students. The Dow Jones Newspaper Fund, long active in this regard, lists in its annual *Journalism Career Guide for Minorities* dozens of scholarships especially designed for minority students—in addition to regular scholarships, grants, loans, and other financial aid available to students in general. There has been some overall increase in numbers of minority students majoring in mass communications, but minority student enrollments remain below their respective percentages in the population. Figures compiled by the Association for Education in Journalism and Mass Communications projected that in the fall of 1992, some 9.2 percent of the nation's 151,740 undergraduate communications majors were African Americans. Latinos accounted for 4.2 percent, a figure that has nearly quadrupled in ten years.

Teaching Idea

Assign students to find out whether your institution's financial aid office offers minority scholarships and, if so, how many and under what conditions. Does your mass communications unit offer minority scholarships?

Teaching Idea

Compare the text's enrollment figures with the students in your class. Do the percentages of students of different backgrounds in your class roughly agree with the national figures?

Asian American communications enrollments also increased; in 1992, they stood at 1.8 percent, while Native Americans comprised less than 0.2 percent.[23]

- *Mass communications training at historically black colleges.* Thirty or more traditionally black colleges and universities, including Grambling, Tennessee State, and Texas Southern, offer at least some mass communications courses. The School of Journalism, Media, and Graphic Arts at Florida A & M University in Tallahassee developed the first such program at a traditionally black institution to earn full national accreditation from the Accrediting Council on Education in Journalism and Mass Communications.

- *Journalism workshops for minority students.* Several universities each year identify a number of talented minority high school students and offer them the opportunity to learn about the newspaper field from journalism faculty, reporters, and editors. The Dow Jones Newspaper Fund initiated the first program of this type in 1968, and since that time its Urban Journalism Workshops and similar programs have enrolled an estimated five thousand minority students for intensive professional training. Many who attend these programs later move into media career fields.

- *Special programs for minorities.* Many newspapers, media groups, and foundations have instigated programs specifically aimed at assisting minority men and women toward mass media careers. The Freedom Forum, as an example, typically contributes $600,000 or more a year in grants to support minority training programs throughout the nation.

- *The Minority Advertising Intern Program.* The American Association of Advertising Agencies (AAAA) has, since 1973, sponsored internships for minority students interested in acquiring the skills and background necessary for successful careers in advertising. Students chosen for this program spend ten weeks in either Chicago or New York, working at assignments that include art direction, account management, copywriting, media planning, market research, and other operations large advertising agencies commonly perform. Besides the AAAA program, many other advertising agencies and departments arrange for individual internships or related opportunities especially for minority students.

- *Minorities in broadcasting.* As with newspapers, many broadcast stations and broadcast groups sponsor minority internships and other recruiting and training programs. Among the prominent leaders in this area is Dwight M. Ellis, vice-president for Minority and Special Services for the National Association of Broadcasters, whose office serves as an information and research clearinghouse for the industry. Through numerous speeches and articles, Ellis heightened broadcasters' awareness of minority issues and helped foster progress toward hiring, retaining, and promoting minorities throughout the broadcast and cable field. The Radio-Television News Directors Association (RTNDA) has also urged its members to enlist more minority journalists. Through its research committee, RTNDA monitors and reports trends in recruitment of minorities and women.

Teaching Idea

Assign students to contact the organizations listed in the box entitled "Plugging into the Network" in this chapter. Have students ask for information about minority opportunities. Discuss the results in class.

No Discrimination, But . . .

Though subtle forms of prejudice may remain, and old stereotypes die hard, it has in fact been a long time since the media of mass communications actively discriminated against members of minority groups. There are occasional reports of a minority or female television anchor being replaced amid charges of racial or sexual discrimination. Often these can be traced to the practices of outside consultants called in to test the "likability" of various on-camera personalities with the viewing audience. Station managements are not required to act upon such subjective recommendations, but a number of them have, especially in smaller markets.

Many talented black and Latino actors have had trouble developing their careers because of the shortage of available parts for them in Hollywood. Those who do work complain of predictable, one-dimensional, and stereotypical roles. On the other hand, some print and broadcast property managements, in their zeal to bring in more minorities, have been charged, informally at least, with reverse discrimination. It may be that if the mass communications media would simply pay higher salaries, talented minorities would be attracted to the field, and the hiring problem would take care of itself as a matter of course.

Annabella Sciorra, director Spike Lee, Wesley Snipes, and architectural consultant Jack Travis discuss an upcoming scene from *Jungle Fever*.

The Images We Present

If you were a black person wouldn't you resent being on TV news programs which showed only negative images of your community? Dr. Louis Sullivan, the Secretary of Health and Human Services, said in a recent speech: "As things stand today a pernicious and harmful stereotype has grown up around the black male. As he typically appears in the media, he's either a jewelry-bedecked drug pusher, a misogynist pimp or a vicious thug. When our young black men see and internalize that stereotype they observe a poison more deadly than any drug they can buy."

"The stereotype," said Dr. Sullivan, "is furthermore a scandalous lie."

I don't think the media are consciously or conspiratorially trying to trash the black community, but they are in fact doing it by not making an effort to show a more representative view of some of urban America's problems. I believe we have to become more sensitive to racial stereotyping and to the images we present.

Carole Simpson, a Washington correspondent for ABC News, in *The Communicator* of the Radio-Television News Directors Association, November 1991.

Role Diversification: TV Versus Real Life

Hit shows like "Murphy Brown," "The Bill Cosby Show," and "Golden Girls" might lead one to think that women, minorities, and senior citizens are doing pretty well on TV. Not so, says a survey released by two actors unions.

Dr. George Gerbner of the University of Pennsylvania's Annenberg School of Communications analyzed 19,642 speaking parts in 1,371 TV shows on ABC, CBS, NBC, Fox, and 11 major cable networks over ten years. . . .

Some of the findings:

• Women play only one of three roles in prime-time TV and one of four in children's programs.

• Seniors and minorities of both genders are greatly underrepresented and seem to be vanishing instead of increasing, as in real life.

• The 43 million disabled Americans are represented by only 1.5 percent of the roles in prime time.

• In daytime programming, the number of women almost equals that of men . . . but nonwhites and the disabled are depicted less than in prime time.

Grandmothers don't have it so easy either, according to actress Geena Goodwin. "The only time they find us interesting is if you've lost all your marbles someplace," she said of TV scriptwriters.

Associated Press dispatch, 16 May 1993.

Success Story: Robin R. Roberts

Since joining ESPN in February 1990, Robin Roberts has been one of the network's most versatile commentators. She anchors SportsCenter, hosts Sunday morning's Sunday Sports-Day, contributes to NFL PrimeTime, and provides reports and interviews from the field.

An outstanding athlete as well as a *cum laude* graduate of Southeastern Louisiana University, where she majored in communications, Roberts has won national awards for her reporting and has been voted the best woman sports commentator on television. In a statement written for this book, she explained her career philosophy:

I will always remember the first time I was referred to as a "two-fer." I was working as a sports reporter for the CBS affiliate in Atlanta, Georgia. I didn't know what the word meant so I asked my mother. She told me because I was both black and a woman that my employer was satisfying two equal opportunity requirements.

It hurt me to know that many people thought that was the only reason I was hired. I knew, however, that I had earned my position. I am currently working at ESPN because I am a qualified and competent journalist. I have never used my color or gender as an excuse not to succeed nor have I pointed to it as the reason for my success.

ESPN's Robin Roberts.

Women in the Media

For **affirmative action** and **equal employment opportunity** purposes "minorities" and "women" are frequently lumped together. Both categories are underrepresented in a field dominated by white males. In most respects, however, the mass media marketplace has been kinder to women than to minorities. Nearly half the country's newspaper reporters and editors are women, and women comprise nearly a third (31 percent) of all broadcast news staffs. As Vernon A. Stone, chairman of the Radio-Television News Directors Association research committee, observes, women on the air were something of a novelty in the early 1970s; they are taken for granted now.[24]

The figures, however, can be deceptive. While 49 percent of newspaper staff professionals are women, only about 10 percent of the news decisions are made by women; men still control 90.4 percent of all top editorships. On large papers, the male dominance is even more pronounced. In broadcasting, more than a third of all television anchors and a fourth of all radio newscasters are women, but only 8 percent of the broadcast companies employ women news directors. Women have moved into the mass communications industry in massive numbers, yet far too many remain at entry-level positions.

Like minority journalists, women sense that they must overcome discrimination in hirings and promotions as well as the subtle

Teaching Idea

The most visible women in news are on network news programs (including CNN and CNN Headline News). Assign students to monitor the network news for one day and report how many women (minority or otherwise) appear as anchors or reporters. Compare these totals with the numbers of local TV news personnel you obtained in response to the first marginal note in this chapter.

Thelma and Louise stars Geena Davis and Susan Sarandon brought a new image of women to movie screens in the early 1990s. The film was controversial but attracted much media attention as well as box office success.

(and at times not-so-subtle) discrimination reflected in mass media content itself. As Dr. Donna Allen, president of the Women's Institute for Freedom of the Press, contends:

> In their employment of women and minorities, media lag seriously behind the U.S. average for all industry. But content and employment go hand in hand. Until the news about this more-than-half-the-population is recognized as "news" progress will continue to be slow. Fortunately, the growing political strength of women in our society is creating a demand for better coverage, and this will require employment of editors and journalists who possess those perspectives and sensitivity. Media that do not reflect all of the public should be, and will be, replaced by other media forms. Much of the pressure for change is coming from the superior news coverage of women in their own, growing and often unique, collective and sharing forms of media.[25]

The "superior news coverage" Allen refers to has, to a great extent, been provided by magazines. Beginning in 1972 with *Ms.,* a number of outspoken, innovative magazines, along with a few older ones that were repositioned editorially, began to speak directly to the concerns of today's complex, sophisticated female audience. "To me, it said *I am,*" asserted Susan L. Taylor, editor of *Essence,* which is targeted at black women. Upon first seeing a copy of the publication, "I kept flipping through the pages and thinking, 'Oh God, a magazine devoted to black women.' I didn't know whether to read it or hug it."[26] Cable television, too, has enhanced opportunities for women's programming. The prime-time success of such programs as "Murphy Brown," which portray the complexities modern women face, along with the respect accorded women television journalists such as Diane Sawyer, Connie Chung, Judy Woodruff, Barbara Walters, and Katie Couric, suggests that a vacuum, which many never knew existed, is at last beginning to fill.

"Murphy Brown" (Candice Bergen), among a number of others, exemplified the changing roles of women portrayed on television.

Women in Media History

Since colonial days, women have managed to cut through political, cultural, and social barriers to make an enduring contribution to the national experience. Here, drawn from *Women in Media: A Documentary Source Book,* by Maurine Beasley and Sheila Gibbons, are a few such individuals and a glimpse at what they achieved:[27]

*   *Mary Katherine Goddard.* Publisher of the *Maryland Journal,* Goddard was chosen by the Continental Congress to do the first official printing of the Declaration of Independence. One of about thirty colonial women who were printers and publishers at the time, Goddard personally developed the *Maryland Journal* into one of the most effective anti-British newspapers— this while serving as Baltimore's chief printer and operating a thriving book business as well. Later appointed postmistress of Baltimore, she became the first woman to hold federal office.
*   *Margaret Fuller.* Arguably the country's first foreign correspondent, Margaret Fuller is known primarily for her work as a transcendentalist philosopher, feminist, critic, and author. Coeditor of *The Dial,* the most influential literary journal in the country during the pre–Civil War era, Fuller later joined the staff of Horace Greeley's New York *Tribune,* which sent her abroad to report on social conditions in Italy, France, and England. Her powerful dispatches deplored the treatment of women in public institutions and the exploitation of women in the marketplace. Killed in a shipwreck just off the New York coast shortly after her fortieth birthday, Fuller did not live to see the reforms she advocated—and through her eloquence made possible—come to pass. Greeley thought her the most remarkable and greatest woman America had yet known.

- *Sarah J. Hale*. For forty years, Hale edited *Godey's Lady's Book,* and she was widely regarded as the foremost woman journalist of the nineteenth century. Hale was no ardent feminist; she stayed well within the conventions of her day. Yet she was able to use her position to campaign for higher education for women, better nutrition and health care, stronger women's property rights, and better opportunities in the marketplace. A widow who entered journalism primarily to support herself and her five children, she quietly encouraged other women writers throughout her long career and, by her own remarkable example, led many into positions of leadership in the communications field.

- *Nellie Bly*. A determined, enterprising, crusading young journalist, Elizabeth Cochrane took the pen name Nellie Bly when she began exposing factory conditions in her hometown, Pittsburgh, in the 1880s. Later moving to Joseph Pulitzer's New York *World,* then the dominant newspaper in the country, Bly quickly established herself as the most famous reporter of her time. Feigning insanity, she had herself committed to Blackwell's Island asylum and then revealed the wretched living and treatment conditions there. This led to a grand jury investigation, dramatic reforms at the institution—and more first-person assignments for Nellie Bly. The most famous of these came in 1889, when she was twenty-four; she raced around the world to beat the record of Phineas Fogg, fictional hero of Jules Verne's *Around the World in Eighty Days.* She made the journey in 72 days, 6 hours, and 11 minutes, all the while dictating her notes for publication in the *World.* It was one of the great publicity stunts of all time. It and the Nellie Bly byline conveyed for millions the excitement and drama of a career in journalism.

- *Ida M. Tarbell*. One of the most relentlessly effective investigative reporters in history, Ida M. Tarbell caused a sensation in 1902 with her massive series of articles on the Standard Oil Company. Through this and similar work, she emerged as a leader among the muckrakers, a small but highly influential band of writers for *McClure's* and other magazines early in the twentieth century. They exposed corruption in government and business, and their faultlessly documented findings led to dramatic local and federal reforms. Tarbell herself later became an owner of the *American* magazine as well as a prominent lecturer and writer on business reform, disarmament, and foreign policy. Her thorough, accurate, and brilliantly researched writing remains, more than three-quarters of a century later, a model of successful investigative reporting.

- *Margaret Bourke-White*. An accomplished photographer and one of the original staff members when *Life* magazine first rolled off the presses in 1936, Margaret Bourke-White became one of the best-known and most-admired correspondents of World War II. Demanding permission to cover the fighting on the same basis as a male correspondent, Bourke-White sent back memorable photos shot under life-threatening conditions. Her peacetime work, especially her photographs dealing with impoverished southern sharecroppers—done in conjunction with novelist Erskine Caldwell, who later became her husband—and her sensational postwar photos for *Life* established her in the front rank of the world's photojournalists.

The pages of *Women in Media: A Documentary Source Book,* contain sketches of many other women who have contributed significantly to communications history and American life. Despite these achievements, much progress remains to be recorded if women are to become fully integrated into positions of communications leadership. The long-term prospects are somewhat encouraging; in 1994, women comprised more than 60 percent of all students majoring in mass communications in

Discussion

Does your department's enrollment reflect this 60 percent figure? Why or why not?

U.S. colleges and universities. About 45 percent of all students in mass communications doctoral programs, the ranks from which future communications professors will be drawn, are women. Numbers of women publishers and broadcast executives, though small, are growing.

The Women's Institute for Freedom of the Press in 1972 adopted its *Associates Statement,* which speaks to present problems as well as outlining an agenda for the future. It says, in part:

> For the right to "freedom of the press" to be meaningful, there must be a realistic means of exercising it—for all of us, not just the multimillionaires among us. . . . We know that changes in the structure of mass communications are going to come; too many people are now being left out. . . . We want to work together to register our unity, to aid each other's media projects, and to secure greater total funds allocated to constructive changes in the world's communications systems. For women to continue to make progress, it is essential that we have a communications system that will enable us to exchange our information with each other and reach the general public.[28]

Largely because of the Women's Institute and other reform and consciousness-raising groups, women are showing up in increasing numbers of media positions, especially in high-visibility television news. "Watching an all-male anchor team these days," Vernon A. Stone observed, "is like going back to 1972."[29] On the other hand, the movement of racial minorities into the industry comes with painful slowness. The American Society of Newspaper Editors' goal of fully integrating the daily newspaper field, as an example, is unlikely to be reached in the near future. Minority hirings by daily newspapers are increasing, but only fractionally, and the broadcasting field's performance is even worse. At that rate, America's daily newsrooms won't be fully integrated—that is, with racial minorities represented on the staffs in the same percentages as the population as a whole—until the year 2055. That's longer than most minorities—or the general public, for that matter—may care to wait.

summary

Despite some impressive recent changes in hiring and promotions goals, racial minorities remain underrepresented throughout the mass communications industry. This is a situation minority groups find doubly depressing: Not only are employment opportunities missed, but so are the chances to educate the white majority about minorities in the United States.

Partly as a result of their historically limited access to the mainstream media, African Americans, Latinos, Asian Americans, and Native Americans have worked to develop their own media outlets. Meanwhile, efforts continue at "fast tracking," scholarships, and other programs designed to involve minorities in the country's major print and broadcast media.

For affirmative action and equal employment opportunity purposes, "minorities" and "women" are frequently lumped together. Both categories are underrepresented in a field dominated by white males. In most respects, however, the mass media marketplace has been kinder to women than to minorities. Nearly half the country's newspaper reporters and editors are women, and women comprise nearly a third of all broadcast news staffs. But once hired, far too many of these women remain in entry-level positions. Only about 10 percent of all top editors of newspapers, and only 8 percent of broadcast news directors, are women. Though the numbers of women in media management positions are increasing—as are the numbers of women enrolled in college and university mass communications programs—the overall demographic profile of the industry shows that much work remains to be done if the mass media are to accurately reflect the diversity of the audiences they serve.

? questions and cases

1. You are managing editor of a midsized daily newspaper with a news staff of 45 persons, all but one of whom are Caucasian. The paper, even in difficult economic times, is quite profitable, and each Christmas since you have become managing editor you have received a performance bonus of more than $10,000. This year, however, your publisher attaches a stipulation: "I think it's time we really got serious about adding more persons from racial minorities to our news staff," he tells you. "I want us to hire four minority staff members as soon as we possibly can. I don't want you to fire anyone just to implement this policy. But the next four persons who leave us—resign, retire, whatever—I want you to replace them with minority people. How you do it is up to you, but your performance bonus will be measured by the progress you make in attaining this minority objective." Outline your plan for identifying and recruiting qualified minority applicants. How will you counter protests from other staff members that your new hiring policy amounts to "reverse discrimination"?

2. One of the new reporters you hire is Latino, and soon after her arrival you assign her to cover a tense, racially motivated protest involving the deportation of some allegedly illegal-alien Latinos in your city. Specifically, you want this reporter, who speaks fluent Spanish, to interview residents of the neighborhood about possible undue harassment from city and state police. The reporter admits she is troubled by the assignment. "How do you *really* want me to cover this story?" she asks. "Am I doing this as a Mexican American or as a journalist?" How do you respond?

3. As managing editor, you are concerned when your circulation department chief tells you the newspaper has little readership in the areas of the city populated primarily by African Americans and Hispanics. "Minorities seem to be getting their news mostly from the radio," the circulation manager explains. "Our paper just doesn't have much appeal to minority readers." What changes might you implement to help remedy this situation?

4. Do you agree with those who contend that the mass media unfairly and unfavorably stereotype minorities and women? Explain your answer, citing as many examples as you can in support of your position.

5. What about other possible stereotypes? For example, are older persons or people with disabilities unfairly depicted in movies and on television? And what about media people themselves: *pushy* reporters, *ambitious* television starlets, *ruthless* editors, *power-mad* film producers and magazine publishers, *unscrupulous* advertising executives, *sleazy* publicity agents? Have any of these portrayals affected how you feel about the mass communications industry?

chapter glossary

affirmative action   A federal government program that promotes hiring minority members.

Asian American Journalists Association   A professional association for Asian American journalists that provides a job network system and scholarships for Asian American mass communications students.

equal employment opportunity   A federal government policy prohibiting discrimination against minorities in any organization's hiring practices.

National Association of Hispanic Journalists (NAHJ)   A professional organization devoted to improving the employment opportunities and professional development of Hispanic journalists.

Native American Journalists Association   A professional association whose primary goal is to provide greater access to news of U.S. and Canadian native populations.

notes

1 Survey conducted by the American Society of Newspaper Editors and reported in the New York *Times,* 30 November 1992.

2 Nolan A. Bowie, *Blacks and the Mass Media* (Aspen, Colo.: Aspen Institute, 1984), 1. For a fuller discussion of minorities and the movies, see Michael Leahy and Wallis Annenberg, "Discrimination in Hollywood: How Bad Is It?" *TV Guide,* 13 October 1984, 6.

3 *Journalism Career Guide for Minorities* (Princeton, N.J.: The Dow Jones Newspaper Fund, 1991), 6.

4 See especially Carter R. Bryan, "Negro Journalism in America Before Emancipation," *Journalism Monographs,* no. 12 (Association for Education in Journalism, 1969).

5 Ibid., p. 19.

6 Quoted in Sharon M. Murphy, "Frederick Douglass," in Perry J. Ashley, ed., *American Newspaper Journalists, 1690–1872* (Detroit: Dictionary of Literary Biography, vol. 43), 163.

7 William H. Taft, *American Journalism History: An Outline* (Columbia, Mo.: Lucas Bros., 1962), 34.

8 *Editor & Publisher International Yearbook,* 1992, I–394.

9 Quoted in Taft, *American Journalism History,* 35.

10 William H. Taft, *American Magazines for the 1980s* (Mamaronek, N.Y.: Hastings House, 1982), 211–33.

11 Ibid.

12 Roger Cohen, "Black Media Giant's Fire Still Burns," New York *Times,* 19 November 1990.

13 George Dullea, "*Essence* Marks 15 Years of Serving Black Women," New York *Times,* 5 April 1985.

14 Bowie, *Blacks and the Mass Media,* 7.

15 Taft, *American Journalism History,* 35.

16 Taft, *American Magazines for the 1980s,* 279.

17 Associated Press, 26 May 1992.

18 Background material furnished to the author by the Native American Journalists Association, 1992.

19 Background material provided to the author by the *Lakota Times,* 1992.

20 James P. Danky and Maureen B. Hady, *Native American Press in Wisconsin and the Nation* (Madison: University of Wisconsin Library, 1982).

21 Background material provided to the author by the Asian American Journalists Association, 1992.

22 Speech to the American Society of Newspaper Editors Minority Conference, Cleveland, 26 October 1984.

23 Gerald M. Kosicki and Lee B. Becker, "Annual Census and Analysis of Enrollment and Graduation," *Journalism Educator,* Autumn 1992, 61.

24 *RTNDA Communicator,* April 1991, 18.

25 Letters to the author, 25 January 1985 and 27 February 1992.

26 Dullea, New York *Times,* 5 April 1985.

27 Published by the Women's Institute for Freedom of the Press, 1978.

28 Excerpted from the Associates Statement, Women's Institute for Freedom of the Press, Washington, D.C., 1985.

29 Vernon A. Stone, "Women Gain, but Minorities Barely Hold Their Own in Their Share of Broadcast News Jobs," *RTNDA Bulletin,* April 1983, 18.

chapter U

International Communications

Objectives

When you have finished studying this chapter, you should be able to:

- Discuss some of the central problems journalists face in reporting the news from abroad

- Analyze the gap between developed and underdeveloped nations in terms of communications resources

- Describe the proposed New World Information Order, and explain why Western communications organizations opposed it

- Discuss current trends affecting international print and broadcast media, international advertising, public relations, and communications research

Mass communications concepts vary widely throughout the world. Consider, for example, the news reporter's critical need to gather facts—the matter of *access,* or getting at news sources. That seems straightforward enough, but in truth, the meaning of journalistic access depends to a great degree on where one happens to be at the time:

- In fully developed nations, access means that news sources and essential documents are open and available. To assure accurate news reporting, source verification is desirable. Indeed, free and easy access to diverse sources is essential to provide accurate and balanced reporting.
- In less developed countries, access means that reporters are permitted to contact official sources only. Often access is denied as a matter of political ideology. At other times, it is argued that the fragile structure of the society or the poorly trained journalists or news sources demand that access to information be controlled.

....
Teaching Idea
Assign students to see what foreign newspapers, magazines, or other materials your institution's library carries. If possible have them bring some to class. Also, if any of your students are from, or have friends or relatives from, former Soviet Bloc or Third World countries, ask them for information about present and former media conditions in these countries.

Highly developed nations such as the United States comprise what is sometimes called the First World, while emerging countries, where two-thirds of the world's population lives, are often referred to as the **Third World.** Between them was the Second World, comprised of communist nations, many of which have since reorganized themselves, dumping Marxism in favor of other forms of government.[1] Within the worlds, and certainly between the worlds, mass communication is burdened with problems—for example,

1 Well over half of the print media throughout the globe, and perhaps three-fourths of the electronic media, are government dominated—governments either control the media outright or possess a significant, and often menacing, voice in what does or does not appear.

2 During a more or less typical year, 1993, at least sixty-five journalists in eighteen countries were killed while attempting to report the news. Seven died during the October uprising in Moscow; ten were killed in Croatia and Bosnia-Herzegovina, five in Somalia, and two in a helicopter crash in Afghanistan. Another forty-five were murdered in fifteen countries by forces opposed to disclosure of the news. About three hundred journalists were arrested in forty-eight nations, and forty-nine journalists were wounded. Since 1988, an average of sixty-six journalists have been killed each year, and an average of 960 cases of free press violations have been reported.[2]

Some governments go beyond censorship, persuading—or ordering—the media of their nations to report the news in a certain way. Propaganda is an article of faith in many lands. More subtle, but equally disturbing, is when a government feeds the media false information in an attempt to influence foreign policy. The U.S. government has at times been accused of just this strategy; it was called "news management" during the 1950s and **disinformation** in the 1990s. As these euphemisms entered the national vocabulary, so did another term, *credibility gap,* describing a situation where the people and the media do not trust the government. The problem is far less serious in the United States than in most of the rest of the world, but the urge of a political administration to try to manipulate the media of mass communications is almost irresistible. The U.S. government, on more than one occasion, has been tempted.

There are essentially two ways that information and ideas can flow throughout the globe. One is for government to control both the content of information and the means of conveying it. The other is to grant professional journalists and others the right to gather the news and circulate it freely. This latter approach, which journalists in the West as well as such countries as India and Japan believe in, meets a chilly reception elsewhere. Third World nations bitterly charge that Western-style media dominate the globe and Western reporting methods depict emerging peoples unfairly.

"Much demonology has grown up on both sides—thoughtless attributions of ill intent by each side to the other," Keith Fuller, former chief of the Associated Press, told the International Press Institute. "I blame most of it on meddling social scientists and government bureaucrats who lack a media background. Let's brush them to one side and search for mutual understanding, speaking as journalists to journalists."[3] Journalists alone, however, won't be permitted to settle international communications problems. The stakes are too high and they transcend "mere" professionalism. Governments will determine their own communications policy—by force, if necessary, thus giving a bizarre new meaning to the very term *communication*. But as A. J. Liebling observed, people are not free if they cannot see where they are going, even if they have guns to help them get there.[4]

In this chapter we shall look at some of the opportunities, and some of the problems, the realm of international communications presents.

Three Global Trends

During the 1990s, in the wake of the sweeping changes in Eastern Europe, much of the world was trying to define, or redefine, press freedom. Formal censorship ended in some formerly communist countries, but many communists remained as editors. They had acquired freedom, but many were unsure as to what it meant or how best to use it. Some, after government funding was cut off, found the free market—having to compete for readers and advertising support—a mixed blessing. Moscow's *Pravda,* which had boasted 13 million circulation before the revolution in 1991, dropped to 2.6 million within a matter of weeks.[5] Many publications folded outright.

As media both inside and outside the former Soviet Union attempted to cope with harsh economic conditions and a wide range of political and social issues, three trends emerged:

1 *Privatization.* With increasing frequency, governments of poorer nations are withdrawing financial support for the mass media, especially the print media, they own. In the former Soviet bloc, *all* media of mass communications were state-owned. In many cases, private interests have been permitted to buy the assets of these media and try to make them pay their own way. This **privatization,** in theory, should in time lead to healthy media competition and a diversity of editorial opinions. But in the short run, many publications are finding it difficult to attract an audience and advertising base and are unable to keep afloat. Beyond that, revenue-starved governments have imposed heavy taxes on the newly free media outlets. In Romania, as an example, the government prepared in 1994 to raise the tax rate to 45 percent on newspapers. In a sense, the government could silence its critics in the press simply by taxing them to death.

Teaching Idea

Assign students to research the press freedom situation today in former Soviet bloc countries (Poland, Hungary, Bulgaria, and so on). Are they following the three "trends" explained in the text?

Censorship in the Korean War

Wire services were the hardest hit by a censorship policy during the Korean War, when General Douglas MacArthur's headquarters required "clearance before transmission" of all press reports, radio broadcasts, and other dispatches related to military operations. Articles could be released, General MacArthur declared, provided that:

1. They are accurate in statement and implication.
2. They do not supply military information to the enemy.
3. They will not injure morale of our forces or our Allies.
4. They will not embarrass the United States, its Allies, or neutral countries.

Would General MacArthur's criteria be challenged today?

From a letter from General Douglas MacArthur to *Editor & Publisher*, 21 January 1951.

2 *More dependence on the broadcast media.* Rising costs and higher prices—required when government no longer subsidizes the media—have rendered newspapers and magazines all but unaffordable in much of the world. As a result, audiences in poorer nations—and most of the world is made up of poorer nations—rely increasingly on radio and television for news and comment. A top editor of the *Moscow News* in 1993 predicted the end of newspapers in Russia, arguing that readers will become solely television viewers because of inflated newspaper and magazine prices.[6] That assessment overstates the case, but his point, that broadcast media will take on even more power in the years ahead, is probably valid. This is a matter of some concern, because broadcast media historically have proven easier for governments to control than newspapers and magazines.

3 *New press laws.* As governments cautiously authorize more private ownership of the mass media, they find it difficult to decide how much freedom to allow. The liberty to speak and write freely is a fundamental human right, but no government enjoys being assailed by the press. Critics of Western-style journalism argue that some legal structure must assure the press's compliance with what is called "the responsible formulation of an opinion." Journalists and government officials often define "responsible" very differently. Such laws must deal with censorship, access to information, protection of national security, public order, public morality, damage to reputation (defamation), invasions of privacy, the protection of journalists. Press freedom, as it is practiced in the West, is not universally accepted as a good idea, and much of the world has never permitted it. The press laws, as governments in Russia, Eastern Europe, and elsewhere rewrite them, pose a monumental challenge in nations where the rule of law, as practiced in the West, has not existed for generations.[7]

Many regard media privatization in Eastern Europe as a mixed blessing. On the one hand, the newspapers are freer. But they must also now pay their own way, through circulation and advertising revenue. The adjustment, after decades of government ownership, is challenging.

But amidst this change one thing remains the same: the disparity between the richer nations and the poorer ones.

"Haves" and "Have Nots"

There are more mass media resources in developed nations than in the rest of the world, an assertion that should come as no surprise. But it may be instructive to examine just how wide the gulf is.

- *Radio.* The most popular and most easily accessible medium of mass communications in the world is radio, yet the Republic of Chad averages only 26 radio receivers per 1,000 inhabitants, and Yemen only 20. In the United States, there are well over 2,000 radios per 1,000 population and, indeed, in 1993 there were an average of 5.6 radio sets per U.S. *household*.

- *Books.* In Peru, 481 titles were published in 1991. In France that same year, the number of new titles was 39,026.
- *Television.* In Guyana, there are 2.5 TV receivers per 1,000 population; in Kenya, 5.9. In the United States there are 812.
- *Newspapers.* In Chad, there are .2 copies of a daily newspaper per 1,000 population; there are only 8 copies per 1,000 in the Ivory Coast. Norway, on the other hand, has 551 per 1,000, Sweden 525, and, in Japan, daily newspaper circulation is 566 copies per 1,000 population. Newsprint is consumed at the rate of 185 pounds per 1,000 population in Algeria, and 54,337 pounds per 1,000 population in Canada.[8]

Teaching Idea

Assign students to check the most recent edition of the *United Nations Statistical Yearbook* for more current figures.

Disturbing as these figures seem, the actual situation is even worse. Many radio receivers in the Third World may be tunable to only one frequency—the government's—and much of the world's press is too poor to gather the news with any degree of completeness. National news agencies and stringers help some, but even so, entire populations simply are not in close and continuous touch with the rest of the world.

Lowndes Stephens and other scholars have compiled persuasive sets of figures that correlate national income level with the degree of freedom accorded the media of mass communications. Their findings: The poorer the population, the less freedom and independence the country's press and broadcasters are likely to have.[9] Economic prosperity and press freedom are linked in nation after nation around the world. Thus, the residents of the poorer countries, who need information and ideas most urgently, are least likely to get them.

What Third World Leaders Want

The lopsidedness of the global communications structure has long been a source of frustration to leaders of developing nations. They claim that a few powerful nations—the United States, Great Britain, Germany, France, and until recently the Soviet Union—monopolize the international flow of news and information and that Third World nations, when publicized at all, are depicted in cruel and unfair images. Third World leaders have claimed that big powerful nations control the wire services and international radio spectrum, that they produce 80 percent of books published each year and dominate the production of television programs and newsfilms, not to mention satellites, fiber optic technology, computers, microprocessors, videotexts and the whole range of advanced communications technology. Add to that dominance of First World, and especially American, movies; in terms of influence and attitude formation, movies may possess more clout than any other medium.

Thus, unable to produce and circulate their own messages, these leaders claim, Third World nations are helpless. All the world can learn about world events is what New York or London or Paris chooses to tell them. If the mass media portray a Third World nation as primitive or politically unstable, then no one is likely to invest urgently needed development capital there. Angry Third World leaders took their case to the United Nations Education, Science, and Cultural Organization (UNESCO), which in 1978 overwhelmingly adopted a declaration calling for "a reduction of existing imbalances as well as current disparities in the facilities available for communications both within countries and between countries." More specifically, this proposed New World Information Order would:

1 Permit each government to approve news reported outside of that country, as well as censor reports coming in.

2 Allow governments to set up regulations regarding the content of material sent from each country (for example, requiring "favorable" articles to balance "unfavorable" ones). Each nation could insist upon a "right to reply" to counter unfavorable reports and alter the reports if necessary or desirable.

3 Call upon industrialized nations to help Third World countries develop and strengthen their own media systems and to support educational programs to provide more trained people for communications work.

UNESCO's then director general, Amadou-Mahtar M'Bow, contended in 1983 that "the establishment of a new information order presupposes both the creation of mass media managed and run by men and women from all regions of the world and a shared sense of professional responsibility, on the part of those who purvey information, toward the values that we all hold in common. Only then will it be possible for reciprocal circuits to be established whereby all peoples will begin to hear their many voices speaking directly and in harmony."[10]

Opposition from the West

Journalists in the United States and other Western nations vigorously opposed the proposed New World Information Order. While applauding UNESCO's goal, "the pursuit of objective truth," free-world journalists cringed at how some governments might define and implement their version of "truth." "We really cannot afford a world of regulated news and views," declared Jerry W. Friedheim, then executive vice president of the American Newspaper Publishers Association. Harold W. Anderson, president of the Omaha *World-Herald,* asserted, "We don't advance the cause of press freedom by joining programs which have the purpose—or are likely to have the effect—of building the propaganda capabilities of an authoritarian government."[11]

In May 1981, leaders of independent news organizations from twenty-one nations, meeting at a Voices of Freedom conference in Talloires, France, synthesized their opposition to the New World Information Order in what they called "The Declaration of Talloires," which said, in part:

1 The people's right to news and information should not be abridged; censorship should be eliminated.

2 Access by journalists and the public to diverse sources of information, official and unofficial, should be without restriction.

3 There can be no international code of journalistic ethics. The diversity of views makes this impossible. Codes of journalistic ethics, if adopted within a country, should be formulated by the press itself and should be voluntary. Official, binding codes cannot be developed or enforced by governments without becoming instruments of official control of the press and therefore means by which to deny press freedom.

4 Members of the press should enjoy the full protection of national and international law.

5 The press's professional responsibility is the pursuit of truth. To legislate or otherwise mandate responsibilities for the press is to destroy its independence. The ultimate guarantor of journalistic responsibility is the free exchange of ideas.

6 All journalistic freedoms should apply equally to the print and broadcast media. Since radio and television are the primary purveyors of news in many countries, there is particular need for nations to keep their broadcast channels open to the free transmission of information and ideas.

In 1985, the United States officially withdrew from UNESCO, an organization it had long supported both spiritually and financially, after extended controversy over press restriction proposals and to protest what U.S. leaders regarded as anti-Western bias. Singapore also pulled out, and the following year so did the British, charging that UNESCO had "become harmfully politicized."

Discussion

Divide students into two groups—one to promote the New World Information Order and the other to oppose it. After the debate, vote on which arguments are the most convincing and why.

In the United States, journalists and scholars challenged the developing nations' view of global news flow. One such study, conducted by Robert L. Stevenson and Richard R. Cole, suggested that "the assertion that the Western agencies ignore the Third World . . . is simply not true." Their analysis of Western news agency coverage found little ideological bias of any kind; any distortions local Third World audiences received was injected, for the most part, by their own government news agencies, which subscribe to the world press services and frequently modify the reports before publishing or broadcasting them. Too, more news does not automatically mean better understanding. "The real task of journalism—one shared by all journalists—" Stevenson and Cole point out, "is to find ways to transform the flood of information into a coherent view of the world that enlightens as well as informs."[12]

UNESCO, meanwhile, has since changed course, toning down its demands for a radical new plan to manage the news around the world. Instead, in 1991, UNESCO member nations adopted what it called the Windhoek Declaration, which declared that "an independent, pluralistic, and free press was essential for democracy." In a speech to the World Press Freedom Committee, director-general Federico Mayor invited the United States to rejoin UNESCO. He asserted that "UNESCO is fully committed to the advance of press and media freedom," adding that "this means leaving codes of journalistic ethics and similar issues in new and emerging democratic systems strictly within the purview of the press and media professionals themselves."[13]

Teaching Idea

Ask students to find out the current status of the United States in regard to UNESCO. Does UNESCO still advocate any press controls?

Foreign Correspondents

The first systematic foreign correspondence may well have come from Cornelius Tacitus, who, about a hundred years before the birth of Christ, traveled from Rome to chronicle the habits and customs of the Germanic peoples. His reports were crisp and insightful and did what the best foreign reporting today attempts to do: make the reader feel a part of the scene. Consider the following, written by an unknown French reporter who covered Napoleon's defeat at Waterloo; his dispatch, reprinted in *The Times* of London on 4 November 1815, began this way:

> It was a dreadful night. The rain fell in torrents and was most oppressive to the troops, bivouacked as they were in the midst of mire, and not having had time to construct any temporary shelter.
>
> Daylight having appeared, the French took their arms and were surprised to perceive that the English remained not only where they had been the night before, but appeared as if resolved to defend their position. Bonaparte, who had been afraid that they would escape during the night, was much pleased at finding them when he awoke and, not being able to restrain his excitement, said to some persons near him at the moment he discovered the enemy:
>
> "Ah! I have them, then—these English!"[14]

Reinventing Foreign Correspondence

It's ideas and the people behind them on which I focus my reporting, not chasing sound bites. The task is not to impress the reader with how important the correspondent is—hobnobbing with all those VIPs—but to persuade the reader, quickly and engagingly, why he should care enough to finish the story.

[Good foreign correspondence] means that everybody you quote has a name, and a face, which you might even describe, if it were possible to do that without being racist, sexist or ageist. Once a character in your story has a name and a face she is no longer a shadowy half-thing called a source, but real: a person. People like to read about persons.

William D. Montalbano, Los Angeles *Times* bureau chief, in *Nieman Reports*, Spring 1994.

James Gordon Bennett was one of the first American newspaper reporters to report from overseas. He covered the coronation of Queen Victoria for the New York *Herald* in 1838. Horace Greeley sent a number of journalists to Europe to report for the New York *Tribune*. The United States' first great foreign combat correspondent was probably George Wilkins Kendall, who covered the Mexican War for the New Orleans *Daily Picayune*. Kendall himself was wounded in the knee during the battle of Mexico City, but he nevertheless charged ahead on horseback to deliver this stirring account, which began:

> CITY OF MEXICO, SEPTEMBER 14, 1847—Another victory, glorious in its results and which has thrown additional luster upon the American arms, has been achieved today by the army under General [Winfield] Scott. The proud capital of Mexico has fallen into the power of a mere handful of men compared with the immense odds arrayed against them, and Santa Ana, instead of shedding blood as he had promised, is wandering with the remnants of his army no one knows whither.[15]

Nineteenth-century leadership in foreign correspondence clearly belonged to *The Times* of London. Its reporters commanded respect, if not fear, throughout the world. Dispatches in *The Times* criticizing the army's handling of the Crimean War in 1855 may have led to the collapse of the cabinet and a reorganization of the military. Prime Minister Disraeli once grumbled that there seemed to be two British ambassadors in every world capital, one sent by the Queen, the other the correspondent from *The Times*.

Early in the twentieth century, a handful of U.S. newspapers likewise developed a distinguished foreign reporting service. Foremost among these was the New York *Times,* whose publisher, Adolph S. Ochs, shrewdly invested much of the paper's resources into creating a world news network. The New York *Herald Tribune,* created when the once-powerful papers begun by Horace Greeley and James Gordon Bennett merged, put together a commendable staff of foreign correspondents, as did the Chicago *Daily News*. Richard Harding Davis, a brilliant, dashing reporter and syndicated columnist, was perhaps the best known American foreign correspondent during this period. Other famous bylines belonged to Irvin S. Cobb of the *Saturday Evening Post* and John Reed, the radical journalist whose coverage of the Russian revolution later evolved into an important book, *Ten Days that Shook the World*. Dorothy Thompson, globe-trotting columnist for the New York *Post* and the *Herald Tribune,* also developed vast followings.

By 1940, radio had emerged as a formidable force; in 1945, one respected survey showed that 61 percent of the population obtained its news primarily from radio, while only 35 percent claimed to rely chiefly on newspapers. Radio networks developed their own overseas bureaus. A talented young team of CBS correspondents, led by William L. Shirer and Edward R. Murrow, shocked American audiences with stark accounts of Nazi aggression in Europe.

The World War II press coverage, in the judgment of esteemed historian Frank Luther Mott, was outstanding in scope, quantity, variety, and reliability—"all things considered, the greatest achievement of the American press in all its history."[16] Hundreds of reporters and photographers traveled with the troops, sending back articles, action photos, and radio actualities produced under combat conditions. Thirty-seven U.S. war correspondents were killed and 112 wounded, a casualty rate four times that of the fighting forces. Most famous of the World War II correspondents was Ernie Pyle, whose folksy, low-key pieces chronicled the lives of ordinary soldiers. He and his colleagues did much to preserve the common morale during those tense hours.

Less well known but equally brave were the correspondents who later reported from combat zones during the Korean and Vietnam wars. Television journalism had by now come of age, and its impact was enormous. A number of scholars consider television's coverage of the Vietnam fighting a decisive factor in formulating

Teaching Idea

Have your class rewrite the 1815 and 1847 dispatches in modern style. Do they lose anything in the process?

Background

Ed Murrow had just begun to recruit reporters for CBS when the war began in 1939. By 1940, both CBS and NBC had several foreign correspondents and daily news broadcasts via shortwave to the United States. After the United States entered the war in 1941, radio became the predominant source for U.S. residents to obtain the latest news. Newspapers prospered also, as readers sought details, maps, and pictures. (Of course, there was no television news until the late 1940s.)

Reporters and photographers bring the war home to U.S. audiences.

Background

While TV news did cover the Korean war from 1950–53, photographers used photographic film, as videotape was not available until well after 1956. The film had to be shipped back to the United States for processing and editing. By the Vietnam war, satellites could instantaneously transmit pictures back to the United States. Portable video cameras and recorders were just coming into use.

Background

CNN correspondent Peter Arnette stayed in Baghdad and reported live during most of the Gulf war. Although he made it quite clear that his broadcasts were censored, some felt he was deliberately sending propaganda.

Background

The alternative to hiring a foreign correspondent would be for a U.S. news organization to rely on local reporters or news organizations. Many of these sources are controlled by their governments in some way.

the general public's attitude toward that unpopular war. More than a dozen reporters and photographers were killed in Vietnam. The press and television journalists earned high marks for the spectacular coverage of the day-to-day fighting and for bringing home to the American public the grim realities of that tragic situation. But the correspondents and their news organizations were criticized, too, especially by those who felt the communications media had neither fully explained the complex motives of the nations involved nor placed the Vietnam war in proper political and historical perspective.

Today's foreign correspondents, superlatively equipped, have instant access to worldwide audiences. The night of 16 January 1991, Gary Shepard of ABC News, telecasting live from the al-Rashid hotel in Baghdad, reported the start of the Persian Gulf war:

> I am looking directly west from the hotel, and through the entire sky there are flashes of light. It appears to be some sort of antiaircraft fire. Couple of flashes on the horizon; something is definitely under way here.[17]

But while the foreign correspondent must be prepared to report from combat zones—most likely in the so-called "brushfire wars" of the Middle East and Latin America—he or she will deal primarily with complicated political, economic, and social issues such as racism, poverty, and terrorism. "An AP foreign correspondent has two jobs," wrote that wire service's foreign editor, Nate Polowetzky. "To cover the events of the day accurately, fairly, and expeditiously, and to give meaning to those events."[18]

Such marching orders—and they apply to all foreign correspondents—are difficult to fulfill. They require considerable intellectual and professional preparation, among such other traits as patience, tolerance, and a capacity for sustained hard work.

Foreign correspondents are expensive. One wire service executive estimated it costs well over $200,000 a year to keep a foreign correspondent operating in a Third World country and traveling within the region.[19] Another problem is finding news editors well prepared to understand and evaluate overseas news, editors who can interpret each dispatch and assign it weight and significance for the audience. Of the more than fifteen hundred daily newspapers in the United States, for example, it has

U.S. newspaper and broadcast audiences overwhelmingly prefer local news to reports of events abroad. Foreign news, except in times of crisis, rarely scores high on readership studies. Indeed, an editor who places a foreign story on page one can reasonably expect it to be the *least* popular story, in terms of the audience it attracts, on the page. "Americans will do anything in the world for Latin America," distinguished New York *Times* columnist James Reston grumbled, "except read about it." His observation, though it came before the civil war in Nicaragua and the drug wars in Colombia, remains on target and applies to other continents as well. So if the wire services and the broadcast networks don't spend more money on foreign correspondents and overseas bureaus than they do, one can perhaps understand why.

been estimated that fewer than one hundred employ a full-time foreign editor with extensive international experience. One implication of this is that the foreign correspondent may not always get the guidance, support, and sensitive editing needed to do the job in the field fully and effectively.

International Broadcasting

As recently as 1950, only 385 international transmitters operated in the world. Now nearly 2,000 crowd the shortwave spectrum with voices from nearly every country of any size in the world. (Satellite technology, to be discussed later, also utilizes radio signals, placing further demands on the electromagnetic spectrum.) Experts believe more than one billion radio receivers operate throughout the globe, and that more than 400 million of these are equipped to receive shortwave.

The Germans began the practice of making daily propaganda broadcasts as early as 1922, and other nations soon followed suit. Now governments of most countries are involved, to at least some degree, in international broadcasting to promote the country's political views, to inform listeners elsewhere about domestic events, to spread a particular culture, and to communicate with friends and allies in distant lands.

The leading U.S. entry in this field is the Voice of America, which in 1994 was broadcasting 1,080 hours of programming a week in forty-six languages to a worldwide audience estimated at 120 million persons. Begun soon after the Japanese attack on Pearl Harbor in December 1941, the Voice of America went on the air to present the policies of the United States, and to present the news as fairly, accurately, and comprehensively as possible. The VOA is thus expected to serve two masters, nationalism as well as professionalism, and that assignment is not an easy one.

Still, VOA broadcasts over the years have won considerable respect for their fairness and honesty. One testament, of a sort, to the Voice of America's effectiveness lies in the fact that the former Soviet Union often deliberately interfered with, or **jammed,** VOA programming. The jamming was done intermittently from the end of World War II, then sustained on a nonstop basis from 1980 to 1987. During that period, experts believe that the Soviets spent more money jamming VOA programs than the United States spent producing and broadcasting them. A considerable portion of the VOA's worldwide audience lives inside what was once the Soviet bloc. VOA jamming ended in 1987, a manifestation of Soviet leader Mikhail Gorbachev's well-publicized campaign of *glasnost* (openness). Then, in the wake of populist revolutions that swept communism out of Eastern Europe, the Voice of America was widely credited with keeping citizens informed and inspired about the upheaval in the region.[20]

The VOA also operates Radio Marti, an anti-Castro station beamed at Cuba from a transmitter in the Florida keys. Begun in 1985, Radio Marti was designed to,

Background

The shortwave radio frequencies lie between 3 and 30 Megahertz (MHz), with much of the action between 5 and 25 MHz. For technical reasons, stations broadcasting on shortwave frequencies can usually transmit over long distances when atmospheric conditions are favorable. (Higher frequencies don't reach as far.)

Teaching Idea

If you or any of your students have a shortwave radio, tune across the bands while recording on an audio cassette, then play the tape in class. Students may hear many different languages as well as a number of English-language broadcasts from foreign nations. (Your library should carry information about stations and frequencies. Note that accurate time signals are available on 2.5, 5, 10, and 15 MHz twenty-four hours a day.)

The Voice of America, this country's government-funded international broadcast service, reaches audiences throughout the world.

according to then President Ronald Reagan, help counteract the "war hysteria" the Cuban government based much of its policy on. Named for José Marti, a poet and Cuban independence hero, the service broadcasts fourteen hours of Spanish-language news, sports, and entertainment programming each day.

Other U.S.-financed international radio operations include Radio Free Europe and Radio Liberty, which broadcast some 900 hours of programs a week in twenty-three languages of Eastern and Central Europe, the Baltic states, and the nations of the former Soviet Union and Afghanistan. Operated by the Board for International Broadcasting and funded largely by intelligence agencies and political activists, these networks are not part of the Voice of America. Their hardline anticommunist stance, which created credibility problems in some quarters, actually worked in favor of Radio Liberty and Radio Free Europe as the Soviet Union began to unravel. By drawing upon their freelance contributors in Moscow and throughout the Soviet Union and on their headquarters staff in Munich, Radio Free Europe and Radio Liberty became a principal means of informing Russians about the drastic changes in their society. As poet Yevgeny Yevtushenko put it, "Radio Liberty was our connection with our own country."[21] Still, as Cold War tensions eased, Radio Free Europe and Radio Liberty may have become victims of their own success; administration officials in Washington were predicting that both broadcast services would likely be phased out before the end of the decade.[22]

The Armed Forces Radio Network reaches U.S. service men and women stationed overseas. Many AFRN broadcasts, especially rock and jazz programs, are popular with foreign audiences also.

The shortwave spectrum is now seriously overcrowded. Emerging nations are requesting new frequencies, while major powers such as the United States and Great Britain (the British Broadcasting Corporation newscasts are especially respected) desire additional channels to make sure their voices are carried around the world. The International Telecommunications Union, which allocates specific channels on shortwave bands, is finding it increasingly difficult to ensure that all countries are heard. As satellite transmissions increase, the Global Village some scholars envision becomes closer and closer to a reality, and competition for the worldwide audience can be expected to intensify still further.

Television

It is one of the ironies of world politics that while America's power to control international events has generally diminished since World War II, American cultural influence continues to grow. The rest of the earth's peoples may not admire U.S. foreign

Teaching idea

Assign students to find out what has happened to Radio Free Europe and Radio Liberty since 1994. Do they now target China?

U.S. Television: From Sea to Foreign Sea

French politicians have complained that there are so many American crime shows on television that French children often know more about the U.S. legal system than about their own. Arrested suspects have been known to show up at police stations demanding rights, such as *habeas corpus*, that do not exist in Napoleonic Code.

America's television heritage is not being lost in the translation. Talbot [Paul Talbot, a legendary pioneer of American overseas television sales] recently bought the rights to the classic series *The Honeymooners* to be remade with foreign actors overseas.

"In television," he says philosophically, his voice carrying the weight of more than forty years experience, "there is your own country, and there are foreign countries like Germany and France and Italy. Then there is this other country that is all in your mind. And that is Hollywood. And Hollywood belongs to everyone."

Rone Tempest, "American TV: We are the World," *TV Guide,* 3 July 1993.

policy or even its form of government, but they love blue jeans and rock music—and most of all, U.S. movies and television programs. The United States exports far more TV shows than any other nation. While some governments denounce what they call American "cultural imperialism," foreign television stations more often than not build their prime-time schedules around TV programs, including soap operas, imported from the United States. Moreover, Madison Avenue's TV marketing techniques, hard-sell and soft-sell, are proving effective in other lands. This is especially true of **public service announcements,** which the world has widely imitated.

Most nations now can offer their people at least some TV programming, though the studios and transmitters may be under tight government control. It's estimated that there are about 250 TV receivers per 1,000 population throughout the globe, although that figure reflects heavy TV penetration in the more industrialized countries and a smattering of well-to-do urbanites in the Third World. Less-developed nations may provide television service for only a few hours in the evening, the schedule consisting of imported shows mixed in among low-budget discussions and similar educational and cultural programs.

Background

For domestic viewers, CNN had (as of 1994) a "World Report" on Sunday afternoons, when it showed tapes produced by several countries, mostly unedited. Overseas, some countries in the Middle East and Asia were attempting to control the number of satellite receivers so their people would not be exposed to Western "propaganda." Also, C-SPAN (in 1994) was showing a rebroadcast of the Moscow evening news in English translation. If it is available to you, this broadcast might be a good audiovisual aid for students.

A Russian version of a U.S. game show.

Coming Clean on Soaps: A View from Mexico

Under the spell of the soap-opera hit of the day, the following exchange took place between my mother-in-law and her seven-year-old granddaughter: "Granny, you're the best cook in the world." "The best cook in the world is Raquel." "But Granny, Raquel is make-believe, and you're real." Raquel, of course, is a character in the soap. Television says more about characters than it does about actors. With movies, nobody talks about the characters, but everybody talks about the actors. For example, in *Viva Zapata*, the audience knows it is seeing not Zapata but Marlon Brando. Television seems to make the characters more intimate. Actually, TV soap operas merely reflect back the simple truisms on which every viewer bases his life, his security, his self-confidence. All the suspense generated by TV soaps relies on and respects those simple truths, just as all the pleasure comes from seeing those truths ultimately vindicated.

Julio Garcia Espinosa, writing in *Nexos* magazine, Mexico City, translated and reprinted in *World Press Review*, June 1993.

Turner Broadcasting System, the Atlanta-based company which revolutionized the cable television industry, in the 1990s saw the emergence of its Cable News Network as a powerful force throughout the globe. CNN travels over foreign cable systems as well as to small satellite dishes that now adorn apartment patios and homes and office building roofs in much of the world. Dramatic new momentum generated from CNN's round-the-clock coverage of the Persian Gulf war, which attracted a foreign audience of 25 million in 130 countries as well as its U.S. audience, which at times reached 60 million. The viewers included chiefs of state and other powerful figures who found in CNN an immediate, effective means of communicating with the rest of the world.

CNN's success has prompted competition from other countries. The respected British Broadcasting Corporation in 1991 launched a twenty-four-hour global news channel and by 1993 could boast an audience of 4 million viewers. And Australian media baron Rupert Murdoch's Sky News, a satellite news channel operating mostly in the United Kingdom, was attracting enough viewers and advertisers to return a profit. Germany's first all-news television channel, n-tv, went on the air late in 1992. This well-financed network, owned in part by U.S. interests (Time Warner), focused on economic and market reports.[23]

The U.S. Information Agency, well-funded during the Reagan years, when its budget was increased from $438 to $837 million, in 1986 launched an ambitious television "superstation" of its own. Called Worldnet, the USIA satellite television system beams several hours a day and, as of 1993, was received in 128 countries. Picked up by cable systems, local stations, individual satellite dish owners, and master antennas in hotels and apartment complexes, Worldnet programming includes talk shows, news, sports, and entertainment broadcasts that attempt to polish America's image abroad and to promote international understanding.

Cable television develops slowly, even in the highly industrialized nations of the world. Some European businesspeople fear that a vast investment in cable could prove disastrous if too few families decide to hook up to the service—or if cable equipment itself is superseded by fiber optics or some other delivery system. Some governments are actively promoting cable, however, preferring it to the ever-increasing numbers of satellite dishes that might bring in programming they consider unsuitable, and over which they could exercise less control than they can over a state-licensed cable system. Cable penetration is currently highest in densely populated countries, such as Holland, and multilingual nations such as Belgium and Switzerland.[24] Other countries approach cable warily; the opportunities cable presents for information and entertainment are balanced in each nation against concerns for cultural sovereignty.

The Print Media

Newspapers

English has become enormously popular around the globe in the years since World War II. An estimated 500 million people now speak English—an astonishing figure, until one realizes that the other 90 percent of the world's peoples speak something else. And well below half of the adults on earth are believed to be able to read, at a functional level, in *any* language. Despite these formidable limitations, the print media do reach many of the world's leaders, giving print an influence far beyond mere numbers of copies circulated.

Most countries have at least one major newspaper people can count upon to discuss current policy intelligently—or, in authoritarian nations, to announce and reflect policy directly. *Renmin Ribao* (*People's Daily*) of Beijing is published with the full weight of China's all-powerful Communist party behind each issue. While not every one of the paper's 7 million readers swallows every propaganda theme, they read the paper anyway, keenly aware that it conveys the official party line, which is itself a good thing to know. *The Times* and *The Guardian* present British viewpoints on world events through thoughtful news and commentary pieces. *Le Monde* of Paris, though considered somewhat leftist by many, publishes brilliant intellectual analyses of world events and trends. Others, such as *The Statesman* in India, the *Neue Zuercher Zeitung* in Switzerland, the Toronto *Globe and Mail* in Canada, and *Corriere della Sera* in Italy, are held in high regard, both within their own nations and by leading journalists throughout the world.

The New York *Times* and the Washington *Post,* among U.S. dailies, clearly belong in any assemblage of global press leaders. Americans abroad keep up with events through the *International Herald Tribune,* published in Paris but owned by U.S. interests. It has a circulation of about 165,000 and sells in many countries of the world. Overseas audiences also widely read *The Wall Street Journal*'s European and Asian editions.

Apart from the prestige press,[25] most of the world's newspapers leave a great deal to be desired. Some—the tabloids of Rio de Janeiro, to cite just one example— are sensationalist sheets, their pages filled with gossipy articles and lurid photographs. A number are untrustworthy reporters of serious news. Often the newspaper staffs, especially in Africa, are poorly trained; moreover, they are obliged to work with obsolete and substandard equipment, with uncooperative news sources, and, in far too many cases, without adequate legal protection to write and comment freely.

Magazines

A number of U.S. magazines publish international editions. The *Reader's Digest,* a pioneer in this field, currently publishes more than 30 editions worldwide, with a combined circulation of well over 25 million. Weekly news and commerce magazines such as *Time, Newsweek,* and *Business Week* also report brisk demand for their international editions, which typically consist of a somewhat condensed version of domestic news and features, plus enhanced coverage of foreign news that includes special reports that overseas bureaus generate. A number of U.S. trade journals boast substantial foreign readership, particularly publications in the petroleum and computer fields. About half of *Scientific American*'s audience lives outside the United States.

Other nations export magazines also. A favorite among journalists everywhere is *The Economist,* a London news magazine justifiably famous for its insights and literary quality. *Der Spiegel* of West Germany, another lively news magazine, enjoys a substantial readership throughout the world, as does *Paris-Match,* which many consider the best picture magazine currently published.

International Advertising

The first American to begin systematic advertising overseas is believed to be J. Walter Thompson, who opened a London branch of his U.S. agency in 1899.[26] Firms in the United States continued to dominate this field by a substantial margin, though British and Japanese agencies, among others, have recorded strong gains in recent years. As with other types of media activity, international advertising exemplifies the startling contrasts in the relative wealth of nations. In the United States, advertising expenditures average an estimated $500 per person per year, while in a number of countries the per capita average is measured in pennies. Despite the obvious differences in income levels, however, U.S. firms have gone after considerable business from overseas customers. Several large U.S. ad agencies report that half or more of their billings (gross sales) come from clients outside the United States. Most of the large U.S. agencies now maintain offices around the world and/or have working agreements with foreign agencies.

Two factors have combined to spur dramatic growth in the international advertising field:

1 *The rise in worldwide brand awareness and availability.* Multinational corporations, both praised and damned throughout the world for the economic and political power they wield, have made certain brand names household words in almost every corner of the earth. Trade agreements and improved transportation and communications systems have accelerated this trend.

2 *Improved living standards.* Without a fair-sized middle class of "cash customers," advertising has little chance for success. Although much of the world exists at or below the poverty level, millions of persons have made significant improvements in the amount of disposable income they have available in recent years.

Some U.S. companies have successfully positioned and advertised products abroad in the same way they do in this country, finding that certain campaign themes and ideas find universal acceptance. Usually, however, they must tailor advertising to a somewhat different audience in each country. A sizable ad campaign failed in Malaysia because it emphasized the color green, which Americans associate with the outdoors and naturalness, but to Malaysians symbolizes death and disease.[27] An advertising

Dunkin' Donuts are popular in South Korea too.

promotion offering the winner a vacation trip for two flopped with Spanish-speaking audiences; research later indicated that a Hispanic winner would want to take along the entire family, so a trip for only two would present more domestic problems than it would be worth.

Just as the creative strategy may differ, so may the media plan. Radio might reach a foreign market better, for instance, than television or print. Few nations have available, or will permit, as many television commercial messages as U.S. audiences endure. In many foreign countries, television commercials are not integrated into regular programming at all; instead, they might be clustered in one or more lengthy breaks during the evening. In any case, international advertising works best when market research precedes it. A sensitive understanding of social and cultural patterns in each nation is also a prerequisite.

International advertising still has its pitfalls. Regulations affecting commerce are different, and usually much more stringent, than in the United States. Some countries virtually outlaw advertising altogether. Even in some of the more developed nations, time and space buyers often bemoan the lack of precise audience measurements and circulation information so readily available in this country. Too, some resent U.S. marketing techniques in general. On the whole, however, advertisers hear relatively fewer charges of "economic imperialism" or "Coca-colonialism," perhaps because they and their audiences continue to grow more cosmopolitan.

Public Relations

The bulk of international public relations activity is devoted to corporate and financial activities: identifying client needs, analyzing problem areas in foreign marketing, and so on. In addition, many public relations professionals deal with foreign governments, helping clients work smoothly with regulatory agencies and legislatures throughout the world. U.S. public relations firms that represent foreign governments, political parties, or companies are required, under the Foreign Agents Registration Act, to register with the U.S. Attorney General's Office. In the highly charged competitive world of the 1990s, foreign organizations hired U.S. public relations firms, as well as prominent officials from previous White House administrations, to

Teaching Idea

Remind students that fluency in a second language can be an advantage when seeking jobs in advertising and public relations.

lobby in their behalf. Charges of "influence peddling" on behalf of foreign interests, notably Japanese companies and Middle East oil empires, grew commonplace and became an issue during the 1992 presidential campaign.

Most international public relations practitioners function less flamboyantly and provoke far less controversy. In any case, lobbying is an inevitable—and, properly conducted, legitimate—part of Washington life. Indeed, international PR lobbyists have argued effectively for human rights, environmental concerns, and numerous other worthy causes.

Skilled U.S. public relations professionals can also pave the way for the introduction of U.S. products to overseas markets. The reorganization of the former Soviet Union and the vast changes in Eastern Europe, for example, resulted in a newfound willingness to accept U.S. products and investment. Many U.S. companies were able to establish a foothold in the former Soviet bloc in the 1990s, as they had in China earlier, largely because of well-conceived public relations efforts.

International Communications Research

U.S. companies that do business overseas are finding it easier in many countries to obtain the market research data they need to plan their marketing and advertising campaigns wisely. Through a network of interlocking private research firms, a manufacturer now has an excellent chance of acquiring the data necessary to chart changes in purchase habits, buying power, attitudes, and images from country to country, and within a given country. Any of several top U.S. research firms can gear up swiftly for overseas studies to reveal:

- Brand share, usage, frequency of purchase, price paid, place of purchase
- Knowledge, awareness of and attitudes toward new or existing products or services
- Pre/post advertising awareness
- Images of products, services, companies
- Concept/product testing[28]

Such companies employ high standards and modern techniques to collect, process, and analyze data. They also ease the difficulties of translation and international coordination. Well-conceived research studies are credited with detecting potential problem areas and providing U.S. business leaders with a heightened awareness of cultural patterns and concerns as they venture into foreign trade areas.

Quite apart from commercially sponsored research, academicians and government investigators perform many other international communications studies. One excellent example is *Circulation of News in the Third World: A Study of Asia,* by two U.S. communications scholars, Wilbur Schramm and L. Erwin Atwood.[29]

Using content analysis and readership study techniques, the authors examined news coverage in a number of Asian newspapers during a given week. They studied which articles were available, how they were developed, which ones various newspaper editors used, which ones readers chose to read, and why. Answers to these and a host of related questions reveal a great deal about the reporters who write from and for that part of the world; about the editors, and their perceptions of the audiences they serve; and, perhaps most important, what readers think is worth knowing about.

A growing number of scholars in political science, sociology, anthropology, economics, and linguistics, as well as those from media-related fields, are engaging in international communications research. The literature that is developing remains to a large extent fragmented and uneven, but it is beginning to shed some light on the complex relationships that exist between peoples—and possibly to dispel dangerous, narrow national stereotypes that hinder common understanding.

The Future

Those who one day write the definitive history of mass communications almost certainly will begin a new chapter with the year 1965, when international transmissions came of age. It was then that the International Telecommunications Satellite Corporation (INTELSAT) blasted its first commercial communications satellite into orbit. Intelsat I, more commonly called Early Bird, became a synchronous satellite: it was guided into an orbit like earth's, remaining in position overhead to relay radio, telephone, television, and other electronic communications throughout much of the world. Intelsat I was later joined by II and III. The three satellites, positioned above the Atlantic, Pacific, and Indian Oceans, could beam toward any point on the globe.

About two hundred communications satellite systems are in operation today. The typical communications satellite contains twenty-four transponders, each with a capacity of 80,000 simultaneous telephone conversations or a television signal. Meanwhile, transatlantic optical fiber cable service, as of 1993, also permitted 80,000 simultaneous telephone calls. The old coaxial copper cables, laid in 1956, could carry only 51 calls at once.[30] Nations have long been able to hear each other's radio broadcasts; now they can more or less routinely watch each other's television programs as well. Relative costs are dropping; once the technology is in place, sending a message halfway around the globe is only a little more expensive than sending it to an adjoining state. The easy access, comparatively low cost, and technical capacity of today's international communications offer grounds for hope—so long as these media remain free and are not regulated into oblivion. But, as Ithiel de Sola Pool points out in his perceptive *Technologies of Freedom,* "Lack of technical grasp by policy makers and their propensity to solve problems of conflict, privacy, intellectual property, and monopoly by accustomed bureaucratic routines are the main reasons for concern." [31]

The problem is not a new one. In the very first message ever dispatched over the just-completed Atlantic telegraph cable, on the evening of 17 August 1858, President James Buchanan congratulated Queen Victoria, praising the cable as

A TRIUMPH MORE GLORIOUS BECAUSE FAR MORE USEFUL TO MANKIND THAN WAS EVER WON BY A CONQUEROR ON THE FIELD OF BATTLE. MAY THE ATLANTIC TELEGRAPH UNDER THE BLESSING OF HEAVEN PROVE TO BE A BOND OF PERPETUAL PEACE AND FRIENDSHIP BETWEEN THE KINDRED NATIONS AND AN INSTRUMENT DESTINED BY DIVINE PROVIDENCE TO PURSUE ITS RELIGION, CIVILIZATION, LIBERTY, AND LAW THROUGHOUT THE WORLD. IN THIS VIEW WILL NOT ALL NATIONS OF CHRISTENDOM SPONTANEOUSLY UNITE IN THE DECLARATION THAT IT SHALL BE FOREVER NEUTRAL AND THAT ITS COMMUNICATIONS SHALL BE HELD SACRED IN PASSING TO THE PLACE OF THEIR DESTINATION EVEN IN THE MIDST OF HOSTILITIES.[32]

By 1914, however, with Europe mobilizing for World War I, the British cut the cables between Germany and the United States leaving only the British lines of communication for news transmission to the United States. U.S. audiences were fed a carefully censored, biased version of events from the Continent, a factor that may have influenced our previously neutral political position. That particular form of interference could not happen today, but other impediments have since emerged.

Years later, governments would begin to flood the airwaves with their own propaganda and disinformation, trying in some cases to jam others' broadcasts. International communications have rarely been, in President Buchanan's phrase of more than a century ago, "sacred in passing to the place of their destination." Satellites, fiber optics, and other innovations have prepared the world technically for the free flow of information and ideas. But whether the world is ready politically and emotionally remains an open question.

Oops!

An error of startling proportions occurred with the following United Press dispatch, which slipped by the military censors and mistakenly announced the end of World War I on 7 November 1918:

PARIS 20
UNIPRESS NEWYORK
URGENT ARMISTICE ALLIES GERMANY SIGNED
ELEVEN SMORNING HOSTILITIES CEASED TWO
SAFTERNOON SEDAN TAKEN SMORNING BY
AMERICANS
HOWARD SIMMS

"Howard" and "Simms" were, respectively, the president of United Press and its chief European correspondent. Their historic bulletin, based on faulty information, touched off hundreds of "extra" editions of newspapers and, according to one historian,

. . . set bells ringing, automobile horns blowing . . . brought business to a standstill, filled saloons, disrupted the stock market . . . snarled traffic, filled the air of downtown New York and Chicago with a ticker-tape and torn paper snowstorm, jammed telephone lines, brought hundreds of thousands capering in the streets and led some men and women into churches to fall on their knees and weep. No other newspaper dispatch ever touched such gigantic explosion.

**Emmett Crozier, *American Reporters
on the Western Front, 1914–1918,*
Oxford University Press, 1959**

Twenty-seven years later, an erroneous message the *other* major U.S. wire service, Associated Press, flashed out prematurely announced the end of World War II.

summary

Well over half of the print media throughout the globe and perhaps three-fourths of the broadcast media are government dominated, making it difficult to sustain a free flow of information and ideas among nations. Censorship and intimidation of mass communications systems are commonplace. Access to media outlets is difficult in much of the world. The gap between the "have" nations and the "have nots" in terms of mass media availability is sometimes enormous.

During the 1990s, in the wake of sweeping changes in Eastern Europe, much of the world was attempting to define, or redefine, press freedom. While newly privatized media in the former Soviet Bloc delighted in their new liberties, they lost the economic support their governments had provided and they had to begin to pay their own way. Many publications folded outright, and millions of consumers simply could not afford to buy newspapers or magazines. Broadcast media were relied upon to an increasing degree. Meanwhile, as governments cautiously authorized more privatization of the media, they developed new press laws to deal with censorship, access to information, protection of national security, and other matters concerning the performance of the mass media.

At the same time, Third World nations continued to object to the lopsidedness of the global communications structure. While the proposed New World Information Order was defeated, Third World leaders still sought for new ways to get their stories to the international community.

Meanwhile, globe-spanning television systems such as the United States Cable News Network began to give the world virtually instantaneous access to fast-breaking news from wherever it happened. International advertising flourished, too, because of the rise of worldwide brand awareness and improved living standards in many countries.

Future trends, including more satellites, fiber optics, and other technological developments, hold dramatic promise for the global community. Easy access, comparatively low cost, and the vast technical capacity of today's international communications offer hope to the world—so long as the mass media remain free and are not regulated into oblivion.

? questions and cases

1. You are a foreign correspondent assigned to cover a summit conference of world leaders in Geneva, Switzerland. As you observe the meeting and begin to write your dispatches, what point of view do you adopt? Do you consider yourself an American first and a journalist second? Or, perhaps, the other way around? Do you see a potential conflict of interest here? What, if anything, could you do about it?

2. If you believe, as most U.S. journalists do, that the New World Information Order would do far more harm than good, what alternatives would you suggest to improve news coverage and understanding of the Third World? How would you implement your suggestions?

3. Interview some international students on your campus. What image of their home countries do they feel the U.S. mass media portray? Do you feel that their attitudes toward the U.S. media are justified?

4. How, if at all, would you change the foreign coverage in the newspapers you read? in the television newscasts you watch?

5. Some scholars believe that the influence of the mass media must be considered in relation to the total environment—that is, to the influences of other forces on the individual. How important do you think the mass media's role is—compared to that of the family, church, schools, and colleges—in determining our attitudes toward people of other countries? Explain.

chapter glossary

disinformation Deliberately providing false information to the press in an attempt to mislead other governments or political adversaries.

jamming Intentionally interfering with radio signals. The former Soviet Union "jammed" Voice of America and other programming by transmitting counter signals on the same wavelengths to render the broadcasts unintelligible.

privatization The process of selling state-owned properties (for our purposes, newspapers and other communications media) to private individuals and companies.

public service announcements (PSAs) Television and radio spot announcements in behalf of nonprofit causes, broadcast in the public interest by individual stations at no charge.

Third World Term used to describe the developing nations of Latin America, Asia, and Africa. The Second World was comprised of former Communist bloc nations, while the First World generally refers to Western nations and developed Pacific Rim nations such as Japan.

notes

1 Leonard R. Sussman, *Glossary for International Communications* (New York: Freedom House, 1984).

2 Sussman, "Press Freedom is Set Back Worldwide," *Editor & Publisher,* 1 January 1994, 28.

3 Address to the International Press Institute, Canberra, Australia, 8 March 1978.

4 Quoted by Marshall McLuhan, *Understanding Media: The Extensions of Man* (New York: McGraw-Hill, 1966). 6.

5 George Garneau, "Left in the Lurch," *Editor & Publisher,* 30 November 1991, 8.

6 Ibid.

7 Sussman, "The Year of Press Law Debates."

8 These figures come from the *United Nations Statistical Yearbook No. 37* (1992).

9 In John C. Merrill, ed., *Global Journalism,* 2d ed. (White Plains, N.Y.: Longman, 1990), 51 ff.

10 "UNESCO Declaration on a Free Flow of World News," *Editor & Publisher,* 2 December 1978, 16.

11 Sheila Norman-Culp, "The Continuing Problem of Overseas Coverage," *AP World,* Fall 1984, 11.

12 Robert L. Stevenson, "The Western News Agencies Do Not Ignore the Third World," *Editor & Publisher,* 5 July 1980, 11.

13 Debra Gersh, "U.S. Urged to Rejoin UNESCO," *Editor & Publisher,* 19 December 1992, 13.

14 Reported in *The Times* (London) 4 November 1815; reprinted in Louis L. Snyder and Richard B. Morris, eds., *A Treasury of Great Reporting* (New York: Simon & Schuster, 1949), 33.

15 New Orleans *Daily Picayune* 14 October 1847; reprinted in Snyder and Morris, *Treasury of Great Reporting,* 72.

16 Frank Luther Mott, *American Journalism* (New York: Macmillan, 1962), 741.

17 Quoted by Lawrence B. Taishoff and Harry A. Jessell, "Television and Radio," *Encyclopedia Britannica, Book of the Year (1992),* 330.

18 Quoted in Norman-Culp, "Continuing Problem."

19 Ibid.

20 Dana Priest, "A Changing World, A Changing Voice of America," Washington *Post,* 28 March 1993.

21 *1992 Annual Report on Radio Free Europe/Radio Liberty, Inc.* (Washington, D.C.: Board for International Broadcasting, 1992), 7.

22 Priest, "Changing World."

23 Jeffrey Scott, "Turner Empire Forcing World to Take Notice," Columbia *State,* 14 June 1992; "Germany Gets All-News TV," New York *Times,* 1 December 1992.

24 Neil Hickey, "Worldnet: USIA's TV Network," *TV Guide,* 2 May 1987, 10; Gary Geipel, "Medienpolitik," *Channels of Communication,* May–June 1985, 42.

25 See John Merrill, *The Elite Press: Great Newspapers of the World* (New York: Pitman, 1968), for full discussion of prestige newspapers.

26 An excellent discussion of international advertising, from which much of this is drawn, is S. Watson Dunn and Arnold M. Barban, *Advertising: Its Role In Modern Marketing,* 6th ed. (Chicago: Dryden, 1986), 757ff.

27 Memo circulated to clients by the public relations firm of Lobsenz-Stevens, quoted in Todd Hunt and Brent D. Ruben, *Mass Communication* (New York: HarperCollins, 1993, 372).

28 Promotional materials supplied to the author by NFO International Research.

29 Published in Hong Kong by the Chinese University Press, 1981, this book reports a high degree of dissatisfaction throughout Asia with the quality of news reporting about that region.

30 Jack Lyle and Douglas McLeod, *Communication: Media and Change* (Mountain View, Calif: Mayfield, 1993), 40ff.

31 Ithiel de Sola Pool, *Technologies of Freedom: On Free Speech in an Electronic Age* (Cambridge, Mass.: Harvard University Press, 1983), 251.

32 Oliver Gramling, *AP: The Story of News* (New York: Farrar and Rinehart, 1940), 33.

chapter V

Technology and the Future

What would an ideal system of mass communications be like? Dr. Leo S. Bogart, one of the wisest of the industry's leaders, thinks that in a perfect world of tomorrow, the mass media system should have:

Objectives

When you have finished studying this chapter, you should be able to:

- Envision some of the opportunities technology will make available to mass media consumers in the years ahead
- Discuss how digital technology will influence specific media of mass communications
- Discuss the potential economic and social impact of conglomerate mergers and media system takeovers on mass media content
- Debate the ethical and legal issues the new technology creates in such areas as privacy protection and falsification

What would an ideal system of mass communications be like? Dr. Leo S. Bogart, one of the wisest of the industry's leaders, thinks that in a perfect world of tomorrow, the mass media system should have:

- *Freedom.* It should permit the expression and examination of every human impulse, experience, and belief without censorship.
- *Range and variety.* It should cover the spectrum of tastes and interests, with the widest possible number of choices in every sector.
- *Balance.* Amid the steady output of entertainment, the mass media system should allow information to find an appropriate place and ensure multiple sources of information and opinion.
- *Innovativeness.* It should permit a constant infusion of new ideas, styles, and formats (not just variations on old ideas) and give them a chance to attract a following.
- *Competitiveness.* The system should be structured to encourage entrepreneurship and discourage monopoly both in delivery and in content.
- *Accessibility.* The mass media should be available to all, rich and poor. This, Bogart adds, might mean expanding the functions of public libraries.
- *Quality.* It should strive to attain standards of excellence in conception and execution, without suppressing expressions that fall short.[1]

Discussion

Ask the class how the mass media can implement each of these qualities. What additional qualities do students believe the system should have?

This last feature, Bogart warns, is the most controversial. Setting "standards of excellence" in the field of information and ideas can be risky. An important idea may be poorly presented, while a flimsy idea, slickly packaged—in a TV sound bite, for example—might be misleading. In a free society there is no anointed authority to pass judgment on what ideas can be offered to the people. But in a perfect media system, the goal would not be to suppress the bad, but to encourage the good.[2]

Discussions of an ideal mass media system have become increasingly pertinent to all of us, for in the last years of the twentieth century we were developing the technology that could assure us virtually whatever kind of mass media system we as a people would choose. Digitalization of data, delivered by dramatic new switching techniques and **fiber optics** to our home or office telephone/television receiver/computer station, can offer us access to almost infinite amounts of material within a matter of seconds. And we can readily store vast collections of books, reference data, manuscripts, movies, tapes, and disks—entire libraries at home, at our fingertips.

But lurking behind the technology lies another issue, larger and of paramount importance to the student of mass communications: the question of content. What will appear on the television screens? Who will write and produce it? How will the

Talkin' High-Tech

Information Highway—The as-yet-nonexistent network of cable and telephone lines that will deliver vast amounts of information directly to consumers' homes.

Internet—An enormous international computer network that links government agencies, universities, corporations, and individuals.

Networking—Technology that connects computers at several different locations and allows communication among them.

Online—A state in which information is accessible electronically, via computers, cable TV, or telephone lines.

Multimedia—Electronic products that use various media (text, graphics, animation, audio) to deliver information. Often these products are also interactive, allowing the user to pick and choose from a variety of information opinions.

Users—An unfortunate word for those who use computers.

Modern Maturity, February-March 1994, 29–31.

Downside? What Downside?

Discussion

In 1994, the U.S. government wanted every telephone and radiotelephone scrambling device to contain a "back door" to allow law enforcement agencies such as the FBI to monitor (eavesdrop, wiretap) conversations. Is this a violation of privacy?

writers and producers assess audience needs and desires? What impact will the new offerings have on traditional media such as magazines, newspapers, books, and even television programs as we know them?[3] These questions, and the many more we could ask, relate to **content**—the cargo that the exciting new vehicles traveling the information superhighway will carry.

And then there are other problems the next generation of mass communicators must deal with to a degree never demanded before in history:

- Legal concerns, such as the protection of individual privacy in an era when it is technically possible to use high-tech communications media as snooping devices.
- Ethical concerns, now that it has become relatively simple to manipulate photographs digitally to make them show whatever we want them to show.
- And a great many other problems that will arise from a nation wired up to **interactive media** of mass communications. Perhaps the greatest problem of all is *what* this new system will communicate. "We believe that we live in the 'age of information,'" writes Bill McKibben, "that there has been an information 'revolution.' While in a certain narrow sense this is the case, in many important ways the opposite is true. We also live at a moment of deep ignorance, when vital knowledge that humans have always possessed about who we are and where we live seems beyond our reach. An Unenlightenment. An age of missing information."[4]

But at no time in the history of human experience have better opportunities existed for filling the gaps of missing information that McKibben calls "Unenlightenment." The tools are at hand. The challenge for those who are in control of the tools, the mass communicators of the future, lies in how to use them wisely. In this chapter, we will begin with a glimpse at some of the technologies that will be available.

The Technologies of Freedom

The Digital Circus

Once communications messages (articles, programs, music, manuscripts, photographs, spoken words, text, graphics, animation, audio) are digitized—reduced to computer codes of zeros and ones—then they can be transmitted through a variety of channels. This means vast change. But the change may not be in the media of mass communications so much as in the digitalization of the content—the form in which the messages are delivered.

As one writer, Nicholas Negroponte, director of the Media Laboratory at the Massachusetts Institute of Technology, explains:

> In the old days, we considered newspapers and television very different media; this is changing rapidly. Newspapers begin as digitized information collected by reporters, edited by editors, and eventually transformed into ink squeezed onto paper. By the turn of the century, all television will also be digital. What is so different about the bit stream that makes a television picture and the bit stream that makes a newspaper? The answer is: nothing. Bits are bits.[5]

Computers will process this information and allow us to interact with it, to have a say in how we want to use the information. With digital technology, we can personalize our own media—calling up on our television screens what we want to see, when we want to see it. Thus, says one writer, "when you wake up in the morning in the year 2000, you will have a section (not the whole paper) called *The Daily Me,* devoted to people, places, and ideas that interest you. When you turn on the car radio, it will automatically play 'important' news. When you want to look at a movie, the system will recommend an excellent one, just as your sister-in-law would have."[6]

Digitalization will affect individual media in different ways. Newspapers, motion pictures, and television will all undergo vast change—but in ways unique to each medium.

Newspapers

The interactive daily newspaper, already taking shape in some U.S. markets, will become increasingly common by the end of the century. The fully interactive newspaper is likely to offer its subscribers such features as:

- Classified ads enhanced to match advertisers and readers. For example, résumés could be forwarded directly via computer to prospective employers, or product inquiries and price offers could be matched to advertisers of merchandise for sale.

Discussion

If you get only information *you* think is important, are you missing information that could be of great value to you?

- Listings of events enhanced to offer seat selection and ticket transaction services. This feature is already available through the Chicago *Tribune*'s "Chicago On Line" service.
- Interactive local advertising and shopping information that allows subscribers who inquire about a product to find out where the product is available, with what models and features, and at what price ranges, and to do comparison shopping without ever leaving home.
- Local news articles enhanced with added background information, depending on the subscriber's wishes.
- Entire newspapers tailored, via computer, to reflect an individual subscriber's desire for greater or lesser amounts of local, state, national, and international news as well as adjusted diets of sports, business, farm, women's, entertainment, and fashion news. The news feeds can be timeshifted and updated throughout the day and night.[7]

In this concept of a newspaper for the future, readers are able to receive the news via their television sets; readers can touch certain portions of the "page" to activate video with sound, obtain further details, and so on. This prototype was developed by Roger Fidler of the Knight-Ridder Information Design Laboratory.

TODAY 2

14

General
Metro
Region
Nation
World
Lifestyle
Obituaries
Opinion
People
Weather

BUSINESS

10

GUIDE

9

SCI/TECH

8

SPORTS

11

WORLD

12

AD INDEX
NEWS INDEX
SEARCH
PREFERENCES
CLOSE

Dow drops 2.94 points to 3,766.35

Preview: The season's best books for kids

A novel way to make screens flat

KNIGHT-RIDDER CURRENT

THURSDAY, MAY 12. 1994, 6:00 AM EDT EDITION

U.N. commander halting attempts to reopen airport

SARAJEVO — The United Nations announced today it was ceasing all attempts to reopen the Sarajevo airport until there was a cease-fire for at least 48 hours. The U.N. commander, Major General Lewis MacKenzie, acknowledged with anger that it was possible the U.N. mission would fail.

'Great powers' may not be able to halt Bosnian conflict

GENEVA — Adopting the language and locale of a bygone diplomatic era, seven foreign ministers met here to argue about whether to impose a settlement in Bosnia, only to concede that the "great powers" of the modern world may be powerless to halt ethnic conflict in the Balkans.

Bihac
Srebrenica
Sarajevo
10 New Regions

Shuttle launch lights morning skies

CAPE CANAVERAL. Fla — The roar of the engines startle cormorants into flight as space shuttle Endeavour clears the launch pad in background during early hours of Thursday morning.

Showdown with Iraq expected later this week

WASHINGTON — An impatient United Nations Security Council has demanded that Iraq comply "fully and unconditionally" with terms of the Persian Gulf War cease-fire resolutions by March 21, or face serious but unspecified consequences. As usual, it is unclear what Saddam intends to do. Deputy Prime Minister Tariq Aziz, was at first defiant but later he seemed to be seeking a way to back down as Iraq has done several times before.

WASHINGTON — First lady Hillary Rodham Clinton testifies before the House Ways and Means Committee yesterday afternoon. Mrs. Clinton asked members of Congress to work with the administration to overhaul the nation's ailing health care system.

Doctor's group offers plan to limit health-care costs

WASHINGTON — The American College of Physicians said today that there should be an overall national limit on health-care spending. The proposal signals a turning point in the debate over the future of the American health-care system because it indicates that significant numbers of doctors now support an approach favored by many labor unions and big businesses.

US Satellite gap limits views of hurricanes

The United States is facing heightened danger from hurricanes because delays in modernizing its fleet of weather satellites are forcing the use of spacecraft so antiquated and poorly positioned that they are raising the risk of forecasting errors.

- Customized coupons delivered electronically.
- "Voice personals," for the lonely-hearts set, allowing subscribers to respond instantly without the barriers associated with letter writing. The system might work this way: The advertiser places a four- or five-line ad in the paper, also recording an accompanying voice "greeting." The paper tags each of the print ads with a number for a voice mailbox. Readers can then browse through the print ads. To hear the advertiser's voice greeting, the reader calls a given telephone number, which then accesses the greeting. The caller may elect to contact the advertiser, or continue browsing through other voice greetings.[8] Voice personals, like other classified ads, could also link subscribers through an electronic network to subscribers of other newspapers across the country.

The newspaper of tomorrow, as Jack Dale writes in *Editor & Publisher,* will be a digital circus. And, he warns, "like all circuses, it contains wizards and magicians, acrobats and high fliers, charlatans and clowns. As from time immemorial, it's not easy to tell the difference." The newspaper industry, he says, "is still powerful, vital and viable. But it's changing."[9]

Motion Pictures

Digitalization technology already developed would permit Hollywood studios to send movies directly to theaters, bypassing altogether the costly business of copying prints and shipping them all over the country. Electronic film delivery, which would save hundreds of millions of dollars in distribution costs each year, would work this way: The movie would be digitally compressed—that is, reduced as to the amount of "space" the data takes up on the transmission medium, making it possible to load far more material on the same signal—then transmitted via fiber optic telecommunication networks to receivers installed in theaters. There, the signal would be decompressed and punched up for showing.

One communications executive compared the momentousness of this breakthrough in film delivery to the change from black-and-white movies to color.[10]

The same technology would allow subscribers at home ready accessibility to movies, live sports events and other attractions, via cable systems.

Indeed, with the astonishing gains in the video rental business—in 1994, movie rentals and sales accounted for *48 percent of all movie studio income*—the digital transmission of films directly to households could make movie theaters themselves nonessential.

Television

Tomorrow's television systems, too, will reflect the digital revolution in a profoundly important way. From computer disks that can store hours of programs as easily as sound bites, television executives are now actively experimenting with digital technology that may one day replace the staple of the industry, videotape.[11] Indeed, some stations, such as WDBB-TV in Tuscaloosa, Alabama, in 1994 were already well along toward bypassing tape altogether in favor of disk-based systems.

Computerized editing machines and their companion computers can store news footage, programs, specials, and commercials in digital form. Digital sound and pictures are crisper and more precise than the analog signal still in wide use.

Broadcast news directors also anticipate a number of other technological developments, such as **on-demand video** services that send additional information—specific services for customers who would pay extra for them—on TV signals, and using video cameras that memorize and store light settings from regularly used locations.[12]

Discussion
Will the newspaper of the future contain any paper, or will it be entirely electronic? Could you clip and save an article, a wedding announcement, a birth announcement, or an obituary?

Extra Information
Film transmission could also take place by satellite, cutting costs even further.

The World Television Market

Meanwhile, efforts to develop worldwide television audiences continue. In 1994, Bill Gates, founder of the computer software giant Microsoft, and Craig McCaw, head of Cellular, the country's largest wireless telephone company, announced one of the most ambitious of such undertakings. Their goal: to create an information "skyway" by placing some 840 satellites into low orbit, forming the first digital, wireless network that could handle telephone calls, interactive television, computer data, TV programs, and movies, transmitting them anywhere on the earth. "It's the information highway without the wires," explained a *USA Today* cover story. "The prime target: customers in remote places that might otherwise be left off an earthbound information highway. The monks of Tibet could use TVs attached to coin-sized antennae and have interactive video conferences with followers around the world. Reindeer herders in Finland could order "I Love Lucy" reruns any time. Oil workers in the Gulf of Mexico could take live video college courses via personal computers linked to the satellite network."[13]

This effort would join those of Rupert Murdoch, whose international holdings include, among much else, British Sky Broadcasting, Asia's STAR-TV and Internet. And it would also join the efforts of Ted Turner, the founder of Cable News Network and a variety of other media systems. "We're all moving at a hundred miles an hour into the future," Murdoch said in 1994, "but nobody knows where we're headed."[14] Wherever the journey leads them, it is certain to result in more global accessibility to international television programming.

Indeed, within this country, these **direct broadcasting satellites (DBS)** may well pose a substantial threat to U.S. television and cable networks, and even to local stations, as still another programming source in competition for viewing time and advertising dollars. These high-powered satellites, locked in orbit above the earth, can beam programming directly into small dishes or antennas throughout a vast region. Overseas, many developing nations perceive them as a potential menace to political and cultural sovereignty.

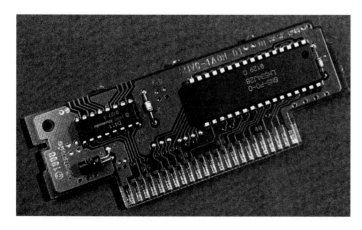

A Nintendo 16-bit game chip.

A high-definition testing lab in Alexandria, Virginia. High definition television, in the works for years, remained an unfulfilled promise in the mid-1990s. Technical problems and high unit costs combined to give HDTV an uncertain future.

HDTV

This stands for *high-definition television*—not, as some tired-of-waiting-for-it cynics have suggested, Humongous Dud Television.[15] HDTV is the digital, wide-screen, ultra-sharp television of the future, where images are as ultra-fine and crisp as on a movie screen. Digital HDTV would mean the images would be received without interference, making the large screen in the living room virtually the household equivalent of a motion picture theater. U.S. manufacturers, who have been locked for years in a tense race with their Japanese counterparts to develop an affordable HDTV system for the vast U.S. market, insist the HDTV revolution is imminent.

Others are less optimistic. Thus far, HDTV unit costs remain prohibitive for mass-market consumer acceptance. And there has been some resistance to the big, unwieldy screen that threatens to overwhelm everything else in the living room. Also, cable TV companies are themselves going digital. A converter box attachment can be plugged into today's TV sets to give them digital capabilities, perhaps making the expensive HDTV purchase unnecessary. Some industry leaders in 1994 were predicting that HDTV's future was, at best, uncertain. Still, the digital possibilities are enormous, with momentous implications for the economies of the nations competing for the best system. So the efforts to make HDTV a realistic consumer bargain will continue.

Background

Presently, consumer TV sets have a picture made up of 525 horizontal lines of information. (Look closely at your TV screen and you will see them.) But the larger the screen, the farther apart the lines are and the poorer the quality. Essentially, HDTV systems add more lines—1050, 1125, or more. The major problems are to develop one international standard and to make the units economically accessible.

More Channels

In the spring of 1994, Time-Warner's experimental Quantum cable television system went online in Orlando, Florida, offering its viewers the possibility of 500 channels. While many of these would be shopping and movie and interactive channels, the prospect of filling 500 channels remained a stupendous one. In the huge New York market, for example, some 150 channels were then in existence. What could possibly fill 500 channels of television programming? One cable industry leader, John Malone, head of Tele-Communications, was not worried. "Walk into a magazine store," he said. "Look at the number of special interest magazines. Count them."[16]

Perhaps he is right. But the real competition ahead in the high-tech world of entertainment and information will be for programming—software. Software can be a TV movie or a talk show, a basketball game or a televised rock concert. The prices for software are soaring. Take just one example: In 1964, CBS paid $5 million to the National Football League for the rights to televise all professional football games, or

Teaching Idea

Ask your students to come up with ideas for additional cable channels. Which seem like the best possibilities?

Stopping the "Clicker": Will Technology Make Things Worse?

> One of the real problems [with television political reporting] that television simply will not come to terms with is that they are an entertainment medium. They are not a news medium. Particularly, when [viewers] are sitting there with their clickers and they've got 69 channels to go around, you've got to stop that clicker, and you've got a second to do it. . . . The problem for us—when I say "us" I'm talking about this society—is that, unfortunately, that's where most of us are getting our information, with that clicker.

Michael Deaver, former White House adviser, quoted in Mathew D. McCubbins, ed., *Under the Watchful Eye: Managing Presidential Campaigns in the Television Era* (CQ Press, 1992).

whatever games it chose. In 1994, the Fox network paid $395 million for the rights to televise just the games from one NFL conference. Johnny Carson—again, for our purposes, he is "content"—in 1964 was paid $100,000 a year to host the highly successful "Tonight" show on NBC. David Letterman's late-night talk show on CBS now lands him a salary of $14 million a year. As one industry analyst, Larry Berbrandt, put it, "Content is the king on the information superhighway."[17]

The mergers in the early 1990s of mass media companies into gigantic conglomerates were driven, to a great degree, by the need for access to, and control of, media content.

Battle of the Giants

The multibillion-dollar merger involving Viacom, Paramount, and Blockbuster was the most spectacular takeover battle of the early 1990s involving the media of mass communications. But there were many others, including, in the summer of 1994, an on-again, off-again merger between CBS and QVC, a home-shopping cable channel. This transaction involved assets valued at $7 billion. In one twelve-month period alone, covering parts of 1993 and 1994, some 160 multimedia deals were made involving more than $75 billion, deals that profoundly changed the multimedia landscape in the United States.[18] The key players are

- Cable companies, who are seizing the opportunities digital compression technology and multiple channels create to achieve greater customer segmentation (**niche marketing**) and encourage higher consumer spending.
- Large electronic equipment manufacturers, worried that cable and telecommunications companies will use their networks and cable delivery lines to bypass VCRs and other stand-alone entertainment systems.
- And content companies, primarily publishers and studios, who understand the need to control talent, books, scripts, and broadcast rights if they are to be able to influence the delivery systems and reach the market.[19]

These intensely competitive companies know full well that the next century, to a degree unheard of in our history, will be an age of multimedia communication, and they will struggle to control the content the new age will require as well as the channels that will deliver this content to the American people.

Owners with New Values? An Issue for Mass Media Consumers

What standards of social responsibility will these new conglomerate owners hold? No one, at this stage, can venture anything more than a guess. But the question remains a vitally important one, because so much is at stake in the answer. One of the

Background

One player not mentioned is the telephone company. When AT&T was broken up in 1984 by federal court order, the seven "baby bells" could not get into the cable business. However, as of 1994, the courts seem to be reconsidering their earlier restrictions. (Researching the phone/cable situation might be a good student project.)

The **Power** of the Mass Media Consumer

Robert Sarnoff (former head of NBC) explained the consumer's power well. Speaking at an NBC affiliates gathering in December 1961, he reiterated the credo of commercial broadcasting, the belief that TV in the United States is what the people want it to be. "It is a mistake to assume that viewing can take place without the consent of the viewers—that a mass audience will just sit there and watch, regardless of what is on the screen," he asserted. "The ultimate decision on what the public sees can come only from the public itself, as long as it is free to watch or not to watch as it pleases."

Quoted by J. Fred MacDonald in *One Nation Under Television: The Rise and Decline of Network TV* (Nelson-Hall, 1990).

industry's most thoughtful observers, Dr. Everette E. Dennis, executive director of the Freedom Forum Media Studies Center, shares his concern:

> There is a justifiable nervousness among people who care about the quality of communication, whether that is translated into violent or sexually explicit content on television and in movies, or is simply shallow, dumbed-down media that no longer seek excellence as a target (not to mention the trend toward tabloid TV sweeping television news in the United States and elsewhere).
>
> The nervousness I speak of—some will call it simple fear—is connected directly to the producers of the news media, of new programming and data services. Where journalistic values and norms have mostly governed the mass media in the United States and the rest of the world for most of this century and where communications companies have a commitment to content for better or worse, it is feared that the new entrepreneurs who come from cable and telecommunications don't share these values or interests. In one scenario, they are simply businesspeople, orchestrating high-stakes enterprises to make a buck, driven more to sell products—whether soap flakes or information—than by a social vision for what communications and information can do for people.[20]

To be sure, there have been charlatans in the mass media field, and a fair number of them are identified in these pages. But the overwhelming majority of those working in mass communications positions in the United States have possessed a dedication that has made the U.S. news media the envy of the world. And they have brought to their work an understanding of the First Amendment and the unique protection it offers. This is not to suggest that entrepreneurs in other fields neglect customer service or professional ethics. But the media of mass communications, constitutionally protected and so vital to the functioning of a democracy, demand a special standard of care. If, as Dennis suggests, "the order of the day is the old 'public be damned' robber-baron attitude, we do have much to fear about who makes our content choices."[21]

Beyond that, the new technology will bring massive ethical and legal issues to bear on those who work in mass communications. For example:

- *How will privacy be protected?* Electronic snooping is far easier in the new age. Interactive newspapers and television sets and computer technology make it relatively simple to monitor not only our most sensitive business transactions but our consumer behavior, a temptation market researchers might find irresistible. (Who responded to what lonely-hearts "voice personal"? Who ordered what porno movies for on-demand home viewing? Who's interested in checking airline ticket prices? Who indicated on an interactive poll his or her political choices?)
- *How will intellectual property rights be protected?* In 1993, a computer was programmed to write a novel (*Just This Once: A Novel Written by a Computer Programmed to Think Like the World's Best-selling Author*) in the style of novelist Jacqueline Susann.[22] Who should benefit from this

Teaching Idea

Assign several students to watch local and network evening news programs, plus "60 Minutes," "20/20," and other news magazine programs. Ask them to discuss whether these programs are more news than entertainment, or vice versa.

publication? The computer programmer? The estate of the author whose style it copied? On a more mundane level, when the user of interactive information applies his or her own additions or changes to it, how can we determine ownership of the resulting material? When someone downloads a book off a CD-ROM disk, how can the author of the original book gain compensation?

Digitalized editing—especially of photographs, to alter them in a misleading and virtually untraceable fashion—and dozens of other ethical matters will face the mass communications media in the years ahead.

Virtual Reality, High-Tech, and Couch Potatoes

Somewhat outside the scope of mass communications, but still very much a part of the technology revolution, is the massive market for video games. Ferocious competition between such industry leaders as Super Nintendo and Sega Genesis has led to technology that makes games more and more lifelike. "We're talking about being able to play a round of golf with Jack Nicklaus," says industry analyst Michael Stanek.[23] Video game sales in 1994 were estimated at a whopping $10 billion in the United States alone.

The technology has enabled the creation of **virtual reality**—an artificial world wherein participants equipped with electronic goggles, earphones, body suits, and gloves can experience and touch computer-created sight and sound environments. Until recently found only in the domain of the high-tech lab, virtual reality has become increasingly more accessible to mass market consumers. Cartridge games for virtual reality systems entered some videogame arcades in 1994. Consumers could use some less elaborate virtual reality systems at home.

And where are we headed with this technology? One distinguished sociologist, Dr. Herbert J. Gans, warns that too much reliance on the information superhighway raises the prospect of becoming a nation of what he calls "electronic shut-ins":

> I use the term shut-ins purposely, for in the past sick and old people imprisoned in their own homes have always been pitied. Pity for shut-ins reflects the fact that we are social animals, requiring a good deal of regular social contact, of various degrees of intensity and closeness, in order to function properly. In fact, other people are good medicine, for we know from health research that adequate "social support" is an important factor in recovering from serious illness, and the lack of such support is correlated with higher rates of mortality.[24]

But another observer, Nicholas Negroponte of the Massachusetts Institute of Technology, also is looking ahead, and he sees far more good than evil:

> Some people say "TILT! I'm not comfortable with personalized media because I may become too narcissistic and lose the common threads of conversation I enjoy when I interact with my friends. How will I know that they know that Israel just signed a peace accord with the PLO?"
>
> You *will* know, because personalization will not be at the expense of headline events. I doubt any profile of me would show deep interest in Mr. [Yasser] Arafat, but I'd be fuming if news of PLO recognition were omitted.
>
> Personalization is not at the expense of common threads of societal awareness—it is a valuable addition.[25]

For the Mass Communications Student

It may be an exaggeration to predict, as Negroponte did, that in the years ahead there could be virtually no difference among the various media because bits of data are bits of data, and they can all be routed effortlessly through a rich variety of communications media. Still, his point is urgent and vital, and the student of mass communications must be aware of it.

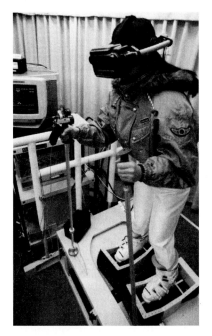

Virtual reality. A computer-simulated experience allows the participant to feel he or she is in an entirely different environment.

Tomorrow's mass communicator may well be less concerned about a specific medium—a newspaper or broadcast or cable vehicle—than about preparing a strong message that can, and will, be presented to the right audience by whatever means are available.

Thoughtful observers predict that the student planning to work in mass communications during the next century can expect to change careers—not jobs, *careers*—perhaps three times. This will require unprecedented flexibility and an adaptability to new circumstances. By way of preparation, such a student should possess, at a minimum:

1 *Clear and effective writing skills.* The technology, no matter how sophisticated, can be no better than the content it transmits.

2 *A familiarity with more than one mass communications medium.* Verbal people must learn to think also in visual terms, while graphics experts must appreciate the context in which pictures and other artworks appear.

3 *A strong set of ethical and professional values.* This last is the most important. The product—the news report, editorial, advertising message, press release—should make a useful contribution to the public good. The central purpose of mass communications in a free society is to spread the truth: truth about a situation, idea, belief, product, or service. Mass communications messages should be truthful, even to the adjectives and adverbs.[26] Communicating the truth has never been easy, and the high-tech world of today and tomorrow will provide a myriad of opportunities, both blatant and subtle, to manipulate and distort the truth. Beyond skill with words and some familiarity with multimedia, the mass communicator in the century ahead will also need to be a fair-minded individual determined to apply that fairness to the day-to-day business of communicating the truth.

The task ahead is a daunting one, but doing it will present breathtaking opportunities for careers in mass communications, for consumer use of mass communications, and even for the country itself.

summary

Digitalization of data, delivered by dramatic new switching techniques and fiber optics to home or office telephone/television receiver/computer station, can offer access to almost infinite amounts of material within a matter of seconds. But along with the technological growth comes another issue, that of content. What will appear on the television screens? Who will write and produce it? What impact will the new "information highway" have on traditional media, such as newspapers, magazines, books, and even television programs as we know them?

Also unknown at this point are the long-term economic and social implications of conglomerate mergers and media system takeovers—the immense concentrations of power a few giant companies will wield in the mass communications industry.

Further concerns include protecting individual privacy; protecting intellectual property (copyright) in the face of interactive media systems; and digital editing, especially of photographs, that can present distorted and misleading images to the public.

For the student of mass communications, the years ahead will offer dramatic opportunities for reaching a sophisticated audience through a variety of media. Tomorrow's effective mass communicator may well be less concerned about a specific medium—a newspaper or broadcast or cable vehicle—than about preparing a strong message that can be delivered to the right audience by whatever means are available. That communicator should possess, at a minimum, strong writing skills, a familiarity with more than one mass communications medium, and a strong set of ethical and professional values.

Discussion

With the new technology, will people still take paperback books to the beach or lake? What do students think of the future of the mass media and their place in it?

? questions and cases

1. Assume for the moment that Professor Negroponte is correct in predicting that writing for all of the mass media of the future will be digitalized and channeled into various forms. Can you still think of specific differences between writing intended for print media and writing intended for broadcast? Discuss.

2. As a mass communicator in the new age of digital technology, what ethical and professional precautions are you prepared to make to preserve an individual's privacy? Can you devise any scenario in which you would, for example, access, without authorization, an organization's electronic database? Are there stories which would justify such behavior? Explain.

3. From your study of the mass communications industry thus far, how would you compare the professional ethics of the industry with those of other industries you are familiar with? Are the mass media's standards for ethical behavior and customer service higher or lower? Explain.

4. As a future consumer in the age of the information superhighway, are you personally concerned about the possibility of becoming what Gans calls "an electronic shut-in"? Has the couch potato mentality already begun to take its toll on American society? Discuss.

chapter glossary

content   For our purposes, the totality of messages (articles, advertising, programming, text, pictures) the media of mass communications present.

direct broadcasting satellite (DBS)   Satellite operating in fixed orbit above the earth that transmits programming directly to antennas or small satellite dishes throughout a region.

fiber optics   Tiny glass strands that transmit digitalized communications messages to receivers that can translate them into light waves depicting images.

interactive media   Telecommunications systems permitting consumers to transmit as well as receive communications messages. Through home computers, interactive media

users can reply to advertising messages, "network" with other users, or participate in surveys, among many other possibilities.

niche marketing   Strategy by which a medium of mass communications or an advertiser cultivates a particular market segment.

on-demand video   Service by which users can arrange their own programming, choosing from an array of movies and other programs available from a vast content base.

virtual reality   An electronic, artificial environment wherein computer users, equipped with special earphones, goggles, body suits, and gloves, can approximate genuine sights and sounds.

notes

1 Leo Bogart, "Highway to the Stars or Road to Nowhere?" *Media Studies Journal* (New York: Freedom Forum Media Studies Center, 1994), 8:1, 11–12.

2 Ibid.

3 These questions and others are dealt with in depth in the *Media Studies Journal* issue cited above.

4 Quoted by Steven Levy, "We Have Seen the Content and It Is Us," *op. cit.,* 160; original from Bill McKibben, *The Age of Missing Information* (New York: Random House, 1992).

5 T. A. Dworetzky, "Roadmap to the Information Highway," *Modern Maturity,* February–March 1994, 27.

6 Ibid.

7 Brendan Elliott and Thomas Miller, "Newspapers and the 'New' Consumer," *Editor & Publisher,* 12 February 1994, 14.

8 Michelle Sagalyn, "Voice Personals: The Cash Cow for Newspapers," *op. cit.,* 22.

9 Jack Dale, "Rumors of the Future and the Digital Circus," *op. cit.,* 8.

10 Paul Wiseman, "Without Film, Would Films Still Be Films?" *USA Today,* 22 March 1994.

11 Jeannine Aversa, Associated Press dispatch, 24 March 1994.

12 Ibid.

13 Kevin Maney and Paul Wiseman, "New Venture Seeks to Cover Earth," *USA Today,* 22 March 1994.

14 Quoted by Richard J. MacDonald, "The Vision Thing," *Media Studies Journal, op. cit.,* 95.

15 Kevin Maney, "HDTV: Clear View but Fuzzy Future," *USA Today,* 24 February 1994.

16 Robert Siegel, "The Yearning Channel," *Media Studies Journal, op. cit.,* 80.

17 Quoted by Kevin Maney, "Info Highway Needs Bait to Lure Traffic," *USA Today,* 17 February 1994.

18 Janice Hughes, "The Changing Media Landscape," *Media Studies Journal, op. cit.,* 53.

19 Ibid.

20 Everette E. Dennis, "An Ethic for a New Age," *Media Studies Journal, op. cit.,* 143.

21 Ibid.

22 Donna A. Demac, "Multimedia and Intellectual Property Rights," *Media Studies Journal, op. cit.,* 59.

23 Mike Snider, "Nintendo Plots Leap Over Sega," *USA Today,* 16 February 1994.

24 Herbert J. Gans, "The Electronic Shut-Ins: Some Social Flaws of the Information Superhighway," *Media Studies Journal, op. cit., 123.*

25 Nicholas Negroponte, "What's in It for Me?" *Modern Maturity, op. cit.*

26 Otto Kleppner, *Advertising Procedure,* 4th ed. (Englewood Cliffs, N.J.: Prentice-Hall, 1950), 701.

credits

Photographs
Chapter A
p. A.2: © SYGMA; **p. A.5:** AP/Wide World Photos; **p. A.7 top:** The Bettmann Archive; **bottom:** © Arlene Collins/Monkmeyer; **p. A.12 left:** © 1994 Cable News Network, Inc. All rights reserved; **right:** © Arlene Collins/Monkmeyer

Chapter B
p. B.4: The Bettmann Archive; **p. B.8, B.16, B.19:** The Granger Collection; **p. B.20:** AP/Wide World Photos; **p. B.21:** © 1991 Cable Network News, Inc. All Rights Reserved

Chapter C
p. C.2, C.11: AP/Wide World Photos

Chapter D
p. D.2: © Margaret Miller/Photo Researchers, Inc.; **p. D.5:** © Spencer Grant/Stock Boston; **p. D.15:** © Toni Michaels

Chapter E
p. E.7: © Arlene Collins/Monkmeyer; **p. E.9 left:** © Martha Stewart/The Picture Cube; **right:** © Toni Michaels; **p. E.11:** © Toni Michaels; **p. E.13:** © Michael Dwyer/Stock Boston

Chapter F
p. F.2, F.5: AP/Wide World Photos; **p. F.10 left:** © Peter Menzel/Stock Boston; **right:** © Rick Smolan/Stock Boston; **p. F.11 all:** © Toni Michaels; **p. F.12:** © Roy Bishop/Stock Boston

Chapter G
p. G.3: © Charles Gatewood/Stock Boston; **p. G.5:** © Culver Pictures; **p. G.7, G.9:** © Toni Michaels; **p. G.14:** © Margot Granitsas/Photo Researchers, Inc.

Chapter H
p. H.2: The Granger Collection; **p. H.9:** © Richard Pasley/Stock Boston; **p. H.10 top:** © Joseph Nettis/Photo Researchers Inc.; **bottom:** © Alexandra Boulat/Sipa Press; **p. H.15:** © Chris Hammond

Chapter I
p. I.3: UPI/Bettmann; **p. I.4:** The Bettmann Archive; **p. I.7:** Culver Pictures; **p. I.8, I.14:** © Photofest

Chapter J
p. J.2: © Arvind Garg/Photo Researchers, Inc.; **p. J.3:** © James Hamilton/SYGMA; **p. J.5:** Culver Pictures; **p. J.7:** AP/Wide World Photos; **p. J.8:** © Christopher Morrow/Stock Boston

Chapter K
p. K.3 left: The Bettmann Archive; **right:** UPI/Bettmann; **p. K.7:** © Dion Ogust/The Image Works; **p. K.8, K.10:** Reuters/Bettmann; **p. K.11:** AP/Wide World Photos

Chapter L
p. L.2: UPI/Bettmann; **p. L.4:** The Kobal Collection; **p. L.9:** © Bob Kramer/Stock Boston; **p. L.12:** © Bob Daemmrich/Stock Boston; **p. L.13:** The Bettmann Archive; **p. L.17:** AP/Wide World Photos

Chapter M
p. M.5: © Photofest; **p. M.6:** The Kobal Collection; **p. M.8:** UPI/Bettmann; **p. M.9, M.13:** The Kobal Collection

Chapter N
p. N.2: AP/Wide World Photos; **p. N.4:** © Toni Michaels; **p. N.5:** AP/Wide World Photos; **p. N.6:** © Richard Lord Ente/The Image Works; **p. N.7:** The Bettmann Archive; **p. N.11:** © Billy E. Barnes/PhotoEdit

Chapter O
p. O.6: Culver Pictures; **p. O.9:** © Toni Michaels; **p. O.10 left:** © Spencer Grant/Photo Reseachers, Inc.; **right:** Courtesy of the Coca-Cola Company; **p. O.14:** Courtesy of the Maytag Company

Chapter P
p. P.3: UPI/Bettmann; **p. P.4:** AP/Wide World Photos; **p. P.6:** © Penny Prince/Gamma Liaison; **p. P.12:** UPI/Bettmann; **p. P.16:** AP/Wide World Photos; **p. P.18:** © Elizabeth Hamlin/Stock Boston

Chapter Q
p. Q.2: AP/Wide World Photos; **p. Q.7:** The Kobal Collection; **p. Q.8, Q.9:** AP/Wide World Photos; **p. Q.12:** © Toni Michaels

Chapter R
p. R.10: © Grant LeDuc/Monkmeyer; **p. R.11:** © Toni Michaels; **p. R.12:** © Steve Goldberg/Monkmeyer; **p. R.14:** Courtesy of Nielsen Media Research; **p. R.16:** Courtesy of JSA Publishing

Chapter S
p. S.7: © Spencer Grant/Monkmeyer; **p. S.9:** © Tim Barnwell/Stock Boston; **p. S.10:** AP/Wide World Photos; **p. S.13:** © Richard Dole Photography; **p. S.15:** © Chris Hammond

Chapter T

p. T.2: © Frank Siteman/Stock Boston;
p. T.3: Courtesy of Wanda Jacobs; **p. T.8:** Courtesy of Don Flores; **p. T.12:** © 1991 Universal City Studios Inc./Photofest;
p. T.13 top: Courtesy of ESPN; **bottom:** © 1991 Pathe Entertainment, Inc./The Kobal Collection; **p. T.14:** © 1993 CBS, Inc./Photofest

Chapter U

p. U.4: © D. Sokolov/Tass/Sovfoto/ Eastfoto; **p. U.9:** © Derek Hudson/ SYGMA; **p. U.11:** © Jean Louis Atlan/SYGMA; **p. U.12:** © N. Malyshev/ITAR-TASS/Sovfoto/ Eastfoto; **p. U.15:** © Bob Daemmrich/The Image Works; **p. U.16:** © Macduff Everton/The Image Works

Chapter V

p. V.4: © Toni Michaels; **p. V.5:** Courtesy of Knight-Ridder Information Design Laboratory; **p. V.7:** © Michael Dwyer/Stock Boston; **p. V.8:** © Philippe Gontier/The Image Works; **p. V.11:** Reuters/Bettmann

index

Your instructor has chosen which chapters to include in your text and the order in which those chapters are placed, so that you and your class can learn mass communication as efficiently as possible. Because there are so many possible options for arranging the chapters, each chapter is page numbered separately, starting over with "1" every chapter. To avoid the confusing situation of having several "page 1's," the page numbers in your text are all preceded by a letter. The letters correspond to all the available chapters your instructor *could have* chosen. Your book will not have a chapter for every letter of the alphabet, and you may not find the letters you do have in proper alphabetical order (for example, you may find that your book starts with page B.1, instead of A.1). Use your table of contents to determine which chapters you do have, which letters identify those chapters, and the order in which the chapters appear. Then you can easily flip to the appropriate letter-number combination when you need to find a certain page in the book.

C

Cablecasting, L.17
Cable News Network (CNN), A.12, C.2, U.13
Cable television networks, L.14
Cablevision, S.16
Campbell, John, B.3–4
Capa, Robert, F.6
Carnegie Commission, L.12
Carrington, Edward, A.7
Carson, Rachel, H.11
Carter, Jimmy, A.4
Cartier-Bresson, Henri, F.6
Cassette recordings, K.4–7
CD-ROM, J.15, K.13, M.13
Censorship (of books), H.14
Channel noise, R.2
Cinemax, L.15
Civil War news reporting, B.13
Clark, Thomas, E.2
Clerk-Maxwell, James, I.2
Clinton, Bill, A.4, Q.8
Cobb, Irvin S., U.8
Cobbett, William, B.6
Codex, H.4
Cole, Richard, U.7
Columbia Broadcasting System (CBS), I.6, I.9
Columbia Journalism Review, Q.12, S.15
Communication theory, R.1–9
    processes and effects of mass
        communication, R.5–9
    theories of diffusion, R.4–5
    theories of mass society, R.3–4
Community press, E.1–13
    approach to the news, E.5–6
    career opportunities, E.11–13
    current operations, E.7
    editorials and columns, E.6
    roles of, E.2–3
    technological change, E.3–4
Community radio, E.7
Compact discs, K.4, K.7, K.13
Compaine, Benjamin, H.2–3
Confidentiality (of news sources), P.15–17
Conrad, Frank, I.3
Contemporary community standards (in
    obscenity cases), P.17
Content analysis, R.15–16
Contract publishing, G.11
Copyright, H.19
Corontos, B.2, B.23
Corporation for Public Broadcasting, J.7
Cosby, Gov. William, B.4–5
Cost-per-thousand (CPM), O.15–16
Creative boutiques, O.7
Creel Committee, N.7–8
Crisis, The, T.5
Crist, Judith, D.2
Cronkite, Walter, R.7
Cutlip, Scott, H.4, H.18

D

Daguerre, Louis, F.3
Dale, Jack, V.6
Dana, Charles A., Q.5

"Dateline NBC," A.11
Da Vinci, Leonardo, F.3
Davis, Elmer, A.9
Davis, Richard Harding, U.8
Day, Benjamin, B.7
Daye, Stephen, H.5
Dayparts, L.22
Deaver, Michael, V.9
Declaration of Talloires, U.6
Defamation, P.1–11
    common law defenses, P.8–9
    defined, P.2–3
    elements of, P.4–6
    fault requirement, P.6–8
    secondary defenses, P.10
De Fleur, Melvin H., R.8–9
De Forest, Lee, I.2, J.12
De Graffe, Robert, H.11
Demographic profiles, O.10
Dennis, Everette, E., V.10
Dependency theory, R.8
Depth interviews, R.14
Designated Market Area (DMA), L.22
Desktop publishing, E.10–11
Dessauer, John P., H.4, H.9
Detroit *Free Press,* D.5
Dial, The, B.18, G.4
Diffusion of innovations theory, R.5
Digital audio broadcasting, K.13
Digital compact cassettes, K.13
Direct Broadcasting Satellite (DBS), V.7, V.13
Disinformation, U.2
Douglass, Frederick, T.3–4
Dow Jones Newspaper Fund, T.10
DuBois, W. E. B., T.5
Duopoly rule, J.10
Dwyer, R. Budd, Q.9

E

Eastman, George, F.13
Ebony, T.6
Economist, The, U.14
Edes, Benjamin, B.5
Edison, Thomas Alva, K.2–3, M.4
Editor & Publisher, S.14–15
Education and Professional Development in
    Mass Communications, S.1–16
    accreditation, S.5–7
    career opportunities, S.11–14
    criticisms and challenges, S.8–11
    early developments, S.2–4
    mass communications schools today, S.7–8
    philosophical problems, S.4–5
    professional journals and trade papers,
        S.14–16
Eisenhower, Dwight, A.4
Electronic Newsgathering Equipment (ENG), F.15
El-hi books, H.7
Eliot, George, Q.2
Eliot, T. S., L.3
Embarrassing facts (in privacy cases), P.13
Emerson, Ralph Waldo, B.18
Essence, T.6
Ethics in mass communications, Q.1–18
    acceptability codes, Q.14
    advertising, Q.13–14

    broadcasting self-regulation, Q.11
    checkbook journalism, Q.8
    computer imaging of photographs, Q.7
    confidentiality, Q.6–7
    conflicts of interest, Q.5
    creative codes, Q.15
    gifts and subsidies, Q.5–6
    "media events," Q.9
    National Advertising Review Board, Q.16
    news councils, Q.9–11
    news leaks, Q.9
    "outing" homosexuals, Q.8
    public relations ethics, Q.16
    relationships with news sources, Q.3
    reporting about AIDS victims, Q.7

F

False light (in privacy cases), P.13
Farm Security Administration (FSA)
    photographers, F.5
Feature syndicates, C.16
Federal Communications Commission (FCC),
    I.6–10, T.7
Federalist, The, B.6
Federal Trade Commission (FTC), Q.13–14
Feshbach, Seymour, R.8
Fessenden, Reginald, I.2
Fiber optics, L.20, V.2
Filler, Louis, B.17
Films, M.1–14
    audience trends, M.2–3
    best pictures, M.7
    career opportunities, M.10–11
    censorship, M.11–12
    early developments, M.2–4
    future outlook, M.12–14
    how movies are made, M.8–10
    ratings and industry self-regulation, M.12
    young people and, M.3
First Amendment, B.6
Fleming, John A., I.2
Flores, Don, T.8
Flowers, Gennifer, Q.8
Flynt, Larry, P.3
Focus groups, R.14
Folio, S.16
Ford, Gerald, A.4
Foreign Agents Registration Act, U.16–17
Fourteenth Amendment, B.6
Fourth Estate, A.2, A.13
Franklin, Benjamin, B.4–5, G.3, H.5, O.4–5
Franklin, James, B.4
Freedom of Information Act, P.14
Freedom's Journal, T.3
Freelancing (for magazines), G.14–16
Frequency (in advertising), O.16
Friedheim, Jerry W., U.6
Fuller, Keith, U.3
Fuller, Margaret, B.18, T.14

G

Gans, Herbert J., V.11
Garrison, William Lloyd, Q.17
Gatekeepers, R.7, R.16–17